SOUTH ASIA DEFENCE AND STRATEGIC YEAR BOOK

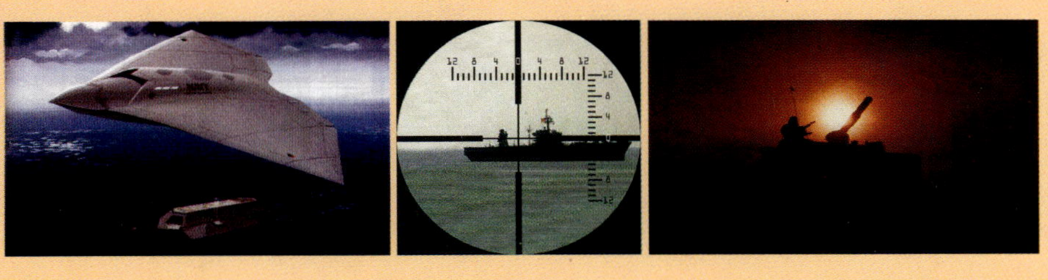

2008

Acknowledgments:

- The data for the Country Studies has been obtained from the US Library of Congress website, CIA handbook website and UNO website, besides other sources.
- The data for the Military Balance has been obtained from the International Institute of Strategic Studies, The Military Balance 2006-2007, US Department of Defense Annual Reports besides other sources.
- Data on Terrorism has been obtained from the South Asia Terrorism Portal website.
- The data for the Trends in Military Technology section has been obtained from published source material of the concerned manufacturers.

SOUTH ASIA DEFENCE AND STRATEGIC YEAR BOOK

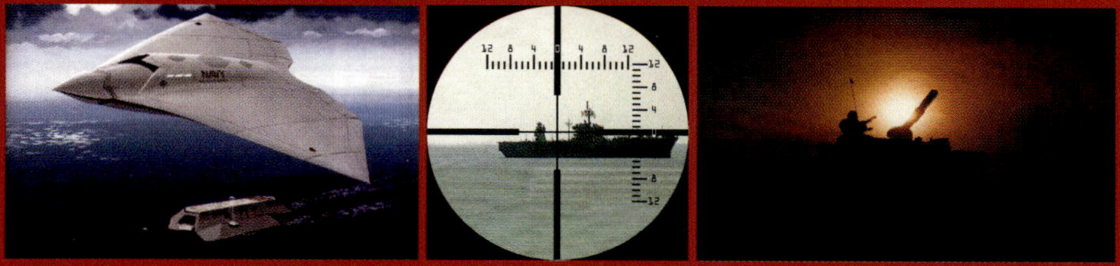

2008

Foreword by
Admiral Sureesh Mehta
Chief of Naval Staff and Chairman, Chiefs of Staff Committee

PENTAGON PRESS

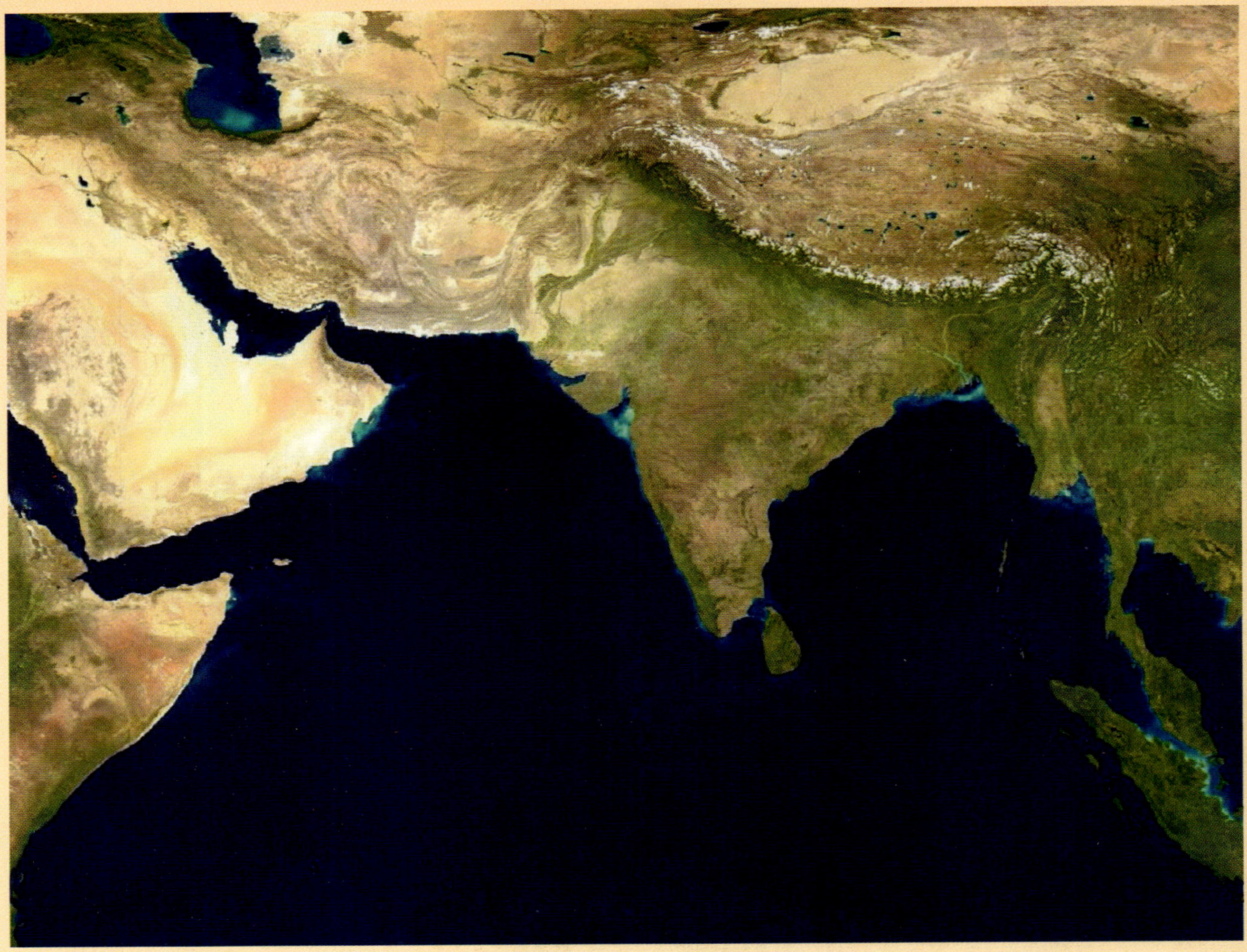

SOUTH ASIA DEFENCE AND STRATEGIC YEAR BOOK 2008

First published 2008

ISBN - 978-81-8274-320-5

Published by

PENTAGON PRESS
206, Peacock Lane, Shahpur Jat
New Delhi-110 049
Phones: 011-64706243, 26491568
Telefax: 011-26490600
email: rajan@pentagon-press.com
www.pentagon-press.com

Design by Artfair, processed, printed and bound at Guide Offset Printer.

Printed on eco-friendly, chlorine free paper.

CONTENTS

एडमिरल सुरीश मेहता
पी वी एस एम, ए वी एस एम, ए डी सी
नौसेनाध्यक्ष

Admiral Sureesh Mehta
PVSM, AVSM, ADC
Chief of the Naval Staff
and
Chairman, Chiefs of Staff Committee

रक्षा मंत्रालय
एकीकृत मुख्यालय (नौसेना)
नई दिल्ली - 110011
Integrated Headquarters
Ministry of Defence (Navy)
New Delhi - 110011

FOREWORD

The opening years of the Twenty-first Century have been characterised by significant and even momentous changes being wrought upon the security fabric of the South Asian Region. As the seventh year of the opening decade of this Century draws to a close, its defining moments in terms of security can best be discerned against the backdrop of the overall regional security environment. It is in this context that the Year Book of the 'South Asia Defence and Strategic Review' assumes particular significance and relevance, for even in this Twenty-First Century, the threat of 'intra-State' as well as 'inter-State' conflict within South Asian Region remains an unwelcome anachronism from an earlier age.

This is a region marked by extreme economic diversities, where some of the fastest-growing economies live cheek-by-jowl with some of the poorest countries of the world. In socio-political terms too, a number of countries of the region have been scarred by the ravages of colonialism and are still struggling to stabilise indigenous socio-political systems that can be inclusive enough for the beneficial aspects of their colonial legacy to be taken advantage of. As a consequence of these and other factors — including, of course, the geo-strategic game-plays of extra-regional powers — South Asia must contend with a variety of security threats that are short of State-on-State conflict, yet present an equal if not greater threat to peace and stability. Today, despite the best efforts of governments, terrorist groups have established deep roots and are operating across national boundaries with increasing impunity and their impact is being felt both, on the land and at sea. The rising trend in incidents of maritime crime, including piracy, is yet another disturbing manifestation of an uneasy security environment. The illegal ingress of arms, drug-smuggling, and, human-trafficking, are generating significant instability in several countries and creating connectivities across the region that law-abiding nation-States can only find disquieting. As if these were not challenges enough, the region is the locus of almost 70% of the world's natural disasters.

Insofar as India is concerned, a fairly constant feature of the past few years has been the growing strength of the Indian economy. It would be fair to estimate that the encouraging nature and speed of this growth will propel the nation to being one of the major 'Asian Poles' (along with China and Japan) in the emerging multi-polar world order. All indicators are that the avoidance of open military conflict will be a high national priority. However, for this very reason, *preparedness* for all eventualities ranging from 'economic competition' to 'military conflict' will be a complementary priority and this realisation will doubtless drive India's security construct.

Yet, the gains from this strong and sustained economic growth have not been inclusive enough to satisfy all sections of the highly pluralistic Indian society and this has, in turn, led to substantial swathes of the burgeoning population falling outside the paradigm of economic growth. Even as the government tries hard to absorb these 'excluded' groups within the ambit of a resurgent economy, there are malevolent non-state actors seeking to drive their own agenda, deeply inimical to that of the Indian State, through these same, disenchanted sections of Indian society. The resultant dichotomous situation, where India is driven by high economic growth while simultaneously being wracked by internal dissent — often fuelled or directed from implacable enmities residing beyond her borders, finds its echoes and reflections in other South Asian societies as well. Thus, Bangladesh, Pakistan, Sri Lanka and Myanmar are also all seemingly poised simultaneously on the brink of great prosperity as well as of disaster. The troubled geopolitical and geo-strategic landscape of Afghanistan dominates the continental outlook of the region and determines the presence of extra-regional military forces on both, land and sea.

In such a situation of regional flux, prudence, if nothing else, demands that all societal sections remain abreast of the developments of the region and mindful of future trends. The succinct statistical and descriptive summaries that define this year's edition of the 'South Asia Defence and Strategic Review' Year Book, serve both these purposes admirably and I am certain that this edition, like its predecessors, will prove both informative and thought-provoking.

Sureesh Mehta

Admiral
CNS & Chairman COSC
31 December 2007

PERSPECTIVE ON SOUTH ASIA

From the Editor's Desk

Introduction

We live in an era of tumultuous revolution in every sphere of human endeavour. Traditional structures are eroding as new forces and trends are sweeping across the world. Yet, in this world of communications, connectivity and convergence, there are deep divisions, as terrorism continues to place its ugly footprint across the globe. Other threats to the hopes of a bright future are aspects of climate change, disease, poverty and malnutrition that continue to haunt us. The forces of globalization and market-economy, coupled with the knowledge revolution are creating new values, attitudes and behaviour, that will shape the direction humanity adopts in the coming years. The past continues to be a matter of dispute when the focus should be on the future. The world thus displays a continuum between aspirations and anguish. Religion and ethnicity continue to divide, while wealth, technology and the free expression of ideas strive to develop unity amongst people. Bridging the divides that fragments humanity remains a great challenge. There are conflicts between national interest and international responsibility, even as traditional barriers to progress are falling. The four dimensions of power—military, economic, technological and cultural are clearly not in balance in South Asia.

The growth rate of the economy has increased steadily, and is today among the highest in Asia. India and to an extent, Pakistan led the growth. Services followed by industry were the drivers of growth. The growth in investments has surpassed that of consumption for the fourth year running. Saving rates, both public and private, and the inflow of capital have also increased. Specifically foreign direct investment has increased, but remains lower than in East and Southeast Asia. The greatest need for governments is to ensure that the fruits of economic growth percolate down and provide tangible benefits to the lowest strata of the population. Resources need to be managed efficiently.

Similar improvements have taken place in the macroeconomic fundamentals (lower inflation, smaller current account deficit, and declining fiscal deficit) and in the integration with the global economy. While developments in India are clearly the predominant factor in the improved economic performance of South Asia, most other countries in the region have been on a similar trend—although their improvements generally are more modest.

Forecasts for growth of South Asia's GDP remain strong at about 7.5%. Risks to this forecast include the volatile oil prices, adjustments of the global payments imbalance, internal political instability and the possible spread of the avian flu. In macroeconomic management, the key areas of concern are inflation and increasing current account deficits. These require slowing down the rapid growth in domestic consumer demand through appropriate monetary and fiscal policies and removing supply side constarints. In addition, action on domestic energy prices is needed to reduce the fiscal burden of the high and rising international oil prices and to improve efficiency of energy use.

Economic Indicators for South Asia[1]

In India, agricultural productivity continues to languish, largely reflecting neglected infrastructure and poor rural extension services. Rising food prices have contributed to inflation. Tensions also surfaced as rapidly expanding industry and services activities encroached on agricultural land. Gaps exist between the more prosperous areas and those in the interior — where population growth is fastest and job creation weak.

In Bangladesh and Nepal, inward remittances reversed trade deficits and generated current account surpluses. Remittances significantly helped the payments positions of Pakistan and Sri Lanka. In Bangladesh much will depend on how the interim Government performs economically, as well as on political developments. Growth in Sri Lanka is expected to consolidate trend performance. If political conditions become more settled, Nepal may reap a modest dividend. Continuing recovery from the tsunami has seen double-digit growth in the Maldives.

South Asia's GDP grew by 7.7% in 2006 (see Table below), having averaged more than 7.5% a year growth since 2003. The GDP of nearly every country in the region grew at over 6.0% in 2006. India had

GDP	2002	2003	2004	2005	2006	2007
South Asia	3.7	7.8	7.4	8.7	8.7	7.7
Afghanistan	28.6	15.7	8.0	14.0	8.0	10.0
Bangladesh	4.4	5.3	6.3	6.0	6.7	6.5
Bhutan	10.0	7.6	6.8	6.5	9.0	18.0
India	3.8	8.5	7.5	9.0	9.2	8.5
Maldives	6.5	8.5	9.5	-4.5	18.2	12.1
Nepal	-0.4	3.0	3.5	2.3	2.3	2.8
Pakistan	3.1	4.7	7.5	8.6	6.6	6.8
Sri Lanka	4.0	6.0	5.4	6.0	7.2	6.1

the highest growth rate of 9.2% among the large economies and the Maldives grew at 18.2%, fastest among the small economies. The services sector contributed most to growth in South Asia, but industry sector growth accelerated in India and Bangladesh, buttressing the sustainability of high growth rates in the future. High levels of consumption and investment boosted growth rates. Domestic demand expanded due to rising incomes, credit expansion, and workers' remittances.

Demand pressures and high world oil and commodity prices led to an increase in the region's inflation rate to 6.0% in 2006. Inflation picked up in Bangladesh, India, and Nepal, but came down in Pakistan and Sri Lanka (though from much higher levels). Government budget deficits remained at elevated levels to reinforce credit expansion, partly because of the increased subsidy to buffer rising oil prices, reconstruction efforts following natural disasters, and high development expenditures.

South Asia's current account deficit increased marginally in 2006 to 2.1% of GDP. Although merchandise exports grew at a robust rate of 18.8%, imports grew at an even higher rate of 24.9%, induced by domestic demand pressures and high world commodity prices. Exports of services and the surge in workers' remittances brought the current account to a narrow deficit. The region's foreign exchange reserves increased because of large net capital inflows.

India, building on its fastest growth in 18 years in 2006, registered growth of 9.3% in the first quarter of 2007. In Bangladesh, political developments continue to dominate, though on the economic front, there has been little change. The textile industry is doing well in the post-quota world and private remittances provide an important source of support for consumption and investment. However, recent measures against corruption and hoarding have added to business sector uncertainty. In Pakistan, growth is at 6.5%, but adverse developments on the political and security fronts could have a crucial bearing on the economy. Growth of 7.0% in 2006 was largely underpinned by expansion in large-scale manufacturing industry and in services. Remittances from Pakistan's foreign-based workers continue to provide substantial support to domestic demand.

Hopes for improvement in Nepal's economic circumstances and performance have so far not been met. In Sri Lanka, real economic growth is expected to hold its course, though the macroeconomic

[1] *Source: Asian Development Bank Outlook - 2007*

situation continues to give cause for concern. In the Maldives, economic rhythm will return to a more settled pace following the spike in 2006 that reflected tsunami-related reconstruction activities. The completion of the Tala hydro-project will give a boost to the income growth of Bhutan's small economy. In Afghanistan, there has been a stronger than expected recovery in agriculture.

The services sector has been the main driver of growth in South Asia. Its shares in the GDP of Bangladesh, India, Pakistan, and Sri Lanka was 49%, 55%, 53%, and 56% respectively in 2006, which is significantly larger than in other countries relative to their respective levels of per capita income and land area. In South Asia the service sector has been performing well recently, with output growing by 10.5% in 2006 led by trade, and transport and communications. The industry sector also expanded rapidly though from a smaller base, with sector growth up by 10.1% buoyed by manufacturing. South Asia's agriculture sector grew by 2.7% during the year.

Despite the reduction in world commodity prices, South Asia's growth of merchandise imports is likely to outstrip exports because of high regional growth rates and lower supply. Vigorous growth in exports of services and workers' remittances is expected to substantially compensate for the trade shortfall, leaving the current account with relatively small deficits of about 2% of GDP for the next 2 years. High growth rates in the region will continue to attract large capital flows. Countries are likely to add to their international reserves and maintain stable exchange rates.

Pakistan

In recent months, Pakistan has witnessed unparalleled political and internal instability with the tragic assassination of Benazir Bhutto as she was leaving an election rally in Rawalpindi barely two weeks before polling day. Its effect on the political dispensation is likely to be substantial even if it takes some time to unravel, complicated by what is seen as the military government's efforts to confuse the situation. This came at the end of a year when the government initially tried but failed to unseat the Chief Justice of the Supreme Court, which was followed by a successful effort to rid the Court of all independent judges late in the year using the device of emergency rule. Militarily and politically, government appears to be losing control over the NWFP, particularly FATA and Waziristan, while Balochistan continues to be in a state of turmoil. Wanton acts of terrorism are commonplace in urban areas and terrorist organisations are gradually gaining strength. General Musharraf has lost credibility and now has only a tenuous hold over power. Major government decisions were being increasingly subjected to judicial scrutiny and review till the judiciary was de-fanged in November. Political agitations are gathering momentum. The extent of mass support that different political parties enjoy is unclear. Independent civil society, especially the legal fraternity, emerged as a powerful force in opposing the government's ham-handed attempts to remove the Chief Justice initially but the limitations of its influence was obvious from the regime's success in finally taming the Supreme Court. Political instability in Pakistan does not augur well for the region.

Although counted as an ally of the US in the war on terrorism, Pakistan cannot easily be characterized as either friend or foe. Indeed, Pakistan has become the major centre of radical Islamist ideas and groups, largely because of its past policies toward India and Afghanistan. Pakistan supported Islamist militants fighting Indian rule in the disputed territory of Jammu and Kashmir and backed the Taliban in its pursuit of a client regime in Afghanistan. The selective cooperation of Pakistan's president and military ruler, Gen. Pervez Musharraf, in sharing intelligence with the United States and apprehending Al Qaeda members has led to the assumption that Pakistan might not be ready to give up its long-standing ties with radical Islam.

Bowing to international pressure, President Pervez Musharraf has restarted an offensive in the remote tribal areas that are rapidly becoming a hub of global terrorism. Yet indications are that, no matter who is in charge, the Pakistani Army is ill-suited - and perhaps incapable - of doing the job. Significant casualties and scant public support for the operation is a major problem. It suggests that America must temper its expectations of what Pakistan can do militarily in the war on terror or risk inflaming the situation further.

For a military revered as Pakistan's proudest institution, such a situation at the hands of non-state actors is symptomatic of a broader malaise. The offensive is almost universally perceived to be an American war contracted out to its Pakistani ally. In the past, perhaps, the Army was willing to play this role - most notably when it bred and supported resistance to the Soviet invasion of Afghanistan in the late 1980s. But now, the Pakistan military is being asked to fight its own citizens in an unpopular counterinsurgency campaign that it has neither the will nor the skill-set to fight.

Pakistan's neighbours, and indeed the world community, have important stakes in its stability, security and prosperity. They are vitally interested in the ability, or otherwise, of its government to contain and eliminate powerful forces of Islamic radicalism that pose a global threat. In case effective measures are not taken, the Talibanisation of Pakistan will become a reality. The problem is that the Pakistan army has no real strategy to combat Islamic radicals and, as Sun Tzu has pointed out, "tactics without strategy is the noise before defeat". This defeat will not be in anyone's interests, least of all India's.

But the true nature of the regime has always been evident and has notable landmarks — the sacking of Supreme Court Chief Justice Saeeduzzaman Siddiqui for not backing the coup in 1999, the unceremonious ouster in June 2001 of President Rafiq Tarrar so that the General could occupy that office, the over-the-top April 2002 referendum, where an alleged 97% voters endorsed his rule, the dismissal of Supreme Court judges who voted against his usurpation and now, the purge of the Supreme Court and High Courts of all judges deemed as not being adequately subservient to the executive.

State power in Pakistan has been concentrated in the hands of a military bureaucratic oligarchy, a tightly knit coterie of mainly (but not exclusively) Punjabi officials who have remained in command of the state apparatus in Pakistan from its inception is directly entrenched in the structure of state power. Constitutionally elected governments, by virtue of their narrow legalistic basis, have felt themselves bound by inherited 'constitutions', which after all were designed by dictators to perpetuate their powers.

Pakistan's relationship with the US has been an uneven and complex one. With the intensification of Pakistan's economic dependence the US has been able to intervene decisively in Pakistan's internal affairs. The US is deeply committed to fighting the drug traffic through Pakistan, its concern heightened by its lack of confidence in the ability or the will of Pakistan authorities to deal with it. It has established its own organization in the country to monitor this and track down offenders. There have been many occasions on which it has had to pressurize the military regime to take action against terrorists. There is also the US concern about Pakistan's nuclear capability, and its danger of falling into the hands of non-state actors.

General Musharraf swore in an interim caretaker government, in December 2007, declaring, "I have actually introduced the essence of democracy in Pakistan, whether anyone believes it or not." The US has given Gen Musharraf considerable slack in meeting his commitments to deal with domestic extremism or his promises to restore authentic democracy. In the ultimate analysis, once in power, the military never has any intention of leaving. Lacking a political mandate to rule Musharraf has consolidated his power base beyond challenge by making the military itself his political constituency. However, it must be realized that, only by destroying itself can the military, and General Musharraf, in particular, hope to establish their own credentials to rule. The main issue in Pakistan is governance. Will ordinary people have a democratic voice in deciding what in the best interest of society? Or will a small ruling elite, meeting in secret and far from public view, be allowed to set the rules that shape the future of the country? It must be realized that there is never a bad time to end dictatorship.

Benazir Bhuttos' assassination on 27 December 2007, as she exited an election rally in Rawalpindi came after decades of surviving rejection from government opponents, threats of violence, failed assassination attempts and other obstacles. No matter what she faced, she supported a form of government she believed would be best for her people. She had twice served as Pakistan's Prime Minister between 1988 and 1996. Earlier she had survived an assassination attempt, on 18 October, when a suicide bomber attacked her cavalcade during a welcome parade at Karachi held in her honour; over 130 people died. She had returned to Pakistan from an eight-year self-imposed exile. Her death raises questions about the ability of Pakistan to confront the terror that faces the country, which is the reason why the military assumed extraordinary powers in the first place.

Pakistan needs a legitimate and popular government and the focus has to shift from personalities to institutions and processes. There has to be a plan, in which the international community should be involved, to bridge this divide. The future course of events in Pakistan needs to be watched carefully. The army has to divest itself from promoting its 'corporate interests'.

Myanmar

Myanmar's 45-year-old tryst with military rule has brought it much misery. General Ne Win, who staged a military coup, declared that his government would follow the "Burmese way of socialism," and started the process of isolating his country from the rest of the world. This bankrupted the country and in 1988, Buddhist monks and students rose up in revolt. The military unleashed a terror campaign in which more than 3,000 people died. Ne Win was replaced by a new military leader, Than Shwe, and his junta, which has ruined the country further.

Under the State Peace and Development Council (SPDC), the ruling junta saw to it that the elected representatives constituted a minuscule minority and the military the dominant majority. Of Myanmar's 52 million people, 75 per cent live below the poverty line. Myanmar is the second largest producer of illegal opium in the world, the first being Afghanistan. The junta has established two mega companies which control almost all economic activities in the country. The military gets 30 to 60% of budgetary resources, to the detriment of other sectors of society. Forced labour is a pervasive problem. The government's most heinous crime has been recruiting children in the Burmese Army. At any given point of time, there are 25,000 such children attached to several battalions. The boys begin military training at the age of seven. They are denied any contact with the outside world.

Roads, electricity, telephones, public transport and other infrastructure facilities are woefully lacking. Since the railway system is in poor shape, inland waterways remain the primary means of long distance transport. Of the total Burmese population, 67% is Buddhist, and the rest divided into seven ethnic minorities. These ethnic minorities are systematically made the targets of violence. Well documented abuses include food and land requisitions, killings, beatings, forced labour and relocations and rapes by the military. It is estimated that there are 453,500 such refugees in Thailand, 15,000 in Bangladesh, 60,000 in India, and 25,000 in Malaysia.

The latest revolt by monks, students and civilians was provoked by the unprecedented rise in fuel prices. The uprising was brutally suppressed; but thanks to the Internet, video, mobile phones and, of course, the enterprising spirit of the patriotic Burmese residing in Myanmar as well as on the Thai border areas, the world could see the non-violent resistance that the Burmese put up and the brutal manner in which the junta responded. This incident has again brought to light the glaring impotence of the international community in reining in the Burmese Army.

Nepal

Political manoeuvres in the power struggle between the Maoists and the Seven Party Alliance (SPA) has been a dominant feature of politics in Nepal during the past year. The framework of a 'peace process' is in place; and the successful attempt of the Maoists to obtain agreement on ending the monarchy after the next elections signals a consolidation of Maoist dominance. The future of the Himalayan country lies in the balance.

India's Emerging Partnership with the US

In recent times, India has hosted most major heads of states and multinational corporations, as well as high-ranking delegations from both the public and private sectors. This constitutes recognition of India's emerging role as an important political and economic player in global affairs. The emerging US-India partnership was sealed in July 2005 with Prime Minister Singh's historic visit to Washington.

India is the world's second most populous nation after China and home to the second largest population of Muslims (that constitute a minority of approximately 12% of India's total population of over 1 billion). India has halved poverty since its independence in 1947. Considering its vast size and complex diversity as the world's most populous democracy, India's relative stability and vibrant civil society remains a monumental achievement. However, sectarianism has not disappeared and its potential for sporadic and violence re-emergence still lurks.

As the geopolitical centre of gravity shifts to Asia in the 21st century, India finds itself in a geographically strategic position at the heart of South Asia and at the crossroads of the economically explosive Far East and the energy-rich regions of the Middle East and the Central Asian republics. Although India's rise is inevitable, it constitutes part of a readjustment to a three century adverse reality which saw western dominance. Now Asia is reclaiming its natural and historic place in the global economy.

Consequently, India is pursuing a policy of strategic pragmatism, exploiting its status as an emerging power to forge relationships of necessity and convenience, based on its basic needs and interests, particularly in the energy sector, which will significantly impact the pace and extent of its immediate and long-term growth. With nuclear-armed neighbours, China and Pakistan, India's policy of pragmatism becomes even more critical.

The commonalities between the US and India include democratic forms of government, language, a shared value for entrepreneurialism and confidence in the future, concern for terrorism and the spread of weapons of mass destruction and a willingness to project power abroad. India is, however, not keen to become embroiled in a balance-of-power game as it would not serve its interests. Although few dispute India's potential for great power status, its path to achieving such status is a long one marked by enormous, but not insurmountable, challenges.

India's long-term interests are more naturally aligned with those of Asia than with those of the distant US. India's main ties to the US are based on trade and security. If the 21st century is to be an 'Asian century,' India's passivity in the international arena has to end.

China and India

Whereas China began its process of economic liberalization under Deng Xiaoping in 1979, India began its opening in 1991 by necessity in reaction to a severe financial crisis. China's astronomical growth over the past 25 years has clearly impacted the Indian psyche and made the desire to "catch up" with China a near national obsession. However, outstanding territorial disputes along the Himalayan borders still exist. Although a silent mutual understanding has emerged in recent years to temporarily sideline such disputes, the lack of precisely defined borders makes the resolution of the border problem difficult. The Tibet issue is covered in three articles in this Year Book.

China has also proven more successful in the competition for energy resources. A memorandum of understanding between India and China was designed to improve cooperation on energy questions, but it realistically amounts to an agreement to combine diplomatic muscle whenever necessary to dictate mutually convenient terms to third party states being targeted for investments in the energy sector. However, competition on the energy front will continue as both states pursue economic growth.

Despite China's spectacular growth and its significant economic and material advantages over India, India retains a long-term political advantage, which is not easily calculable in the short-term. India's economic reforms, however slow, are taking place within a democratic framework; the institutions of civil society are established and continue to strengthen as economic change takes place. Considering the magnitude of India's size, population and diversity, the Indian process of reform is a significant achievement, particularly in light of a multi-party coalition government.

China is attempting to increase transparency and accountability at the local level in order to reduce corruption, principally regarding infrastructure development projects that impact the livelihood of ordinary citizens, and to narrow the gap between urban and rural and coastal and interior regions. However, this does not emanate from a deliberate choice to reform but rather the fear and threat of domestic instability and internal strife in terms of violent protests that could result in civil disorder and fragmentation. Reports of tens of thousands of protests in China's rural regions have further fuelled these fears.

Once regarded as a liability, India's enormous and continuously growing population is now considered an economic asset set to overtake China as the world's most populous nation. As a result of years of strict policies to control population growth in China, the ratio of the working population to total population will diminish in the future. For many in international business, China is the world's blue-collar workforce and India is the world's white-collar assembly line. However, both countries are seeking to improve capabilities in different fields. China is trying to improve its Information Technology sector and India is focusing beyond IT to push growth of its manufacturing and agricultural sectors. This necessitates greater deregulation and massive investments in developing infrastructure, principally in the transportation system. Today, China spends nine times more than India on infrastructure.

It remains in the long-term mutual interests of China and India that they continue to develop ties, cultivate relations and increase cooperation on all fronts in order to ensure uninterrupted and peaceful economic growth and global stability. Their bilateral trade is set to surpass $30 billion this year and the two countries would achieve the 2010 target of $40 billion much before that date.[2]

[2] *http://www.ians.in/loginexists-news.php*

Peace and Security

Nation-building in South Asia has been very fractured and difficult. No other part of India or South Asia has been subjected to such a prolonged violent struggle, which has held development for ransom as the Northeastern region of India. Violent and vociferous demands by various ethnic groups for independence and for new states have been occurring over the past five decades. The fire of insurgency has long engulfed this strategic region making it one of South Asia's most disturbed areas. Bound by four countries (Bhutan, Bangladesh, China and Myanmar), the region has immense geopolitical significance. There are a large variety of conflicting dynamics in the North East, ranging from insurgency for secession, to insurgency for autonomy, from sponsored terrorism to ethnic clashes, to problems of continuous inflow of migrants and the fight over resources.

Illicit trafficking in small arms is closely aligned with that of narcotic drugs. Arms are usually exchanged for drugs, which can lead to far larger profits and can also be used for laundering money and enriching individual fortunes. The Golden Triangle, the largest drug producing area outside Afghanistan where illicit opium production and refining takes place has close proximity with this region. The North Eastern region has a 1,643 kilometre border with Myanmar, the main source of the opium trade. Myanmar produces 80% of the heroin in South-East Asia and is responsible for 60% of the world's supply. Northeast India furnishes trafficking routes for Myanmarese heroin as many heroin labs are located near the border. There are more than 19 trafficking routes from Myanmar to the North East.

Small arms proliferation and narcotics impedes development, which breeds the discontent that feeds insurgency. It is the reality of today's world that small arms have emerged as weapons of mass destruction, killing half a million people globally each year. South Asia has seen a massive proliferation of small arms in the last two decades. Armed violence has become an everyday reality in the region which, ironically, introduced the concept of Ahimsa (non-violence) to the world. The damage done by small arms ranges from outright killings to maiming and mutilation, from rape to all possible violations of human life. Young boys brandishing small arms kidnap, extort, and loot innocent civilians to buy their weapons and then live off them. In addition to the enormous, critical damage done to the education system, the development of resources and of infrastructure has been crippled by insurgency.

The fact that large expanses of territories in so-called failed states escape government control need no longer be considered a regrettable feature of the post-modern world, but rather a strategic challenge that should be addressed urgently. The longer Pakistan's military runs the country, the more it alienates itself from the people it has sworn to protect. The situation in the North West Frontier Province and the Federally Administered Tribal Areas in Pakistan (adjoining Afghanistan) is a major problem that requires surgical action. There are two levels of conflict. First, is between the state and the illegal armed groups, and second between the Taliban leaders and the local administration and tribal elders.

The longer most leaders stay in power, the more their record is likely to become tarnished. General Pervez Musharraf has been in charge of Pakistan for eight years - a longer period than any other leader except for Zia-ul-Haq and Ayub Khan. The essence of representative government and checks against abuse of power are an independent judiciary, an independent media, and political parties that chose their own leaders and that are held accountable by the electorate for their shortcomings. Pakistan cannot become the moderate, progressive, enlightened state that Musharraf and the Qaid-i-Azam have envisioned unless these conditions are met. Dictatorships, essentially, rob people of their future.

In the political sphere, Bhutan is scheduled to change from a monarchy to a two-party democratic system in 2008.

Climate Change

Most climate projections indicate increasing monsoon variability, resulting in increases in both flood and drought intensity in South Asia. Some of the most vulnerable regions in the world to sea level rise are in South Asia, along the coasts of Pakistan, India, Sri Lanka, Bangladesh, and Myanmar, with the Maldives being particularly threatened. Almost 40% of the regions population lives within 50 kilometres of its coastline. About 10% of Bangladesh lies within three feet above mean sea level. Over the next century, population rise, land scarcity and frequent ?ooding, coupled with increased storm surge and sea level rise could cause millions of people to cross the border into India. Migration across the border to India is already such a concern that India is building a fence to keep Bangladeshis out. Water availability a?ecting agricultural productivity and increased e?ects of infectious disease are other primary climate e?ects expected to cause problems in South Asia.

India and Pakistan have long, densely populated and low-lying coastlines that are very vulnerable to sea level rise and storm surge. Studies have predicted that by the end of this century, due to the rise in sea levels —ranging anywhere between 0.18 and 0.59 metres— South Asia will witness an increase in soil salinity and erosion of agricultural land, which will affect thousands of people living in the coastal areas. Possible increases in the frequency and intensity of storm surges could be disproportionately large in heavily developed coastal areas and also in low-income rural areas, particularly such low-lying cities such as Mumbai, Dhaka and Karachi.

By 2050, South Asia, which is dependent on glacial melting for water may face serious consequences from vanishing glaciers on the Tibetan plateau, could be among the hardest hit regions. The Gangotri glacier is receding at a rate of 17.15 metres per year (1971-2004) and suffered a retreat of 12.10 metres during 2004-05. Scientists believe that the recession of glaciers in the area cannot be checked due to various reasons, including pollution, lack of economic feasibility and the nature of the Indian Himalayan glaciers. The situation appears to be rather grim.[3]

Defence Expenditure

The defence expenditure of countries covered in this Year Book, as well as other high-bracket countries, is given in the table below:

Rank	Country	Military expenditures (USD)		Date of information
	World	Total	1,200,000,000,000	2007 (estimate)
	NATO	Total	849,875,309,000	
	European Union	Total	300,745,000,000	
1	United States		553,000,000,000	2007
2	United Kingdom		72,894,000,000	2007
3	France		67.640,000,000	2007
4	Germany		52,100,000,000	2007
5	Japan		49,100,000,000	2007
6	China		45,000,000,000	2007 (official figures)
7	Russia		32,400,000,000	2007
8	Italy		32,093,537,000	2006 (estimate)
9	Saudi Arabia		31,255,000,000	2007
10	South Korea		26,050,000,000	2005
11	India		21,330,000,000	2007
12	Australia		18,200,000,000	2007
13	Canada		16,900,000,000	2007
14	Spain		15,792,207,000	2006
15	Turkey		15,166,000,000	2007
22	Singapore		7,053,000,000	2007
28	Pakistan		4,800,000,000	2006
47	Thailand		1,775,000,000	NA
48	Malaysia		1,690,000,000	NA
53	Indonesia		1,300,000,000	2004
58	Bangladesh		1,008,000,000	2005
72	Sri Lanka		606,200,000	2005
109	Afghanistan		122,400,000	2005
115	Nepal		104,900,000	2005
132	Maldives		45,070,000	2005
138	Myanmar		39,000,000	NA
163	Bhutan		8,281,000	2005

[3] *Asian Age; New Delhi; 31 March 2006*

ISSUES

INDIA AND THE WORLD BALANCE OF POWER

Dr K Subrahmanyam
Former Director, IDSA, New Delhi

Balance of Power before Nuclear Era

Throughout history, rulers have resorted to balance of power as a strategy to augment their own interests and security. This was so before the concept of nation state developed and continued thereafter. The 18th and 19th centuries demonstrated how the balance of power game was played in Europe and finally brought to an end the Napoleonic wars with the Congress of Vienna. 19th century Europe saw a number of balance of power wars and finally resulted in the emergence of Germany, France, Russia, Austria-Hungary and Britain as the major balancers. That balance of power broke down with the outbreak of the First World War. After an interim pause of 20 years the Second World War broke out, which ended with the total victory of Western alliance and emergence of nuclear weapons as an ultimate weapon.

The balance power in the pre-nuclear era was not a permanent phenomenon. It was usually an attempt by states to develop alliance relationships which would be beneficial to them if a war broke out. A common misperception is that balance of power led to stability and peace over a period of time. This was not entirely true. During the 19th century, when Balance of Power was being pursued by major nations in Europe there were wars between Prussia and Austria, Prussia and France; war to unify Italy, wars in the Balkans and the Crimean war. These wars were fought between Armies and civilian casualties hardly occurred.

This situation changed with the First World War when wars engulfed civilian populations. During this period, Nations tended to form alliances to strengthen their respective positions and bargaining power and capabilities to fight wars, if necessary. The First and Second world wars were fought between two alliances. With the introduction of aerial bombing and large mechanized armies, wars became total and tended to cause civilian casualties exceeding military casualties. The end of the Second World War saw the development of the atom bomb which was intended to be and was used as a weapon of mass destruction.

The end of the Second World War coincided with the emergence of two adversarial ideologies – Democracy and market capitalism as against centralized socialist planning and communist party dictatorship. The end of the war also triggered off decolonisation and development of a universal nation-state system of the United Nations expanding from 51 members in 1945 to 192 at present. The conflicting ideologies led to two confronting military blocs with the newly-emerging ex-colonial nations staying out of the military blocs and forming the non-aligned movement.

A widespread understanding developed over decades that the nuclear weapons were the ultimate weapons and any war using them would not result in victory to one or the other side but in unacceptable casualties and damage to both. Therefore, for the first time in history, two confronting military blocs armed to the teeth with weapons that could have destroyed the human civilization several times over, after an eyeball to eyeball confrontation of four decades decided to sit across the table and conclude a peace agreement and cut their forces. This happened on 19 November 1990 at Paris and had no historical precedence.

The Cold War ended with the Paris agreement. Up to that point of time the Western European nations, Japan, Australia and even China relied on the US for their security and the Eastern European nations looked to the Soviet Union for their security. This was termed a bipolar world and their confrontation from 1949 to 1990 was called the Cold War since no direct hostilities took place between the two sides.

After the Cold War

The Western Cold War strategy was based on a thesis first advocated by the US diplomat, George Kennan. He argued that it was counterproductive to fight a war with the Soviet Union and instead, a better strategy would be containment in which the Soviet Union was contained by the Western alliance politically, militarily, economically and technologically. If that happened over a period of time, internal pressures that would be generated within the Soviet Union would result in its collapse. Though it took some 44 years George Kennan's thesis worked and the Soviet Union collapsed in 1991.

With the dissolution of the Soviet Union, its ideology – communism – also collapsed. In the other major communist power China, the leadership under Deng Xiao Peng had started dismantling the communist ideology from 1979 onwards. While one party dictatorship under the Communist Party was sustained, the economic philosophy and practice of communism was abandoned. Following this development, major democracies no longer felt any threat from Communist powers and did not feel the need for reliance on the US for security as they did in the previous four decades. They did not, however, give up their military alliances, NATO, the ANZUS Pact, the security treaty between Japan and US and the military pact between US and South Korea. These alliances continued though the major powers started asserting their autonomy increasingly.

The result of this development is a new balance of power system. In the earlier eras aggressive nations felt that territorial acquisition was essential to have access to raw materials. Hitler invaded Russia to take possession of Ukrainian wheat fields and Caucasian oil wells. European countries acquired empires to exploit and base their own development on the exploited wealth. The wars in Vietnam, Afghanistan and Iraq prove that, while more sophisticated and better equipped armies can defeat local armies in battles, it is not possible to occupy a country with a population opposed to the occupation and keep it under occupation at an acceptable cost. This is especially true of medium-sized (Iraq and Afghanistan) countries. Only countries with very small populations like Panama and Grenada are vulnerable to occupation.

During the latter half of the 20th century, which was the Cold War period, the currency of international power was nuclear weapons. In the 21st century this is no longer so. The two major powers have cut down their nuclear arsenals and no longer flaunt them as they used to, during the Cold War. Excepting for US, China and Japan most of the Western countries, including Russia, cut back on their military expenditures. The 21st century is considered a period in which knowledge will be the currency of power and a nation's standing in the international hierarchy will be measured by its economic and technological power.

This new international system was described by Prime Minister Manmohan Singh in his address to the Combined Commander's Conference on 20 October 2005:

> "The end of the Cold War, increasing global interdependence, and the global nature of many threats has made strategic concepts developed in a bipolar world irrelevant. The United States has emerged as the dominant economic, military, technological and cultural power. However, the European Union, Russia, China, Japan and India will consolidate their individual position and will be required to play a global role. We must evolve a new paradigm of security cooperation relevant to an emerging multipolar world in which global threats will require global response ..... major powers will seek normal and mutually beneficial relations with the United States. They will also seek to improve bilateral relations with each other, independent of their relations with US. Our strategic policy must orient itself to this new

complexity. We must shed our Cold War shibboleths, rework our relationships with all major powers and emerging economies and improve our relations with all our economic partners and neighbours".

Dr Manmohan Singh's view is not a utopian view. The neo-conservative US Secretary of State, Dr Condoleezza Rice, writing in The Washington Post of 11 December 2005 said, "*For the first time since the peace of Westphalia in 1648, the prospect of violent conflict between Great Powers is becoming ever more unthinkable. Major states are increasingly competing in peace and not preparing for war. To advance this remarkable trend the United States is transforming our partnership with nations such as Japan and Russia, with the European Union and especially with China and India. We are building a more lasting and durable form of global stability, a balance of power that favours freedom.*"

Underlying these perceptions is the worldwide realisation that a nuclear war cannot be won and should not be initiated—a declaration made by President Ronald Reagan of US and General Secretary Gorbachev of the Soviet Union in 1985. Long ago, in the forties, the American strategic thinker, Bernard Brodie analyzing the implications of the nuclear weapons in international relations said that the role of the military was no longer to fight and win wars but to prevent wars from breaking out. The history of the last 60 years has proved Bernard Brodie right. Nuclear deterrence has persevered peace. This was also the reason why India, though a strong advocate of a nuclear weapon-free world, finally found it necessary and compelling to conduct nuclear tests and declare itself a nuclear weapon state. This decision to acquire nuclear weapons was taken by Prime Minister Rajiv Gandhi in 1989 after he failed to persuade the international community to listen to his call for a phased programme of nuclear disarmament in the special session of the UN General Assembly for disarmament in June, 1988. Ironically enough, four US statesmen who have contributed significantly to the evolution of US nuclear strategy, former secretaries of state Dr Henry Kissinger and George Schultz, former Defence Secretary, William Perry and former chairman of the Senate Armed Services Committee, Senator Sam Nunn, in a joint article published in the Wall Street Journal on 4 January 2007 have referred to Rajiv Gandhi's plan for nuclear disarmament and have called on the US to take the initiative to move towards a nuclear weapon free world.

The Present Era

In today's world no rational nation would think of embarking on a course of aggressive action that might lead to nuclear war because no strategic, political or economic objective is worth the damage likely to be caused to the initiator of the nuclear war in terms of human casualties and economic and environmental damage. There are very serious doubts about the practical feasibility of war termination once a nuclear exchange is initiated. It is against this background that US strategists have concluded that the prospect of violent conflicts among the major powers has become increasingly unthinkable. It should be noted carefully that while wars among major nuclear weapon powers is ruled out wars between major and medium powers (US-Iraq war, US-Afghanistan war) between medium powers (Indo-Pakistan and Iraq-Iran war) and small powers and bigger powers (Kuwait and Iraq) could occur. Balance of power is among the major powers. They will continue to play the game of acquiring influence over medium and smaller powers to gain advantage for themselves vis-à-vis their major power rivals. That is an inherent part of international politics.

At the same time it should be clearly recognized that military power has diminishing utility. The problem of military occupation has already been referred to. In addition, there are difficulties in developed countries in raising large armies. Conscription has become unpopular and most of the industrialized countries have abandoned it. Populations are also unwilling to see their sons and daughters killed in distant lands for causes not immediately related to their own national security. Thus, one sees the mighty US, which once could field its NATO forces in central Europe and field 500,000 men in Vietnam, now finding itself overstretched with less than 150,000 men in Iraq.

There is also increasing recognition all over the world that there are new international threats. They are international terrorism, religious extremism, proliferation of weapons of mass destruction, pandemics, organized crime, narcotics and human trafficking, climate change etc. These threats cannot be handled by any single power, however mighty it may be. In addition there is the threat posed by failing states which become launching pads for many of the above threats.

India's Situation

This is the international milieu in which India has made its entry as the last member of the balance of power. There is a tendency, in some quarters in our country, to regard that it was our inherent right to be a major player in the international system ever since we became independent-based on the size of our country and our population. The world did not recognize us to be such a major player. India was importing food and was dependent on foreign aid. Our military weakness was exposed in 1962. There were widespread doubts, both within India and abroad, whether this highly diversified country with so many religions, languages, ethnicities, largely illiterate, growing at the annual rate of measly 3.5 percent would be able to survive as an integrated and united country or would break up. Excepting for Pakistan and China the rest of the world was sympathetic to the Indian experiment but did not think of India as a major power entitled to have its say as a major player in the international system.

That started changing after the end of the Cold War and after India launched on its economic liberalization in 1991, after coming very close to bankruptcy. That unleashed the Indian entrepreneurship. India attempted to integrate itself with the international system, economically and politically. India became an Information Technology power; Indian growth rate rose firstly to six percent and then climbed on to 8 and 9. India conducted nuclear and missile tests. Militarily, India forced Pakistan to vacate the Kargil intrusion without escalating the conflict. Indian companies became global. India became a major market in the world with the prospect of potentially becoming the 5th or 4th largest market in the world. Now along with China, India with its high growth rate is regarded as a likely engine of global growth, even as the industrialized economies slow down. Consequently, the world took notice of India as it did of China in the eighties.

As other countries like Brazil, South Africa, Indonesia, Mexico, South Korea and Nigeria grow and their share in the international economic pie increases in size they too will become balancers. But that is some time away. The engine of growth today is young skilled working population and application of technology and organizational skills. The key to this growth is education, health and infrastructure.

India has certain advantages, as well as problems, in growing further as a major economic and technological power rivaling China. The crucial advantage India has is of a young population. In other major powers China, Japan, Russia and European Union the population is ageing and soon they will reach an unfavourable position of a relatively smaller working population having to support a much larger sized non-working aged population. In such circumstances their growth rate is bound to fall. Only India and US have populations still relatively young. The US Under Secretary of State, Nicholas Burns gave the US assessment of the future in 21st century in his speech in the Asia Society on 18 October, 2005. He said *"India is a rising global power. Within the first quarter of this century, it is likely to be numbered among the world's five largest economies. It will soon be the world's most populous nation and it has a demographic structure that bequeaths it a huge skilled and youthful workforce."*

As nations develop, China with its over ten percent annual growth rate is expected to overtake US in terms of gross national product (GNP) in terms of purchase parity prices (PPP) in the next couple of decades. China is also engaged in a major effort to out produce US in terms of engineers, technicians, scientists, doctors and biological scientists. The US, which has been the preeminent global economic, technological and military power, has reasons to worry about China overtaking it not in GNP in PPP terms but also in technological and economic terms.

The US is also aware that the global economic centre of gravity is shifting from the trans-Atlantic area where it had been situated for the last four centuries to the Asian Pacific region. Five out of six balancers of power China, Japan, Russia, European Union and India are in Eurasia. There are worries among US, Japan, European Union and Russia that China would emerge as a pre-eminent power in Eurasia. Therefore, all the powers other than China would prefer India to grow rapidly not to be against China militarily or to contain China but to balance China.

Similarly the other major powers of the world China, Japan, Russia and the European Union would like the pre-eminence of US to be balanced to the extent possible by the combined weight of other powers. Therefore, they would be in favour of the growth of India, Presently, and that of Indonesia, Brazil and South Africa, in future, so that the US share in the global economy and technology will progressively decline.

A Prognosis

This is where a basic difference in the world views of Prime Minister Manmohan Singh and a large number of other political leaders, still in the grip of Cold War thinking, emerge. Dr Manmohan Singh is convinced that in the new balance of power situation the global forces are favourable to India's rapid growth and development. Those with Cold War mindset believe that there are other powers who are hostile to India's growth (China is usually cited) and others believe that US wants to make India a subordinate partner to contain China. There will no doubt be competition and cooperation among the major powers with the object of advancing their respective self-interests. Whether it is in a bilateral relationship or one involving a larger number of major nations, each power will attempt to maximize its benefits. When it comes to economic and technological transactions or to politics, every power will attempt to increase its influence in as many countries as possible. That is what the balance of power is all about!

Since there is an inherent competition between US and China, the US will be looking for partners who can help it to sustain its technological pre-eminence. India shares its value system (democracy and market-based economy) with the US and is an English speaking country. In the last three decades, when Indo-US relations for most of the period were not cordial, an Indo-American community was built up in US and it has now reached 3 million. This community consists to a significant extent of highly skilled personnel. Indians in US are said to constitute the first or second ethnic community in terms of high income. The Indian contribution to US technology has been so significant that captains of industry like Bill Gates are pleading with the US Congress to allow immigration of Indian technicians without any ceiling in quotas. Many major US industries have been outsourcing their business processes and component and subsystem manufactures to India. In addition, many top US industrial establishments are opening R&D centres in India. In a competitive global economy US is compelled to off-source services and manufacture to India to reduce its costs and remain competitive in the international market.

Given these circumstances, Washington is bound to prefer the buildup of the Indian community in US. Already Indians make the largest student community and are next only to the Mexicans in seeking visas to US. In that sense there is a better natural affinity between India and US than there is between India and any other major power. This relationship at the popular level is bound to grow irrespective of the relationship between the Governments.

India does not have a clash of national interests with the European Union, Russia and Japan. The past unhappy relationship of US with India was due to US reliance on Pakistan as an ally, first during the Cold War, then as a go-between to China and later during the anti-Soviet war in Afghanistan. With China, India has territorial disputes. China has armed Pakistan with nuclear weapon technology missiles and sophisticated conventional arms. China has also encouraged other neighbours of India in their unfriendliness towards this country. Therefore, India's problems in playing a sophisticated balance of power game to its advantage are in respect of China and US. As it happens, these two are potential rivals. US is looking to India as a partner in helping it to sustain its technological lead over China in the long run. China is attempting to block India from cooperating too closely with the US to its disadvantage. China is also trying to use its ideological friends in India to oppose enhancing Indo-US ties.

The US currently needs Pakistan in the global war on terrorism. Yet it has decided to de-hyphenate India and Pakistan and deal with India independent of its policy towards Pakistan. The US, after six years of treating Pakistan as a partner in the war on terrorism, is openly expressing disillusionment. As of now the US has not gained fully India's confidence to be a strategic partner. Indians complain that the terrorism in India, originating from Pakistani entities, has not been condemned adequately by US. Also, US military aid to Pakistan has gone far beyond its legitimate requirement to fight terrorism. There has been a recent change in Pakistani policy as its forces are engaging the Taliban *jehadi* militias in direct combat.

China did not believe that India would survive united, in the fifties and sixties. Thereafter China tried to use Pakistan as a surrogate nuclear threat to India and fully exploited US-India estrangement. After Indian economic liberalization, China used to refer to India's role as a regional player, refusing to acknowledge India as a global power. However, China quickly changed its stance soon after US announced its intention to help India in its efforts to become a world class power. China took the initiative to improve its commercial and political links with India. At the same time it has not yielded any ground on the territorial dispute.

There has been growing tension between US and Russia, mostly due to US attempts to increase its influence in the former Soviet republics, the US attempt to set up missile defence in Eastern Europe and the expansion of NATO. Russia is the only power which has capabilities comparable to US in the field of strategic weapons. The Russians feel that the US has tended to take them for granted and not displayed adequate sensitivity to Russian concerns in their own neighbourhood. The US is also trying to wean away the former Soviet Republics around the Caspian Sea with oil and gas reserves.

In turn, Russia has joined the China-sponsored Shanghai Cooperation Organisation (SCO). Russia and China have conducted joint military exercises along with other SCO countries, Kyrgyzstan, Kazakhstan, Tajikistan and Uzbekistan. India, Pakistan, Iran and Mongolia have been attending the SCO as observers. Russia, China and India have also trilateral consultations on a regular basis.

Russia is the largest arms supplier to China and India. In turn, it needs these markets if it is to develop and produce modern weapons. India has an agreement with Russia to produce the fifth generation combat aircraft. Russia has also agreed to lease out to India two nuclear propelled submarines. Russia is constructing two nuclear reactors in India and has expressed its willingness to construct four more after India gets the Nuclear Suppliers Group waiver.

India has had a traditional defence relationship with Russia going back to Indo-Soviet MiG agreement of 1962. India concluded with the Soviet Union a peace and friendship treaty to countervail the US-Pakistan-China axis during the Bangladesh war. But till the end of the Cold War, presumably in line with its non-alignment policy, India did not have any military exercise with any country, not even with the Soviet Union from which it derived 70 percent of its equipment. After the end of the Cold War, India started holding military exercises, starting with naval exercises, in the Arabian Sea with the US Navy. In a balance of power world India must hold exercises with all major powers. The criticism from certain quarters about the Quadrilateral Naval exercise of India, US, Japan and Australia as one intended against China is meaningless in the balance of power world. The Indian Ocean area is the sea way to large amount of energy traffic. It is subject to threats of piracy and there are fears of maritime terrorism. The US, Australia and India are Indian Ocean powers. With the US Navy the largest, Japan is a major stakeholder in respect of energy traffic. Therefore such quadrilateral exercises are logical and not directed against any other nation.

Conclusion

In playing the role of a balancer of power, in the current six-nation balance of power, India will have both opportunities and challenges. Such a balance of power game in a world in which war among major powers is of extremely low probability because of the existence of nuclear weapons is historically unprecedented. India as well as other powers are still learning to play the game. However, one elementary principle stands out. The bargaining strength in this balance of power vis-à-vis a particular major nation depends to a large extent on the maintenance of good relations with the competitors of the concerned power. India's relations with China, Japan and ASEAN improved as India enhanced its relations with US. Identifying very closely in political terms with any major power limits the manoeuvrability for a player. So does a palpable adversarial attitude towards any of the powers. People tend to forget that non-alignment was balance of power in a bipolar world where the two major powers were unable to go to war with each other because of the existence of nuclear weapons. That was non-alignment, as a strategy, as formulated by Jawaharlal Nehru. Unfortunately non-alignment as interpreted by many in the country was a kind of isolationalism and neutralism.

India, is recognized by the world as a rising power with potential to become one of the leading markets of the world. Many Indian companies have global footprints and the Indian diasporas has a significant role to play. India represents one sixth of the global population. Thus India is going to play a global role. That role cannot be a subservient role to any other power. Therefore, it can only be as a major balancer in the global balance of power.

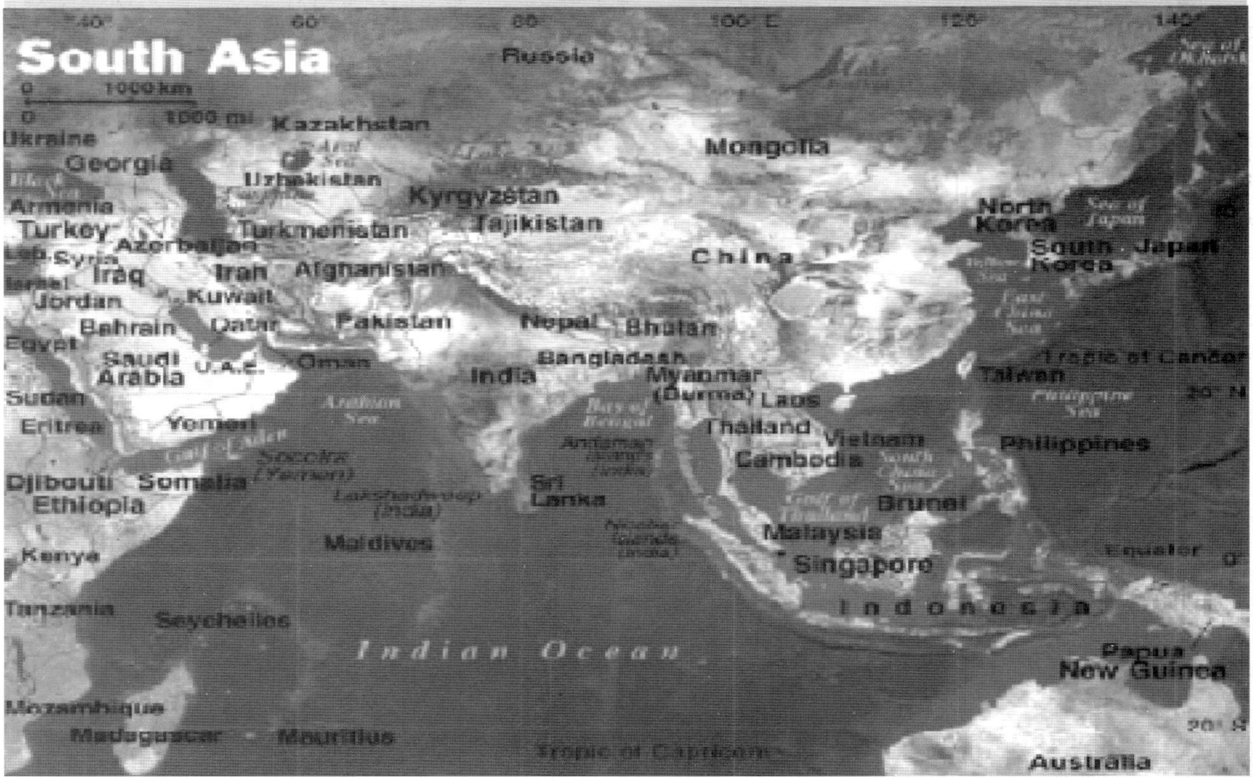

CONFLICTS AND COOPERATION IN SOUTH ASIA

Kalim Bahadur

Former Professor, Jawaharlal Nehru University, New Delhi

The South Asian Region

The South Asian region comprises of eight[1] countries and occupies a strategic location in Asia. It is also one of the poorest, illiterate, malnourished, least gender sensitive and deprived region of the world. It comprises about 22% of the world's total population. Nearly 40% of the world's poor live in this region. About 35% of the population is living with daily income of less than one dollar. Almost all the countries of this region are facing problems of poverty, illiteracy, unemployment, diseases, income inequality, low productivity and dependence on agricultural sector. Thus the socio-economic condition of this region as a whole is in shambles.[2]

Most of these countries have a history of direct or indirect colonial rule and also have a history of common struggle against imperialism. India, Pakistan, Bangladesh, Sri Lanka and Maldives were formally under direct British rule. India and Pakistan emerged out of the first partition of India and Bangladesh seceded after a freedom struggle from Pakistan, in 1971. Nepal, Bhutan and Afghanistan were formally independent but were under the British sphere of influence. Because of the common history, religion and culture and also of the economic and social problems inherited from their colonial past it was hoped that the countries of South Asia after gaining freedom would come together, cooperate, reconstruct and rebuild their countries for the benefit of the entire region.

All the countries of South Asia are multi-ethnic, multi-linguistic and multi-religious societies. However, various problems which have been the legacy of imperialism have led to bitter rivalries and conflicts among them. Nevertheless, there are some unique features of the South Asian region which have led to conflicts and also make cooperation amongst them an urgent necessity. The eight countries of South Asia are not even roughly equal in size, population and economic development. India dominates the region and is larger than all the other countries combined in size, population and economic strength. Almost all the countries of South Asia have a common border with

---

[1] *Afghanistan became the 14th SAARC Summit held in New Delhi on 3 April 2007*

[2] *Greater Kashmir; Srinagar; (Online Edition); 28 October 2007*

India, or have direct access to it, except Afghanistan which has a common border with Pakistan but not with India. The difference in size of India with other South Asian countries is so large that it creates a psychological barrier between India and its neighbours e.g. the population of India is estimated to be 1,129 million, within an area of 1,269, 338 square miles, whereas the population of the Maldives is estimated to be 300,000, within an area of 400 square miles.[3] Because of the big difference in size and power in comparison with other smaller states, identification of common interests in the region is most difficult.[4]

There is no doubt that the economies of the South Asian countries have tremendous potential which, if properly directed, can lead to the benefit of the entire region. Since 1996 the GDP growth rate in Bangladesh, Bhutan, India, Maldives, Nepal, and Sri Lanka has exceeded 5 percent a year. Pakistan has been growing at that pace since 2000. Afghanistan's economy has been set back because of prolonged civil war, foreign invasions and insurgencies. During the past two years India and Pakistan have grown at 7 percent. In order to remove poverty they will have to raise and sustain growth at 8-10 percent per year.[5]

Internal Conflicts

The conflicts in South Asian are broadly of two kind's viz. domestic and international. These conflicts also include foreign interventions e.g. the Soviet and American intervention in Afghanistan and the Indian peacekeeping venture in Sri Lanka. Domestic conflicts are mainly ethnic, linguistic and religious. They are mainly the legacies of the colonial past. These conflicts are fallout of the failure of the nation building by the ruling classes after freedom from foreign rule.

India has a variety of ethnic, social, and political conflicts. The insurgencies in Assam, Manipur, and Bodoland have not been resolved. In the eighties the ethnic movement in Punjab developed into a separatist movement which led to the tragic events at the Golden Temple in 1984. The socio-economic movement, also called the Naxalite movement in Bihar, Jharkhand and some districts of Andhra is also a major flash point for violence. Religion-based communal movements in India have assumed violent forms.

In Bangladesh democracy has been fragile. There have been frequent military coups and martial law regimes. The insurgency in the Chittagong Hill Tracks is a source of instability. Democratization in Bangladesh has been an intermittent byplay of confrontationist and constitutional politics.[6] The recent postponement of elections and the intervention of the military in the political domain could explode into a mass movement for the restoration of democracy if elections continue to be put off on one excuse or the other. Bangladesh may be in for tenure of military rule?

Nepal is also undergoing political upheaval ever since the assassination of the late monarch, King Birendra along with some of his family members, in 2001. Whereas the Maoists seem to threaten the weak roots of democracy, King Gyanendra assumed autocratic powers to restore absolute monarchy, which was resisted by the people. He was forced by the popular movement to hand over power to the elected representatives of the people. However, due to the inability of the political parties to reach a consensus on the fate of the monarchy, and the contours of the new constitution, normalcy has yet to be restored in Nepal. The situation is still uncertain in Nepal as reflected by the recent postponement of the election.[7]

The ethnic conflict in Sri Lanka has grown into a civil war which has eluded a solution over two decades. Sinhalese and Lanka Tamils have lived in the island for more than two thousand years, whereas the Tamils of Indian origin were brought there by the colonial rulers, mainly as indentured workers on British-owned plantations. The Muslims migrated to Sri Lanka from West Asia and India and formed an ethno-religious community in pre-colonial times. The Lanka Tamils, most of who live in the northern region, have experienced discrimination for several decades. In the national elections of 1977, they voted overwhelmingly for the Tamil United Liberation Front (TULF), an alliance of all the parliamentary parties of the north, which had concluded that the Tamil national question could not be resolved within a unitary state and therefore demanded a separate Tamil state called Eelam. The Sinhalese nationalist forces and the Tamil nationalist groups came to regard armed confrontation as the only possible mechanism to resolve ethnic antagonisms. This led to the armed struggle to achieve

---

[3] *www.ifoplease.com/ipa/A0004379.html*

[4] *Kh Atiar Rahman; "The Conflicts of Ethnic Groups of South Asian Region." www.articlebase.com/print/227473 Accessed on 13/10/07*

[5] *http://web.worlbank.org/*

[6] *Kumar Rupsinghe and Khawar Mumtaz; (Eds.); Internal Conflicts in South Asia; 1996; London; Sage Publications Ltd; p. 109*

[7] *"Editorial", Rising Nepal; Khatmandu; 10 October 2007*

a separate Tamil state. Another political conflict within the Sinhalese society, the JVP led political campaign, ended only with the annihilation of the JVP. The LTTE led insurgency goes on unabated.[8] The TULF had envisaged the path to Eelam as peaceful and non-violent.

Internal conflicts in Pakistan threaten the very existence of the country. Some of them have implications for Pakistan's external relations. At present the country is facing both ethnic and Islamic extremist insurgencies. The insurgency in Balochistan broke out some years ago mainly when the people demanded a greater share in decision-making on development plans in their own province. Their major grievance was that Balochis did not benefit from the gas and oil in their province and also against the extremely low representation of the Balochis in government service, as well as police and the armed forces.[9] In August 2006 the Balochi leader Akbar Bugti was killed by the army. Since then the violence has aggravated. The state's writ no longer runs in large swathes of Pakistan territory in Chitral, Swat, Waziristan and Balochistan. Islamic militancy which was given governmental encouragement during Pakistan's intervention in the war in Afghanistan in the 1980's is coming back to haunt Pakistan's ruling classes. It is clear that religious extremism has become a major threat to internal stability in Pakistan. It is not easy for the military regime to control the situation. One major problem is that the extremists are not organized under one party but are a variety of tribal and ethnic-based groups with different agendas and different interpretations of Islam. The situation is further complicated by the rise of sectarian conflicts, e.g. Shia versus Sunni and Deobandi versus Barelvi, and the recent incident in July 2007 when a group of hard-line militants holed themselves in the Lal Masjid in the centre of Islamabad and attempted to blackmail the administration to accept their demands in the name of religion. They could be removed only after army action with heavy loss of life.

Afghanistan, which is new member of the South Asian family, is a multi-ethnic and multi-language nation though almost 99 percent of the population is Muslim. The country has been facing political instability ever since the overthrow of the King Zahir Shah in 1973 by his cousin Sardar Mohammad Daoud, who was himself toppled by the leftist Khalq party in 1978.The left regime suffered from factionalism, from within, and the violent hostility of its opponents, from without. The Soviet intervention in 1979 turned the country into a war zone through their proxies when the United States decided to jump into the fray on behalf of the Mujahideen. The withdrawal of the Soviet forces did not bring peace to the country. The US and Pakistan fought the war in the name of Jihad but the Jihadis were unable to give the country a united government. In the early nineties Pakistani agencies promoted a new extremist militant group, called the Taliban. This group hosted the al Qaida leader, Osama Bin Laden. The United States invaded Afghanistan in the wake of 9/11 in October 2001 and decimated the Taliban. The country is now facing war from the resurgent Taliban which the NATO forces do not appear to be winning. The Karzai regime does not have the legitimacy or the popular support to overcome the challenges it is facing.[10]

Intra Regional Conflicts and Foreign Powers

Some South Asian countries have used close relations with outside powers to use them in case of need against India. Nepal has often used the China card against India. The Myanmar military junta also uses the China card similarly. Pakistan's military alliance with the US since the early fifties was obviously directed against India. This alliance failed Islamabad during the 1971 war with India. Since then, Pakistan has sought close relations with the Peoples Republic of China. India's 1971 Treaty of Friendship and Cooperation with the Soviet Union was mainly aimed against American intervention on the side of Pakistan during the war in East Pakistan. The Soviet Union intervened in Afghanistan to protect the leftist regime, leading to Pakistan joining hands with the US to support the Mujahideen's Jihad against the Soviet army.

India-Pakistan Relations

Intra-regional conflicts in South Asia could be divided into two categories -between India and Pakistan, and between India and other the South Asian countries.[11] A recent conflict is the one between Pakistan and Afghanistan. The most important conflict is between India Pakistan, where hostility has persisted for the

[8] *Rupsinghe and Mumtaz; n. no. 6; p. 119*
[9] *Kalim Bahadur; "The Turmoil in Balochistan"; Aakrosh; New Delhi; July 2005; Vol. 8;.No. 28; p.45*
[10] *Barnett R. Rubin; "Saving Afghanistan"; Foreign Affairs; January-February 2007*
[11] *Kanti Bajpai; "Crisis and Conflict South Asia after September 11, 2001" in South Asian Survey; Volume 10; Number 2; July-December 2003; New Delhi; p. 197*

last sixty years. Its importance is reflected by the widespread belief that all efforts for South Asian cooperation have come to naught because of this root tension and conflict, which are deep rooted in history and religion.[12]

The partition of the subcontinent, in 1947, was enforced amidst bitter controversies and its aftermath laid grounds for many more. The partition itself led to the largest migration in history because of religion. India and Pakistan were at war within a few weeks of independence in October 1947. India had almost 560 princely states and their relations with British were different from that of rest of India which was called the British India. The partition plan had made no specific provision for the future of these states except that each state will have to accede to either India or Pakistan which meant that no princely state could be independent. Moreover, the decision for accession to either of the two dominions would be made only by the ruler. Three accessions became controversial. These were three princely states of Jammu and Kashmir, Junagarh and Hyderabad. The states where the majority of population was Hindu and the ruler was a Muslim - in Hyderabad and Junagarh or where the population was Muslim and the ruler was Hindu - in Jammu and Kashmir.

A condition had been attached to the accession of states. They had to take contiguity into consideration. This meant that a princely state located inside the territory of one dominion could not accede to the other dominion. Hyderabad and Junagarh were located inside the territory of India whereas Jammu and Kashmir was contiguous to both India and Pakistan. The anti-feudal movement in Jammu and Kashmir had been led by Sheikh Muhammad Abdullah, leader of the Jammu and Kashmir National Conference which was ideologically close to the Indian National Congress. The leaders of the Muslim League believed that the Maharaja would not accede to Pakistan and therefore, in a preemptive attempt to stall the accession of the state to India, Pakistan sponsored the invasion of the state by the tribal volunteers who were joined by personnel of Pakistan army.[13] This was the first India-Pakistan war which broke out within the first few weeks of independence. Pakistan has since then claimed Kashmir as the unfinished agenda of partition. The two neigbouring countries have gone to war over the issue of Jammu and Kashmir in 1965 and in 1999.

The princely state of Junagarh was another dispute on the pattern of Jammu and Kashmir. The majority of the people of the state were Hindu but the ruler was Muslim. Pakistan objected to the accession of Jammu and Kashmir to India because of its being a Muslim majority state but had no compunction in accepting the accession of the Hindu-majority state of Junagarh to Pakistan.[14] The people of Junagarh revolted against the ruler and Junagarh remained a part of India.

India-Pakistan conflicts are not confined to Kashmir alone. There were claims and counter claims about the divisions of assets and demarcation of boundaries. Pakistani leaders accused India of trying to undo Pakistan. This mutual perception of hostility was transferred to the respective country's belief of the other as a threat to its sovereignty and territorial integrity. Moreover, leaders of Pakistan failed in the task of nation building and have used the image of a hostile India to unite and integrate the people. The failure of nation building and national integration has led to the emergence of centrifugal tendencies in Pakistan. The failure of democracy and long periods of centralised military rule have fuelled regional separatist movements. The domination of the political system by Punjabis and the suppression of regional languages and cultures promoted strong ethnic movements in East Pakistan, Balochistan, Sind and the North Western Frontier Province.

The inability of the military and bureaucratic rulers of Pakistan to address the ethnic aspirations led to the growth of the separatist autonomy movement in East Pakistan which culminated in the famous Six-Point programme of the Awami League. The military ruler Gen Yahya Khan refused to honour the popular mandate of the 1970 election which had gone in favour of the Awami League, led by Sheikh Mujibur Rahman. This led to the secession of East Bengal in 1971 and the emergence of Bangladesh in the third India- Pakistan war, in that year.

Pakistan under General Zia ul Haq declared that Kashmir was the 'core issue' and in the late seventies sponsored the terrorist campaign in the state of Jammu and Kashmir in the name of Jihad. Initially the

---

[12] *Lt. Gen. Talat Masood, (Retd.); "Kashmir and Indo- Pak conflict."; South Asian Journal; Lahore; August-September 2003; No 1; p. 32*

[13] *Mirza Shafiq Hussain; Azad Kashmir, ek Siyasi Jaeza 1947 ta 1975; Islamabad; 1990; Idara barai Tehqiq wa Saqafat; p. 112*

[14] *Lars Blinkenberg; India –Pakistan: The History of Unsolved Conflicts; Munksgaar; 1972; Dansk Udenigspolitisk Instititutsskrifter 4 p. 98*

movement was started by the Jammu and Kashmir Liberation Front (JKLF) but General Zia turned it into an Islamic movement when several Islamic militant groups were inducted into Jammu and Kashmir in the name of Jihad. After the withdrawal of the Soviet forces a large number militants from other countries which were also inducted into the state of Jammu and Kashmir.[15]

Pakistan-Afghanistan Relations

Afghanistan has been accepted as a member of the South Asian Association for Regional Cooperation (SAARC). This has added another dimension to international relations amongst the South Asian family. Earlier it was the conflict between India and Pakistan which played an important role in determining the activities of SAARC. Pakistan's relations with Afghanistan have also been conflict ridden ever since Pakistan came into being in 1947. Pakistan had assumed that after independence it will inherit the same relationship with Kabul as the British had. Afghanistan voted against the membership of Pakistan in the United Nations. Kabul argued that large chunks of Afghanistan territory had been forcibly transferred by the British imperialist rulers into British Indian territory under a Treaty in 1893 and a new boundary line was imposed upon the country, which was called the Durand line.

The Durand line has divided the Pushtun people and it was never accepted by any of the Afghan regimes that came to power in Kabul. The Pushtun people of the Frontier province had participated in the Indian National movement against the British, under the leadership of Khan Abdul Ghaffar Khan and Mahatma Gandhi. They had been infused with the spirit of non-violence while participating in the freedom struggle. The people of the North Western Frontier Province had been given the option of deciding in a referendum whether they wanted to join Pakistan or India. However, the leaders of the Pushtun people led by Khan Abdul Ghaffar Khan decided to boycott the referendum as they had not been given the option of independence. It is for historians to decide whether that decision to boycott the referendum was correct. Had the people voted for joining with India probably the history of the region would have been different. The Khan Brothers had given the call for uniting the Pushtun people on both sides of the border in Pushtunistan. However, Pakistan projected the idea of Pushtunistan as an example of Indian design to undo Pakistan. The concept of Pushtunistan was never spelt out in detail. Whether it meant the formation of an independent state by uniting the Pushtun population on the both sides of the Durand line, or that the Pushtuns of Pakistan would join Afghanistan or the other way round.

Afghanistan, being a landlocked country, was dependent on Pakistan for access to the outside world. Pakistan used this to browbeat Kabul. Several times during the last sixty years Pakistan has blockaded Afghanistan's trade through Karachi. Pakistan opposed the leftist takeover of Afghanistan in the late seventies and hosted Afghan rebels, Gulbuddin Hekmatyar and late Ahmed Shah Masood, even during the regime of President Mohammad Daoud. Some of the rebel leaders led the fight against the leftist regime in Kabul.

General Zia teamed up with the Americans in their bid to turn Afghanistan into the Soviet Union's Vietnam. Pakistanis were not told that, turning the country into a proxy battlefield between the two superpowers would entail more than just receiving F-16 aircraft. It meant opening the door for all types of militants from different parts of the world to flock to Peshawar on their way to Afghanistan. In October 2001 Pakistan once again lined up with the United States in the latter's 'war on terror'. Ironically, at present, the Musharraf regime is hunting down people who are the children of the Reagan-Zia Jihad. As a result of the Zia and Musharraf policies, the country has become a turf for vicious wars fought over matters that are not solely Pakistan's concern.[16] The Saudis were funding the Jihad, Americans were supplying the weapons and Pakistani agencies were distributing them to favoured Jihadi groups. The Jihad in Afghanistan helped General Ziaul Haq assume the leadership of the Islamic world while before that he was an international pariah for toppling an elected Prime Minister Zulfikar Ali Bhutto and hanging him later. Militants from all over the world mobilized to fight in Afghanistan and Jihad became permissible activity.

Pakistan's foreign policy has been India-centric.[17] All its major foreign policy moves have an India dimension, including the Pakistani Afghan policy and

[15] *Zahid Hussain; Frontline Pakistan: The Struggle with Militant Islam; New Delhi; 2007; Penguin/Viking; p. 25*
[16] *Haider K. Nizamani; "Al Qaida Comes to Pakistan." Dawn; Karachi; 27 October 2007 Online Edition*
[17] *Khaled Ahmed; "Hindrances to Cooperation"; South Asian Journal; August- September, 2003; No.1; p. 12*

attempts to build a Muslim bloc. It is said that Pakistan objective in Afghanistan was to gain strategic depth. Pakistan's lack of depth led to their strategic belief about the fusion of the defences of Afghanistan and Pakistan. Islamabad wanted a regime in Kabul which would be under its influence. Pakistan offended Afghans by attempting to dictate their policies and by positioning itself as a major player in the contemporary version of the Great Game.[18]

India's conflicts with its smaller neighbours like Nepal, Bangladesh and Sri Lanka have been relatively minor issues like river water distribution, border smuggling, and minor territorial disputes. Many of them have been resolved. For example the Mahakali Treaty and the Trade and Transit Treaty with Nepal, the 1996 Treaty on sharing of Ganga waters with Bangladesh and the India Sri Lanka Treaty on Boundary demarcation in the Palk strait. India's intervention in Sir Lanka in 1987 is held to be a mistake which was corrected by withdrawing the army in 1990.

Cooperation in South Asia

There is no gainsaying the fact that there has been a great need for cooperation amongst the countries of South Asia to benefit the people of the region in their social, economic and political development. Any cooperation will have to take into account the peculiar ethnic, geographical, and economic conditions of the region. Ethnic identities in South Asia are not restricted to national frontiers. They spill over across the entire region. Various nationalities are not confined to one country alone. In many cases they are spread over several countries of South Asia and even outside the region. Bengalis not only inhabit Bangladesh but are also present as a major nationality in India. Tamils live in India and Sri Lanka. Same is the case with Muslims, Sikhs, Gurkhas, Sindhis and so on.

The imperative of cooperation among the South Asian countries can be understood by the socio-economic conditions of the people of the region who constitute 25% of the world's total population. Nearly 40% of the world's poor live in this region. All the countries face similar problems like poverty, illiteracy, unemployment, diseases, income inequality, low productivity and dependence on agricultural sector. In order to deal with such challenges SAARC was formed in 1985 and hailed as a major diplomatic breakthrough. But SAARC's slow progress and modest achievements over the past decade have evoked different reactions.

The aim behind the formation of this regional grouping was to strengthen the relationship, on social, cultural, economic and scientific fronts among the seven member countries and thus pave a new way for peace, progress and prosperity in the region.[19] Since the ground situation within which various regional associations work differs, comparison of SAARC's performance with other regional associations will have to be done with caution.[20] There is no doubt that SAARC has not as yet become a cohesive group because some countries have strong suspicions about Indian motives. The controversy about an Indian initiative to form a sub-regional group with Nepal, Bangladesh and Bhutan points to this lack of trust. Though the "growth quadrangle", as the foursome has been called, is aimed essentially at bringing about greater intra-regional cooperation, Pakistan demurred at it just because the initiative came from India.[21] The focus of SAARC was initially to focus on:

1. Agriculture and Rural Development.
2. Health and Population Activities.
3. Women, Youth and Children.
4. Environment and Forestry.
5. Science and Technology and Meteorology.
6. Human Resources Development.
7. Transport.[22]

Later, the SAARC Preferential Trading Arrangement (SAPTA) was signed in 1993 for giving preferential access to exports of the member countries in a limited way. The SAPTA framework provided for periodic rounds of trade negotiation for the exchange of trade concessions on tariff, and para tariff using a combination of negotiating approaches.[23] Following this, during the SAARC Summit in January 2004, an

---

[18] *Husain Haqqani; "The Wind Blows Another Way at the Durand Line"; Indian Express;' New Delhi; 15 March 2006*

[19] *Kishore .C. Dash; "The Political Economy of Regional Cooperation in South Asia"; Pacific Affairs; Vancouver; Vol. 69; No.2; Summer 1996; www.motholyoke.edu/acad/intel/dash.htm*

[20] *Padmaja Murthy; "Relevance of SAARC". Strategic Analysis; New Delhi; Vol; XXXIII; January 2000*

[21] *Indian Express; New Delhi; 15 May 1997*

[22] *www.SAARC-sec.org/main.php?t=2*

[23] *Vijay Katti; "India and the Regional Economic Integration in South Asia:"; India Foreign Affairs Journal; New Delhi; Volume 2, No 4; October-December 2007; p. 94*

agreement on a South Asia Free Trade Area was signed. It was hoped that through SAFTA some of the problems in the intra-regional trade would be removed. However, Pakistan ratified the SAFTA on the condition that free trade with India would not be allowed. According to a Pakistani economist, there was a strong lobby in Pakistan which wanted concessions from India on Kashmir as a price for its entry in SAFTA. On the other hand India would have welcomed Pakistan into SAFTA but would not have regretted if it had it kept out.[24] During the SAARC Summit in New Delhi Pakistan Prime Minister of Pakistan Shaukat Aziz repeatedly hinted that promoting trade with Pakistan was connected to progress in talks on Kashmir.[25]

The founders of the SAARC were mainly moved by the desire to promote cooperation in the socio-economic field and the organization was designed to complement both bilateral and multilateral relations of the SAARC states. The poor performance of SAARC can be attributed to two major factors. One relates to inherent problems in the region, which are not favourable for the promotion of an effective regional grouping in South Asia. These problems are deep historical and cultural differences, and very restricted trade in the region due to competing structures of their economies. However, the scenario in South Asia is not all that pessimistic. India-Pakistan relations, in spite of tensions, are on the upswing. Restrictions and reservations notwithstanding, and without the grant of the most favoured nation status to India by Pakistan, trade between the two countries in 2006-2007 crossed the $ 1 billion mark (almost the double of 2003-2004), and informal trade was $ 2 billion.[26]

Conclusion

There are some inherent economic, political and economic difficulties in developing cooperation in South Asia, some of which have been pointed out. However there have been some achievements also in the cooperative endeavours of the region. Some of the major disputes among the South Asian countries on the distribution of river waters have been resolved. The peace process between India and Pakistan has been progressing at a steady pace and many confidence building measures have improved the general atmosphere in the region. The free trade agreements among some countries in the region have improved the intra-region trade. The proposals for a common market in South Asia and also the suggestion for a South Asian Parliament, if it finds acceptance, will go a long way in promoting peace and cooperation in the region.[27]

[24] *Shahid Javed Burki; "Safta Needs a Patron"; www.dawn.com.pk/2006/2/21/index/htm accessed on 21 February 2006*
[25] *Daily Jang; Karachi; 3 April 2007 Online Edition*
[26] *Daily Times; Lahore; 20 March 2006 Online Edition*
[27] *S.D. Muni; "A South Asian Parliament;" South Asian Journal; No. 6; October-December 2004*

FAILING STATES OF SOUTH ASIA

PR Chari

Research Professor, Institute of Peace and Conflict Studies, New Delhi

Some Theoretical Perspectives

Any discussion of failing or failed states requires the concept of 'state' to be understood; it derives from the 'social compact' entered by an individual with the larger human assembly for mutual benefit. Rousseau defines this 'social compact' thus:

> "*Each of us puts his person and all his power in common under the supreme direction of the general will, and, in our corporate capacity, we receive each member as an indivisible part of the whole*...This public person, so formed by the union of all other persons, formerly took the name of *city,* and now takes that of *Republic* or *body politic;* it is called by its members *State* when passive, *Sovereign* when active, and *Power* when compared to others like itself. Those associated in it take collectively the name of *people,* and severally are called *citizens,* as sharing in the sovereign authority, and *subjects,* as being under the laws of the State."[1] [Emphasis in original.]

Rousseau was agnostic about the longevity of the State, believing that an inherent tension existed between the 'particular will' of the Prince, more broadly, the ruling dispensation of the State, and the general will embody the People. Sooner or later, he argued, the Prince "must inevitably suppress the Sovereign and break the social treaty. This is the unavoidable and inherent defect which, from the very birth of the body politic, tends ceaselessly to destroy it, as age and death end by destroying the human body."[2]

From a realist perspective State power flows out of its monopoly over the legitimate use of organized violence to defend itself and its citizens. Morgenthau notes: 'State' is but another name for the compulsory organization of society—for the legal order that

[1] *Jean-Jacques Rousseau, The Social Contract and Discourses, (London: Everyman's Library, 1982 Reprint), p. 175*

[2] *Op. cit. p. 232*

[3] *Hans J. Morgenthau, Politics Among Nations: The Struggle for Power and Peace, Fifth Edition, Indian Edition, (Calcutta: Scientific Book Agency, 1973), p. 487*

determines the conditions under which society may employ its monopoly of organized violence for the preservation of order and peace."[3] In other words, a successful state maintains its monopoly over the legitimate use of force within its territory, and that monopoly cannot be challenged with impunity by militias, insurgents, terrorists, warlords and so on. Morgenthau approvingly cites Quincy Wright to conclude that the preservation of domestic peace is of the essence; this is evident from the course of history, which reveals that civil wars "were costly both in lives and in economic losses far in excess of contemporary international wars."[4] Indeed, the annual statistics on major armed conflicts compiled by the Stockholm Peace Research Institute (SIPRI) make clear that the majority of these conflicts are taking place *within* and not *between* States, placing a heavy premium thereby on State failures occurring.[5]

The enabling factors that predicate state failure are apparent, and include the infiltration of ruling elites to create a lawless regime, high levels of corruption, feeble exercise of sovereignty or state power, and so on. When a state is deemed to be failing and when that process ends in state failure is difficult to ascertain at the margins, but objective criteria are available to undertake this estimation. A state tending towards failure is unable to enforce its laws, displays high crime rates, political corruption, an impenetrable bureaucracy, judicial ineffectiveness, military interference in politics, with traditional leaders wielding more power than the state. A 'failed state' is recognizable by its central government losing control over its territory; serious communal and ethnic divisions dividing its population; rent-seeking elites dominating the regime; a collapse of the rule of law; and pervasive corruption.

A study analyzing the links between regime failure and resource scarcity, population growth, pollution and environmental factors was supported by the US Central Intelligence Agency in the early nineties. This State Failure Project correlated several non-traditional security variables with political instability. The most robust model focused on "three critical variables: the vitality of democratic institutions, the openness of the regime to international trade, and the "quality of life" (best measured by infant mortality) but also reflecting a number of environmental factors."[6]

The Failed States Index 2007

Attention might be drawn now to the annual "failed states index," drawn up by the Fund for Peace, a US think-tank, which is published by *Foreign Policy* in Washington.[7] For ranking nations on this index 12 determining factors were identified and awarded 10 marks each like mounting demographic pressures; massive movement of refugees and internally displaced peoples; legacy of vengeance-seeking group grievances; chronic and sustained human flight; uneven economic development along group lines; sharp and/or severe economic decline; criminalization and de-legitimization of the state; progressive deterioration of public services; widespread violation of human rights; security apparatus becoming a 'state within a state'; rise of factional elites; and the intervention of other states or external actors. Scoring on these determining factors for the 2007 Index was then effected from 12,000 publicly available sources over May-December 2006, allocating separate marks for each factor and aggregating these marks for individual countries. A list of the 60 most vulnerable countries was then drawn up.[8] It is noteworthy that countries that rank high among the failed states rank low in the Human Development Index, but rank high in the listing by Transparency International of corrupt countries.

Are any empirical linkages possible between state failure and objective factors in their polity and economy? The Fund for Peace study published by *Foreign Policy* relates state failure negatively with religious intolerance e.g. Sudan and Iraq; bad and entrenched leadership e.g. Robert Mugabe in Zimbabwe has remained in power for 27 years; proneness to disaster induced by environmental deterioration, which will accelerate in future due to climate change e.g. China. Religious intolerance and the persecution of minorities correlate strongly with failed states e.g. Bangladesh. State success is related positively to the holding of elections, despite the

[4] *Quincy Wright, A Study of War, (Chicago: University of Chicago Press, 1942), Vol. I, p. 651*

[5] *For instance, in 2004 there were 19 armed conflicts in 17 locations around the world. None of them were interstate conflicts; all of them were within states, and were either concerned with control over the government or over territory. SIPRI Yearbook 2005: Armaments, Disarmament and International Security, (Oxford: Oxford University Press, 2005), p. 121*

[6] *Robert Chase, Emily Hill, Paul Kennedy, (Eds) The Pivotal States: A New Framework for U.S. Policy in the Developing World, (New York: W.W. Norton and Company, 1999), p. 294*

[7] *Cf. The Failed States Index 2007, http:// www.foreign policy.com accessed on 7 September 2007*

[8] *Op. cit. p. 8*

existence of high poverty levels e.g. India; combating endemic corruption by taking action against high-ranking officials e.g. Bangladesh is making a serious attempt here.

Of interest in this ranking of failing states is that Sudan, Iraq and Somalia head this list, Afghanistan ranks eighth; but, apart from Iraq and Afghanistan, the other first ten failed states in this list are located in sub-Saharan Africa. Significantly, the instability factor of 'external intervention' scores the maximum of 10 points for Iraq (United States), Somalia (Ethiopia, encouraged by the United States), and Afghanistan (United States).[9] In other words, the empirical evidence suggests that a strong reason for state failure is intervention by external powers, especially the United States, which seriously questions the Bush administration's policy of interventionism. Clearly, the American misadventure in Iraq is traceable to President Bush's decision to invade that country in 2003, remove Saddam Hussein from office, disband the Iraqi armed forces, and dismantle its Ba'athist administration. The U.S. has now entered a quagmire of sectarian quarrels and animosities. Ironically, the disaster which befell Saddam Hussein's impetuous invasion of Kuwait in 1990 now threatens the US intervention in Iraq in 2003. Future historians will note that a price must be paid to initiate conflict, but a larger price must be paid for extrication from that conflict.

With "an absolute deficit of political accountability, [and] still no effective system of policing or jurisprudence"[10], Iraq exhibits the attributes of a failed state. Much the same could be said of Afghanistan, which has endured conflicts and instabilities since the soviet invasion at the end of 1979; it is currently facing a civil war between competing ethnicities, foreign armed forces and indigenous militias. Currently, the United States is unwilling to negotiate with the resurgent Taliban forces, but several of its NATO allies favor negotiating with the Taliban on strictly utilitarian considerations.

The internal dynamics within a failing state like Iraq and Afghanistan are of serious consequence for the human security of their people. But the incipient dangers to the international system from failing states also need recognition. For one, instability can spread to their neighbors due to cultural affinities, familial linkages, and illegal migration. The classic example would be Sudan where the violence in Darfur has led to a massive forced migration of its population into neighboring Chad and the Central African Republic, thereby destabilizing these countries.

A space is also created thereby for transnational criminal and terrorist organizations to entrench themselves in the territory of failing states, which provides an opportunity for these organizations to organize training camps and replenish their ranks from the population owing loyalty to narrow religious and tribal structures woven together by hatred towards their ruling elites. These organizations can be utilized to provide economic support for religious or political reasons to desperate people by luring them into smuggling arms and drugs, human trafficking, and armed violence.

It has been perceptively held that: "Despite their internal decay and instability, failing states retain the outward instruments of sovereignty such as diplomatic recognition and membership in the United Nations and protection under its Charter. These diplomatic realities can serve as severe impediments to counter-terrorist operations, particularly in cross-border operations to eliminate terrorist networks".[11] Thus failing states are a danger to themselves, but also to the international system, and this reality must be appreciated by the international community to take remedial steps in their own enlightened self-interests.

Does the Failed States Index exaggerate the situation obtaining in the international system? Has 'failed state,' which gained currency after 9/11, become a synonym for 'rogue' states or 'states of concern.'? Has 'failed state' become another pejorative term like 'superpower'? Indeed, Naom Chomsky believes that[12] the United States routinely concocts categories of states like 'terrorist' (Reagan), 'rogue' (Clinton) and now 'failed' (Bush) to justify its interventionist policies to either subjugate them (Iraq) or save them from themselves (Haiti). A less evangelical approach towards newly decolonized Third World countries would appreciate that they were born economically weak and politically disunited. They are in various

---

[9] *The external intervening countries responsible for the state failing are placed within brackets*

[10] *Peter Beaumont, "Iraq still looks much like a failed state," The Hindu, September 3, 2007*

[11] *Stefan M. Aubrey, "The New Dimension of International Terrorism" (Zurich: Vdf. Hochschulverlag, 2004), p. 138, cited in Andrea Plebani, "Attractiveness of WMD for Radical Islamist Movements: Ideological Constraints, Black-Spots, and Failed-Weak States", Strategic Insights, Volume VI, Issue 5 (August 2007)*

[12] *See transcript of interview. http://www.democracynow.org/article.pl?sid+06/03/31/148254#transcript accessed on 15/9/07*

stages of state formation, being forcibly integrated. Decolonization increased existing strains in their body politic due to grinding poverty, exacerbated by the media-fed revolution of rising expectations, fomenting discontent. Long-subsisting ethno-political tensions also surfaced, aggravating the problems of national integration. Basic institutions like the bureaucracy, judiciary, and law enforcing machinery were unable to cope with these huge problems leading to bad or no governance.

How far would it be fair, therefore, to castigate these states as failed and docket them within an index? These are valid arguments, highlighting the need for strong states to address the multitudinous problems confronting newly emerged nations to ensure their national and human security, and retain their integrity. Proceeding further, the quality of governance and the capacity to provide good governance lies at the root of the ability of states to address these basic problems. The Failed States Index enumerates the factors that underline misgovernance, and estimates individual incapacity to reverse this situation by providing good governance. The Index only adjudges the descent of countries on a viability scale taking into account relevant factors threatening their very existence. In other words, their vulnerability to internal violence and societal collapse is being evaluated.

What about South Asia?

How do the South Asian countries fare on the Failed States Index? Including Afghanistan, which has now joined SAARC, it is disconcerting to find that, except for India and the Maldives, the other six SAARC countries are listed among the first sixty states in the Index. Their respective rankings are Afghanistan (8), Pakistan (12), Bangladesh (16), Nepal (21), Sri Lanka (25) and Bhutan (47). Significantly, Afghanistan, Pakistan and Bangladesh are also listed as 'critical' countries; Nepal heads a second list of countries 'in danger'; and Bhutan falls in a third list of borderline states.[13] All these countries display a paucity of good governance among their major factors of instability.

Paradoxically, a marked diminution in inter-state conflict in South Asia has occurred, but intra-state tensions and instabilities have greatly increased, adding to the vulnerability of these failed states in the region. The Pakistan-Afghanistan border region is currently witnessing Taliban resurgence, and a loss of control by both countries over this swathe of territory might lead, as Sleigh Harrison believes, to the emergence of an "Islamic Pashtunistan" comprising the Pashtun-dominated areas on both sides of the Durand line. Nepal is also attempting a difficult transition to democracy by incorporating the resurgent Maoists into its parliamentary system. Bangladesh is seeking to reconcile democratic practice with accountability by its political class. In Sri Lanka, dialogue has been the first casualty of a virtual breakdown in its peace process to end its long ordeal of ethno-political violence and conflict.

Do these countries display any common characteristics relevant to their status of being failed state? At least four unique features can be recognized.

- First, they have either been subjected to external intervention in the past or are vulnerable to it. The American intervention has aggravated prevailing instabilities in Afghanistan. The American presence in Pakistan is a political issue, worsening its existing instabilities. Indian interventionism–overt or insidious—is a contentious issue in the plebiscitary politics of Bangladesh, Nepal and Sri Lanka, with great political energy being dissipated in debating its malefic influence on their domestic polity. These features of South Asian politics arise from its unique geography, characterized by a large stable India being encircled by weak and failing states vulnerable to external intervention.
- Second, it is evident that the diffusion of communications and information technology shrinks geographical and intellectual spaces. Adverse developments in one country spill over porous borders affecting stability in the neighborhood. The resurgence of the Taliban in the tribal belt straddling Afghanistan-Pakistan constitutes a cancerous node in South Asia; it could spread engendering instability in Central Asia, but also in Pakistan, fuelled by the drug economy established in these lawless areas. Another example is forced migration into neighboring states due to environmental causes, natural disasters and internal conflicts. India is the haven for refugees from Burma, Sri Lanka and Bangladesh for reasons of proximity, cultural and familial linkages, but also its stability.

[13] *International Herald Tribune, August 1, 2007. Selig Harrison's argument is that, in the conventional wisdom, either Islamist or Pashtun identity will triumph in this conflict, but the more plausible alternative is the emergence of an "Islamic Pashtunistan"*

Unsurprisingly, such migratory movements, forced or voluntary, have profound implications for the security of West Bengal, the Northeastern states, Tamilnadu and the southern states of India.

- Third, an aspect of failed states requiring greater attention is the belief that the multinational al-Qaeda wishes to acquire weapons of mass destruction (WMDs). It had established several research facilities in Afghanistan, contacted experts in the field and procured some basic components for manufacturing WMDs. Incidentally, the angst that failing states and irresponsible non-state actors might acquire WMDs had inspired American military intervention in Iraq and Afghanistan. Coincidentally, Pakistan and North Korea have nuclear weapons, and are 12th and 13th respectively in the listing of failed states. A bipartisan survey among foreign policy experts by the Centre for American Progress reached the alarming conclusion that "Pakistan is the nation most likely to transfer nuclear technology to terrorists in the next three to five years."[14] This threat was linked to Pakistan's internal stability, and highlighted the dangers from its turbulent political system.
- Fourth, South Asia highlights the phenomenon of failed states displaying a functioning central authority, strong military, effective paramilitary and police forces and a stable leadership, but failing in parts. Several areas in South Asia exhibit partial state failure characterized by weak spots within their territory. One such weak spot is the area around Peshawar, which provides refuge for al-Qaeda and Taliban elements; it has an international arms bazaar, where all types of arms can be freely bought and sold, and is also the distribution centre for opium and its derivatives for supply to the world market. Other weak spots are the Affine peninsula, the Chittagong Hill Tracts, northwestern Nepal, parts of Kashmir and the northeast Indian states and, the rapidly growing area in central and eastern India (172 out of some 600 plus districts) that are coming under Naxalite control. Strenuous efforts are naturally made by states to regain their control over these weak spots, which then exhibit the unleashing of great violence and the brutalities of civil war, generating conditions for intensifying state failure. The coexistence of functioning national and provincial authority with loss of control over swathes of its territory distinguishes several countries in South Asia. Can these situations extend further into South Asia? A Peshawar-like scenario could be replicated elsewhere in the region presaging a spillover of instability, destabilization of contiguous areas in the country and the region, heightening the dangers of WMD proliferation, and creating a milieu propitious for external intervention.

These pessimistic prognostications are derived from the verity that regional conflicts in South Asia have deep roots embedded in ethno-political animosities that weaken State authority, and enable the nurturing of criminal and terrorist organizations. It can be rationally presumed that central authority in any country will not countenance their territory being used by such organizations to launch extra-territorial attacks unless this embodies state policy; otherwise, they would fear that such insouciance would invite severe external reactions. Pakistan has discovered, incidentally, that its long-standing policy of joining the American war on terror in Afghanistan, but promoting terrorism in Kashmir had inherent contradictions, which has manifested now with al Qaeda and Taliban turning against Islamabad. Furthermore, the limited resources of failing states in South Asia are greatly eroded by corruption; the consequent weakening of governance further erodes their capability to deal with criminal and terrorist organizations in their territories.

What does all this mean for India? The wisdom has yet to dawn on India's governing elites that the failing states on its security horizon constitute a new threat to national security. Surrounded by failing states, it should have a vested interest in their stability. Contingency planning is required; hence it must evaluate the nature of these threats with greater precision. Are they likely to arise from increased terrorist attacks, WMD proliferation, surge migration, or in other exotic ways? How could they be countered? Apropos, there is little appreciation in India's security establishment of the value of 'soft power' to sanitize its neighborhood. Hard power and the acquisition of military and nuclear muscle claim their attention, but have little relevance to this new range of threats from failing states. There is nothing to suggest that SAARC is cognizant of these threats, the declarations issued after its Summit meetings seem more concerned with drafting anodyne statements

[14] *Jon Fox, "Pakistan Said Most Likely to Give Nuclear Tech to Terrorists," Global Security Newswire, http://www.nti.org/d_newswire/issues/print.asp?story_id accessed on 22/8/07*

than addressing the real problems of South Asia. The evolution of a more informed and relevant neighborhood policy has become too urgent to be ignored much longer.

Conclusion

The foregoing analysis paints a gloomy picture of state failure in South Asia. But, can failing states reverse this trend, mitigate instability, and halt their further slide into state failure? A counsel of wisdom suggests that they should rebuild their organizational capacities, which requires rebuilding their primary institutions of governance like the public and civic services, judiciary, law and order machinery, and the armed forces. The natural inclination of failed states is to announce new development schemes and sweeping reform measures as the mantra for lulling critical public criticism. Thereby, they also subscribe to the general delusion that reduction of poverty levels is required, but that the reduction of inequalities and the sense of injustice this generates is not very relevant. Greater honesty is needed to realize that announcing development programs and reform measures is not enough; their implementation and monitoring is essential to ensure that the touted advantages reach the intended beneficiaries. Ensuring this simple, but politically courageous policy—since powerful vested interests are involved—is the most effective means to reverse the current trend of state failure in South Asia. We come up here against the familiar problem of a lack of political will afflicting South Asia's ruling elites, and India is no exception to this general rule.

This is not a counsel of despair. Arguably, India provides a fair example of a state that has drawn itself back from the brink of joining the failed states. The end of the Cold War and the disintegration of the Soviet Union in the early nineties left India bereft of its chief strategic ally; in the economic sphere, years of profligacy by earlier governments had left only two weeks of foreign exchange reserves in its national exchequer; internally, the country was being excoriated by a serious insurgency movement in Punjab and Kashmir. The reversal of these dangerous trends over the past decade and a half suggests that failed states and those on the brink of failure can reverse these trends, provided an enlightened leadership takes the unpopular decisions required. It is arguable that India's democratic structure provides the space to dither and postpone unpleasant decisions without a political upheaval, despite tensions remaining due to disparities and inequalities. A minimal appreciation has also accrued that a multi-religious and multi-ethnic society can be knit together by delegating more power to state and lower administrative echelons.

There is, however, another aspect to this problem in South Asia that applies to India, and is best encapsulated in the conundrum that a state can fail in parts? There is little doubt that the writ of several South Asian states is limited, and does not run over their entire territory. The best example is Afghanistan, which provides currency to the *bon mot* that its government's writ runs over only Kabul and that too, only during the day! But, more seriously, the writ of the Pakistan government no longer runs over the FATA region, especially over Waziristan. Neither does the Sri Lankan government's writ run over its Jaffna area, which is controlled by the Tamil Tigers. This is also true for the government of Nepal. For that matter, it is questionable whether the writ of the Indian government runs over the whole of Jammu and Kashmir or the northeastern states or the steadily enlarging area in the country that has passed under the control of the Naxalites and other left extremist organizations?

The phenomenon of states having a stable central authority but parts of the state passing out of its control to exhibit state failure exists in many parts of the world; hence, the threats to regional and global polity arise from state failure in localized areas that have the dangerous potential to spread outwards in concentric circles. The significance of this phenomenon for South Asia suggests the need for evolving a sectional Index to incorporate partial State failure, and pinpoint the dangers to the stability of national and regional entities from sub-national state failure.

REGIONAL RESPONSE TO TERRORISM

General VP Malik
Former Chief of the Army Staff, India

Introduction

There is rarely a lucky day in South Asia these days when our people are not confronted with an act of terrorism; somewhere or the other, in some form or shape, for some reason or another. Terrorism in South Asia ebbs and flows.

Terrorism now is neither definable within geographical boundaries, nor within the traditional moulds of rationality. Terrorist groups do not owe loyalty to any national flag, religion, or even ethnic society. They extinguish innocent lives as legitimate victims. They seek martyrdom in suicide missions. The terrorists' threat is not only through ground actions. It is further magnified by their acquiring aerial capability. And there are very real prospects of such groups acquiring higher technology, and even Weapons of Mass Destruction in the pursuit of their endeavours.

Before proceeding further, it needs emphasis that the so-called war on terrorism is a misnomer: terrorism is neither state specific nor an ideology. *It is a method of employing political violence in pursuit of an ideology.* The Second World War was not against blitzkrieg, but against Nazism which used blitzkrieg to overrun Europe. The war on terrorism is just a mobilizing term. It can not achieve success unless there is a comprehensive grand strategy that is implemented in letter and spirit to eradicate it.

Role of the United Nations and Democratic Nations

In the last 44 years, starting September 1963, the United Nations has adopted 12 conventions concerning counter-terrorism. The number of signatories kept increasing with each successive convention, which indicates that whenever the international community feels a real threat to most of its members, it tends to unite and find the best ways to protect the security and well being of the world population.

The UN Security Council Resolution 1373, condemned the attacks on 9/11 unanimously and unequivocally, and expressed its determination to prevent all such acts. It urged the member states to work together urgently, to prevent and suppress terrorist acts. It also decided that member states should 'deny safe haven to those who finance, plan, support, or commit terrorist acts.' It called upon member-states to find ways of intensifying and accelerating the exchange of operational information regarding actions of terrorists or their networks; traffic in arms, explosives or sensitive materials; use of communication technologies and the threat posed by the possession of weapons of mass destruction by terrorist groups.

Resolution 1373 was further reinforced in Resolution 1456 when the United Nations decided to monitor its implementation and establish a committee with the assistance of appropriate expertise. Unfortunately, these provisions have not been translated into effective mechanisms for monitoring and enforcing compliance so far. It is for this reason that Al-Qaeda, Lashkar-e-Taiba, LTTE and other such terrorist groups have over the years developed the ability to finance their activities, and continue to do so, through charities, drug trade, and gun running. The nexus between drug smuggling and terrorism, the organized flow of arms from East and West into South Asian nations, by seas and across land borders, resulting into increasing terrorists' activities is self-evident.

It is a recognized fact today that the more likely targets of terrorism are democratic societies. That is so because pluralism, peaceful co-existence, dialogue as the basis of resolution of differences, adult franchise as the optimal means of organizing internal affairs of the nations: these are an anathema to the terrorist groups. Such democratic societies challenge the very cause and rationale of the terrorists' existence.

For this very reason, democratic nations have a more significant role than other nations of the world. They would more naturally develop the multi-lateral institutions and multi-national coordination required to counter terrorism. They would not get bogged down in definitional or causal arguments. Blocking financial supplies, disrupting networks, sharing intelligence, simplifying extradition procedures: these are preventive measures which can only be effective through international cooperation based on trust and shared values. Therefore, institutions like the Counter Terrorism Committee of the United Nations should comprise only the hard-core democratic nations.

Counter Terrorism in South Asia

Geo-politically, South Asia represents an integral security zone. And in that, India has special ties with each of her neighbours—of ethnicity, language, culture, common historical experience, or of shared access to vital natural resources of a degree of intensity that is not shared by any two others.

Currently, the whole of South Asia—India, Nepal, Bangladesh, Sri Lanka, Maldives, Afghanistan and Pakistan -is going through internal unrest and upheavals due to ethnic conflicts, religious fundamentalism, or just cussed political polarizations that encourage and use terrorism. The terrorists' activities have a history of crossing national boundaries, often leading to inter-state tensions. The terrorist situation in South Asia has deteriorated, primarily due to lack of political consensus, a comprehensive collective strategy, a will to implement, and adequate capacity building.

Despite committing themselves to the SAARC Regional Convention on Suppression of Terrorism - 1987, the Eleventh SAARC Summit Declaration adopted at Kathmandu on 6 January 2002, and the Additional Protocol to the SAARC Regional Convention on Suppression of Terrorism of 6 January 2004, which recognized the importance of updating the Convention to meet the obligations devolving in terms of Security Council Resolution 1373 (2001); many SAARC nations continue to provide direct or indirect support to terrorists' organizations.

A few nations in South Asia still carry the belief that someone's terrorist can be someone else's freedom fighter. Such a notion is puerile. Any pre-meditated and unlawful act of violence against innocent people or non-combatants, irrespective of its cause and motive is nothing but terrorism. Such notions and advocacy reflect lack of commitment to the war against terror. *'Terrorism is a double-edged weapon. It is like a wicked dog, which often bites the hand that feeds it.'* Further, *'a proxy or sub conventional war due to terrorists' activities can easily escalate into a conventional war.'*

The most important requirement to counter terrorism in South Asia is for all nations to raise the level of trust and confidence. South Asian nations should take voluntary action against terrorists' activities on their soil rather than complain, or wait and respond to complaints from each other. South Asian nations need to stand together, and cooperate as counter terrorism partners. Cooperative regional efforts only can produce genuine security improvements—particularly in securing borders, transportation, enhancing document security, disrupting of terrorist financing, and restricting their movements.

A New Approach and Strategy

Terrorists' activities anywhere will stop only when their fuel runs out. There is a need to combat and defeat the menace in all its manifestations. We need a regional strategy and cooperation, but essentially local operatives and doctrines. A few important points need to be highlighted.

One! At the ideological level, this war is between terrorist groups which do not believe in values of democracy, multi-culturalism, ethnic and religious tolerance. The counter terrorism grand strategy followed in many countries, with preponderance of Defeat, Deny and Defend elements, is far too militarist and operationally focused. It does not cover the ideological milieu adequately. A pure military approach, given the fragility of institutional framework in operational areas and volatility of developments, can easily descend into anarchy. Long term ideological and politically sensitized counter terrorism elements must play a more dominant role. There must be support for all those who believe that 'ideologues' should be included in the strategy and operational fight against terrorism.

Two! We need to devise collaborative strategies at the highest level. However, a uniform top-down strategy must not be applied everywhere. Counter terrorism operational strategies and action plans should be worked out for each region and each location. They must take into cognizance the more important indigenous and local factors to neutralize terror networks. The terrorists do have ideological, doctrinal and sectarian differences; even ego clashes arising from different cultural and national backgrounds. We need to take advantage of these differences. This can be done only if we attempt to analyze them properly. How they are linked? How they are financed? How do they operate? It is important that each country facing the problem analyzes it independently, and then we pool this information. We need to build on elements of stability, nurture democratic impulses, nudge regimes to provide greater socio-political and socio-economic justice, and engage in dialogues. Partners in the campaign to isolate terrorism should, as far as possible, be regional, with leadership that emanates through domestic democratic processes.

Three! Counter-terrorism strategy and cooperation should deal with all aspects of international terrorism: its linkages with transnational organized crime, illicit drugs, money laundering, illegal arms trafficking, and proliferation of nuclear, chemical, biological and other potentially deadly materials and their means of delivery. It should seek a firm commitment, and action, to meet cross-border threats posed by the terrorists.

Four! Terrorism is not just a military problem. It is primarily a socio-political and socio-economic problem. In the counter terrorism strategy, besides checking violence, we must combat and isolate the *ideology* that is irrational and is not acceptable to modern society. We have to use all elements of national power; not just military but political, economic and other kind of persuasion and pressures. For this, we need both hard power as well as soft power: hard power to deal with violent armed terrorists, and soft power to deal humanely with societies, their culture, traditions and ethos. The intellectual and psychological dimensions of the terrorists' threat and counter terrorism are as important as its physical dimension. Youth organizations, educational networks, women's empowerment, and local development initiatives should all play a role, with government as a supportive partner.

Some important elements of the collective strategy and action plan would have to be:

- Establishment of a Regional Counter Terrorism Centre with *experts* from different countries, to work under a common umbrella, to provide professional guidance and secretarial support to the SAARC political leadership, and to monitor implementation of their Resolutions in letter and spirit.
- Capacity building in combating terrorism by intelligence, police, para military and military in each other's schools of instructions; thus learning from varied experience. To combat terrorists, force multipliers for surveillance, night fighting and precision targeting are more important than heavy weapons.
- Greater liaison and coordination for planning and execution of counter terrorism operations. This would require certain amount of inter-operability. The backbone of such inter-operability is joint training, sets of common inter-operable communication systems and operating procedures.
- A common data-base at the regional level, a multilateral/bilateral intelligence sharing, and a mechanism for joint interrogation of important suspects and terrorist leaders.
- Trust and transparency of action against terrorists' sanctuaries in foreign territories, and also against States sponsoring terrorism.
- Effective joint action against terrorist-funding, gun running and narcotics production and smuggling.
- Legal assistance to each other in matters relating to investigations and prosecution.

The Indian Experience

India has a population of over 1 billion spread over 3.1 billion square kilometres. It has people speaking 16 major languages and 200 dialects. There are a dozen ethnic groups, seven major religious communities with several sects and sub sects, and 68 socio-cultural sub regions: all part of a developing, semi-literate society. There are rapidly rising social, political and economic aspirations of groups in its multi-ethnic, lingual, cultural and communal social structure. The ancient, multi-ethnic and multi-cultural diversity has its plus and negative points, which makes India's national security quite complex.

India has been one of the longest victims of terrorism. But it has also handled terrorism successfully in Mizoram, Punjab and several other parts of the country. More importantly, it has not allowed terrorism to politically or economically destabilize the nation.

India adopts a comprehensive approach to counter terrorism. Counter-terrorism can be effective only if there is a multi-pronged approach, based on a national consensus. India's counter-terrorism approach treats terrorism as a phenomenon with political, economic, social, perceptual, psychological, operational and diplomatic aspects, all of which need equal and simultaneous attention. It seeks a holistic approach to all these dimensions. Therefore, it has a system of unified command in terrorist affected areas, under a Governor or the Chief Minister, with committees made up of all the earlier mentioned functionaries.

India believes in and encourages a healthy, well-functioning democracy, good governance, and a secular and liberal mind-set, which makes no distinction between the majority and the minority, and treats everyone equal in the eyes of the law. Firmness and determination in action, tampered by a civilized, democratic and patient behavior by the State, have been the hallmark of India's counter-terrorism policy.

The aim of the security operations is only to isolate, arrest, or eliminate hardcore secessionist elements, and to deter their supporters. The security forces use a stick and carrot approach. They employ the principle of 'use of minimum force' during such operations; not the overkill required in a war. The security forces not only fight militants and anti-social elements, but also reassure innocent people feeling insecure, or neglected, due to inadequate civil administration.

Tough measures lead to increasing alienation. Conversely, politically expedient attempts to appeasement carry the risk of being read as a sign of weakening resolve. The need is to find the right balance.

With experience, India has realized that we need specially organized, equipped and trained, areas-oriented security forces to deal with insurgencies and terrorism. Special Forces, Rashtriya Rifles, Assam Rifles, Rapid Reaction Force: these are some examples. These forces, and those who work alongside, need training for local terrain, people, their language, customs, and traditions. Special training schools have to be established for this purpose. The Army insists that every soldier, deployed for such operations, carries a Do's and Dont's card on his person.

During sustained operations, the security forces involve senior and respected citizens, and professionals, as a link between them and the locals. They also form citizens' committees to learn about their difficulties, hold meetings with them as frequently as possible. Along with military operations, small and large-scale civic action programmes are undertaken. In some areas, the Indian Army has formed Army Development Groups and launched Operation Sadbhavana (Goodwill). The overall aim is to win the hearts and minds of the populace. It would be counter productive to alienate hundreds and thousands of 'fence sitters' in order to kill a suspect.

At no stage can a nation afford to give a full license to the security forces to operate freely. There is a requirement to define clearly; their responsibility, authority, legality, and accountability.

Conclusion

There are no quick-solutions to counter terrorism. It is a long process. Also, there is no military solution to a terrorist, insurgency or secessionist problem. The military can only create conditions wherein the adversary is inclined to, or feel it necessary to come to the negotiating table. Ultimately, the solution lies in the political domain; within existing national constitutions, and sometimes with slightly modified constitutions.

Counter terrorism in South Asia needs a comprehensive strategy that encompasses political, economic, social, psychological, operational and diplomatic issues. The operations have to be primarily regional, or country specific with local players.

The key success factor, however, is the commitments by South Asian nations to work with each other. It is essential for the governments of the region to cooperate, build trusted networks, seek informed support from their people, provide responsive, legitimate and effective governance, and engage closely with international community. Only then would they be able to eliminate terrorism, prevent instability, and avoid conflict in the region.

DEFENCE ECONOMIES OF SOUTH ASIA : AN ANALYSIS

Maj Gen (Retd) Jatinder Singh
Defence Analyst

Introduction

At the present time defence spending and the awarding of defence-related contracts are major tools at the disposal of governments for supporting and stimulating local economies. Another important issue at the present time is conflict of land use between defence requirements and growing commercial demands. Defence is a costly business. Over the past few years, the Indian Ministry of Defence (MoD) has significantly altered the way it acquires weapon systems. In particular, initiatives like offsets, transfer of technology (ToT), involving private sector into these acquisition and manufacture processes. The impetus for these changes has come from a natural push within the government and from the industry to improve processes and partly from the squeeze of budgetary pressures.

In Pakistan, General Musharraf inherited an economy in crisis. Shackled by sanctions and parched of capital, Pakistan had defaulted on foreign debts. He ensured that the country did what the International Monetary Fund (IMF) told it to do, and ended the crisis. Partly due to continued fiscal prudence and some sensible reforms, Pakistan has notched up an average growth rate of 7% plus over the past few years. It also helped that after the attacks on America on 11 September 2001, General Musharraf decided to stop supporting the Taliban government in next door Afghanistan and grant America access to airbases from which to fight it. The benefits have not been confined to a surge of American aid dollars that boosted the growth figures. Having joined the "war on terror" the General then surprised many by throwing himself into peacemaking with India. This is encouraging. But a bigger concern for most Pakistanis is the state of their broken and predatory institutions, which have helped to make Pakistan unstable and prone to extremism.

The Indian government is debating whether to increase its $ 21.8 billion defence budget from 2.2% of Gross Domestic Product (GDP) to 3%, which would mean another $ 50 billion over next five years. India, where the overall economy is growing at 9% per year, wants to maintain its position as a big regional power. It perceives the Chinese build up as a prelude to increase its own spending.

In Search of Value for Money

In their pursuit of prudent financial management, the Ministry's of Defence (MoD's) in the various South Asian countries have been encouraged to base procurement decisions on securing value for money. This means looking at capability, availability and lifetime costs of maintaining the equipment. This after all, is the requirement of suitable defence economy; to ensure the armed forces are equipped with weapon systems they need, when they need it and at an affordable price. But how is value for money defined? And do we have a meaningful approach to measuring it?

Modern warfare is now increasingly focused on an effects–based approach that de-emphasises destruction and emphasises results, or outcomes, through better integration of different military assets. The approach necessarily involves a complex and interconnected system or network of military assets. In procuring these assets, there are inevitably complex trade-off decisions to be made in order to determine the optimum combination of assets that deliver the effect. This requires a better understanding of how to quantify military capability and, therefore, understand the trade-off between capability, availability dates and the cost of acquisition. A further factor that complicates value for money assessments in defence is the recognition that defence spending affects not only the equipment the armed forces receive but also has a broader impact on the nation's economy as a whole.

There is, first, the important aspect of supporting a defence industrial strategy. Every nation needs a certain defence capability for which it would rather not be dependent on others. Where there is such a strategic requirement, it is clearly important that value-for-money judgements take into account the value of procurement decisions on sustaining the strategic industrial base. Second, there is the impact that defence procurement decisions have on the broader industrial base of the country. Finally, there are a whole host of other ways in which defence economy affects the economic and social status of a country. It leads to job creation, valuable know-how intellectual property rights, ToT and skills training. Thousands of combatants leave the armies each year and go into the economy, usually well-trained and well-disciplined. They are a huge benefit to their companies.

Taking account of the kinds of factors described above, how does one assess the value for money involved in defence spending? They are, inevitably, subjective judgements to be made as to, for example, the likely level of exports to be achieved, the strategic importance of a capability, the value of the intellectual property to be developed and so on. There are also judgements to be made, which may fall well outside the procurement perspective, as to the need to generate wealth in a particular region of the country. In its pursuit of better financial management, MoDs are seeking to be rigorous in prioritising how to spend limited resources in order to make the structural changes and investments in new equipment the services need. It has set the principle of competition at the heart of procurement strategy. Few would quarrel with the concept of competition as a basis for allocating resources, but the global defence industry is far from being a level playing field

In defence terms, South Asian countries defence markets are not truly open markets and in fact have been promoting protectionism of their reasonably pathetic defence manufacturing Public Sector Undertaking (PSU) or the Ordnance Factories Board (OFB). On the contrary, it is in everybody's interest to have open markets that can involve the private sector and sustain real competition and benefits to the tax payer. However, the reality is that the international defence market is going to shrink. If the South Asian countries are serious about building and retaining a strong defence industrial base, the industry needs to be given a clear understanding of what the government/MoD's long -term requirements and its acquisition criteria are likely to be. This calls for increased clarity over those areas that the government considers strategically important to the nation in the long term and better collaboration with industry to make sure that the country stays in the premier league in those areas. There is a need for a better framework for measurement. There is also a need to recognise that decisions, based on competition alone, may not always deliver the best value for money to the nation.

It seems that in the South Asian context modernizing of the armed forces is taken as just adding the latest armament to the forces inventories. The political class and even the bureaucracy lack an understanding of the concept of modernisation. Directions are given by Cabinet Committee on National Security (CCNS) on proposals put up by service Headquarters (HQ). The three services generally work in watertight compartments thereby resulting in no single service HQ formulating comprehensive and balanced proposals for modernization in today's global security environment, where military operations are optimally carried out through integrated operations of the three services.

Such integrated/joint planning is nearly non-existent due to the absence of a functioning National Security Council (NSC) which could deliberate on modernisation and arrive at pragmatic economic decisions. To achieve optimum defence economics, the CCNS needs to communicate to the Defence hierarchy the strategic threats which should be taken into consideration, for the immediate, mid-term and long-term future. This is a basic requirement in national security decision-making and management in all modern defence economics. India has managed to create aberrations. The previous National Democratic Alliance (NDA) government rendered the threat assessment mechanism, the Joint Intelligence Committee (JIC), dysfunctional by loading it with the secretarial duties of the NSC which was never convened. The likelihood of a full scale, high intensity war lasting several weeks is not very high in the near future. This has to be kept in mind by the defence hierarchy and the defence economy should be so planned so as to concentrate on removing existing deficiencies in the inventory and modernising low intensity warfare fighting capability inventory rather than going overboard on legacy systems like tanks and guns.

For medium and long-term threat management and modernisation there has to be a pragmatic assessment of the nature of future wars in the South Asian environment. Joint and integrated warfare is the order of the day and as also into the future. Defence modernization should lead to reduction in manpower and expansion of critical assets which are force multipliers in all types of conflict e.g. armed helicopters, protected vehicles, electronic warfare assets etc. A comprehensive threat assessment of the South Asian environment would suggest that most security threats are likely to be from within or the immediate neighbourhood due to terrorism, left-wing extremism, communal and caste tensions, bad governance, unrest in tribal areas and various kinds of secessionism. The defence economy should cater for the modernizing of paramilitary forces and intelligence services. Having insurgents/terrorists better armed than the paramilitary forces in trouble spots is a recipe for disaster.

Indian Defence Economy – Budgeting System

The defence budgeting system in India has been following the legacy left by the British. There has been very little effort to incorporate efficiency and accountability. The defence budget is presently allocated as follows:[1]

- Major Head 2076 – Revenue Expenditure: Army (Demand No. 23)
- Major Head 2077 – Revenue Expenditure: Navy (Demand No. 24)
- Major Head 2078 – Revenue Expenditure: Air Force (Demand No. 25)
- Major Head 2079 – Revenue Expenditure: Defence Ordnance Factories (Demand No. 26)
- Major Head 2080- – Revenue Expenditure: Defence Service Research & Development (Demand No. 27)
- Major Head 4076 – Capital Expenditure; Defence Services (Demand No. 28).

The revenue expenditures of the Directorate General of Quality Assurance (DGQA) and the National Cadet Corps (NCC) form part of the Army revenue budget. The Army budget also accounts for the Ex-servicemen Contributory Health Scheme (ECHS), which covers the medical expenses of ex-servicemen of all the three services. The revenue expenditure of joint staff, which takes care of HQ Integrated Defence Staff (IDS), the Andaman and Nicobar Tri-service Command and the Strategic Forces Command, is under the Navy's budget. A point of interest is that the entire capital expenditure of the defence services is covered under one major head. The existing budget is divided into Revenue and Capital expenditure. Revenue Expenditure comprises Pay and Allowances, Transportation, Stores, Revenue Works and Miscellaneous Expenditure. Capital Expenditure covers Land, Works and Acquisition of Equipment (including aircraft and vehicles).

While allocations in 'Revenue' are based primarily on the trend of expenditure in the past, capital budget is limited by allocations made by the Government. The process of the budgetary system has remained unchanged over the past few decades. The budget caters for requirements of one financial year and therefore the commitments for the future, arising out of a deal or a contract in a particular financial year are made without reference to the likely availability of funds in future years. These commitments then become obligatory in the ensuing financial years, and sometimes result in a situation where the limited budget does not allow new projects or schemes to be undertaken. The Armed Forces are therefore, never

[1] *"Defence Budgeting System: Need for Change"; Pravin Joshi; "Strategic Analysis, New Delhi; Oct-Dec 2005*

clear what their allocation for capital expenditure would be for the next few years. If one of the three services can somehow get a major project started with low cash outgo in the initial years, then it has automatically assured for itself a larger share of the capital budget in later years, starving projects of the other services, which may be equally critical.

Defence Planning. This focuses mostly on threat assessments. Resource assessment pertaining to manpower, technology and equipment over the coming few years is rarely carried out. Mid-course revision of the budget has become routine. The five year defence plans have lost their utility for resource planning. It is the task of the Government to carry out resource allocation and the service HQ cannot do this without the Government indicating the basis of what might be available. India's defence planning has suffered adversely from the consequences of inability or unwillingness to commit to long-term allocation of resources. Weapon systems and military equipment have a life of 15-25 years before they are due for replacement. Similarly, manpower is inducted in India's case for a period of 17-30 years, but funding for defence is carried out on an annual basis with a mid-year review to revise estimates of expenditure. The MoD has burdened itself with house-keeping functions of the armed forces which are best left to them since the MOD is not trained to think through long-term perspectives based on the geo-strategic scenario.

In August 2004, the Standing Committee on Defence, while examining the Demand's for Grants 2004-05, expressed serious concern that half of the period having already elapsed, the 10th Defence Plan (2002-07) had not been finalised. The MoD passed the buck to Ministry of Finance for not committing on fund availability. The committee also expressed displeasure with the MoD for the sketchy reasons advanced for the delays and as also the planning mechanism. The committee recommended that the MoD should prepare a 15 years roadmap with a long-term strategic perspective. This was to be updated periodically for modernization and acquisition plans for the defence services. It would also indicate the budgetary support required so as to enable the Finance Ministry to appreciate the long-term objectives of defence preparedness.

Sub Allocation to the Services. The apportionment of the defence funds between the services and amongst the various arms / capabilities within the individual service is being carried out according to ratios established long ago. This resulted in lopsided expenditures and in the building up of certain specific capabilities at the expense of other equally, if not more important force multipliers. A rigid budget together with the allocation to each service diminishes the returns which can be gained from flexible combined services and, within services a combined arms approach. The result is that each service demands its own perceived share of the budget and until pressurised by MoD spends funds on what it considers important, regardless of overall defence policy and the operational requirements of other services.

Defence Services Estimates (DSE). A feature of the defence budget is the absence of any supporting documents along with the DSE. The DSE, presented during the budget session, lists out the allocation of funds for the relevant financial year. Also listed are the allocations for the previous financial year and expenditure of financial year prior. One can compare the allocations and expenditure merely in arithmetical terms. In fact a meagre increase over the previous year's allocation or expenditure is considered appropriate and no explanations are sought. However, reductions or large increases draw a lot of explanations. Though Minor Heads and Detailed Heads are listed, the real purpose for allocations, primarily in the stores in Revenue and the entire capital budget is not reflected. From financial year 2003-04, an expanded version of the DSE i.e. Volume II, is being published. This contains command-wise allocations, under certain heads, and user-wise allocations under the stores head. However, it has not been able to reflect any programmes or objectives.

Indian Defence Economy under United Progressive Alliance (UPA) Government. Indian defence procurement has been rather tardy since the past three years. Very few request for proposals (RFP) have been issued. The Army has been at the receiving end of this lethargy since several key projects pertaining to acquisition and firepower resources have not moved, giving a setback to the combat readiness of the service. Initially the efforts of the UPA were to unearth any lingering defence scandals from the previous government, a step that has brought proposed overseas procurements under the microscope. The UPA has been harking on the fact that it wants the process of defence procurement to be more transparent. This resulted in the cancellation of a deal with South Africa's Denel for 180 self propelled Howitzers, one of the Army's priority programmes.

MoD sources indicate that defence planners are studying China's defence economy and wondering how to keep up with the perceived long term Chinese threat. The government is debating whether to increase its $ 21.8 billion defence budget from 2.2% of GDP to 3% which would mean another $ 50 billion over next five years. The armed forces purchase plans include a major deal to acquire 200 combat multi-role aircraft for the Air Force; about 150 helicopters, Unmanned Aerial Vehicles (UAV) and additional Airborne Warning and Control Systems (AWACS). The acquisition plans for the Navy include 30 warships over the same time, including stealth frigates, and two more aircraft carriers. The army's plan for purchase includes 200 helicopters, UAVs, guns and equipment to modernize the infantry. The MoD has planned to expedite its spending on Anti Ballistic Missile (ABM) systems and as also cruise and ballistic missiles. The armed forces need to replace or upgrade most of the erstwhile Soviet Weaponry acquired during 1960s and 1970s[2]. Upgrading it would cost about $ 20 billion. Some planners want to replace this equipment with western (read USA) equipment. This, in view of the present status of the proposed nuclear deal, is in a stage of limbo and therefore, a growing feeling that there is no alternative but to refurbish and use the existing Russian equipment with selective acquisition of present generation aircraft, helicopters etc. from Russia.

Recent Defence Finance Reforms in India

Enhancement of Delegation of Financial Powers. In 2001, the existing financial powers of various authorities in the services were enhanced by four to ten times. This gave the services greater responsibility along with more satisfaction.

Defence Procurement Organisation (DPO). Consequent upon the recommendations of the Group of Ministers (GoM) in 2001, a DPO comprising the Defence Acquisition Council, Defence Procurement Board (DPB), Defence Research and Development Board and the Acquisition Wing has been constituted. The DPB was constituted with the objective of bringing efficiency into procurements. While the Board oversees all acquisition activities, it has no financial power to sanction any projects. Even under the fast track procedure, the role of the DPB is recommendatory in nature. In the report of the Standing Committee on Defence (2004-05) on demands for grants of the MoD, DPB seems to have added one more tier in clearance of defence proposals, causing further delays in procurement of defence equipment. The committee recommended that a study group be constituted to examine the entire gamut of defence economy.

Defence Finance Management Strategy. Need for programme budgeting to provide a framework for applying cost-benefit or cost-effectiveness analysis in which individual and alternative force structures e.g. fighter squadron are cost analysed, related to benefits, outputs, or effectiveness of each force structure. Thus, programme budgeting draws attention to important trade-offs in defence choices. Programme budgeting is not without its limitations. It should be seen as an information system for planning and evaluation, but it does not remove the need for individuals to make decisions. Some of these limitations have led to new defence budgeting initiatives.

Sri Lanka

The Srilankan government plans to increase defence expenditure by nearly 20% to 166.4 billion rupees ($ 1.48) from 139.6 billion rupees in 2007. In 2006, the budget military expenditure surged by 44%. The government increased defence expenditure by $ 70 million to a total of $ 718 million (52.4 billion rupees) which is higher than the combined spending on education and health of just $ 470 million.

Over the past few years, the defence budget has been supplemented regularly with additional allocations to meet the escalating cost of the ongoing war with the Liberation Tigers of Tamil Eelam (LTTE). Sections of big business are pushing for an end to the 17-year war due to the economic hardship. Military expenditure now consumes nearly 25% of government revenue and has undermined efforts to reduce budget deficit as demanded by the IMF. Despite cutbacks to other departments, military spending has soared and the deficit stood at 8% for 2006. The government plans to raise overall spending in 2008 by 11% over levels budgeted for 2007, which analysts say will result in higher corporate taxes and cuts in capital projects. This increase in defence spending is as a result of the escalation of the conflict.

According to the appropriation bill for 2008, the total projected recurrent expenditure for Sri Lanka Army will be 6,618, 80, 00,000 rupees. The total projected

[2] *"India May Increase Defense Spending" by Vivek Raghuvanshi. Defense News – Sep 07*

capital expenditure for the SLA – 6,50,00,00,000 rupees. The Sri Lanka Navy will receive 1,917,40,00,000 as recurrent expenses and 800,00,00,000 rupees as capital expenditure. The Sri Lanka Air Force projected recurrence expenses 1,356,00,00,000 and projected capital expenses are 600,00,00,000 rupees.

Bangladesh

In Bangladesh, the budgetary provision for the defence services for fiscal year 2007 was 5,397 crore Takas. For 2008, this has been increased to 5, 469 crore Takas (an increase of 1.3%).[3] This amounts to 6.3% of the total budget. While the government did not expand defence budget in a major scale, defence expenditure is normally increased through different ministries.

The defence services received 9.8 per cent of the total non-development budget for 2007. Alongside, the development budget for Defence is set to grow by 61.3% in 2008. Defence expenditure for Bangladesh in 2007 stood at 1.15% of GDP. This is lower than the comparable spending in Pakistan (2.84%) and India (1.81%).

Bangladesh has about 11,000 troops on UN missions today and this constitutes one of their main source of funds. Bangladesh also has an Army Welfare Foundation (Sena Kalyan Sangstha) which is into the hotel business. The Foundation also runs a number of other manufacturing industries. The Khulna shipyard and Machine Tool Factory have also been taken over in the name of discipline and efficiency.

Nepal

The economic survey had estimated that GDP growth rate would reach 4.5% in the current fiscal year. Owing to the lack of visible improvement in the law and order situation and investment climate, and also due to adverse weather, the production of major crops declined, resulting in the estimated GDP growth rate of only 2.5%. Problems of law and order exist. Tasks such as bringing Maoist cantonment management to a completion, returning seized properties and rehabilitating the internally displaced people remain incomplete. Problems long suppressed are now unfolding. Demands for right to development are increasingly vocal. The government policies relating to the management of cantonments for Maoist combatants, reintegration and rehabilitation of the Maoist combatants, democratization of the Nepal Army, utilization of the properties of late King Birendra and his family is being implemented on a time-bound basis.

A sum of Rs. 10 billion and 890 million has been allocated for Nepal Army's regular operations. Necessary amounts required for the Nepal Army to be involved in the protection of national parks and wildlife conservation, and for development works to be implemented by Nepal Army, has been provisioned in concerned ministries. In comparison, only Rs. 2 billion has been allocated for agriculture.

Myanmar

The military of Myanmar is officially known as Tatmadaw. The military expenditure for fiscal year 2005 was 7.07 billion US $, which as a percentage of GDP came to 19%. The Myanmar Defence Industries is the lifeline of their armed forces. There are 13 major factories throughout the country that produce 70 major products for the Army, Navy and Air Force. The main products include automatic rifles, machine guns, Anti-Aircraft guns etc. For 2007, the defence budget is pegged at 8.2% of GDP.

Pakistan

Shortly after his coup in 1999, General Musharraf unveiled a "seven point agenda" to save the nation. He vowed to do all the right things; revive a sick economy, reduce corruption, rebuild national confidence and so on. But a year later he had made so little progress that 'The Economist' labeled him a "useless dictator". Seven years on, General Musharraf is still in charge and the economy has been transformed. In the financial year to mid-2005 it grew by 8.6%, the highest figure for two decades; followed by a 6.6% rise in the following year. The Pakistani rupee is stable. The irony is that it was probably the cascading effect of the 11 September 2001 terrorist attack on USA wherein America wanted Pakistan as an ally and was prepared to pay. It gave $ 600 million straight up, promised to forgive $ 2 billion of debt and persuaded other creditors to go easy. Some of Pakistan's debt was already due to be rescheduled; America ensured that the terms were generous[4].

---

[3] *http://www.cpd-bangladesh.org/Budget%20analysis_FY08.pdf*

[4] *"Changing Its Stripes" – The Economist, July 6, 2006*

In December 2001 the IMF agreed on a $ 1.3 billion facility. Meanwhile remittances rocketed, especially from Pakistanis in America, reflecting fears that Christian countries might freeze Muslim assets. Remittance flows also became more visible as America cracked down on the informal hawala money-transfer system, which it thought was being used by terrorists. This fiscal reprieve, combined with sensible reforms in the banking sector and plenty of spare capacity, provided the basis for Pakistan's burst of growth. But the country has been here before. In both the 1960's and the 1980s, the economy sustained annual growth of over 6%. These periods too, saw military rule which brought relative stability and lashings of aid dollars. The first general in charge, Ayub Khan managed the economy well, the second, Zia-ul-Haq, did not, but was also blessed with a rush of remittances, from the Middle East. Both periods were followed by a decade of civilian misrule during which donors and investors withdrew, growth dropped to 4%, and millions of people were pitched into poverty. Will General Musharraf leave behind a more solid basis for growth? He might. Since 1999 his government has privatized $ 5 billion worth of assets. It has doubled the number of taxpayers, albeit from a low base of 1 million. To sustain 7% growth, Pakistan will need much more foreign investment.

Military Inc – Inside Pakistan's Military Economy "by Ayesha Siddiqa is a detailed exposition of the business and commercial empire run by the Armed Forces.[5] The Central argument of the book is that Milbus (combining the words military and business) perpetuates the military's political predatory style. Ms. Siddiqa defines Milbus as military capital used for the personal benefit of the military fraternity. It refers to all activities that transfer resources from the state to an individual or group within the military. These activities do not figure in the defence budget. There are various invisible benefits of the activities of Milbus, such as using contacts in the military to swing business opportunities. Defence contracts are the most common. Ms. Siddiqa cites the example of the former ISI boss Lt Gen Hamid Gul's daughter running a private bus company, which was able to get preferential access to bus routes between Islamabad and Rawalpindi.

The military describes its commercial empire as "welfare" activities but the book questions this by pointing out that the main beneficiary is the officer cadre. It justifies this in terms of its role as the saviour of the nation, posturing an external threat from India so great that over the years, 'national security has developed into a dogma at par with religious ideology". The external threat is also used to include internal security matters. With their eyes on getting elected, politicians are loathe to challenge this national security agenda. For observers of the India- Pakistan peace process, the book resurrects an old question. If the external threat on Pakistan's eastern border is so necessary for the military to maintain its internal supremacy, which includes its political and economic domination, would it ever allow or enable fully normal relations with India?

Faced with the problem of defence against a much larger potential adversary - India from a relatively limited resource base, the military claims a large share of the nation's resources even to maintain a minimal effective defence capability. From 1958 to 1973, the defence budget accounted for nearly 60% of the total government expenditure. Since 1973, this percentage has been reduced by half due to growing inflation and foreign military aid. In 2006, Pakistan defence accounted for nearly a quarter of the national budget. It spent $ 4.26 billion (ranked 39th in defence spending) which is 4.5% of the GDP.

Pakistan, as part of its defence economy, is trying its hand at exports. In fact it has been trying to palm off substandard military equipment to some countries including Sri Lanka. Pakistan and interested parties in the Sri Lankan Army are understood to be pushing for the sale of Al Zarrar tanks, though Colombo had earlier rejected the offer since it preferred to buy T-72 tanks from Belarus, which are technically superior and nearly four times less than the price of the Pakistani Al Zarrar. The Pakistani defence establishment has gone into an overdrive to clinch the deal. They look at Sri Lanka as a major arms market and several other systems are up for sale. These proposed deals amount to more than $ 200 million. There seems to be discontent in the lower levels of Sri Lankan army as they had to struggle with equipment supplied by Pakistan such as radio sets, battery chargers etc. Most of the defence dealers from the two countries are mainly retired armed forces officers, which allowed them easy accessibility to top ranking decision makers.

---

[5] *"Military Inc – Its big business in Pakistan"; Nirupama Subramanian. 'THE HINDU' April 19, 2007. Se also Ayesha Siddiqa, Military Inc.; Pluto Press, London, 2007*

The Bush administration has provided nearly $ 11 billion in aid to Pakistan since 2001, most of it in military hardware and cash support for the country's operating budget. But frustrations are rising among military officers on both sides because the aid has produced neither battlefield success nor great trust. Western experts are suggesting that Pakistan seems to be utilizing most of the aid on large weapon systems and not on counter insurgency systems. In addition no other country receives more assistance from Washington for military training. Since 2001, Pakistan has received more than $ 6 billion from the coalition support fund. The fund reimburses US allies for costs incurred in fighting global terrorism.

Conclusion

The absence of a well-defined defence economy planning has serious implications for defence budgeting. The existing budget structure of the defence economy is merely allocation of funds without co-relating to long-term threat assessment. Perspective planning is carried out in water tight compartments in various agencies dealing with defence e.g. OFB, DRDO and the services in the case of India.

The defence budgets of both India and Pakistan are of a very large magnitude. Due to an upsurge in the national economies of both these South Asian countries, their defence economics have grown by five to six times over the past decade. As components of their respective national budgets these continue to be the largest i.e. in India about 16% and in Pakistan about 20-25% including the hidden expenditure. Both the countries defence economy has not had the benefit of having a performance budget component. Allocations of funds for defence continue to grow from year to year, especially in view of the large costs involved in the purchase of weapon platforms like aircraft and ships. This warrants the need for better financial information systems to ensure accountability and 'value for money'. Information technology systems and a computer savvy nation can facilitate the correction of this anomaly.

CENTRAL ASIA'S ENERGY RESOURCES: AN INDIAN AND PAKISTANI PERSPECTIVE

Nirmala Joshi
Director, India – Central Asia Foundation, New Delhi

Introduction

Among the several issues confronting mankind today, the issue of ensuring energy security has acquired a critical significance. In the past it was the industrialized nations of the West that were the chief consumers of energy. Today, it is both the industrialized nations and the developing countries whose demand for energy is rising at a phenomenal rate. Apart from the rising demand for energy the politicisation of the issue has complicated the demand. An element of uncertainty was injected in the aftermath of the oil crisis of 1973, when energy was used as a tool to achieve political goals. In the changed context of the present day world, it is important not only to secure energy for economic advancement but it is, perhaps, more important to ensure uninterrupted and predictable supply of energy. The essence of energy security was aptly stated in the New US-Russian Energy Dialogue of May 2002, where it was stressed "successful development of the global economy depends on timely and reliable energy delivery".[1]

The break up of the Soviet Union in 1991 drew the attention of the world to the energy resources of the Central Asian region. The three states of Central Asia, namely, Kazakhstan, Turkmenistan and Uzbekistan are richly endowed with natural resources including energy—oil and natural gas. The Kazakh and Turkmen sectors of the Caspian Sea are also rich in energy and the possibility of unexplored reserves being high is equally real. It would not be wrong to say that the energy resources of the Central Asian region became one of the factors that brought about a shift in international politics from Europe to Asia.

Since the shift in focus, there has been an intense competition among major powers; the United States of America and the European Union (EU) on the one hand and the Russian Federation on the other to control this vital resource. In fact, many analysts

[1] *Bush-Putin Joint Statement on New US-Russian Energy Dialogue, 24 May 2002. Issued by the International Information Programmes of the US Department of State*

believe that the ongoing competition is reminiscent of the 19th century "great game" between the Tsarist and British empires for the control of Afghanistan and the perceived access to the warm waters of the Indian Ocean. This time, instead as one perceptive observer noted: "the new great game is all about oil and gas. The imperial soldiers and spies of a bygone era have given way to engineers and deal makers as the States jockey for the lucrative business of building pipelines to tap the vast resources of the landlocked region".[2] An additional factor that has complicated the energy scenario of Central Asia is its geopolitical location in the centre of Eurasia. The Central Asian region flanks Russia in the North, China in the East, the Middle East and Afghanistan in the South.

In South Asia the demand for energy is also growing. Domestic sources of energy are not able to keep pace with the rising demand. They are also looking to external sources to fulfil their requirements. Due to their geographical proximity to Central Asia it is realistic for India and Pakistan to seek Central Asian energy. However, we find that, even in South Asia, the energy issue has got intertwined with differing strategic concerns of both India and Pakistan. These varying perspectives have, to an extent, cast a shadow on efforts to acquire Central Asian energy. Before we examine Indian and Pakistani perspectives on the energy issue, it is essential to have a brief overview of the estimated energy wealth of the region and also to understand the dynamics that are at play in Central Asia.

Central Asian Energy Scenario

Though the Central Asian energy reserves are not comparable to that of the Persian Gulf and the Middle East, estimated to be between 450 and 530 billion barrels, they nevertheless do constitute a significant alternative. In Kazakhstan, proven oil reserves are 10 billion barrels and possible reserves are estimated at a whopping 85 billion.[3] The Kashagan oil field on the Caspian sector of Kazakhstan is considered as the largest field outside the Middle East. Kazakhstan also has enormous reserves of natural gas and the Karachaganak gas field is estimated to contain vast quantities of this fuel. The figures for oil production for October 2007 showed that its growth is modest for the present. It stood at 44.7 million tonnes which translates into 1,372,000 barrels per day (b/d).[4] The development of the Karachaganak gas field has led to an increase in gas production as compared to oil. While the climate for foreign investors in the energy sector is friendly, as compared to the other Central Asian States, the passage of recent amendments to the law on subsoil resources could be a dampener in future. The amendments, approved by the Parliament in September 2007, empower the authorities to amend terms of contracts with investors, where Kazakhstan's economic interests or national security are deemed to be jeopardized.[5] A case in point is the problems between the government and the AgipKCO, a consortium that is developing the Kashagan offshore oil fields. Negotiations to settle the problem appear to be continuing.

Turkmenistan is also extremely rich in energy resources, particularly natural gas. It is the fifth largest depository of natural gas in the world. Its proven oil resources are 1.5 billion barrels and possible estimated at 32 billion barrels. Gas resources, including proven and potential deposits, are at 8.9 trillion cubic metres (tcm).[6] After assuming office in February 2007, President Gurbanguly Berdymukhammedov announced ambitious production targets of extracting 80 billion cubic metres (bcm) of natural gas in 2007 and 10.4 million tonnes of crude oil. But these targets can be fulfilled only if Turkmenistan is able to attract foreign investments. There has been renewed interest by Western multinationals in Turkmen gas, but the operating climate is even more difficult than it is in Kazakhstan. A coherent energy policy has yet to be worked out.[7] So far the only major step taken by the President is to reaffirm the earlier agreement for building a gas pipeline directly from Turkmenistan to China.

Uzbekistan's energy wealth is modest. It has confirmed oil deposits of 0.2 billion barrels and potential deposits estimated at 1 billion barrels. Natural gas deposits both proven and possible are estimated at 3.1 trillion cubic metres.[8] The business

[2] *The Times of Central Asia (Bishkek), 29 November 2001*

[3] *Raja Menon, "Treacherous Terrain: The Political and Security Dimension of Energy Development in the Caspian Sea Zone", NBR Analysis, vol. 9, no. 1, February 1998, p. 11. Quoted by R.G. Gidadhubli, "Oil Politics in Central Asia", Economic and Political Weekly, 30 January 1999*

[4] *The Economist Intelligence Unit (EIU)(London) Country Reports – Kazakhstan October 2007, p. 27*

[5] *Ibid., p. 28*

[6] *Ariel Cohen, Testimony Before the Subcommittee on Asia and Pacific, United States House of Representatives, 17 March 1999*

[7] *EIU, Country Reports – Turkmenistan, April 2007, p. 22*

[8] *EIU, Country Reports – Uzbekistan, September 2002, p. 28*

climate in Uzbekistan is difficult. Foreign investments, especially from the West are limited, probably because of political reasons. Uzbekistan has, however, permitted small scale investment in the exploration field. Russian monopoly Gazprom has made a modest investment involving exploration of seven blocs on the Usl-Yurt plateau.[9]

While estimates of various studies about the Central Asian energy reserves may vary, they all, however, agree that reserves are substantial to make a difference. "It (Central Asian energy) could play a significant role as a marginal supplier in arresting a jump in the price of oil in a high price environment and diversifying supplies".[10] One daunting factor unique to Central Asia is that the region is landlocked and Uzbekistan is doubly landlocked. Even the Caspian Sea is a closed one. Central Asian energy to reach world markets, therefore, requires an excellent and an efficient pipeline infrastructure. After the break up in 1991 one major pipeline, namely the Caspian Pipeline Consortium (CPC) has been constructed which carries Kazakh oil from its massive oil field Tengiz to the Russian Black Sea port of Novorossisk. The Central Asian States are dependent on Russia to transport their energy to world markets. It is only in late 2006 that a pipeline from Atasu in Central Kazakhstan to Alashankou in Western China, bypassing Russia, was constructed. Plans are already afoot to extend this pipeline to the Caspian Sea. Kazakhstan has also entered into swap deals with Iran whereby it would send oil to the northern port of Iran through the Caspian Sea and in turn Iran would export an equivalent quantity of oil from its southern port on the Persian Gulf.[11] But this arrangement was subsequently discontinued. Reports suggest that this arrangement could be revived. A small pipeline carries Turkmen gas to northern Iran – the Korpedzhe-Kurt Kui pipeline. The bulk of Turkmen gas is, however, sold to Russia.

The western route which could transport Central Asian energy to European markets appears a distant possibility for the present. The unresolved legal status of the Caspian Sea has hindered efforts by Central Asian States to reach European markets. In the absence of a settlement of the legal basis of the Caspian Sea, the other best option is via Iran. The Iranian corridor would provide access to the Persian Gulf, but this route is not favoured by the US. The potential for exploring the southern route to South Asia is high and worth pursuing.

Role of Major Powers

The issue of energy security sparked off an intense competition among the major powers for control of this strategic resource. Linked to the issue of providing several options to the landlocked states of Central Asia was the geopolitical and strategic interest of the West, particularly the US. The energy issue provided the West with an opportunity to advance their geopolitical and economic interests and enhance its own influence. The American strategy aimed to reduce the Russian influence by making the post-Soviet states independent and prosperous. In this context, the issue of building a pipeline infrastructure, as mentioned, assumed tremendous importance. While planning the transport routes for energy, efforts were made to bypass Russia, and the Russian monopoly had to be challenged. In this regard the "contract of the century" was signed in Baku, Azerbaijan between the State Oil Company of Azerbaijan Republic and a consortium of companies led by British Petroleum on 20 September 1994. The route was from Baku to Ceyhan in Turkey via Tbilisi in Georgia (BTC). The BTC has become operational since late 2005.

On the other hand, the CPC formed by Russia, Kazakhstan and Oman, in which the American oil companies Chevron-Texaco also have a major share, is a venture supported by Russia. Thus in no time pipeline politics had emerged in a big way, with symbolic rivals, the BTC versus CPC. Meanwhile, Russia has skillfully used the advantages that have accrued to it because of high oil prices and Russian near monopoly over the pipeline infrastructure, especially in Central Asia, to regain its waning influence there. The approach of Russia is to ensure that the energy policy of the Central Asian States is in tandem with its own. Russia would like to retain its status as a leading "energy power".

Kazakhstan and Turkmenistan are eager to diversify their supply routes and not be dependent on one route, which is the Russian one. The two countries are in the midst of their systemic transition and are fragile nation-states. The best option for Kazakhstan and Turkmenistan to export their oil and gas to Europe would be to join the BTC, and a parallel pipeline

[9] *Ibid., Country Reports – Uzbekistan, June 2007*

[10] *Kapil Kak, "India's Strategic and Security Interests in Central Asia", in Nagendra Rao and Mohammad Monir Alam, eds., Central Asia: Present Challenges and Future Prospects (New Delhi, Knowledge World, 2005), p. 218*

[11] *R.G. Gidadhubli, "Oil Politics and Central Asia", Economic and Political Weekly, January 30, 1999, p. 262*

being thought about for gas. Kazakhstan has agreed in principle to be associated with BTC but plans to build pipelines along the floor of the Caspian have met with Russian objection on ecological grounds. The Kazakh representative, Erik Ultembayev, on the Caspian Basin Talks made a perceptive remark when he said that he does not see any difference between Russia's plans to build a pipeline across the floor of the Baltic and Caspian Seas.[12] Kazakhstan is considering the option to transport oil to Azerbaijan via tankers across the Caspian Sea, but waters around its Caspian port of Aktau are shallow. A special fleet of shuttle tankers to handle large scale oil traffic would be required.

The resolution of the Caspian Sea legal tangle would require Russian agreement. It is also true that when pipelines pass through more than two or three countries securing each country's concurrence is by no means an easy task. According to a pre-feasibility study conducted on "North-South Energy Corridor: Kazakhstan-Iran-India" by the ORF Centre for Resources Management in April 2006, the BTC pipeline which involved inter-governmental agreements between four countries took all of four years to get the 17,000 signatures (one signature for every ten metres of the pipeline) required for financial closure of the project.[13] Moreover Kazakhstan and Turkmenistan are located in a region that is also rich in energy sources. Russia and Iran are leading producers of oil and natural gas. Therefore, "Turkmenistan's two easiest routes to markets are through large gas producing states, Russia and Iran, and both these countries have a strong interest in harnessing Turkmenistan's reserves only insofar as they amplify the value of their own gas assets".[14] In view of their difficult geographical location and internal weaknesses, Kazakhstan and Turkmenistan have adopted pragmatic energy policies. For now, Russia is simply the most useful.

Besides the danger of these countries being destabilized by non-conventional challenges such as religious extremism, international terrorism, aggressive nationalism and drug trafficking is also an important factor to reckon with. More so, when we discuss the Indian and Pakistani efforts to secure Central Asian energy.

Indian and Pakistani Engagement with Central Asian Energy

Over the years, as mentioned, Indian and Pakistani demand for energy has been growing at a rapid rate. Their respective domestic production is unable to keep pace with the rising demand. Reports suggest that seven years on and India would be one of the highest consumers of energy. Importing energy has already become a major component of India's policy for energy security, while this aspect is acquiring a new significance for Pakistan.

In the Indian hydrocarbon scene "The Hydrocarbon Vision 2025" published by the Government of India, in February 2000, clearly highlighted the predicament faced by the country in ensuring energy security. India's oil self sufficiency declined from 63% in 1989-90 to 30% in 2000-01. India's demand for oil is expected to increase from 122 million tonnes in 2001-02 to 196 million tonnes in 2011-12 and 364 million tonnes in 2024-25. Domestic production during this period would increase, but would not be able to keep pace with the demand. It is predicted that by 2024-25 oil sufficiency would be a mere 15%. Similarly, India's requirement for natural gas would increase and is expected to rise from 49 bcm in 2006-07 to 125 bcm in 2024-25.[15] Another estimate by the Tata Energy Research Institute has predicted an even more dire situation. According to their estimates, India's import dependence in crude oil is expected to touch 80% by 2010 and in natural gas 77%. Supplies are expected largely from the Persian Gulf, Central Asia and Southeast Asia.[16]

In the case of Pakistan, its energy needs were succinctly stated by Mukhtar Ahmed, Energy Advisor to the Pakistan Prime Minister. He said, while addressing the "Conference on Fuelling the Future: Meeting Pakistan's Energy Needs in the Twenty First Century", on 21 June 2006, that "over the next twenty years the country's overall demand for energy will increase by 350%. During this period the percentage

[12] *Current Digest of Post Soviet Press, 2006, vol. 58, no. 21, p. 13*

[13] *Quoted in meeting with Kaz Munay Gaz, October 2005, "North-South Energy Corridor: Kazakhstan-Iran-India", A Pre Feasibility Study, April 2006 (ORF Centre for Resources Management, Delhi), p. 32*

[14] *Martha Brill Olcott, "International Gas Trade in Central Asia: Turkmenistan, Iran, Russia and Afghanistan" in David G. Victor and others, eds., Natural Gas and Geopolitics from 1970 to 2040 (Cambridge, University Press, 2006), p. 227*

[15] *Talmiz Ahmad, "Oil Diplomacy for India's Energy Security", in Atish Sinha and Madhup Mohta, eds., Indian Foreign Policy: Challenges and Opportunities (New Delhi, Academic Foundation, 2007), p. 1093*

[16] *Quoted by Kapil Kak, n. 10, p. 218*

of Pakistan's total energy needs met from indigenous sources will fall from 72 to 38%.... Pakistan has given high priority to tapping the energy resources in the region and several projects for import of natural gas from the gas rich countries in the Middle East and Central Asia have received serious attention.[17] Incidentally Pakistan is placing greater emphasis on natural gas and hopes to make it "the fuel of choice" for future.

What are the options that India and Pakistan can pursue vis-à-vis Central Asia? The first and perhaps the best option for natural gas is the Turkmenistan-Afghanistan-Pakistan-India (TAPI) gas pipeline. The TAPI project was initiated in October 1995 by President Saparmurat Niyazov when he signed an agreement with Unocal and its partner in the project Delta Oil of Saudi Arabia. The project had the full backing of the US. It is believed that in their drive to launch this project some American multinational companies had negotiated with the Taliban.

The 1680 kilometre long pipeline is expected to transport natural gas from the Turkmen gas field at Daulatabad in the western part of the country via Herat and Kandahar in Afghanistan to Quetta and Multan in Pakistan and then to Fazilka in India. Unocal withdrew from the project in 1998 perhaps due to difficulties raised by the Taliban government. In the wake of the defeat of the Taliban, the TAPI project has once again been revived. It has received the strong backing of the US and recently, the Asian Development Bank (ADB) has taken the initiative to re-launch the project.

In the early years of the TAPI project India was not at all enthusiastic about it. In the Annual Report of the Ministry of Defence for the year 2000-2001 it was clearly stated that "energy cooperation and sharing arrangements only with countries whose actions do not undermine India's security and which have demonstrated a willingness to cooperate meaningfully with India".[18] Since the ouster of the Taliban, India's approach to the TAPI project has undergone a positive change. The geopolitical change in India's neighbourhood and partly the increasing urgency to ensure energy security made India to see the situation differently. It is plausible that Indian perception of Pakistan using its leverage as a transit country over India, especially during a crisis situation, could have been reconsidered. India is now all set to formally join the project at a Steering Committee meeting called by the project sponsor ADB at Islamabad on 28-29 November 2007. The four countries would be signing the Project Heads of Agreement and a Gas Pipeline Framework Agreement. At the meeting Turkmenistan is expected to make a presentation on the potential of its reserves and volumes available for export. Once operational, the TAPI is expected to provide India 40 Million Standard Cubic Meters Day (MSCMD) during the first four years and 31 MSCMD in the next 26 years.[19] There are, however, still doubts in some quarters whether Turkmenistan has sufficient gas for TAPI as large quantities of gas have already been committed to Russia and China.

Pakistan on the other hand, had always been a strong supporter of the project. In September 1997 Unocal and Pakistan concluded a thirty year gas pricing agreement. Apart from meeting its own rising demand for gas, "the fuel of choice", Pakistan also has larger interests at stake. The Turkmen-Afghanistan-Pakistan (TAP) project was envisaged by Pakistan as part of its attempts to emerge as the gateway to Central Asia and as a hub linking the Middle East, Central Asia and China. In this regard the TAP project had three phases in the Pakistani perception. In the first phase, the gas pipeline would reach Multan; in the second it would be extended to Gwadar port for onward export of gas to Japan and other Far Eastern countries; and in the third phase it would be extended to India.[20] Pakistan's ambition to emerge as a hub for energy, trade and transport for the Central Asian countries is uncertain for the present. But if it does succeed in its ambition, the political fall out for Pakistan in terms of leverage would be tremendous. For the present, however, Pakistan's main concern is the disruption of energy supplies threatened by a growing wave of terrorism both within the country and from the neighbouring country. It is also possible, as some analysts opine, that the threat of disruption of energy supplies could promote greater cooperation among the states of the region. Such cooperation would undoubtedly require tremendous political will.

The second option is the Iran-Pakistan-India (IPI) pipeline project. The IPI project was launched in 1994. The 2600 kilometre long pipeline is expected

[17] *www.wilsoncenter.org/events/docs/Text of Keynote address. Accessed on 6 November 2007*

[18] *Annual Report of the Ministry of Defence, Government of India, 2000-01, p. 11*

[19] *Indian Express (New Delhi), October 11, 2007*

[20] *Dr. Maqsudul Hasan Nuri, "The Afghan Corridor: Prospects for Pak-CAR Relations Post Taliban?", Regional Studies (Karachi), vol. 20, no. 4, 2002, p. 36*

to transport Iranian gas to Pakistan and India. Discussions on the project have however dragged on. Contrary to the prevailing view, India has been interested in the project. Prime Minister Dr. Manmohan Singh said in reply to a question whether the pipeline was a good idea, "We are in dire need of energy and we are keen on carrying out this project. The negotiations are proceeding".[21] The cost of the pipeline is expected to be US $7.4 billion. Earlier, the Russian gas monopoly Gazprom had acquired a 10% stake in the project, but it seems that it has withdrawn from the project. It is not clear who the supporters of this pipeline project would be.

From the Indian perspective, the biggest impediment is the periodic price revision the supplier would undertake after every three years. The price fixation would depend on the prevailing international prices for natural gas. In the case of TAPI the price has been fixed for thirty years. Besides the Turkmen government has allotted a gas field for TAPI, while Iran has yet to allocate a field for the IPI project. Apart from economic considerations, political calculations have also weighed in the Indian decision to adopt a cautious approach towards this project. Given the continuing tensions over Iran on the nuclear issue, the IPI project may not be easy to implement. Recent reports suggest that Iran and Pakistan have finalized the contract which is likely to be signed within a month. India still remains a potential participant of the deal.

It is possible that, if the IPI becomes operational and the Iranian nuclear issue is sorted out, Turkmenistan could be a potential party to the deal. Russia and Kazakhstan, who would like to diversify their markets, could also join the project. In February 1997, a tripartite agreement between India-Iraq-Turkmenistan was signed to promote economic interaction. The agreement envisaged a combination of rail and sea routes. According to the agreement a railway line from Sarakhs in Turkmenistan would reach the Iranian border town of Meshad, and then to Chah Bahar port on the Persian Gulf, and then by sea to Mumbai. This route holds the promise for transporting energy as well. The swap deals of Kazakhstan would also get an impetus. The effectiveness of this option would depend largely on the resolution of the Iranian nuclear issue.

Apart from these two southern routes, another possibility that is being discussed is transporting Central Asian energy to India and Pakistan via China. According to the ORF Pre Feasibility Study a gas hub could be created at Urumchi and Kashgar in China. This gas hub could connect supplies from Central Asia and Siberia from where they could diverge into two branches, one to south reaching northern India and second one in the eastward direction. Crossing the Karakoram mountain ranges would be a technological challenge.[22] An equally daunting task would be to procure the cooperation of China for this venture. The contentious border issue between India and China needs to be settled especially if Aksai-Chin is projected as the area for its entry into India. For the present it seems that it could be simpler to ship oil by sea. Some analysts are of the view that given the high degree of pragmatism in Chinese thinking, it is possible that the authorities could agree.

At the wider level India has kept out of the Central Asian great game, but neither did it have its own approach to the issue of energy security. It was only a couple of years ago that India made a proposal for an Asian gas grid—the objective being to link energy producing and consuming regions to one another. It seems that the objective was to forge some kind of an understanding with China on the energy issue instead of being competitors. Such an approach came in the wake of the Indian fiasco in the Petro Kazakhstan deal, which was lost to China. A ministerial meeting to promote the idea of an Asian Gas Grid was held in New Delhi in November 2005. At the meeting two important suggestions were put forward. One, that the BTC oil be brought to India via tankers from Saudi Arabia and second that the TAPI project originate in Azerbaijan. Nothing further was heard about these ideas. The Chinese preference would be for promoting such ideas through the Shanghai Cooperation Organization (SCO). At the latest SCO summit at Bishkek, in August 2007, President Nursultan Nazarbaev put forward a proposal for the formation of an "energy club", and suggested a meeting of producing, transporting and consuming countries. India and Pakistan, as countries with Observer status in the SCO, stand to benefit if the idea takes off. Similar ideas were mooted at the recent trilateral meeting of India-Russia-China in Harbin, China, in October 2007. But these ideas are still in the realm of the conceptual stage.

Indian efforts to secure energy related contracts are not as vigorous as they should be, and the Central

[21] *Hindu (Chennai), February 17, 2007*
[22] *n. 13, p. 32*

Asian responses to Indian efforts are also lukewarm. It is as President Vladimir Putin says "a seller's market". In 2005, India lost the bid to buy Petro Kazakhstan to China. Media reports suggests that negotiations for giving ONGC Videsh equity in a lucrative Caspian oil field would depend on India's support on the issue of Kazakhstan joining the world trade body.[23] During Prime Minister Manmohan Singh's visit to Uzbekistan, in April 2006, a Memorandum of Cooperation between the Gas Authority of India Ltd. and Uzbekneftgaz was signed. So far there appears to be no follow up action, and the reasons for this delay are not known. Apart from lack of geographical connectivity which acts as a major impediment in transporting energy, Indian involvement is needed in related areas such as acquisition of assets abroad, equity participation in prospecting fields, exploration and production participation in downstream projects (refineries and petrochemicals), finalisation of long term L.N.G. contracts and setting up of trans-national gas pipelines.[24] This will give India an opportunity to enhance its leverage in the energy sector.

Conclusion

The Central Asian energy issue has been caught in the vortex of international politics—the great game. An intense competition, accompanied by a vigorous diplomacy to control this vital resource has made energy a seller's market issue. Initially; the Indian approach to the Central Asian energy issue was not as dynamic as it should have been, perhaps lack of direct connectivity may have acted as an impediment. The Indian approach, however, is now proactive. Given India's high level of technical skills and vast experience, Indian involvement in energy related areas holds immense promise. Such a presence would help India in harnessing the Central Asian hydrocarbon reserves.

[23] *Times of India (New Delhi), October 14, 2006*

[24] *Talmiz Ahmad, n. 15, p. 1086*

TIBETAN PARADOX

Brigadier (Retd) VP Malhotra
Defence Analyst, Author of "Tibetan Conundrum"

Tibet is a landlocked, high altitude country with an average altitude of 4,000 metres. The country is bounded by the Himalayas towards the south and by the Karakoram and Kunlun mountains in the west, and the Kunlun, Altyn and Quilion ranges in the north. It generally slopes from west to east with prominent openings in the east and northeast. Western Tibet is desert and sparsely inhabited with its population density increasing towards east. Eastern Tibet is wooded and relatively prosperous. Tibet and Tibetan ethnic areas are a source of major rivers feeding South and South East Asia. Tibet is a plateau distinct from the neighbouring regions.

Brief History

Till the 9th century Tibet was a warrior expansionist nation and maintained an army of 200,000. The Tibetan empire had expanded to include parts of China, Central Asian Republics and Ladakh. So much was the military glory of Tibet that it is said that the Caliph of Baghdad had to go in for a treaty arrangement with the Emperor of China against Tibet. Around the 9th century Tibet came under Buddhist influence and by the 13th century, almost entire Tibet converted to Buddhism.[1] The hand that held the sword was now supporting a prayer wheel. A warrior nation had turned pacifist.

The Mongols conquered Tibet in the 13th century and, in the 16th century, the Tibetan Lamas formally went in to an arrangement with the Mongol rulers known as *Cho Yon* meaning Patron-Priest relationship. The Lama became the spiritual and temporal head in Tibet, albeit with foreign support. The concept of Dalai Lama, which was Mongolian in origin, also came in to being during this time.[2] Tibet's troubles seem to have started with the Lama getting used to ruling with foreign support. The security sector was totally neglected with far reaching consequences in 1950-51.

Tibet was an independent state till the 14th century despite the *Cho Yon* arrangements with the Mongols. China misled the world to its advantage when China and Tibet were being ruled simultaneously by the Mongols from the Mongol seat of power in Beijing.

---

1 *Warren W. Smith, Jr, Tibetan Nation, HarperCollins Publishers, India, p. 82*
2 *ibid. p. 106*

Also the intra and inter faction intrigues in Tibet brought in the foreign influence more prominently. Tibet became an area of interest in the great power game between the British, Russia and China in late 19th and early 20th century. China became a major player but Tibetan sovereignty was never lost to China nor did Tibet ever become a vassal of China. As the Qing dynasty in China collapsed in the early 20th century, Tibet severed all its relations with China, expelled all Chinese troops, declared independence and remained so till invaded by China in 1950.[3]

When the Chinese invaded Tibet in 1950-51, the Tibetan demand was complete independence as was prevailing till then over the centuries. The 17-Point Agreement between Tibet and China was signed under duress when the former had been subdued militarily. The uprising against Chinese rule, which started in 1956, culminated in the escape of the Dalai Lama along with 80,000 followers to India in 1959. The precise stand of the Dalai Lama and his Government-in-Exile was their demand of complete independence and nothing less.[4] The demand was based on the historical facts and international law.

The Dalai Lama now operates from a foreign land and has not succeeded in achieving his Government's stated goal of total independence. His absence from Tibet for over 48 years has led to the complete cultural and demographic transformation of Tibet. Against the original population of 6 million Tibetans in Tibet, China has settled 7.5 million Hans, thus changing the demographic ratio in favour of China. The process continues without any interference or resistance. Because of absence of their temporal and spiritual head for nearly five decades, China is in full control of Tibetan affairs. It is a case of national submission.

Strategic Importance of Tibet. With Tibet becoming part of China, the buffer between China and South Asia has disappeared with far reaching security implications for South Asian countries. The military deployment in Tibet provides China with a military mounting base for engaging the South Asian region.

The Siling-Gormo railway line was completed in 1979 and became operational in 1984. The 550 kilometre Gormo-Lhasa railway became operational in 2006. The train crosses an altitude of 17,000 feet with howling winds. The complete traction, rolling stock, fuel etc. has been tailor manufactured for operations in high altitudes. The railway line is planned to be further extended to Shigatse and connected to Yunnan via Nyingtri.

The occupation of Tibet by China has increased China's reach into the South Asia with conventional as well as nuclear-tipped missiles. With strategic missiles deployed in Tibet, all value objectives in South Asia can be engaged to devastating effect. The airfields in Tibet facilitate mid-air refueling to mount air attacks on value objectives in South Asia as also support a ground offensive. With further development these airfields could act as main airfields distinct from the forward airfields.

China has already gained access to the Indian Ocean with the construction of the Karakoram Highway and the projected development of a road from Yunnan through Myanmar. Her access to the Indian Ocean has further improved with the occupation of Tibet. While such a gigantic effort will contribute to the economic exploitation of Tibet by China, the infrastructural up gradation will also contribute to its strategic and political aims. As for India, Tibet must be denied as

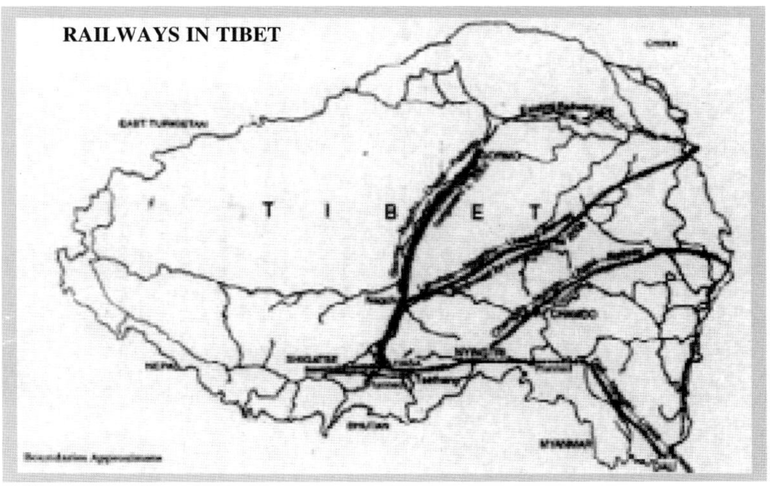

[3] *Dawa Norbu, Tibet The Road Ahead, HarperCollins Publishers, India, p. 60*

[4] *His Holiness, the Dalai Lama's Press Statements and Speeches in 1959. Statement made to New York Times*

a vantage point and a mounting military base to any foreign power. The Dalai Lama's proposal to declare it a zone of peace should be supported. The militarisation of Tibet propels India to deploy more than ten mountain divisions along its northern borders leading to a sizeable economic drain of scarce resources. For India, tranquil northern borders are most desirable. There are other emotive issues like religion, culture, traditions and ethnicity which compel India to exercise her responsibility towards Tibet. The Mansarovar Lake and Mount Kailash, which are considered sacred in India, are located in Tibet.

Natural Resources

Tibet and its ethnic areas are rich in unexploited strategic mineral resources.[5] Through diverse sources the Tibetan mineral resources have been estimated at 40% of China's reserve of chromites and over 14% of copper reserves are located in Tibet and its ethnic areas. Tibet also has substantial reserves of uranium, plutonium, cesium, strontium, gold, oil and natural gas.

The Water Tower of Asia

Tibet and Tibetan ethnic areas are endowed with the greatest river system in the world. Its rivers supply fresh water to 80% of Asia's population and approximately 45% of the world's population. Three of the world's major rivers (Yarlung Tsangpo or Brahmaputra, Yangtze and Mekong) have their source in Tibet or the Tibetan ethnic areas. The Indian subcontinent is nourished by the perennial flow of four major rivers originating from different directions of the Kailash Range in western Tibet. Other mighty rivers flowing from Tibet such as the Yangtze, Yellow, Salween and Mekong sustain the lives of millions in China, Myanmar, Laos, Cambodia, Thailand and Vietnam.

The Yarlung Tsangpo or Brahmaputra runs 2057 kilometres in Tibet and then makes a U-turn (Great Bend) to enter India in the Siang district of Arunachal Pradesh, flows through India and Bangladesh and drains in to the Bay of Bengal. 33% of its water is collected in catchments in Tibet. Its valleys in India and Bangladesh are fertile farmlands with thick forest coverage, crops of tea, rice, jute and rare flora and fauna. The river is crucial to the economy of the entire region. It is reliably reported that China proposes to build the world's largest dam with a capacity of 40,000 MW[6] of power, in the next 15-20 years, in the area of the Great Bend. Since the plan will influence the life of millions of people in Tibet, India and Bangladesh, a detailed study is recommended to be carried out by the lower riparian countries so that the project proceeds in accordance with established international norms. A similar approach would need to be adopted by the lower riparian countries with regard to the other Tibetan rivers namely Karnali, Yangtze, Yellow, Mekong and Salween, flowing in to Nepal, Myanmar, Thailand, Laos, Cambodia and Vietnam.

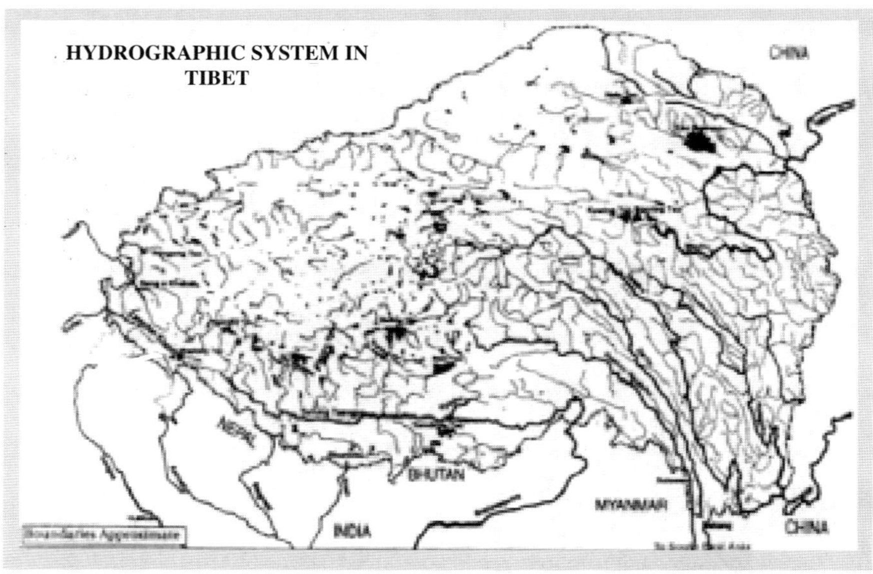

[5] *A scientific survey conducted by Swami Parnavananda in 1930s and 1940s revealed gold, radium, iron, titanium and emery in the area of Lake Mansarovar and Mt Kailash. A report of the investigating teams of the Chinese Academy of Science, soon after the occupation of Tibet, also revealed existence of substantial strategic minerals*

[6] *http://www.rediff.com/news/2003/oct/27spec.htm*

Lebensraum

The issue of Tibet should be seen with the issues of other nationalities viz. Sinkiang, Inner Mongolia and Manchuria. In order to provide 94% of the Han population, who were occupying only 40% of the territory, space to live, the living space of the minority nationalities (6%) who are occupying 60% of the territories that is rich in sub-surface wealth, was required. It is also relevant that China proper has only 20% cultivable land and the rest is mountains, deserts and swamps.

Legal Status of Tibet[7]

The essential ingredients for statehood in international law are population, territory, a government exercising effective control over that population and territory, and the capacity to enter into relations with other states independently and sustain them. The latter is most important.

When the PLA entered Tibet in 1950, Tibet presented all attributes of statehood. Tibetans are a distinct population in a distinct territory. Tibet had a fully functioning government headed by the Dalai Lama which administered the country through civil, judicial, taxation, post and telegraph services, and had a separate currency (comprising of numismatic paper money and coinage). The country had defined borders (even though some border disputes existed) and issued passports to its people, which were recognized internationally. In 1948, France, Great Britain, India, Italy, and with reservation, the United States accepted the Tibetan passports.

Tibet concluded treaties, as a sovereign nation, with other states which included British India, China, Mongolia, Ladakh and Nepal. Tibet negotiated a treaty as an equal sovereign with China and Great Britain at Simla in 1913-14. The very fact that, in 1956, China abrogated all past treaties between Tibet and Nepal goes to prove further that Tibet has been an independent country and was concluding international treaties.

Historical evidence demonstrates that Tibet has always been an independent state, despite periods during which it was influenced to varying degrees by foreign powers. By the 8th century, Tibet had become the most powerful nation in Asia, and had conquered several Chinese provinces. In the 13th century, Tibet came under Mongol dominance decades before the Mongols conquered China. Tibet was administered separately by the Mongols through local Tibetan rulers, in contrast to China which the Mongols ruled directly. Tibet also was declared independent 18 years earlier than the Chinese in the 14th century. Tibet was a distinct country and was treated as such by the Mongols.

The Chinese argument that they were maintaining military posts and advisers in Tibet and that a large number of Tibetans were regularly visiting China to pay tribute to the Chinese ruler is not borne by records held with China or Tibet. During the visit of the Dalai Lama to China in 1653, the Chinese Emperor rode out of the city to receive him and accorded him the highest honour as an equal. The Chinese argument that the Dalai Lama performed *kow-tow* as if he was heading a Chinese vassal is far from truth and is not borne by record.

From 1349 to 1642, Tibet was a secular kingdom, free from Mongol and Chinese control. Emperors of the Chinese Ming Dynasty, however, nominally granted titles to certain Tibetan officials but exercised no effective control over Tibetan affairs. In 1720, Manchu troops entered Tibet to expel the Mongols and to protect the Dalai Lama. The Chinese claim that the troops were accompanied by a team of cadres from the imperial administration to reorganise the Tibetan administration. The Chinese further claim that the Tibetan Kashag (Parliament) and the Kalons (Members of Parliament) reported to the two Chinese Ambans for all matters including defence and foreign affairs. According to the Fourteenth Dalai Lama the role of the Ambans was only to keep the Emperor informed of the happenings in Tibet (an ambassadorial role), supervise the defence of Tibet and keep the Mongols at bay. They were not involved in the proceedings of the Kashag (Parliament).

In 1792 Emperor Qianlong sent troops to Tibet to repel the Nepalese invasion which indicates that China exercised some kind of control over Tibetan foreign policy during this period. It could be concluded that China would be exercising a fair amount of administrative control over Tibet as well. It appears that Tibet was heading towards becoming a Chinese satellite when Qianlong died and the Qing court became unable to protect Tibet against foreign invasions. The Qing Emperors provided no military assistance in Tibet's wars with the Dogras (1841-

[7] *An Inquiry Committee of Tibet headed by Shri Purshottam Trikamdas, Findings of International Commission of Jurists. (Historical facts verified)*

1842), the Gorkhas (1855-1856), and against intrusion by British India (1903-1904). The wars ended with peace treaties signed by the Dogra and Tibetan plenipotentiaries in 1842 and between Nepalese and Tibetan plenipotentiaries in 1856. Under the treaty, Nepal extracted a form of tribute from Tibet and assumed a protectorate role over it. When Kalon Shatra established a new Government in Tibet in 1862, he looked to the Nepalese Court for official recognition, not to Peking. By the middle of the 19th century, therefore, the Qing Empire did not exercise effective control over Tibet, even to the limited extent of securing its borders.

By the beginning of the 20th century, Tibet had become a focus between China, Britain and Russia. On the pretext of sending a trade mission to Tibet, British troops entered Tibet resulting in loss of life and conclusion of a Treaty in 1904 between Tibet and Britain. Obviously the treaty was concluded on unequal terms. China played the role of a bystander totally ignoring her responsibility, if any. The treaty was bilateral and clearly signified the independent status of Tibet. The Manchu court refused to countersign the treaty as it failed to recognize Chinese suzerainty over Tibet. On protracted negotiations China concluded a treaty in 1906 with Great Britain which prevented Tibet from concluding direct negotiations with any foreign power without the consent of China. China, however, was excluded from the category of foreign powers. An Anglo-Russian Treaty signed in 1907 also accepted a measure of Chinese suzerainty over Tibet. Both London and Moscow undertook to refrain from violating Tibet's territorial integrity and interfering in her internal affairs. Both parties were precluded from entering in direct negotiations with Tibet except through the good offices of China. Nothing can be read in these bilateral treaties among Great Britain, China and Russia. They could not legislate or decide pertaining to a third country behind its back. These were intrigues of power in the region promoting their interests or forestalling perceived threats.

In 1911 the Chinese revolution swept the country and the Qing dynasty fell. Tibet decided to make a clean break with China. The Chinese troops including the Ambans were expelled from Tibet. In 1913, the Dalai Lama, who had earlier escaped to India, returned to Tibet and declared independence. Information in this regard was sent to India, Great Britain and Russia. Distinctive Tibetan currency and postage stamps were ordered. Tibetan currency remained in circulation till 1959.

During World War II, Tibet remained neutral, and it insisted on that neutrality despite pressures from China, Great Britain and the United States. Tibet refused to permit the construction of a road through its territory to carry military supplies from British India to China. These were the acts of a functioning independent state. Thus, Tibet was an independent country at the time of Chinese invasion in 1950 with a government headed by the Dalai Lama.

The Present Status

After the signing of the 17-Point Agreement, Tibet became an integral part of China with promise of near complete internal autonomy. The promise was not kept. The Chinese also sought to impose their systems which ran counter to the Tibetan way of life and religion. The widespread riots which started in 1956 culminated into repressive policies and escape of the Dalai Lama to India in 1959, from where he runs his Government-in-Exile.

In the absence of the Dalai Lama in Tibet, the Chinese are changing the face of Tibet from one which was conservative, religious, traditionalist, ritualistic and non-materialistic, transitioning to declining religious values and traditions, and materialism. Also the Chinese will be tenacious to retain Tibet in order to exploit its economic potential, engage South Asian countries and to improve her access to the Indian Ocean.

The Chinese population transfer policy has been applied to all minority areas uniformly. In erstwhile Manchuria there are 75 million Chinese against 2-3 million Manchus. In Sinkiang there are 7 million Chinese out of total population of 14 million. In Inner Mongolia, Mongols have been reduced to 2.5 million against 8.5 million Chinese. In Tibet 7.5 million Chinese have been settled reducing the Tibetans to a minority in their own country.

There are 500,000 Chinese troops and a quarter of China's nuclear arsenal located in the Tibetan Autonomous region (TAR). It is estimated that there are 6-8 ICBMs, 60-70 Medium Range Ballistic Missiles (MRBMs) and 20-25 Intermedium Range Ballistic Missiles (IRBMs) located on Tibet's soil. 15 radar stations and 14 military airfields in TAR and ethnic areas support the Chinese military might in Tibet.[8]

[8] *An assessment of the author*

With the changing demography, sociology and militarisation of Tibet, the Dalai Lama who insisted on the 'pre-1950 Status' till 1959 has already scaled down his demand in 1987, to:

- Transformation of the whole of Tibet in to a Zone of Peace.
- Abandonment of China's population transfer policy.
- Respect for the Tibetan people's fundamental human rights and democratic freedom.
- Restoration and protection of Tibet's natural environment and the abandonment of China's use of Tibet for the production of nuclear weapons and the dumping of nuclear waste.
- Commencement of 'earnest negotiations' on the future status of Tibet and of relations between the Tibetan and Chinese peoples.

These proposals were rejected by China in totality. The demand was further scaled down by the Dalai Lama in 1988 during an address to the European Parliament in Strasbourg, to:

- Tibet would comprise of *Cholka Sum* (T'sang, Chamdo and Amdo) and should become a self governing democratic political entity in association with PRC.
- The self governing democratic political entity would comprise of an elected chief executive, a bicameral legislative branch and an independent judiciary.
- The new government would have powers to decide on Tibet and Tibetans.
- The Foreign Affairs could be retained by PRC. The Government of Tibet should however, develop and maintain relations through its own Foreign Affairs Bureau in the fields of religion, commerce, education, culture, tourism, science, sports and other non-political activities.
- Tibet should be declared a Zone of Peace, however, China could maintain a small force for defensive purposes, the size of which could be decided through mutual consultations.

USA and European countries would not take any direct initiatives which would ruffle China. No country has formally questioned the status quo and the issue is being kept alive only as a handle to embarrass China, when required. The proposals should have been accepted, at least for discussion, since the Dalai Lama has consented to remain part of PRC. As for India, His Holiness the Dalai Lama is a respected guest of India and the Government of India cannot even think of asking him to leave Indian territory. However, the Government of India's official political stand is that Tibet is a region of China.

Tibetans in exile are stateless people. Over 1,000 escapees add to the original exiled population, every year. Their escape and escape routes are harsh accompanied by the exploitation by touts and authorities *en route*, in Tibet, Nepal and in India. For those seeking independence for Tibet or owing allegiance to the Dalai Lama and the Panchen Lama, if caught *en route*, the weight of oppression can be heavy in deed. Lately, Nepal has denied the Tibetans permission to transit through their country in order to appease China and possibly India as well. On arrival at the Tibetan camps they are well received and their stay is managed to the extent of their rehabilitation. Not all are political escapees. Some come to seek the blessings of the Dalai Lama and go back. Others come to escape from the harsh living conditions created by the Chinese, never to return. There are yet others who come for economic reasons or for education in the environment provided by the Tibetan Government-in-Exile. Since their expectations are high, some are not satisfied with the cost and risk in escaping to India. Thus their experience of exile is rather complex and deserves sympathy and international support.[4]

India is not a signatory to the UN Refugee Convention and does not have national legislation regarding refugees. However, India considers Tibetans and Sri Lankans in camps to be *prima facie* refugees, but regards most other groups as economic migrants. As such, most Tibetans hold Indian Residential Certificates. Tibetans do not enjoy the same rights as Indian citizens, such as formal participation in Indian politics or grant of a legal Indian passport, but are free to work and own property.

The endeavour of the Tibetans to protect their cultural and religious identity has so far faced minimal opposition from their Indian hosts, barring a few minor incidents. For the past 50 years, the Fourteenth Dalai Lama has kept alive their dreams of survival as a distinct entity. However, as the number of Tibetan refugees swells, the Tibetan administration faces the growing challenges of their settlement and also preserving their religious identity, from the onslaught of modern society in India.

---

[9] *Interview of a few recent escapees by the author at Dharamshala in 2004*

An important question also arises, "What after the present Dalai Lama?" The Dalai Lama feels that, whether the institution of the Dalai Lama remains or not, depends entirely on the wishes of the Tibetan people. At the present moment, the Dalai Lama's institution is useful to the Tibetan culture and the Tibetan people. Thus, the Tibetan people should choose to have another Dalai Lama. The usual search would take place for a reincarnation, using the traditional mixture of omens, guidance from senior lamas and physical search. The Dalai Lama has said he expects his successor to be found in a "free country", so he can carry on what he calls his "unfulfilled mission". But if the Fourteenth Dalai Lama were to be allowed to return to Tibet within his own lifetime, the Fifteenth would be found there.

The long stretch between the death of one Dalai Lama and the adulthood of the next has always been a time of political weakness and exploitation. Many fear that his death will rob them of their last chance of any genuine self-rule, independence or autonomy. Others predict confusion, chaos and/or bloodshed. Tibetan youth might finally feel free to resort to a freedom struggle, a mix of non-violence and violent agitation.

It is prudent to presume that either the democratically elected Prime Minister of the Tibetan Government-in-Exile or a Kashag appointed Regent will guide the Tibetans in Tibet and those in exile, till the re-incarnate reaches adulthood. The Chinese will also choose their own Dalai Lama or his re-incarnate, like they chose their own Panchen **Lama. It is** highly unlikely that China would accept someone from beyond its borders. But China selecting its own Dalai Lama will have far reaching implications.

Environmental Issues

Any nation which undertakes abrupt modernization traumatizes the environment. This is more so when the modernization is motivated to meet the requirements of another nation or of an occupying nation or a nation which has been absorbed as result of a treaty like the 17-Point Agreement.

Grassland Degradation. The Kham areas alone, in the eastern Tibetan Plateau, had forest cover of more than 10 million cubic metres. Deforestation for the benefit of the mainland led to the devastating floods in 1998 in China. The policy had to be reversed and reforestation of the slopes and erstwhile forests has been undertaken by migrant Hans leading to restricted use of land for grazing. Herdsmen and their cattle have been fenced in order to progress reforestation. Then was the requirement of meat in the mainland. The size of herds was quadrupled leading to further pressure on the grasslands. Deforestation, reforestation and over grazing are leading to disappearance of the grasslands, desertification, unemployment and severe economic and social pressure on the traditional nomads.

Bio-Diversity Degradation. Bio-diversity in Tibet is under tremendous strain because of population growth and economic development. It has been severely affected by increased human activity like deforestation, over-exploitation of animal and plant resources, pollution and introduction of invasive species. Han-isation and modernization has reduced the area available for flora and fauna from the pre-1950 level. Hunting and poaching activity is being encouraged to attract tourists.

Mineral Exploitation. Massive investments for creating infrastructure to extract gas, copper and chromites have been made in north and north east Tibet. Chromites are much needed for the expanding car industry in China. Asbestos mining, aluminum smelters, lead and zinc mining are expanding in the area. Exploitation of the salt lakes is necessary to manufacture plastics and chemical fertilizers. Oil fields in Tsaidam pump two million tons of crude to the nearby refineries. There are hardly any safeguards to ensure environmental regulation. The pollution is causing flourisis both in the human beings and animals.

The Road Map

Tibet faces two paradoxical issues. First, it has been occupied by China, who could either be evicted by force or through negotiations. Second, Tibet is a Buddhist state and is headed by the Dalai Lama. He must not use or advocate violence, he must adopt non-violent means like diplomacy, negotiations, *satyagraha* (peaceful agitation based on truth) or persuasion. His two hats prevent him from adopting direct measures.

Peaceful Agitation

A peaceful agitation for resolution of the Tibetan issue would be time consuming and in the meanwhile Tibet may transform the way Manchuria has lost its original identity. The major advantage of this course of action is that the Dalai Lama can and has mustered international support against human rights violations in Tibet. The Dalai Lama's non-violent approach to violence and illegal occupation of Tibet has precedence in Gandhi's non-violent agitation which contributed to hastening of independence in India in 1947. The difference however is that Gandhi was leading the movement from within India whereas Dalai Lama is operating from another country, with restrictions. There were other contributing factors to the independence of India. In the case of Tibet, China is a mighty power and within its striking distance. Chinese are more direct and ruthless in dealing with dissensions. A non-violent approach is unlikely to succeed.

Democratisation of China

Pursuing the non-violent course, Tibet can hope for a favourable resolution of the issue if China goes democratic. There are Chinese, in and out of China, who aspire for democratic form of governance. Such groups are suppressed in China but the Chinese in exile are rather vocal. The 'Federation for Democracy in China (FDC)', operating in western countries, advocates that China should become a genuine democratic federation. Under the proposed form of governance, a great deal of autonomy other than defence and foreign affairs would be assured. The aspect of self-determination is inherent in any democratic set up, but that should lead to genuine autonomy as part of a federated China. Genuine autonomy would imply freedom to choose form of governance, fundamental human rights, and freedom of belief and protection of culture. It is further stated by the FDC that independence for Tibet or Taiwan would be a disaster, both for these territories and China. Tibet would have a 'Tibet specific' form of governance and not necessarily like Taiwan, Hongkong, Hainan or any other province of China. The Dalai Lama, however, would have a mammoth task at hand to transform Tibet from autocratic governance to devolution of authority to the people.

Also, the Han settlers would have to be managed democratically. Tibet's borders could be re-negotiated around the concept of *Cholka sum*. If the moderates come in a position to assert themselves, and the Chinese diaspora plays its role, China could go democratic and the resolution of minority aspirations would then be addressed appropriately. But that is hard to come by. It is a policy of inaction, wait and watch. With the existing form of governance and deployment of the Chinese Military Regions, it is unlikely that democratic transformation will be allowed to take place in the foreseeable future. The conflict in the minds of Tibetan youth will grow simultaneously with transformation of Tibet in to a materialistic state. The status and role of the Dalai Lama prevents him from approving action one way or the other.

Non-Violent Action

Short of direct action, a very innovative and effective option can be exercised which would meet the requirements of the non-violent philosophy of the unquestioned leader of all Tibetans and Buddhists, the Dalai Lama. Under the guidance of the Holiness, all Tibetans should revert back to their country without indulging in any violence or offence. Tibetans, as refugees, have the right to return to their homeland without conditions. Seventy five to hundred thousand refugees returning to their homeland in unison could be very effective even in the face of most ruthless authorities. Tibetans, following their philosophy of non-violence, compassion and sacrifice, must be prepared to sacrifice their lives non-violently for the sake of the future generations. Silently they would demand the rightful status of their country. The world would not only sympathise with them but would respect them as an intelligent, organized and committed race.

Tibet is a compact society. The Chinese cannot afford to captivate its leader, His Holiness the Dalai Lama or their Prime Minister and members of Kashag as it would amount to captivity of the Tibetan society as a whole, with far reaching consequences. The Tiananmen type of atrocities cannot be inflicted in the present times with prevalence of media transparency, human right conventions and international organizations. Effective and committed leadership would emerge to guide the Tibetan masses. At the least, the Tibetans would be in their own homeland to decide and fight for their future. The entire non-violent operation would have to be planned in precision and in unison. The author has interviewed a large number of escapees from Tibet, both at Dharamshala and at New Delhi. The response to any kind of action is mixed. While a large number is looking for a leader to guide them achieve their mission, yet there are those who are mortally scared of the Chinese.

In a meeting of the author with the Prime Minister of Tibet's Government-in-Exile in 2004, it was revealed that only non-violent course will be adopted and they hope to succeed. He further revealed that the non-violent course is quite dynamic and not passive as perceived by some. He, however, conceded that there is a considerable difference in opinion with regard to the modus operandi of the Tibetan freedom struggle. There is a considerable number who think that a non-violent course will not lead to freedom of their homeland. They are impressed with the way the Indian freedom movement was conducted. They believe in direct action. During a briefing at the Tibetan Youth Congress (TYC) HQ at Dharamshala in 2004, it was brought out to the author that their main aim is to achieve independence at all costs but only through peaceful means. TYC has 78 Chapters spread in 11 countries with 25-30,000 members.

Mr. Lhasang Tsering, the former President of the TYC, feels that no useful purpose would be served by seeking autonomy within the Chinese framework as the autonomy promised in the 17-Point Agreement was not granted. Tibetans, as such, would become second-grade citizens in their own country. He said that the middle path is immoral, undemocratic and anti-Buddhist. The Tibetan Government-in-Exile would fail in its mission if it settles for autonomy as autonomy was already promised in the 17-Point Agreement in 1951. He believes that the Tibetan authorities are not on the right lines and their struggle to achieve independence through Ahimsa (non-violence) will not succeed. He elaborated that non-violence implies action rather than being passive and hoping for things to happen. He is a proponent of action and was an activist in the Mushtang Camp in Nepal for operations in Tibet, which was being funded by the CIA. He is of the opinion that the Tibetan youth is prepared to struggle but they require leaders.

The Dalai Lama has also stated that he may choose his successor during his life time. He may even choose a woman as the 15th Dalai Lama. Either of the statements, if implemented, will cause confusion and disunity among the Tibetans and may seriously impair the campaign for the Tibetan cause.

Struggle

China is a mighty country, a nuclear power and cannot be evicted from Tibet employing traditional military means. Tibet and Tibetans have no means to fight an expensive battle. Only a 'low cost-no cost' option with human grit and commitment could be employed and that too without the express permission of their head of the state, the Dalai Lama. Such an option would require international support by way of donations, aid in kind or currency and training facilities. It would not come from Tibet's neighbouring countries for they have their own internal and external predicaments as would be evident from the quality of support they provided for the Tibetan cause in the United Nations. A few private parties and NGOs in USA and Europe however would support the Tibetan cause. Technical support could also be expected from Taiwan, Japan and South Korea, and constructive sympathy from the Republic of Mongolia. There are, over 100 offices and NGOs the world over who are Tibet-sympathisers. There are 29 such organisations in USA itself. Some governments may also provide the organisational support surreptitiously as was done in 1950s and 1960s.

At the end of the Afghan war the Uighurs, Muslims and the Turks are known to have gone to Afghanistan and Pakistan for jihad training and yearn for independence the same way as the Central Asian Republics who broke away from the Soviet Union in the late eighties. Tibetans may have already made a common cause with the neighbouring Uighur Autonomous Region and launch a common or overlapping movement. Once a decision has been taken or the intentions converge it would turn in to an insurgency scenario with a protracted time frame. Tibetan youth may not settle for any solution short of independence. At the face of it, it does not seem achievable, but commitment to righteousness, Tibetan cause, self confidence of the people of Tibet, their self esteem, human grit, endurance and tenacity would be good enough rallying points to operate on.

In a meeting with the Tibetan youth which included veterans from the 1956-59 uprising, a veteran briefed on how Algeria, South Africa, India, East Timor and some other countries achieved independence pursuing both violent and non-violent movements. During the discussion it emerged that the Tibetan youth would settle for genuine autonomy in the intermediate time frame but once the foothold is gained the youth has designs to press for independence. Genuine autonomy would be based on the Dalai Lama's Five Point Proposals.

The Hans would be forced to recoil and the Chinese forces compelled to deploy in high altitude making their occupation of Tibet prohibitively expensive. The mega projects of Golmo-Lhasa pipeline, railways, airfields, industry, timber export and so on would be severely interdicted. As more and more Chinese forces are inducted in Tibet, offers of negotiations would be conveyed to achieve the intermediate aim. The time frame for achievement of the intermediate aim and the ultimate aim will depend upon the determination and motivation of the people of Tibet, the mobilization of foreign support, employment of science and technology in prosecution of the insurgency operations and the internal state of China. The movement may spread its tentacles in other minority nationality areas, besides creating support offices in other countries.

Keeping the ultimate aim and ground reality in view, it appears that some kind of liberation organisation has already been carved out by the Tibetan youth to be put in to execution at an appropriate time, possibly awaiting a dynamic leadership to emerge. To this end, the 'International Campaign for Tibet' annually organizes leadership training camps in the United States and Europe. The Tibetan flag and an appropriate logo would be a rallying point. The nucleus would be provided by a few dedicated leaders, some of these may be veterans.

Tibetan liberators will be operating on high altitude, and weapons, ammunition and equipment would *per force* need to be 'high altitude and desert proof'. The youth realizes that the procurement of arms and ammunition would need lobbying, convincing, finance and *quid pro quo*. Weapons and equipment are available in plenty in the grey markets in the countries where armies have been demobilized, areas where insurgencies have terminated or in drug economies. Closer home, weapons and ammunition are available in Afghanistan (Taliban and Al Qaeda), Golden Crescent (Afghan-Pakistan-Iran border), Golden Triangle (Laos-Myanmar-Thailand borders), North West Frontier Province of Pakistan, Cambodia, Vietnam and Philippines.

Keeping the aim in view, enclaves would be liberated which would continue to expand till they draw military response by the occupying Chinese forces. Similar situations perpetually created, would lend respectability to the resistance movements leading to negotiations. The best scenario for Tibet would be if similar movements start fermenting in other minority nationality areas as well. It would be prudent to presume that South Asia's northern borders are likely to witness a flare up despite the desire of tranquility by India and the Dalai Lama. The scene may shift from the Pacific to China's west.

Conclusion

Tibet is strategically important to China for reasons of its location, natural wealth and its space. It is expedient to dig out and devise arguments which can be advanced to prove that Tibet was part of China. However, such argument should be weighed against overwhelming proof in history that Tibet was an independent country. There is no doubt that somewhere along the passage of time, particularly during and after the Mongol rule of both China and Tibet, the country went into some kind of a subordinate role to China while maintaining its internal sovereignty. A nebulous relationship of equality, suzerainty, vassalage, tributes and *Cho-Yon* was found to be good enough excuse for invading and subjugating Tibet.

A democratic administration in exile was set up at Dharamshala, India with assistance from the Government of India. The Tibetans have kept alive in India what was almost totally destroyed or sinocised inside Tibet. Credit for the success of the Tibetan community at Dharamshala and elsewhere undoubtedly goes to the democratic vision, foresight and leadership of His Holiness the Dalai Lama. Today, the Tibetan issue is well known internationally.

The ultimate goal of the Tibetan freedom movement would be to make the people of Tibet pursue their traditional way of life in Tibet. The fundamental characteristic of Tibet as a nation has been peace, compassion, non-violence, spirituality and democracy. In the Tibetan philosophy, political freedom is only a means and not the end. The Dalai Lama, his Government and Tibetans would endeavour to undo the obliteration of their country by peaceful means, according to Buddhist traditions. But like any other youth, the Tibetan youth is getting restless and is convinced that non-violent means are being seen as Tibetan weakness and would not lead to any tangible results. The Tibetan community is at a crucial time in its history, awaiting leadership to emerge.

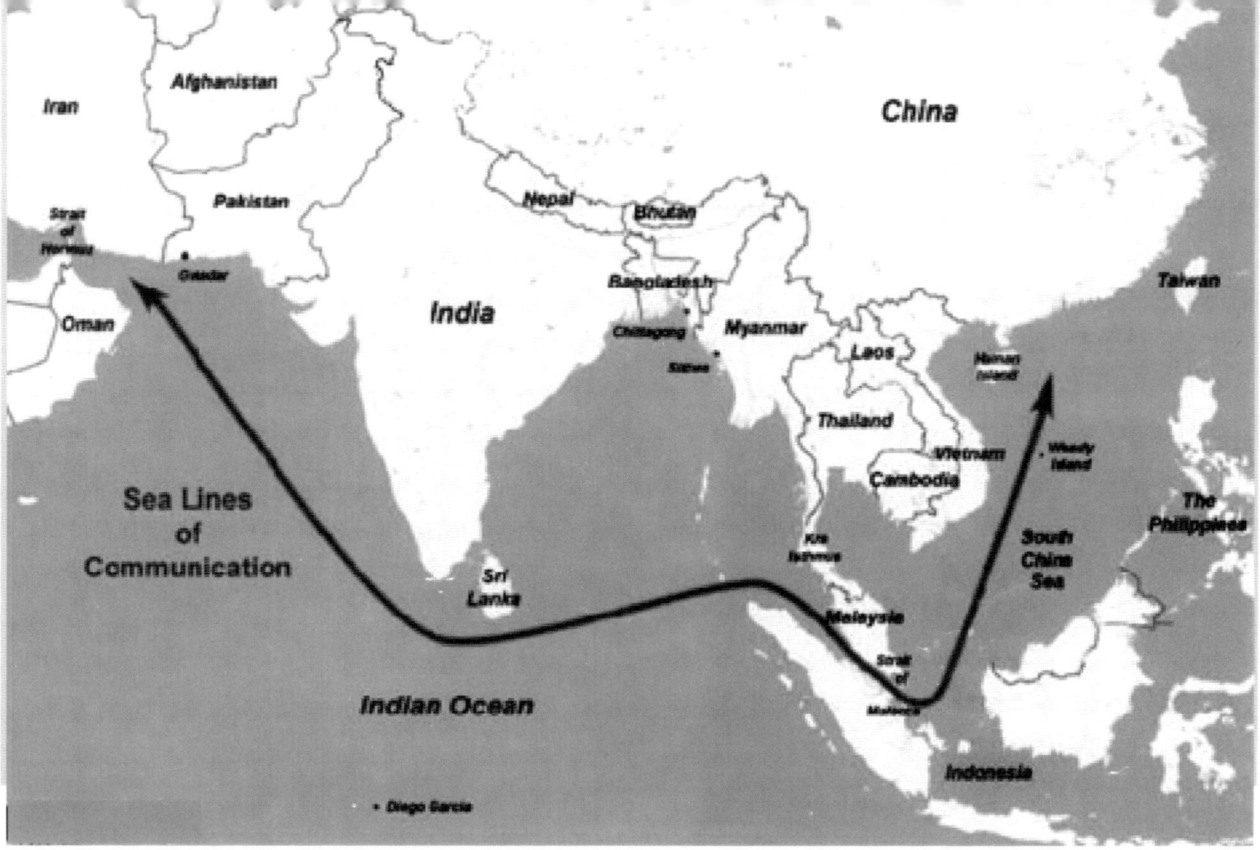

THE INDIAN OCEAN REGION IN THE WORLD ENERGY SCENARIO

Cmde Rajeev Sawhney
Executive Director, National Maritime Foundation, New Delhi

Major powers have historically sought to establish dominance over areas rich in resources so as to enhance or sustain their national power. This quest was the rationale for the European colonisation of Asia and Africa which provided the critical inputs for western industrialisation. This pursuit frequently also led to competition between the then major powers, often ending in conflict during the 18th and 19th centuries. Since the discovery of oil as an energy resource in the early 20th century, hydrocarbon energy has been the main driver of global economic growth and industrialisation. The two world wars in the last century saw a significant manifestation of this trend and this has continued during the latter half of the century. The Persian Gulf emerged as the most significant source of hydrocarbons which thus saw great powers jostling for influence in the region. Growing global economic growth has increased the importance of hydrocarbons and consequently those countries that possess large reserves of this valuable resource. Emerging economies such as China and India have thus joined the existing major powers in the pursuit of securing their supplies of hydrocarbon energy.

The Indian Ocean Region

At the outset it would be relevant to define the Indian Ocean Region (IOR) to place the ensuing discussion in the correct perspective. The IOR is considered to include the region stretching from the Suez in the East to the Malacca Straits that connect the Indian Ocean to the South China Sea and the Pacific. Bounded in the north by the South Asian landmass and in the South by the Antarctic Continent, the Indian Ocean roughly covers an area of about 736 million square kilometres. The countries that border this region include a large and diverse collection, ranging from those that are industrialised to emerging economies, such as India and the countries of South East Asia, to those in Asia and Africa that are still underdeveloped and in need of considerable development. The population of this region includes almost two thirds of humanity. In terms of energy security too there is considerable diversity, while some IOR states are energy deficient, others possess important energy surpluses. In an era of depleting global energy reserves in a context of rapidly increasing demand, the location of such surpluses have become sites for competition, between the energy deficient North and the development deficient South.[1] In the future, the Indian Ocean Region will remain increasingly important to any discussion of energy security, not only because of the critical importance of regional states as energy suppliers, but also because of the essential role of the Ocean as an energy route.

Global Energy Demand

In the 21st century too, hydrocarbons retain their significance since for the sustenance of economic growth, the new determinant of national power, assured access to adequate energy has become critical. The globalisation phenomenon that has shrunk the globe has largely been driven by the significant advances in information technology and communications. This has enabled industry to seek the most cost effective locations for setting up production centres, leveraging modern transportation systems to run their critical supply chains. In the long term, between 2004 and 2030 World Gross Domestic Product (GDP) growth rates are forecast to grow at between 3.8% and 4.1%, led by the rising economies of China and India. Bloomberg[2] quoting the IMF's 2007 World Economic Outlook reported that the global economy would grow by 4.9% in 2007, following a 5.4% growth in 2006[3] while projecting that this would be sustained at the same rate in 2008. The report however added a caveat on the possible impact of higher oil prices, something that has since occurred, with global oil prices touching nearly US$ 100. A US recession, which accounts for one fifth of global output, it states could result in a global slowdown, however any such slowdown should be balanced by growth in the rest of the world, which would be accompanied by a surge in energy consumption.

According to the US Energy Information Administration's (EIA) World Energy Outlook 2007,[4] global energy use is projected to rise sharply over the next three decades as shown in Figure 1.

As can be seen, this demand for oil and natural gas combined is projected to grow from 7 billion tonnes of oil equivalent in 2005 to over 10 billion by 2030. The major portion of this demand growth would be of fossil fuels with natural gas consumption increasing from 100 to 163 trillion cubic feet between 2004 and 2030. Similarly in the case of fluids,[5] worldwide liquid consumption is projected to rise from 83 million barrels per day (bpd) in 2004 to 97 bpd in 2015 and 118 bpd by 2030. See Figure 2.

Liquids comprise the major fuels for transportation, which comprises 68% of the overall fluids consumption. According to the EIA's World Energy Outlook 2007[6] as well, the world's primary energy needs in the Reference[7] Scenario are projected to grow by 55% between 2005 and 2030, at an average annual rate of 1.8% per year. Demand reaches 17.7 billion

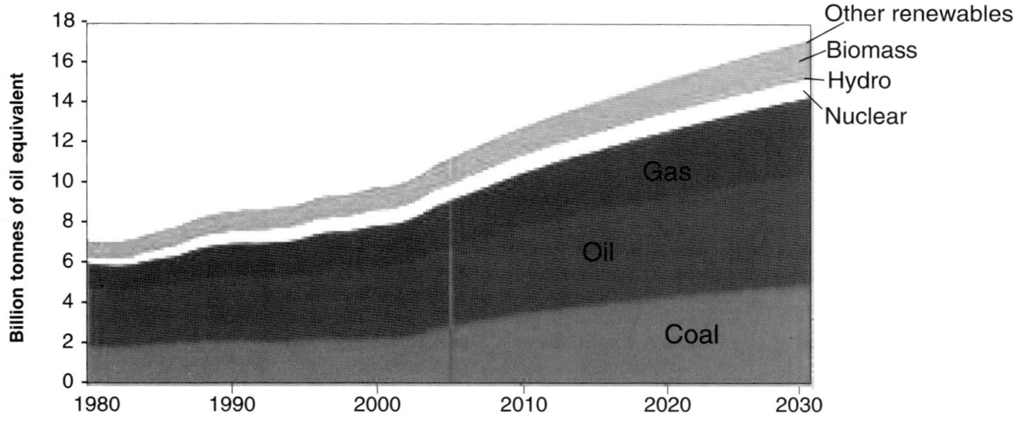

Figure 1. World Energy Demand

[1] Introduction, p 1, Energy Security and the Indian Ocean, Ed Rumley & Chaturvedi, South Asian Publishers, 2005

[2] William Mcquillan, World GDP to grow 4.9%, weather US slump says IMF, 11 Apr 2007, www.bloomberg.com, accessed 20 Nov 2007

[3] The July update to this figure released by the IMF has upped this figure to between 5.2-5.3% for 2007 & 2008. www.imf.org

[4] World Energy Outlook 2007, Office of Integrated Analysis and Forecasting, EIA , www.eia.doe.gov.oiaf.ieo, accessed 16 May 2007

[5] As per EIA, Fluids refer to all conventional crude oil as also other liquid substitutes such ethanol, coal to oil and gas to liquids expressed in million barrels oil equivalent per day

[6] Executive Summary, World Energy Outlook 2007, www.eia.doe.gov

[7] The 2007 WEO is worked out for three different scenarios. The Reference Scenario that lays out the energy trends to 2030 based on existing policies. The Alternative Policy Scenario describes what will happen if stronger action is taken to curb demand and develop alternatives. The High Growth Scenario details the consequences of such growth for energy demand, imports, investments and CO_2 emissions

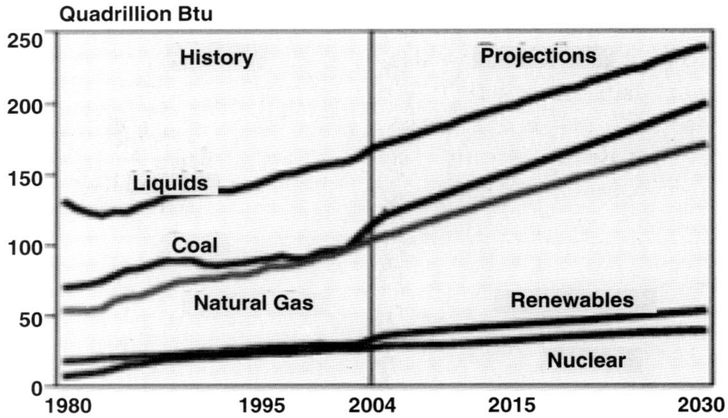

Source: *History*: Energy Information Administration (EIA). *International Energy Annual* 2004 (May-July 2006). Web site www.eia.doe.gov/iea. Projections: EIA, System for the Analysis of Global Energy Markets (2007).

Figure 2. World Marketed Energy Use by Fuel – 1980-2030

tons of oil equivalent (toe), compared with 11.4 billion toe in 2005. Fossil fuels remain the dominant source of primary energy, accounting for 84% of the overall increase in demand between 2005 and 2030. Oil remains the single largest fuel, though its share in global demand falls from 35% to 32%. Oil demand is expected to reach 116 million barrels per day in 2030, or 37%, up on 2006. Thus it is evident that global dependence on hydrocarbons fuels is not about to reduce; indeed consistent growth is the prediction. Evidently, this sustained demand would reinforce the importance of the regions that contain the world's major hydrocarbon reserves.

The World Energy Outlook 2007 also states that energy developments in China and India, the emerging giants of the world economy and international energy markets are transforming the global energy system by dint of their sheer size and their growing weight in international fossil-fuel trade. Similarly, both countries are increasingly exposed to changes in world energy markets. The staggering pace of Chinese and Indian economic growth in the past few years, outstripping that of all other major countries, has pushed up sharply their energy needs, a growing share of which has to be imported.[8]

The IOR and Global Hydrocarbon Reserves

Oil and the Persian Gulf.[9] The presence of oil in the Gulf region had been known for centuries, however commercial discovery of oil in the region first occurred in 1907 in Iran at Masjid-i-Suleman. By the early 20th century the entire Gulf was found to be flooded with this newfound wealth. However, during colonial rule foreign companies controlled oil exploration, transportation and trading and the Anglo-Persian Oil Company established in 1909 cemented British control over the natural resources of the Gulf. Oil assumed strategic importance during the two World Wars and retention of control over the region was considered to meet the Allied Powers' demand for energy resources. American oil interests in the area resulted in international economic competition, but Britain retained more than 50% of the holdings in all joint ventures. Later a British-based international consortium, the Iraq Petroleum Company, paved the way for a number of joint ventures in the Persian Gulf, in which British, American, French, and Dutch interests were represented. Post World War II, the new Gulf governments nationalised their oil reserves. This action challenged Western interests in the region as did the creation of the Organisation of Petroleum Exporting Countries (OPEC) in 1960. With a majority of Gulf States becoming OPEC members, this freed the oil industry from Western control. Furthermore, the spectacular growth of the oil industry and increasing dependence on the Middle Eastern oil imports of Europe, Japan and the US added strategic dimension to oil production in the Gulf region.

In the wake of the three oil shocks of 1973-74, 1979-80, and 1990-91, the entire focus of Western strategy was to ensure the free flow of oil at reasonable prices from the region. A US recession followed each of these shocks and one assessment is that during the past 30 years, the US has suffered about $ 7 trillion in total economic costs. Gulf oil thus became a fundamental

[8] *Executive Summary, WEO 2007, www.iea.org, accessed 07 Nov 2007*

[9] *Israel, the Middle East and the Great Powers, Eds by Israel Stockman-Shomron, Trans Publishers 1984*

US national security policy objective and has continued to influence her global policies and role. It is also believed that the US-led war against Iraq in 1990-91, was motivated by the oil factor. A look at the oil and gas reserves of the Persian Gulf Region as estimated in 2006 by the US EIA clearly brings out the ample hydrocarbon resources in the region:

- **Oil**. In 2006, the Persian Gulf countries (Bahrain, Iran, Iraq, Kuwait, Qatar, Saudi Arabia, and the United Arab Emirates) produced about 28% of the world's oil, while holding 55% (728 billion barrels[10]) of the world's crude oil reserves.

Table 1: Persian Gulf Countries Petroleum Statistics (2006)

Persian Gulf Countries Petroleum Statistics (2006)[11]

Country	*Reserves (Total Liquids - billion bbl)*	*Capacity (Total Liquids - Mn bbl/d)*	*Production (Total Liquids - Mn bbl/d)*	*Consumption (Total Liquids - Mn bbl/d)*	*Net Exports (Total Liquids) Mn bbl/d*
Saudi Arabia	262.3	12.1	10.7	2.1	8.7
Iran	136.3	4.3	4.1	1.6	2.5
Iraq	115.0	2.0	2.0	0.6	1.4
Qatar	15.2	1.2	1.1	0.1	1.0
UAE	97.8	3.1	2.9	0.4	2.5
Kuwait	101.5	2.8	2.7	0.5	2.2
Bahrain	0.1	0.1	0.05	0.03	0.02
Total	728.0	23.6	23.6	5.3	18.2

In 2006, the Persian Gulf countries together exported 18.2 million barrels per day (bbl/d), representing roughly one-fifth of world oil supply. The group exported the remaining oil via pipelines through Turkey to the Mediterranean and Saudi Arabia to the Red Sea. The region currently produces over 23 million barrels per day of total liquids and is expected to increase its market share over the next two decades. According to the EIA's *International Energy Outlook 2007*, Persian Gulf oil production is expected to moderately grow and reach 26 million bbl/d by 2015, nearly 30 million bbl/d by 2020, and over 38 million bbl/d by 2030, compared to over 23 million bbl/d in 2006. This would increase the share of Persian Gulf oil production to 33% of the world total by 2030, up

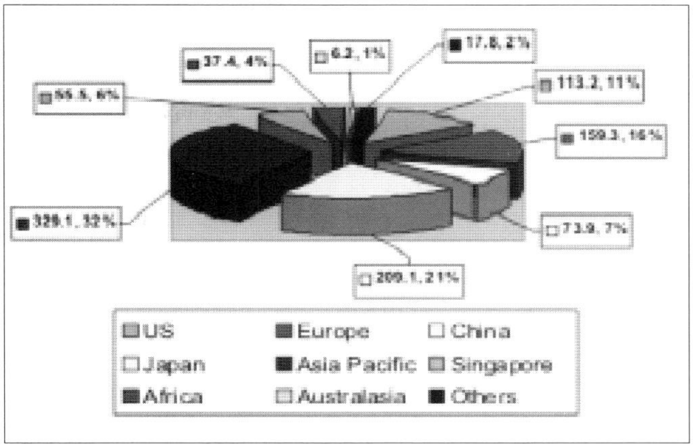

Figure 3. Persian Gulf Oil Exports 2006 (Million Tons)

from 28% in 2006. The breakdown of the oil exports from the region are as shown in Figure 3. These provide a good indication of the significance of the region for meeting global energy demand.

- **Natural Gas**. The Persian Gulf region, particularly Qatar and Iran, contains significant reserves of natural gas (2,509 Tcf)[12] amounting to over 40% of the world's total and the region exports about 18% of the world's LNG production. Iran, Qatar, Saudi Arabia, and the United Arab Emirates hold the world's second, third, fourth, and fifth-largest reserves (behind Russia), respectively. Persian Gulf natural gas will become increasingly important in coming years, as both domestic gas consumption and gas exports (by pipeline and also by liquefied natural gas (LNG) increase. The main LNG exporters from the Persian Gulf are Qatar and the United Arab Emirates sending out about 18% of world LNG shipments in 2005 according to Cedigaz, the international association for natural gas.[13] The region's market share could increase in the next decade as Qatar expands its LNG capacity. Iran is another potential LNG exporter, and its South Pars gas field contains at least 280 Tcf of reserves.

Importance of the Indian Ocean Region. The IOR is thus the most significant in this context considering that it contains the major portion of global hydrocarbon reserves. Most of these are in the Persian Gulf Region

[10] *As per Wikipedia, a barrel(bbl) of petroleum or related products represents 42 US gallons or 158.987 litres. This measurement originated in the early Pennsylvania oilfields which permitted both British and American merchants to refer to the same unit, based on the old English wine measure, a cask called the tierce*

[11] *Source: EIA Short Term Energy Outlook*

[12] *There is a slight variation from the figures in the statistical data available in the EIA's data giving the World Proven Natural Gas Reserves, January 1, 1990 - January 1, 2007 Estimates, updated on 12 Mar 2007*

[13] *www.cedigaz.org*

Table 2: Persian Gulf Natural Gas Statistics

Persian Gulf Countries Natural Gas Statistics[14]

Country	Reserves (Natural Gas - Tcf) 2006	Production (Dry Natural Gas - Tcf) 2005	Consumption (Tcf) 2005	LNG Exports (Tcf) 2005
Saudi Arabia	240	2.5	2.5	—
Iran	974	3.6	3.6	—
Iraq	112	>0.1	>0.1	—
Qatar	910	1.6	0.7	1.0
UAE	214	1.7	1.5	0.3
Kuwait	55	0.4	0.4	—
Bahrain	3	0.4	0.4	—
Total	2,509	10.3	9.1	1.3

or West Asia as is clear from Figure 4 which gives the 2007 status of proven global oil reserves.[15] With 55% of these reserves being in West Asia, the attention paid to events in this sub-region of the IOR should come as no surprise. The status with regard to natural gas reserves is also similar with the major portion of the estimated reserves lying once again in the IOR as shown in Figure 5.[16] Further, if we examine the status of hydrocarbon reserves within the IOR, Figures 6 and 7 clearly indicate the primacy of West Asia with 96 and 82% of its Oil and Natural Gas Reserves respectively. Effectively therefore it is the Gulf that should be the focus of any study of hydrocarbons for the IOR.

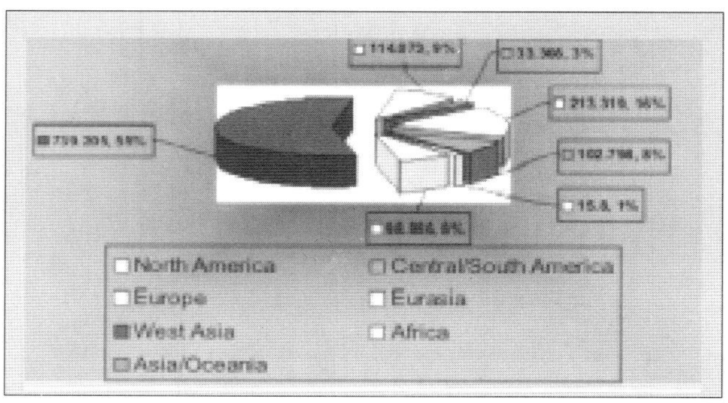

Figure 4. Proven Global Oil Reserves – 2007 (Billion Barrels)[17]

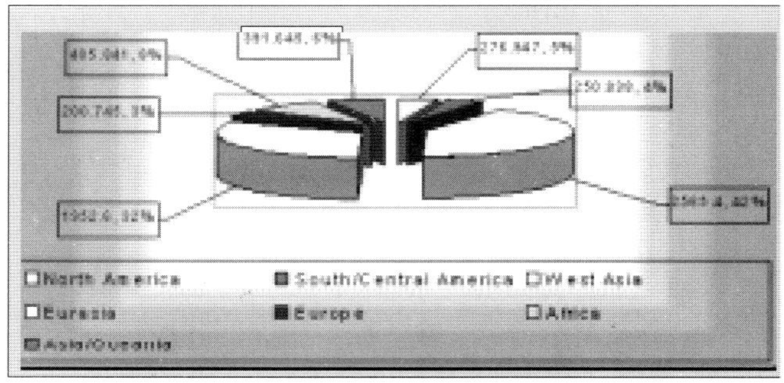

Figure 5. Global Natural Gas Reserves – 2006 (Trillion Cubic Feet)[18]

Gobal Dependencies on Gulf Hydrocarbons

Considering that the Persian Gulf is the source for a significant portion of the global energy supplies it would be pertinent to examine the dependence of the various countries/regions on this hydrocarbon reserve.

- About 40% of the energy consumed by the United States comes from oil. The United States, with about 5% of the world's population, is responsible for 25% of the world's oil consumption while only having 3% of the world's proven oil reserves.[19] US gross oil imports (mostly crude) from the Persian Gulf averaged 2.2 million bbl/d during 2006. The majority of Persian Gulf oil and petroleum products imported by the United States came from Saudi Arabia (66%), with significant amounts also coming from Iraq (25%), Kuwait (8%), and small amounts (less than 1% total) from Qatar and the United Arab Emirates. Iraqi total liquids exports to the United States reached 553,000 bbl/d in 2006. Saudi exports fell from 1.54 million bbl/d in 2005 to 1.46 million bbl/d in 2006. Overall, the Persian Gulf accounted for about 18% of US net oil imports and approximately 11% of US oil demand in 2006. As is evident from the Figure showing the distribution of exports from the Gulf in 2006, the US received 11% of the exports from this region.
- Western Europe (defined as European countries belonging to the Organization for Economic Cooperation and Development (OECD) averaged

[14] *Source: Cedigaz*

[15] *The figures indicate the reserves for North America as being 213.319 Bn Bbls; these include 178.792 Bn bbls that are estimated as being in Canada. Over 95% of Canada's reserves are the oil sands deposits in Alberta. Estimates of global oil reserves that do not take these into account thus show the Persian Gulf states as having about 65% of the world's reserves of oil*

[16] *Source: World Crude Oil and Natural Gas Reserves, January 1, 2006, EIA*

[17] *Data Source: EIA, Posted 21 Jun 2007, from Oil & Gas Journal*

[18] *Data Source: EIA, Posted 21 Jun 2007, from Oil & Gas Journal*

[19] *http://en.wikipedia.org/wiki/United_States_oil_politics*

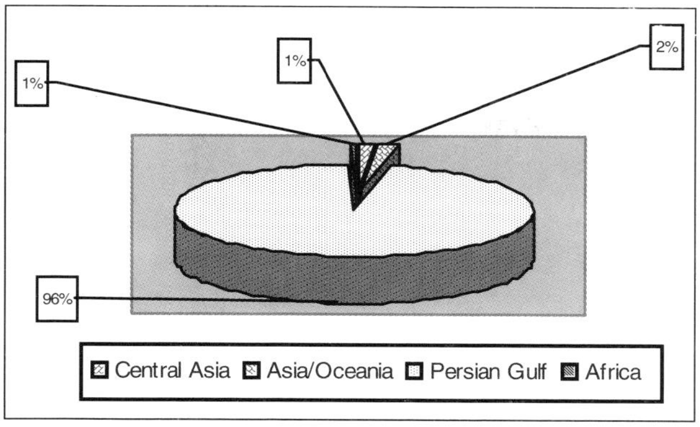

Figure 6. Indian Ocean Region Oil Reserves – 2006 (Billion Barrels)

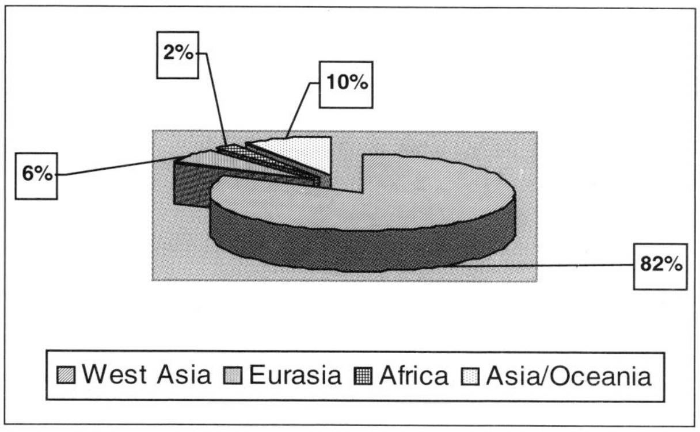

Figure 7. Indian Ocean Region Natural Gas Reserves – 2006 (Trillion Cubic Feet)

2.8 million bbl/d of oil imports from the Persian Gulf during 2006. The largest share of Persian Gulf oil exports to Western Europe came from Saudi Arabia (44%), with significant amounts also coming from Iran (33%), Iraq (13%), and Kuwait (7%). Overall, 16% of Persian Gulf Exports in 2006 were to Europe.

- Japan averaged 4.4 million bbl/d of net oil imports from the Persian Gulf during 2006. This constitutes 21% of overall exports from the Gulf in 2006. Japan's dependence on the Persian Gulf for its oil supplies has increased sharply since the low point of 57% in 1988 to a high of 83% in 2006. About 35% of Japan's Persian Gulf imports in 2006 came from Saudi Arabia, 29% from the United Arab Emirates, 12% from Iran, 12% from Qatar, 10% from Kuwait, and over 1% from Bahrain and Iraq combined. Japan's oil imports from the Persian Gulf as a percentage of demand continued to rise to new highs, reaching 80% in 2006.[20] This

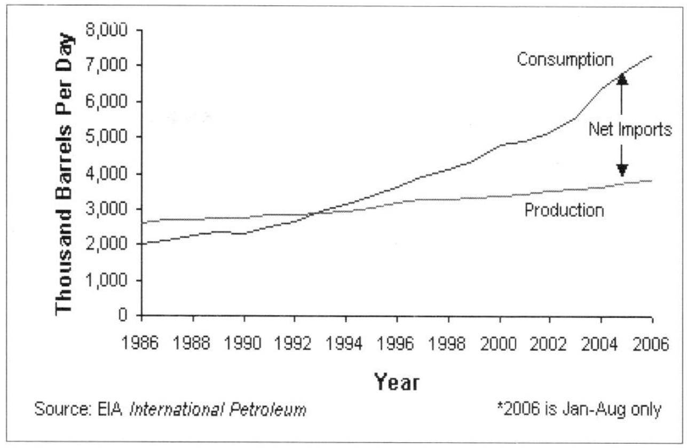

Figure 8. China's Oil Production and Consumption, 1998-2006

explains her involvement both in the Gulf region as also in the Malacca Straits through which most of this energy flows transit.

- China, the world's second largest consumer of primary energy is a key player in world energy markets, accounting for more than 10% of the world's total energy demand. Though the Chinese economy is very dependent on coal, of which it possesses large reserves, but the share of natural gas, oil and nuclear in the primary fuel mix will grow. By 2030, net oil imports are expected to reach almost 10 mb/d - more than 8% of world oil demand. Imports will also have to meet 30% of the country's natural gas needs in 2030. These trends will make China a strategic buyer. China's rapid economic growth, with GDP increasing at over 10%, would only be sustained if it has an assured supply of hydrocarbon energy. Already this growth has seen her become a net importer of oil since 1993 and the demand supply gap is growing steadily since production has plateaued whereas demand is booming, as is evident from Figure 8 showing a graphical representation of China's Oil Production and Consumption between 1986 and 2006 (Insert Fig. 8 here). The gap in 2006 was estimated by EIA to be over 3 million barrels per day, and growing. Much attention has been given to China's national oil companies investing in oil exploration and production assets overseas. However, so far these acquisitions have contributed relatively little to China's oil imports as per EIA. However what is significant is that in her efforts to reduce her dependence on the Gulf, China has increased her sourcing from alternative

[20] *Source: World Crude Oil and Natural Gas Reserves, January 1, 2006, EIA*

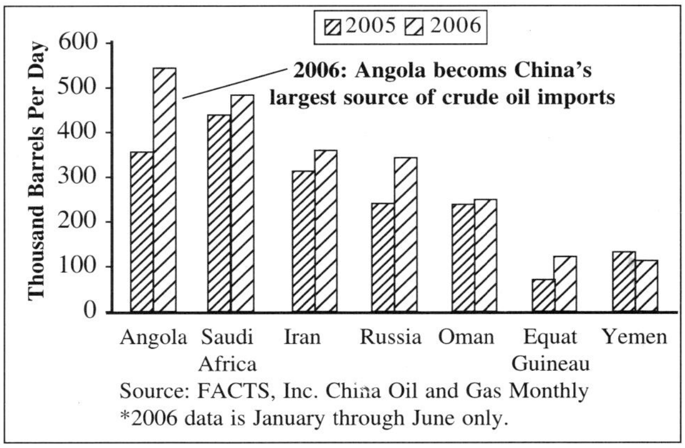

Figure 9. China's Crude Oil Imports, 2005-06

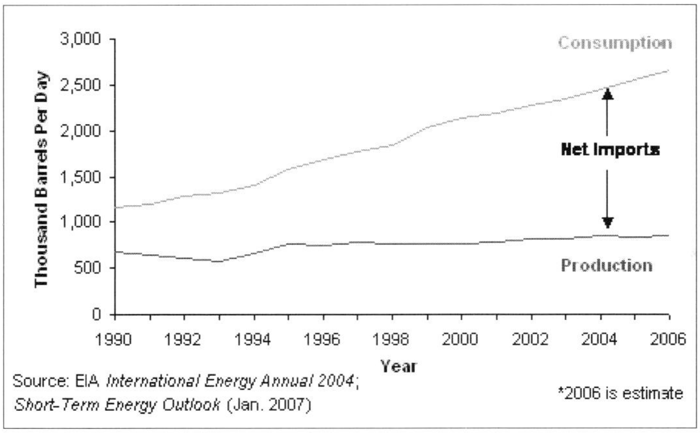

Figure 10. India's Oil Production & Consumption, 1990-2006

regions such as West Africa. As a result, in 2006, Angola overtook Saudi Arabia as China's largest single source of oil imports, as can be gauged from Figure 9 which shows the top sources of China's crude oil imports. (Insert Figure 9) Overall though the Gulf retains its position as the main source for meeting China's energy needs. However, the oil sourced from Africa still needs to transit the IOR and this has led to concerns regarding her energy vulnerability and various overland pipeline initiatives have resulted, though these are likely to meet only a modest proportion of her demand.

South Asian Perspective[21]

More than one-fifth of the world's total population lives in South Asia. However, the nations in the region have among the lowest per-capita incomes in the world. The South Asian region (Bangladesh, Bhutan, India, the Maldives, Nepal, Pakistan, and Sri Lanka) is notable for its large and rapidly growing population (more than one-fifth of the world total). Despite rapid economic growth during the 1990s, the nations in the region have among the lowest per capita incomes in the world. India is by far the largest South Asian country in terms of population, GDP, and land area, followed by Pakistan and Bangladesh. In 2005, India had an estimated growth rate in real GDP of 7.2%, while Pakistan and Bangladesh had estimated growth rates of 8.4% and 5.4%, respectively. India's GDP is projected to grow 6.8% in 2006, with Pakistan's growth at 6.4% and Bangladesh's growth at 5.1%. South Asia is in a period of transition as it strives to implement effective economic, political, social, and legal structures to support sustained growth.

Energy Demand/Supply Situation. Economic and population growth in South Asia have resulted in rapid increases in energy consumption in recent years, well above rates seen in the OECD. Energy Information Administration (EIA) estimates of South Asia's primary energy consumption showed an increase of 52% between 1993 and 2003.[22] Despite this growth in energy demand, however, South Asia continues to average among the lowest levels of per capita energy consumption in the world, but among the highest levels of energy consumption per unit of GDP.[23] Discounting "non-commercial" sources of energy including animal waste, wood, and other biomass, South Asia's commercial energy mix in 2003 was 44% coal, 35% petroleum, 13% natural gas, 6% hydroelectricity, 1% nuclear and 0.3% "other." There are, however, significant variations within the region. Bangladesh's energy mix, for example, is dominated by natural gas (67% in 2003), while India relies heavily on coal (52% in 2003). Sri Lanka and the Maldives are overwhelmingly dependent on petroleum (84% and 100%, respectively); Pakistan is diversified among petroleum (38%), natural gas (41%), and hydroelectricity (14%). South Asian nations are faced with rapidly rising energy demand coupled with increasingly insufficient energy supplies. Let us take a closer look at the hydrocarbon demand for the region:

- **Oil**. South Asian oil imports are expected to increase in the next few years, with the Middle East being a primary source for the oil imports. South Asia contains reserves of only 6.2 billion barrels of oil, around 0.5% of world reserves. In 2005, South Asia consumed around 3.09 million barrels per day (bbl/d) of oil, and produced

21 EIA Country Briefs, South Asia Overview, www.eia.doe.gov, Last Updated: March 2006, accessed 11 Nov 2007
22 In 2003, South Asia accounted for approximately 4.0 % of world commercial energy consumption, up from 3.1% in 1993
23 Ibid

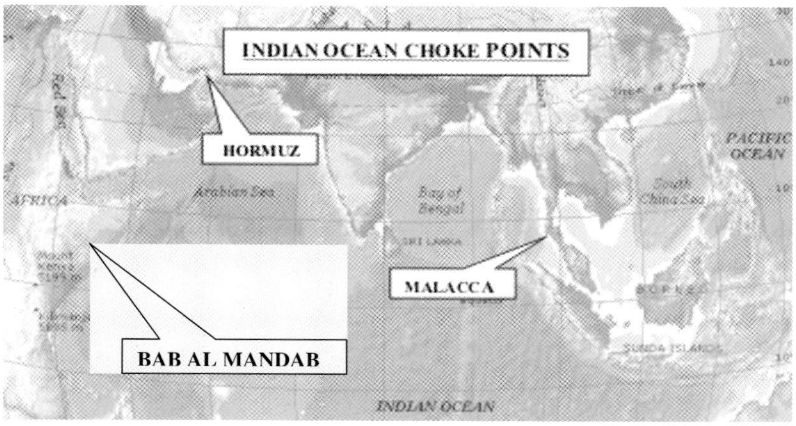

Map Showing Indian Ocean Choke Points

approximately 0.93 million bbl/d, making the region a net oil importer of around 2.2 million bbl/d. The majority (around 858,000 bbl/d in 2005) of South Asia's oil production comes from India, whose offshore Bombay High field accounts for approximately one-third of total Indian oil output. Most of the remainder of South Asia's oil production comes from Pakistan (around 62,000 bbl/d in 2005). Growing demand for transportation fuels and industrial power has been a major factor behind the growth in South Asian oil consumption. Between 1990 and 2005, South Asian oil consumption, led by India, grew by about 111%. India's oil consumption is forecast to grow another 10% by 2010, reaching 2.8 million bbl/d (up from 2.5 million bbl/d in 2005). India's domestic oil production has flattened at around 33 mmt[24] (of which 2/3rd is from offshore areas), with the demand – supply gap steadily rising as is evident from the graph alongside.

Thus her dependence on imports is projected to rise from the present 60-70% to over 90% by 2025.[25] In Sri Lanka, where oil is the dominant source of energy, consumption more than doubled between 1990 and 2005. In 2005, Sri Lanka, whose oil consumption was 87,000 bbl/d, imported all of its crude oil, using it largely for electricity generation and transportation. In recent years, Sri Lanka has further increased oil imports in an effort to avoid over reliance on hydroelectricity. South Asia's oil imports are projected to more than double by 2020 with the Middle East being the primary source for oil imports.

- **Natural Gas**. In January 2006, South Asia's proven natural gas reserves were estimated at 62.1 trillion cubic feet (Tcf), approximately 1% of the world total, with potentially larger resources suspected but unproven. India's and Pakistan's reserves are 38.9 Tcf and 28.2 Tcf, respectively, while the only other South Asian country with reserves, Bangladesh, contains approximately 5.0 Tcf. Foreign energy companies including Shell and Unocal believe that Bangladeshi reserves may be higher than the official figure. The US Geological Survey estimates that Bangladesh contains 32.1 Tcf in additional "undiscovered reserves." If the higher estimates prove to be correct, Bangladesh could become a major gas producer and supplier to the potential market in neighboring India. All natural gas production in South Asia is consumed domestically. Natural gas is seen as playing an important part in supplying new power plants in the region and diversifying from expensive oil imports. As a result, natural gas usage has increased rapidly in South Asia over the last decade, growing about 67% between 1993 and 2003. In 2003, the region produced and consumed around 2.2 Tcf of natural gas. Around 43% was consumed by India, 38% by Pakistan, and the remaining 19% by Bangladesh. Indian consumption of natural gas has risen faster than that of any other fuel in recent years and accounts for approximately 7.0% of the country's energy demand. At nearly 1.0 Tcf in 2003, Indian gas demand is projected to significantly and rapidly increase, reaching 2.5 Tcf in 2025. Bhutan, the Maldives, Nepal, and Sri Lanka do not currently produce or consume any natural gas.

Summary. South Asia's extreme dependence on imports to meet its rapidly growing demand is evident, a majority of it being from the Gulf Region. Though India, the major consumer of energy in the region is pulling out all stops and attempting to reduce her

[24] *Presentation by Director Gen Hydrocarbon on India's Oil & Gas Industry, accessed from GH website, www.dgh.gov.in*

[25] *India's Energy Dilemma, CSIS South Asia Policy Monitor No 98, Sep 2006, www.csis.org*

vulnerability, this does not appear to be forthcoming. Within the region too, the lack of political convergence and domestic politics are inhibiting cooperation in this area. Thus Bangladesh is not only reluctant to sell its gas to India but is also not willing to permit transit passage for Myanmar's gas to India. This ideal avenue of reducing the regions dependence on external imports is therefore not being realized. Significant energy flows from the Persian Gulf are thus likely to continue for the foreseeable future.

Concerns on Sustainability of Hydrocarbon Reserves and Energy Security

As we look at the growth in global demand for hydrocarbon energy the inevitable question that arises is that of continued availability. Rising global energy demand poses a real and growing threat to the world's energy security.[26] China's and India's combined oil imports are projected to surge, from 5.4 mb/d in 2006 to 19.1 mb/d in 2030 – more than the combined imports of Japan and the United States today. Ensuring reliable and affordable supply will be a formidable challenge. Inter-regional oil and gas trade grows rapidly over the projection period, with a widening of the gap between indigenous output and demand in every consuming region. The volume of oil trade expands from 41 mb/d in 2006 to 51 mb/d in 2015 and 65 mb/d in 2030. IEA's World Energy Outlook for 2007 highlights the consuming countries' growing reliance on oil and gas imports from a small number of producing countries and states that this threatens to exacerbate short-term energy-security risks. Much of the additional oil imports are likely to come from the Middle East, the scene of most past supply disruptions, and will transit vulnerable maritime routes to both eastern and western markets. The potential impact on international oil prices of a supply interruption is also likely to increase: oil demand is becoming less sensitive to changes in price as the share of transport demand – which is price-inelastic, relative to other energy services – in overall oil consumption rises worldwide.[27] The world's energy resources are however, considered adequate to meet the projected growth in energy demand at least for the next three decades. Increased production in the Middle East and the former Soviet Union, which has massive hydrocarbon resources, will meet much of the growth in the world oil and gas demand. OPEC producers, particularly those in the Middle East, will meet most of the projected 60% increase in global oil demand in the next three decades.[28]

Energy trade is consequently likely to expand rapidly in the coming years and, in particular, the major oil and gas consuming regions will see their imports grow substantially. This trade will increase mutual dependence among nations, but will also intensify concerns about the world's vulnerability to energy supply disruption, as production is increasingly concentrated in a small number of producer countries. As such, supply and price security has moved to the top of the energy policy agenda. The governments of oil and gas importing countries will need to take a more proactive role in dealing with the energy security risks inherent in fossil fuel trade. They will need to pay more attention in maintaining the security of international sea-lanes and pipelines, and they will have to look anew at ways of diversifying their sources of fuels, as well as the geographic resources of those fuels.[29]

The Importance of Maritime Trade

The 2006 UNCTAD review of world maritime transport has assessed that world seaborne trade grew at 3.8% in 2005, at 7.11 billion tons of loaded goods. This trade has been driven by an average growth of 6% in the volume of world exports, critical to the global economy.[30] The global merchant fleet has also grown by 7.2% to 960 mn DWT to cater for this growth, a net gain of 64.2 mn DWT. There is widespread consensus on the need to ensure that trade flows remain uninterrupted. Global dependence on hydrocarbon energy to sustain economic growth also predicates that these supplies flows are not disrupted.

IOR Shipping Routes and Choke Points[31]

Three fifth of global oil trade of 43 million barrels of oil moves by sea[32] with tankers being the most cost

[26] *World Energy Outlook 2007: Fact Sheet Oil*

[27] *Summary IEA's World Energy Outlook 2007*

[28] *Usman Aminuddin, Note 2*

[29] *Usman Aminuddin, Opportunities In The Development Of The Oil & Gas Sector In South Asian Region, Islamabad Papers, www.issi.org.pk/islamabad_paper_htm*

[30] *UNCTAD Review of world maritime transport 2006*

[31] *World Oil Transit Chokepoints, EIA Nov 2002. www.eia.doe.gov/cabs/World_Oil_Transit_Chokepoints/Full.html, accessed Nov 2007*

[32] *As per UNCTADs 2006 Review of World Maritime Transport, Tankers comprised 36.9% of the global shipping Fleet totalling 354,219,000 DWT(Growth of 5.4%). To this one could add the 22,246,000 DWT of LNG ships that make up 2.5% of the total(Growth of 7.5%). Thus almost 40% of the global shipping fleet is involved in the transportation of hydrocarbons*

effective means of transporting cargo being low cost, efficient and extremely flexible. Though the oceans are vast and vessels could travel as they please, in effect they move along fixed maritime routes. These are of course established by custom, primarily being dictated by commercial considerations which require the shortest route to be chosen from origin to destination. This results in a concentration of maritime traffic along routes that are called Sea Lanes of Communication or SLOC's, akin to highways across the oceans. However, whilst transiting from one ocean/sea body to another, shipping is constrained to transit the narrow straits, termed as choke points, which connect these. These effectively constrict maritime traffic travelling along various routes; this bunching imparts a vulnerability to maritime trade that needs to be addressed.

The Indian Ocean has a number of choke-points that control access into/out of the IOR

With the Persian Gulf region containing over 55 of the proven oil reserves, tanker traffic from the gulf is obviously considerable with roughly half of the world's top 20 busiest crude oil-exporting ports are located in the Persian Gulf. A look at the energy flows through these strategic choke points:

- **The Straits of Hormuz**. As there are only a handful of conduits allowing oil exports to leave the Persian Gulf and bypass the Straits of Hormuz, the vast majority (about 93%) of oil exported from the Persian Gulf transited by tanker through the Straits of Hormuz. This strait thus plays an exceedingly important role in Persian Gulf oil and gas transportation, for moving these products to global markets.[33] Oil flows through the Straits of Hormuz account for roughly two-fifths of all global crude oil and petroleum product tanker shipments. This consists of 2-mile wide channels for inbound and outbound tanker traffic, as well as a 2-mile wide buffer zone and at its narrowest point is only 34 miles wide. Approximately 17 million bbl/d of crude oil and refined products transit the Straits of Hormuz, going both east to Asia (especially Japan, China, and India) and west (via the Suez Canal, the Sumed pipeline, and around the Cape of Good Hope in South Africa) to Western Europe and the United States. In addition, over 3.5 Bcf/d of natural gas travels through the Straits of Hormuz via LNG tankers in route to Asia, Europe, and North America.
- **Bab al Mandab** This strait connects the Gulf of Aden to the Red Sea thus is the main transit for all oil moving west from the gulf to Europe, the US and the western parts of Asia via the Suez Canal. The alternate routing would be around the Cape of Good Hope, greatly adding to transit time and costs, as occurred after the 1973 West Asian Conflict.
- **Straits of Malacca**. The Straits of Malacca connect the Indian Ocean to the South China Sea and through it the Pacific. Countries such as China, South Korea and Japan as also other Pacific Rim countries are dependent on the 11.7 mn bbl/day (2004) of oil that pass through these straits. Over 60,000[34] ships pass through this 500 nm passage which is merely 1.5 nm wide at its narrowest point in the Singapore Straits. This includes 30% of world trade and 50% of world energy needs. Should the Straits not be available for any reason, this would entail a considerable diversion for ships using this passage incurring significant costs in terms of both time and money.

Threats to Maritime Trade in IOR

Though no authenticated figures appear to be available on the maritime traffic in the Indian Ocean, some estimates[35] indicate that this numbers over 100,000 ships annually or over 250 ships per day. Contemporary threats to maritime trade basically arise from piracy and terrorism, both of which are perpetuated by non state actors that operate freely across national boundaries as also the largely unregulated areas of the oceans that are not under national jurisdiction. Such threats to maritime trade resuit in insurance companies levying higher rates for ships passing through areas that are at higher risk, thus increasing the costs of transportation. The consequence is higher prices of commodities that in the case of hydrocarbons have a cascading effect on the global economy. The stakes in maintaining stability along these sea-lanes are thus high and have been the subject of much discussion in the region. A quick look at these threats and how they could impact shipping would be appropriate at this stage.

---

[33] *Bateman, Raymond and Joshua Ho, Safety and Security in the Malacca and Singapore Straits-An Agenda for Action, IDSS report May 2006*

[34] *Ibid.*

[35] *Considering that the figure of 63,000 ships transit the Malacca Straits annually is authenticated, it would appear that this figure is in fact an underestimate. This is based on the fact that other than those ships that pass through the choke points, there is considerable intra IOR traffic*

- **Maritime Piracy**. The age old menace of piracy saw a revival in the 20th century and in the IOR this was predominant in South East Asia and the Malacca Straits. This resulted in enhanced insurance rates and global concern for security of international shipping especially energy saw the littorals initiate cooperative measures to combat the threat. These have seen a dip in incidents however the threat remains a concern. RECAAP's[36] latest quarterly report[37] issued by indicates that the first nine months of 2007 saw 77 incidents of piracy in the region. This was a drop from the 118/107 incidents reported in the same period in 2005/2006 respectively. Of these 77, whilst 59 were actually carried out, 18 were attempted acts of piracy. Though a majority of 2007's incidents occurred whilst ships were at anchorage / in port, a significant number (20) took place whilst they were steaming. Further, the recent trends seem to indicate that tankers were at greater threat with 31 of 77 attacks experienced in 2007 being on tankers. This would clearly indicate the extent of the vulnerability of the platforms feeding the energy lifelines in the region. The International Maritime Bureau, in its latest report on piracy[38] has indicated a 37% increase in the second quarter of 2007, with a majority of the increase being accounted for by incidents off the Somali Coast. In fact some of these attacks occurred well out to sea with one even being attempted 315 miles offshore. The problem has become so acute that the IMO in Jun 2007 asked the US Security Council to implement measures to intervene, as the rising attacks were not only affecting the delivery of humanitarian aid, but putting international shipping in the area at risk.[39] Piracy is thus clearly one of the major threats that maritime traffic faces in the IOR, right across from the east coast of Africa to the South China Sea.
- **Maritime Terrorism**. The new threat to world shipping is that from maritime terrorism. The hijacking of the Italian cruise ship Achille Lauro by a team of Palestinian terrorists in Oct 1985 was the first recorded incident of Maritime Terrorism in recent history. Subsequently there have been a series of attacks on maritime targets, notable being the one on the USS Cole in the Port of Aden in 2000 by the Al Qaeda. In October 2002, al-Qaeda using a boat packed with explosives rammed and badly holed a French supertanker Limburg[40] off Yemen. A 2004 study by the Institute for the Analysis of Global Security[41] reveals that terror organizations have planned several attacks against oil tankers in the Arabian Gulf and Horn of Africa. According to FBI Director Robert Mueller, "There have been any number of attacks on ships that have been thwarted."[42] Many terror experts have expressed concern that Al-Qaeda might seize a ship and crash it into another vessel or into a refinery or port. There is no doubt that al-Qaeda is intent on hurting the west economically by interrupting the flow of oil to American, European and Asian markets. Al-Qaeda leaders have vowed numerous times, to cut the "economic lifelines" of the world's industrialized societies as such attacks would not only disrupt life in the west but also weaken and perhaps topple Gulf oil monarchies heavily dependent on oil revenues for their survival.

There is a view that despite the isolated incidents of maritime terrorism and the predictions of worst case scenarios, maritime terrorist attacks are, and have remained, quite rare, as such attacks constitute only 2% of all international terrorist incidents over the last three decades. While a number of terrorist organisations have the desire or motivation to carry out maritime attacks they accepted, their contention is that there is still currently a lack of capability in this area of operation and that this is likely to remain so in the immediate future. Attacks against maritime targets require specialized equipment and skills they say; it also requires some knowledge of local shipping

36 RECAAP is a 16 nation grouping of states that was set up in 2006 to combat the piracy threats by agreeing to share information. An Information Sharing Centre has been established at Singapore and the reports cover a wide swath of area from the IORs Arabian Sea & Bay of Bengal to Japan. See ww.recaap.org for more information

37 RECAAP ISC Quarterly Report – 01 Jan to 30 Sep 2007, www.recaap.org. Viewed 29 Oct 2007

38 cargosecurityinternational.com,GLOBAL: IMB report cites spike in piracy, 12-07-2007. The IMB Piracy Reporting Centre (PRC) is the only operation of its kind in the world, offering Ships' Masters the ability to report attacks of piracy from any location, at any time. The work of PRC is funded by 22 organisations including P&I Clubs, ship owners and insurers

39 Stefano Ambrogi, IMO asks Security Council to act on Somalia piracy, 28 Jun 2007, Reuters Alertnet, accessed 23 Nov 2007

40 The 158,000-tonne Limburg, Figureered to the Malaysian oil firm Petronas, was approaching the Yemeni port of Mina al-Dabah when the explosion occurred at about 9.15am local time on 06 Oct 2002. All but one of the ship's 25-strong French and Bulgarian crew were accounted for after the explosion, which blew a gaping hole in the side of the tanker. The crew saw a high-speed vessel approaching on the starboard side _ an explosion followed." He added it was thought there were explosives aboard the small boat. http://www.guardian.co.uk

41 Threats to Oil Transport, www.iags.org/oiltransport.html, accessed 26 Nov 2007

42 In June 2002, a group of al-Qaeda operatives suspected of plotting raids on British and American ships and tankers passing through the Strait of Gibraltar were arrested by the Moroccan government

patterns, boat operation and maintenance, and most importantly boarding techniques. Notwithstanding these arguments, no security manager would be so imprudent as to ignore the threat. Numerous inputs are available to suggest that many terrorist groups are in fact acquiring maritime capabilities. Taped statements by two top leaders of al-Qaeda post the 2001 Bali Bombings alluded to attacks on "economic lifelines", obviously a threat to maritime trade.[43] According to an Israeli report, Jemaah Islamiyah and the Abu Sayyaf Group (both considered to have close links to al Qaeda) have also developed maritime capabilities, provided by the LTTE. It is also stated that much of the expertise acquired by both groups were passed on by al-Qaeda's maritime-operations commander Abdul al-Rahim al-Nashiri before his capture in Aden in November 2002. The US assessment also estimates that the Jemaah Islamiyah is actively pursuing the acquisition of a maritime terrorism capability, including diving and mining training. Terrorist attacks on maritime transportation carrying hydrocarbons would have considerable impact on the costs of sourcing energy and impact economies worldwide. A report[44] prepared for the US Congress states that the *Limburg* bombing caused insurance rates among Yemeni shippers to rise 300% and reduced Yemeni port shipping volumes by 50% in the month after the attack.

Conclusion

The world economic outlook for 2007 has projected a steady expansion of the global economy led by the rapid growth in China, Russia and India. Considering that economic growth is dependent on the steady availability of energy resources, this growth will see continued demand for hydrocarbon resources. The World Energy Outlook 2007[45] forecast that that the world's energy needs would grow by 55%, at an annual growth rate of 1.8%, by 2030, with fossil fuels remaining the dominant source of energy. Thus the importance of the Persian Gulf, as the holder of the world's largest hydrocarbon reserves, to the global economy would continue to be significant. Developing countries it is reported, whose economies and populations are growing the fastest, will contribute 74% of the primary energy usage with China and India accounting for 45% of this increase. Domestic production is unable to keep up with the burgeoning demand and this gap between demand and output will catapult India to one of the largest consumers of crude oil along with China. The increase in China's energy demand between 2002 and 2005 was equivalent to Japans current annual energy use as per the 2007 World Energy Outlook. As for India, it is set to become the worlds third largest oil importer after the US and China by 2025.

The obvious question therefore would be to ask whether the available reserves would be able to meet this growing demand. The theory that the world's hydrocarbon reserves are finite and that production has reached a peak has been belied by the regular discovery of fresh reserves. It does appear that hydrocarbons are not about to run out in the short term. The World Energy Outlook 2007 states that "*The world's remaining oil resources are expected to be sufficient to meet rising demand over the next two and a half decades. Much of the increase in demand will come from China and India, driven largely by the rapid growth in demand for mobility. As much of their incremental oil needs will have to be imported, the reliance on a small number of major oil exporters – notably in the Middle East – is set to grow, raising concerns about energy security.* Global oil demand is projected to reach 116 million barrels per day in 2030– 32 mb/d up on 2006 with fast growing energy demand for transport being the main driver. Today, there are about 900 million cars and trucks on the world's roads; by 2030, the number is expected to pass 2.1 billion. Some 42% of the increase in global oil demand by 2030 comes from China and India. China accounts for the biggest increase in oil demand in absolute terms of any country or region.[46] OPEC's share in meeting this demand is projected to rise from the present 42% to 52% by 2030. Since a majority of these countries lie in the IOR,[47] the significance for the region is obvious.

With over 55% of the world's hydrocarbon reserves, the Indian Ocean Region is clearly vital to global energy supplies. The dependence of most major economies

[43] *In a recent article a Pakistani analyst has rightly highlighted ocean borne terror threats are an enduring danger to ports worldwide as well as to global trade. Al Qaeda, he writes has a declared commitment to undertaking maritime acts of terror. Cdr Muhammad Azam Khan PN (Retd), The US, the North Arabian Sea and Pakistan, May 2007, USNIPs*

[44] *Paul W. Parfomak and John Frittelli, Congressional Research Service Report for Congress on Maritime Security:Potential Terrorist Attacks and Protection Priorities, 09 Jan 2007*

[45] *WWW.worldenergyoutlook.org/quotes, accesses 03 Dec 2007*

[46] *Ibid*

[47] *The Organization of the Petroleum Exporting Countries (OPEC) consists of Algeria, Angola, Indonesia, Iran, Iraq, Kuwait, Libya, Nigeria, Qatar, Saudi Arabia, the United Arab Emirates, and Venezuela. Regional Definitions, EIA International Energy Outlook 2007, p 220*

on Persian Gulf Oil and Gas, most of which transits by sea, results in there being great global interest in the security of these energy lifelines. With the interdependencies that have been generated by globalisation, there is wide agreement that inter-state conflicts are unlikely. Modern economies are greatly dependent on uninterrupted supply chains most of which use maritime transportation. The primary focus of most states being on improving their economic wellbeing is another argument against the possibility of any such conflict. Further, there is a shared concern for the security and safety of the SLOC's, as also for their energy lifelines in the IOR. This concern for ensuring maritime security could be translated into cooperation towards tackling the threat posed by maritime terrorism and piracy, both of which are prevalent in the region. This is due to the fact that their perpetuators being non state actors do not respect national boundaries. Experience in other areas has shown that the adoption of a cooperative approach could successfully tackle this threat, since such activities, if left unchecked, could seriously damage global economic wellbeing, not a prospect that is in any nation's interest.

India's strategic location in the IOR dominates the shipping routes that pass through the region. This gives her the opportunity to act as a stabilising force in the region provided that it develops adequate maritime forces to undertake this task. As one of the worlds emerging economies, aiming to be a global leader, India needs to take on a lead role towards achieving regional security. Such a course would also serve the purpose of securing India's own growing energy needs, which are increasingly going to be sourced from abroad.

INTEGRATED SECURITY - NEED OF THE HOUR

Air Marshal RS Bedi (Retd)

Former Director General, Defence Planning Staff

India has been in a state of war ever since its independence in 1947. Its armed forces, particularly the army have fought more wars and internal security operations than any other military elsewhere in the world. And what's more surprising is that both the external aggressions, as also the internal security challenges have been met without any noteworthy inter-service jointness, integration or even political direction. It is not far off the mark to say that having come up independently and nursed their primary roles all along, the idea of jointness receded from their thinking altogether. Each of them fought the wars individually in pursuance of their own objectives, without sharing plans or resources. Wherewithal and resources were made available to each other only if found spare. Service sovereignty was paramount. "The full potential of military strength has not been realized due to lack of synergy between political, diplomatic, economic and military strengths and absence of jointness and integration between the three services and between the service and the Ministry of Defence, as each service has developed independently."[1]

In today's context, no single service can guarantee the country's security all by itself, its individual strengths notwithstanding. Without adequate integration of multiple government agencies, it is not possible to ensure requisite synergy and thrust for realizing national security objectives. The joint approach therefore must start at the top and go down to the bottom of the hierarchy in order to ensure total integration and harmonization of all elements of national power. That is the only way to ensure synergy and resource optimization.

"The keystone to joint operations is not structure but synergistic thinking. In the Second World War, Japan's jointness was hampered by lack of coordination between the Japanese Navy and the Army. Military policies were also inconsistent with the foreign policies of the time. The army and the navy had their own foreign policies in accordance with their respective views and aims."[2] Fortunately, the Indian armed forces operate strictly under the political leadership, albeit, without much direction as regards the aims and the objectives to be achieved and

---

[1] *Maj Gen Ashok Mehta, The Tribune, Chandigarh, August 27, 2007*

[2] *Wg Cdr Sartaj Bedi, Air Power Journal, Volume 2, No. 4, Winter 2005 (Oct-Dec)*

the manner of doing so. The services thus left to themselves grew independent of each other. And that is what has led to the paramountcy of individual approach over jointness.

Since each service grew in isolation to fight its own version of the war, its performance was less than optimum. Nor did any government ever make any serious attempt to reform the higher defence organization to enable the services to reap the benefits of jointmanship or, for that matter, issued any directive as to what were their aims and the objectives during peace and war, except for the brief instructions issued during Mr R Venkataraman's tenure as Defence Minister in 1987. This political void led each service to evolve its own threat perception and the corresponding strategy to meet it without any input from the government or interaction with any other service. Unless the government issues a clear mandate as to what precisely is expected of them during peace and war, no joint directive or jointmanship can be worked out. "The singularity of aim and each service's contribution towards the same is however, of utmost importance, irrespective of the type of war. A political aim must necessarily evolve into a joint military aim, before individual service aims come into being."[3]

In fact, the concept of jointmanship has not been quite understood. For it to be meaningful, plans have to be fully integrated, but unfortunately the services are still hesitant to share them with each other. The tendency is to try and obtain maximum resources from the other without giving much in return. "Unfortunately, the face that jointmanship is assuming is that of how best to integrate the assets of other service(s) into one's own plans and strategies. As a result, each service would perhaps still fight the way it deems best albeit, with a more assured assistance from the other(s)."[4]

It is interesting to note that the Parliamentary Committee on Defence for the year 2007 has observed that there is no 'jointness' in the armed forces. The committee found total lack of synergy between the three services, as was the case during the Kargil conflict years ago. Even amongst the tri- service organizations like the Andaman and Nicobar Command, it was found to be far from satisfactory, with each service operating in water tight compartments, without much jointness of command and control. After the Kargil conflict, the Group of Ministers had recommended a number of measures to rejuvenate the higher command of the three services with a view to bring about requisite synergy but as always the most crucial of the recommendations have remained unimplemented, to date.

The lack of synergy between the services, and the inherent flaws in the functioning of the Chiefs of Staff Committee (COSC), demand urgent action on part of the government to streamline the higher defence organization. "The functioning of the COSC has to date revealed serious weaknesses in its ability to provide single–point military advice to the government, and resolve substantive inter-service doctrinal, planning, policy and operational issues."[5] After September 2001, an attempt was made to strengthen it, albeit marginally, by giving it some additional responsibilities, but it has continued to suffer on account of inherent drawbacks present in any committee system. The committee system that works on a majority vote is not suitable for expeditious decision making. It delays and dilutes the nature of decisions.

"In India, the effort to set up a modern system since 1947, on the basis of the historical experience of others (since we lacked our own experience in modern times) remained deficient in structure as well as in institutionalizing what was set up in the beginning itself, and what was left was soon dissipated, leaving the key level of the COSC hanging in a virtual vacuum. Our own system set up since then (1947) has never laid down a mandate for the COSC to provide 'single point' military advice to the political executive authority."[6] At best, this apex forum can provide collective advice to the government.

Integration between the three services and the Ministry of Defence to constitute a composite body which would take all decisions jointly cannot be avoided for long. In fact, certain amount of integration with the Ministry of External Affairs would also be essential to ensure comprehensive synergy between national security and foreign policy. The Chief of Defence Staff, in such a scenario, would thus advise the political leadership on matters of military strategy and the Defence and the Foreign secretaries on matters of politico-military relevance.

---

[3] *Ibid*

[4] *Ibid*

[5] *GoM's Report after Kargil " Management of Defence" (New Delhi, GoI, Feb 2001) page 97*

[6] *Jasjit Singh, Air Power Journal, Volume 3, No2, Summer 2006 (April-July)*

Unfortunately, there is no consensus amongst the armed forces on this issue, nor for that matter is there any consensus amongst the political parties. The fear that the unity of command and control (power) thus invested in one (uniformed) individual may prove inimical to the national interest, though unfounded, is proving to be a major stumbling block. Although, the Defence Minister, Mr. AK Antony sent out a letter in August 2007 to various political parties, seeking their views on the issue of a Chief of Defence Staff (CDS), the truth is that neither the political establishment nor the bureaucracy is comfortable with vesting too much power in the hands of an armed forces' official. The bureaucracy, opportunistic as it is, is exploiting this uncertainty for fear of being relegated from a position of primacy to that of second fiddle. The politico-bureaucratic culture in India is known for deferring uncomfortable decisions, particularly on matters military.

Ever since the debate on jointness started, it was largely the Indian Air Force and, to some extent, the Navy that opposed the concept of the CDS, because of some past prejudices. But the Army has all along been vehemently in favour of it. Six years after the Group Of Ministers (GoM's) recommendation submitted to the Prime Minister in February 2001, to create the post of the CDS, the army has sprung a surprise on the nation. The outgoing Chief of the Army Staff, Gen. JJ Singh, in August 2007 said "the time is not ripe for the creation of CDS. The concept of CDS was 'early in its time' in the Indian context and it would come about only after the country's border problems are resolved and the internal security situation stabilized. The current challenges before the nation are single service specific."[7]

The Army Chief seems to prefer integration of men in uniform with experts from the Ministries of Defence and External Affairs as the first step prior to the creation of CDS. In his perception, integration of the country's security and foreign policy for total synergy in future conflicts is an important pre-requisite. "Intermingling and cross postings of officers, as happens in other democracies, would bring about complete synergy in future conflicts and would eventually pave the way for the CDS who would then be a single window advisor to the government on strategic matters."[8] The Army Chief's argument that the present challenges before the country, like terrorism, insurgency and disputed borders require boots to be on the ground, though not denied cannot be accepted as being in the army's exclusive domain. The role of the navy and the air force has, in fact, acquired much greater salience than ever before. With the army now coming out with such arguments for the first time, prospects for the appointment of a CDS have further receded.

In reality, the role of the armed forces is gradually getting transformed. Although, all out conventional war is not very likely in the nuclear backdrop, fighting a war across the spectrum of conflict, including asymmetric warfare in the ongoing Revolution in Military Affairs (RMA) and ever increasing technological means, pose a serious challenge to any modern armed forces. This would, needless to say, call for a tri-service approach with each service having an enhanced qualitative rather than quantitative capability to form a fully integrated force structure, capable of operating from land, sea and air. A joint military doctrine, together with a clear cut defence policy, enunciated by the government would be necessary if the requisite strategic capability and reach is to be ensured. In the light of the fast changing strategic and technological environment, there is an inescapable need for a dynamic defence policy and doctrine. It cannot be achieved without unifying various elements of national security.

It is rather unfortunate that in the 60th year of our independence, we continue to follow the adhoc security framework bequeath by Lord Ismay who was Mountbatten's Chief of Staff and at one time that of the British prime minister. In the light of the highly disturbed conditions prevailing in India, as also in the armed force at the time of partition, Lord Ismay perhaps tried to avoid any radical re-organization and instead went in for a committee system. He recommended the creation of the COSC with multiple subcommittees to ensure coordination between the services, quick decision making and above all, civil supremacy. It was almost a replica of the COSC comprising the Chief of General Staff (CGS), the Flag Officer Commanding Royal Indian Navy (RIN) and the Air Officer Commanding (AOC) India, which was set up by the British in India in the mid-20th century. Lord Ismay's recommendations, based on this framework, were formalized through a cabinet resolution on 5 September 1947. Unfortunately, civil supremacy was soon replaced by 'bureaucratic control' by simply designating the Armed Forces HQ

[7] *Gen. J.J. Singh, Hindustan Times, August 28, 2007*
[8] *Ibid*

as attached offices of the Department of Defence, instead of retaining them as independent departments of the Government of India. The military leadership, at the time, was too inexperienced to realize the implications of this seemingly minor amendment. It did not take long for the powers of the service chiefs, status of service HQs and the committees to erode.

Later, whilst announcing the abolishment of the title of Commander-in-Chief in the parliament in 1955, Prime Minister Nehru stated that a Board and a Council would be set up for the purpose of planning and management of defence policy but it never came about. Sadly but true, whatever security structure was passed on to us, even that was allowed to degenerate with passage of time. The national leadership did not understand the nuances and the intricacies of national security management. In fact, as of now, we hardly have any higher defence organization to manage the country's security. All existing arrangements are adhoc to say the least. India's higher defence management is in urgent need of meaningful reforms.

The last few decades have witnessed revolutionary changes in the nature and the characteristics of modern day warfare. Threat perceptions have changed with the changing modus operandi of achieving political and military ends. Other means of war are being constantly evolved. Limited war, low intensity conflict, terrorism and religious extremism have taken the place of long drawn conventional war. Non-state actors have become unseen warriors that have emerged as a major threat to the nation. Nuclear wars are, in any case, unthinkable. Technology is playing an important role in this revolution. Information technology, and cyber space has opened new vistas to warfare. Thus, modern warfare is progressively becoming multi-faceted, inter-dependent and multi-service specific. Response to aggression, whatever is its form, has to be prompt and multifarious. Air power, because of its inherent characteristics of flexibility and promptness, has assumed greater significance. Without its support, other services will find themselves inadequately prepared to meet these new challenges. Integration, not only within the services but also with other government components has also become unavoidable. A mechanism in consonance with the current situation is the need of the hour.

An attempt was first made in 1987 by Arun Singh the then Defence Minister under Rajiv Gandhi. Arun Singh was able to carry the three Chiefs with him on the issue of the CDS. But as the relations between the school days buddies soured, the intelligence establishment was able to persuade Rajiv Gandhi to shelve the proposal. The reform process started yet again with K Subrahmanyam's Kargil report of 2001 but then Prime Minister Atal Behari Vajpayee, for some reason hesitated to accord approval, despite the strong recommendation of his own Home Minister in favour of the CDS. The GoM's argument favouring the CDS was that he would provide single-point military advice to the government, administer the strategic forces, optimize the planning process through inter-service dialogue and last but not the least ensure requisite jointness amongst the services. It is understood that Mr. Vajpayee was swayed by the air force's vehement opposition in the light of their experience with Gen JN Chaudhuri and Field Marshal Manekshaw, besides the advice given by former Prime Minister Narasimha Rao and former President Venkataraman to go slow.

It is time the politico-bureaucratic hierarchy overcomes the mental block and reforms the long overdue security apparatus in keeping with the dynamic environment. The changing dynamics of the security situation calls for a continuous review of the country's security structure. With its gradually rising status in the comity of nations, India would be required, sooner or later to play the role of a peacekeeper in the region. To ensure peace and stability in the immediate and distant neighbourhood, as also in Asia in the near future, India's security structure has to be well equipped to meet these challenges effectively. Unfortunately, we hardly have any worthwhile security structure. We allowed what little we inherited to degenerate with passage of time. There is no option but to make a fresh start.

Since we have little to learn from our own past, taking the cue from other advance democracies will be unavoidable, and a lesson in some cases. It is interesting to note here that even a country like the US hardly reviewed its security structure for decades. It entered World War II with the Departments of Army and Navy virtually autonomous and organizationally belonging to George Washington vintage. The Navy's concept of independent command at sea and decentralized organization was in total contrast to the Army's penchant for highly centralized command and control, as a result of its experience in World War I and the Spanish wars. The first reform itself came about circumstantially when, during the war, an interface with the British COSC had to be created. The US formed an adhoc committee called the Joint Chief of Staff (JCS) for the duration of the war. The political authorities later felt the need to bring about substantial organizational reforms in order to streamline the security organization, stop inter-service rivalry and thus improve the armed forces' overall potential. The National Security Act of 1947 established the National Security Council, Central Intelligence Agency and National Military Establishment headed by a political authority called the Secretary of Defence. The Joint Chief of Staff was also accorded formal approval.

Despite periodic attempts at reforming the system in 1949, 1953 and1958, the problems could not be surmounted in entirety or for that matter requisite jointmanship achieved. The USAF, Navy and the Marines remained at loggerheads all the time. Realizing the inescapable need for yet another major reform in the interest of optimizing of armed forces' potential, the Goldwater-Nichol Defence Reorganization Act of 1986 was passed. It made the Chairman of JCS, the highest ranking military officer and the principal military advisor to the President. It also assigned military forces drawn from various services under command and control of a C-in-C who would be directly responsible to the Secretary of Defence. The Chiefs of Staff in this system were thus reduced to controlling organizational, training and logistic aspects only.

Let it be said here that despite all this, inter-service rivalry or individual service primacy surfaced its ugly head during the Iraq war. The remedies applied by the Goldwater-Nichol Act to defence management and administration in 1986 were not able to overcome the problem in its entirety. Defence organization needs continuous and innovative application of mind so as to remain in harmony with the prevailing security environment. In this regard, the British remained well ahead of every one. They had created the COSC soon after World War I. They have a codified Joint Allied Doctrine since 1994. Even Pakistan has a system akin to the CDS. It must however be remembered that each of these models is nation-specific and cannot be applied blindly in an alien environment.

The armed forces in India face a major problem, in that "our polity does not have the comprehension of defence matters.The armed forces by themselves at present lack the institutional will and vision to bring about any meaningful changes on their own. Therefore, regrettably, we have to wait for some external agency or personality to initiate a political intervention in our cause." [9] Our politico-bureaucratic combine suffers from some unfounded old biases which despite the prevalent circumstances continue to be played up within the government hierarchy. Notwithstanding this, if India has to become a reckonable power, as it aspires, it must pay as much attention to building security infra structure as it does to building its economy. Both are complementary and not mutually exclusive. The answer lies in integrating all agencies that have anything to do with national security. We need a holistic approach, not piecemeal and half-hearted measures.

[9] *Vice Admiral Arun Prakash, PVSM,AVSM,VrC, VSM, Journal of the USI of India, Volume xxxII, No550, Oct-Dec,2002*

POLITICAL VIOLENCE AND HUMAN SECURITY IN NORTH EAST INDIA

KS Subramanian
Former member of the Indian Police Service;
Author of "Political Violence and the Police in India" (Sage 2007)

Political violence in the northeast of India is having a huge impact on the 'human security' of ordinary people in the region. This aspect is often ignored in discussions on security issues. 'Human security' as a concept is dealt with in detail in many UN documents. In this paper, a brief assessment of the impact of political violence on human security in the selected northeastern states of Manipur, Nagaland and Tripura is being done. The three states, along with Assam, are currently affected by political violence. The region is inhabited by a large number of tribal communities. The selected states are those in which the author has had professional working experience.

The whole of Nagaland and Manipur and the entire area under 22 police stations and parts of 5 other police stations in Tripura have been for long under the draconian Armed Forces (Special Powers) Act, 1958 as amended in 1972. The law empowers 'any commissioned officer, warrant officer, non-commissioned officer or any other person of equivalent rank in the Armed Forces' to shoot to kill on suspicion, destroy armed dumps, arrest any persons without warrant and search any premises without warrant. No prosecution, suit or any legal proceeding against any such officer shall lie without the previous sanction of the central government. The normal operation of the law and order and development machinery cannot take place in such conditions. Human rights violations are common. It is noteworthy that paramilitary forces, excluding army units, deployed in the region outnumber the civilian police forces.

The northeastern states comprise of Arunachal Pradesh, Assam, Manipur, Meghalaya, Mizoram, Nagaland and Tripura. Recently, Sikkim has been added to the list. The region is sensitive and strategic, bordering Nepal, Bhutan, China, Myanmar and Bangladesh. With a total population of about 38 million (2001 census), the northeastern states have about 4% of India's population and about 7% of its land area. Assam, with a population of over 26.5 million, constitutes about 70% of the total population of the region.

Manipur

Manipur borders the Indian states of Nagaland, Assam and Mizoram towards the north and west and with an extensive border with Myanmar to the east and south. Along with Nagaland, Assam and Tripura in the region, Manipur has experienced political violence arising from the confrontation between armed opposition groups and government forces. This has led, among others, to serious violation, by both state and non-state agents, of the rights of ordinary people including women and children

In 1980, the whole of Manipur was declared a "disturbed area" under the Armed Forces (Assam and Manipur Special Powers) Act, 1958. The Act confers broadly defined powers to shoot to kill on government armed forces. This law is perceived to foster a climate in which the agents of law enforcement use excessive force with impunity. A pattern of apparently unlawful killings of suspected members of armed opposition groups has resulted from the systematic use of lethal force as an alternative to arrest by the security forces. Civilians, including women and children have been among the victims of killing and wounding. All children born after 1980 in the state have been innocent victims of a state of siege and have never known the meaning of peace. In 1997, the Supreme Court of India (SCI) upheld the validity of the law but human right agencies hold that it violates Article 6(1), 9 and 14 of the International Covenant on Civil and Political Rights (ICCPR).

Redress for victims of human rights violations, including a growing number of children, has, for many years, been impossible to obtain in Manipur, although the SCI had suggested a few measures of protection against human rights violations under the law afore-mentioned. This state of affairs, like in other conflict-affected states of the region as well as in Jammu & Kashmir, fundamentally erodes the human rights of ordinary people, guaranteed under the laws of India.

Despite its small size and population, Manipur has a rich heritage of history and culture. The population of Manipur (about 2 million) can be divided into two main groups, the Meiteis and the hill tribes. Most of the Meiteis live in the smaller valley area of the state, while the hill tribes live in the surrounding, much larger hill areas. The hill people can again be subdivided mainly into the Nagas and the Kuki-Chins or the Kuki-Mizos (together consisting of 29 major and 14 minor tribes). The Thangkul, Mao, Maram, Anal, Kabui, Maring and others belong to the Naga group while the Hmar, Paite, Zou, Thadow, Gangte, Simte and others belong to the Kuki-Mizo group. A large number of different groups of tribal people have also migrated, especially into valley region from neighbouring states.

The state has eight districts, three in the valley and five in the hills. The valley districts are Jiribam, Thoubal and Bishnupur. The hill districts are Churachandpur, Chandel, Ukhrul, Senapati and Tamenglong. 30administrative sub-divisions and 31 community/tribal development blocks exist. The density of population is 579 per square kilometre in the valley and 34 in the hills. The Autonomous District Councils under the Indian Constitution administer the hill districts while the decentralized Panchayat Raj Institutions (PRIs) have been set up in the valley region. The hill areas has a difficult terrain and are part of the Himalayan foothills extending into the Bay of Bengal. Rain-fed agriculture is the mainstay of the valley economy, while traditional shifting cultivation is more common in the hill areas. About 37% of the nearly 2 million people are children up to 14 years of age.

The Meiteis, originally perhaps a tribal community, had constituted the ruling establishment in the former princely state of Manipur. Following their conversion to Hinduism in the 18th century and assimilation into the newly independent state of India in the late 1940s, the Meiteis were deprived of the benefits available to tribals in the reservation policies adopted by the Government of India. The hill tribes, on the other hand, received such benefits. This led to a feeling of discrimination and generated bitterness on the part of the Meiteis, now transformed from being rulers into the ruled, in Manipur. Historical memories of past glory, delay in the formation of the new state of Manipur (which came into existence only in 1972 as against Nagaland which became a full-fledged Indian state as early as 1963) added to the discontent. A militant revivalist movement premised on the state's return to its pre-Hindu identity arose, coupled with a demand for secession from India. Population growth and a struggle for an adequate means of livelihood compounded the scenario. Electoral politics has led to endemic political instability and opportunistic alliances in government. The hill region inhabited by the Nagas and the Mizos has had it no better, given the background of militancy in neighbouring Nagaland and Mizoram. Manipur thus witnesses the spectacle of over 30 (major and minor) armed opposition groups operating against government forces.

The United Liberation Front (UNLF) of Manipur was founded in the sixties by Samarendra Singh to achieve an independent, socialist state. A breakaway group, led by O Sudhir Kumar, set up a government in exile in neighbouring East Pakistan (later Bangladesh), called the Revolutionary Government of Manipur (RGM), with the objective of liberating the state by armed struggle. Following the liberation war of Bangladesh in 1971, the Meitei secessionist groups received a setback. Some accepted the amnesty offered by the state government but some others, led by N Bisheswar Singh, went to China in 1975 in search of support. On his return in 1978, Bisheswar Singh set up the People's Liberation Army (PLA), to achieve independence by armed struggle. Other armed underground organizations also came into existence in the late seventies and the early eighties, such as the people's revolutionary Party of Kangleipak (PREPAK) and the Kangleipak Communist Party (KCP). Militant activities were stepped up. The government imposed the Armed Forces (Special Powers) Act, 1958 in the valley. While some of the militant groups suffered temporary setbacks, the late eighties witnessed a revival of Meitei militant groups, especially the PLA, which set up camps in Myanmar and Bangladesh. It also launched a campaign against social evils. The Meitei militant groups espouse a pan-Mongoloid identity, reject the Bengali script for the Manipuri language and have revived practices of the old Meitei religion, Senamahi. A campaign was also launched against "mayangs" (outsiders) settled in Manipur.

The Naga militant groups, mainly the National Socialist Council of Nagaland (Muivah) remain strong in the hill region inhabited by the Nagas, adjoining Nagaland. An ethnic conflict has erupted between the Nagas and Kukis mainly over the land issue. A number of Kuki militant groups have emerged, especially the Kuki nationalist Army (KNA) and the Kuki national front (KNF). Other groups such as the Paites, Hmars and Vaipheis launched identity-based struggles. Thus, the entire state has come to be divided along ethnic lines. Human rights violations perpetrated by these groups as well as by the armed forces of the government aggravate the distress of the common people, especially women and children.

The uninterrupted enforcement of the Armed Forces (Special Powers) Act, since 1980, has profoundly compromised the implementation of the provisions of CRC in Manipur. Every person born after 1980 has lived under this Act, which is considered a violation of international humanitarian law. Children have been witnesses, survivors and direct victims of armed conflict between the State and the various armed opposition groups. Civilians, not engaged in armed conflict, have been frequent casualties. Pre-school education, the responsibility of the Social Welfare Department, is affected by poor functioning of schools, especially in remote areas. Funds for teaching aids are disbursed infrequently. The right of the indigenous children to receive education in their own languages, to be familiar with their own histories and cultural values, has been denied. The violent political context affects the implementation of an entire range of educational, nutritional, health and other services. Funds earmarked for nutritional supplements have not been disbursed for years.

It is difficult to imagine the situation of children who are born and have had to grow up in an atmosphere of violence, terror and intimidation. Since 1992, ethnic clashes over the land question among different communities have led to families being rendered destitute and homeless. These clashes occur usually in the remote regions of the state where access to services is difficult. Displaced persons are housed in makeshift camps or have to take shelter with better-off members of the family. Children are the most badly affected. No general education or education on drugs, sexual health and other harmful practices are available. Suicides among the adolescent and the youth are said to be increasing. Growing drug addiction, psychosocial problems, unemployment and lack of basic services characterize the child welfare scenario. Increase in child labour has also been witnessed. With easy availability of cash through child labour, children fall a prey to drug abuse. The largest number of new drug addicts is said to be working children and juveniles.

Nagaland

Nagaland, an important state in the northeastern region of India, is unique for its enduring insurgency, which has had a deeply damaging impact on the security, survival, development and participation of children and women (not to speak of their health, education and nutrition). The conflict between the Indian government and the militants in this tribal-dominant state originated as soon as the Indian state came into existence in 1947 and has lasted to this day, albeit in an attenuated form. The circumstances of the induction of the Indian army into Nagaland have been well brought out in some studies.

The Naga people were never part of the freedom struggle launched by the Indian nationalists. Historically, they had enjoyed a separate identity even during British occupation of India. This experience, coupled with considerable Indian nationalist misunderstanding is seen by many to be at the bottom of the trouble between India and the Naga people. The history of the conflict between India and the Naga movement for independence is a complex and tortuous one. Several factors have contributed to the persistence of the conflict even after the formation of the state of Nagaland in 1963; introduction of a democratic setup in the state; and the holding of regular elections.

No comprehensive study has yet been made of the impact of the insurgency on ordinary people including women and children. However, anecdotal and journalistic accounts reveal a serious picture. Women and children became the main victims, when in the past, village after village was burnt down, and concentration camps set up, forced labour imposed and large scale internal displacement of population with incidents of torture, rape and killings.

The Nagas comprise some 17 major tribes and over 20 sub-tribes spread over several states of the northeast and the neighboring Myanmar. The major tribes include the Ao, Angami, Sema, Lotha, Thangkul, Konyak, Rengma and Mao. Each tribe and sub-tribe speaks its own language, as part of the Tibeto-Burmese group of languages. The Nagamese language, on the lines of Assamese (the language of the neighbouring Assam State), has emerged as the local lingua franca. The state has a population of about 1.2 million in a total population of over 40 million in the region and an area of over 16, 000 square kilometres in a total area of over 255,000 square kilometres. There are seven districts and forty-eight rural development blocks. About 88% of the population is 'Scheduled Tribes', listed in the Constitution of India, with a literacy rate of over 61%.

In 1947, Angami Zapu Phizo, the top leader of the Naga National Council (NNC) unfurled the banner of revolt against India. He was arrested along with his associates in 1948. Upon release in 1949, Phizo became president of the NNC. The NNC publicly resolved to establish a sovereign Naga state. In May 1951, the NNC held a 'referendum' on the issue and claimed about 99% support for Naga independence from India. The 1952 general election was boycotted and a violent movement launched. In 1956, Phizo set up an underground Naga Federal Government (NFG) and a Naga Federal Army (NFA). The same year, a military crackdown by the government of India took place. The Armed Forces (Special Powers) Act, 1958 was enforced in the state. However, Phizo managed to escape to UK.

In 1963, Nagaland attained full statehood under the Indian Union. This was followed by a serious attempt to bring about a political settlement with the Naga underground. A Peace Mission in 1964 resulted in the suspension of military operations. Six rounds of talks between the government and the militants ended in failure and the Peace Mission was wound up in 1967. In 1972, the Government of India banned the NNC, NFG and NFA as 'unlawful associations'. A massive military operation was followed by the resumption of dialogue. The Shilling Accord, as it was called, was signed between the antagonists in 1975. The NNC-NFG agreed to ratify the Indian Constitution and decided to lay down arms.

A section of the Naga underground, which had gone on a training mission to the People's Republic of China, however, repudiated the Shillong Accord and refused to lay down arms. A new underground organization called the National Socialist Council of Nagaland (NSCN) under the leadership of T Muivah, Isak Swu, and SS Khaplang was formed in Myanmar in 1980. The NSCN became the most powerful militant outfit in the region fighting for the Naga cause. As the Nagas have always been divided along clan and tribal lines; the rank and file of the NSCN came from the Konyak tribe; and the command structure was dominated by the Thangkul, internal organizational divides emerged. Coupled with apprehensions among the Konyaks that the dominant Tangkhuls were striking a deal with the Government of India, a vertical split took place in the NSCN in 1988. A breakaway Konyak faction led by K Konyak and SS Khaplang, a Hemi Naga from Myanmar, emerged. Isak Swu, a Sema from Nagaland and T Muivah, a Tangkhul from Manipur led the Tangkhul faction. Severe inter-factional clashes, which followed, resulted in the killing of hundreds of activists of both factions.

With the death of Phizo in 1990, another split occurred in the NSCN. Phizo's daughter Adino, an Angami, and K Nanthan, a Sema, set up rival factions. The latter joined the Muivah-led NSCN in 1996. The Government of India, under the Unlawful Activities (Prevention) Act, 1967, banned all factions of the NSCN. The NSCN (Muivah) has stressed that the Naga region was never part of India and was, therefore, not 'inherited' by India from the British, as claimed by Indian nationalists.

Since 1997, a cease-fire and a peace process have been underway between the Government of India and the two main factions of the NSCN, the NSCN (Muivah) and the NSCN (Khaplang). Efforts are also on to extend the peace process to the other underground organizations in the region. The outcome remains to be seen.

The Naga struggle has had as its prime motivating factor neither regional disparity nor uneven development, as elsewhere, but the idea of an independent

Naga homeland in which the Naga "way of life" could be preserved. Unlike other regions where ethnic movements may have arisen as a consequence of a skewed development process, historical and cultural factors played a big role in the Naga region. At independence, the Nagas were not psychologically prepared to enter into a union with free India. The brutal military crackdown in the 1950's, led to a prolonged human and social tragedy widening the gap between India and the Naga people. The formation of a full-fledged state of Nagaland within the Indian Union in 1963 did not compensate for this tragedy and suffering. In its subsequent attempts to win over the Nagas, the Indian State has poured huge sums of cash into the state in the name of development without always making adequate institutional arrangements for their proper utilization. The benefits failed to percolate to the masses but helped create and legitimize a political and business class with a stake in the Indian market and dependence on the Indian State.

The growth of market forces has won the battle for India in its struggle to retain Nagaland. The emergence of a vocal section of Naga society made up of the urbanized middle class does not favor secession from India today. However, the threat of secessionism does constitute a useful bargaining counter in the game of pan-Indian democracy.

The village of Khonoma, not far from the state capital Kohima, gave birth to perhaps the greatest Naga leader of modern times, Angami Zapu Phizo. It is estimated that about 70 men of the village, mainly in the age group of 25-45, were killed in the hostilities during 1956-1975. Assuming that, on an average, each man killed left behind a young widow and three children (that is, four dependents in all) who had to eke out a living anyhow, a figure of 280 dependents emerges for the village. Even if one assumes a plot of land with each such family for its survival, the figure of 280 dependents is still too large for a single village to support. Multiply this by 1056 villages in state as a whole and the figure of dependents in the state becomes 95,680 (or 73,920 households). This figure relates only to the period 1956-1975. The years following the Shillong Accord of 1975 (which was not accepted by some Naga groups) have, however, seen further large scale killings as result of the fratricidal blooded-letting among the Naga underground factions which emerged.

The impact of all this on the Naga family structure was as follows:

- While the 'woman of the house' is highly regarded and is the mainstay of the traditional family economy, in the event of the sudden death of the husband, she has to shoulder the entire family burden, which reduces her to a life of hardship. Most of these women are young widows and despite some help from the clan, they feel bound to rear their children the way their late husbands would have liked.
- The lack of a father affects the children in the pursuit of their deepest longings. They feel bound to respect their fathers' memory and their 'sacrifice 'for the cause. They thus become rebels and live by the memory of their fathers and consider the Indian security forces as their main enemy. Many young men, hardly in their teens, take to the gun and join the underground, entering a vicious cycle of killing and getting killed.
- After the fighting, some men find it necessary to go to work on land, while others would need to go school. Still others end up as illiterates.
- Internal displacement, resulting from the conflict, forces many to live in the jungle. They are unable to retain their traditional loyalty to their home village and become disoriented. Loss of cultural ethos of their home village results in a sense of loss of identity.
- The struggle for survival after a life of conflict results in many becoming victims of diseases: beriberi, diarrhea, water-borne illnesses, and typhoid swelling of the joints and vitamin deficiencies. Salt is a difficult item to get for those forced to live in the jungle. Eating cold and uncooked food in order not attract enemy attention, causes many to suffer from vitamin deficiencies.

The splintering of the underground movement, which began in the 1980's leading to fratricidal killings, has had its own distinct consequences. One estimate reports the loss of life as a result the conflict during 1997-99 as 440, abductions as 211 and defections from one faction to another as 470. Another estimate places the figure of killings during the 1990's, at about 2,000. Assume two children per victim and a total 4,000 youths are fast growing up to 'take their place' in society. Many of those killed were potential leaders at the village, district, and state levels. In a state with a total population of only about 1.2 million, can one estimate the loss of leadership potential this implies?

The dependents of those killed in the conflict during 1956-75, could somehow adjust to their loss and grief in the name of the ideology of freedom for which their lives were sacrificed. But those killed in the subsequent fratricidal fighting of the 1980's and after had no such ideological moorings to help them cope with the aftermath of conflict. Then again, some Nagas with a belief in non-violence were often forced to support government forces. Their children become confused when they see the children of those who opposed the government 'yesterday' but are 'today' are enjoying the perks and privileges of state support available to them. The collective anger of this and other sections of frustrated youths is a decisively negative force. Unable to work with their own hands on land, these children either become 'professional students' occupying positions in student organizations or join a Naga faction and take to extortion for a living and get emotional satisfaction in their new-found 'respectability'.

The worst victims, however, are the women and children who suffer silently and with dignity. Those who have already died 'suffer no more', but those who live, have to suffer a 'living death'. Some victim families fall back on ancestral land but this is not always sufficient to take care of their needs all the year round. They, therefore, have to rely on the collection of minor forest produce to eke out a living or turn into daily wagers. Benefits of government projects do not always percolate down to the needy. However, a reassuring feature is that some of these kids do come up by their own effort and hard work and manage to outshine those who benefit from government patronage. The future of Naga society may well lie in the hands of these shining examples of self-help.

Tripura

Tripura is a hilly state in the northeastern region of India with an area of 10,486 square kilometres. The state has a mix of hills, valleys and dense forests. It is bounded by Bangladesh in the north, west and south; and by the Indian states of Assam and Mizoram in the east. The maximum length of the state from north to south is 183.5 kilometres and the maximum breadth from east to west is 122.7 kilometres. The international border with Bangladesh is 832 kilometres long. In 1991, the population of the state was 2.8 million of which nearly 31% consisted of indigenous communities. Only 15% of the population resides in urban areas. The economy is predominantly agricultural. The Tripuri maharajas ruled the state for about 1300 years. After partition of the Indian sub-continent, the state formally acceded to the Indian Union in 1949. It became a Union Territory in 1956 and a full-fledged state in 1972. The people of the state practiced a self-sufficient subsistence economy. There has been a gradual shift towards settled agriculture. Industry is conspicuous by its absence. The government is the main employer. Starting initially with one district and ten sub-divisions, Tripura now has four districts, 15 sub-divisions and 29 development blocks. Development activities are being decentralized through local self-governing institutions, i.e. Panchayati Raj Institutions (PRIs) and Autonomous District Council (ADC) in tribal areas. The two main groups of people who reside in the state are the Bengalis and the indigenous communities belonging to over 18 categories such as Tripuri, Reang, Jamatia, Noatia, Halam, Chakma, Mog, Kuki, and Lushai.

Tripura, along with Manipur, Nagaland and Assam faces the problem of an armed tribal militancy directed at the state government. More than half the total area of the state has been declared as "disturbed" under the Armed Forces (Special Powers) Act, 1958. The administration is largely dominated by non-tribal interests and is seen as biased against tribals in the framing of policies and their implementation. An example often cited relates to the Dumbur Hydro-electric Project, which led to large-scale displacement of tribal families due to submergence of good tribal land to generate a few megawatts of electricity for urban areas with non-tribal concentrations. Anti-poverty programs have not resulted in the reduction of tribal poverty. These factors have led to divisions among the state's residents along tribal/non-tribal lines and the raising of issues of ethnicity, identity and sub-nationalism by tribal youth. The political framework within the state has not provided an effective platform for expression of these issues, and insurgent groups in nearby states have become role models for local tribal youth.

Migration, mainly of Bengalis, into Tripura can be traced to the period of British ascendancy in the region (late 19th century) and the moves in favour of modern judicial and administrative systems. The people with education and experience to administer these systems were outsiders from the neighbouring province of Bengal, who were encouraged to settle in the state through preferential access to land and senior posts in the government. The initial influx of outsiders was followed by a deluge at the time of India's partition in 1947 and again in 1971 with steady streams in between which continues even today. As a result, a tribal majority state has been transformed into a tribal minority state.

Most commentators identify land alienation as the root cause of unrest among indigenous communities in Tripura. Alienation has resulted from the influx of immigrants from erstwhile East Pakistan (now Bangladesh) since 1947. It is estimated that 609,998 people migrated to Tripura between 1947 and 1971. This resulted in less land being available for tribals to cultivate and in their indebtedness to moneylenders and traders.

The former princely rulers of Tripura had constituted Tribal Reserved Areas within the state under Tribal Reserve Orders of 1931 and 1941 for settlement of five specified tribes. These areas covered 42% of the total area of the state. Transfer of land to persons other than members of these indigenous communities was banned. However, with the heavy influx of immigrants after the merger of Tripura in the Indian Union, no immediate measures were taken to protect the interests of the tribals. On the contrary, an area of 777 square kilometres was de-reserved 1948 with a view to increase the land revenue and to solve the rehabilitation problem that the state faced after partition.

It was only in 1960 that the Tripura Land Revenue and Land Reforms Act was brought into force. The Act imposed restrictions on transfer of land from tribals to non-tribals. It was first amended in 1974 to provide for restoration of illegally transferred land. In reality, land alienation is known to be more widespread than as revealed by official statistics. The rural tribal people in general have little knowledge of the intricate process of litigation. Approaching the courts for redress is also beyond their economic capacity. In order to protect the interests of the tribal people, the Autonomous District Council and Village Councils were set up in 1982 under the Sixth Schedule of the Constitution.

As a result of the demographic upheaval, a new agrarian structure emerged. The immigration of Bengalis and their settlement in Tripura slowly replaced the tribal communal mode of production with production based on private ownership of land. The migration of Bengali peasants increased the area of settled agriculture. The authorities discouraged the tribals from practicing shifting cultivation and increased the area of reserved forest in the state. The resulting sharp fall in the area available for shifting cultivation coupled with continued unproductive cultivation of the same old lands for years exposed the tribals to exploitation by moneylenders and businessmen. This opened the floodgates for the transfer of tribal lands to non-tribals, which became the most potent cause of ethnic conflict. The developing rural stratification also led to increase in the agricultural labour force.

The demographic and socio-economic changes gave rise to a complex interplay of class and ethnicity, tribal and Bengali. While the scope for class-based political mobilization of Bengali and tribal poor increased, the dramatic growth in the Bengali population and the diminution of the tribal population gave rise to an anti-Bengali Tripuri ethnic consciousness. From the 1940s onwards, a series of ethnic movements emerged to articulate the tribal cause. The limited expansion of educational opportunities in the 1940s created a new group of educated tribal youths, discontented over denial of posts in administration. The princely state had preferred the employment of Bengalis. Tribal youth organizations emerged and they served as a vehicle for the development of Tripuri nationalism and communism.

Tribal discontent with the communists' inability to comprehend the nationality issue in the framework class analysis led to increasing dissident activity. In 1967, a new tribal youth organization, the Tripura Upajati Juba Samithi (TUJS), was formed. It demanded, among other things, the introduction of an autonomous district council for the tribal people, the recognition of Kok Borok, the indigenous language, as an official language and the restoration of tribal lands alienated to non-tribals. In 1977, the TUJS became an electoral force to reckon with. It did well in the elections in 1982 and 1985 for the Tribal Autonomous District Council (formed in 1979). Later, it provided impetus to the formation of a guerilla group, Tripura National Volunteers (TNV), headed by Bijoy Hrangkhal, which became the fountainhead of the two main militant groups operating in Tripura today: the All Tripura Tiger Force (ATTF); and the National Liberation Front of Tripura (NLFT). The setting up of the Tribal Autonomous District Council resulted in an anti-tribal uprising in 1980 in which over 2,000 persons (mainly tribals) were killed. In the subsequent period, despite the strengthening of the Tribal Autonomous District Council to empower the tribals, tribal discontent has not been assuaged, mainly on account of political failures. Recent years have seen an increasing number of violent incidents perpetrated by various militant outfits such as killings, kidnappings for ransom. The Government of India has had to deploy hundreds of central military and paramilitary units in the state.

The two main national political parties, the Indian National Congress (INC) and the Communist Party of India (Marxist) which have formed successive state governments in Tripura since 1972, have been largely ineffective in addressing the basic issues behind the tribal protest in the state. There is a serious paucity of information and analysis on the status of children affected by conflict in Tripura. Many studies are available on its nature and causes of the insurgency.

However, none exists as regards its impact on women and children. The State Social Welfare department is yet to undertake a serious study. During a brief visit, the following insights could be gathered:

- The high points of the conflict saw large scale burning of houses and other dwelling units, resulting in serious displacement and dislocation of people, especially women and children. Children have had to be put up in make shift camps for long periods with an adverse impact on their schooling, food security, health and so on. The impact of the conflict on the health of children has been serious.
- The children of the indigenous communities, always neglected, have been very badly affected. The psychological and economic impacts have been significant. Field level studies are needed to assess the situation.
- Cerebral malaria is a major affliction among women and children. The armed conflict situation prevents access to medical care.
- The central paramilitary forces deployed in the state have recently launched a community action programme, including visits by medical and paramedical staff, which has been welcomed, especially in interior tribal habitations. However, many tribal habitations are inaccessible due to the difficult terrain as well as the adverse security scenario.

Tripura is the only state in the northeast where the indigenous tribal people, once the majority population, have been reduced to a minority as a result of massive influx of refugees from Bangladesh. The indigenous people, who accounted for 95% of the population in the 1931 Census, were a mere 31% in the 1991 Census. In addition to land control and monopoly of trade and business, the immigrants also dominate government jobs. The conflict situation, relating basically to the land issue, has persisted from around the 1940's. Demographic and political forces have further conspired to thrust political power firmly into the hands of the non-tribal immigrants. The aggravated disadvantage lends a sharper edge to the ongoing indigenous communities' militancy. These developments have had an adverse impact on women and children. There is a particular need and scope for a comprehensive study of this impact.

A study concludes that geographically, politically and culturally the people of Tripura have been affected by insensitive governments, lop-sided development, opportunities lost to the migrant majority and the brutality they have faced at the hands of the police, paramilitary and armed forces, whose presence and powers have only grown with the passage of time. The all-pervading powers of the armed forces are the outcome of the provisions of the special security legislations imposed on the state.

Conclusion

Many studies exist on the nature and causes of the violence in the northeast. There is also a large and state-centric literature on the strategic issues in the northeast. However, only a few human rights organizations have bothered to examine the impact of political violence on the lives of the ordinary people, especially women and children. Security analysis today is a complex subject and must include the human rights of women and children, not just security of the State. In the northeastern context, there has been an excess of political violence and human rights violations.

References

1. *Baruah, Sanjib (2005)* Durable Disorder: Understanding the Politics of Northeast India, *Oxford University Press, New Delhi*
2. *Bhattacharyya H (1999)* Communism in Tripura *(Ajanta Publications), New Delhi*
3. *Chasie, Charles (2000)* The Naga Imbroglio: A Personal Perspective, *(United Publishers), Guwahati*
4. *Hazarika, S. (1994)* Strangers in the Mist, *New Delhi*
5. *Hazarika S. (2000)* Rites of Passage: Border Crossings, Imagined Homelands, India's East and Bangladesh, *Penguin*
6. *Mahbub ul Haq Human Development Centre (1999),* South Asia Human Development Report, *Islamabad*
7. *Mullik B.N. (1971, 1972, 1972a)* My Years with Nehru *(Allied Publishers, New Delhi)*
8. *Manipuri Students Association (2004),* Support Manipuri People's Resistance Against the Armed Forces Special Powers Act, 1958
9. *National Campaign Committee Against Militarization (1997)* 'Where Peacekeepers have declared war': Report on Violation of Democratic Rights by Security Forces in the Northeast, *Green Park, New Delhi*
10. *Oommen, T.K., (2006)* Understanding Security: A New Perspective, *Macmillan, New Delhi*
11. *Rustomji, Nari (1973, 1983)* The Enchanted Frontiers and The Imperiled Frontiers, *Oxford University Press, New Delhi*
12. *Subramanian, K. S. (2000)* Employment Generation in the Northeast, *Kurukshetra, Monthly Journal of the Ministry of Rural Development, New Delhi Volume 48 No. 10 (July)*
13. *Subramanian K.S. (2001)* Human Rights of the Tribal People: The Basic Issue in Tripura, *Mainstream, Republic Day Special Number, January*
14. *Subramanian K. S. (2003)* Development Policies and Programmes in the Northeastern Region: A Case Study of Tripura, *(Institute of Applied Manpower Research), New Delhi*
15. *Subramanian, K. S. (2004)* Manipur Fiasco and the Crisis of Human Rights in the Northeast" *(Mainstream) New Delhi, September 18.*
16. *Subramanian K. S. (2004)* Human Rights of Women and Children in Nagaland *(Mainstream) New Delhi, November 7.*
17. *United Nations Development Programme (UNDP) 1990, 1994, 2005,* Human Development Reports.

THE "TIBET ISSUE" IN SINO-INDIAN RELATIONS

Professor Li Tao
Executive Director, Institute of South Asia Studies, Sichuan University

"The 21st century will be the Asian century". The study on relations between the two major powers in Asia—China and India—is assuming increasing importance. As an important part of India's national security strategy and the Indian Government's policy toward China, the "Tibet issue" inevitably becomes a focal point of consideration. An in-depth analysis of the issue can help us understand Sino-Indian relations in a correct perspective and help develop Sino-Indian relations.

I. The Indian Government's Tibet-related Policies

The Indian Government's Tibet-related policies have undergone a four-phased development:

Phase One: From Independence to the Lhasa Rebellion (1947-59)

In 1947, the newly independent Indian Government carried on many measures of the colonial British Raj and kept the former "British Office" in Lhasa with its representative, Hugh E. Richardson, and his team. A series of events promoting Tibetan independence occurred.[1] There was the separate Tibetan delegation sent to New Delhi for the "Pan-Asian Conference",[2] the "Reting Incident", the so-called "Tibetan Trade Delegation" in India, the "Driving Han people out of Tibet" movement,[3] and so on. During this period, the Indian Government only recognized China's suzerainty over Tibet, and demanded the transfer of all special rights and interests enjoyed by British-Indian authorities in Tibet to independent India.[4] Meanwhile,

[1] *Tibet and Peace in South Asia, National Committee for Tibet and Peace in South Asia, New Delhi, 1991, pp. 46-47*
[2] *Selected Tibet Historical Information, Sanlian Bookstore, 1973, p. 357*
[3] *Guo Guanzhong, Truth about Tibet Incident on July 8, 1949, Ethnic Studies 1990, No. 2*
[4] *Dawa Norbu, Tibet in Sino-Indian Relations, Strategic Digest, April 1998*

the Indian press vilified the PLA's peaceful liberation of Tibet, and even reported Indian military interference.

In 1950, the Indian Government delivered three diplomatic notes to the Chinese Government on 21 October, 28 October, and 1 November respectively, accusing the People's Liberation Army (PLA) of invading Tibet. In 1951, with the support from the representative of Indian Office in Lhasa, the Tibetan separatists gathered in Dekyi Lingka, where the office was located, to hold the so-called "General Assembly of Tibetan Deputies".

On 29 April 1954, the Chinese Government and the Indian Government signed the "Agreement on Trade and Transportation between India and the Tibet Region of China", which invalidated all of the privileges enjoyed by British-India in Tibet.

In 1956, when the 14th Dalai Lama and the 10th Panchen Lama went to India to attend the 2500th Anniversary of SakyaMuni, Prime Minister Nehru formally announced that Tibet was a part of China. However, he also showed sympathy to the "Tibetan People's quest for Autonomy" in his address to the Indian Parliament. He met the Dalai Lama on several occassions.

In 1956, the Indian Consulate General in Lhasa played certain roles in the disturbance caused by Khargya. In 1958, while visiting Bhutan, Prime Minister Nehru made an extraordinary inspection tour to Yadong (Dromo in Tibetan).[5] In March 1959, a rebellion broke out in Lhasa. It is believed that, apart from the CIA, the Indian Consulate General was also involved covertly.

For the benefit of the bilateral relations between India and China, the Nehru administration correctly relinquished its colonial legacy in Tibet. The Indian Government did not vote for "Tibet independence" in the UNO, though it was very critical of the PLA's presence in Tibet. In principle, the Indian Government recognized China's rightful control over Tibet, both politically and militarily. But at the same time, taking advantage of the close religious, cultural and economic ties between India and Tibet, the Indian Consulate General in Lhasa maintained special relationship with some Tibetan leaders who were dissatisfied with the democratic reform of Tibet, which was tantamount to secret support. There were instances of helping Tibetan separatists for traveling to the US for military training and smuggling them back into Tibet to organize armed rebellion. In such operations, the Indian Consulate General provided intelligence to the separatists, facilitated their passages to the US and Taiwan, and helped the separatists to establish bases for "Tibet independence" in Kalimpong in India.

Phase Two - From Granting Refuge to the Dalai Lama to the Return of the Ambassadors (1959-76)

After 1959, India actively tried to turn Tibet into a real buffer zone between the two countries. The Indian administration supported some Tibetan leaders with their separatist activities on the one hand, and began to implement the "forward policy" along the Sino-Indian border on the other hand. This inevitably brought an end to the Sino-Indian honeymoon.

Granting refuge to Tibetan rebels in India: In April 1959, Nehru met with the Dalai Lama and granted political asylum to him. In the meanwhile, the Indian Government established the "Central Tibetan Relief Committee", which included the "Tibetan Resettlement Office". Subsequently, the Indian Government helped the Dalai Lama establish the "Tibet Government in Exile" (TGIE), and allocate funds, materials and land to construct the "refugee camps", which were later called the Tibetan settlements.[6] The TGIE came into existence in Dharamsala in 1960. Although the TGIE was not officially acknowledged by the Indian Government, Tibetans were allowed to hold public assemblies, protests and other activities championing Tibetan independence. Anti-China slogans have been displayed at Dharamshala and other Tibetan centres.

Territorial disputes: On 22 March 1959, Prime Minister Nehru wrote to Premier Zhou Enlai, reiterating that the Sino-Indian boundary should follow the high watershed in Himalaya, and that China should confirm various agreements between India and Tibet signed in the past.

Establishment of Tibetan military forces against China: Through the activities of the Indian intelligence agencies, and with the involvement of Gyalmo Thundup (the Dalai Lama's elder brother) who acted as an intermediary between the US and the Indian intelligence agencies, the "Indian Tibetan Special Border Troops" and the "Indo Tibetan Border Police Force" were created, and the Tibetan army called

[5] *Yang Gongyuan, 90 Years' vicissitudes – Memories of a Diplomat, Hainan Publishing House, January 1999, pp. 253-254*

[6] *Gyatso Tenzin, Beyond Dogma, Freedom in Exile: The Autobiography of the Dalai Lama, London: Hodder and Stoughton Ltd. 1990*

"Chushi Gangdruk" (Religious Guards of the Four Rivers and Six Ranges) was re-established and strengthened. In addition, the Indian Government allowed the CIA to fly armed personnel and weapons through Indian airspace to Tibet.

Support of pro-Tibetan resolution in the UNO: In the 20th UN General Assembly held in 1965, the Indian Government voted in favor of the resolution tabled by El Salvador, Ireland and Malaysia, condemning China's "violation of human rights and freedom in Tibet".[7] But with the normalization of US-China relations (coinciding with the CIA's termination of the assistance to the Tibetan subversive army), especially after the "Chushi Gangdruk" was totally defeated in Nepal in 1974, India gradually stopped providing support to the Tibetan guerrillas. In July 1976, China and India decided to restore their diplomatic relations at the Ambassadorial level, signaling a thaw of the icy relations between India and China.

Phase Three: Transformation of India into a Nuclear Weapon State (1976-98)

In 1976, China and India restored diplomatic relations at the Ambassadorial level, and bilateral relations gradually warmed up. In 1988, Prime Minister Rajiv Gandhi's visit to China further promoted the development of Sino-Indian relations. Under this circumstance, the Indian authorities once again clarified its stand on the "Tibet issue". To be exact, India accepted Tibet as an autonomous region of China, Tibetans were not allowed to carry out anti-China political activities in India, and the Tibet issue was categorically the internal affair of China. From 1989 onwards, there has been a decrease in donations and funds to the Tibetans in India and four hospitals that had been providing free medical treatment to the Tibetan refugees were closed down. Furthermore, the Indian Government stopped allocating additional land to the expanding Tibetan population. In 1993, Prime Minister Narasimha Rao reiterated the above-mentioned Indian stand on Tibet during his visit to China. The Indian government adhered to its new policy towards Tibet as witnessed by the curbing of Tibetan separatists' activities during Premier Li Peng and President Jiang Zemin's visits to India.

However, due to its strong wish to turn Tibet into a buffer zone between India and China, which had never diminished all those years, the Indian Government was quite incapable of discarding its double-edged Tibet policy. From the mid-1980s onwards, the US and western countries were expecting a drastic social change in China, and the Tibetans abroad tried to internationalize the "Tibet issue", it was at this juncture that the negative side of India's Tibet policy was exposed. To be specific, the Indian Government openly called upon the Chinese Government to start negotiations with the Dalai Lama as soon as possible, and turned a blind eye to various Tibetan separatist activities within India, such as the celebration of the International Year of Tibet, the peace march campaigns, the referendum, fast-to-death hunger strikes, etc.

More noteworthy was the emergence of a pro-Tibet surge from all walks of life in India during this period, which exercised a direct influence over the Indian Government's Tibet policy and boosted the morale of the Tibetan separatist activities. First of all, there were a variety of anti-China groups in India sympathetic to Tibetan secessionism, which included the "All Party Indian Parliamentary Forum for Tibet", "India Tibet Friendship Society", "Students for a Free Tibet", and "Himalayan Committee for Action on Tibet", etc. These groups were urging the government to recognize the TGIE and render support to "Tibetan independence". They even staged a number of street demonstrations for this end.[8] Second, the Indian Parliament's support to Tibet independence could no longer be ignored, especially after the riots in Lhasa in the late 1980s. Many members of the Indian Parliament requested the government to re-examine its policies vis-à-vis the "Tibet issue" and support the Dalai Lama's "five-point peace plan".[9]

Phase Four: During the Turn of the Century (1999 – to date)

Along with the improvement of the bilateral relations and deepening of Sino-Indian cooperation, the Indian Government's Tibet policy is changing for the better, despite some residual uncertainties.

In the wake of the Indian nuclear tests in May 1998, Sino-Indian relations suffered a major setback. It was the Indian Foreign Minister Jaswant Singh's visit to China, in June 1999, which put the briefly derailed bilateral relations back on track. With great efforts by

[7] *Anand Kumar (Ed.), Tibet : A Sourcebook, Radiant Publisher, New Delhi, 1995, pp. 163-167*

[8] *Referring to Tibetan Review?www.xizang-zhiye.org at the same period*

[9] *George Fernandes, Member of Parliament and Leader of Samata Party, on Tibet. Keynote address delivered at the International Convention on Tibet and Peace in South Asia, New Delhi, 12-14 August,1989. Referring to INDIAN LEADERS ON TIBET, Dharamsala, 1998*

both sides, there were improvements in the bilateral relations and mutual cooperation despite all the difficulties, China and India have turned a new page in their mutual ties since the beginning of the 21st century. Improvement of the bilateral relations was shown in the following areas: significant increase in high level visits; regular strategic dialogues and military exchanges; the speedup of the border negotiation; agreement on political principles on border disputes and the establishment of a bilateral negotiation mechanism at the high level of the special representatives; increase in cultural and economic exchanges. On 6 July 2006, the re-opening of the Nathula Pass promoted the border trade activities to a new high.

The warming up of the bilateral relations makes it impossible for the situation of the "Tibet issue" to return to Phase Two, when confrontation was at its worst. In general, the "Tibet issue" is no longer the greatest concern or the main obstacle hampering the development of bilateral relations. In short, the importance of the import of the "Tibet issue" in the context of Sino-Indian relations has significantly diminished. In the Sino-Indian Joint Declaration signed in June 2003, India for the first time explicitly recognized Tibet as a part of China, which served to narrow down the space of the "Tibet issue" and weaken its negative impact on bilateral relations. During Premier Wen Jiabao's visit to India in 2005, the Indian Government reiterated that the Tibet Autonomous Region was a part of the territory of People's Republic of China, and India would not allow Tibetans to engage in anti-China political activities on Indian soil. The government of the ruling alliance led by the Indian Congress Party has approved the Tibet policy of its predecessor government led by the BJP, demonstrating the continuity of the Tibet policy of the Indian Government in the changed political context.

II. Anatomy of the Indian Government's Tibet Policy

1. Geostrategy, the Decisive Factor in the Indian Government's Tibet Policy

Geopolitics is an indispensable element in any country's foreign policy. The Indian leadership and strategists have always regarded Tibet as a part of its sub-continental strategy—treating it as a buffer between China and India. This is not only a historic legacy, but also a consideration of practical interest. From the ancient Maurya Dynasty down to the Mughal Empire, India could be conceived as a vast territory. During the colonial period, the British Indian authorities expanded its rule to Afghanistan and part of Tibet to the north, the Indian Ocean to the south, and Southeast Asia to the east. Since India achieved independence in 1947, the ambitious Indian leadership headed by Jawaharlal Nehru has cherished a delicate "security strategy of the Himalayan Barrier", with superpower status as the ultimate goal of the national strategy. Within just a few years time, by employing diplomatic measures, India successfully brought neighbouring countries and regions such as Bhutan, Nepal, and Afghanistan under its control, and secured an absolute leadership in the sub-continent. As an essential part of India's national security system, Tibet is of great importance to the Indian authorities. It has always been a strategic thought in India's Tibet policy to maintain a buffer zone between India and China, and to foster a pro-India governing power on that land. For a long period, India only accepted Tibet as an "autonomous region" of China, implying its special status and "buffering" role, which was apparently aimed to eliminate the threat to India caused by the so-called Chinese presence in Tibet.

2. The "Passion for Tibet" and the "China Threat Theory", their impact on the Tibet policy of the Indian Government

There is a long historical relationship between India and Tibet. The Dalai Lama has repeatedly stated in public that "one Bodhi tree has two branches, i.e. India and Tibet." Tibetans regard India as a "Holy Land". Similarly, Indians take Tibetan culture and religion as the legacy of the ancient Indian civilization, believing that "Tibet preserved and helped spread the mystique Indian tradition in the world".[10] Some Indians are even concerned that the extinction of the Tibetan way of life will make "Indian characteristics" face the same fate. Especially in recent years, with the revival of Buddhism in India, Tibetan Buddhism and the Dalai Lama have become more and more attractive to the Indian public, scholars and the media.[11] The "China Threat Theory" which originates from the Indian concern over the emergence of a mighty neighbor, has further strengthened Indian public's sympathy and support to the Tibetan exiles. It is why the Indian Government's Tibet policy enjoys broad public support.

---

[10] *Gyaneshwar Chaturvedi;"India's Tibet Policy" Tibet Bulletin, January-February 2005*

[11] *Claude Arpi, Cultural Relations between India and Tibet : An overview of the light from India, Dialogue, Vol. 6, No. 2, 2004*

3. Tibetan propaganda in India, the Crucial Influence on the Indian Government's Tibet Policy

Since the Lhasa rebellion in 1959, tens of thousands of Tibetans have fled abroad. According to the TGIE's statistics in 2004, a total of 138,000 Tibetans are scattered all over the world, of whom over 110,000 are in India. The exiles have set up their own "Government in Exile", more than 100 schools, 500 or so monasteries and cultural centres, a number of farms, factories and hospitals in India. Tibetan settlements can be found in over 10 Indian states both in the North and the South.

The impact of Tibetans in India has many ramifications, such as:

a) as a religious and political leader, the Nobel Laureate Dalai Lama's intervention into religious strives enhances the publicity of the "Tibet issue";
b) the Tibetan residents' close relationship with both central and local Indian government officials, many Tibetans have become Indian citizens and joined Indian government services;
c) frequent lobbying campaigns in asking for support of the Indian Parliament for Tibet;
d) cooperation with various NGOs on Tibet-related seminars intended for influencing the "Tibet issue";
e) launching boycott Chinese goods campaigns, protests, hunger strikes, assault on the Chinese Embassy in New Delhi, etc.

4. The International Impact on India's Tibet Policy

In spite of its "non-aligned" and "neutral" foreign policy, India's Tibet policy is not immune to the frequent changes in the international situation and Sino-Indian relations. Independent India's affinity with the British colonial rule and its innate pro-West stances positioned the Indian Government in the Western camp during the early stages of the Cold War in the 1950s and 1960s. The US alliance with Pakistan in the early 1950s (1954) stimulated the fast development of Sino-Indian relations.[12] From the late 1950s to the 1960s, with the escalation of the Cold War, shift of the strategic focus of the US and Soviet Union, and warming up of the Sino-Pakistan relations, India reversed its Tibet policy, which aggravated the deterioration of Sino-India relations and finally triggered the border war in 1962. After the Cold War ended, India aligned with the US-led western countries to criticize China in the name of "democracy" and "human rights" vis-à-vis the "Tibet issue".

III. Prospects of Indian Tibet Policy in the New Era

After more than half century's ups and downs, Sino-Indian relations are gradually normalized. Through the learning process from the past lessons and the quest for the common ground, both of the governments are committed to strengthening mutual friendship. Along with changes of the international situation and progress of the "Sino-Tibetan talks", new prospects of the Indian policy on Tibet may be expected in the context of Sino-Indian relations.

1. Irrevocable Progress towards an all-round Cooperation between China and India relating to the "Tibet Issue"

In the first place, a stable and healthy long-term Sino-Indian relationship is in the interest of socio-economic development for both the countries. After a bumpy past, both countries have settled down to tackle the fundamental issue, i.e., to develop the national economy. Both China and India have the common desire to maintain a stable and peaceful international and domestic environment. At the same time, with increasingly enhanced national strength, both countries are hoping to alter the existing international order making it more just and equitable, reflecting the right international status commensurate with their strength. China and India also share common views on the international code of conduct, e.g. the "Five Principles of Peaceful Coexistence" (Panchasheela). Both countries are advocates of "independence", and opposed to hegemonic, unilateral power politics and interference in other country's internal affairs. Moreover, Sonia Gandhi, the President of the Congress Party and Chairperson of the Indian ruling alliance has made several visits to China, and the Congress-led Indian government since the regime of Rajiv Gandhi has attached comparatively great importance to Sino-Indian relations. In this sense, the dominant friendly atmosphere in Sino-Indian relations will not be blown away.

Second, the complementarities between China and India in the fields of trade and commerce have much room for greater economic cooperation. The economies

[12] *Robert J. McMahon, U.S.Policy Toward South Asia and Tibet during the Early Cold War, Harvard University International Conference—The Cold War And Its Legacy In Tibet : Great-Power Politics And Regional Security, 2002*

of China and India are complementary instead of competitive, and each has its own preponderant industries in international trade. India occupies the leading place in the high-tech departments of the software industry, while China is robust in "hardware" manufacturing industry. In addition, there is huge potential for cooperation between China and India in the fields of agriculture, energy, health care, etc.

Third, the paradigm of "geostrategy" that used to hinder the development of Sino-Indian relations has been fading in the changing global context. Far back in the 1940s, K.M. Panikkar, later Indian Ambassador to China, had already pointed out that "with the growth of airpower, the Himalayas were no longer the impenetrable barrier to prevent the potential enemies from the north".[13] Along with the improvement of the weapons, especially the nuclear arsenal of both countries, the geostrategic paradigm based on the Himalayas as well as the "Tibet issue" have largely become irrelevant. Besides, considering the different defence priorities of the two countries, China has to focus more attention on the US-Japan Joint Defense System and the Taiwan secessionist movement, and India, for quite a long time to come, will still be preoccupied by the intra-South Asian rivalry.[14] Therefore, an all-round cooperation is in the best interest of both countries.

2. The "Sino-Tibetan Talks", a new cushion for the Sino-Indian relations

With the rise of China's international status and rapid progress in the socio-economic development in China's Tibet Autonomous Region and the neighbouring Tibetan-inhabited areas, the international outlook of the "Tibet issue" is changing.[15] The international community is increasingly poised to a more objective and fair view on the "Tibet issue", which will undoubtedly facilitate understanding between Tibetans and Chinese both at home and abroad, conducive to the dialogue between Beijing and Dharamsala, and, most important of all, the final resolution of the "Tibet issue". Since the reform and opening up, the central government of China has invited several "Tibetan delegations" to visit the homeland. Under the complicated international situation, however, those visits did not deepen mutual understanding, but resulted in more disputes than before. A new round of "talks" has been initiated since the beginning of the 21st century. Up till now, the central government has made six "contacts" with the representatives of the Dalai Lama.

3. Changing tactics of the Tibetan Separatist Movement and Impact on India's Domestic Politics

Fearing the improvement of Sino-Indian relations, the Dharamsala clique has changed its separatist strategy. The tightening of restrictions by the Indian Government on the activities of the radical anti-China Tibetan exiles, such as assaults on the Chinese Embassy etc., the Dharamsala clique has decided on a changed tactics of appealing to the "grass-roots", so as to exercise greater influence over Indian people and the public opinions on the Tibet issue. Tibetan exiles have set up, reorganized and expanded various organizations to promote Indo-Tibetan relations. In June 2005, Indo-Tibetan Co-operative Societies were set up in over 10 Tibetan settlements in India. In 2002, the dying "All Party Indian Parliamentary Forum for Tibet" was revived with the help of Tibetan exiles. A number of organizations such as the "Core Group for Tibetan Cause", "India Tibet Coordination Office" and "India Tibet Friendship Society" became backbones in supporting the "Tibet issue".

Second, the connection between the "Tibet issue" and India's national security was emphasized on various occasions. In recent years, the number of seminars on the "Tibet issue" in Sino-Indian relations held all over India has increased drastically. From 2003 to 2005, there were more than a dozen large-scale seminars (with over 100 attendants) held on "Turning Tibet into a Non-violent District", "Sino-Indian Relations and Tibet Issue" and "Himalayas and National Security". In addition to this, media personalities and members of Indian parliament were invited to visit the Tibetan settlements and Dharamsala during the so-called "Tibet Year 2004". It was remarkable that the Dalai Lama also showed his "care" for India in a very clear way by attending various religious rituals and secular ceremonies.

---

[13] *Karunakar Gupta, translated by Wang Hongwei, Wang Zhiting, The Secret History of the Sino-Indian Border, China Tibetan Study Publishing House, December 1990, p. 56*

[14] *Tsering Shakya, India's Tibet Policy in the Post-Cold War Era: Foundations in Nationalism and Ideology, Harvard University International Conference—The Cold War And Its Legacy In Tibet: Great-Power Politics And Regional Security, 2002*

[15] *Li Tao, Impact of US Tibet-Related Media on Sino-US Relations, Chinese Governance in Border Area (quarterly) No. 158, (Taipei) China Border Governance Magazine, June, 2004*

In short, thanks to the separatist activities of Tibetans in exile, it has become a distinct phenomenon that Indian political leaders would always be overwhelmed by waves of anti-China and pro-Tibet appeals before they embark on trips to China. In a nation harassed by such complicated religious and ethnic minority issues,[16] the "Tibet issue" has become a bargaining chip of the political parties in their fight for governing power, and the Indian Government's Tibet policy will undoubtedly be adversely affected.

4. Impact of the Changing International Situation on the "Tibet Issue"

Against China's rising economic and military power, the United States has taken pains to contain China. Since 2006, the US has upgraded its ties with Taiwan and strengthened cooperation with Japan and Australia. During the US-Japan-Australia security talks in March 2006, "emerging China" became the main concern.[17] At the same time, the US began to show greater interest in India. It seems that the "stable economic recession" of EU and Japan, the traditional allies of the US, has suddenly put India - the rising democratic country with rapid growth rate second only to China in Asia - to the front stage for containing China. Naturally, the US could not wait to offer the preferential treatment and good will to India, the important ally with great potential in rivalling China. During his trip to India in 2006, President Bush signed the agreement on nuclear cooperation with India, which considerably enhanced the strategic relationship between the US and India. As the "Tibet issue" has always been of great concern to the US and other Western countries, on which India and the US share a common interest, the changing international situation is bound to affect the "Tibet issue" in Sino-Indian relations, albeit it may not be a decisive factor.

IV. Conclusion

Over the past 50 years, despite the changes of the ruling parties and the different characteristics of the Indian Government's Tibet policy at different times, there has been a consistent posture on the "Tibet issue":

1) The Indian Government's Tibet policy changed with the changes in Sino-Indian relations.
2) The Indian Government's Tibet policy is highlighted for its dual nature.
3) India's Tibet policy basically remains consistent despite minor differences of specifics.
4) There seems to be an Indian motivation to use the "Tibet issue" to checkmate China.
5) Decades of hard encounters proved that the friendly relations and peaceful development are not only beneficial to both countries, but also helpful for the resolution of the "Tibet issue".

The US has turned the "Tibet issue" into a strategic tool to contain and distract China. Therefore, India's maintaining a correct stand vis-à-vis the US-led anti-China coalition on the "Tibet issue" is vital to the interest of Sino-Indian relations. Any ruling alliance that governs India in future will continue to tolerate the Tibetan exiles and their political manoeuvres for a considerable period of time, and the intensity of the secessionist activities will vary according to the ups and downs of Sino-Indian relations. It is unrealistic to expect the total disappearance of the Tibetan secessionist activities even after the decease of the Dalai Lama. In the foreseeable future, the Indian Government will not abandon the dual nature of its Tibet policy completely. India will continue to keep the pressure on China through the "Tibet issue" while at the same time clarify its unchanged position of recognizing Tibet as part of China and put restraints on "Tibetan separatist" activities. In order to make this practice perfect, India may need to keep a proper distance from the US-led western alliance on the "Tibet issue" keeping aloof from their anti-China manoeuvres.

[16] *Sun Shihai, Sino-Indian relations in the 21st century, Asia Report 2000, 01, Changchun Publishing House*
[17] *AFP, Sydney, March 15, US-Japan-Australia Security Talks Focused on China, Reference Information, March 16, 2006*

INDO-US STRATEGIC PARTNERSHIP: RAMIFICATIONS OF US INVOLVEMENT IN AFGHANISTAN AND IRAQ

Lt Gen RK Sawhney (Retd)
Former Deputy Chief of Army Staff, India

After the airborne strikes that killed nearly 3000 people in the United States (US) on 11 September 2001, President George W Bush transformed America's global posture and refashioned his government's international relationship. This has had a substantial effect on the sub-continent. The attack on the twin towers of the World Trade Centre and the 13 December 2001 attack on the Indian Parliament impacted on the nature of US relations with India and Pakistan as well as the bilateral engagement between the two neighbours.

But five years on, the initial gains of the war on terror seem fragile at best, with fighting crackling in Afghanistan, parts of Iraq paralyzed by violence and the legal pillars of the US-led offensive crumbling. After 9/11, the entire world stood with the US and supported its goals of eliminating terrorism. Today, that grand coalition is badly fragmented. West Europe, Russia and China, which supported the US in the wake of 9/11, are now making detrimental efforts to limit its presence in Iraq. Insofar as India is concerned, the last five years have given rise to new security cooperation with the US in the war on terror. Paradoxically, however, we find Pakistan (the epicentre of terrorism) emerging as the principal beneficiary in the war against terrorism. After the military showdown between India and Pakistan as an aftermath of the 13 December 2001 attack on Parliament, US involvement led to de-escalation and establishment of the basis for a new dialogue on Kashmir. There exists, however, a deep trust deficit in India against Pakistan, which is likely to persist even if democracy is re-established in Pakistan.

Afghanistan

Till 2005 there were hopes for optimism about the situation in Afghanistan. There were signs of planned renewal, maintenance, construction and investments, at least in Kabul and parts of Northern Afghanistan. This was a welcome change after the wanton destruction and inactions of last two decades which left both hard and soft infrastructure totally dilapidated. The United Nation Development Programme (UNDP) rated Afghanistan as the country next-to-last in the entire world in 2002 in its Human Development Index. To be fair, the last three to four years support by the US and international regional players (including India) did help bring about installation of a new government, introduction of new currency, establishment of a measure of macro-economic stability, adoption of a new Constitution, and the conduct of a reasonably fair election that chose a President and subsequently the Parliament.

There were, however, signs of security issues not being addressed adequately. It was being wrongly assumed that stability would come in with more development. The process of raising the National Army and tackling of the regrouped Taliban and Al Qaeda elements was not being give due attention by the US, International Security Assistance Force (ISAF), or the North Atlantic Treaty Organisation (NATO) troops. Keeping in view the dismal state of affairs in Iraq, the Americans were deliberately underplaying their problems in Afghanistan and trying to wish away the activities of the regrouped Taliban and Al-Qaeda. The dubious and dangerous role being played by Pakistan was being tolerated by the US, despite repeated warnings by their own envoy in Kabul. Although Pakistan was supposed to have deployed approximately 80,000 troops in its border with Afghanistan, they are still to produce any credible results. Half-hearted operations did get launched but got no substantial results. If all this was not enough, Afghanistan was emerging as the main producer of opium and its derivatives, accounting for almost 80% of world's annual supply.

The Current Scenario

It appears that the worst case scenario has become a reality in Afghanistan. The Southern provinces, bordering Pakistan have become the epicentre of a Taliban resurgence that has doubled the American casualty rate country-wide this year. Across Afghanistan, roadside bomb attacks are up by 30 percent, and suicide bombings have increased 100 percent. Statistically it is now nearly as dangerous to serve in Afghanistan as it is in Iraq. The problem began in 2002 when US Defence Department opposed a request by Afghanistan's new leadership for a sizable peace keeping force and deployed only 8,000 American troops. During the first 18 months after the invasion, the US-led coalition deployed no peace-keepers outside Kabul, leaving the security of the provinces to ill-led, ill-equipped and barely trained Afghan security forces. The international community and the US both came up short on the security aspect and took it for granted. This was a blunder which is now coming back to haunt not only America but the whole region.

It is not only the security but also economic aid which has not been provided to this country in adequate measure. The Afghan economy continues to subsist on international as well as US aid and which comes in driblets. American officials have said the country was more destitute than they had envisaged, yet the $ 909 million they provided in assistance in 2002 amounted to one-twentieth of the $ 20 billion allocated to post-war Iraq. Americans quintupled assistance to $ 4.9 billion by 2005, but then reduced it by 30 percent in 2006. The Taliban leadership meanwhile found safe haven in neighbouring Pakistan. President Karzai quite rightly feels that there is some sort of Pakistani connivance with Taliban / Al Qaeda which has helped them regroup and enhance their effectiveness to the present dangerous level. There is no evidence that Pakistan is about to sever all links with Taliban or give up its dreams of a client state in Afghanistan. The peace deal signed by Musharraf's government with the Pakistani Taliban was a pointer in this direction. The treaty signed in the tribal area of North Waziristan created a refuge for Taliban and their Al Qaeda allies.

One can not help but think that Afghanistan, US and other NATO troops fighting the Taliban insurgency just across the border, are looking askance at Pakistani's stance wherein they have ceded North Waziristan to the Talibans. Accusations refuse to go away that Pakistani agents are supporting the insurgency with training, arms and cash as part of a strategy to gain influence in Afghanistan. President Bush has refused to see this dubious peace deal in this light, as probably he did not want to destabilize a valued ally. The US media and the strategic community, however, have not been so kind to Musharraf. Seth G Jones, a political scientist at the RAND Corporation averred that Pakistani agents have helped the Taliban leader Mullah Mohammad Omar hide and tipped his fighters on movements of the US-led forces. Keeping these trends in view one cannot help be pessimistic about Afghanistan's future. As large segments of Afghan territory came under Taliban influence, development would cease, schools (opened with great difficulty) would get converted into *madrassas* and the countryside once again turn into a *Jihadi* factory producing brainwashed terrorists out to create trouble once again in the region. India would be directly affected by such a fall out. One does not visualize any improvement in this situation, even with the possible future changes in the political set up of Pakistan after the next election.

A Possible Multilateral Approach to Deal with Afghanistan

It is time the international community helped Afghanistan break away from the stranglehold of Pakistan, who would like to treat the country as their strategic backyard. The American establishment is doing nothing to discourage this process for their own shot-term gains. Afghanistan's geographical position places it on the cross roads between the Middle East and Asia as well as Europe and the Indian Sub-Continent. It also links Europe, Russia and Central Asia with the Indian Ocean. Thus, its location is such that it must be deemed a part of Central Asia rather than South Asia. Pakistan is just one of its neighbours and can not, therefore, be allowed to take over the role of mentor especially keeping in view its destructive and destabilizing role in Afghanistan.

The Central Asian Republics to the North of Afghanistan as well as countries like Russia, China, Iran and India have legitimate interests and concerns in this country. These must be acknowledged, understood and respected by the US as well as the rest of the international community. Instability in Afghanistan, whether caused by drug trafficking, Islamic extremism or political breakdown would have global ramifications and most adversely affect the internal environment of the aforesaid countries. The international community must, therefore, induce the American Administration for taking a lead in creating an active forum or an organisation to give practical reason to these countries to assist the US in bringing permanent peace in Afghanistan as well as its extended neighbourhood. Pakistan, which is a part of the problem rather than solution, must also be included in this group so as to encourage it to be more responsible, accountable and transparent in dealing with Afghanistan. Inclusion of Iran, though quite important, may not be possible at present due to the prevailing state of US-Iran relations.

Iraq

The war on terror, as it has unfolded, has become a prime example of politics governed by gullibility. The invasion of Iraq was a direct consequence of one the most astounding political fantasies seen in a modern democracy. Saddam had no links with Al Qaeda and certainly no weapons of mass destruction to threaten the US or Western Nations. The US Administration told their public and the world that in addition to the afore-mentioned reasons (which were actually non-reasons) the war on Iraq was also being undertaken to remove Saddam and in his place install a tolerant, pluralistic, democratic society in the heart of the Arab-Muslim world as a part of broader war of ideas against violent radical Islam. The US, however, acted as if this process would be easy and sacrifice-free. They were naïve enough to believe expatriates, like the infamous Ahmed Chalabi, who convinced them that the US invasion would be welcomed by the suppressed Iraqis who would rise in support of the American troops. Thus, the very basis of planning for Iraq was faulty.

Further, just enough troops were sent out to topple Saddam with no capability of either sealing the borders or controlling the internal situation subsequent to taking over another country. If this was not enough, the complete Iraqi armed forces, better part of the police and the administrative services were disbanded in one go. All these well trained / equipped, but disgruntled, elements promptly turned into the most formidable insurgency force seen in modern times. Results of this stupidity are there for everyone to see. In two months, in Baghdad, alone 3,200 people died in fierce fighting, according to Iraqi figures – a sum in excess of the total death toll of 9/11. More than 2,600 US troops have also died since the conflict began in March 2003.

It was somewhere in mid 2003, that the US started searching for countries which would contribute to counter-insurgency operations in Iraq. India, emerging as a strategic partner was approached. As is normal with the Americans, a lobbying effort both within and outside India was launched to convince it of the benefits of contributing to the aftermath of this ill-planned and botched up war in Iraq. Regretfully, quite a few senior members of the Cabinet as well members of the strategic community became vocal supporters of sending troops to Iraq. Thankfully, the then PM remained sceptical and took the advice of the then Army Chief and turned down this request. One shudders to think of the consequences had India agreed to this suggestion. This is not to say that India is not concerned with Iraq. It has always had good relations with Iraq and, as a matter of fact, trained their armed forces in the 1980s. India also has stakes in insuring stability in Iraq as well as the whole of Middle-East and the Gulf Region. India imports 80 percent of its energy requirements from the region and a huge number of Indian expatriates work there, whose security is matter of great concern to India. Realistically, however, India's capacity to contribute towards it is very minimal. However, India can at least join in the international initiative for rebuilding the destroyed infrastructure, in humanitarian projects, and providing scholarships for higher studies including in specialist fields.

Outlook for the Future

The short history of the Iraq war is that Sunnis in Iraq, and the nearby Arab states, refused to accept the concept of one-man, one-vote, because it meant bringing the Shiite majority to power in Iraq for the first time. The Sunni mainstream believes that Shiites are lesser Muslims and must never be allowed to rule Sunnis. For two years the Shiite centre in Iraq put up with Sunni violence that the US could not stop because it did not have enough troops. But eventually the Shiites snapped, formed their own death squads and turned to Iran for military aid. They focused more on communal survival than on making Iraq's democracy work.

Today, we have Shiite and Sunni parties in the Iraqi cabinet, with their own private militias—exactly like in Lebanon during its civil war. In the meanwhile, the US military leadership in Iraq is talking about Iraqi forces taking on responsibility for national security with 'very little coalition support' within a year to 18 months. They have not talked about parallel withdrawals of US troops. Instead, the American-led coalition troops would pull back into large bases and provide support before leaving. The US military leadership appears to be rather optimistic. Earlier predictions that US military presence would be reduced from about 1, 30,000 to 1, 00,000 by the end of last year, proved to be wrong. Strategic analysts, on the other hand, believe that there is little prospect of Iraqis taking over in the near future. 2, 60,000 Iraqi troops can at best expand their role. They, however, have a weak structure and without air power or heavy weapons, do not have the capacity or capability of dealing with the prevailing insurgency as well as the real risk of civil war. The Americans, before they throw up their hands, can make one more effort to produce a more stable accord amongst Shiites, Sunnis and Kurds over power-sharing and oil revenues as well as demobilize their respective militias. Whether they can achieve this aim, only time will tell.

BANGLADESH: DEMOCRACY UNDER THREAT

Dr. Sreeradha Datta

Research Fellow, Institute for Defence Studies and Analyses, New Delhi

Introduction

During the last sixteen years the model of democracy that Bangladesh has followed has been rather interesting. It sought to overcome the prevalent deep political mistrust and the problem of governmental interference in elections through the introduction of a neutral caretaker government. This unique constitutional provision of 1996 was to ensure conduct of free and fair *Jatiya Sangsad* (parliament) elections and hand over power to an elected government within ninety days of its tenure. The most recently retired chief justice of the Supreme Court is mandated to head it as its Chief Advisor and is to be assisted by a nominated team of ten advisors. However, ever since the Bangladeshi Nationalist Party (BNP) coalition government completed its term in October 2006, rather than a smooth transition to a caretaker government, Bangladesh has been embroiled in ongoing political crises. Beginning with the political stalemate over the post of the Chief Advisor of the caretaker government, a number of unprecedented events occurred. Presently, the second consecutive caretaker government led by Chief Advisor Fakhrudin Ahmed has promised to hold the postponed 9th *Jatiya Sangsad* elections by 2008. The last fourteen months of political uncertainty and almost a year of the interim government has laid bare the fragility of Bangladesh's democratic structures.

The introduction of this second caretaker government averted the near civil war situation that had arisen out of the heightened political tension between the two opposing alliances one led by the Awami League (AL) and other by the BNP. Near breakdown of governmental control made the imposition of another unelected administration inevitable, which with large measure of support from the army, soon stabilized a very violent nation. The caretaker government having taken complete control of a rather difficult situation outlined its reform programme of restoring stability by end of 2008.

After its secession from Pakistan in 1971, Bangladesh has witnessed various forms of government. After the short-lived socialist experiment of its founding father, Sheikh Mujibur Rahman, it endured fifteen years of military rule, which was successfully overthrown in 1990. The parliamentary democracy that has existed since 1991 was disrupted with the introduction of an interim government, since January 2007. These events have led many analysts, within Bangladesh and outside, to question not only the nature of the unelected government led by a technocrat, but also what these developments portend for the future of democracy in Bangladesh.

This paper will briefly outline the nature of the present caretaker government in Bangladesh; the thrust of the reforms that have been undertaken by the interim government, the possibility of Bangladesh returning to electoral democracy, and its implications for India.

The Pre-2007 Phase

A brief preview of Bangladesh before October 2006 portrays a nation that had made a successful transition from successive authoritarian regimes to a functioning democracy. An electoral democratic system had been in place since 1991 and the last two elected governments had successfully completed their full term. Bangladesh enjoys a multi-party system that has been dominated by two major political parties, AL and BNP, with smaller parties like *Jaitya Party* as well as religious parties like *Jama'at-i-Islami* and *Islami Oikya Jote* playing a pivotal role.

Elections have been held on schedule, with a considerable strength of voters, and have largely been contested freely and fairly in the presence of international monitors. Over the last few years the economy has improved significantly, recording a near 6 per cent growth rate annually, in the process attracting some foreign direct investment as well. More significantly, the armed forces after a long stint in power went back to the barracks. During the last decade and a half, despite being called on few occasions to support the elected government the army had not shown any overt political ambitions. The presence of a strong vibrant civil society and an independent and non-partisan media had lent Bangladesh a distinct character that had set it apart from other developing Islamic nations in the region.

Notwithstanding its considerable achievements, Bangladesh has not been able to reinforce the democracy that was ushered in 1991, after overthrowing its military president Ershad. The elected governments did not encourage democratic traditions and institution to be strengthened leading to non-democratic tendencies, not only within the political parties but also in the *Jaitya Sangsad*. Bangladeshi political leaders have failed to strengthen democratic governance with major political parties been run like serfdoms. The state has, over the years, retreated from virtually every sector of governance, education, health and social welfare, infrastructure development as well as law and order. Arguably the lack of a long-term vision of its leaders has allowed violence to grip the state. The limited evolution of institutions, during the last decade and a half, did not allow democracy to take roots leading to the present crises. Having once triumphed over its military leaders, Bangladesh is once again poised at a critical juncture.

The Political Crises

The crisis was imminent from the time the BNP-led government was preparing to demit power. Besides other election engineering machinations one of the most blatant moves involved increasing the retirement age of the judges of the Supreme Court from 65 to 67 years. This effectively meant that Justice K M Hasan, the last retired Chief Justice of the Bangladeshi Supreme Court, would head the Caretaker Government and not Justice Syed J R Mudassir Hussain who would continue to be the Chief Justice of the Supreme Court. The opposition's main objection to Justice Hasan's candidature was that not only was he a party functionary of the BNP but had also headed the foreign affairs cell of the party. Given his past association with the BNP, Justice Hassan could not be considered as impartial, a pre-requisite for the post of Chief Adviser. The 14-party opposition alliance led by the AL was able to garner enough support from the people to compel Justice Hasan to decline the post, hours before he was scheduled to do so. This sudden turnaround led to President Iajuddin Ahmed assuming the office of the chief advisor. Although not strictly a legal transgression President Ahmed resorted to this without exhausting other constitutional alternatives provided for in the event of such an eventuality.

While the 14-party opposition alliance, led by the AL, accepted this Presidential move, it continued to voice its grievances against the chief election commissioner MA Aziz. Aziz had not only published (in defiance of High Court orders) an inaccurate voters list with over 12 million fake names but had also declared an election date by early November despite inadequate progress in dialogues taking place between the government and the opposition parties on electoral reforms. This further deepened the political tension that was brewing for long between the two opposing political groups. In view of the increasing show of street protests and mass violence by the opposition alliances, the President-cum-Chief Advisor decided to send Aziz on long leave and appointed Mahfuzur Rahman as acting Chief Election Commissioner (CEC). This belated conciliatory move in November was not sufficient to placate the oppositions as it was increasingly becoming obvious that Iajuddin led caretaker government under the influence of the BNP was unlikely to accede to any of the opposition demands. It was increasingly become clear that under the prevailing circumstances there was no scope for any level playing field for all contesting candidates.

The deep schism between the AL-led Grand alliance and BNP-led coalition, deepened in the months prior to the elections, especially over the issue of electoral reforms. The confrontation between the two main opposition groups led to daily street violence, *hartals*, and mass strikes. As the election date of 22 January 2007 approached, the standoff between the two main camps acquired menacing overtones. The AL's threat to lay siege to the President's house was the last straw. In the wake of withdrawal of the United Nations (UN) election observers, the civil society with considerable pressure from the international community was galvanised into action. It led to the dissolution of the Iaujuddin-led caretaker government, proclamation of emergency and installation of the caretaker government headed by a neutral candidate, economist Fakhruddin Ahmed.

The Interim Administration

The prolonged innings of the caretaker government in Bangladesh is a unique development. Soon after taking over office, Fakhruddin Ahmed undertook sweeping reforms and a widespread crackdown on corruption. By all accounts this interim eleven-member government of technocrats was initially well received and people were looking forward to the army-backed civilian administration to bring in some fundamental reforms and place the nation on a firm democratic footing. In his first nationwide telecast on 22 January, the Chief Advisor outlined a comprehensive seven-point 'reform' programme which aimed at meeting 'people's demand' of uprooting corruption, introduction of ID cards and use of transparent ballot boxes to ensure 'an election participated by and acceptable to all.'[1] The road map outlined by the caretaker government has promised all necessary support to the Election Commission for holding parliamentary elections by October 2008.[2]

Paradoxically, an emergency called in by a civilian government for the first time in the history of Bangladesh was welcomed by most. Despite the suspension of civil liberties, people were relieved to be able to walk the streets freely after months of continued unrest and violence. Within hours of the declaration of emergency, as part of the anti corruption drive initiated by the government, the security forces carried out simultaneous midnight raids and arrested many political leaders especially those belonging to the BNP and AL. It also levelled corruption charges against several high profile bureaucrats and businessmen. Much of what the caretaker government has been able to accomplish in demolishing unauthorised structures, unearthing stolen relief supplies, and retrieving illegal vehicles, was largely due to the support provided by the armed forces.

The active role of the army in the caretaker government gave rise to speculation about its role in the polity. The Chief of Army Staff, Lt Gen Moeen U Ahmed's political articulation on the failure of the nation to 'recognise' the 'father of the nation' and forwarding his idea of indigenous 'democracy' evoked strong fears of a more active role, if not a coup, by the military.[3] Susceptible to either the visible factions within the armed forces, or sensitivity towards disapproving public reaction or the strong disapproval of the western community, Moeen had to reassure them by admitting that 'the army is not the proper institution for governing the country.'[4]

Indeed, many politicians tired of their authoritarian leaders welcomed the internal reforms initiated within the political parties. Besides financial transparency, registration of the elected party leaders is now a prerequisite to ensure their participation in the *Jatiya Sangsad* election. Attempts to bring the political parties within the purview of public scrutiny and initiation of internal reforms within political parties have been widely lauded. The political parties are now required to complete elections to their central and grassroots committees in accordance with their constitutions before applying for registration of their elected leaders with the Election Commission.

[1] *CA vows to transfer power through polls at earliest, Daily Star, (Dhaka) January 22, 2007*

[2] *Shakhawat Liton, 'Voter list by Oct '08, poll by Dec,' Daily Star, (Dhaka) July 16, 2007*

[3] *Moeen U Ahmed, 'The challenging interface of democracy and security,' Daily Star, (Dhaka) April 4 2007*

[4] *No chance for military involvement in politics, Daily Star, (Dhaka) May 24, 2007*

The caretaker government apart from its reforms measures has also endeared itself to the masses with few populist measures:

- It executed six leaders of the extremist group Jama'atu Mujahideen Bangladesh on 29 March 2007 before the scheduled date given by the High Court.
- The Chief Advisor paid homage at the grave of Bangabandhu Sheikh Mujibur Rahman on his birth anniversary, and at the grave of Shaheed President Ziaur Rahman on his death anniversary.
- Former army officer Mohiuddin Ahmed, a condemned killer of *Bangabandhu* Sheikh Mujibur Rahman, was deported by the US Homeland Security to Bangladesh.
- The judiciary was separated from the executive to maintain its independence.
- The Election Commission was reconstituted and a proposal to grant it independence from the Executive was approved.
- The Anti-Corruption Commission was reconstituted with Hasan Mashhud Chowdhury, a retired lieutenant-general as its head.
- *Upazila* elections were announced.
- Numerous reforms were implemented in the garment and other local industries.
- The process for corporatisation of Nationalised Banks was initiated.
- The Chittagong Port was privatised.
- The interim government has also seriously considered activating the National Security Council, which includes the chiefs of the three armed forces, even though it is headed by a civilian. Although details are not yet known it is clearly a move which is likely to strengthen the control of the military over civilian governments.
- The interim government has also announced that it would ratify the United Nations Convention against Corruption (UNCAC) which would allow Bangladesh to benefit from a comprehensive international cooperation framework for mutual law enforcement assistance, especially in extradition and investigations. Various independent task forces with over arching powers are being constituted as a part of the anti corruption drive.

Many of these actions, and the promise to deliver electoral reforms including the preparation of flawless voters' list, introduction of voter ID cards, and use of transparent ballot boxes entrusted to the newly constituted Election Commission have received widespread support both at home and abroad. According to a Bangladeshi editor, this caretaker government found favour with Bangladesh as means to underpin democracy but its lack of accountability could very well change that opinion.[5]

The only reason that the caretaker government has survived in power, and the chief advisor acknowledges it every time an occasion arises, is because the general public think of it as an instrument to strengthen democracy. But now if this very instrument of 'strengthening democracy' becomes a symbol of mindless and arbitrary use of power, then how will the public distinguish it from such previous abusers of power and continue to lend it support?

Certainly people's support has accorded this government with legitimacy, and bestowed it with authority that it constitutionally lacks.

Extra-constitutional Acts

Notwithstanding its success in stabilising a deteriorating political situation, arguably the caretaker government has acquired a character completely disparate to its original nature envisaged in the constitution. Its charter according to the constitution is to provide "to the Election Commission all possible aid and assistance that may be required for holding general elections ....',[6] it has clearly gone far beyond its mandate and has taken upon itself a task that is usually discharged by a full-fledged functioning government, not one which is essentially temporary in nature. It led to the ushering in of the second caretaker government, continued prolongation of emergency and its consequent ban on political activities and deferring of parliamentary elections. Signing of various contracts, reconstitution of institutions, various foreign policy decisions have all been outside the purview of the caretaker government. The caretaker government has clearly acquired a character completely disparate to its original nature envisaged in the constitution.[7]

[5] *Mahfuz Anam, 'This is no way to strengthen democracy Just as "command economy" failed, so will "command politics,' Daily Star(Dhaka) July 17, 2007*

[6] *The Constitution of the People's Republic of Bangladesh Article 58D (2)*

[7] *For detail reading, Sreeradha Datta, ' Bangladesh : amidst constitutional crisis,' ed SD Muni, IDSA Asian Strategic Review 2007, Academic Foundation, New Delhi, 2007, pp105-116*

Contrary to the constitutional stipulation of the caretaker government handing over powers to an elected popular government within 90 days after the dissolution of the previous parliament, this interim government even after eleven months has continued with the imposition of emergency and ban on political activities. It has assumed powers of an elected government and gone to the extent of presenting a populist budget, and taking various foreign policy initiatives.

The caretaker government has been trying to strike a fine balance with a combination of popular reforms package and introducing legal orders tailored to meet its requirements. This includes the promulgation of the ordinance disallowing bail or any other legal remedy from any higher court until the corruption cases are resolved in a trial court. This denies the accused any legal reprieve. Interestingly this ordinance came into effect from 13 February, although it was issued on 22 March, which clearly brought accused Tarique Zia arrested on 6 March, as well as other high profile political as well non-political personalities under its purview.

In the initial days the government received not only large scale domestic support but also widespread international backing. The western powers dominated by USA, UK and the EU had been urging the caretaker government led by President Iajuddin to undertake significant electoral reforms to enable a level playing field for the elections. While they were earlier applauding the caretaker government on its achievements, they are presently critical of the human rights violations and unrestrained use of power by the security forces. Pressure to lift the ban on political activities is slowly building up within and outside Bangladesh. Apart from the Commonwealth Secretary-General, Don McKinnon, various western Ambassadors based in Dhaka have also urged the interim government to remove the state of emergency and ban on political activities. In their opinion, there can be no free and fair parliamentary elections without political parties becoming the dialogue partners of the Election Commission.

While internal reforms within the political parties were a positive measure, the caretaker government's attempts to weaken the two main political parties are being viewed with great suspicion. Its 'minus two' formula of forcing Khaleda Zia to go into exile and not allowing Sheikh Hasina to return to Bangladesh was strongly challenged.[8] Notably, in a clear defiance of the ban on political activity, people turned out in hundreds on the streets of Dhaka to welcome Hasina on her return from the USA in May. The subsequent arrests of Hasina and Khaleda on corruption charges have not been without ulterior motives. By especially targeting these two party leaders the government is attempting to split the political parties which together command bulk of the electoral support. The leadership vacuum, as well as the demands to undertake reforms, has deepened the schism within the political parties. Both the BNP and AL are under pressure both from inside and outside to restructure their organisation. In the absence of Khaleda Zia, the BNP is on the verge of disintegration and the AL is struggling to hold itself together after Hasina's arrest.

Surge of Islamic Militancy

One of the main concerns that continue to preoccupy Bangladesh ever since the caretaker government has taken over centres around the role of religious political parties and their various affiliates. It has been well established over the last five years of BNP coalition rule that the religious political parties especially the *Jamaat-i-Islami* has been patronising religious militant groups which led to an unchecked reign of terror in recent years. One of the earliest populist measures the caretaker government undertook was the execution of the Jamaat-ul-Mujahideen Bangladesh (JMB) militants on 29 March 2007 in its drive against terrorism. Despite some arrests of *Hizbut Tahrir* and *Jama'atul Mujahideen* militants, there has not been any breakthrough in unearthing the militants responsible for creating havoc in Dhaka during the last five years, except in the case of the attack on Humayun Azad and a blast at a cultural festival. On the contrary according to media reports the JMB cadres have regrouped with the militants of *Insaf* and *Allar Dal*. The two attacks on 11 April 2007 on the prosecutor of the case of executed terrorists, and three near-simultaneous explosions at railway stations in Dhaka, Chittagong and Sylhet on 1 May 2007, pose a grave challenge to the present interim government, particularly when the government machinery has a considerable support base in the Islamic groups.

Closely connected to the question of reining in of the Islamic militants is the role of the religious parties in the polity. The electoral strength of religious political

[8] *NM Harun, 'Minus-two' formula: a bitter concoction of an 'idea,' New Age, (Dhaka) July 22, 2007*

parties has been far outweighed by their overall importance as coalition partners and is a clear reflection of ground realities in Bangladesh. The fewer members of *Jamaat* or other religious groups coming under the caretaker government's scanner has been justified on the grounds that they are less corrupt, as compared to mainstream politicians. The caretaker government not only views them as less of a political threat but also is unwilling to confront them as they wield considerable influence.

One of the first dialogues the CEC initiated with the political parties led to the issue of the pro-liberation forces and anti-liberation forces. Three and a half decades after the Liberation War, this question is still hotly debated in Bangladesh. In recent times it has assumed significance in the face of fresh demands initiated by smaller parties like *Krishak Sramik Janata League* and Communist Party of Bangladesh before the CEC, to bring those opposed to the liberation war to task and disallow them from assuming political positions.[9]

The Road Ahead

With an aim of holding 'free fair and acceptable' elections by 2008, the caretaker government has initiated electoral dialogues with fifteen political parties from September 2007 onwards, whilst simultaneously lifting the ban on indoor politics in Dhaka. The three-month long dialogue process is to enable the finalisation the draft of the electoral reform proposals in preparation for the *Jatiya Sangsad* elections. It would also make public personal details like academic qualification, profession, source of income and criminal records of an aspirant seeking votes.

Bangladesh's return to parliamentary democracy through elections, at the earliest, is the best possible option. For many Bangladeshi the avoidance of one-sided farcical elections in January 2007 and the arrest of high profile corrupt people would not have been possible without the installation of the caretaker government and support of the army. But prolongation of emergency laws and non-transparency of the present administration have not added to their credibility. The caretaker government's initial popularity has seen a dip in recent months, especially over the treatment of leaders like Sheikh Hasina, Khaleda Zia and other political/religious leaders.

Given the growing impatience among the people, there is every likelihood of a multi-party election taking place in 2008. To avoid further delays in *Jatiya Sangsad* elections, parties will be forced to undertake reforms and in the absence of their leaders AL and BNP both would realise the need to maintain internal cohesion. Splinter groups have very little chance of any major electoral gains. Despite general disappointment with their leaders, developments over the last few months have significantly changed the public mood given the travails that the leaders have had to undergo. The caretaker government's harsh treatment of Sheikh Hasina and the positive High Court ruling in her favour would indeed buttress AL supporters.

The probability of the caretaker government continuing beyond 2008 is real. Notwithstanding it's idealistic pro-reform posturing, its obvious ambition for power and authority is not lost on any observer. It would not let go any opportunity to continue its smooth run at the helm of affairs. Arguably, many of present problems in Bangladesh have their origin in dynastic politics which has led to nepotism and entrenched corruption but the blatant targeting of the two families could be reflection of the government's long term political ambition. While the arrest of Tarique Rahman, son of the former prime minister was applauded, but the move to press extortion charges against Sheikh Rehana, a non-political person and one of the surviving members of *Bangabandhu's* family, seems rather out of proportion. Having gone through the façade of preparing for elections, it may not be completely unexpected if the caretaker government resorts to some guise to cancel elections citing inappropriate conditions to do so. The political parties sensing this possibility are likely to get their act together to ensure that the road map outlined by the Chief Advisor is not derailed.

The possibility of the Army taking over is often a point of speculation. Given the immediate tasks that the caretaker government had on hand, the army was needed to assist it to carry out extensive reforms and the anti-corruption drive. Unlike the past fifteen years, the army's involvement is pervasive in this administration. Within weeks of the caretaker government taking charge the army chief, Moeen U Ahmed, was openly charging political leaders of failing the nation and was seen stepping into sensitive areas like 'politicians divisive policies.' Though, sensing public disapproval, he was swift to reassure that the

[9] *Kader Siddiq, 'Wants Jamaat to make public apology before EC registration, New Age (Dhaka) September 17, 2007*

Army was not harbouring any political ambition. It has also been argued by many that the UN threat of removing Bangladesh peacekeeping troops from its blue helmet duties as well as the pressure of the western donor nations to get Bangladesh on a democratic track, have been the reasons behind the Army downplaying its real role. Given the military's past history the possibility of them usurping powers and assuming complete political control will always be speculated on.

Although the military has established itself as one of the most stable functioning organisations in Bangladesh, because of the civilian façade that the caretaker government has strongly maintained, the people have accepted its recent resurgence. Given Bangladesh's past experience of military rulers, unless there is a serious crises pointing towards a complete break down of governmental machinery, Bangladeshi will not allow the army to assume sole control of the government. The present situation in fact is one that imminently suits the military establishment. They are in a position to command and direct the government without assuming any public responsibility for their actions.

Implications for India

From Indian point of view the changed political condition in Bangladesh has far reaching implications. An overturn of democracy in the neighbourhood has an immediate repercussion on political and economic interactions and more importantly portends directly on security concerns.

Given the unexpected political developments in Dhaka, India saw an opportunity in strengthening its relations with an apolitical government and towards that end made positive overtures which were duly reciprocated by Bangladesh. The Indian position of treating the developments as 'an internal matter of Bangladesh' was well received in Dhaka. While India did suggest the need for early elections to the *Jatiya Sangsad*, it simultaneously expressed its appreciation of the Herculean task that was facing the interim government.

High profile Indo-Bangladesh political contacts had been limited in the last five years of the BNP coalition government. Beginning with the visit of India's Minister for External Affairs, Pranab Mukherjee to Dhaka, soon after Fakruddin Ahmed assumed office in February 2007, there has been rapid progress at normalising relations. The Indian move of offering trade sops impressed upon Bangladesh to commit to taking bilateral relations to an "irreversible higher trajectory." Apart from the Bangladesh Rifles Director General, Shakil Ahmed's, Indian visit in March 2007 the meeting of the Foreign Secretaries - Shivshankar Menon and his Bangladeshi counterpart Md. Touhid Hossain, which took place after a gap of two years, was seen as a very successful one. Various outstanding issues including security, trade imbalance, peaceful border management and cooperation in management of water resources were covered in these talks. The Indian decision to left a ban on rice exports and a proposal to pay for the rebuilding of ten villages affected by cyclone Sidr announced by Mr. Pranab Mukherjee on his visit to Dhaka on 1 December 2007 was very well received.

On the economic front, both Indian and Bangladeshi leaders initiated various measures that resulted in number of agreements taking place. They include:

- New Delhi agreed to purchase two million pieces of readymade garments every year without any duties;
- The pact on inland water transit was renewed and would now remain in force till March 2009;
- Bangladesh has offered to resume the Sealdah-Joydebpur passenger train service suspended since 1965. A trial run of *Moitree* took place on 9 July 2007. India has also offered US $ 150 million credit line to Bangladesh to upgrade railway tracks within its territory.
- India has agreed to allow duty-free access to more Bangladeshi products.
- Bangladesh would import 120,000 tones of diesel per annum from the Numaligarh Refinery in Assam;
- Bharat Heavy Electricals Limited has secured a Rs 55 crore contract for setting up a sub-station in Bangladesh. It would construct and commission a 230 KV substation at Baghabari and also expand the Ishurdi substation.[10]
- Both sides agreed to jointly combat terrorism;
- The Mittal Group has signed a memorandum of understanding on investments, which includes $300 million for mine development, $100 million for oil exploration and production, $500 million for power plants, $1.5 billion for petrochemicals and $500 million for liquefied natural gas (LNG) and related projects.[11]

---

[10] *Indian BHEL gets 240MW Siddhirganj power plant job, New Age, (Dhaka) February 1, 2007*

[11] *Mittal Group keen to invest in Bangladesh, New Age, (Dhaka) July 10, 2007*

Although many bilateral meetings have taken place, where some commitments have been made to address India's security concerns, most of the decisions taken in these meetings are yet to be implemented. As a result, core Indian security concerns vis-à-vis Bangladesh remain unaddressed. Recent assurances by Bangladesh about addressing Indian security concerns are yet to be followed up by any tangible actions. The issue of safe havens for North Eastern militants, and illegal migration, both of which are core concerns for India are not the issues that Bangladesh will address. Indeed it is reasonable to suggest that, given the limited leverage that Bangladesh has over India, the raison d'être behind its activities will always outweigh the incentives it would have to enter into a meaningful partnership with India.

As mentioned earlier, the former is the only source of advantage Bangladesh has over India and similarly India's limited leverage over Bangladesh will ensure that the continuation of this practise will never become too costly for Bangladesh. So far as the illegal migrants are concerned, Bangladesh even if they wanted to, which is not the case; they do not have any control over its mobility. With increasing water levels in the Sunderbans and growing paucity of land, Bangladesh is unable to offer any genuine persuasion that would hold back its impoverished population from crossing the border into India.

Despite the argument of elected leaders being required to toe the populist line, the return of democracy in Bangladesh will always find favour with India. Arguably, electoral compulsions often hinder effective resolutions of sensitive issues, Indian experience with the present unelected government has not been without its pitfalls either. Evidently, the present non-political government have also had to tread softly vis-à-vis India. Indeed, given the nature of Indo-Bangladesh bilateral ties, an elected government in Bangladesh will have greater leverage to strengthen bilateral ties in the long term.

Although India has refrained from propounding democratic values to its neighbours and maintains bilateral ties with unelected governments, return of democracy in Bangladesh is a prospect that India keenly awaits.

Conclusion

Irrespective of the nature of the government in Bangladesh, there is very little room for manoeuvre that India will have in the short term in Bangladesh. For long, their relations have been hostage to political suspicion and mistrust, which cannot be addressed in the short term. Notwithstanding the increased people to people contacts and increasing cultural and social and economic interactions, Bangladesh will continue to be a security threat to India. For India, the best option would be to engage Bangladesh at multilateral forums and keep its bilateral interactions limited and allow for Bangladesh to desire stronger bilateral ties with India. Apart from the bilateral meetings, multilateral forums can be exploited for developing various types of engagements.

Bangladesh's desire to have democracy is indisputable but its ability to develop democratic institutions and practices is questionable. Bangladesh is in need of a government that can promote independent institutions which can complement each other in its effort to strengthen a democratic and pluralistic polity. If the recent predicament can nudge the Bangladeshi leaders in truly reforming their autocratic tendencies and push them to work towards a system that genuinely has the benefit of the general population as a goal then Bangladesh would have once again triumphed over another crisis successfully.

RISING CHINA: WHAT IT MEANS FOR THE WORLD

Srikanth Kondapalli
Associate Professor in Chinese Studies, Centre for East Asian Studies, School of International Studies, Jawaharlal Nehru University, New Delhi

Introduction

One of the major features of 21st century is the rise of China, after it declined, like in the case of Mughal India, from Qing Dynasty onwards in 19th century. Starting from the late 1970s China's focus on economic and military modernisation programmes has elevated the country's profile among not only the Asian countries but also at the global level. While the concept of "peaceful rise", or in its latest variant "peace and development" gained currency among officials and scholars in China from about 2003, China's rise in several indicators can be seen from about the 1978 Four Modernisations programme and specifically to the late 1980s and 1990s. Not only did China consistently post near double-digit economic growth rates, specifically after Deng Xiaoping's famous southern China tour of 1992, but also has become a favourite destination for foreign direct investment from other countries. Trade increased by leaps and bounds and constitutes more than half of the gross domestic product (GDP). Joint venture companies and reform of the state industrial policies have contributed to the phenomenon of China as one of the largest manufacturing hubs of the world. The entry of China into World Trade Organisation in 2001 opened up new opportunities.

Economic & Military Rise

By 2007 China became the fourth largest economy and one of the largest traders of the world. In 2008, it is estimated to surpass the German GDP levels. Its trade volume crossed $ 1.4 trillion, while its GDP figures are rising to more than $ 2.4 trillion. China plans further economic progress as President Hu Jintao mentioned in his address to the Bo Ao Forum for Asia in April 2004, the Chinese government intends to "quadruple the 2000 GDP to 4 trillion US dollars with per capita GDP of 3,000 US dollars". Further at the 17th Party Congress in October 2007, Hu declared that China would make efforts to enhance the GDP figures. China's foreign exchange reserves have increased to nearly $1.2 trillion, making it the largest such reserves in the world. China has embarked on developing its infrastructure and started the East-West oil and gas pipeline from Shanghai to Urumqi (and extended to Kazakhstan), railway line from Golmud to Lhasa (and being extended to Xigaze), river diversion projects, etc. In addition, it has plans to connect the country with Russia and Central Asia with energy pipelines. The 2008 Olympics and 2010 Shanghai Expo are poised to further add to the lustre of a rising China.

Another important dimension of China's rise is its military modernisation programme, which was enhanced after the People's Liberation Army (PLA) suffered losses in the 1979 Vietnam War. The 1985 "structural reorganisation" plan has relatively succeeded in putting the rank and file of the PLA on the road to a "lean and mean" armed force. Hardware and software modernisation of the PLA and double-digit increases in the defence budget allocations, throughout the 1990s, and in the subsequent period, were to make it one of the forces to contend with in the region. It is generally recognised that by 1999, the PLA was making a turn around from a large infantry-based armed force to that of gradually acquiring the potential to project power abroad. This was part of the strategy to transit from mechanisation to information-based warfare. On 11 January 2007, China conducted an anti-satellite test with a ground-based missile destroying one of its retired Fengyun satellites located about 860 kilometres away, in orbit. In addition, in December 2006, the PLA has also indicated in its white paper that China would increasingly deter regional conflicts from breaking out and would manage conflict in the short to medium term.

Official Injunctions

These two major changes – in the economic and military fields- can be said to be the basis for the current rise of China, although there has also been considerable rise in the "soft power" of China in the last decade, as a nation of industrious peoples and a rational actor. These have considerably elevated the profile of China in not only Asia but also in the world.

Against this generalised introduction, the concept of "peaceful rise" was proposed by Zheng Bijian, vice president of the Chinese Communist Party (CCP) Central Party School at the Bo Ao Forum for Asia in 2003. However, a year before this speech, nearly twenty Chinese scholars, reportedly, worked out the major arguments of this thesis to systematically attempt to counter the security concerns expressed by China's neighbours and those in the West. Premier Wen Jiabao, in his address to Harvard University in late 2003, stated that China's rise is bound to be peaceful. However, Zheng Bijian in his speech at the Boao Forum of Asia on April 25, 2004 observed candidly that China's rise may usher competition in the Asia-Pacific region, but argued that such competition would take the path of "friendship, cooperation, mutual benefit and win-win, not competition of arms build-up, or competition for spheres of influence or hegemony". He also advocated establishing "communities of common interests" in East Asia and "sub-regional mechanisms with different functions and features, and conduct flexible cooperation to achieve marked results".

Subsequently, as the following section indicates, several officials and scholars in China have reflected on this phenomenon. However, to ward off any negative connotations that "rise" indicates in the discourse of late has been a tendency to rephrase the phenomenon as merely "peace and development". By December 2006, reinforced at the October 2007 17th Party Congress, this took the dimension of building a "harmonious society".

Overall, two broad schools of thought emerge on the China rise debate. One calls for restraint, focus on economic development, not contending for hegemony with either the US or other rising countries but enhancing the countries soft power. Another trend of thought is calling on the Chinese leadership to initiate pro-active foreign policies, enhance comprehensive national strength and focus on defence modernisation. It appears China is undergoing a transformation between these two trends with increasing focus on pro-active foreign policy strategies. Premier Wen Jiabao, for instance, reportedly issued an article on 26 February 2007 titled "A Few Issues About the Historical Tasks in the Initial Stage of Socialism and Our Country's Foreign Policy" in which he mentioned that China should follow Deng's injunctions on "economics at the centre", although it appeared that instead of "concealing one's capabilities", Wen mentioned the need for "initiative and aggressiveness in diplomatic work". China's active involvement in Sudan's Darfur crisis, the Iranian and North Korean nuclear issues, multilateral involvements in Central Asia and East/ Southeast Asia is a pointer in this direction. More could be expected in the near future.

Impact on Asia

The rise of China has impacted Asia and beyond in several ways. Essentially, China's rise has been a domestic feature as several Chinese scholars and officials have noted. However, it has resonations outside China as well. Following the overall guidelines of the CCP, China has made major efforts on how to seize the strategic initiative in not only economic aspects but also play a pro-active role in the regional and global contexts with the bottom line of not getting entangled in a war on issues other than those related to core Chinese sovereignty claims.

One major effect of the increase in China's trade is the increasing dependence of the Asian region on China. By 2007, Japan, South Korea, the ASEAN countries and others traded more with China than with the US or with the European Union. While China enjoys trade surpluses with the US (of about $300 billion), it has relative trade deficits with a number of Asian countries. In strategic terms, this relationship is poised to be more enmeshed than in a number of centuries before. At one level, China's trade has opened up several vistas to a number of Asian countries, at another level it has the potential to replace the US from the region and create a long-term structural dependence on China.

At a more positive level, China's rise is accompanied with increasing economic accommodation shown by China to its neighbours. In Asia, China supported an Asian Monetary Fund (although no investment funds have been allocated so far) and during the financial crisis of 1997 it came to the rescue of the affected countries. China has also been actively involved in multilateralism in a departure from its previous position of interacting only at the bilateral level. China has signed a treaty of amity and code of conduct with ASEAN countries (as was done by other countries), participated in regional security forums and proposed new security initiatives, even as the main problems on clashing sovereignty claims in Taiwan, South China Sea, Senkaku Islands, border dispute with India and Bhutan, etc. were relegated to the background.

In other parts of Asia also, China has expanded its multilateral efforts such as in the Shanghai Cooperation Organisation (SCO), become an observer at the 14th South Asian Association for Regional Cooperation summit meeting held at Delhi in 2007, argued for ASEAN+3 as the leading group in the two East Asian Summits held in December 2005 and January 2007 (though it finally acceded to the Japanese and Singapore pressure to accommodate India, Australia and New Zealand), and has worked out sub-regional cooperation arrangements such as in the Tumen River in East Asia, Mekong delta in Southeast Asia, Kunming Initiative, etc.

China's relations with the US would be crucial as several officials and scholars have mentioned. China is engaged in consultations with the US on non-proliferation, counter-terrorism campaign and bilateral military cooperation. Recently China has conducted a strategic dialogue with the US and a naval exercise in 2006, while joining the eight-nation multilateral exercise conducted by Pakistan in 2007 in the Arabian Sea. With other countries as well, China has become increasingly engaged in security dialogues and has been moving towards multilateralism in joint military cooperation, especially with Russia (with which it had signed a strategic partnership and cooperation agreement and has launched joint exercises in August 2005), the Central Asian Republics ("Friendship" and "Peace Missions"), France, the United Kingdom, Pakistan and India in the fields of maritime search and rescue and counter-terrorism campaigns.

The PLA has also stepped up its United Nations peacekeeping efforts across the globe and has increased military exchanges with and visits to other countries. These have contributed to relative transparency and exposure of Chinese military personnel to the outside world, although one of the reasons for such "military diplomacy" is also to scour through advanced weapon systems and technologies.

Obstacles

The rise of China is not expected to be a smooth transition. Indeed, several Chinese officials and scholars have pointed to the potential roadblocks to such rise, foremost among which are the US opposition, Taiwan, Japan, India and other countries. Of these, Taiwan and possible US military support to Taiwan was mentioned as crucial. It appeared in the last one decade and more, as Taiwanese businesses increasingly indicated preference to China trade (with more than $280 billion in investments, nearly 500,000 Taiwanese residing in Chinese cities and probable strengthening of "three links" after the "three mini links" were opened) and as important Taiwanese political leaders visited China in the last two years, the strategic scenario in the Taiwan Straits appears to be tilting towards China. Nevertheless, PLA military deployments in the region, including ballistic missiles (estimated at about 900 and increasing according to US Department of Defence estimates) are posing security and stability challenges in the region.

The responses of the PLA, as reflected in the six White Papers it issued from 1995-2006, indicate the extent of tension on this issue. The 2004 White paper considered the "vicious rise" of independence forces in Taiwan as posing a serious threat to China. The 1998 paper, coming as it were after the 1995-96 Taiwan Strait missile crises, has been the most extreme, of all the papers, in its position on Taiwan. It argued: "In deciding which way to deal with the issue of Taiwan, the Chinese government has no obligation to make a commitment to any country or any person attempting to split China." While China perceives Taiwan as its internal matter, in the globalization era in which China actively participates and is integrated, this position would be reckless with regard to international shipping, insurance rates, stock exchanges, environmental fallout and other factors. The 2000 paper refers to possible "drastic measures" by the Chinese government on Taiwan if the latter were to "refuse, sine die, the peaceful settlement of cross-Straits reunification through negotiations." This provision may have been incorporated at the behest of the then military commission chairman Jiang Zemin in whose regime it was believed that several intimidating military exercises and postures were made.

Another related issue on Taiwan is the Chinese refusal to continue participation in the UN Register of Conventional Arms after 1997 to protest against "a certain country ... [which] began to register its arms sales to Taiwan in the form of a footnote to its national report". To cap these, in 2005 China approved an anti-secession law which explored "non-peaceful means" to solve the Taiwan issue. This has irrevocably changed the Taiwan Straits scenario from one of peaceful resolution to forcible resolution. With Taiwan's ruling and opposition parties deciding to introduce referendum on whether Taiwan can join the UN, the situation in the Taiwan Straits could harden with possible Chinese military actions between 22 January and 22 March 2008.

Adjusting to Multiple Rises

Another major hurdle for China's rise is similar "multiple rises" of other countries. In such a case, China may be looking into how to convert this challenge into an opportunity. Some in the PLA noted that China may derive sustenance from other rising powers. One may surmise that China may get latest military technologies such as from Russia (which is rising under President Putin as the Goldman Sachs report on BRIC countries indicated), from the European Union countries (which plan to open the arms bazaar to China) or from Japan (which is experiencing a "hollowing out" effect to China), or even from India (in terms of IT software from Bangalore and predominantly raw materials imports, specifically iron ore). China has shown a voracious appetite to consume a variety of raw materials from across the world with Asia, Africa and South America topping the list. This is expected to continue with further Chinese forays into these regions.

A second major possible hurdle for China's rise is its dispute with Japan which has intensified in the last four years. Japan has already exhibited its economic and technological prowess for quite some time now, despite its economic slowdown in the 1990s. It has the second largest foreign exchange reserves and first rate science and technological capabilities with dual-use facilities. Mutual suspicions about military build up, political troubles about historical relationships and sovereignty disputes about the Senkaku Islands have contributed to a decline in bilateral relations, though Japan has invested heavily in China leading to "hollowing out" of its economic and technological aspects to China.

There has also been a feeling that Japan has lost out to China in Southeast Asia with the latter proposing a "new security concept" of enhancing mutual trust and mutual cooperation for mutual benefit of the concerned parties. Several recent incidents have also indicated to such loss for Japan. The first came with the 1997 financial crisis in which even as Japan doled out an estimated $45 billion, it was China which received much of the Southeast Asian political support. China has extended only about $ 500 million during this crisis. Another incident, involving the United States surveillance plane EP-3 incident in April 2001, indicated to the increasing chasm between the US and Southeast Asian countries, with the latter supporting the Chinese cause.

On the counter-terrorism issue as well, China has exhibited a nuanced position closer to the ASEAN (specifically Indonesia and Malaysia) positions. More importantly, given the strategic rise of China in the region with its free trade area proposals and the like, the region is poised to come more under Chinese influence to the detriment of Japan (and the US). This is one of the factors of Japanese suspicions on the proposed ASEAN+3 (Association of South East Asian countries, Japan, China and South Korea) or East Asian Community idea. These issues are compounded with increasing Chinese naval activities in the regions close to Japan, partly because of energy security issues and the Chinese urge to enter the Pacific Ocean.

Thirdly, while China has agreed to the Code of Conduct on South China Sea, since it is a non-binding declaration, the affected countries are wary about

China's stance on the dispute. The Philippines Navy and Vietnam have expressed concerns on the Chinese naval build-up and exercises as posing challenges to their security. Wary of the growing Chinese influence in the region, Singapore leaders have called for balancing China by inviting India into the region in economic and military aspects. With India's suggestions in 2006 (and repeated in 2007) to ameliorate the Malacca Straits security situation, several ASEAN countries have been exhibiting interest in India.

Fourthly, a rising India could turn out to be either of sustenance or competitor to China's rise in the future. While the two countries have initiated normalisation mechanisms and strategic dialogues (with the May-June 2006 defence ministers agreement on expanding military exchanges and annual dialogue yet to be implemented), the pace of normalisation of relations is slow and complicated, as it were also with Chinese nuanced position on the Indian bid for UN Security Council membership and the on-going Indo-US nuclear deal issue.

The points of contention between the two countries related to the unresolved border dispute (even after three rounds of talks in 1960, seven rounds in 1981-87 and 15 rounds of joint working group meetings in 1988-2005 and then 11 rounds between Special Representatives between 2003 and 2007), China-Pakistan continuing cooperation in strategic weapons, China's arms transfers and pro-active role in other Southern Asian countries (Nepal, Bangladesh, Myanmar and Sri Lanka) raise concerns in India. Besides, China's Western Development Campaign of improving infrastructure projects in Tibet and other western regions, especially the railway line, roads, airfields expansion and laying of fibre optic lines are viewed with concern by the Indian Defence Ministry which has also expressed that the Chinese missiles in Tibet are targeting several Indian cities. It appeared that raising 11 mountain divisions, the plan to operationalise and deploy enhanced Agni-III intermediate-range ballistic missiles, construction of 12 strategic roads in the border regions and the plan to deploy long-range fighter aircraft by India was a response to counter such challenges. The recent Chinese naval "string of pearls" concept has enhanced Chinese reach in the Indian Ocean region, especially up to Gwadar in Pakistan, Great Cocos, Hyangyyi, Mergui and other ports in Myanmar.

Assessment

China's rise has been a major event of the 21st century. It has impacted on Asia and beyond in economic, strategic and military terms. As the hard and soft power components of China expanded in the last few years, the country's stock has increased enormously. It appears China is in the midst of transitions between a "soft rise" to that of possibly a "hard rise" in future. China is currently able to reshape the regional order in Asia to an extent through economic and military nudges.

Through multilateral arrangements and active participation, China has been able to expand its influence in all the five major parts of Asia. In East Asia, it has the most dynamic economy and military modernisation and proposes economic integration; in Southeast Asia it has become the dominant power; in South Asia, through proxies like Pakistan and Bangladesh, it has acquired major stakes; in Central Asia, it is leading the SCO (although Russian President's visit to the Caspian Sea for energy deals in 2007 may change equations here) and in West Asia, it is becoming a major power through close links with Iran and free trade area proposals with the Gulf Coordination Council countries. An interesting situation is that, coinciding with the US soft power decline after the 9/11 events, that of China increased in the recent period. If the recent Chinese desire is to "squeeze" the US out of Asia, it has relatively succeeded if we go by the some of recent ASEAN, SCO responses. Some argue that as the US was busy with its campaigns in Afghanistan and Iraq after 9/11, China found nearly six years to consolidate its position in the region.

However, at a different plane, there has also been a lot of hype, and some reality, in the increase in Chinese influence or its effective impact on the international power structure. China's (inadequate) role was tested in the tsunami case in Asia, as with the 1997 financial crisis, counter-terrorism, Iraq war parleys at the UN, dependence on Malacca Straits and West Asian oil without a military ability to ensure supplies, etc. Although some argue that China, given its burgeoning economy and global reach, should shoulder "responsible stakeholder" status, no major explicit Chinese posture is forthcoming in this regard. This needs to be seen as the international strategic situation changes.

China has argued that it is opposed to hegemonism and power politics and also the threat or use of force in international relations and advocates the settlement of international disputes through peaceful means. Laudatory as these statements are and, if implemented sincerely by China or other countries most of the conflicts that afflict the world could be resolved. Nevertheless, the track record of China in this regard is inconsistent and contradictory, if not suspect. Several examples may be cited regarding the threat or use of force by China to solve disputes.

While China argues that resolving the Taiwan issue is its internal matter, in the age of globalization, it is difficult to conceive of a subject as purely internal, especially as armed preparations are being made to resolve issues. The 1995-96 events are a pointer that many countries of the region may be affected in terms of trade, shipping, insurance, stock exchange and environmental security. It is likely that China may use force between 22 January and 22 March 2008, as noted by Taiwanese experts, on the issue of referendum in Taiwan.

China's stance on the South China Sea dispute, likewise, is contradictory and intrusive. While China has stated that it is ready to postpone the settlement of the sovereignty dispute, this, nevertheless, did not prevent it from employing its naval forces in interfering constantly in the region as the Philippines Navy has pointed out. Vietnam is wary of Chinese intentions and capabilities as well in the Paracels, though it has signed an agreement on the Gulf of Tonking issue and is willing to work with China. China has also concluded a trilateral agreement with the Philippines and Vietnam to share maritime resources in the region.

China's threat of use of force during the Indo-Pakistan conflicts of 1965, 1971, 1999 is well recorded. China's arms sales to several countries in South Asia, Southeast Asia and the Middle East, though on a smaller scale as compared to other countries, are detrimental to regional stability. Fresh sales of F-22P frigates and licence manufacturing of JF-17 fighters (with Russian made RD-33 turbofan engines) to Pakistan, MiG-23 fighter sales to Bangladesh and Myanmar, etc pose "security concerns" for neighbours like India. Continuing transfers of weapons of mass destruction or technologies from China to Pakistan or other countries, despite signing and agreeing to abide by international arms control and disarmament treaties, has not only exposed Chinese claims to be a "responsible" stakeholder and rising power but has also raised concerns among neighbouring countries.

The 11 January 2007 anti-satellite test of China also destabilises outer space in terms of space debris damaging civilian satellites and potentially threatening other countries space-based assets. China's arms sales to both the warring states of Iran and Iraq at the same time during the 1970s are inexplicable and opportunistic. This has been the context for the growing suspicions of its neighbouring countries about the nature and dynamics of the Chinese defence sector and also the launch of the "good neighbour" policy, the sincere implementation of which will be watched closely by all concerned neighbours.

SRI LANKA: THE WAY FORWARD

Dr. K Sarveswaran
University of Colombo, Sri Lanka

Introduction

The decade's long ethnic conflict in Sri Lanka has reached to a new height, both in terms of destructive power of the conflicting parties, and in terms of active involvement of the international community. The major impact of the involvement of the international community is that it brought about the Cease Fire Agreement (CFA) signed between the Liberation Tigers of Tamil Eelam (LTTE) and the Sri Lankan Government (SLG) in 2002. It was facilitated by Norway, backed by the international community particularly the co-chair and India.

However, considering the Sri Lankan Government's (SLG's) declared "war against terrorism" and the subsequent acceleration of offensive in the Northeast province against the sprit of CFA on the one hand, and the LTTE's deployment of air power[1] and commando operations such as Anurathapura air base attack in response to the SLG's drive for a military option on the other, shows that the undeclared Eelam war IV began.[2] It began without withdrawal from the CFA by the parties, which is still holding its validity. In addition, the international monitoring mission [Sri Lanka Monitoring Mission (SLMM)] mandated to monitor the CFA is still functioning. While the SLG and the LTTE do not want to adhere to the CFA they also do not want to undermine the international community for opposing reasons.

The inability of the international community in enforcing the CFA, in its words and spirit, shows their limitations in dealing with the conflict. In a real sense the international community is in a quandary between the much hyped stance of 'drive against terrorism'[3] and the unprecedented humanitarian and human rights violations of the Sri Lankan state under the pretext of

[1] *LTTE's light aircrafts converted as bombers had successfully bombed twice in Colombo, once in Palaly air base and once on Anuradapura air base in support of commando attack*

[2] *See for details Sunday Times Colombo, 28 October 2007. Many Colombo-based news papers between 23 and 27 October 2007 confirmed that 18 aircrafts were fully destroyed. According to the defence columnist of Sunday Times 'Iqbal Athas' a total of twenty-four aircrafts were damaged. Former minister Sripathy Sooriyarachi said only one out of 27 aircrafts could be used. The other 26 aircrafts are fully or partly damaged and cannot be used. The monetary loss is estimated at US $ 226 million*

[3] *Subsequent to the 9/11 attack on the Twin Towers by Al Qaeda, the US declared its policy to drive out terrorism in the globe*

'war against terrorism.'[4] Since major countries such as UK, USA and India have branded the LTTE as a terrorist organisation and are committed to fight against terrorism, these countries obliged to help the Sri Lanka state to defeat the LTTE. They can not neglect or reject the just cause of the Tamil's struggle for sixty years or be blinded to the anti-Tamil laws and practices[5] merely for the reason that the LTTE is leading the struggle. The cause and the demand is well within the internationally accepted norms and theories but the international community can not justify or at least openly support a military solution of the problem. Exploiting the policy dilemma of these countries, the SLG and the LTTE wanted to meet their respective ends.

The SLG wants to reap maximum benefit from the campaign for an anti-terrorist drive by the international community. It has adopted a strategy to masquerade the ethnic conflict as a terrorist problem in its campaign in and out of the country. On this premise it is justifying unprecedented violations against human rights and humanitarian laws and pursuing the international community to furnish support to win its goal (terrorism). Parallel to the military option, the SLG has shattered the foundations laid by the peace process of the past by bifurcated the Northeast province that was established by the India-Sri Lanka agreement. Highlighting the violations, and other anti-Tamil laws and practices against internationally accepted norms, the LTTE has adopted a strategy of unmasking the SLG and the Sinhalese polity at large to the international community, and is pursuing them to support a solution based on recognition of sovereignty of the Tamil's (as a nation).

The LTTE firmly believes that an assured solution to the Tamil problem is a divided Sri Lanka. For the Sinhalese polity in general and the SLG in particular, the solution should be within the frame work of a unitary Sri Lanka to ensure the supremacy of Sinhalese. The dominant section of the international community believes that a federal Sri Lanka would end the conflict and suggests that the SLG find a solution based on 'power sharing' that could 'satisfy all the segments of the people' of the island. Each one's proposal for a solution seems unacceptable to the rest.

This scenario virtually raises the following questions:

1) Why is the Sinhalese polity/SLG adamantly opposing a federal system for six decades?
2) How far can a power sharing/federal solution be sustainable and realistic to end the conflict for ever?
3) What may be the realistic approach that could deliver sustainable peace?

This article intends to explore the core issues for the conflict on the part of the Tamils and to explore the real causes that prevent the Sinhalese polity from devolution of power. Understanding and assessment, based on internationally accepted theories and norms are necessary to suggest any long lasting resolution. The author also intends to evaluate the suggestions of the international community, based on the understanding derived from the above mentioned studies.

Understanding Sinhala Nationalism and the Conflict

The conflict is fundamentally a clash between historically evolved Tamil and Sinhala nations. Different scholars identify different dates to mark the beginning of the conflict (political division along ethnic lines). However, the author finds the date of competing and contradictory demands of territorial representation[6] vs. communal representation[7] between the Tamils and Sinhalese at the turn of the 2nd decade of the 20th century. The ongoing conflict originated in the 1910s and has grown for nearly a century. In other words the conflict is passing through the 4th generation of Sinhalese and Tamils. Except few aberrations, nearly ninety years of ethnic divide can be broadly classified in three stages; the first thirty years until 1947 marked by lobbying for communal/ equal representation based

[4] See the reports of Human Rights Watch, International Amnesty and the United Nations Human Rights Commission on Sri Lanka 2000-2007

[5] Almost all the western countries and India are experiencing the spillover effect of the anti-Tamil rule of the Sri Lanka state for nearly a quarter century

[6] Territorial representation means electing representatives through territorially demarcated electorates in which distribution of population would be almost equal. The British colonial government created a state council to govern the island from 1833. It used to appoint one Tamil and one Sinhalese member to the council to address domestic issues. This equal representation maintained a historic mindset of co-possessors of the island and equal authority over the affairs over the island. But when the Sinhalese found that they are majority in number and a head count is the major tool of democracy, they demanded territorial representation to get more representation than the other community

[7] Opposed to territorial representation Tamils demanded that the principle of equality be maintained to elect representatives based on ethnic identity and equality

on the principle of 'non-domination'.[8] The next thirty years until 1977 marked the Gandhian movement for a federal system.[9] The last thirty years until the present time (2007) marks the struggle for separate state.

Even after 60 years of ethnic strife within the unitary system, the belief of the Sinhala-Buddhist nation in the unitary system is crucial for their survival and has not changed. The Jathika Hela Urumaya (JHU)[10] in a statement signed by the party's General Secretary Ven. Omalpe Sobhitha Thera thanked the President for amending the ruling Sri Lanka Freedom Party's (SLFP) proposal mean to solve the conflict that upholds country's 'unitary status' and 'pride of place to Buddhism'. The UNP, the main opposition party, declared that they do not subscribe to a federal system as a solution. The Sinhala-Buddhist Marxist party, the JVP, propaganda secretary and parliamentarian Wimal Weeravansa requested the ruling regime to defeat terrorism and not to think of sharing power with the Tamils. JHU not only appreciated the SLFP for it's resolution to maintain the unitary system but went further and confessed it's stance, or rather reflected the dominant stance of the Sinhalese polity, by stating that this country belongs to the Sinhalese. Tamils and Muslims can live in this country but should not assert for rights. If the Tamils want a separate state they can do it in India. This implies that the Sinhalese are the sons of the soil and all others are migrants or aliens. This is not just the JHU's stance, but reflects the Mahavamsa mindset of the entire Sinhala polity.

Previous president Chandrika Bandaranaike Kumaratunge (SLFP), in the late 1990s, while visiting South Africa stated in a television interview that, *"your problem is different because this is your country* [South African aboriginals...sic] *but the Tamils are not like you"*. This implied that the Tamils are migrants and they do not have the legitimacy to fight for their rights or freedom. Her predecessor Wijetunga (UNP) like JHU openly said, *"Sinhalese are like trees and the Tamils are like parasites. They should live dependent on Sinhalese."* This implied that they should not claim rights or power. They could not be given nor are they not entitled to autonomy. His predecessor R. Premadasa (UNP) openly opposed the India-Sri Lanka agreement that presented a much weaker decentralization of power to the provinces, within the unitary system.

The first president J. R. Jayawardane (UNP) in 1985 said, *"I would not hesitate to have a relationship even with devil to wipe out terrorism* (Tamil struggle for separate state)". This too implies that in his thought Tamils are secondary citizens, not equal to the Sinhalese and subject to the rule of the Sinhalese hence, he did not want to recognize the grievances of the Tamils. The list would extend down to the mindset of the first prime minister of the country, Dudley Senanayake, who promised to maintain the status-quo of the minorities just before the end of colonial rule. Disowning his words after the departure of the colonial rulers, he made more than one million Tamils stateless by one act. His aim was to reduce the representation of the Tamils and mute their voice as much as possible. By keeping them almost as slaves, the government wanted to weaken any potential political and economic challenges from the Tamils and to ensure that their own are not affected.

The entire Sinhalese leadership of independent Sri Lanka cut across all the Sinhalese parties in the mindset that the Sinhala-Buddhists are the 'sons of the soil' and have the sole authority over the land, wealth and power of the island. The concept of 'sons of the soil' is one of the fundamental and potential elements of the construction of Sinhala identity and nationalism. Other aspects of nationalism were built up over this foundation. Sinhala-Buddhist nationalism, propounded by the revivalist Anagarika Dharmapala, emphasizes blend of pre-eminence of Sinhalese in the entire helm of affairs of the island and considered the Tamils and Muslims as aliens.

The Sinhala-Buddhist revivalist leader Anagarika Dharmapala gave impetus to this notion of Sinhala nationalism by constructing the ingredients for Sinhala nationalism. He gave new interpretations to Mahavamsa, a Buddhist chronicle. The Saiva-Tamil revivalist movement led the campaign against the conversion to Christianity and tried to protect and promote Tamils against increasing domination of

---

[8] Non-domination was the principle based on which the Tamils demanded communal representation to the State Council in 1910s. It further developed as 50:50 on the same principle. (50% representation for the Sinhalese and 50% for all other minorities)

[9] Failure of the 50:50 representations led the Tamils to demand for a federal system to protect their social, economic and political life. This struggle continued until the 1976 Vaddukoddai resolution of the TULF for separate state

[10] JHU is a political party formed mainly by Buddhist monks and Buddhist fundamentalist with the aim of purifying politics from corruption and nepotism. But in practice they are almost fully engaged in opposing any power sharing exercise and encouraging the war to defeat the LTTE

English. This movement never indulged in any hate campaign against pre-colonial religions or people. Contrarily, the approach of the Sinhala-Buddhist revivalist movement led by Anagarika Dharmapala spread venom against all non-Sinhala, non-Buddhist people especially, the Tamils. He led the movement between 1903–05 and 1911–14. He dubbed Ceylon Tamils and Muslims equally with Europeans as aliens and exploiters. Jayewardene was quoted as saying: 'Look at the administration report of the General Manager of Railways...Tamils, Cochins and Hambankarayas are employed in large numbers *to the prejudice of the people of the Island*—sons of the soil, who contribute the largest share.'

In Anagarika Dharmapala's thinking, 'people of the Island' and 'sons of the soil' meant exclusively Sinhalese-Buddhist.[11] Anagarika's racial and religious chauvinism was much stronger than his anti-imperialism. It brought the Sinhalese more into conflict with Tamil and Muslim traders.[12] Despite the fact that the Sinhalese are a highly mixed community, he launched a strong campaign to stimulate anti-south Indian and anti-Tamil feelings that Sinhalese are Aryans and Tamils are Dravidians.[13] He wanted a 'Buddhist State and the Governor, the Colonial Secretary, and all other high officials should be Buddhist'.[14] When the Sinhala politicians today resuscitate the image of Anagarika Dharmapala and echo his slogan *Sinhalayanee nagtiv* (Sinhalese arise!), they are recognising in him their true ancestor.[15] No doubt, the racial discourse of Anagarika and the movement laid strong imprints in the minds of a cross-section of the Sinhala people and leaders. 'Majoritarianism' and 'exclusionism' that began to rule the Island since the turn of 1900s is the core of the legacy of Anagarika Dharmapala and the core cause of the present conflict.

Mahavamsa, the Buddhist chronicle written by a Buddhist monk, is the main source for Sinhala-Buddhist revivalism. It is like the Hindu epic Ramayana, a blend of elements of fact with mythical and imaginative stories aimed at glorifying and propagating the Buddhist past in the island. The origin of the Sinhalese race itself mythical. According to the chronicle the race was born from a 'lion and a princess' in the present Orissa – West Bengal region. The campaign to construct a Sinhala identity and nationalism for more than a century, based on this chronicle, and to masquerade it as 'Sinhala-Buddhist history' has a strong anti-Tamil content.

From its origin, Sinhala nationalism defies the rights of non-Sinhala-Buddhists.[16] From this understanding it could be said that the Sinhala-Buddhist revivalism brought about Sinhala chauvinism in place of nationalism. It is this well entrenched chauvinistic mindset that naturally created a mental block to refuse to appreciate the diversity and accept the multi-ethnic and multi-cultural social reality. The psychological division was manifest in the process of transfer of power from the colonial rulers, isolated the Tamil leadership and undermined the interests of Tamils. This continued in the post independence era with increasing vigour as the Sinhalese gained absolute ruling power, which is now being challenged by the Tamil leadership.

Evolution of the Tamil and the Sinhala Nations in the Island: A Glance

Contrary to the basis of the Sinhalese's construction of their identity and nationalism, scholars trace Tamils as the earliest migrants from South India to the Island, or aborigines of the Island who had constant connections with South India. Also, they indicate historical causes and factors that determined the growth of Sinhalese population. The earliest inhabitants of Sri Lanka were a tribe called 'Nagas' who had the 'Saiva Tamil civilisation'. Later, some of them embraced Buddhism and contributed to the growth of both religions. Nagas, according to Mahavamsa, 'inhabited the northern and western parts of the Island in the 6th century B.C. (before Vijaya's entry to the Island), and continued to inhabit these areas until the 1st century A.D.'[17] Archaeological surveys reveal that Nagas were living as early as 500 B.C. in Jaffna.[18] Historian Paul Pieris observed: *Naga people, like the Tamil speaking Dravidians of South India, had continued to worship God Siva...they constructed a number of Siva*

[11] *Kumara Jayewardene, Seminar paper on "Nationalism, Revivalist Movements and Ethnic Consciousness in Sri Lanka" quoted in Reggie Sriwardena, Lanka Guardian, Vol. 3, No. 3, 15 August 1980, p. 14*

[12] *Ibid, p. 16*

[13] *Ibid, p. 14*

[14] *Ibid*

[15] *Gunadasa Amarasekara, "Anagarika Dharmapala Marxvadhee dha?" Pamphlet, in Sriwardena, No. 29, p. 14*

[16] *See for details Wickramasinghe Nira "Ethnic conflict in the colonial era" Konark, New Delhi, 1998?*

[17] *Chelvadurai Manogaran, The Untold Story of Ancient Sri Lanka (Chennai: Kumaran Publishers, 2000), p. 42*

[18] *Ibid, 42–44*

temples...most of these temples were built at coastal locations...long before Vijaya arrived on the Island.[19]

Even 'the *Mahavamsa*, like the *Ramayana*, mentions prosperous kingdoms, townships, and rural settlements in the Island when the Sinhalese [Vijaya] arrived'.[20] Citing various dimensions of historical studies, Manogaran concludes that the Island was called *Illam* (Eelam) during the *Sangam* Period, (3rd century B.C. to 1st century A.D.), and was originally settled by Dravidian-speaking people who had migrated from South India from pre-historic times.[21] The Sinhalese believed themselves to be the descendents of Vijaya, based on the Buddhist chronicle, *Mahavamsa*, according to which Vijaya came to Sri Lanka with seven hundred of his male friends and intermarried with the Tamils of the Pandyan kingdom of Madurai (present Tamil Nadu). Moreover, they brought thousands of families belonging to various guilds from the same place at their every visit and this practice was continued for centuries. War between Sinhalese kings led them to invite south Indian kings for their support and a section of the warriors stayed back and were given an area to settle down and have their own rule. This resulted in waves of migrations from South Indian's, largely from the Pandians state, in present Tamil Nadu.

Buddhism was introduced to Sri Lanka much later, from the Vijaya period. Buddhist clergy generated the concept of a Sinhalese kingdom, or society, only after the 4th century A.D.[22] Later, there were huge Buddhist migrations from present Tamil Nadu and other parts of South India due to the anti-Buddhist 'Bhakti movement'. They too were assimilated with the Sinhalese Buddhists. Enhancing these views, P.B.J. Hevawasam observes that Hindu worship and deity system prevailed until the introduction of Buddhism. Those who embraced Buddhism, incorporated many of their Hindu deities, traditions and practices which are still prevalent.[23]

The burden of history of pre-colonial Sri Lanka has contributed immensely in escalation of the present ethnic conflict. Scholarly studies suggest that the pre-Buddhism society shared common deities and language which was dominantly Saiva-Tamil until commencement of colonialism.[24] There is hardly any trace to prove that the war between the Sinhalese and Tamils was an ethnic war. Rather, they were aimed at expansion of territory and increasing their power.[25] Even after they evolved as two distinct communities with the introduction of Buddhism, Tamils and Sinhalese had a cordial relationship, even at times of rule of the one over the other.[26]

The Cause of Conflict: An Understanding of Tamil Mindset

Tamils played a leading and pioneering role in the affairs of the island all through history. Three kingdoms existed in Ceylon at the introduction of colonialism - Kotte, Kandy and Jaffna. Except Kotte, rest were ruled by Tamil kings. Jaffna was ruled by Sankili Kumaran and Sriwickrama Rajasinghan ruled Kandy.[27] The last five rulers of the Kandyan kingdom belonged to the Madurai Nayakkar dynasty until it fell to British colonialists. Bandara Vanniyan was the chieftain of Vanni who was defeated subsequent to the rise of the Kandyan kingdom. Rule of the Tamils in the island continued until 1815. In the early 1500s, when the Portuguese tried to capture the Kotte kingdom, Sankilikumaran, the Jaffna king in solidarity with the Kotte king brought reinforcements from South India and sent them to Kotte to fight the Portuguese. He also killed many Tamil fishermen of Mannar who bowed to the threats of the Portuguese and converted to Christianity.

Tamils are aborigines and immensely contributed to the protection and development of the island in all spheres of its life including development of the Sinhala-

---

[19] *Paul E. Pieris, "Nagadipa and Buddhist Remain in Jaffna", Journal of Royal Asiatic Society (Ceylon Branch), Vol. 28, n. 70, pp. 17–18, quoted in, Manogaran, n. 3, p. 46. These oldest temples are called as 'five Eeswarams' situated along coastal lines of the Island from South western coast of Chilow (silapam) to eastern coast of Batticaloa (Mattakizhappu)*

[20] *N D Vijesekara, The People of Ceylon (Colombo: M.D. Gunasena & Co. 1965) p. 60*

[21] *Manogaran, n. 3, p. 52*

[22] *Ibid, p. 53*

[23] *P.B.J. Hevawasam, "Images of Hindu Gods in Buddhist Temples in the Southern and Western Coasts of Ceylon", paper read at the Second International Conference Seminar on Asian Archaeology held in Colombo in 1969, Colombo, Tribune, 22 October, 1977, p. 12*

[24] *Ibid, and Selvadurai Manogaran, n. 3*

[25] *The famous battle between Duttagamini and Ellara was not a Sinhalese–Tamil ethnic fight in modern terms as there were Tamil soldiers in Duttagamini's army and Sinhalese soldiers in Ellara's army. Ibid, pp. 23–24*

[26] *Manogaran, n. 3, pp. 60–63*

[27] *There was an agreement signed between the Kandyan king and the British colonialist subsequent to the defeat of the Kandyan kingdom. Sriwickrama Rajasinghan signed the document in Tamil*

Buddhist civilisation. They prevented the colonialist from entering into the island and fought to protect their kingdoms from them. The Tamil nation, and the kings, treated the Sinhala-Buddhist as brothers and fellowmen of the island. They viewed the conquerors as a common enemy of the island. Their thoughts and deeds reflected a wider perspective that was in the interests of the entire island and not merely in terms of their own community. As rulers of the island, they never perceived themselves as a minority; instead they felt it their responsibility to protect the co-possessors of the island i.e. the Sinhalese. The solidarity shown to the Kotte king and their stiff resistance to the conquerors for more than 300 years is one of the striking manifestations of patriotism in its real sense, contrary to colonial and post-colonial masqueraded claims of Sinhala patriotism as Sri Lankan patriotism. In spite of the fact that Tamils are aware that they are the aborigines, their attitude and approach towards the other communities was inclusive and accommodative. They never had doubts or confusion about their identity and nationalism. In sum, the authoritative mindset of the Tamils over the island has emerged as a historical evolution and not constructed by myths and stories. It was this mindset that was manifested when dealing with the colonial rule.

The mindset of the Sinhalese, as noted by acclaimed political science scholar of Sri Lanka Uyangoda, "*Sinhalese have inferiority complex.*"[28] The reason for such complex as historian Nira Wickramasinghe observed was due to historic defeats and a dependency mentality in relation to Tamils.[29] It has led to inherent jealousy that used to look for an opportunity for vulnerability to establish control over the perceived superior and to enjoy or exercise superiority over them. The defeated mindset has an inherent revenge attitude in it. Sinhala-Buddhist revivalism propped up the concept of Sinhalese as 'sons of the soil' and the Tamils as migrants. Politicisation of this concept gave the Sinhalese a new dimension and reactivated their zeal to "re-conquer the Tamils".[30]

It was only Tamil leaders who agitated in the State Council for certain rights or grievances that were of the interest to the Sinhalese too.[31] They made the colonialists accept full-moon days as holy days.[32] Sir. Pon. Ramanathan's meeting with the Queen for release of the Sinhalese leaders arrested in the anti-Muslim riots of 1915 is also an example of this. The Sinhalese leaders gave a great reception on his arrival from London. They put him in a decorated cart and themselves pulled the cart through the streets of Colombo to respect his service. Tamil leaders pioneered and lead political activities as Ceylonese patriots. They initiated the formation of Ceylon National Congress (CNC) and the Jaffna Youth Congress, and successfully organized boycott of state council elections in protest against the Donughmore Constitution, as it failed to deliver full independence.

After the failure of the CNC, the core of the entire movement was led by the Jaffna Youth Congress to evolve a Ceylonese national movement and Ceylonese nationalism. But when the process for gradual transfer of power from the colonial rule began, Sinhalese leaders demanded territorial representation contrary to the existing practice of communal and equal representation to the Tamils and the Sinhalese. The issue of territorial representation continued to develop and gained increasing momentum for nearly three decades from 1910s to the Soulbury Commission of 1947. In this duration, the colonialists gradually increased the number of local representatives based on territorial elections.

The Present Conflict: Origin and Development

Since Sinhalese are the majority in number, the territorial representation system would present a majority of Sinhalese representatives to the State Council. Even at the beginning of constitutional reform movement, the Sinhalese elites demeaned, individually and collectively, to the colonial rulers for territorial representation. They represented exclusively the interest of the Sinhalese. The intention of the move was to "re-conquer the Tamils" for ever. They failed to demonstrate as leaders of all the communities. This approach pushed the other communities, especially the Tamils, to address their issues separately with the colonialists.

The attitude and demands of the Sinhalese was to reduce the Tamils to a minority in the State Council,

[28] *Uyangoda Jayadeva, 1999, Civil rights in Sri Lanka, International Centre for Ethnic Studies, Colombo*
[29] *Wickramasinghe Nira, 1998, Ethnic Conflict in the Colonial Era, Konark, New Delhi*
[30] *De Silva K.M., The History of Sri Lanka*
[31] *See for details K.M. De Silva*
[32] *All the full moon days are holy days for the Buddhist*

and thus put an end to the primacy of place they enjoyed in the affairs of the island's history. Tamil leadership realized the impending danger that this system would place them subject to the rule of the Sinhalese forever. Asserting for their due place in the governance of the country, the Tamils demanded communal representation based on the principle of "non-domination", to restore their independency and primacy in the affairs of the island. Based on such status, they were prepared to share rule with the Sinhalese. But the dominant Sinhalese polity was rigid in their aim and wanted to exploit the proposed Westminster system. Sinhalese leadership convinced the colonialists, through manipulation and manoeuvre, that power could be transferred to them. They also agreed to protect their interests in the island. Contrary to the prevailing status of a separate kingdom/ administrative unit, when they conquer the island, the British rulers transferred powers to the Sinhalese with a territorial representation system to the parliament. This transfer of power to the Sinhalese was perceived by the Tamils as illegal and arbitrary.[33] The sovereignty of the Tamil nation was snatched by the Sinhalese leadership through surreptitious means through the British rulers and is considered by the Tamils as sheer betrayal on part of the Sinhala leadership.

The transfer of power left the Tamils with a betrayed mindset. The mandate of Tamils in the entire post-independence parliamentary and other elections in the north and the eastern province proved beyond doubts that Tamils never delegated their sovereignty to the Sinhala dominant state[34] and confirmed that they would not compromise their historic authority over their traditional homeland. Tamil nationalism, while asserting its position vehemently, appreciates Sinhalese nationalism but not chauvinism. Until the 1970s they adopted the Gandhian way of asserting their rights. Contrarily, Sinhala Nationalism (in content and manifestation - chauvinism) out rightly defies Tamil nationalism. The Sinhala polity consistently adopted constitutional, legal and practical measures to ensure that the Tamils would not and should not be allowed any space to have even meagre power. The Sinhala revivalist movement strongly believes in establishment of the entire island as a pan-Sinhala-Buddhist state. Implementing this policy, the predominantly Sinhala state employs strategies of assimilation and annihilation.[35]

In response, the Tamil leadership propped up the Tamil's assertion for a federal system and then for a separate state. The Sinhala state used the Tamil struggle to accelerate their project. While the Tamil speaking community is 27% of the total population, more than 99% of the armed forces and police are Sinhalese. Except teachers, among administrative staffs nearly 95% are Sinhalese. The anti-Tamil war devastated the Tamil society immensely in all spheres. More than hundred thousand Tamils have been killed, more than a million Tamils driven out from the country, and more than six hundred thousand Tamils uprooted from their domicile, and made refugees within the country. It was this mindset that humiliated the Tamils and Tamil leadership repeatedly. Thus, the state compelled the Tamils to adopt an armed struggle since the 1980s, which produced the LTTE.

Approaches to Resolution: Dilemma of the International Community

It is in this light that peace makers, especially the International community, should see the attitude and the approach of the present government and the LTTE towards the ethnic conflict and conflict resolution. President Mahinda Rajapakse who is heading the SLG said in different jargons, *"we will continue to pursue the war until we completely wipeout the LTTE"*, *"we will wipe out the terrorism to its roots"* and *"we will liberate the northern Tamils from the clutches of LTTE terrorists like we have done in the eastern province"* expresses his pledge to go for an absolute military solution.[36] Even after the debacle of Anuradhapura air base, the President vowed that the attack would not deter the existing SLG moves to wipeout terrorism to its roots. As a parallel move in this direction he has bi-furcated the Northeast province. The merged Northeast province was the major achievement of the India-Sri Lanka agreement in 1987. (The Tamils have demanded, from 1950 onward, that the North and

---

33 While the colonialist capture the Island Tamils lived in their own kingdom, but while leaving they transferred the ruling power of the Tamils to the Sinhalese against the will of the Tamils

34 The first election of 1947 vast majority of Tamils voted against the Soulbury Constitution, subsequently up to 1970 they voted for federal system and then till today for separate state or alternate to separation. All these issues were addressed by Tamil parties

35 Sri Lankan state tried to cripple the Tamils voice by constitutional and legal means such as citizenship law, Official language act and 1972 Republican Constitution aimed at assimilate them into the majority Sinhalese community. When these all resisted by them aggressively government took rather annihilation approach to achieve the same

36 See for details text of the speech made by the President of Sri Lanka in the 62nd General Assembly meeting in United Nations and many of the Colombo based news papers for last six months including Veerakesari, Colombo, 26.10.2007

Eastern provinces be recognized as their 'traditional homeland').

The international community is repeatedly suggesting to the SLG to present a peace proposal that would satisfy all. It seems that the international community has failed to understand the core of the conflict adequately. Lack of an understanding of the anti-Tamil Sinhala 'nationalism' raises the question whether any compromising formula is realistic within the framework of a predominantly Sinhalese state, as suggested by the international community. Any solution must cater for the suppressed and not the suppressor. Nearly after a quarter century of their anti-Tamil drive, the SLG is not less than genocide.[37] Endorsing this attitude of the SLG, B. Raman observes: *"Make no mistake about it. President Mahinda Rajapakse and other Sinhalese leaders are no lovers of Tamils. They may smile and smile, but they would like nothing better than to crush LTTE even as a political organization so that the Tamils could be ultimately reduced to the status of the red Indians in the US."*[38]

Hence, psychologically, logically and practically the Sinhalese polity can not willingly present any devolution of power to the Tamils. The 1958 Bandaranaike-Chelvanayakam pact to the 2004 PTOMS signed between the SLG and the LTTE have been disowned by the various Sinhalese party leaders and not the Tamil leadership. It is an illusion to believe that there can be a solution acceptable to all. If the international community uses its influence to impose a federal solution it would add one more to the number of failed exercises. The treatment to the much weaker Provincial Council system by the SLG, the fanatic campaign of the JVP and JHU to wipe out Tamils under the guise of fighting terrorism and the UNP's declaration that they never advocated a federal system as a solution shows the unchangeable chauvinistic mindset of the Sinhalese. Any national community in the world would not be willing to compromise its nationalism. The Sinhalese are no exception. Considering the fact that they project and practice Sinhala chauvinism as nationalism, substantial power sharing would seriously undermine Sinhala 'nationalism'.

Conclusion

Considering the stark reality that the entire Sinhala and Tamil communities are polarized on ethnic lines in every aspects of their life, it is clear that there is no mechanism within the country capable of negotiating between the two parties. The international community, while dealing with the conflict resolution, seems to be a facing serious dilemma between their commitment to wipeout terrorism and the commitment to protect the contents of the United Nations Charter (Right to Self-Determination to the Nations), human rights and international humanitarian law.

The CFA was signed between the SLG and the LTTE 'terrorist'. The international community always suggests that the SLG negotiate with the LTTE. Therefore, the LTTE is recognized as the official representative for any negotiations. Contrarily, justifying fighting terrorism and the LTTE shows the serious and dangerous dilemma of the international community. The European Union (EU) exerted pressure on the LTTE by banning its functions in the EU countries. On the other hand, when the Sri Lankan state forces are uprooting nearly three hundred thousand Tamils from their homes; making them nomads by starving and shelling them, goes against the spirit of the CFA, human rights and humanitarian law. The international community has failed to take any effective measures to prevent the destruction and despair of these Tamil civilians. The international community is, therefore, facing a serious challenge on its stance regarding the LTTE.

Despite the limitations of the international community, they still hold leverage in influencing the warring factions. The depth of the conflict suggests for need of a paradigm shift in the approach to the resolution of the conflict. A new approach should restore the lost rights of the Tamils. Considering the innate inability of the Sri Lankan state to accommodate the Tamils, restoration of lost rights should be based on the recognition of the sovereignty of the Tamils.

[37] *See for definition of genocide, United Nations document on genocide*

[38] *B.Raman. Director Institute for Topical Studies, India, Morning Leader Colombo, 14.11.2007*

THE PROBLEM OF (IN) KASHMIR

Seema Mustafa
Resident Editor, Asian Age, New Delhi

Kashmir, it is said, is the unfinished legacy of partition, the issue that continues to divide India and Pakistan and makes peace an elusive goal. It is the emotional chord on which Pakistan based its independence, and India its secularism. War, terrorism, violence, unrest has not been able to resolve the issue with neither Islamabad nor New Delhi quite willing to give up their claim over this land that continues to agitate minds and inflame passions.

The Indian government, after 60 long years, has changed its policy to admit that the problem is of Kashmir, and not just within Kashmir. This concession has allowed the peace process with Pakistan to be institutionalised, in that both countries have been going through tedious rounds of the composite dialogue in which Kashmir is now firmly on the table. Not much headway has been made on any one issue, but at least the talks have allowed a certain rapport with New Delhi and Islamabad using the channels of contact to often work out a common response, or sort out what officials like to term as "misunderstandings."

The Indian government has allowed its policy on Kashmir to shift to a point where, like Pakistan, it agrees that peace between the two neighbours is now dependent on their ability to resolve the issue of Kashmir. And note, the problem is of Kashmir and not in Kashmir, and hence New Delhi is able to take the position that there is little for it to do within Kashmir, as its only the dialogue with Pakistan that can eventually lead to a final solution and final peace. The people of Kashmir who are clamouring for attention, and insist that they are being ignored by the two governments, are also giving credence to the argument that the problem is of Kashmir and not in Kashmir. The 'of' makes it an external problem, the 'in' makes it a problem between New Delhi and Kashmir. The last was what successive governments tried to handle with a level of dishonesty and incompetence that is history and the first is what governments in recent years have now decided to opt for.

The contention of this article is that the problem, even today, is not of Kashmir as much as it is in Kashmir. And if that is clearly understood, there is a great deal that a government can do to make it acceptable to the people of that state. It can begin, as it has managed, to ensure free and fair elections. It can work to make all sections of society, be they militants, separatists or others, contest the elections. It can recognise and respect the government that comes to power. It can develop a border policy, based on a strong federal foundation, to ensure that states like Jammu and Kashmir are ensured a certain status that will defeat those seeking to destabilise elected governments and take law into their own hands. It can address the aspirations of the people through regular contact and dialogue. It can ensure that its actions and its policies towards the state are not blunted by prejudice and discrimination. Withdrawal of troops, release of prisoners, end to human rights violations are all just part of this larger approach. These are not an end in itself as many even in Kashmir have started to believe, but manifestations of a change in policy that starts recognising the sensitivities of the people and working to create an infrastructure that gives this true expression.

A case in point is the intervention of New Delhi to overthrow governments elected by the people of Jammu and Kashmir in good faith, and the arrest of leaders like Sheikh Abdullah on highly flimsy grounds. It was these actions that were seen as a betrayal by the people of this border state, with the anger being compounded by the increasingly graphic display of incompetence and prejudice in New Delhi. Pakistan that had been looking for an opportunity found it in the growing disaffection of the Kashmiris in the 1980's and directed its extremists to Jammu and Kashmir in the knowledge that the militants would be protected. The years of militancy, the deaths, the destruction, the anger, the alienation, and human rights violations are now part of the records of the history of Jammu and Kashmir, as governments in New Delhi refused to recognise the suffering of the people, and on occasion even tried to turn it to communal advantage in other parts of India.

There is no doubt that a pause has been provided by the peace process. It is no secret that both India and Pakistan were 'nudged,', 'shoved', 'pushed' to the negotiating table by the United States (US) that did not want a war breaking out between the two nations. It had enough troubles in the region already. It is also no secret that both are still talking because of the US pressure, and while there are many in each establishment who would like to see an end to this dialogue, the peace process appears to have indeed become irreversible. This is again largely because of domestic reasons: Pakistan is in a mess and cannot afford a war; India does not want anything to come in the way that could retard its growth and development goals. The Kashmiris, fed up with militancy, are looking at peace as the only option and while not happy with the local government or with the way the talks between the two governments are proceeding, have decided to wait it out rather than encourage those elements that could take the state back to the militancy decade of the 1980's. The price they paid with their blood was more than any human being could afford.

It is for all these reasons that the current phase in Jammu and Kashmir marks a strong departure from the past, even from the recent past. It constitutes that moment in history that comes once in a long while, and if not recognised goes into the annals as a missed opportunity for which peoples and nations pay a heavy price. It is that phase where the people of the state, after having supported militancy have rejected it completely. The extremists function without support as the Kashmiris are fed up of violence and desperately want peace. It is that phase where the people of the Valley in particular have rejected US initiated peace proposals, supported by Pakistan, seeking to trifurcate Jammu and Kashmir along religious and ethnic lines. Kashmiriyat remains important, and communalism a doctrine that has not taken hold except in a few pockets of Jammu. It is that phase where the Kashmiris are fed up of their own separatist leadership, seeing them as agents of either New Delhi or Islamabad or as in some cases, of both. These leaders do not have a greater say than the elected representatives of the political parties in the state, and that constitutes a major shift in public opinion.

But most important of all, the extended honeymoon with Pakistan is under strain and the Kashmiris do not see a state torn apart by its own problems and with a future as uncertain as theirs, as being able to resolve their problems. Kashmiris do not hesitate to point out that Pakistan President Pervez Musharraf is extremely unpopular in the Valley, and his proximity to the US as well as the military operations against his "own people" have lost him his support base in the Valley. Delhi can see the General's preoccupation with his internal crisis, and the fact that he and Pakistan are not going to emerge from this mess in the near future, as an opportunity to shift its position from looking at the problem of Kashmir to the problem in Kashmir and working out a solution that would be acceptable to the people of the state.

Pakistan had always wanted to be key to Jammu and Kashmir. But as pointed out earlier, it is only now that the governments in India have agreed to legitimise the Pakistani position through the peace process that is discussing Jammu and Kashmir as the problem that needs to be resolved. This became necessary, as the matter was complicated by governments here that had stopped even trying to deal with Jammu and Kashmir and the problems within. India, under international pressure to resolve the issue with Pakistan, recognised Pakistan's argument that Kashmir was an unfinished business of partition, and embarked on a peace process that did lower the temperature between New Delhi and Islamabad but did little to improve life for the Kashmiris on both sides of the border. This was because the talks were not directed at resolving Kashmir but in bringing the two warring sides closer together. So while Lahore and Amritsar embraced each other in a new burst of understanding, there was little to bring the Kashmiris together except the Srinagar-Muzaffarabad bus that was a good initiative but got entangled in a web of bureaucratic controls.

There is need for the government now to recognise this moment in history and take hold of it. And that does not need detailed never-ending dialogue with Pakistan, except to ensure that the solution addresses its part of Kashmir as well. It does need detailed dialogue with the people of Jammu and Kashmir, however, but this has not even got off the ground. For the first time in decades, there is a general consensus from within Jammu and Kashmir for a solution resting on the pre-1953 formula for autonomy. That will basically give the state a prime minister and jurisdiction over all subjects except finance, defence and external affairs. There is no need to go into the details in this article, except to say that the autonomy proposal will have to be fine tuned to meet the requirements of both the state and the centre. A close study of the Sarkaria commission report will answer many of the queries that are being raised by both sides at present. Of course, it will require a great deal of work by the centre and by the government, political parties, individual leaders and the people of Jammu and Kashmir to become acceptable to all concerned. The government at Delhi will have to take the separatist leaders on board, and that makes a dialogue with them even more necessary. All doors will have to be opened, without fear and favour, and all sections of society involved in what could be made into the most important dialogue in the chequered history of the state. The people of Jammu and Kashmir are willing to examine the autonomy formula, and it is for New Delhi now to make it palatable.

The government probably knows this, as well as others outside the loop. But for some reason, probably based on the usual levels of prejudice and distrust, it has decided to ignore it. The Kashmiris who did attend the roundtable meetings convened by Prime Minister Manmohan Singh communicated this willingness on their part, but unfortunately nothing has come out of the meetings but the same promises that the Kashmiris have been listening to for six decades. The recommendations were not taken seriously by the government, and progress to even examine the issue from within is stalled. India appears to be waiting for Pakistan to settle its problems, instead of looking upon the current turmoil in the neighbouring state as an opportunity to reach an acceptable settlement with the Kashmiris. There is a certain reluctance in government to look at Kashmir as a problem within India, with the result that the political process between New Delhi and Srinagar is virtually dead.

The problem is in Jammu and Kashmir. It has to do with non-governance, corruption, poor administration and all the issues that affect the common man in any state, in any country. It has, however, also to do with the far more complicated issue of status in which is combined a desire for respect and dignity. The Kashmiris do not want to be part of a system that has not been able to understand and respect Kashmiriyat, that has hesitated and at times aggressively refused to accommodate their sensitivities, that has not hesitated to use the Hindu-Muslim card to invoke communal passions, that has shown scant interest in the development of the region, and that has revoked their preferences and choices at every available opportunity. This is not an exaggeration, and it is important for New Delhi to realise that border states, including the north east region, cannot be dealt in the same manner as the central parts of India. This is because the external influences are many, the options encouraging secessionist forces exist, and the interests of neighbouring countries can complicate matters to a point where bloodletting becomes the only option, for the peoples and for the militaries.

"The disillusionment with Pakistan, born of recent developments there, provides an opportunity to engage in meaningful discussions with the people of Jammu and Kashmir. The Hurriyat leadership with the exception of the hardliners as well as the mainstream political parties like the People's Democratic Party and the National Conference have begun to talk again of the pre-1953 option. And this can provide a starting point for an engagement between New Delhi and the people of Jammu and Kashmir to find a solution to the problems of the state that would meet the aspirations of the people. But it is imperative that any solution to the problems of the state, where it involves a change in the relationship between the State and the Union of India, must be endorsed not only by the people of the State but also by the people of the rest of India. If indeed one accepts, as one has argued in the case of the nuclear deal with the United States of America, that Parliament represents the will of the people of India, then a first step should be the setting up of a Parliamentary committee of all parties to debate the various options that are available to peacefully resolve the Kashmir issue and redress the grievances that have turned a paradise into a violent hell. It is evident to that moderate opinion in Jammu and Kashmir, particularly in the valley, is seeking a way out of the vortex of violence. It is imperative that India, particularly the central government, takes immediate steps to capitalise on the sentiment and provide a healing touch to the state. A process of dialogue and discussion, not secretive, and not limited to selected interlocutors, but open and with the involvement of all the people of India and the people of Jammu and Kashmir needs to be started. The Hurriyat through its recent comments appears to be again opening the door to dialogue. In one sense it is Pakistan today that is isolated and preoccupied with its own domestic turmoil. The average Kashmiri is politically savvy and realises that the evolution of India holds far greater promise for the future generation of Kashmiris than the turbulence in Pakistan which is beginning to destroy Pakistan's social fabric and promises continuing turbulence with possibly an increasing climate of extremism. Wisdom and the welfare of India both demand that the government of India does not let this opportunity slip by.

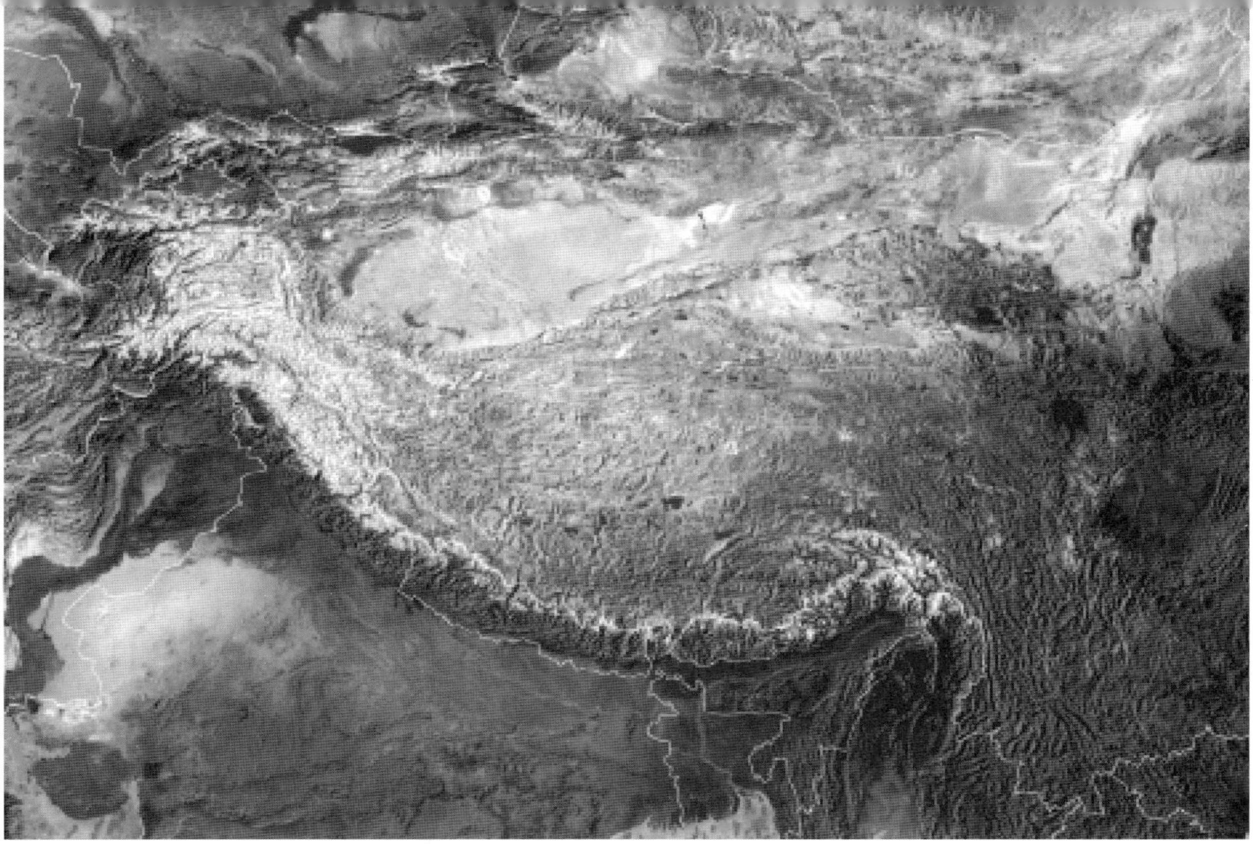

CHINA AND TIBET IN THE EARLY 1950S: THE LIBERATION AND AFTER

Prof PL Mehra

Formerly Professor and Chair of the Departments of History and Central Asian Studies, Panjab University, Chandigarh (India);

Author of Studies in Frontier History: India, China and the Disputed Border

I

Over the past half a century and more since Tibet's fateful 'liberation', mounted by Mao and his men in October1950, a lively, if also not a little controversial —and veritably unending—debate has raged over the role New Delhi, as successors to the Raj, played in the events leading to, and resulting from the Chinese assault. By no means less important was the reaction in Whitehall which until a few years earlier had been dealing with Lhasa and its affairs. And whose officer on duty, H E Richardson, then British Trade Agent at Gyantse—after August 1947 he had stayed in, ad interim, as independent India's representative—was still in Lhasa when news of the People's Liberation Army (PLA) units' attack on Tibet's eastern provinces were received in a jittery Tibetan capital.

Developments in the months that followed are too well-known to need reiteration. Briefly the youthful Dalai Lama who had a little earlier assumed full powers as his country's ruler fled his capital and headed for Yatung, a stone's throw from the Indian frontier, where he and his officials now camped. In a bout of frenzied activity the Tibetan government made a number of moves in New Delhi, London, Washington - to garner some support - more material than moral, to push the invaders back. As if to exhaust all his avenues, the Dalai Lama made a fervid if desperate appeal to the world body in New York to heed his feeble voice as a victim of blatant aggression. Sadly nothing much seemed to avail. The world, its tub thumping and lip sympathy apart, was much too busy with its own affairs and offered little solace: Tibet was far too remote and inaccessible to receive help and the new Chinese People's Republic far too close- and important - to annoy. In the final count, after a great deal of to-ing and fro-ing of the Lama's representatives he had perforce to conclude a 17-Point Agreement with Beijing. The latter has insisted all along that Lhasa's representatives had a free hand in conducting the parleys, a claim the Dalai Lama and his people have stoutly contested.

A distinguished Chinese-American academic, Professor Qiang Zhai who teaches at Harvard has in a well-researched article re-lived those momentous years and highlighted the role of China, the US and British governments. India too comes in, in a big way. The exercise has drawn heavily on source material in archives in London and Washington and also such Chinese archival sources as are now ready to hand. The present writer had a very welcome opportunity to comment on Professor Zhai's excellent piece and the following pages are, with slight changes, a reproduction of what the *Journal of Cold War Studies* carried. It would have been ideal if the reader had a good hard look at all that the Professor had to say; regrettably, this was found to be a little impractical. In its absence the opening paragraphs in the rejoinder (II) offer a faithful albeit brief summary statement of the main points of his argument. This, hopefully, should make the succeeding text (III) answer to its principal objective of putting the record straight, especially in the context of New Delhi's alleged sins of omission and commission.*

II

A summary statement of Qiang Zhai's detailed presentation will help put its major thrust into sharper focus. Washington was keen to help Tibet but keener still that the "primary responsibility" of supporting Tibet's cause be taken up by India—and the United Kingdom. It made a number of suggestions starting with the proposal that New Delhi serve as the venue for a United States-Tibet dialogue. Later, it was prepared for "procurement and financing" of military aid - provided New Delhi would ensure delivery across its territory. More, it was ready to cooperate with India "in every possible way" to forestall a Chinese conquest of Tibet and proposed inter alia joint New Delhi-Western operations. Although it would not lodge any formal protest it was less than happy when India and the UK managed to get a discussion of the Chinese aggression in Tibet off the United Nations agenda.

Reactions in South Block and Whitehall were, for most part, in consonance. Nehru responded by underlining that talks in New Delhi between the US and Tibet would be counter-productive. They would attract wide publicity and only "speed up" Beijing's plans for a take-over. Off its own bat, the U.S. had dissuaded Lhasa from dispatching a mission to its shores.

For his part the Indian prime minister was strongly persuaded that good relations with the People's Republic of China "outweighed" any obligations New Delhi had inherited from the British concerning Tibet. US - UK suggestions for Indian arms to help Tibet were ruled out. The US was less than clear if Tibetan leaders had "any military plans" to offer resistance while the British were certain that such arms could not halt a Chinese invasion and would best serve only as a morale-booster. Any joint New Delhi-Western operations were ruled out as "politically undesirable." Failure to obtain Indian cooperation had "dimmed" US enthusiasm while it was reasoned that Western non-involvement might work for "indefinite postponement" of Beijing's armed assault. Whitehall was persuaded that any attempt to intervene would be both "impracticable and unwise"; it was "not sufficiently interested" in Tibet either to embroil itself with China or get "out of step" with India.

China's PLA units attacked Tibetan positions at Chamdo (05 October) and took strong exception to the Indian protest note, insisting Tibet was part of Chinese territory. Mao indicated that while Tibet might/might not negotiate, he would not tolerate any "foreign" influence in Tibet's affairs. Clearly the Indian stance had irritated the Chairman and reinforced his distrust of Nehru. Meantime Tibet apart, Washington was uneasy about Chinese dealings in Korea and Vietnam. New Delhi responded by suggesting that it would be "most helpful" to do nothing for any US backing of Tibet would lend credence to Beijing's charge that the Great Powers had been intriguing in its affairs.

On 07 November Tibet appealed to the UN to "restrain Chinese aggression"; ten days later the youthful 14th Dalai Lama took over as his country's ruler. His assumption of power has been viewed as an indication that Lhasa deemed it was "a little too early" to compromise with Beijing. At the UN, the British delegate indicated that since India entertained "strong doubts" about the absolute independence of Tibet and there was a "preponderance" of Indian interest in the matter, Whitehall would not take any initiative. As in the case of according recognition to the PRC, there was a great deal of "sensitivity" to New Delhi's opinion.

El Salvador sponsored the Tibetan appeal. During the General Committee's session both the British and Indian delegates sought to avoid debate, indicating that

* *Qiang Zhai. "Tibet and Chinese-British-American Relations in the Early 1950s", Journal of Cold War Studies 8:3 (summer 2006): 34-53. Doi: 10.1162/jcws.2006.8.3.34.Reviewed by Parshotam Mehra. Panjab University in Chandigarh (India) Published by H-Diplo on 9 September 2007 under the caption H-Diplo Article Review Mehra on Zhai*

the chances for a peaceful settlement still existed. Insofar as New Delhi was most directly involved, everybody, including the US, fell in line. If India had acted otherwise, the US later averred, it would have put the item on the agenda.

Meanwhile Tibet slowly but surely succumbed to Chinese pressures that brought about "negotiations" in Beijing and the conclusion of the 17-Point Agreement (May 1951) which laid down inter alia that the Tibetan people "shall return to the family" of the People's Republic of China and that the Central People's Government "shall conduct the centralized handling" of all external affairs of Tibet.

In sum, Qiang Zhai concludes, Tibet was primarily an issue of Indian concern while Britain was preoccupied with safeguarding its interests in China - and Hong Kong. Nehru, eager to play the peacemaker in Korea, was less than willing to confront Beijing openly on the issue of Tibet. Washington's principal preoccupation was to contain communism, even though it was eager to salvage the Tibetan cause. Its major hurdles: Tibet's geography - too remote and isolated - and the unwillingness of its non-communist neighbour, India, to alienate China by owning Lhasa's cause. For the US, Korea and Taiwan remained primary issues of contention, Tibet relatively less so. Mao suspected the British of manipulating India behind the scenes and feared a pro-British-American faction behind Lhasa's decision to explore the possibility of the Dalai Lama seeking refuge in India or outside.

III

For a proper perspective on some of the major themes Qiang Zhai has touched upon, a few relevant aspects of the Tibetan situation need careful scrutiny. To start with, Whitehall had fought shy of any overt intervention to bolster the Dalai Lama's regime in the opening decades of the 20th century and left the latter more or less to his own devices. It may be recalled that before the runaway 13th Dalai Lama set foot in Yatung (February 1910), Indian policy towards him had remained "unformulated" and the Viceroy was "unsure" of how to proceed. At his interview with the Tibetan ruler in Calcutta (April 1910), Minto "firmly though politely" rejected his major demand for a British protectorate even as he had done so in the case of the 9th Panchen Lama earlier in 1906. When the Lama's request for the British "to intervene directly" to halt Chinese aggression in his country failed, he began to beg for "any kind of help."[1]

In Beijing the Dalai Lama was viewed "as a barrier" to successful Anglo-Chinese relations. To safeguard its interests against a resurgent China, India decided to develop closer ties with Nepal, Bhutan, and Sikkim. In 1910, the Kashag had told "Britain and Ministers of Europe" that "big worms are eating little worms."[2] The Laden La mission (1912) was designed to accompany the refugee Dalai Lama on his return journey home as well as help in the evacuation of the rebellious Chinese soldiery holed up in Tibet, especially in Lhasa. More, it was to ensure that the fragile cease fire between the rump of the Chinese army and an aroused Tibetan populace baying for its blood held and became permanent. Sadly, Whitehall, hypersensitive on its policy of non-intervention in China's affairs, put its foot down on this venture. As a compromise, Laden La was to stay put in Gyantse from where he was to act as "a long-distance advisor" to the Lama.[3]

About this time (ca. 1914) the Dalai Lama had given Bell to understand that he wanted Tibet to be "entirely independent" but would consult the British government "whenever necessity arises."[4]

In June 1919 Jordan, the British Minister in Beijing reported Chinese "willingness" to debate the boundary issue (Tibet was to be kept out) that had remained unresolved at the tripartite Simla Conference (1913-4). The August talks in the Chinese capital appeared "reasonable" to start with when these were suddenly terminated.[5] Broadly, British policy in Tibet was "sterilisation" and isolating the country "as far as possible". Bell's Lhasa mission (1920-21) was demonstrative of "a more liberal approach" and a broad decision against posting a permanent British representative in Lhasa where he may not have been easy to protect.[6] All the same, Curzon, now foreign secretary in the British government, wanted "a firm line" yet "an open attitude" regarding China on Tibet.[7]

---

1 *Wendy Palace, The British Empire and Tibet 1900-1922, (London: RoutledgeCurzon, 2005): 65-6, 69*

2 *Wendy Palace: 70*

3 *Nicholas and Deki Rhodes, A Man of the Frontier: SWLaden La (1876-1936), His Life and Time in Darjeeling and Tibet (Kolkata, 2006), Chapter 7 "The Dalai Lama Returns to Tibet", 23-27, gives a vivid description of the British "volte face". Understandably Laden La was "very disappointed"*

4 *Wendy Palace: 126*

5 *Parshotam Mehra, The McMahon Line and After (New Delhi: Macmillan, 1974): 330-343*

6 *Parshotam Mehra, The McMahon Line: 356-369*

7 *Wendy Palace: 141-142*

Professor Qiang Zhai's meticulous data on Washington's efforts to persuade the British and the Indian governments to stand up for Tibet at the UN and render it all help including men and munitions makes for impressive reading. For the record though, American interest in Tibet's affairs goes far back to the opening decade of the 20th century when Rockhill, the American Minister in Beijing, acted as an unofficial advisor to the 13th Dalai Lama and helped him negotiate with the Qing court (1908). The Minister noted that the Tibetan ruler, while ill-treated by the Dowager Empress and the youthful Emperor would not cooperate in the difficult task they now propose to undertake of governing Tibet like a Chinese province.[8]

Long after the 13th Dalai Lama had retired to the heavenly fields (1933) and there was an imminent danger of an armed Chinese escort for the 9th Panchen Lama, by then a confirmed Chiang protégé, crossing over into Tibet (1936-7) with the unambiguous objective of restoring the Lama - and suborning the rickety, regent-led Lhasa regime to Chinese ends in the bargain - the British government in India held back and refused to lend any material help barring diplomatic support. More, it refused to counsel the Tibetan government offering any armed resistance to the Chinese onslaught. The British mission's report is clearly demonstrative of the Tibetan regime's thinking and of the Raj's own predilections. The Regent's attitude, the report heavily underlined, did not indicate that the Tibetans would put up much, if any resistance nor is it at all certain that we should want them to do so especially as it is possible that the Chinese might make it a pretext for a more serious invasion.

It does not seem at all certain that this (active resistance to Chinese escort) would be the wisest course for the Tibetan government to adopt, if ... in any case it seems desirable to avoid any risk that the Tibetan government on the departure of the (Gould) mission from Lhasa, might be left under the impression that His Majesty's Government (HMG) would encourage such a course.[9]

The state of Tibet's defences and the leadership of its "army" were summed up neatly in Brigadier Neame's report (1936) that was not exactly complimentary.[10] In Lhasa, it revealed, there were only 600 troops of the Bodyguard regiment, 400-armed police and 300 soldiers from regiments stationed in Kham. There were six mountain guns in the Tibetan capital (of which two were "dangerous to fire"), 2 Lewis guns and 6,000 modern rifles. Neame indicated that in his considered judgment:

> Tibetans as a nation are absolutely non-military .... Tibetan government and officials concerned with army have absolutely no idea of sound military organization, administration or training .... troops employed on active service in East Tibet are incapable of firing with effect and waste ammunition when in action.

In the event, the Brigadier concluded that:

> It is justifiable to say that except for the fact that they possess a certain number of modern weapons, which few of them know how to use; the army has advanced little from its condition in 1904 when the British Mission advanced to Lhasa...

And one may be sure that no significant change, qualitative much less quantitative, for the better would have taken place in the decade or so that elapsed between 1936 and 1950. It should follow that short of an armed intervention by New Delhi/Britain or the US, singly or in unison, there was no stalling or halting the progress of the Chinese Peoples' Liberation Army in October 1950.

It is pertinent to add that British efforts to help in the modernisation of Tibet were minimal at best. With the Lama himself beating a hasty retreat in the wake of the monks' rebellion (1921), they held their hand. Charles Bell and some "do gooders" in Lhasa notwithstanding, the mantra was sterilisation of Tibet, its complete isolation. Moreover, in Whitehall, relations with China, especially on the commercial plane, were rated far more important. No wonder that in Beijing's British Legation, Tibet was viewed as a drag, a particular nuisance.[11]

Later whatever the compulsions of China in its inability to exercise any meaningful authority in Lhasa for the years the 13th Dalai Lama was alive (d. 1933) and for almost a decade and a half thereafter, it refused to yield

---

[8] *Parshotam Mehra, From Conflict to Conciliation: Tibetan Polity Re-visited, Harrassowitz, (Wiesbaden: Harrassowitz, 2004): 33, 35*

[9] *Parshotam Mehra, Tibetan Polity: 76*

[10] *Alastair Lamb, Tibet, China and India, 1914-1950 (Hertingfordbury: Rockford, 1989): 274. See also Melvyn C. Goldstein, A History of Modern Tibet 1914-1951 (Indian Edition, New Delhi, 1933): 287.*

[11] *Wendy Palace: 55*

any ground on its theoretical claims to Tibet as an integral part of the mainland, and mounted tireless efforts to give these shape and form. The idea of war supplies, via Tibet, to a beleaguered Chinese regime or massing of troops in the provinces bordering on Tibet or planning airfields there to pressurize Lhasa were part of the same plan. Some of the 1943-44 exchanges, briefly reproduced below, in which both Whitehall as well as the State Department were involved, demonstrate that even a hard-driven Guomindang regime was uncompromising in its resolve to incorporate Tibet into the larger whole of the motherland

> HMG do not feel themselves committed to regard China as the suzerain unless she in turn agrees to Tibetan autonomy. If the Chinese government contemplate withdrawal of Tibetan autonomy HMG and the Government of India must ask themselves whether in the changed circumstances of today it would be right for them to continue to recognize even a theoretical status of subservience for a people who desire to be free and have in fact maintained that freedom for more than thirty years. (British Foreign Office, 22 July 1943)

> There have been increasing indications in recent months that the Chinese Central Government desires, and as soon as it is in a position to extend its control over Tibet by force of arms. It is almost a foregone conclusion that Tibet will resist such encroachment by all means at its command including, presumably, appeals to Great Britain and the US. (Charge in China, Chungking, to the Secretary of State, 20 September 1943)

> Chinese regard Tibet as an integral part of China; regard relations with Tibet as an internal problem... in their study of geography the Chinese have long been taught that Tibet is a part of China ... Politically and in law Chinese claims regarding Tibet stand on far firmer ground than do British claims. (Acting Secretary of State to Ambassador in China, 29 September 1943)

> Recent additional troop concentrations on the Tibet-Chinghai border and that the Chinese possibly for the purpose of "pressure" to be applied later on is constructing some airfields there. .... it was curious how much trouble was taken over outlying regions such as Tibet and Outer Mongolia, which are of absolutely no economic value to China. (Ambassador in China to Secretary of State, 4 October 1943)

> Major Tolstoy believes that it would take from six to eight months from the Indian border to China for a shipment to go through even under adverse conditions; that it would be necessary to have our representatives accompany the shipments; and that the entire transportation could be handled by certain responsible Tibetan traders who are either in India themselves or who have their representatives on the Indian border. (William J Donovan, Washington, April 14, 1944)[12]

In the light of the above it should follow that neither for Generalissimo Chiang Kai-shek in the mid-1940s nor yet for Chairman Mao at the end of the decade was there any question of a negotiated settlement. According to Michael Sheng, Mao believed that China "must assert control" over Tibet "as soon as possible"; more, that the use of military force was inevitable and the only question was "how much force to use and when." He was also convinced that Britain, India, and the U.S. were "forging an anti-Beijing front". Mao succeeded largely because of the superiority of the Chinese army, the insularity of Tibet's polity and, lip sympathy apart, the indifference of the rest of the world.[13]

Earlier as Hopkinson, the British Political Officer in Sikkim, was to put it (1948) the plain objective Chiang kept in view was "nothing short of complete Tibetan surrender" to the wishes of the Chinese government. Nor was that all. For in the course of his review of developments for the years August 1945-August 1948, the British officer revealed inter alia that T L Shen, the Guomindang Chinese representative in Lhasa, had told him (1945) that the real obstacle to a settlement in Tibet was the "likelihood" of British aggression and the Chinese fear thereof. Hopkinson's own considered view was that a Chinese-Tibetan settlement was impossible because of "Chinese intransigence for ignoring such facts as Tibet's refusal to surrender its hard-won independence" over the past thirty odd years and demand for Lhasa's complete capitulation. Indian independence, Hopkinson stressed, "made no

[12] *For the fuller text see Parshotam Mehra, The North-Eastern Frontier: A Documentary Study, 2 vols,*

[13] *Michael M. Sheng, "Mao, China, Tibet and the Korean War," Journal of Cold War Studies 8:3 (Summer 2006): 15-32, cited in James Matray's H-Diplo review, at http://www.hnet. org/~diplo/reviews/PDF/Matray-Sheng.pdf .*

difference" to Chinese "claims to Indian territory in Assam."[14] (Polity, 90) Was it any wonder then that New Delhi's later efforts, as revealed in the October-November (1950) diplomatic exchanges with Beijing, drew a blunt, if spirited, rebuff? [15] A few of the more relevant excerpts reproduced below spell out their respective positions and make for sober reading.

New Delhi-Beijing, Memorandum, 21 October 1950:

> The Government of India feels that the time factor is extremely important. In Tibet there is not likely to be any serious military opposition and any delay in settling the matter will not therefore affect Chinese interests, or a suitable final solution. ...... (Government of India's) interest in this matter ... is to see that the admission of the People's Government to the UN is not postponed .... A peaceful solution is sought while military action may cause unrest and disturbances on her own borders.

New Delhi-Beijing, Note, 28 October 1950:

> In the present context of world events, the invasion by Chinese troops of Tibet cannot but be regarded as deplorable and, in the considered judgment of the Government of India, not in the interest of China or of peace.
>
> ..... deep regret that in spite of the friendly and disinterested advice repeatedly tendered by them...the Chinese Government seek a solution of the problem by force instead of the slower and more enduring method of peaceful approach.

Beijing-New Delhi, Note, 30 October 1950:

> The People's Republic of China would "like to make it clear: Tibet is an integral part of Chinese territory and the problem of Tibet is entirely a domestic problem of China. The Chinese PLA must enter Tibet, liberate the Tibetan people and defend the frontiers of China. This is the resolved policy of the Central People's Government.

New Delhi-Beijing, Note, 1 November 1950:

> Beijing's charge that India's representation "affected by foreign influences hostile to China" and categorically repudiate it. The Government of India's policy has been entirely independent and directed solely towards a peaceful settlement of international disputes and avoidance of anything calculated to increase the present deplorable tensions in the world.
>
> A settlement of the Tibetan problem ... by peaceful negotiations adjusting legitimate Tibetan claims to autonomy within the framework of Chinese suzerainty. Tibetan autonomy is a fact which the Chinese Government was themselves willing to recognize and foster.

Beijing-New Delhi, Note, 16 November 1950:

> But regardless of whether the local authorities of Tibet wish to proceed with peace negotiations and regardless of whatever results may be achieved by negotiations, no foreign intervention will be permitted. The entry into Tibet of the Chinese PLA and the liberation of the Tibetan people are also decided.
>
> Deeply regret that the Indian Government in disregard of the facts has regarded a domestic problem of the Chinese Government - the exercise of its sovereign rights in Tibet - as an international dispute calculated to increase the present tensions in the world.

Soviet Russia's role in Tibet's "liberation" makes for interesting reading. It is clear that Stalin saw the land of the lama as a Western stooge, and lent Mao and his men not only considerable moral support in the task of "liberation" but also, in the initial stages, tangible armed assistance and training of personnel. Tibet, it appears, emerged as a major subject during Mao's official visit to Moscow (December 1949 - January 1950). When the Chairman asked Stalin to continue Russian air support rendered in the case of Sinkiang

[14] *Parshotam Mehra, Polity, 90, n. 205. Review, August 1945 to August 1948 by A J Hopkinson, Political Officer in Sikkim, India Office Records. Mss Eur D 998/23, para 18. It may be of interest to note that both Hopkinson's official "review" as well as Richardson's annual report for 1947 had reached Whitehall through a devious channel and not through Government of India in New Delhi. Hopkinson, it would appear, had kept copies of these reports which he was "good enough to loan" to the Commonwealth Relations Office in London when he visited there "to see us". A note in the CRO, Pol. Est. 6120/49 dated 19 January 1949, addressed to one H S Shattock in the UK High Commission's Office in New Delhi while forwarding copies of these reports revealed that the Government of India "seemed to have kept (these reports) to themselves". For details PRO, FO 371/76315*

[15] *For the full text, Parshotam Mehra, North-Eastern Frontier, II, "New Delhi-Beijing exchanges, October-November 1950": 155-64*

for Beijing's impending attack on Tibet, Stalin's response: "It is good you're getting ready for the attack. Tibetans should be taken in hand." Liu Shao-chi in a memorandum to Stalin (late 1949) expressed the view that "the question of Tibet should be solved by political means and not by military force." Three years later (1952) Peking asked Moscow for help "in establishing control over Tibet."[16]

Stalin told Mao that Tibet is "a part of China" and therefore Chinese troops "should be stationed" in Tibet. Chou En-lai affirmed that keeping Chinese troops in Tibet was "indisputable." The Soviets held Mao's absorption of Tibet to be justified and underlined the urgency of its "peaceful liberation" from western imperialism. The historian Leontiev (1958) expressed the view that Tibet had been turned into a "semi-colony of British imperialism, an agrarian and raw material appendage for the imperial powers."[17]

The Russian author is categorical in his assertion that Stalin's counseling strongly affected decision-making by Beijing on the Tibetan issue in the years 1949-52. More, that Stalin gave Mao the "go ahead" for Tibet's military occupation by the PLA in October 1950. Apart from considerable diplomatic support, Stalin also rendered some tangible help in building transport communications between China and Tibet and training of PLA units in the early1950s. Moscow was certainly not interested in an independent Tibet; the latter it feared would "most likely" ally itself with the "imperialist West" rather than the "communist East"[18].

It is in this context that US interest in persuading Whitehall or Nehru's India to render both moral and material support needs to be viewed. In an era of mounting cold war tensions, US support of the Tibetan cause via El Salvador came to be viewed for all that was worth: a clever tactic by Uncle Sam to score an important victory against its ideological adversaries. New Delhi's efforts to bring about a cease-fire in Korea- where in October 1950 Chinese "volunteers" joined the North Korean army to invest the south-synchronized with events leading to and following Tibet's "liberation" by the Peoples' Liberation Army made things a lot more complicated. Odd as it may sound, a decade or so later the Cuban missile crisis ran pat into Beijing's massive armed assault on India's land frontiers (October 1962) making a difficult situation far worse. History unfolds itself in strange, inscrutable ways!

A word on the proposed or projected aid for Tibet may not be out of place. According to Carole McGranahan, the Americans were "mainly interested in preventing the spread of Communism rather than providing serious and committed aid to Tibet." Kenneth Knaus has cited the Tibetan ruler to the effect that the U.S. had "used Tibet as a pawn in the Cold War" and he no doubt resented it. Young though he was, the Lama was not naïve. For while at Yatung, in 1951, the youthful ruler had much hoped that "some help" would be forthcoming from Britain and the U.S. And "it did not come". All that he received was "one letter from the American consul in Calcutta"! New Delhi too, he had "calculated", would not be "happy" if he crossed over. Later he could quite see that such US support as was forthcoming in the 1950s was "not out of moral principle or sympathy but because of the world wide anti-Communist policies." More, it was "not genuine support for the restoration of Tibetan independence."[19]

Two major criticisms of Qiang Zhai's extremely well researched presentation may be in order. To start with, a slight imbalance in favour of US - and to an extent British - source-material is noticeable. And in the bargain there is a relative neglect of Indian and Chinese sources. For the US the temptation to use the excellent, extremely valuable if informative volumes in the Foreign Relations of the United States series is understandable.

So also the rich and well-preserved British Public Record Office archives (The National Archives of the United Kingdom) in London. As to Chinese sources this reviewer has no competence to comment but a word or two on the Indian sources may be of interest. Here there is a problem no doubt about New Delhi's short-sighted if also ill-advised policy of sitting tight on its archival records and even though a 30-year limit is said to be operative, in actual fact it is observed more in the breach than compliance. The above notwithstanding, there is no dearth of first-rate primary sources in the plethora of letters/private papers/

[16] *Alexandre Andreyev, Soviet Russia and Tibet: the debacle of Soviet Diplomacy 1918-1930s (Leiden: Brill, 2003): 385*

[17] *Andreyev, 387*

[18] *Parshotam Mehra, Polity: 95*

[19] *Carole McGranahan, "Tibet's ColdWar: the CIA and the Chushi Gangdrug Resistance 1956-1974," Journal of Cold War Studies:8.3 (summer 2006): 102-30. See also Kenneth Knaus, Orphans of the Cold War, America and the Tibetan Struggle, (New York: Public Affairs, 1999) both cited in Tom Grunfeld's Article Review, JCWS, 8.3 (summer 2006). For the Dalai Lama's stay at Yatung see Thomas Laird, The Story of Tibet: Conversations with the Dalai Lama (London: Atlantic Books, 2006): 300, 310*

correspondence relating to the 1950s in the printed volumes of Jawaharlal Nehru's works and a host of secondary sources dealing with the then-prime minister's foreign policy especially in the realm of his relations with China.

Another significant omission in this reviewer's opinion is the relative neglect of the Indian viewpoint, all the more so in that New Delhi's role—on the author's own showing—was pivotal. That Nehru reacted the way he did is important but even more relevant is to pry deeper to find out why he behaved the way he did. And here the British legacy he inherited comes in for proper scrutiny. The Raj's policy towards Tibet was ambivalent at best. And it succeeded largely because it faced - thanks to a moribund, weak and invertebrate Guomindang regime in China - no major crises.

As political legatees of the Raj, Nehru's India understood, if not perhaps always appreciated, the various compulsions in which its policy was formulated and executed. This would go far to explain why more often than not there was a close liaison, and a singular identity of views on major issues, between New Delhi and Whitehall—much more so than between either of them and the White House in Washington. Not unlike New Delhi, Whitehall too was allergic to supplying Lhasa with arms—and armed men! In the unlikely event that they did, results would have been chaotic, both in, and outside of, Tibet. Nor would men and munitions have been of any help in the circumstances in which Lhasa was placed. The clearest demonstration of a New Delhi-Whitehall nexus was their decision—sad and unfortunate as it proved in retrospect—to put off the debate on Tibet at the UN in the hope that a negotiated settlement with Beijing would emerge.

In the light of the important role New Delhi played in the evolving situation in those fateful years it stands to reason that the author may perhaps consider recasting his title. His text has, as it stands, apart from the "Conclusions", two sub-sections: "The Role of Britain" and "The Role of the United States." How about carving out a third: "The Role of India", on which he has expatiated at some length and in some detail.

A small error in mixing up KPS. Menon with VK Krishna Menon has no doubt inadvertently crept in. The former, a distinguished diplomat, was independent India's first foreign secretary; the latter, long in public life, was defence minister in the Indian government in the early 1960s.

NATIONAL GOVERNANCE AND INTERNAL SECURITY

N N Vohra

Former Defence and Home Secretary, Government of India and Principal Secretary to the Prime Minister

There is a crucial link between National Governance and Internal Security. If Internal Security is not maintained Governance cannot be delivered and there would be grave threats to the very unity and integrity of the country. Likewise, Internal Security cannot be safeguarded if Governance is delivered by an inefficient and corrupt administration.

It is perhaps not necessary to define Governance. However, in the simplest terms, governance relates to the effective management of national affairs at all levels of functioning; guaranteeing the country's unity and integrity and securing the safety and overall welfare of its people. For the attainment of these objectives it would be essential that political, economic, executive and judicial authority is exercised in a manner which ensures that the people are enabled to enjoy their rights, discharge their obligations and resolve their disputes within the parameters of the Constitution and the Rule of Law.

The exhaustive Constitution of India provides the basis of the relationship between the Union and the States and delineates the Legislative, Judicial and Executive framework within which the Union and the States shall discharge their respective responsibilities for delivering governance. The Preamble to the Constitution provides the key to its philosophy: it enshrines the sovereignty of the people and envisions a socialist, secular, democratic republic based on justice, liberty, equality and fraternity.

The principles of governance of India are excellently enunciated in the chapter on Directive Principles of State Policy in the Constitution. It has been laid down (Article 37) that the provisions contained in this chapter shall be "fundamental in the governance of the country" and that it shall be the "*duty of the State* to apply these principles in making laws".

The founding fathers of the Constitution of India were acutely aware that political democracy would have no significance unless it was accompanied by social and economic democracy. It was their belief that, within the democratic framework, clean and efficient governance would transform the social, economic and political life of our people and build a strong, prosperous and vibrant nation. The Directive Principles, described as the 'core' or the 'conscience' of the Constitution, provide the goals and guidelines which, if vigorously pursued and timely implemented, would have led to removing the inequalities and disabilities suffered by large segments of our society and thus paved the way for the achievement of social and economic justice.

We have still to traverse a very long distance to achieve our nation-building goals. About a quarter of our population still lives below the poverty line. The persistence of large-scale poverty and illiteracy, the lack of employment, shelter, clean drinking water, basic sanitation and health care, food and nutrition, and the yawning gaps in the achievement of various other vital developmental targets manifest the serious failures of national governance. The default in achieving social and economic justice has perhaps been the most signal failure.

The failures of governance have led to the recognition that governance shall become honest and effective, and inequalities shall start reducing, when the people are empowered and communities are enabled to manage their own affairs. In this context, the 73rd and the 74th Amendments to the Constitution provide the constitutional mandate for the provision of self-governance through the establishment of duly empowered rural and urban local self governing institutions. It is a matter for deep regret that the States have still to evince the required political will to effectively pursue the path of democratic decentralization.

Thus, today, in large parts of the country, the people's sovereignty still means no more than the right to exercise their vote whenever elections are held. It is however a matter for enormous satisfaction that, despite failures on various fronts and despite the serious shortcomings of the electoral processes, the spirit of democracy stands deeply rooted in India.

Among the many reasons for the continuing failures of governance a significant factor has been the instability of the political regimes in the States from around the late 1960s and at the Centre in the past decade and a half. From 1989 onwards, there were six governments at the Centre in less than a decade. It has also been seen that frequent elections have not invariably engendered conclusive outcomes. In recent years no single party or pre-poll alliance of parties has succeeded in securing a clear majority. Unstable coalition governments in the States, perennially occupied in combating threats to their survival, have failed to deliver effective governance.

It may be relevant to observe that, over the years, the politicization of caste and communal identities has led to divisiveness and disruption of the national ethos. The failure of the electoral system to prevent anti-social, communal, undesirable and even criminal elements from contesting and winning elections has contributed to the progressive decline of the polity and the consequential failure of the State Assemblies and the Parliament to effectively discharge their vital constitutional roles.

Consequent to the 1993 serial bomb blasts in Mumbai, on the direction of the Prime Minister, a Committee was established to enquire into certain aspects of the bombings. In September 1993 this Committee, generally referred to as the Vohra Committee, had reported the existence of a deep nexus between political personalities, public servants and crime syndicates. As per the Director CBI's report to this Committee "all over India crime syndicates have become a law unto themselves. Even in the smaller towns and rural areas, muscle men have become the order of the day. Hired assassins have become part of these organizations. The nexus between the communal gangs, police, bureaucracy and politicians has come out clearly in various parts of the country". Quoting the Director Intelligence Bureau, the Committee reported that the Mafia network is "virtually running a parallel government, pushing the State apparatus into irrelevance" and that in certain States "these gangs enjoy the patronage of local politicians, cutting across party lines, and the protection of functionaries . . . Some political leaders become the leaders of these gangs/armed *senas* and, over the years, get themselves elected to local bodies, State Assemblies and the national Parliament". By all accounts, over the past decade and a half, this criminal nexus has enlarged and extended its reach.

Governance has been adversely affected also because political leaders remain incessantly preoccupied with the narrow, sectarian and partisan interests of their parties and the pursuit of day-to-day political gains and have no time or patience to attend to the crying needs of the common man. The failure of the political executive to devote sustained attention to its constitutional responsibilities has led to governmental functioning in the States being marred by gross delays, inefficiency, insensitivity, unaccountability and pervasive corruption.

Today, thanks to the information technology revolution and the fast spreading reach of the media, the awareness and expectations of the average citizen have been significantly enhanced. This has, correspondingly, generated much deeper dissatisfaction with the failures of governance. Unless urgent and ruthless steps are taken to check maladministration and corruption the anger and disgust of the common people, particularly the disadvantaged and oppressed elements, it could lead to their alienation. And past experience has shown that alienated elements can be easily lured to adopting the gun culture and joining unlawful networks whose activities cause serious public disorders.

In the past decade and more, despite the constraints of governance under coalition governments, the rate of the country's economic growth has been consistently higher than at any time in the past. It is heartening to observe that the new economic strength is being utilized to significantly enhance the investments in human development and poverty eradication programmes and for the execution of varied schemes for improving the quality of life of the common man.

In the obtaining environment of steady economic growth and dynamism the interest of foreign governments, companies, investors and entrepreneurs has been growing steadily. Quite understandably, foreign investors would keep a close watch on the situation in India, to be assured of the security of their assets and holdings. In this context, national governance has the super-added responsibility of ensuring that internal security is effectively maintained to promote our growing international trade and business interests which are vital for the steady growth of our economy.

Let us now take a quick look at the constitutional position in regard to national security management in our country.

The safeguarding of national security encompasses eternal vigilance to meet every threat to the Indian State from every possible source within the country and from anywhere across its land or sea borders or from across the air space.

Broadly speaking, national security would comprise *external security* i.e. safeguarding the realm against any external threat, and *internal security* i.e. maintenance of security within the entire country. National security management would also encompass employment, food, water and shelter security; fiscal and economic security; energy, science, technology and environment security; cyber security, et al. However, in this paper, only issues relating to internal security management are dealt with.

For appreciating the implications of internal security it may be useful to keep in mind the physical parameters of our concerns which, while being generally well known, are invariably forgotten.

India is the seventh largest country in the world with an area of about 33 lakh square kilometres. It has land boundaries of 15,200 kilometres, over 600 island territories, a coastline of over 7,500 kilometres and an EEZ of 25 lakh square kilometres. We have land frontiers and maritime boundaries with half a dozen neighbouring countries. Except some of our hinterland States, e.g. Haryana and Madhya Pradesh, all other States and some of the Union Territories have one or more land or sea borders which require to be guarded. Our borders with Pakistan and China are militarized; those with Pakistan have generated a variety of threats ever since Independence.

While discussing India's security concerns it would be also useful to remember that the country represents an immense cultural and geographical diversity and socio-religious traditions which go back to 5,000 years of recorded history. The well over a billion people of India comprise multi-racial, multi-religious, multi-lingual and multi-cultural societies. India has 22 major languages and over 1,500 dialects. Every major religion in the world is practiced in India. The roots of India's secular and pluralistic traditions are imbedded deep in our ancient history.

India's internal security problems, arising from varied sources, are influenced by a host of factors among which are its past history, geography, colonial legacy, a burgeoning population, sharp social and economic disparities and complex socio-cultural and ethno – religious traditions which interplay freely in our secular democracy. As events in the past decades have shown, regional and global developments have also been impacting significantly on India's security concerns.

Under the Constitution, "Public Order" and "Police" are included in the State List (List II, Seventh

Schedule). Consequently, for maintaining internal security the States have exclusive powers [Article 246(3)] to make laws and take all necessary executive action in respect of both the aforesaid subjects. Thus, in the normal circumstances, the States are responsible for maintaining internal security within their jurisdictions.

As regards the Centre's responsibility, the Constitution prescribes [Article 355] that it shall be the *duty* of the Union to protect the States against *external aggression* and *internal disturbances* and to ensure that the governance of every State is carried on in accordance with the Constitutional powers, failing which Presidential Rule may be imposed [Article 356] in the defaulting State, till constitutional functioning can be restored. The Constitution also provides [Article 352] for the enforcement of Emergency if a situation exists or there is an imminent danger of the security of India being threatened by *war* or an *armed rebellion.*

Looking back, from 1947 onwards, India has faced varied internal security problems. Some of the more serious threats have emanated from Pakistan's unceasing efforts to seize Jammu and Kashmir (J&K) and its sustained strategy to create chaos and disorder to de-stabilize and "break up" India.

India has been facing increasing internal security threats in the past years and, as today, the public order in about 40% of the districts is seriously affected by insurgencies, terrorist activities or political extremism. From around the early 1980s the Pakistan Inter-Services Intelligence (ISI) succeeded in launching terrorist activities in Punjab which suffered enormous human and economic loses for over a decade, till the situation was normalized. Benefiting from the experience gained from its foray into Punjab, Pakistan launched a proxy-war in J&K in end 1989. Over the past nearly two decades now, the continuing wave of terrorism has resulted in the loss of thousands of innocent lives, ruined the economy and, worst of all, shattered the historical secular fabric of Kashmir. In the North East (NE) region, several States have continued to face varying insurgencies, many of which have been accentuated by Pakistan's ISI cross-border networks. The illegal immigration from Bangladesh has led to a demographic upheaval and generated serious communal, political, social and economic tensions and conflicts in several areas of the NE region.

Instigated by the Pakistan ISI, and spurred by domestic factors, there has been a steady increase in the growth of pan-Islamic militant outfits which have been preaching fundamentalism and spreading subversion and violence. Over the years, the reach of these networks has spread to areas in Central and South India.

The Left-Wing extremist groups, specially the People's War Group and the Maoist Communist Centre, have been continuing to enlarge their violent activities which have progressively spread to cover vast tribal areas in several States.

Several organized crime and mafia groups have linked up with Pakistani ISI supported networks and progressively extended their criminal, subversive and communal activities. The narcotics and drug mafia outfits, also involved in the smuggling of weapons, RDX and other materials for causing death and destruction, have been carrying out large scale *hawala* and money laundering operations. The enormous funds generated by the unlawful activities of these groups have been utilized for spreading Islamic fundamentalism, creating violence and executing terrorist activities. Serious threats to internal security have emerged from the Pakistani ISI linking up with organized crime and mafia outfits and exploiting this nexus to organize major violent incidents in various cities of India, virtually at their will.

For the past nearly three decades now, ever since Pakistan's initial venture to foment militancy in Panjab, the Centre has been kept incessantly engaged in dealing with serious internal security problems in the North East region, Panjab, J&K, in the various States affected by the activities of the Naxalite groups and in all the areas affected by violence caused by Islamic fundamentalist groups. The restoration of normalcy in any disturbed area has inescapably involved the application of coercive power which, in other words, means the deployment of the required strength of Central Police Forces and, as required, contingents of the Indian Army.

From the experience gained in combating militancies, insurgencies and terrorist activities in the past years it has become abundantly clear that the responsibility of the disturbed States does not end merely with the deployment of State or Central Police Forces, or even the Army, to restore the disturbed area to normalcy. The Armed Forces of the Union are deployed in aid of the civil authority and, constitutionally, the concerned State remains entirely responsible till normalcy is fully restored.

It is necessary to recognize that the deployment of Central Police Forces, or the Army, for carrying out anti insurgency/terrorist operations may not yield the expected outcome unless the entire State administrative machinery, led by the Chief Minister, devotes continuous organized attention to sensitively dealing with the root causes which contributed to the break down of the public order. Time bound initiatives would need to be implemented to identify and resolve the social and economic problems or the political demands and aspirations of the agitating groups. Simultaneously, the entire State administration apparatus would require to devote close and continuous attention to providing effective governance, systematic attention being paid to resolve the day-to-day difficulties faced by the common man, particularly those which may have emerged on account of the ongoing disturbed situation. Instead of slackening its functioning on account of the prevailing disturbed environment the administrative apparatus shall need to work overtime to ensure that all socio-economic development and poverty alleviation programmes are implemented with high efficiency and honesty and within an urgent time frame.

To timely deal with arising internal security problems, the State Governments need to exercise constant vigilance, particularly in regard to the restoration of complex pending issues, and launch prompt initiatives to open meaningful dialogues with the leaders of the aggrieved groups or communities. Past experience has shown that very high human and economic costs have to be paid if there is a failure to timely deal with issues which can lead to conflicts and violence. The situation is further complicated when a violent agitation, arising from a sensitive demand, is dealt with merely as a law and order problem and the disturbance sought to be quelled with the application of force. In many such cases the agitating elements are supported and incited by adversary external agencies and, when this happens, it is the beginning of much larger problems.

The deep despair and consequent alienation of the disadvantaged communities is heightened by the social, economic and political exploitation to which they are subjected. Feudal systems continue to exist in several parts of India where the much needed land, agrarian and other reforms have still to be carried through. It is indeed most unfortunate that despite the economic disparities and severe disadvantages from which they suffer, the neglected and oppressed segments of society are further subjected to continuing harassments which arise from the various political parties exploiting religious, ethnic and caste factors merely to secure electoral gains.

Besides the gross failures of governance to pursue the avowed welfare-state goals and deliver social and economic justice to the masses, there has also been failure to timely and sensitively respond to the felt needs and aspirations of ethnic and tribal communities, most of whom live in remote, difficult and harsh areas. The demands of such neglected communities have been ignored for prolonged periods and if and when any ameliorative action has been taken it has happened essentially to secure an envisaged electoral gain for the party in power. Such failures of governance have promoted enhanced distrust and alienation among the neglected communities, which no longer have any faith or trust in their State Governments.

The poor and neglected people have many other reasons to be angry and frustrated. For example, the large outlays provided to the States for poverty alleviation schemes are not timely or fully utilized. In many cases, the funds are diverted to other purposes or even embezzled. Such gross failures result in despair, cynicism and deep seated alienation among the poorest segments of society.

Failures of this kind arise from continuing mal-administration, unaccountability and corruption. Despite endless public criticism in the past several decades effective steps have still to be taken to deal with corruption at the highest levels and to enforce efficiency, honesty and accountability in the functioning of governmental and public institutions. The Lok Pal Bill has been awaiting enactment for the past nearly four decades now and the functioning of the Lok Ayukts, established in many States, has still to see even the known crooks being brought to book. Needless to stress, if good governance is to be delivered perhaps the most crucial challenge shall be to restore ethical and moral values to public life in our country.

Corruption erodes and weakens the very foundations of the administrative and legal framework and disrupts the Rule of Law. Thus, internal security cannot be safeguarded unless the governmental apparatus is rid of corruption.

Corruption has the subversive affect of destroying discipline. And indiscipline leads to the unaccountability which has permeated the administrative apparatus and also led to the growth of the threatening politico-bureaucratic-criminal nexus about which a reference was made earlier.

Efforts to reduce corruption do not invariably yield the expected outcome as most of the tainted elements enjoy the patronage and protection of their political masters who have placed them in key positions and continue to use them for the execution of their unlawful behests. As stated earlier, from the perspective of effective internal security management it is a matter for deep concern that even persons of highly questionable integrity, who may have close linkages with criminal and anti-national elements, could continue to hold responsible positions in the administrative system. The potential of such elements subverting national interests from within the system poses a most serious threat to the security of the State.

The continuing determined efforts of adversary external agencies to destabilize India by spreading religious fundamentalism, inciting tensions which lead to conflicts, and perpetrating violence and subversion, have generated challenges which impinge on issues of external security management. In this context it needs being recognized that issues relating to the management of internal and external security have got inextricably interwoven and, as such, the Centre would need to evolve an holistic approach to internal security management, in close coordination with the States. In the security scenario which has evolved over the past three decades and more, it would be impractical, in fact extremely hazardous, to deal sectorally with the management of internal and external security issues.

Internal security cannot be maintained satisfactorily in the country unless the States effectively discharge their constitutional duty of maintaining peace and public order in their realms. The States cannot pass on this crucial responsibility to the Centre, as has been the continuing trend in the past years. A signal failure of the States has been the continued neglect and the political exploitation of their Police organizations. This has most adversely affected the discipline, morale, efficiency, honesty and trustworthiness of the constabulary. It is essential that every State undertakes a time bound programme to enlarge, train and equip its Police to effectively manage the existing and emerging challenges as well as to provide very strong support for the implementation of the Centre's initiatives to maintain public order in the entire country.

A stable security environment cannot be engendered merely by promulgating new laws. In the ultimate analysis every citizen must discharge his duty to uphold and protect the sovereignty, unity and integrity of the country. It is indeed unfortunate that while the vast majority of educated people are concerned only about their Fundamental Rights there are not very many who are even aware of their Fundamental Duties, laid down in Article 51A of the Constitution. Even if action were to be taken to enforce the Fundamental Duties of our citizens it would be unsound to assume that the citizenry of India shall be overnight imbued with patriotic feelings to protect national interests if the environment in which they live and work continues to be vitiated by discrimination, corruption and injustice. The requisite environment can be engendered only if the States perpetually demonstrate and ensure that the laws of the land apply equally to the rich and influential and the highest placed public servants. Side by side, it must be particularly ensured that no injustice is done to the poor and the disadvantaged segments of society as this would result only in promoting distrust and despair among the masses and further eroding their loyalties.

In the aforesaid context it has also to be noted that lawlessness cannot be controlled and internal security maintained unless the entire framework of the criminal justice system functions with speed, fairness and transparent honesty. In 2005, of the over 23 million cases awaiting disposal in the country over 7 million Indian Penal Code crime cases were pending trial. The ever increasing number of criminal cases awaiting investigation and trial and the correspondingly declining conviction rates has generated the growing public perception that crime is a "low-risk, high-profit business".

Besides the enormous logistical inadequacies in the justice delivery system the integrity of the magistracy and the subordinate judiciary is seriously tainted. In the recent past serious allegations of questionable integrity have been raised even against those who man the superior echelons in the judicial structure. Needless to say, the most urgent measures need to be taken to clean up the justice administration apparatus and enlarge and strengthen it to deliver speedy and effective justice. Another cause for serious concern is that while India continues to have hundreds of altogether obsolete and irrelevant laws, most of which were enacted during the colonial period, it does not have an adequately stringent law, applicable all over the country, which can effectively meet the requirements of dealing with terrorist offences, cyber crimes and the fast growing areas of organized criminality which pose a grave threat to national security. India also does not have a Federal Crime Agency which can deal with the serious offences committed by criminal networks whose activities may spread across the States, across the entire country and across various foreign lands. India also needs a comprehensive law for dealing with serious economic offences which, if not timely checked, have the potential of disrupting the national economy. Today, terrorist and criminal networks operate in a border-less world and, needless to say, the grave challenges posed by their activities cannot be tackled if the various concerned law enforcing agencies continue to operate within their respective limited jurisdictions. What is urgently required is an appropriate legal framework and an extremely well considered strategy which is executed in the most effective coordination between the Centre and the States, to deal with each and every aspect of internal security management.

Another matter for serious concern relates to the failure, over the past six decades, to develop a pool of functionaries who have been especially trained to manage the security apparatus at the Centre. Only the Intelligence Bureau has a sub-cadre of deputationist Indian Police Officers who, after acquiring the required experience, comprise the core of the Bureau and can spend their entire careers in this agency. Research and Analysis Wing (R&AW), the agency for external intelligence, has been facing serious personnel problems and recently there have been a number of incidents of grave professional failures. As per the continuing practice, the officers assigned to posts in the Home Ministry, drawn from various services and cadres, are not required to possess any past experience in the field of security management. The situation in the States is much worse. It is a matter for deep concern that despite the serious challenges to national security faced by India it has still not been recognized that security management cannot any longer be entrusted to persons who have no training or experience in this field. It is also no longer viable to entrust the work of Intelligence agencies only to officers of one particular service. It is necessary that very high priority is accorded for raising a pool of adequately trained and trusted officers who can be assigned to posts in the Intelligence Agencies and the Departments and Ministries which are responsible for managing internal and external security.

In the aforesaid context, particularly keeping in view that even key posts in the Home and Defence Ministries and their related agencies are, on many occasions, assigned to functionaries who have no prior experience of working in the security administration arena, I had proposed (in the Task Force Report on Internal Security, September 2000) that Government may consider the establishment of a dedicated Security Administration Cadre which is comprised by officers selected from among volunteers from the Civil and Police Services, Defence Services, Defence Science Research Organisation, Science and Technology, Information and Communication Technology, Broadcasting and Media and other relevant areas.. It was envisaged that such a pool of officers, in various age groups, would be properly trained and assigned to posts in the security management machinery. After critically assessing their performance, the selected officers could be allowed, as is done in the Intelligence Bureau, to enjoy open-ended tenures so that, over time, they acquire the much needed professional expertise which is sorely lacking in the existing set-up. It was projected that, once such a dedicated cadre gets adequately established, Government would be able to select the most suitable officers, from within this pool of officers, to man posts at given levels in the Union Home Ministry, the Intelligence Agencies, National Security Council Secretariat, Ministry of Defence and other security management related areas. Side by side, the States could be provided required support, particularly well designed training facilities, to raise similar cadres. The Government had approved the aforesaid approach in early 2001. Nearly seven years have since elapsed. It is apparent that Government does not intend to terminate the continuing practice of even the top most posts in the security apparatus being filled by persons who have no past experience in security management.

In conclusion, considering the extremely worrying scale and pattern of the internal security failures in the recent past, the Centre shall need to significantly enlarge the capacity of its Intelligence agencies, and to also ensure that the States take similar action, so that a constant vigil can be effectively kept across the length and breadth of the country. The Centre would also need to most vigorously pursue the States to ensure that the functioning of their Police forces is completely depoliticised and their autonomous working entrusted to the best available officers, known for their integrity and professionalism. The speediest possible measures must also be taken to revive the criminal justice system and restore its credibility. It is equally important that the State Chief Ministers urgently bring themselves around to fully understanding the altogether grave consequences if they fail to maintain peace and order within their jurisdictions or dither in providing total support and coordination to the Centre's initiatives to make the management of internal security more effective.

Finally, effective enforcement of the Rule of Law is crucial to the maintenance of national security and delivery of good governance. Any threat to the constitutional values shall pose a threat to the very foundations of the polity and society and, consequently, to the very unity and integrity of India.

COUNTRY STUDIES

AFGHANISTAN

Afghanistan recognizes its independence day as 19 August, the date in 1919 when the country became fully independent of British rule. The background of the Afghan flag is three equal vertical sections of black, red, and green from left to right. In the centre of the flag in yellow is the national coat of arms, which portrays a mosque with a banner and a sheaf of wheat on either side. In the upper-middle part of the insignia are the lines "There is no God but Allah and Muhammad is his prophet." and "Allah is Great." together with a rising sun. The word "Afghanistan" and the year 1298 (the Muslim calendar equivalent of the year of independence, 1919) are located in the lower part of the insignia.

History

Archaeological evidence indicates that urban civilization began in the region between 3000 and 2000 B.C. Between 330 and 327 B.C., Alexander the Great defeated the emperor Darius III and subdued local resistance in the territory that is now Afghanistan. Alexander's successors, the Seleucids, continued to infuse the region with Greek cultural influence. Thereafter, the Mauryan Empire of India gained control of southern Afghanistan, bringing with it Buddhism. In the mid-third century B.C., nomadic Kushans established an empire that became a cultural and commercial centre. From the end of the Kushan Empire in the third century A.D. until the seventh century, the region was fragmented and under the general protection of the Iranian Sassanian Empire.

After defeating the Sassanians at the Battle of Qadisiya in 637, Arab Muslims began a process of conquering the Afghan tribes and introducing Islam. The Ghaznavid Dynasty became the first great Islamic dynasty to rule in Afghanistan. In 1220 all of Central Asia fell to the Mongol forces of Genghis Khan. Afghanistan remained fragmented until the 1380s, when Timur consolidated and expanded the existing Mongol Empire. Timur's descendants ruled Afghanistan until the early sixteenth century.

In 1504 the region came under a new empire, the Mughals of India, who for the next two centuries contested Afghan territory with the Iranian Safavi Dynasty. With the death of the great Safavi leader Nadir Shah in 1747, indigenous Pashtuns, who became known as the Durrani, began a period of nominal rule in Afghanistan that lasted until 1978. The first Durrani ruler, Ahmad Shah, known as the founder of the Afghan nation, united the Pashtun tribes and by 1760 built an empire extending to Delhi. The empire fragmented after Ahmad Shah's death in 1772.

In 1826 Dost Mohammad, the leader of the Pashtun Muhammadzai tribe, restored order. Dost Mohammad ruled at the beginning of the Great Game, a century-long contest for domination of Central Asia and Afghanistan between Russia, which was expanding to the south, and Britain, which was intent on protecting India. During this period, Afghan rulers were able to maintain virtual independence, although some compromises were necessary. In the First Anglo-Afghan War (1839–42), the British deposed Dost Mohammad, but they abandoned their Afghan garrisons in 1842. In the following decades, Russian forces approached the northern border of Afghanistan. In 1878 the British invaded and held most of Afghanistan in the Second Anglo-Afghan War. In 1880 Abdur Rahman, a Durrani, began a 21-year reign that saw the balancing of British and Russian interests, the consolidation of the Afghan tribes, and the reorganization of civil administration into what is considered the modern Afghan state. During this period, the British secured the Durand Line (1893), dividing Afghanistan from British colonial territory to the southeast and sowing the seeds of future tensions over the division of the Pashtun tribes. Abdur Rahman's son Habibullah (ruled 1901–19) continued his father's administrative reforms and maintained Afghanistan's neutrality in World War I.

In 1919 Afghanistan signed the Treaty of Rawalpindi, which ended the Third Anglo-Afghan War and marks Afghanistan's official date of independence. In the inter-war period, Afghanistan again was a balancing point between two world powers; Habibullah's son Amanullah (ruled 1919–29) skillfully manipulated the new British-Soviet rivalry and established relations with major countries. Amanullah introduced his country's first constitution in 1923. However, resistance to his domestic reform program forced his abdication in 1929. In 1933 Amanullah's nephew Mohammad Zahir Shah, the last king of Afghanistan, began a 40-year reign.

After World War II, in which Afghanistan remained neutral, the long-standing division of the Pashtun tribes caused tension with Pakistan, founded on the other side of the Durand Line in 1947. In response, Afghanistan shifted its foreign policy toward the Soviet Union. The prime ministership of the king's cousin Mohammad Daoud (1953–63) was cautiously reformist, while strengthening ties with the Soviet Union. However, in 1963 Zahir Shah dismissed Daoud because his anti-Pakistani policy had damaged Afghanistan's economy. A new constitution, ratified in 1964, liberalized somewhat the constitutional monarchy. In the ensuing decade economic and political conditions worsened. In 1973 Daoud overthrew the king and established a republic. When economic conditions did not improve and Daoud lost most of his political support, communist factions overthrew him in 1978.

In 1979 the threat of tribal insurgency against the communist government triggered an invasion by 80,000 Soviet troops, who then endured a very effective decade-long guerrilla war. Between 1979 and 1989, two Soviet-sponsored regimes failed to defeat the loose federation of mujahideen guerrillas that opposed the occupation. In 1988 the Soviet Union agreed to create a neutral Afghan state, and the last Soviet troops left Afghanistan in 1989. The agreement ended a war that killed thousands, devastated industry and agriculture, and created 5 to 6 million refugees.

The 1988 agreement did not settle differences between the government and the mujahideen, and in 1992 Afghanistan descended into a civil war that further ravaged the economy. Among the leaders of the warring factions were Ahmad Shah Massoud, an ethnic Tajik; Gulbuddin Hekmatyar, a Pashtun; and Abdul Rashid Dostum, an Uzbek. Despite several temporary alliances, struggles among the armed groups continued until one Islamic fundamentalist group, the Taliban, gained control of most of the country in 1996. The Taliban used an extremist interpretation of Islam to assert repressive control of society. The economy remained in ruins, and most government services ceased. The Taliban granted the al Qaeda the right to use Afghanistan as a base. al Qaeda is responsible for the terrorist attacks on the United States on 11 September 2001. Subsequently, the Taliban rejected international pressure to surrender al Qaeda leader Osama bin Laden. When the United States and allies attacked Afghanistan in the fall of 2001, the Taliban government collapsed, but Taliban and al Qaeda leaders escaped. A United States-led International Security Assistance Force began an occupation that is still in place.

In December 2001, Afghan leaders in exile signed the Bonn Agreement, forming an interim government, the Afghan Interim Administration, under the leadership of the Pashtun moderate Hamid Karzai. In 2002 Karzai was selected president of the Transitional Islamic State of Afghanistan, whose ruling council included disparate leaders of the anti-Taliban Northern Alliance. A new constitution, written by a specially convened Loya Jirga, or constituent assembly of regional leaders, was ratified in early 2004. In October 2004, an overwhelming popular vote elected Karzai president of the Islamic Republic of Afghanistan.

Regional warlords and large areas of Afghanistan remain beyond the control of the Karzai government. Despite substantial international aid, the Afghan government, which included representatives from many factions, is unable to address numerous social and economic problems. The parliamentary elections of September 2005 gave regional warlords substantial power in both houses of the National Assembly, further jeopardizing Karzai's ability to unite the country. The Bonn Agreement lapsed after the 2005 elections. The agreement's successor, the Afghanistan Compact, went into effect in January 2006 to set forth goals for international assistance in economic development, security, protection of human rights, and the fight against corruption and drug trafficking through 2010. In the meantime, the Taliban has intensified terrorist activities in areas beyond government control.

Geography

Afghanistan is landlocked country with a size of approximately 647,500 square kilometres, is located in Central Asia, north and west of Pakistan, east of Iran, and south of Turkmenistan, Uzbekistan, and Tajikistan. The narrow Wakhan Corridor extends from northeastern-most Afghanistan to meet with China. Afghanistan has borders with China (76 kilometres), Iran (936 kilometres), Pakistan (2,430 kilometres), Tajikistan (1,206 kilometres), Turkmenistan (744 kilometres) and Uzbekistan (137 kilometres). Afghanistan has a boundary dispute with Pakistan over the Durand Line, where there are ongoing incursions, smuggling, and terrorist movement.

The terrain of Afghanistan is dominated by rugged mountain ranges, which generally run from the northeast to the southwest. Mountains occupy all but the north-central and southwestern regions of the country, which are dominated by plains. Nearly half the country has an elevation of 2,000 metres or more, and the highest peaks in the northeastern Hindu Kush range exceed 7,000 metres. Historically, mountain passes along the northeastern border with present-day Pakistan have been of great strategic importance. Significant parts of the southwestern plains region are desert.

Afghanistan's main rivers are the Amu Darya (800 kilometres), the Harirud (850 kilometres, the Helmand (1,000 kilometres) and the Kabul (460 kilometres). The chief tributaries to the Amu Darya, which forms much of the country's northern border, are the Koshk and the Qonduz. The climate generally is of the arid or semi-arid steppe type, featuring cold winters and dry, hot summers. The mountains of the northeast have sub-arctic winter conditions. Farther south, monsoon effects moderate the climate near the Pakistan border and increase rainfall as far inland as central Afghanistan. The highest precipitation occurs in the Kabul region of the northeast. The highest temperatures and lowest precipitation are in the southwestern plains region, where summer temperatures reach 49° C. Low temperatures in the northeastern mountains range from –15° C in winter to 0° C in summer. The climate of the north-central Turkistan Plain is increasingly arid closest to the northern borders with Turkmenistan, Uzbekistan, and Tajikistan.

Agricultural resources are primarily grazing land; fertile crop-growing land is concentrated in Kondoz Province in the north and Helmand Province in the south. Afghanistan is known to have major deposits of chrome, coal, copper, iron, and salt, as well as lesser amounts of a wide variety of minerals including gold, silver, and uranium. Natural gas is the most abundant hydrocarbon resource. Substantial oil deposits are recognized but not yet quantified. Water for all purposes is in critically short supply. Some 12.1% of Afghanistan's land is classified as arable; however, in the early 2000s a four-year drought cut that figure in half. Only 0.2% of the total is planted to permanent crops.

Although little studied before recent times, the environment of Afghanistan is assumed to have been spared large-scale disturbances until the Soviet invasion of 1979. Since that time, however, numerous events have caused severe damage. Afghanistan, which has no appreciable bodies of water, suffers from a limited freshwater supply that makes potable water unavailable to more than half the population. In recent years, groundwater quality has deteriorated because of agricultural and industrial runoff, and water quantity has been diminished by large-scale land clearing and desertification. Because of insufficient water treatment, the incidence of water-borne diseases is very high. Widespread overgrazing, soil erosion, salinization, and water logging have reduced agricultural productivity. Although Afghanistan has little industry, particulate pollutants from the Aral Sea and industrial complexes in Iran, Turkmenistan, and Uzbekistan contaminate the atmosphere in northern Afghanistan. Chemical use and physical destruction in recent military conflicts have damaged the environment, and landmines and unexploded shells are residual hazards endangering an estimated 4 million Afghanis in 32 provinces.

Society

Population. Assessment has been difficult because many people have not had fixed residences. In 2006 the estimated population was 31.1 million. The population growth rate was 2.7% per year. The population is approximately 75% rural; in 2004 the six most populous cities accounted for less than 10% of the population. In 2006 net out-migration was 0.4 per 1,000 population. After heavy out-migration and internal displacement in the 1980s and 1990s, an estimated 2.5 million Afghans returned to Afghanistan in 2003–4 before the numbers began to decrease. In 2005 about 1.2 million Afghans were living in Pakistan and Iran, the main recipient countries for Afghan refugees

Demography. In 2006 some 44.6% of the population was younger than 15 years of age and 2.4% was older than 64. The estimated birthrate was 46.6 per 1,000 population, and the estimated death rate was 20.3 per 1,000 population. The infant mortality rate was 160 deaths per 1,000 live births. Life expectancy was 43.1 years for males and 43.5 years for females. The fertility rate was 6.7 children born per woman.

Ethnic Groups. The main ethnic groups are Pashtun (42%), Tajik (27%), Hazara (9%) Uzbek (9%) Aimak—a Persian-speaking nomadic group (4%), Turkmen (3%) and Baloch (2%). The largest remaining nomadic group is the Kuchis, a Pashtun group whose population has dwindled to about 1.5 million since 1979. The Pashtuns are the major ethnic group in the south and the east, the Tajiks in the northeast. The predominant groups in north-central Afghanistan are the Hazaras, Tajiks, and Uzbeks.

Languages. More than 30 languages are spoken in Afghanistan. The official languages are Dari (Afghan Persian) and Pashtu. Dari is spoken by 50% of the population, and Pashtu is spoken as a first language by 35%. Turkic languages (primarily Turkmen and Uzbek) are spoken by 11% of the population. Of the languages spoken by smaller segments of the population, the most important are Balochi and Pashai. Many Afghans speak more than one language; Dari is the most common second language.

Religion. Virtually the entire population is Muslim. Between 80 and 85% of Muslims are Sunni and 15 to 19% Shia. The minority Shia are economically disadvantaged and frequently subjected to discrimination. Small numbers of Hindus and Sikhs live in urban centers.

Education and Literacy. Despite substantial improvements during the reign of Mohammad Zahir Shah (ruled 1933–73), in 1979 some 90% of Afghanistan's population remained illiterate. Beginning with the Soviet invasion of 1979, successive wars virtually destroyed the education system. Most teachers fled the country during the Soviet occupation and the subsequent civil war. By 1996 only about 650 schools were functioning. In 1996 the Taliban regime banned education for females, and the madrassa (mosque school) became the main source of primary and secondary education. After the overthrow of the Taliban in 2001, the interim government received substantial international aid to restore the education system. In 2003 some 7,000 schools were operating in 20 of the 34 provinces, and 27,000 teachers were teaching 4.2 million children (including 1.2 million girls). Of that number, about 3.9 million were in primary schools. In 2004 and 2005, informal community education programs began in nine provinces. When Kabul University reopened in 2002, some 24,000 students, male and female, enrolled. In the early 2000s, the rehabilitation of five other universities progressed very slowly. Since the end of the dogmatic Taliban era in 2001, public school curricula have included religious subjects, but detailed instruction is left to religious teachers. In 2003 an estimated 57% of men and 86% of women were illiterate, and the lack of skilled and educated workers was a major economic disadvantage.

Health. Beginning in 1979, military conflict destroyed Afghanistan's health system. Most medical professionals left the country in the 1980s and 1990s, and all medical training programmes ceased. In 2004 Afghanistan had one medical facility for every 27,000 people, and some centres were responsible for as many as 300,000 people. In 2004 international organizations provided a large share of medical care. An estimated one-quarter of the population had no access to health care. In 2003 there were 11 physicians and 18 nurses per 100,000 population, and the per capita health expenditure was US$28. At the same time, the physical and psychological effects of war have substantially increased the need for medical care. Infant, child, and maternal mortality rates are among the highest in the world. In rural areas, one in five children dies before reaching age five. Because of poor sanitation and insufficient potable water supply, infectious and parasitic diseases such as malaria and diarrhea are very common. Malnutrition and poor nutrition also are pervasive. The drought of 1999–2002 exacerbated these conditions. An estimated 800,000 Afghans are disabled. In 2006 the United Nations Development Programme estimated that an HIV/acquired immune deficiency syndrome (AIDS) epidemic could occur in Afghanistan because of the high incidence of intravenous drug use, unsafe blood transfusion procedures, and large numbers of refugees, poor health facilities, and illiteracy. Inspite of large-scale international assistance, the World Health Organization does not expect Afghanistan's health indicators to improve substantially for at least a decade.

Welfare. Largely because of protracted military conflict, Afghanistan in 2004 had the highest proportion of widows and orphans in the world. Large numbers of disabled individuals and former members of regional militias also lack a means of support. In 2004 the World Bank estimated that 20% of families lacked a secure food supply and another 50 to 60% were on the verge of severe poverty. The government provides very little welfare protection. Most of the welfare activity in the country has been provided by international nongovernmental organizations (NGOs), such as the Afghan Health and Development Services, Afghan Women's Education Center, and Humanitarian Assistance for the Women and Children of Afghanistan, and by United Nations organizations. Several NGOs also work with Afghan refugees in other countries, especially Pakistan.

Economy

Overview. Economic statistics for Afghanistan traditionally are inexact. Afghanistan's economy, which always has been heavily agricultural and one of the poorest in the world, was shattered by wars in the past two decades. Industry, much of which depended on agricultural output, suffered as well. Some small-scale trade in urban centers and agriculture in some regions has revived. However, damage to the infrastructure will take much longer to repair. The 2004 International Conference on Afghanistan pledged US$8.3 billion for economic infrastructure reconstruction during the following three years. At the 2006 London Conference on Afghanistan, international donors pledged US$10.4 billion to the Afghanistan National Development Strategy, which includes economic and social components, during the ensuing five years. In 2006 some 22 provincial reconstruction teams led by Western civilian and military personnel were working to restore economic infrastructure and security in Afghanistan. A major economic problem is replacing the income generated by opium production, which in 2005 yielded an estimated 52% of the country's gross domestic product (GDP). Smuggling, particularly across the Pakistan border, is an important part of the "black economy." In 2005, a significant regional step was the establishment of an economic coordination council by the governors of four provinces in resource-rich and strategically vital eastern Afghanistan.

Gross Domestic Product. Excluding illegal poppy production, Afghanistan's GDP is estimated at US$5.22 billion or US$232 per capita. Agriculture contributes an estimated 38% to the GDP, services 38%, and industry and mining 24%. Following the economic standstill of the late 1990s, GDP growth rates in the early 2000s have been very high: 28.6% in FY 2002– 3, 16% in FY 2003–4, and 8% in FY 2004–5. However, the starting points upon which such figures are based were very low.

Government Budget. In the early 2000s, Afghanistan's ratio of revenue to gross domestic product, 4%, was one of the lowest in the world, and domestic revenues are not expected to match the government's operating costs. For FY 2004–5 the government's operational budget was US$561 million, and the revenue for that budget period was US$269 million. Under the pro-Soviet regimes of the 1980s, inflation was high but limited by government controls. Inflation reached 150% per year during the civil war of the early 1990s, and it is believed to have remained high under the Taliban. After the currency reform of 2002, inflation averaged about 10% per year for the first two years, but it rose to 16.3% in 2005.

Agriculture. It is traditionally the foundation of Afghanistan's economy, employing as much as 80% of the workforce and contributing at least half of the GDP. Because of the poor quality of most agricultural land, subsistence agriculture predominates. Although many displaced Afghan farmers have returned to their land, land mines and the destruction of irrigation systems has made much agricultural land unusable. Livestock, a vital part of the agricultural economy, was similarly affected as grazing land disappeared. The drought of 1999–2002 and an infestation of locusts devastated the rural population and further reduced agricultural output. The nomadic Kuchis were forced to find sedentary occupations. Because of limited water supplies, half of Afghanistan's arable land is uncultivated. Beginning in 2003, agricultural output increased because of international aid and increased rainfall, except in the south where the drought continued into 2004. The area under cultivation rose significantly in 2004: it decreased by 21% in 2005, but productivity increased. The main legal crops are wheat, vegetables, grapes, rice, barley, corn, fruits, and potatoes. The main types of livestock are cattle, sheep, and goats. The internationally supported programme to replace poppies with legal crops showed some progress in 2005. Between 2004 and 2005 the area under poppy cultivation decreased by 21%, but production declined by only 2.4%. By contrast, between 2003 and 2004 the area under poppy cultivation had tripled, and the estimated value of the poppy crop more than doubled as output reached 4,200 tons. As cultivation of poppies was discouraged, crop diversification increased somewhat, although poor transportation and irrigation infrastructure restricted the expansion of some perishable crops.

Forestry. Most of Afghanistan's mountains are barren rather than forested. In the mid-1990s, an estimated 2.9% of the land was forested, but war, illegal exploitation, and the need for firewood have removed an estimated 50% of that resource. There is no programme of forest preservation or commercial exploitation. In 2003 an estimated 3,150 tons of timber products were harvested, about half for fuel.

Mining and Minerals. Most of Afghanistan's mineral resources, which are believed to be substantial, remain unexploited. Among resources identified are bauxite, emeralds, gold, iron, lead, magnesium, mercury, silver, sulphur, tin, uranium, and zinc. Because of transportation problems and insufficient investment, however, only barites, chromium, coal, copper, natural gas, and salt have been extracted commercially. The largest coal mining operation is at Karkar Dodkash in north-central Afghanistan.

Industry and Manufacturing. Before the wars of the late 20th century, industry was based on the processing of local agricultural products, including textiles, sugar, and chemical fertilizers made from natural gas or coal. The main manufacturing centre was the Kabul region. In 2004 all of Afghanistan's industrial sector had stopped producing or was producing at a substantially reduced rate. The reasons for this reduction in productivity are war damage, shortages of raw materials and spare parts, and the postwar priority of rebuilding overall infrastructure before industry. In the early 2000s, foreign investment in the industrial sector focused on small and medium-sized enterprises, predominantly in telecommunications. Revival projects have concentrated on agricultural processing and carpet enterprises. Some small plants in Herat, Kabul, and Mazar-e Sharif produce textiles, leather goods, and processed foods. Because of war damage, the construction sector expanded rapidly in the early 2000s and was seen as an important economic driver for the ensuing decade. However, that sector of the economy suffers from substantial corruption.

Energy. War damage depleted Afghanistan's energy generation infrastructure, particularly generators and power lines. In 2004 energy shortages were a critical obstacle in resuming economic activity, but in 2005 the electricity supply improved significantly under Minister of Water and Energy Ismail Khan. Given adequate extraction and distribution infrastructure, Afghanistan's domestic coal, natural gas, and oil resources can meet its energy needs, and the Kunar River provides untapped hydroelectric potential. In 2002 Turkmenistan signed an agreement to provide natural gas and electric power to Afghanistan, and Tajikistan and Uzbekistan also send power to some northern regions. In 2004 an international consortium completed an evaluation of Afghanistan's energy potential, focusing on natural gas and recommending future energy policy. Some natural gas wells and 31 oil wells that were active during the Soviet occupation have remained capped since that era. In 2004 natural gas reserves were estimated at 5 trillion cubic feet. Oil reserves were estimated at 95 million barrels and coal reserves at 73 million tons. Although Afghanistan is a natural pipeline route between Central Asian natural gas fields and the Arabian Sea and the often-discussed Trans-Afghan Pipeline clearly would be an economic boon, security issues have prevented construction. Afghanistan's domestic pipelines connect gas fields only with local consumers.

Services. Afghanistan's banking system, which collapsed during the civil war of the early 1990s, was limited to financial transactions supporting retail commerce. With the collapse, moneychangers became the main source of financing, and opium and wheat became the primary forms of capital for the agricultural population. Elimination of poppy cultivation means destitution for farmers relying on opium for credit. Since 2002 the government has encouraged recovery of a formal banking system. A set of commercial banking laws was passed in 2003, and banks from Britain, India, and Pakistan have opened branches in Kabul. In mid-2004 the Afghanistan International Bank (AIB) began operating with the backing of the Asian Development Bank and 75% ownership by Afghan businessmen and started making corporate loans. Smuggling and other illegal economic activity that were pervasive during the war periods left a very strong residual black-market economy specializing in moving goods illegally into Pakistan and moving illegal drugs northward into Central Asia and ultimately Russia and Western Europe. Opium production supporting the latter activity remains very high in 2005 (accounting for between 75 and 87% of the world supply), despite government efforts to reduce it. Because security conditions in Afghanistan have remained inadequate, especially outside Kabul, the formerly prosperous tourism industry has not revived, despite a government program to establish 20 tourist sites by 2010. Meanwhile, dangerous conditions have spurred the growth of private security services that protect government officials and business people.

Labour. Because of the very large black-market economy, statistics on the labour force are incomplete. In 2004 the labour force in the legitimate economy was estimated at 15 million. Conflict has seriously depleted the supply of skilled labour. About 80% of the workforce is in agriculture, 10% in industry, and 10% in services. Although accurate statistics on unemployment generally have not been available, 2005 estimates were 50%. No minimum wage has been set. Existing labour laws are little observed, and unions have not played a role in protecting workers' rights.

Foreign Economic Relations. In 2004 the United States signed a bilateral Trade and Investment Framework Agreement, which will increase trade levels with Afghanistan. The European Union also gives Afghan products preferential trade status. Trade with Iran has increased substantially. Iran has given Afghanistan the use of its Arabian Sea port at Chabahar under favorable conditions, despite U.S. objections. In 2003 Afghanistan, Iran, and Uzbekistan established a trans-Afghan trade corridor linking Uzbekistan with Chabahar and Bandar-e-Abbas. Uzbekistan's border procedures have slowed commerce along the route, however. Trade with Pakistan is complicated by a high level of smuggling across the border; in 2004 an estimated 80% of goods entering Afghanistan from Pakistan were subsequently smuggled back into Pakistan. In 2002 the two countries revived their Joint Economic Commission, which had been moribund for 10 years, in order to improve commercial relations. The main purchasers of Afghanistan's exports in order of volume are Pakistan, India, the United States, and Germany. The main suppliers of Afghanistan's imports in order of volume are Pakistan, the United States, India, Germany, Turkmenistan, Kenya, the Republic of Korea (South Korea), and Russia. Aside from opium, the main export commodities are fruits and nuts, carpets, wool, cotton, hides and pelts, and precious and semi-precious gems. The main imports are capital goods, food, textiles, and petroleum products. In the fiscal year ending in March 2005, Afghanistan's exports (including re-exports) were worth US$1.7 billion, and its imports were valued at US$3.9 billion, creating an unfavorable trade balance of US$2.2 billion.

External Debt. In 2004 Afghanistan had US$8 billion in bilateral debt, owed mainly to Russia. Some US$500 million also was owed to multilateral development banks. Both bilateral and multilateral debt figures increased significantly in 2005.

Foreign Investment. To encourage foreign investment, in 2002 the government began allowing 100% foreign ownership of Afghan enterprises, offering substantial tax benefits and unlimited transfer of assets out of the country. The Afghanistan Investment Support Agency was established in 2003 to centralize foreign investment activities. However, Afghanistan's highly corrupt and inefficient bureaucracy has limited investment, and there is no legal system for adjudication of commercial disputes. In addition, the liberalized policy does not apply to investment in pipeline construction, telecommunications infrastructure, the fuels and minerals industries, or other heavy industry where state-owned enterprises predominate. Likely future investment sectors are telecommunications, energy, mining, agricultural equipment, and health care systems. In 2004 foreign direct investment totaled an estimated US$351 million. The largest investors are Pakistan, Iran, China, the United Arab Emirates, Central Asian countries, members of the European Union, and the United States.

Infrastructure

Overview. Afghanistan's transportation system, which prior to 1979 was rudimentary except for a modern system of main roads, suffered severe damage during the ensuing two decades. In the early 2000s, the road system, which provided the only transport in most parts of the country, has been an urgent reconstruction project. Some 79% of public transport expenditures for the period 2005–11 were earmarked for road improvement. No rail system exists. After suffering damage to most airports during the wars, the air transport system has been reviving in the early 2000s. Because landlocked Afghanistan has been very dependent on routes through Pakistan, with which relations have been tense, a top priority is diversifying Afghanistan's access to seaports and to new markets in India by making new bilateral transportation agreements.

Roads. The main internal road system that was built in the 1960s included about 2,000 kilometres of roads. In 2003 Afghanistan had 8,200 kilometres of paved roads and 26,600 kilometres of unpaved roads. Heavily damaged in the 1980s and 1990s, the main arteries connect the cities of Ghazni, Herat, Kabul, and Kandahar with roads crossing the Pakistan border. Critical commercial and military roadways through the Salang and Tang-e-Gharu mountain passes, respectively north and east of Kabul, were badly damaged during the Soviet occupation and ensuing conflicts. A new highway connects Kabul with Kandahar, and in 2004 work began on a connector between Kandahar and Herat. Germany is financing a road connecting Jalalabad with the Pakistan border. India, Iran, and Pakistan are constructing roads connecting Afghanistan with their respective national road systems. Provincial roads, which also received heavy damage during conflicts of recent decades, generally have not been repaired since the end of hostilities. In 2003 only about 28,000 vehicles were licensed privately; the government's goal was to increase that number to more than 100,000 by 2010. In 2002 some 33,500 taxicabs were in operation.

Railroads. Afghanistan has no functioning railroads. For a variety of geopolitical and practical reasons, numerous plans for a trans-Afghan line failed to materialize in the 19th and 20th centuries. Only five short domestic lines were built, including one line passing across the Friendship Bridge into Uzbekistan. Otherwise, lines built toward Afghanistan by surrounding countries stopped at the border. A new line to link the major cities of Afghanistan with the Iranian port of Bandar-e Abbas and with Pakistan is under construction. Road building is a much higher priority of infrastructure restoration than is railroad building. In 2006 plans called for five new freight dispatch stations along the borders to link domestic roads with railroad lines from neighboring countries.

Ports and Inland Waterways. Afghanistan is landlocked; the main ports along its chief waterway, the Amu Darya River, are Kheyrabad and Shir Khan. The most important inland waterway is the Amu Darya River, whose 800 kilometres along Afghanistan's border can accommodate vessels up to 500 deadweight tons.

Civil Aviation and Airports. Some 46 airports are in operation; 10 have paved runways, but only three runways longer than 3,000 metres. Nine heliports also are in operation. In 2005 Kabul International Airport, the only destination for international flights into Afghanistan, was renovated. Connections to Kabul were made via Delhi, India; Islamabad, Pakistan; and Baku, Azerbaijan. Airports at Herat, Jalalabad, and Mazar-e Sharif also were renovated. The military conflicts destroyed many of the aircraft of the national line, Ariana, and damaged most of the civilian airports. After a series of crashes in 1998–99, Ariana lost its international flight status; the airline regained approval for international flights in 2002. In 2004 Ariana began regular flights to Delhi, Dubai, Frankfurt, Islamabad, Istanbul, and Moscow. In 2003 the first private airline, Kam Air, began flights. However, both Ariana and Kam are rated as having poor safety regulations. Afghanistan has received substantial foreign assistance; India has trained flight staff and contributed three Airbuses.

Pipelines. Afghanistan has 387 kilometres of natural gas pipelines.

Telecommunications. Afghanistan has an estimated 80,000 main telephone lines and 800,000 cellular phones. In 2002–3 two foreign-owned mobile telephone companies began operations, bringing investment commitments of US$180 million and heralding a significant improvement in national telecommunications. Both cellular networks were unreliable in their first years of operation. In the early 2000s, expansion occurred almost entirely in mobile phones. The number of Afghans with Internet access increased rapidly between 2000 and 2005, multiplying from an estimated 1,000 to 25,000. Public Internet facilities are available in Herat, Kabul, Kandahar, and Mazar-e Sharif. However, Internet cafés in Kabul are increasingly targeted by terrorist attacks.

Government and Politics

Overview. The adoption of a new constitution in January 2004 and the election of Hamid Karzai as president in October 2004 were considered major advances in Afghanistan's fragmented political life. However, day-to-day control of the provinces proved difficult both before and after the election, and substantial regional power centres remain. After the first National Assembly was seated in December 2005, the balance between the executive and legislative branches remained uncertain, and Karzai was obliged to name key regional warlords to his new cabinet in 2006. The role of Islamic precepts in governance remains extremely controversial particularly in the judicial branch. In March 2006, the United Nations renewed for one year the mandate of its Assistance Mission in Afghanistan (UNAMA), designed to provide political and strategic guidance.

Executive Branch. The president and two vice presidents are elected as a ticket by popular vote to five-year terms. The first such election under the 2004 constitution occurred in October 2004. President Hamid Karzai is both chief of state and head of government. The president appoints ministers, subject to the approval of the Wolesi Jirga (People's Council), the lower house of the National Assembly. The government includes 25 ministries. Appointments to these ministries have been distributed among influential regional and military groups. The National Defense Commission, headed by Karzai, is a six-member advisory board that includes leaders of the main regional groups.

Legislative Branch. The constitution calls for a bicameral legislature, the National Assembly. Members of the lower house, the 249-member Wolesi Jirga (People's Council), are elected directly for five-year terms. The Wolesi Jirga, whose geographical distribution is determined by population, has 249 seats. Some 68 seats are designated for women and 10 for the Kuchis. The 102 members of the upper house, the Meshrano Jirga (House of Elders), are appointed by provincial councils (one member for each of 34 provinces, serving four-year terms); by district councils (accounting for another 34 members, each serving three-year terms); and the president. The constitution specifies that the 34 presidential appointees, who serve five-year terms, be one half women and include two representatives of the Kuchis and two representatives of the disabled. Members of the Meshrano Jirga are appointed after the elections for the Wolesi Jirga. The government can convene a Loya Jirga (Constituent Assembly) to decide urgent matters of independence, national sovereignty, and territorial integrity. Such an assembly, which can amend the constitution and bring charges against the president, must include members of the National Assembly and chairpersons of the provincial and district councils. A 1,650-member Loya Jirga chose the transitional government that took office in 2002, and a second one formulated the 2004 constitution.

Judicial Branch. Afghanistan's judicial branch deteriorated during the Soviet occupation, and justice was administered by strict Islamic law during the Taliban era (1996–2001). To replace the ad hoc system in place under the transitional government, the constitution of 2004 stipulated that the Supreme Court include nine justices appointed by the president, with approval of the Wolesa Jirga, for 10-year terms. These justices have particular importance because they are responsible for managing the personnel, budgets, and policy decisions of the entire national, regional, and local court system. At the urging of his Western partners in the 2006 Afghanistan Compact, President Karzai replaced several Supreme Court justices in 2006. However, the head of the court, responsible for appointing judges of the other national courts, is the ultraconservative Fazel Hadi Shinwari, a staunch advocate of Islamic law. Below the Supreme Court are high and appeals courts. A National Security Court handles cases of terrorism and other threats to national security.

Administrative Divisions. The major sub-national administrative division is the province (*velayat*), numbering 34 in 2006. Two new provinces were added in 2004. Each province has between five and 15 districts; and some 361 districts are in existence. Each province has one designated provincial municipality;

some but not all provinces also have a single rural municipality. The municipalities fall under the direct jurisdiction of the Ministry of Interior.

Provincial and Local Government. According to the constitution, provinces, districts, and villages are governed by directly elected councils. The first elections for those councils, for 420 seats, were held concurrently with the national parliamentary elections of September 2005. The chief executive at the province level is the governor, who is appointed by the president. As is the case with the national cabinet, the president has distributed governorships among influential regional and military groups. Province and district administrations have the same basic structure as the national government. According to the constitution, the central government, which theoretically stands at the centre of a highly centralized system, delegates authority to the sub-national jurisdictions in (unspecified) matters where local or regional action is more efficient. In actuality, the structure and government of the provinces have varied greatly; in most cases, provincial governance is based on the financial and military strength of local leaders as well as personal and tribal loyalties.

Judicial and Legal System. Although every province has a lower and a higher court, judicial procedures are influenced by local authorities and traditions. The supply of trained jurists is very limited. An education programme has been run by Italian judicial experts to prepare judges, prosecutors, and defense lawyers. The majority of local court officials came from Muslim religious schools and lacked judicial skills. The respective roles of Islamic and secular law in the new national judicial system have not been well established; a large portion of the current law code is based on laws passed under the last king, Mohammad Zahir Shah (ruled 1933–73). In rural areas, where local elders and tribal authorities resolve criminal cases, Taliban laws have remained in effect. In all provinces some 90% of local cases are based on Islamic and tribal law.

Electoral System. Suffrage is universal for male and female citizens 18 years of age and older. A new electoral and political party law went into effect in May 2004. About 77% of registered voters participated in the direct presidential election of 2004, the first since 1969. That election was managed by the Interim Election Commission appointed by Hamid Karzai, then the head of the interim government. Although some incidents of intimidation were reported in elections for the constitutional Loya Jirga in late 2003, the constitutional referendum of January 2004, and the presidential election of October 2004, monitors found those voting processes to be basically fair. In 2004 Karzai appointed an 11-member Joint Electoral Management Body to permanently oversee election registration and procedures. The first parliamentary and local elections were held in September 2005 after being postponed for nearly a year for security reasons; technical assistance was provided by the Organization for Security and Cooperation in Europe (OSCE). Although the election commission ostensibly disqualified individuals commanding armed groups from the parliamentary elections, several of the most powerful regional warlords gained seats. The complex voting system for those elections, in which about 50% of eligible voters participated, received substantial criticism. Because all candidates ran as individuals and no party representation was allowed, substantial fragmentation resulted.

Politics and Political Parties. The Political Parties Law of 2003 requires that all political parties be registered with the Ministry of Justice and observe the precepts of Islam. In 2005 some 43 parties had gained such recognition, but party identification was not allowed for candidates in the 2005 parliamentary elections. Most political groupings are based on alliances that formed during the military struggles of 1979–2002. The Northern Alliance is an influential loose confederation of several Hazara, Tajik, and Uzbek groups who fought against the Taliban. Factions of the alliance were key forces in the parliament of 2006. At the time of the 2004 presidential election, the largest individual parties were the Islamic Party of Afghanistan, the National Congress Party of Afghanistan, the National Islamic Movement of Afghanistan and the National Movement of Afghanistan (a coalition of 11 parties known variously as the Afghan Nationalist Party and the Afghan National Understanding Front. Other major parties are the Afghan Social-Democratic Party, the Communist Party of Afghanistan, the Liberal-Democratic Party of Afghanistan, the Revolutionary Association of Women of Afghanistan, and the Socialist Nationalist Afghan Party. President Karzai has declined to form a party to advance his programmes. Important non-party political pressure groups are the Society of Islam under former president Burhanuddin Rabbani and the Islamic Union for the Liberation of Afghanistan under military leader Abdul Rasul Sayyaf. The two groups are allied. The first parliament featured a broad division between leaders of previous military conflicts and younger "modernists" who emphasized future development of the country. Another important division of political power is between the Pashtun-dominated south and the Tajik- and Uzbek-dominated north.

Mass Media. Afghanistan has an estimated 45 FM radio stations and about 10 television stations. Radio is the most widespread source of information. A government-run national television station and seven radio stations are located in Kabul, and nine provinces have regional television stations. Most of the electronic news media are government-owned. The state-owned Radio Television Afghanistan is the most powerful broadcast outlet. Four cable stations appeared after the overthrow of the Taliban, carrying Indian and U.S. programmes. However, in 2003 the Supreme Court banned cable television on moral grounds. The circulation of independent print publications has been confined to the Kabul region. The 2004 media law requires registration of periodicals with the Ministry of Information and Culture. In 2005 some 250 periodicals were registered. The principal daily newspapers are the state-owned *Anis*, *Arman-e Melli*, *Eslah*, and *Kabul Times* and the privately owned *Eradeh*, *Hewad*, *Ittefaq-e Islam*, and *Shari'at*. Because of financial difficulties, all independent print media are dependent on the government or another faction.

Foreign Relations: Traditionally a neutral country, Afghanistan mirrored the foreign policy of the Soviet Union during the decade of Soviet occupation. Neither the Soviet-supported regimes in Afghanistan nor the Taliban regime received wide international recognition. After the fall of the Taliban in 2001, Afghanistan established diplomatic relations with most countries of the world. In December 2002, the six nations bordering Afghanistan signed a "Good Neighbor Declaration," guaranteeing the country's independence and territorial integrity. Since its establishment in 1948 on Afghanistan's southeastern border, Pakistan has been a key neighbour with which Afghanistan has substantial differences. During the Soviet occupation, Pakistan was the main supply point for the mujahideen insurgency. In the late 1990s, Pakistan supported the Taliban regime, reversing its support only after the Taliban refused to surrender Osama bin Laden in late 2001. Relations between Afghanistan and Pakistan have been strained by the ongoing separation of the Pashtun tribes and by disagreements on border procedures and smuggling. A United States-sponsored Tripartite Commission is the main arena for discussion of these issues. Major current issues are the continued presence of Taliban and al Qaeda forces in Pakistan's border provinces and Afghanistan's willingness to have closer relations with India. Both partners have a vital stake in friendly relations: for Afghanistan, Pakistan remains a vital corridor to the Arabian Sea, and for Pakistan, Afghanistan is a vital connection to the hydrocarbon and other resources of Central Asia. In the early 2000s, India moved aggressively by offering a range of assistance projects worth US$600 million and establishing diplomatic missions throughout Afghanistan. India further expanded the assistance package in 2006. Relations with Iran generally have been positive. Iran opposed the Soviet-backed and Taliban regimes in Afghanistan, and it has actively supported reconstruction efforts of the early 2000s. Trade relations also have improved in this period. The main bilateral issue is Iran's long-standing claim to share the water resources of the Helmand River, which irrigates Afghanistan's southern agricultural region before flowing into Iran. Other issues are the ongoing presence of Afghan refugees in Iran, Iranian support for certain warlords in Afghanistan's border provinces, and Iranian concerns for the Shia minority in Afghanistan. Beginning in 2005, the Karzai government felt substantial Western pressure to eschew closer relations with Iran, which in turn endeavored to create new bilateral links. Russia has viewed Afghanistan as a vital region since the early nineteenth century. Relations with the Soviet Union were close until the invasion of 1979, which aroused lasting hostility on the Afghan side. In the early 2000s, official

relations have improved as Russia pledged assistance in building Afghanistan's military and business establishments, clearing landmines, and developing oil and gas extraction. However, residual mistrust and issues such as outstanding Soviet-era debts to Russia, which Afghanistan has not officially recognized, have limited improvement. Relations with post-Soviet Tajikistan were complicated by Afghanistan's role in its neighbor's long civil war of the 1990s. Tajik insurgents used Afghanistan as a base for military operations, and about 100,000 Tajiks took refuge in northern Afghanistan in the early 1990s. In the early 2000s, Afghanistan has sought improved commercial relations; a planned bridge over the Amu Darya River will enhance the trade route north into Tajikistan. Relations with Uzbekistan have been limited by the harsh border controls enforced by Uzbekistan to prevent the entry of narcotics smugglers and Islamic fundamentalists from the south and by Uzbekistan's ongoing support for Abdul Rashid Dostum, the Uzbek warlord who controls parts of northeastern Afghanistan. Afghanistan became an important region for the United States because of the Soviet invasion of 1979, but the Soviet occupation, ensuing civil war, and Taliban regime made normal relations difficult or impossible until the fall of the Taliban in late 2001. Since that time, the successive Karzai governments have received substantial U.S. support to reestablish the infrastructure and strengthen government control of outlying regions. The United States has granted Afghanistan considerable preferential trade treatment. Since entering Afghanistan in late 2001, the U.S. military's Operation Enduring Freedom has pursued its objectives of eliminating Taliban and al Qaeda forces from Afghanistan and providing humanitarian assistance.

National Security

The aim of the Karzai government's national security policy is to establish a credible armed force, the Afghan National Army (ANA), and a national police force that will represent all the major ethnic groups in Afghanistan and provide all conventional aspects of domestic security. Some 24,000 soldiers have been trained by US forces and participated in counterterrorism operations, but the air force is still in the planning stage. The long-term goal is to prepare an army of 70,000 (in five corps), an air force of 8,000, a border guard force of 12,000, and a police force of 62,000. 10,000 militia organizations exist, many of them commanded by regional warlords. Some militia personnel have been integrated into the ANA and the police forces, but the disbanding of militias remains an elusive goal of the central government. Large areas remain outside government control and are dominated by narcotics traffickers, tribal leaders, and terrorist groups. Trafficking and terrorist groups in the south have increased their activity.

Foreign Military Relations. Afghanistan has depended almost entirely on US and North Atlantic Treaty Organization (NATO) forces to provide security in and around Kabul. Some 19,000 U.S. troops and 1,500 troops from other countries make up the US led Operation Enduring Freedom. The International Security Assistance Force, which since 2003 has been under the rotating command of officers from NATO countries, includes 9,000 troops from 36 countries. In 2005 Afghanistan received an estimated US$396 million in foreign military assistance. The Organization for Security and Cooperation in Europe (OSCE), of which Afghanistan became a cooperative partner in 2003, provides expertise on border security.

External Threat. The only external threat is the movement of hostile forces and terrorists from staging areas across the porous Pakistan border.

Police. Plans called for Afghanistan to increase its police force, the Afghan National Police (ANP), to 62,000, including conventional, border, highway, and counter-narcotics police to be trained with substantial German assistance. Although the police officially are responsible for maintaining civil order, local and regional military commanders continue to exercise control in the hinterland. Police have been accused of improper treatment and detention of prisoners. The mandate of the International Security Assistance Force extended into several new provinces, but local militias maintained control in some areas unoccupied by those forces. Because the NATO force has not assumed counter-narcotics or border control functions, serious gaps exist in those aspects of security. Troops of the Afghan National Army have been sent to quell fighting in some northern regions lacking police protection.

Internal Threat. A large part of the country remains without adequate security, and armed bands launch attacks in regions not controlled by the central government. Several extremist anti-government groups maintain a substantial presence in Afghanistan. They included surviving members of the Taliban, al Qaeda operatives, and the Hezb-e Islami Gulbuddin, led by warlord Gulbuddin Hekmatyar. Elements of the formerly anti-Taliban Northern Alliance reportedly are supplying arms to the Taliban. International non-governmental organizations have periodically suspended operations. A major internal security factor has been criminal activity associated with the prosperous drug trade. Drug processing laboratories are located throughout the country, traditional informal financial networks launder narcotics profits, and some provincial and national government officials have been implicated in the drug trade. Afghanistan's estimated opium output makes it by far the largest global producer of the drug. The government programme lacks national scale, opium growers often are not compensated for lost crops, and strong regional leaders profit from the drug trade. Cultivation has expanded significantly in provinces such as Badakhshan, which is located on the main trafficking route into Tajikistan. Incidents of abduction, violence, and terror continue, particularly in regions not under control of the national government. A government programme to disarm 100,000 militia personnel resulted in disarming an estimated 11,000. Abdul Rashid Dostum (who also is deputy defense minister), Water and Energy Minister Ismail Khan, Abdul Rabb al-Rasul Sayyaf, Atta Mohammad, and former Defense Minister Mohammed Fahim have been particularly intransigent warlords. Local fighting also has persisted over land resettlement questions. The Afghan government has decommissioned more than 60,000 former combatants and collected more than 35,000 weapons under the Disarmament, Demobilisation and Reintegration program. A new effort, the Disarmament of Illegal Armed Groups (DIAG), has been launched.

Terrorism. President Karzai has suffered several assassination attempts and some government officials have been assassinated. Small-scale attacks on villages have been common. Large-scale terrorist attacks have increased in the south and southeast and are expected to increase in the southern territory dominated by insurgents and narcotics traffickers. In an effort to split the Taliban movement, President Karzai has offered amnesty to members of the former Taliban regime and current fighters.

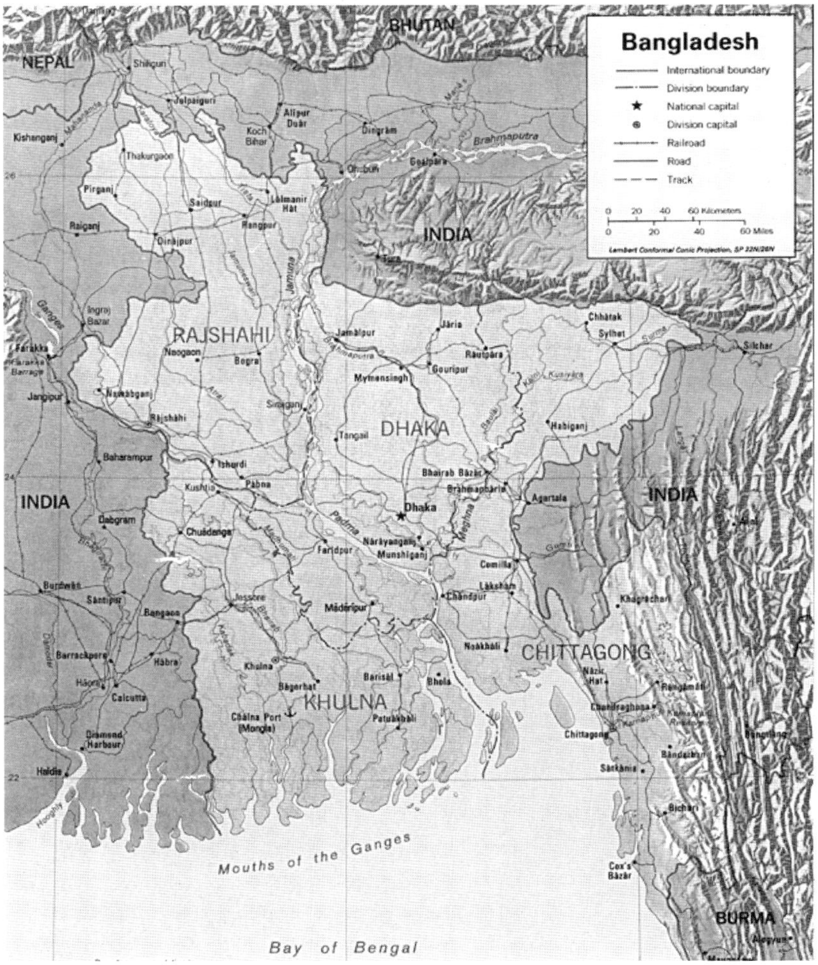

BANGLADESH

Bangladesh, formerly the East Wing of Pakistan, emerged as an independent nation in December 1971. The exclamation on the occasion—"Joi Bangla!" (Victory to Bengal!) was a collective cry following a particularly bitter and bloody struggle for freedom. These words echoed the cultural and ethnic disposition of the new state—in short, the ethos of the people—that Bangladesh was to be a culturally and linguistically cohesive unit. Pakistan was divided into two wings, separated by 1,600 kilometres of Indian territory, with Islam only a tenuous link between the two wings. Of paramount importance to East Pakistanis was the Bangla language and culture, a consideration not appreciated by the West Wing of Pakistan.

The first national leader of Bangladesh was Sheikh Mujibur Rahman (Mujib). Yet the future of the country enshrined in the 1972 Constitution as nationalism, socialism, secularism and democracy, was uncertain. By1975 Mujib was discredited for presiding over a bankrupt and corrupt regime, and assassinated along with most of his family. In the ensuing years, a number of regimes rose and fell in the violent legacy of Bangladeshi politics. Authoritarian and military rule has dominated the short history of Bangladesh. But Bengali society is known for its mercurial politics, and popular demands for a more open government in Bangladesh, has continued unabated.

History

Bengal was loosely associated with the Delhi Sultanate, established in 1206, and paid a tribute in war elephants in order to maintain autonomy. In 1341 Bengal became independent from Delhi, and Dhaka was established as the seat of the governors of independent Bengal. Turks ruled Bengal for several decades before the conquest of Dhaka by the Mughal emperor Akbar in 1576. Bengal remained a Mughal province until the decline of the Mughal Empire in the 18th century.

Bengal was, however, never truly subjugated. Being remote from the centre of government in Delhi and because lines of communications were poor, local governors maintained their independence. Although Bengal remained provincial, it was not isolated intellectually, and Bengali religious leaders from the 15th century onward have been influential throughout the subcontinent. Bengal prospered over the centuries and trade developed making Dhaka a centre of textile trade.

In 1905 the British governor general, Lord George Curzon, divided Bengal into eastern and western sectors in order to improve administrative control of the huge and populous province. In 1912 the British voided the partition of Bengal, a decision that heightened the growing estrangement between the Muslims and Hindus in many parts of the country. The reunited province was reconstituted as a presidency and the capital of India was moved from Calcutta to New Delhi.

Pakistan was born in bloodshed and came into existence on 15 August 1947, confronted by seemingly insurmountable problems. One of the most divisive issues confronting Pakistan in its infancy was the question of what the official language of the new state was to be. Jinnah yielded to the demands that Urdu be Pakistan's official language. In East Pakistan, the dissatisfaction quickly turned to violence. (The Bengalis of East Pakistan constituted an estimated 54% of Pakistan's entire population). Jinnah visited East Pakistan on only one occasion after independence, shortly before his death in 1948. In the Constituent Assembly frequent arguments voiced the fear that the West Pakistani province of Punjab would dominate the nation. An ineffective body, the Constituent Assembly took almost nine years to draft a constitution, which was never put into effect.

At a 1966 Lahore conference of both the eastern and the western chapters of the Awami League, Mujib announced a controversial six-point political and economic programme for East Pakistani provincial autonomy. He demanded that the government be federal and parliamentary in nature, its members to be elected by universal adult suffrage with legislative representation on the basis of population; that the federal government have principal responsibility for foreign affairs and defence only; that each wing have its own currency and separate fiscal accounts; that taxation would occur at the provincial level, with a federal government funded by constitutionally guaranteed grants; that each federal unit could control its own earning of foreign exchange; and that each unit could raise its own militia or paramilitary forces.

Mujib's six points ran directly counter to greater national integration. It would divide Pakistan by encouraging ethnic and linguistic cleavages in West Pakistan, and would leave East Pakistan, with its Bengali ethnic and linguistic unity, by far the most populous and powerful of the federating units. It was tantamount to a call for independence.

On 25 March 1969 General Yahya Khan placed under martial law and assumed the titles of chief martial law administrator and president. He announced elections to take place on 7 December 1970 and East Pakistan was awarded 162 seats out of the 300-member National Assembly. On 12 November 1970, a cyclone devastated an area of almost 8,000 square kilometres of East Pakistan's mid-coastal lowlands and its outlying islands in the Bay of Bengal. It was perhaps the worst natural disaster of the area in centuries. As many as 250,000 lives were lost. Two days after the cyclone hit, Yahya arrived in Dhaka after a trip to Beijing, but he left a day later. His seeming indifference to the plight of Bengali victims caused a great deal of animosity.

The elections on 7 December 1970 were the first in the history of Pakistan in which voters were able to elect members of the National Assembly directly. In a convincing demonstration of Bengali dissatisfaction with the West Pakistani regime, the Awami League won all but 2 of the 162 seats allotted to East Pakistan in the National Assembly. Bhutto's Pakistan People's Party came in a poor second nationally, winning 81 out of the 138 West Pakistani seats in the National Assembly. The Awami League's electoral victory promised it control of the government, with Mujib as the country's prime minister, but the inaugural assembly never met.

Yahya and Bhutto vehemently opposed Mujib's idea of a confederated Pakistan. Mujib was adamant that the constitution be based on his six-point programme. Bhutto, meanwhile, pleaded for unity in Pakistan under his leadership. As tensions mounted, Mujib suggested he become prime minister of East Pakistan while

Bhutto be prime minister of West Pakistan. It was this action that triggered mass civil disobedience in East Pakistan. Yahya decided to ignore Mujib's demands and on 1 March 1 postponed indefinitely the convening of the National Assembly.

West Pakistani troops were sent to East Pakistan as tensions rose. Talks between Yahya and Mujib collapsed, and on March 23 Bengalis following Mujib's lead defiantly celebrated "Resistance Day" in East Pakistan instead of the traditional all-Pakistan "Republic Day." Yahya decided to "solve" the problem of East Pakistan by repression. On 25 March the Pakistan Army launched a terror campaign calculated to intimidate the Bengalis into submission. Within hours a wholesale slaughter had commenced in Dhaka, with the heaviest attacks concentrated on the University of Dhaka and the Hindu area of the old town. Bangladeshis remember the date as a day of infamy and liberation. The Pakistan Army came with hit lists and systematically killed several hundred Bengalis. Mujib was captured and flown to West Pakistan for incarceration.

The West Pakistani press waged a vigorous but ultimately futile campaign to counteract newspaper and radio accounts of wholesale atrocities. The civil war was played down by the government-controlled press as a minor insurrection quickly being brought under control. After the tragic events of March, India became vocal in its condemnation of Pakistan. An immense flood of East Pakistani refugees, between 8 and 10 million according to various estimates, fled across the border into the Indian state of West Bengal. In April an Indian parliamentary resolution demanded that Prime Minister Indira Gandhi supply aid to the rebels in East Pakistan. She complied but declined to recognize the provisional government of independent Bangladesh.

On 4 December 1971 the Indian Army, far superior in numbers and equipment to that of Pakistan, executed a 3-pronged pincer movement on Dhaka launched from the Indian states of West Bengal, Assam, and Tripura, taking only 12 days to defeat the 90,000 Pakistani defenders. On 6 December, India became the first nation to recognize the new Bangladeshi government.

At independence, Bangladesh was scarred by civil war. The number of people killed, raped, or displaced could be only vaguely estimated. The task of economic rehabilitation, specifically the immediate goal of food distribution to a hungry populace, was frustrated by crippled communications and transportation systems. The new nation faced many other seemingly insurmountable problems inhibiting its reconstruction. One of the most glaring was the breakdown of law and order. In the wake of the war of independence, numerous bands of guerrillas still roamed the countryside, fully armed and outside the control of the government.

Despite substantial foreign aid, mostly from India and the Soviet Union, food supplies were scarce, and there was rampant corruption and black marketeering. Mujib's economic policies also directly contributed to his country's economic chaos. His large-scale nationalization of Bangladeshi manufacturing and trading enterprises and international trading in commodities strangled Bangladesh entrepreneurship in its infancy. However, at the time of the first national elections held in 1973 the Awami League won 282 out of 289 directly contested seats. After the election, the economic and security situations began to deteriorate rapidly, and Mujib's popularity suffered further as a result of what many Bangladeshis came to regard as his close alliance with India.

On the morning of 15 August 1975, Mujib and several members of his family were murdered in a coup engineered by a group of young army officers, most of whom were majors. The diplomatic status of Bangladesh changed overnight. One day after Mujib's assassination President Bhutto of Pakistan announced that his country would immediately recognize the new regime and offered a gift of 50,000 tons of rice in addition to a generous gift of clothing. India, however, suffered a setback in its relations with Bangladesh.

After several coups Ziaur Rahman, the Chief of Army Staff became the Chief martial Law Administrator of Bangladesh in November 1976. Zia made repatriate Major General Hussain Muhammad Ershad the deputy army chief of staff. Having consolidated his position in the army, Zia became president on 21 April 1977 and seemed to be supported by a majority of Bangladeshis.

In May 1977, with his power base increasingly secure, Zia drew on his popularity to promote a nineteen-point political and economic program. Zia focused on the need to boost Bangladeshi production, especially in food and grains, and to integrate rural development through a variety of programs, of which population planning was the most important. He heeded the advice of international lending agencies and launched an ambitious rural development program in 1977, which included a highly visible and popular food-for-work program.

One of the most important tasks Zia faced was to change the direction of the country. Zia altered the Constitution's ideological statement on the fundamental principles, in particular changing the Mujibist emphasis on secularism to "complete trust and faith in almighty Allah." While distancing Bangladesh from India, Zia sought to improve ties with other Islamic nations. Throughout his regime, Zia pursued an active foreign policy, and the legacy of his efforts continued to bear fruit in the late 1980s. In 1980 Zia proposed a conference for the seven nations of the subcontinent (Bangladesh, Bhutan, India, Maldives, Nepal, Pakistan, and Sri Lanka) to discuss the prospects for regional cooperation in a number of fields. This initiative was successful in August 1983 when the South Asian Association for Regional Cooperation (SAARC) was established.

In April 1978, Zia announced that elections would be held to "pave the way to democracy," adding that the Constitution would be amended to provide for an independent judiciary as well as a "sovereign parliament." Zia also lifted the ban on political parties. He was supported by a "national front," whose main party was the Jatiyo Ganatantrik Dal (National Democratic Party). As the candidate of the Jatiyo Ganatantrik Dal-led Nationalist Front, Zia won overwhelmingly, taking 76.7% of the vote. After campaigning by Zia, the Bangladesh Nationalist Party won 207 of the 300 seats in Parliament with about 44% of the vote.

Zia was assassinated in Chittagong on May 30, 1981, in a plot allegedly masterminded by Major General Manzur, the army commander in Chittagong. The army, under its chief of staff, Major General Ershad, remained loyal to the Dhaka government and quickly put down the rebellion, killing Manzur. In the trials that followed, a sizable number of officers and enlisted men received the death penalty for complicity.

After Zia's assassination, Vice President Sattar became acting president and, as the Constitution stipulates, called for new elections for president within 180 days. Although there was some speculation that Zia's widow, Begum Khalida Ziaur Rahman, and Mujib's daughter, Sheikh Hasina Wajed, would be candidates, Sattar ran against a number of political unknowns in the November election and won the presidential election with two-thirds of the vote. Immediately following the 1981 election, Ershad pushed Sattar for a constitutional role for the military in the governance of the country. On 24 March 1982, Ershad dismissed Sattar, dissolved the cabinet and the Parliament, and assumed full powers under martial law.

In January 1985, it was announced that parliamentary elections would be held in April, to be preceded by a partial relaxation of martial law: the Constitution was to be fully restored after the elections. In order to be eligible to contest the elections as a candidate in the presidential election in October 1986, Ershad Joined the Jatiya Dal, being elected as Chairman of the party and nominated as its presidential candidate. In the presidential election, which was boycotted by both the Bangladesh Nationalist Party (BNP) and the Awami League (AL), Ershad won an overwhelming victory.

In the Parliamentary elections, which were held in February 1991 the BNP alliance won an overall majority and, following discussions with the Jamaat-e-Islami, as a result of which the BNP was ensured a small working majority in the Jatiya Sangsad, Begum Khaleda Zia assumed office as Prime Minster. In September the BNP had gained an absolute majority in the Jatiya Sangsad, following the party's victory in a number of by-elections.

The main political parties are the Awami League and the Bangladesh Nationalist Party (BNP). The AL, which spearheaded the war of independence under Sheikh Mujib, is now led by his daughter, Sheikh Hasina. The differences between the AL and the BNP in terms of official economic policy have largely disappeared. While AL plays on its leading role during the war of liberation in 1971 and attacks those who opposed it, the BNP appeals more broadly to nationalist forces, drawing support from forces that had been on both sides of the liberation war.

Other parties active in Bangladesh include the Jatiya Party (JP), led by the deposed president, General Ershad. It has experienced several damaging splits since 1997 owing to its alternating support for the AL and the BNP. The Jamaat-e-Islami (Jamaat) is a fundamentalist party that espouses an Islamic state. In recent years it has come under a severe onslaught for its pro-Pakistan stance in 1971. The Islamic Oikyo Joite (IOJ), a member of the BNP four-party alliance, also seeks to implement Islamic doctrine, but draws more support from extremist elements of society. There are several leftist parties, including a communist party, which has entered a variety of shifting alliances for electoral purposes.

The results of the general elections over the years, in terms of number of parliamentary seats, have been as under:

Party(s)	1979	1986	1988	1991	1996 Feb	1996 Jun	2001
AL	39	76	—	96	—	146	63
BNP	207	—	—	139	272	116	191
JP	-	153	251	35	—	31	14
Jamaat	-	10	—	18	—	3	17
Others	54	61	49	12	—	4	13

In January 2007, following widespread violence, a caretaker government was appointed to administer the next general election. The country has suffered from extensive corruption, disorder and political violence. The new caretaker government has made it a priority to root out corruption from all levels of government. To this end, many notable politicians and officials, along with large numbers of lesser officials and party members, have been arrested on corruption charges. The caretaker government claims to be paving the way for free and fair elections to be held before the end of 2008.

Geography

Bangla Desh is a country of 144,000 square kilometers with a land area 133,910 square kilometers. Its topography is of a broad deltaic plain besides the Chittagong Hills in the southeast, low hills in the northeast and modest-elevation highlands in the north and northwest.

Bangladesh is located in the low-lying Ganges-Brahmaputra River Delta or Ganges Delta. This delta is formed by the confluence of the Ganges (Padma), Brahmaputra (Jamuna), and Meghna rivers and their respective tributaries. The Ganges unites with the Jamuna (main channel of the Brahmaputra) and later joins the Meghna to eventually empty into the Bay of Bengal. The alluvial soil deposited by these rivers has created some of the most fertile plains in the world. Bangladesh has 58 trans-boundary rivers, making water issues politically complicated to resolve—in most cases as the lower riparian state to India. Most parts of Bangladesh are less than 12 metres (39 ft) above sea level, and it is believed that about 50% of the land would be flooded if the sea level were to rise by 1 metre.

The highest point in Bangladesh is in Mowdok range at 1,052 metres in the Chittagong Hill Tracts to the southeast of the country. A major part of the coastline comprises a marshy jungle, the Sundarbans, the largest mangrove forest in the world and home to diverse flora and fauna, including the Royal Bengal Tiger. In 1997, this region was declared endangered.

Straddling the Tropic of Cancer, Bangladeshi climate is tropical with a mild winter from October to March, a hot, humid summer from March to June. A warm and humid monsoon season lasts from June to October and supplies most of the country's rainfall. Natural calamities, such as floods, tropical cyclones, tornadoes, and tidal bores occur almost every year, combined with the effects of deforestation, soil degradation and erosion. Cox's Bazar, south of the city of Chittagong, has a beach that stretches uninterrupted over 120 kilometres.

In September 1998 Bangladesh saw the most severe flooding the modern world has seen. Although only 1,000 people were killed, 30 million were made homeless and 130,000 cattle were killed, 50 square kilometres of land were destroyed and 11,000 km of roads were damaged or destroyed. 66% of the country was underwater. There were several reasons for the severity of the flooding. Firstly, there were unusually high monsoon rains. Secondly, the Himalayas shed off an equally unusually high amount of melt water that year. Lastly, trees that usually intercept rain water were cut down for fire wood or to make space for animals.

Population

With a population of about 159 million, it has the eighth largest population in world, with an annual growth rate of 3.6%. About 82% live in rural areas, 18% in urban areas. Its population density of 821 per square kilometer is the highest in world. Over 98% of the population are Bengalis. Others include about 600,000 Biharis (Urdu-speaking, non-Bengali Muslims) and 900,000 members of tribal minority groups. The main tribal group are Chakmas, living primarily in Chittagong Hills Tracts. Bangla is the official language and English is widely used by educated elite. Arabic is used in many Muslim homes. There are also various tribal languages. The religion is nearly 83% Muslim, 16% Hindu, less than 1% Buddhist, Christian, and tribal religions.

Education

Education based on the British system: five years primary, five years lower secondary, and two years higher secondary. Higher education includes 758 general colleges, 7 universities, and 50 professional

Bangladeshi defense planners have long regarded India as a regional bully, a perception shared by the Bangladeshi public. Bangladesh has been the object of three main Indian security concerns since independence: Bangladeshi internal stability, its strategic position in relation to China, and Dhaka's alleged involvement with Indian tribal insurgents. These security concerns were compounded by Indian charges that Dhaka turned a blind eye to Indian tribal insurgents using safe havens in eastern Bangladesh and allowed a tide of Bangladeshi emigrants to move into the Indian states of Tripura and Assam. India also expressed the concern that serious instability in Bangladesh could trigger another exodus of refugees into India.

Pakistan. Pakistan was hostile to Bangladesh in the early 1970s, but by 1974 it was apparent that the new nation would stand on its own, and Pakistan recognized Bangladesh. Diplomatic relations were established in January 1976, followed by the reestablishment of communications and transportation links. As Bangladesh subsequently adopted a cooler stance toward India, moved closer to China and the West, and stressed its Islamic cultural heritage, its interests are similar to those of Pakistan and both have a wide variety of bilateral agreements.

Two major areas of disagreement remained between Bangladesh and Pakistan stem from the dislocations resulting from the independence struggle. The first concerned the finances of united Pakistan. After the war, Bangladesh claimed that it deserved a share of the US$4 billion worth of pre-independence exchange, bank credit, and movable assets protected in West Pakistan. In a 1975 agreement, Bangladesh accepted half of Pakistan's pre-1971 external debt, but asset sharing issues remain unresolved. The second issue concerns the emigration of nearly 540,000 Biharis (non-Bengali Muslims) to Pakistan after the war.

Bangladesh enjoys good relations with the other nations of South Asia. Bangladesh has made strenuous efforts to extend cooperation with these nations through the South Asian Association for Regional Cooperation.

Burma. It is the only nation besides India that shares a border with Bangladesh. Relations between the two countries have generally been cordial, but relations deteriorated in 1978 and 1979 when 150,000 Bengali-descent Muslims flooded into Bangladesh from Burma. It brought to light anti-Bengali feelings in western Burma. Intervention by the UN a led to a negotiated repatriation of the refugees and the reestablishment of good relations. Later talks led to the demarcation of the land boundary between the two countries. Bangladesh and Burma settled their maritime boundary.

China. Bangladesh enjoys relatively warm ties with the People's Republic of China which has, particularly in the past decade, increased economic cooperation with it. Between 2006-07, trade between the two nations rose by 28.5% and there have been agreements to grant various Bangladeshi commodities tariff-free access to the Chinese market. Military cooperation between the Military of Bangladesh and the People's Liberation Army is also increasing, with joint military agreements signed and Bangladesh procuring Chinese arms which range from small arms to large naval surface combatants such as the Chinese Jiangwei Class Missile Frigate.

Security Environment

Bengalis have been opposing governments since those imposed by the Mughals in the sixteenth century. Bengali secession movements, first from Britain and then from Pakistan, were violent struggles that exacted an enormous human toll. This legacy of violence, coupled with the propensity to organize the population into mass movements to overthrow governments, has carried over into the present.

Probably the longest running source of domestic violence has been the tribal insurgency that has festered in the remote Chittagong Hill Tracts since the late 1970s. Spearheaded by the predominantly Chakma guerrillas with an estimated strength of 2,000 lightly armed guerrillas known as the Shanti Bahini (Peace Force), the rebels are seeking autonomous status for the Chittagong Hills, the expulsion of Bengali settlers from traditional tribal lands, the restoration of tribal rights and privileges enjoyed under British and

Pakistani rule and subsequently repealed by the Mujib government, and the withdrawal of the army from the Chittagong Hills. Bangladesh has frequently asserted that India has aided the Shanti Bahini by offering arms assistance, military training, and bases. India has denied the charges and has countered that Bangladesh Army operations in the Chittagong Hills have precipitated a massive exodus of Chakma refugees into the Indian state of Tripura.

Bangladesh's borders encompass five Indian states i.e. West Bengal, Assam, Meghalaya, Tripura and Mizoram. It is virtually impossible to completely seal the porous international border, which passes through very difficult terrain. The issues which impact Bangladesh security environment with India are:

- Illegal immigration from Bangladesh, which is estimated at approximately 300,000 annually. The total number of Bangladeshi nationals in India is estimated at 15 to 17 million. There is hardly any state in India, where Bangladeshi nationals are not residing. This has the makings of a crisis in the years ahead.
- There are a number of Indian insurgent groups camping in the Chittagong Hill Tracts of Bangladesh and some insurgent leaders are operating with impunity from Dhaka.
- Bangladesh territory has become a conduit for weapon smuggling for Indian as well as Myanmar insurgents. The Cox's Bazaar coast offers convenient landing points for arms smugglers. Besides arms-dealing and gun-running, there is a high degree of piracy and armed robberies. The Bangladesh-Myanmar border area is also home to nearly 100,000 Muslim refugees and migrants i.e. the Rohingyas from Arakan (Rakhine) state of Myanmar.
- The growth of Islamic fundamentalism in Bangladesh has been given a modicum of legitimacy by the inclusion of fundamentalist Islamic groups/parties in the government. This does not augur well for the containment of extremism.
- About 70% of the arms inventory of the Bangladesh military is of Chinese origin. China has made inroads into other economic and infrastructural projects. This is viewed with concern by India.
- The separation of India and Bangladesh based on religious lines is not consistent with geography and deep cultural affinities. The cooperative mechanisms between the two countries are hostage to misplaced distrust. In 1999, Bangladesh agreed to examine the proposal to allow transshipment of Indian goods through its territory. However, this proposal sparked off a major controversy and opposition on the grounds that it would jeopardize the security of Bangladesh.
- Bangladesh has proven gas reserves of about 150 billion cubic meters. It currently consumes 9.9 billion cubic meters annually. Gas exploration and production is being done in partnership with the western companies, for which Bangladesh has to defray the cost. Export of gas can substantially offset the financial burden. India is the most accessible and cost effective market for supply of gas through a pipeline. However, there has been little progress towards finalizing a deal.
- Bangladesh's strategic location with respect to the narrow Assam corridor, which links the Indian heartland with its northeast, is a strategic irritant if not a threat.
- The naval bases in Bangladesh by virtue of their location, strategically dominate the Bay of Bengal. There have been reports alluding to overtures by the US to seek a maritime foothold in that region.
- Bangladesh has many unresolved border disputes with India, especially with regard to the adverse possessions and enclaves that were to be exchanged consequent to the 1974 land boundary agreement between Sheikh Mujibur Rahman and Smt. Indira Gandhi. Border issues with India have led to several incidents.

The big brother syndrome is a powerful influence on Bangladesh's security thinking and its threat perceptions are more imagined than real. For India, Bangladesh is one of its seven neigbouring countries. For Bangladesh, India is the only major neighbour. Therefore, there is a tendency to exaggerate apprehensions or fabricate threats from India. This has given rise to an anti India lobby within the Bangladesh populace and polity, which has impaired and inhibited some mutually very beneficial cooperative proposals and ventures between the two countries, e.g. the granting of a transit route to northeast India through Bangladesh territory.

In most of its military training institutions and military exercises, India is referred to as an enemy. Bangladesh is conscious of the fact that it is not capable of undertaking any offensive against India, given the huge mismatch in the size and military capabilities of the two countries. It has, therefore, adopted a wholly defensive strategy around debilitating an Indian offensive by the use of numerous rivers and other obstacles, and preventing the fall of Dhaka for a sufficiently long period to allow the international community to intervene. It also factors in the use of guerrilla warfare in its defence strategy against an Indian offensive.

Bangladesh perceives that although there are no major contentious issues with Myanmar, yet some have the potential for escalation. The bilateral relationship between the two countries has been acrimonious over the issue of alleged support by Bangladesh to Myanmarese insurgents belonging to groups like the Rohingya Solidarity Organisation and the Arakan Rohingya Islamic Front. The Myanmar authorities accuse Bangladesh of providing sanctuaries to the insurgents in Rohingya refugee camps on its territory. Myanmar has in fact laid minefields along some portions of its border with Bangladesh to restrict the movement of insurgents. In recent times, there have been some clashes between NASAKA (the border force of Myanmar) and the Bangladesh Rifles.

When Bangladesh joined the community of nations, it was at first recognized by only India and Bhutan. With its fragile and underdeveloped economic infrastructure under extreme duress, its law and order situation challenged by numerous well-armed contingents of unemployed former freedom fighters, its impoverished population agitated by the unfulfilled promise of rising expectations, Bangladesh was, in international circles, given the label of "international basket case."

Environmental Challenges

Threats to the environmental security of Bangladesh are a cause of concern. They are floods, salinity, siltation, and cyclones. The dry season leads to recession of water in the Ganges, which affects Khulna and other neighbouring districts causing increased salinity in the rivers and streams, posing a serious threat to agriculture and industrial activities. Salinity also affects the flora and fauna in the Sunderbans forests. According to experts, the soil character of Bangladesh is undergoing changes because of siltation and salinity. Bangladesh views construction of barrages in India upstream of the river have aggravated the situation.

Periodic floods also cause destruction to agriculture, roads and human lives affecting the economic and social life of Bangladesh. Also, the level of arsenic in the ground water has reached a dangerous level. According the experts Bangladesh is in the midst of the biggest mass poisoning in history, having more than five times the amount considered acceptable in 46 districts.

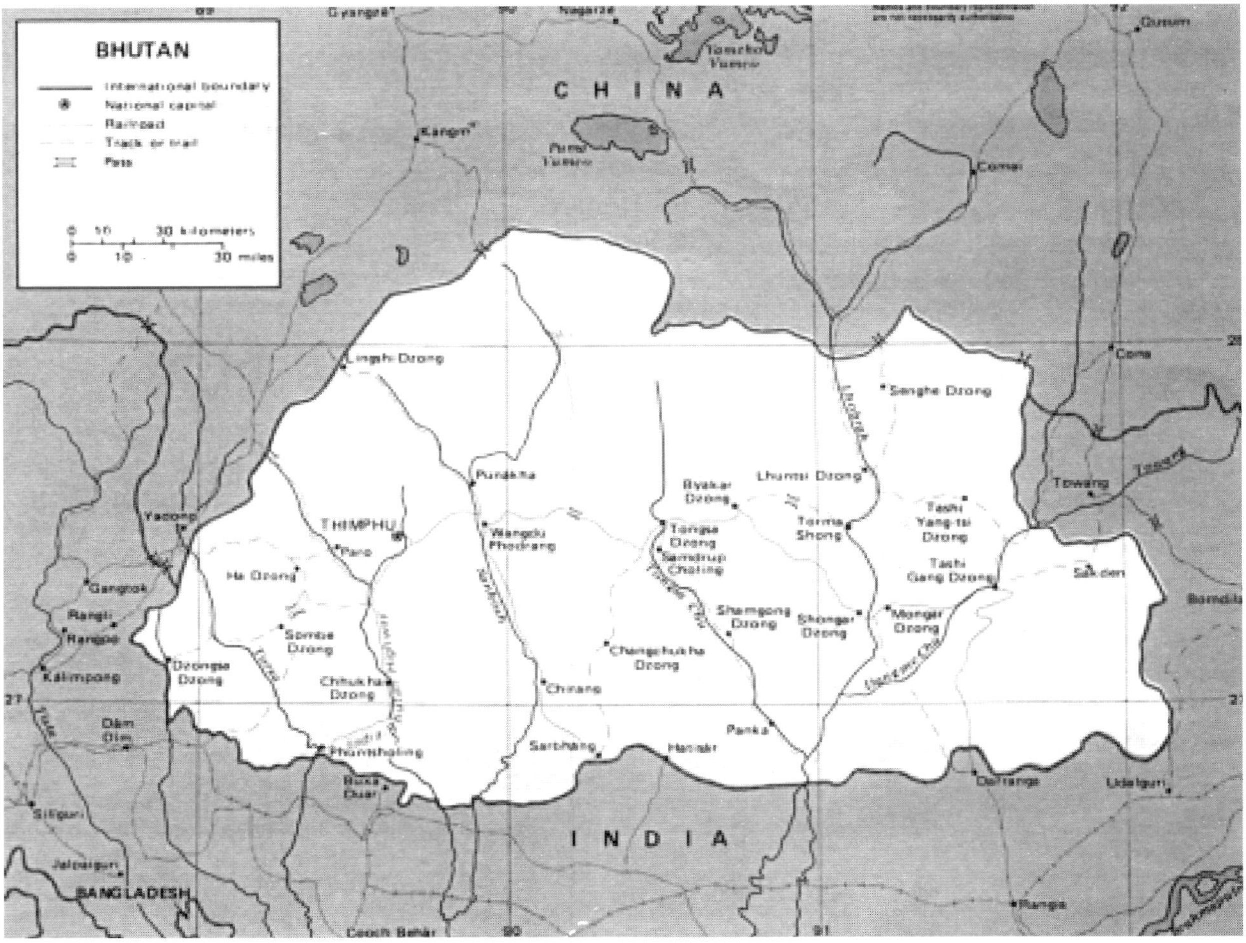

BHUTAN

The Kingdom of Bhutan is a landlocked nation in the Himalaya Mountains, sandwiched between India and China in South Asia. The Bhutanese call their country 'Druk Yul'(land of the thunder dragon). The origins of the name Bhutan are unclear; historians have suggested that it may have originated in variations of the Sanskrit words Bhota-ant (the end of Bhot—another word for Tibet), or Bhu-uttan (highlands). The word Bhutan as a name for the country dates from the late 19th century.

The Kingdom of Bhutan has its capital at Thimphu. Its flag is rectangular and divided diagonally from the lower left side corner. The upper part is yellow, symbolizing the secular power of the king, while the lower part is orange, representing the Buddhist religion. Across the middle a white dragon (druk) is depicted, which symbolizes purity. The jewels held tightly in the dragon's claws symbolize wealth. The roaring mouth represents the strength of deities protecting the country. The yellow colour with a dragon in the flag of Bhutan shows a close relation with the emperors of China whose earlier flag was golden yellow with a dragon.

Variations of the Sanskrit words Bhota-ant (end of Bhot, an Indian name for Tibet) or Bhu-uttan (meaning highlands) have been suggested by historians as origins of the name Bhutan, which is used only in English-language official correspondence. The traditional name of the country has been Drukyul—country of the Drokpa, the Dragon People, or the Land of the Thunder Dragon—a reference to the country's dominant Buddhist sect.

Bhutan has an area of 47,000 square kilometers and a land boundary of 1,075 kilometres (China 470 kilometres, India 605 kilometres). Bhutan is one of the most isolated and least developed nations in the world. Nonetheless, it has been described as the happiest least developed country on earth. Foreign influences and tourism are heavily regulated by the government to preserve the country's traditional culture and national identity. The landscape ranges from subtropical plains in the south to the Himalayan heights in the north, with some peaks exceeding seven thousand metres. Mahayana Buddhism is the state religion and the population is predominantly Buddhist, with Hinduism being the second most dominant. Thimphu is the capital and largest city.

History

Bhutan's early history is unclear, because most of the records were destroyed after fire ravaged Punakha, the ancient capital in 1827. By the 10th century, Bhutan's political development was heavily influenced by its religious history. Various sub-sects of Buddhism emerged which were patronized by various Mongol and Tibetan overlords. After the decline of the Mongols in the 14th century, these sub-sects vied with each other for supremacy in the political and religious landscape, eventually leading to the ascendancy of the Drukpa sub-sect by the 16th century.

Until the early 17th century, Bhutan existed as a patchwork of minor warring fiefdoms when the area was unified by the lama and military leader Shabdrung Ngawang Namgyal. To defend the country against intermittent Tibetan forays, Namgyal built a network of impregnable dzong (fortresses), and promulgated a code of law that helped to bring local lords under centralized control.

In the 18th century, the Bhutanese invaded and occupied the kingdom of Cooch Behar to the south. In 1772, Cooch Behar appealed to the British East India Company who assisted them in ousting the Bhutanese, and later in attacking Bhutan itself in 1774. A peace treaty was signed in which Bhutan agreed to retreat to its pre-1730 borders. However, the peace was tenuous, and border skirmishes with the British were to continue for the next one hundred years. The skirmishes eventually led to the Dooar War (1864–1865), a confrontation over who would control the Bengal Dooars. After Bhutan lost the war, the Treaty of Sinchula was signed between British India and Bhutan. As part of the war reparations, the Dooars were ceded to the British in exchange for a rent of Rs. 50,000. The treaty ended all hostilities between British India and Bhutan.

During the 1870s, power struggles between the rival valleys of Paro and Trongsa led to civil war in Bhutan, eventually leading to the ascendancy of Ugyen Wangchuck, the ponlop (governor) of Tongsa. From his power base in central Bhutan, Ugyen Wangchuck defeated his political enemies and united the country following several civil wars and rebellions in the period 1882–1885.

In 1907, an epochal year for the country, Ugyen Wangchuck was unanimously chosen as the hereditary king of the country by an assembly of leading Buddhist monks, government officials, and heads of important families. The British government promptly recognized the new monarchy, and in 1910 Bhutan signed a treaty which "let" Great Britain "guide" Bhutan's foreign affairs. In reality this did not mean much. It also did not seem to apply to Bhutan's traditional relations with Tibet. The greatest impact of this treaty seems to be the perception that it meant Bhutan was not totally sovereign. After India gained independence from the United Kingdom on 15 August 1947, Bhutan became one of the first countries to recognize India's independence. A treaty similar to the one of 1910 was signed on 8 August 1949 with India.

When the Chinese People's Liberation Army entered Tibet in 1951, Bhutan sealed its northern frontier and improved bilateral ties with India. To reduce the risk of Chinese encroachment, Bhutan began a modernisation programme that was largely sponsored by India.

In 1953, King Jigme Dorji Wangchuck established the country's legislature—a 130-member National Assembly—to promote a more democratic form of governance. In 1965, he set up a Royal Advisory Council, and in 1968 he formed a Cabinet. In 1971, Bhutan was admitted to the United Nations, having held observer status for three years. In July 1972, Jigme Singye Wangchuck ascended to the throne at the age of 16 after the death of his father, Dorji Wangchuck.

In the 1980s, in order strengthen Bhutan's identity as a nation, the "one nation, one people" campaign was started to foster greater integration of the peripheral ethnic and cultural groups into main stream Bhutanese society. The age old code of conduct, known as Driglam namzha and usage of the official national language Dzongkha was promoted. Around the same time, a nation wide census revealed a huge influx of illegal immigrants of Nepali origin, into Southern Bhutan. When the government attempted to remove the illegal settlers, there was a violent backlash; numerous acts of terrorism were carried out against government schools, hospitals, offices and neutral Southern Bhutanese. In order to re-establish order in the south, the government was forced to draft many young men and able bodied civil servants into a militia force. Eventually order was restored; along with the illegal settlers, a number of political dissidents and Southern Bhutanese who had rebelled against the country, fled to Nepal, where they were admitted into United Nations run camps and given refugee status. Despite the best efforts of the governments of Bhutan, Nepal and India, as well as out side parties such as the United Nations, European Union and the United States, a viable solution to this problem proves to be still elusive.

In 1998, King Jigme Singye Wangchuck introduced significant political reforms, transferring some of his powers to the Prime Minister and allowing for impeachment of the King by a two-thirds majority of the National Assembly. In late 2003, the Bhutanese army successfully launched a large-scale operation to flush out anti-India insurgents who were operating training camps in southern Bhutan.

In 1999, the government lifted a ban on television and the Internet, making Bhutan one of the last countries to introduce television. In his speech, the King said that television was a critical step to the modernization of Bhutan as well as a major contributor to the country's Gross National Happiness (Bhutan is the only country to measure happiness) but warned against the misuse of television which may erode traditional Bhutanese values. Some believe it has indeed affected Bhutan in a negative way.

Bhutan is a predominantly Buddhist country, with the religion forming an integral part of everyday life. A new constitution was presented in early 2005 which will be put up for ratification by a referendum before coming into force. In December 2005, His Majesty Jigme Singye Wangchuck announced that he would abdicate the throne in his son's favour in 2008. On 14 December 2006, he announced that he would be abdicating immediately. Bhutan will now enter a new era of democracy, starting with its first elections in 2008. Despite the popular appeal of the King to the people of Bhutan and general reservations towards the politics of democracy, it is by royal decree that the country will undergo this drastic change in its political system.

On 8 February 2007, the Indo-Bhutan Friendship Treaty was substantially revised. Whereas in the Treaty of 1949 Article 2 read as "The Government of India undertakes to exercise no interference in the internal administration of Bhutan. On its part the Government of Bhutan agrees to be guided by the advice of the Government of India in regard to its external relations." In the revised treaty it now reads as "In keeping with the abiding ties of close friendship and cooperation between Bhutan and India, the Government of the Kingdom of Bhutan and the Government of the Republic of India shall cooperate closely with each other on issues relating to their national interests. Neither Government shall allow the use of its territory for activities harmful to the national security and interest of the other." The revised treaty also includes in it the preamble "Reaffirming their respect for each other's independence, sovereignty and territorial integrity;" an element that was absent in the earlier version. The Indo-Bhutan Friendship Treaty of 2007 strengthens Bhutan's status as an independent and sovereign nation.

Geography

The northern region consists of an arc of glaciated mountain peaks with an extremely cold climate at the highest elevations. Most peaks in the north are over 23,000 feet (7,000 m) above sea level; the highest point is claimed to be the Kula Kangri, at 24,780 feet (7,553 m), but detailed topographic studies claim Kula Kangri is wholly in Tibet and modern Chinese measurements claim that Gangkhar Puensum, which has the distinction of being the highest unclimbed mountain in the world, is higher at 24,835 feet (7,570 m). Watered by snow-fed rivers, alpine valleys in this region provide pasture for livestock, tended by a sparse population of migratory shepherds.

The Black Mountains in central Bhutan form a watershed between two major river systems: the Mo Chhu and the Drangme Chhu. Peaks in the Black Mountains range between 4,900 feet and 8,900 feet (1,500 m and 2,700 m) above sea level, and fast-flowing rivers have carved out deep gorges in the lower mountain areas. Woodlands of the central region provide most of Bhutan's forest production. The Torsa, Raidak, Sankosh, and Manas are the main rivers of Bhutan, flowing through this region. Most of the population lives in the central highlands.

In the south, the Shiwalik Hills are covered with dense, deciduous forests, alluvial lowland river valleys, and mountains up to around 4,900 feet (1,500 m) above sea level. The foothills descend into the subtropical Dooars plain. Most of the Dooars is located in India, although a 6–9 mile (10–15 km) wide strip extends into Bhutan. The Bhutan Dooars is divided into two parts: the northern and the southern Dooars. The northern Dooars, which abuts the Himalayan foothills, has rugged, sloping terrain and dry, porous soil with dense vegetation and abundant wildlife. The southern Dooars has moderately fertile soil, heavy savannah grass, dense, mixed jungle, and freshwater springs. Mountain rivers, fed by either the melting snow or the monsoon rains, empty into the Brahmaputra river in India. Data released by the Ministry of agriculture showed that the country had a forest cover of 64%.

The climate in Bhutan varies with altitude, from subtropical in the south to temperate in the highlands and polar-type climate, with year-round snow, in the north. Bhutan experiences five distinct seasons: summer, monsoon, autumn, winter and spring. Western Bhutan has the heavier monsoon rains; southern Bhutan has hot humid summers and cool winters; central and eastern Bhutan is temperate and drier than the west with warm summers and cool winters.

Government and Politics

Politics of Bhutan takes place in the framework of an absolute monarchy developing into a constitutional monarchy. In 1999, the fourth king of Bhutan created a ten member body called the Lhengye Zhungtshog (Council of Ministers). The 'Druk Gyalpo'(King of Druk Yul) is head of state. Executive power is exercised by the Lhengye Zhungtshog, the council of ministers. Legislative power is vested in both the government and the National Assembly. On the 17th of December 2005, the 4th King announced to a stunned nation that the first general elections would be held in 2008, and that he would abdicate the throne in favour of his eldest son, the crown prince. Now as the country is preparing to usher historic changes by introducing the parliamentary democracy in 2008, works are in full swing and political parties are now legal. The new democratic system will comprise an upper and lower house, the latter based on political party affiliations. There are currently two political parties, following a recent merger. Elections for the upper house begin in October 2007. The Judicial power is vested in all the courts of Bhutan. The Chief Justice is the administrative head of the Judiciary.

Economy

The Ngultrum is the currency of Bhutan and its value is pegged to the Indian rupee. The rupee is also accepted as legal tender in the country. Incomes of over Nu 100,000 per annum are taxed, but very few wage and salary earners qualify. Bhutan's inflation rate was estimated at about 3% in 2003. Bhutan has a Gross Domestic Product of around USD 2.913 billion (adjusted to Purchasing Power Parity), making it the 162nd largest economy in the world.

Though Bhutan's economy is one of the world's smallest, it has grown very rapidly with about 8% in 2005 and 14% in 2006. As of March 2006, Bhutan's per capita income was US$ 1,321 making it one of the fastest growing in South Asia. Bhutan's standard of living is growing faster than that of its neighbouring countries and is one of the highest in South Asia.[citation needed] Bhutan's small economy is based on agriculture, forestry, and the sale of hydroelectric power to India. Agriculture provides the main livelihood for more than 80% of the population. Agrarian practices consist largely of subsistence farming and animal husbandry. Handicrafts, particularly weaving and the manufacture of religious art for home altars are a small cottage industry and a source of income for some.

A landscape that varies from hilly to ruggedly mountainous has made the building of roads, and other infrastructure, difficult and expensive. This, and a lack of access to the sea, has meant that Bhutan has never been able to benefit from significant trading of its produce. Bhutan currently does not have a railway system, though Indian Railways plans to link up southern Bhutan with its vast network under an agreement signed in January 2005. The historic trade routes over the high Himalayas, which connected India to Tibet, have been closed since the 1959 military takeover of Tibet (although smuggling activity still brings Chinese goods into Bhutan).

The industrial sector is minimal, production being of the cottage-industry type. Most development projects, such as road construction, rely on Indian contract labour. Agricultural produce includes rice, chilies, dairy (yak) products, buckwheat, barley, root crops, apples, and citrus and maize at lower elevations. Industries include cement, wood products, processed fruits, alcoholic beverages and calcium carbide.

Per capita income is around $1,400 (•1,170), ranked 124th. Government revenues total •122 million ($146 million), though expenditures amount to •127 million ($152 million). 60% of the budget expenditure, however, is financed by India's Ministry of External Affairs.[8] Bhutan's exports, principally electricity, cardamom, gypsum, timber, handicrafts, cement, fruit, precious stones and spices, total •128 million ($154 million) (2000 est.). Imports, however, amount to •164 million ($196 million), leading to a trade deficit. Main items imported include fuel and lubricants, grain, machinery, vehicles, fabrics and rice. Bhutan's main export partner is India, accounting for 87.9% of its export goods. Bangladesh (4.6%) and the Philippines (2%) are the other two top export partners. As its border with Tibet is closed, trade between Bhutan and China is now almost non-existent. Bhutan's import partners include India (71.3%), Japan (7.8%) and Austria (3%).

The existing paper currency is being revised and new notes are developed to replace the existing old ones. As of now, denominations of Ngultrum one and Ngultrum five have been introduced. Coins are also very much in use in Bhutan.

In a response to accusations in 1987 by a journalist from UK's Financial Times that the pace of development in Bhutan was slow, the King said that "Gross National Happiness is more important than Gross National Product." In a recent survey organized by the University of Leicester in the UK, Bhutan was ranked as the planet's 8th happiest place.

Demographics

Among the Bhutanese people, several principal ethnic groups may be distinguished. The second dominant group is the Ngalops, a Buddhist group based in the western part of the country. Their culture is closely related to that of Tibet. Much the same could be said of the Sharchops ("Easterners") the dominant group, who are associated with the eastern part of Bhutan (but who traditionally follow the Nyingmapa rather than the official Drukpa Kagyu form of Tibetan Buddhism). They are called the Eastern Bhutanese and Western Bhutanese respectively. In modern times, with improving transportation infrastructure, there has been much intermarrying between Easterners and Westerners, due to the closeness of their cultures and traditions. In the early 1970s, intermarriage between the Lhotsampas and main stream Bhutanese society was encouraged by the government.

The national language is Dzongkha, one of 53 languages in the Tibetan language family. The script, here called Chhokey ("Dharma Language"), is identical with the Tibetan script. A number of Nepali dialects are spoken in parts of southern Bhutan. Khengkha is spoken in central Bhutan. In the schools English is the medium of instruction and Dzongkha is taught as the national language. There are 24 languages currently spoken in Bhutan, all of them in the Tibeto-Burman family, except Nepali, an Indo-Aryan language. Till the 1980's the government sponsored the teaching of Nepali in schools in Southern Bhutan. However, after the violent insurgency in the south, Nepali was removed from the curriculum. The languages of Bhutan are still not well-characterized, and several have yet to be recorded in an in-depth academic grammar. English now has official status as well.

The literacy rate is only 42.2% (56.2% of males and 28.1% of females), 14-year olds and younger comprise 39.1%, while people between 15 and 59 comprise 56.9%, and those over 60 are only 4%. The country has a median age of 20.4 years. Bhutan has a life expectancy of 62.2 years (61 for males and 64.5 for females) according to the latest data from the World Bank. There are 1,070 males to every 1,000 females in the country

Districts

Bhutan is divided into four dzongdey (administrative zones). Each dzongdey is further divided into dzongkhag (districts). There are twenty dzongkhag in Bhutan. Large dzongkhags are further divided into subdistricts known as dungkhag. At the basic level, groups of villages form a constituency called gewog and are administered by a gup, who is elected by the people. The Dzongkhags (districts) of Bhutan are:

1. Bumthang
2. Chukha
3. Dagana
4. Gasa
5. Haa
6. Lhuntse
7. Mongar
8. Paro
9. Pemagatshel

10. Punaka
11. Samdrup Jongkhar
12. Samtse
13. Sarpang
14. Thimphu
15. Trashigang
16. Trashiyangste
17. Trongsa
18. Tsirang
19. Wangdue Phodrang
20. Zhemgang

Culture

Bhutan has a rich and unique cultural heritage that has largely remained intact due to its isolation from the rest of the world until the early 1960s. One of the main attractions for tourists is the country's culture and traditions. Bhutanese tradition is deeply steeped in its Buddhist heritage. Hinduism is the second dominant religion in Bhutan, being most prevalent in the southern regions. Both religions co-exist peacefully and receive support from the government, and enjoy royal patronage. The government is increasingly making efforts to preserve and sustain the current culture and traditions of the country. Due to its largely pristine natural environment and cultural heritage, Bhutan has aptly been referred to as the Last Shangri-la.

While the Bhutanese are free to travel abroad, Bhutan is seen to be inaccessible to many foreigners. There is a widespread misperception that Bhutan has set limits on tourist visas. However it is the high tourist tariff and requirement to go on packaged tours that makes Bhutan a difficult tourist destination.

The National Dress for Bhutanese men is the gho, which is a knee-length robe tied at the waist by a cloth belt known as the kera. Women wear an ankle-length dress, the kira, which is clipped at one shoulder and tied at the waist. An accompaniment to the kira is a long-sleeved blouse, the toego, which is worn underneath the outer layer. Social status and class determine the texture, colours, and decorations that embellish the garments. Differently coloured scarves and shawls are important indicators of social standings, as Bhutan has traditionally been a feudal society. Jewellery is mostly worn by women, especially during religious festivals and public gatherings. To strengthen Bhutan's identity as an independent country, Bhutanese law requires all Bhutanese citizens to wear the national dress in public areas and as formal wear.

Rice, buckwheat, and increasingly maize, are the staple foods of the country. The diet also includes pork, beef, yak meat, chicken, and mutton. Soups and stews of meat and dried vegetables spiced with chillies and cheese are prepared. Ema datshi, made very spicy with cheese and chilis, might be called the national dish for its ubiquity and the pride that Bhutanese have for it. Dairy foods, particularly butter and cheese from yaks and cows, are also popular, and indeed almost all milk is turned to butter and cheese. Popular beverages include butter tea, tea, locally brewed rice wine and beer. Bhutan is the only country in the world to have banned the sale of tobacco.

Bhutan's national sport is archery, and competitions are held regularly in most villages. It differs from Olympic standards not only in technical details such as the placement of the targets and atmosphere. There are two targets placed over 100 metres apart and teams shoot from one end of the field to the other. Each member of the team shoots two arrows per round. Traditional Bhutanese archery is a social event and competitions are organized between villages, towns, and amateur teams. There are usually plenty of food and drink complete with singing and dancing. Wives and supporters of the participating teams cheer. Attempts to distract an opponent include standing around the target and making fun of the shooter's ability. Darts (khuru) is an equally popular outdoor team sport, in which heavy wooden darts pointed with a 4 inch nail are thrown at a paperback-sized target ten to twenty metres away.

Another traditional sport is the digor, which can be best described as shot put combined with horseshoe throwing. Football is an increasingly popular sport. In 2002, Bhutan's national football team played Montserrat—billed as 'The Other Final', the match took place on the same day Brazil played Germany in the World Cup Final, but at the time Bhutan and Montserrat were the world's two lowest ranked teams. The match was held in Thimphu's Changlimithang

National Stadium, and Bhutan won 4-0. Rigsar is the new emergent style of popular music, played on a mix of traditional instruments and electronic keyboards, and dates back to the early 1990s; it shows the influence of Indian popular music, a hybrid form of traditional and Western popular influences. Traditional genres include the zhungdra and boedra.

Characteristic of the region is a type of castle fortress known as the dzong. Since ancient times, the dzongs have served as the religious and secular administration centres for their respective districts.

Chaam, sacred masked dances, are annually performed during religious festivals. Bhutan has numerous public holidays, most of which centre around traditional seasonal, secular and religious festivals. They include the winter solstice (around January 1, depending on the lunar calendar), the lunar New Year (February or March), the King's birthday and the anniversary of his coronation, the official start of monsoon season (September 22), National Day (December 17), and various Buddhist and Hindu celebrations.

Masked dances and dance dramas are common traditional features at festivals, usually accompanied by traditional music. Energetic dancers, wearing colourful wooden or composition facemasks and stylized costumes, depict heroes, demons, death heads, animals, gods, and caricatures of common people. The dancers enjoy royal patronage, and preserve ancient folk and religious customs and perpetuate the ancient lore and art of mask-making.

Inheritance in Bhutan generally goes in the female rather than the male line. Daughters will inherit their parents' house. A man is expected to make his own way in the world and often moves to his wife's home. Love marriages are the norm in the urban areas nowadays but the tradition of arranged marriages is still common in the villages. Although uncommon, polygamy and polyandry are accepted; often being a device to keep property in a contained family unit rather than dispersing it.

Military and Foreign Affairs

The Royal Bhutan Army is Bhutan's military service. It includes the Royal Bodyguard and the Royal Bhutan Police. Membership is voluntary, and the minimum age for recruitment is 18. The standing army numbers about 6,000 and is trained by the Indian Army. It has an annual budget of about US$13.7 million—1.8% of the GDP.

Though the 1949 Treaty with India is still sometimes misinterpreted to mean that India controls Bhutan's foreign affairs, Bhutan today handles all of its foreign affairs itself including the sensitive (to India) border demarcation issue with China. Bhutan has diplomatic relations with 22 countries, including the European Union, with missions in India, Bangladesh, Thailand and Kuwait. It has two UN missions, one in New York and one in Geneva. Only India and Bangladesh have residential embassies in Bhutan, while Thailand has a consulate office in Bhutan.

By a long standing treaty, Indian and Bhutanese citizens may travel to each other's countries without a passport or visa using their national identity cards instead. Bhutanese citizens may also work in India without legal restriction. Bhutan does not have formal diplomatic ties with its northern neighbour, China, although exchanges of visits at various levels between the two have significantly increased in the recent past. The first bilateral agreement between China and Bhutan was signed in 1998, and Bhutan has also set up consulates in Macau and Hong Kong. Bhutan's border with China is largely not demarcated and thus disputed in some places.

On 13 November 2005, Chinese soldiers crossed into Bhutan under the pretext that environmental conditions had forced their retreat south from the Himalayas. The Bhutanese government allowed this incursion (after the fact) on humanitarian grounds. Soon after, the Chinese began building roads and bridges within Bhutanese territory. Bhutanese Foreign Minister Khandu Wangchuk took up the matter with Chinese authorities after the issue was raised in Bhutanese parliament. In response, Foreign Ministry spokesman Qin Gang of the People's Republic of China has said that the border remains in dispute (completely ignoring the original official pretext for the incursion) and that the two sides continue to work for a peaceful and cordial resolution of the dispute.

Security Issues

Bhutan is bounded on three sides by India. From east to west, the Indian states of Sikkim, West Bengal, Assam, and Arunachal Pradesh border Bhutan. In view of the long-standing political disputes and border confrontations between India and China, Bhutan has long been part of India's strategic defense plan. In the view of some Indian strategists, Bhutan is a weak link in India's defense against China.

The key document guiding relations with India is the Treaty of Friendship between the Government of India and the Government of Bhutan of 1949. The ten-article treaty, in force in perpetuity, calls for peace between the two countries and assures Indian non-interference in Bhutan's internal affairs in return for Bhutan's agreeing "to be guided by the advice of the Government of India in regard to its external relations". It also guarantees free trade between the countries and duty-free transit across India of Bhutan's imports. Furthermore, the treaty assures the rights of citizens of each country and the extradition of criminals seeking refuge in either country.

Events in Tibet have had causal effects on Bhutan-Indian relations. The Indo-Bhutanese border was delineated in the Treaty of Peace of 1865 between Bhutan and Britain, but it was not until the period between 1973 and 1984 that a detailed delineation and demarcation was made. Border demarcation talks with India generally resolved disagreements except for several small sectors, including the middle zone between Sarbhang and Geylegphug and the eastern frontier with Arunachal Pradesh.

Historically, Bhutan's foreign relations were limited to contacts with Tibet, India and Britain. In the 1960s Bhutan joined international organizations. It first became a member of the Colombo Plan in 1962, which put the kingdom into contact with member states throughout South Asia and Southeast Asia for fostering cooperative economic development. UN membership was achieved in 1971, followed by seats in the UN's agencies, including the International Monetary Fund and the World Bank. A founding member of SAARC in 1983, Bhutan has also established relations with the Coordination Bureau of the Nonaligned Countries (the headquarters of the Nonaligned Movement), the Group of 77, the Asian Development Bank, and the European Community. In 1975 Bhutan and four other landlocked Asian countries (Afghanistan, Laos, Mongolia, and Nepal) were granted a special status as "least developed landlocked countries" by the UN Economic and Social Commission for Asia and the Pacific (ESCAP) in coordination with the United Nations Conference on Trade and Development (UNCTAD) and UNDP. Despite these organizations' intentions to assist Bhutan and the other countries in dealing with international transit problems, Bhutan declined to participate in their work.

Perhaps the most significant international participation Bhutan embarked on in the 1980s was membership in SAARC. Bhutan became involved in useful working group discussions on agriculture and livestock, rural development, meteorology, telecommunications, science and technology, health and population, transportation, postal cooperation, and trade and industrial cooperation. In Bhutan's extensive multilateral diplomatic activities, officials see their country emerging as an "Eastern Geneva" providing a "venue for peace-making efforts in South Asia."

CHINA

The outbreak of revolution on 10 October 1911 signaled the collapse of the Qing Dynasty (1644–1911), which was formally replaced by the government of the Republic of China on 12 February 1912. The People's Republic of China was officially established on 1 October 1949, replacing the Republic of China government on mainland China.

The flag of China is red with a large yellow five-pointed star and four smaller yellow five-pointed stars (arranged in a vertical arc toward the middle of the flag) in the upper hoist-side corner. The color red symbolizes the spirit of the revolution, and the five stars signify the unity of the people of China under the leadership of the Chinese Communist Party. The flag was officially unveiled in Beijing's Tiananmen Square on 1 October 1949, the formal announcement of the founding of the People's Republic of China.

History

The intersection of migration, amalgamation, and development has characterized China's history from its earliest origins and resulted in a distinctive system of writing, philosophy, art, and social and political organization and civilization that was continuous over the past 4,000 years. Since the beginning of recorded history the people of China have developed a strong sense of their origins, both mythological and real, and kept voluminous records concerning both. As a result of these records, information concerning the ancient past, not only of China but also of much of East, Central and Inner Asia, has survived.

The Chinese polity was first consolidated and proclaimed an empire during the Qin Dynasty (221–206 B.C.). Although short-lived, the Qin Dynasty set in place lasting unifying structures, such as standardized legal codes, bureaucratic procedures, forms of writing, coinage, and a pattern of thought and scholarship. These were modified and improved upon by the successor Han Dynasty (206 B.C.–A.D. 220). Under the Han, a combination of the stricter Legalism and the more benevolent, human-centered Confucianism—known as Han Confucianism or State Confucianism—became the ruling norm in Chinese culture for the next 2,000 years.

Another recurrent historical theme has been the unceasing struggle of the largely agrarian Chinese against the threat posed to their safety and way of life by non-Chinese peoples on the margins of their territory. For centuries most of the foreigners that China's officials saw came from or through the Central and Inner Asian societies to the north and west. This circumstance conditioned the Chinese view of the outside world. The Chinese saw their domain as the self-sufficient centre of the universe, and from this image they derived the traditional (and still used) Chinese name for their country—Zhongguo, literally Middle Kingdom or Central Nation. Those at the centre (*zhong*) of civilization distinguished themselves from the "barbarian" peoples on the outside (*wai*), whose cultures were presumed to be inferior by Chinese standards.

Starting in the pre-Qin period, Chinese states built large defensive walls that, in time, composed a "Great Wall." The Great Wall is actually a series of noncontiguous walls, forts, and other defensive structures built or rebuilt during the Qin, Han, Sui (A.D. 589–618), Jin (1115–1234), and Ming (1368–1643) periods, rather than a single, continuous wall. The Great Wall reaches from the coast of Hebei Province to northwestern Gansu, officially 6,000 kilometres in length, although unofficial estimates range from 2,700 kilometres to as many as 50,000 kilometres, depending on which structures are included in the measurement.

It was in the 19th century that China first clashed with the European nations. The Manchu had conquered China and established the Qing Dynasty (1644–1911), ushering in a period of great conquest and a long period of relative peace. When Europeans began arriving in increasing numbers, Chinese courtiers expected them to conduct themselves according to traditional tributary relations that had evolved over the centuries between their emperor and representatives of Central Asian states who came via the Silk Road and others who came from Southeast Asia and the Middle East via the sea trade. The Western powers arrived in China in full force at a time of tremendous internal rebellion and rapid economic and social change. By the mid-19th century, China had been defeated militarily by superior Western technology and weaponry, and the government was plagued with ever mounting rebellions. By 1911 the millennia-old dynastic system of imperial government was toppled as a result of the efforts of a half century of reform, modernization, and, ultimately, revolution.

The end of imperial rule was followed by nearly four decades of major socio-economic development and socio-political discord. The initial establishment of a Western-style government—the Republic of China—was followed by several efforts to restore the throne. Lack of a strong central authority led to regional fragmentation, warlordism, and civil war. The main figure in the revolutionary movement that overthrew imperial rule was Sun Yatsen (1866–1925), who, along with other republican political leaders, endeavored to establish a parliamentary democracy. They were thwarted by warlords who resorted to assassination, rebellion, civil war, and collusion with foreign powers (especially Japan) in their efforts to gain control. Sun Yatsen eventually turned to the new Soviet Union for inspiration and assistance. Soviet advisers helped the Guomindang establish political and military training activities. A key individual in these developments was Jiang Jieshi (1888–1975; Chiang Kai-shek in Yue dialect), one of Sun's lieutenants from the early revolution days. But Moscow also supported the new Chinese Communist Party (CCP), which was founded by Mao Zedong (1893–1976) and others in Shanghai in 1921.

The Soviets were prepared for either side to emerge victorious. The struggle for power in China began between the Guomindang and the CCP as both parties also sought the unification of China. Sun's untimely death from illness in 1925 brought a split in the Guomindang and eventually an uneasy united front between the Guomindang and the CCP. Jiang Jieshi trained a new generation of officers who would soon embark on the Northern Expedition. Zhou Enlai (1898–1976), who later become premier of China under the communists, was a political commissar at this time. Jiang, who succeeded Sun Yatsen, broke with his Soviet advisers and with the communists and by 1927 was successful in defeating the northern warlords and unifying China. The years 1928 to 1937 are often referred to as the Nanjing Decade because of the national development that took place under Jiang's presidency before World War II when China's capital was in Nanjing (Southern Capital). The Northern Expedition had culminated in the capture of Beijing, which was renamed Beiping (Northern Peace). Thereafter, the Nanjing government received international recognition as the legitimate government of China.

With the 1927 split between the Guomindang and the CCP, the CCP began to engage in armed struggle against the Jiang regime. The Red Army was established in 1927, and after a series of uprisings and internal political struggles, the CCP announced the establishment in 1931 of the Chinese Soviet Republic under the chairmanship of Mao in Jiangxi Province in south-central China. After a series of deadly campaigns by Jiang's armies, the Red Army and the CCP apparatus broke out of Jiangxi and embarked on their epic 12,500-kilometre Long March of 1934–35 to a new stronghold in Shaanxi Province in the north. During the march, Mao consolidated his hold over the CCP when in 1935 he became chairman, a position he held until his death in 1976.

Japan invaded Manchuria in 1931, established the puppet government of Manchukuo in 1932, and soon pushed south into North China. The 1936 Xi'an Incident—in which Jiang Jieshi was held captive by local military forces until he agreed to a second front with the CCP—brought new impetus to China's resistance to Japan. However, a clash between Chinese and Japanese troops outside Beiping on 7 July 1937 marked the beginning of full-scale warfare. Shanghai was attacked and quickly fell. An indication of the ferocity of Tokyo's determination to annihilate the Guomindang government is reflected in the major atrocity committed by the Japanese army in and around Nanjing during a six-week period in December 1937 and January 1938. Known in history as the Nanjing Massacre, wanton rape, looting, arson, and mass executions took place, so that in one horrific day, some 57,418 Chinese prisoners of war and civilians reportedly were killed. Japanese sources admit to a total of 142,000 deaths during the Nanjing Massacre, but Chinese sources report upward of 340,000 deaths and 20,000 women raped. Japan expanded its war effort in the Pacific, Southeast, and South Asia, and by 1941 the United States had entered the war. With Allied assistance, Chinese military forces—both Guomindang and CCP—defeated Japan. Civil war between the Guomindang and the CCP broke out in 1946, and the Guomindang forces were defeated and had retreated to a few offshore islands and Taiwan by 1949. Mao and the other CCP leaders reestablished the capital in Beiping, which they renamed Beijing.

The communist takeover of the mainland in 1949 set the scene for building a new society built on a Marxist-Leninist model replete with class struggle and proletarian politics fashioned and directed by the CCP. The People's Republic of China was barely established when it perceived a threat from the United States, which was at war in North Korea, and elected to support its neighbour, the new communist state, the Democratic People's Republic of Korea. The Chinese People's Volunteer Army invaded the Korean Peninsula in October 1950 and, along with its North Korean ally, enjoyed initial military success and then a two-year stalemate, which culminated in an armistice signed on 27 July 1953. Meanwhile, China seized control of Tibet. It also had embarked on a political rectification movement against "enemies of the state" and promoting "class struggle" under the aegis of agrarian reform as part of the "transition to socialism."

Periods of consolidation and economic development facilitated by President Liu Shaoqi (1898–1969) and Premier Zhou were severely altered by disastrous anti-intellectual (such as the Hundred Flowers Campaign, 1957), economic (the Great Leap Forward, 1958–59), and political (the Great Proletarian Cultural Revolution, 1966–76) experiments directed by Mao and his supporters. During this time, China had broken with the Soviet Union by 1959, fought a border war with India in 1962, and skirmished with Soviet troops in 1969. Less radical leaders such as Zhou and Vice Premier Deng Xiaoping (1904–97), who had been politically rehabilitated after his disgrace early in the Cultural Revolution, asserted some control, and negotiations were initiated with the United States, ending a generation of extreme animosity toward Washington. The 1976 death of Mao ended the extremist influence in the party, and, under the leadership of Deng Xiaoping and his supporters, China began a period of pragmatic economic reforms and opening itself to the outside world.

Reform-era activities began in earnest in 1978 and eventually made China one of the largest world economies and trading partners as well as a regional military power. The Four Modernizations (agriculture, industry, science and technology, and national defence) became the preeminent agenda within the party, state, and society. The well-being of China's people increased substantially, especially along coastal areas and in urban areas involved in manufacturing for the world market. Yet, politics, the so-called "fifth modernization," occurred at too slow a pace for the emerging generation. China's incipient democracy movement was subdued in 1978–79 at the very time that China's economic reforms were being launched. As Deng consolidated his control of China, the call for political reform came to the fore again in the mid-1980s, and pro-reform leaders were placed in positions of authority. Zhao Ziyang (1919–2005) was appointed premier, and Hu Yaobang (1915–89) CCP general secretary. Deng himself, satisfied with being the "power behind the throne," never held a top position. The democracy movement, however, was violently suppressed by the military in the 1989 Tiananmen incident.

In the years after Tiananmen, conservative reformers led by Deng protégé Jiang Zemin (later to become president of China) endured and eventually overcame world criticism. When Deng went into retirement, the rising generation of technocrats ruled China and oversaw its modernization. Political progress gradually occurred. Term limits were placed on political and governmental positions at all levels, succession became orderly and contested elections began to take place at the local level. Tens of thousands of Chinese students went overseas to study; many returned to participate in the building of modern China, some to become millionaires in the new "socialist economy with Chinese characteristics." As a sign of its emerging superpower status, in October 2003 China launched its first "taikonaut" into space on a 22-hour journey. The second space launch, with two taikonauts, took place in October 2005 and involved a 115-hour flight. In the next stage of space exploration, China plans to conduct a space walk, rendezvous docking in orbit, launch a moon-orbiting unmanned spacecraft and to land an unmanned probe on the moon.

As the 21st century began, a new generation of leaders emerged and gradually replaced the old. Jiang Zemin gradually gave up his leadership role and moved into a position of elder statesman, still with obvious influence exerted through his protégés who were embedded at all levels of the government. Hu Jintao emerged—by 2004—as the preeminent leader (president of China, chairman of both the state Central Military Commission and party Central Military Commission, and general secretary of the CCP).

Geography

China has a total area of nearly 9,596,960 square kilometres. From east to west, the distance is about 5,000 kilometres from the Heilong Jiang (Amur River) to the Pamir Mountains in Central Asia; from north to south, the distance is approximately 4,050 kilometres from Heilongjiang Province to Hainan Province in the south and another 1,450 kilometres farther south to Zengmu Shoal, a territorial claim off the north coast of Malaysia.

China has a total of 22,117 kilometres of land boundaries with 14 other nations. These borders include. Afghanistan (76 kilometres), Bhutan (470 kilometres), Burma (2,185 kilometres), India (3,380 kilometres), Kazakhstan (1,533 kilometres), North Korea (1,416 kilometres), Kyrgyzstan (858 kilometres), Laos (423 kilometres), Mongolia (4,677 kilometres), Nepal (1,236 kilometres), Pakistan (523 kilometres), Russia (4,300 kilometres), Tajikistan (414 kilometres), and Vietnam (1,281 kilometres). China's coastline extends 14,500 kilometres from the border with North Korea in the north to Vietnam in the south. China's coasts are on the East China Sea, Korea Bay, Yellow Sea, and South China Sea. China claims a 12-nautical-mile territorial sea, a 24-nautical-mile contiguous zone, a 200-nautical-mile exclusive economic zone, and a 200-nautical-mile continental shelf or the distance to the edge of the continental shelf. China is involved in a complex dispute with Malaysia, Philippines, Taiwan, Vietnam, and possibly Brunei over the Spratly (Nansha) Islands in the South China Sea. China also occupies the Paracel (Xisha) Islands, which are also claimed by Vietnam and Taiwan, and asserts a claim to the Japanese-administered Senkaku Islands (Diaoyu Tai) in the Pacific Ocean.

Most of the mountainous and militarized boundary with India is in dispute, but Beijing and New Delhi have committed to its resolution with discussions on the least disputed middle sector. China's de facto administration of the Aksai Chin section of Kashmir (which is disputed by India and Pakistan) is the subject of a dispute between China and India. India does not recognize Pakistan's ceding lands to China in a 1964 boundary agreement. In October 2004, China signed an agreement with Russia on the delimitation of their entire 4,300-kilometer-long border, which had long been in dispute.

Topography. Mountains cover 33% of China's landmass, plateaus 26%, basins 19%, plains 12%, and hills 10%. Thus, 69% of China's land is mountains, hills, and highlands. China has five main mountain ranges, and seven of its mountain peaks are higher than 8,000 metres above sea level. The main topographic features include the Qingzang (Qinghai-Tibet) Plateau at 4,000 metres above sea level and the Kunlun, Qin Ling, and Greater Hinggan ranges. In the Himalaya Mountains are Mount Everest (known in China as Qomolangma) at 8,844.4 metres (based on new official measurements) and K–2 at 8,611 metres, shared with Nepal and Pakistan, respectively. The lowest inland point in China— the second lowest place in the world after the Dead Sea—is at Turpan Pendi, 140 kilometres southeast of Urumqi, the capital of Xinjiang Uygur Autonomous Region, at 154 metres below sea level. With temperatures that have reached 49.6 C, it also ranks as one the hottest places in China.

Principal Rivers. China has 50,000 rivers totaling some 420,000 kilometres in length and each having a catchment area of more than 100 square kilometres. Some 1,500 of these rivers each have catchment areas exceeding 1,000 square kilometres. Most rivers flow from west to east and empty into the Pacific Ocean. The Yangzi (Changjiang or Yangzte River), which rises in Tibet, flows through Central China, and, having traveled 6,300 kilometres, enters the Yellow Sea near Shanghai. The Yangzi has a catchment area of 1.8 million square kilometres and is the third longest river in the world after the Amazon and the Nile. The second longest river in China is the Huanghe (Yellow River), which also rises in Tibet and travels circuitously for 5,464 kilometres through North China before reaching the Bo Hai Gulf on the north coast of Shangdong Province. It has a catchment area of 752,000 square kilometres. The Heilongjiang (Heilong or Black Dragon River) flows for 3,101 kilometres in Northeast China and an additional 1,249 in Russia, where it is known as the Amur. The longest river in South China is the Zhujiang (Pearl River), which is 2,214 kilometres long. Along with its three tributaries, the Xi, Dong, and Bei—West, East, and North—rivers, it forms the rich Zhujiang Delta near Guangzhou, Zhuhai, Macau, and Hong Kong. Other major rivers are the Liaohe in the northeast, Haihe in the north, Qiantang in the east, and Lancang in the southwest.

Climate. Most of the country is in the northern temperate zone. There are complex climatic patterns ranging from the cold-temperate north to the tropical south, with sub-arctic temperatures in the Himalaya Mountains, resulting in a temperature difference of some 40° C from north to south. Temperatures range from –30° C in the north in January to 28° C in the south in July. Annual precipitation varies significantly from region to region, with a high of 1,500 millimetres annually along the southeastern coast and a low of fewer than 50 millimetres in the northwest. There is an alternating wet monsoon in the summer and a dry monsoon in winter. North China and southward are affected by the seasonal cold, dry winds from Siberia and the Mongolia Plateau between September/October and March/April. Summer monsoon winds bring warm and wet currents into South China and northward.

Natural Resources. China has substantial mineral reserves and is the world's largest producer of antimony, natural graphite, tungsten, and zinc. Other major minerals are bauxite, coal, crude petroleum, diamonds, gold, iron ore, lead, magnetite, manganese, mercury, molybdenum, natural gas, phosphate rock, tin, uranium, and vanadium. With its vast mountain ranges, China's hydropower potential is the largest in the world.

Land Use. 14.86% (about 1.4 million square kilometres) of China's land is arable. About 1.3% (some 116,580 square kilometres) is planted to permanent crops. With comparatively little land planted to permanent crops, intensive agricultural techniques are used to reap harvests that are sufficient to feed the world's largest population and still have surplus for export. An estimated 544,784 square kilometres of land is irrigated.

Environmental Factors. The major current environmental issues in China are air pollution (greenhouse gases and sulfur dioxide particulates) from over reliance on coal, which produces acid rain; water shortages, particularly in the north; water pollution from untreated wastes; deforestation; an estimated loss of 20% of agricultural land since 1949 to soil erosion and economic development and desertification. Deforestation has been a major contributor to China's most significant natural disaster—flooding. China's national carbon dioxide (CO_2) emissions are among the highest in the world and increasing annually. The CO_2 emissions are estimated at 2.8 billion tons. These amounts cited by the UN are more than double those of India and Japan but still less than half those of the United States. China's ozone depleting potential also is high. The CO_2 emissions are mostly produced by coal-burning energy plants and other coal-burning operations. Better pollution control and billion-dollar cleanup programmes have helped reduced the growth rate of industrial pollution.

Time Zone. Although China crosses all or part of five international time zones, it operates on a single uniform time, China Standard Time (CST; Greenwich Mean Time plus eight hours), using Beijing as the base.

Society

Population. Government sources put the population at an estimated 1,313,973,713 in July 2006. The annual population growth rate was estimated at 0.59% (2006 estimate).The nation's overall population density was 135 persons per square kilometer in 2003. The most densely populated provinces are in the east. Jiangsu (712 persons per square kilometer), Shangdong (587 persons per square kilometer), and Henan (546 persons per square kilometer). Shanghai was the most densely populated municipality at 2,646 persons per square kilometer. The least densely populated areas are in the west, with Tibet having the lowest density at only 2 persons per square kilometer. Sixty-two% of the population lived in rural areas in 2004, while 38% lived in urban settings. About 94% of population lives on approximately 46% of land. In the long term, China faces increasing urbanization; according to predictions, nearly 70% of the population will live in urban areas by 2035.

Demography. China has been the world's most populous nation for many centuries. When China took its first post-1949 census in 1953, the population stood at 582 million; by the fifth census in 2000, the population had almost doubled, reaching 1.2 billion. China's fast-growing population was a major policy matter for its leaders in the mid-20th century, so that in the early 1970s, the government implemented a stringent one-child birth-control policy. As a result of that policy, China successfully achieved its goal of a more stable and much-reduced fertility rate; in 1971 women had an average of 5.4 children versus an estimated 1.7 children in 2004. Nevertheless, the population continues to grow, and people want more children. There is also a serious gender imbalance. Census data obtained in 2000 revealed that 119 boys were born for every 100 girls, and among China's "floating population" the ratio was as high as 128.100. These situations led Beijing in July 2004 to ban selective abortions of female fetuses. Additionally, life expectancy has soared, and China now has an increasingly aging population; it is projected that 11.8% of the population in 2020 will be 65 years of age and older. Based on 2006 estimates, China's age structure is 0–14 years of age—20.8%; 15–64 years—71.4%, and 65 years and older—7.7%. Estimates made in 2006 indicate a birthrate of nearly 13.3 births per 1,000 and a death rate of 6.9 per 1,000.

Migration. In 2006 it was estimated that China was experiencing a –0.39 per 1,000 population net migration rate. Of major concern in China is its growing "floating population" (*liudong renkou*), a large number of people moving from the countryside to the city, from developed economic areas to underdeveloped areas, and from the central and western regions to the eastern coastal region, as a result of fast-paced reform-era economic development and modern agricultural practices that have reduced the need for a large agricultural labor force. Although residency requirements have been relaxed to a degree, the floating population is not officially permitted to reside permanently in the receiving towns and cities. As early as 1994, it was estimated that China had a surplus of approximately 200 million agricultural workers, and the number was expected to increase to 300 million in the early 21st century and to expand even further into the long-term future. It was reported in 2005 that the floating population had increased from 70 million in 1993 to 140 million in 2003, thus exceeding 10% of the national population and accounting for 30% of all rural labourers. According to the 2000 national census, population flow inside a province accounted for 65% of the total while that crossing provincial boundaries accounted for 35%. Young and middle-aged people account for the vast majority of this floating population; those between 15 and 35 years of age account for more than 70%. Other migration issues include the more than 2,000 Tibetans who cross into Nepal annually, according to the United Nations High Commissioner for Refugees (UNHCR). The government tries to prevent this out-migration from occurring and has pressured Nepalese authorities to repatriate illegal border-crossing Tibetans. Another activity viewed as illegal is the influx of North Koreans into northeastern China. Some 1,850 North Koreans fled their country in 2004, but China views them as illegal economic migrants rather than refugees and sends many of them back. Some of those who succeed in reaching sanctuary in foreign diplomatic compounds or international schools have been allowed to depart for South Korea.

Ethnic Groups. Besides the majority Han Chinese, China recognizes 55 other nationality or ethnic groups, numbering about 105 million persons, mostly concentrated in the northwest, north, northeast, south, and southwest but with some in central interior areas. Based on the 2000 census, some 91.5% of the population was classified as Han Chinese (1.1 billion). The other major minority ethnic groups were Zhuang (16.1 million), Manchu (10.6 million), Hui (9.8 million), Miao (8.9 million), Uygur (8.3 million), Tujia (8 million), Yi (7.7 million), Mongol (5.8 million), Tibetan (5.4 million), Bouyei (2.9 million), Dong (2.9 million), Yao (2.6 million), Korean (1.9 million), Bai (1.8 million), Hani (1.4 million), Kazakh (1.2 million), Li (1.2 million), and Dai (1.1 million). Classifications are often based on self-identification, and it is sometimes and in some locations advantageous for political or economic reasons to identify with one group over another. All nationalities in China are equal according to the law.

Languages. The official language of China is standard Chinese or Mandarin (Putonghua, which means standard speech, based on the Beijing dialect). Other major dialects are Yue (Cantonese), Wu (Shanghaiese), Minbei (Fuzhou), Minnan (Hokkien-Taiwanese), Xiang, Gan, and Hakka (Kejia). Because of the many ethnic groups in China, numerous minority languages also are spoken. All of the Chinese dialects share a common written form that has evolved and been standardized during two millennia and serves as a unifying bond amongst the Han Chinese. The government has aggressively developed both shorthand Chinese and Pinyin (phonetic spelling) as ways to increase literacy and transliterate Chinese names. The Pinyin system was introduced in 1958 and was approved by the State Council in 1978 as the standard system for the romanization of Chinese personal and geographic names. In 2000 the Hanyu (Han language) Pinyin phonetic alphabet was written into law as the unified standard for spelling and phonetic notation of the national language.

Religion. The traditional religions of China are Confucianism, Daoism, and Buddhism. Confucianism is not a religion, although some have tried to imbue it with rituals and religious qualities, but rather a philosophy and system of ethical conduct that since the 5th century B.C. has guided China's society. Kong Fuzi (Confucius in Latinized form) is honored in China as a great sage of antiquity whose writings promoted peace and harmony and good morals in family life and society in general. Ritualized reverence for one's ancestors, sometimes referred to as ancestor worship, has been a tradition in China since at least the Shang Dynasty (1750–1040 B.C.). In 2005 the Chinese government acknowledged that there were an estimated 100 million adherents to various sects of Buddhism and some 9,500 and 16,000 temples and monasteries, many maintained as cultural landmarks and tourist attractions. Approximately 8% of the population is Buddhist, approximately 1.5% is Muslim, an estimated 0.4% belongs to the government-sponsored "patriotic" Catholic Church, an estimated 0.4 to 0.6% belongs to the unofficial Vatican-affiliated Roman Catholic Church, and an estimated 1.2 to 1.5% is registered as Protestant. Most adherents of Islam are members of the Uygur and Hui nationality people. The Falun Dafa (Wheel of Law, also called Falun Gong) quasi-religious movement based on traditional Chinese *qigong* (deep-breathing exercises) and Daoist and Buddhist practices and beliefs was established in 1992 and claimed 70 million to 100 million practitioners in China in the late 1990s. Because of its perceived antigovernment activities, Falun Gong was outlawed in China in April 1999, and thousands of its practitioners were arrested and sentenced to "re-education through labour" or incarcerated in mental hospitals. The constitution grants citizens of the People's Republic of China the freedom of religious belief and maintains that the state "protects normal religious activities," but that no one "may make use of religion to engage in activities that disrupt public order, impair the health of citizens or interfere with the educational system of the state."

Education and Literacy. Education in China is the responsibility of the Ministry of Education. The population has had on average only 6.2 years of schooling, but in 1986 the goal of nine years of compulsory education by 2000 was established. The education system provides free primary education for five years, starting at age seven, followed by five years of secondary education for ages 12 to 17. At this level, there are three years of middle school and two years of high school. The Ministry of Education reports a 99% attendance rate for primary school and an 80% rate for both primary and middle schools. Since free higher education was abolished in 1985, applicants to colleges and universities compete for scholarships based on academic ability. Private schools have been allowed since the early 1980s. In 2003 China supported 1,552 institutions of higher learning (colleges and universities) and their 725,000 professors and 11 million students. While there is intense competition for admission to China's colleges and universities among college entrants, Beijing and Qinghua universities and more than 100 other key universities are the most sought after. The literacy rate in China is 90.9%, based on 2002 estimates.

Welfare. In pre-reform China, the socialist state fulfilled the needs of society from cradle to grave. Child care, education, job placement, housing, subsistence, health care and elder care were administered through state-owned enterprises and agricultural communes and collectives. Article 14 of the Constitution stipulates that the state "builds and improves a social security system that corresponds with the level of economic development." Social security reforms since the late 1990s have included unemployment insurance, medical insurance, workers' compensation insurance, maternity benefits, communal pension funds, and individual pension accounts.

Economy

Overview. By 2005 China's economy had become the second largest in the world after the United States when measured on a purchasing power parity (PPP) basis. The government has a goal of quadrupling the gross domestic product (GDP) by 2020 and more than doubling the per capita GDP. Central planning has been curtailed, and widespread market economy mechanisms and a reduced government role have prevailed since 1978. The government fosters a dual economic structure that has evolved from a socialist, centrally planned economy to a socialist market economic system, or a "market economy with socialist characteristics." Industry is marked by increasing technological advancements and productivity. People's communes were eliminated by 1984 and the system of township-collective-household production was introduced to the agricultural sector. Private ownership of production assets is legal, although some nonagricultural and industrial facilities are still state-owned and centrally planned. Restraints on foreign trade were relaxed when China acceded to the World Trade Organization in 2001. Joint ventures are encouraged, especially in the coastal special economic zones and open coastal cities. A sign of the affluence that the reformed economy has brought to China might be seen in the number of its millionaires (measured in U.S. dollars)—a reported 236,000 millionaires in 2004, an increase of 12% over two years earlier. Chinese officials cite two major trends that have an effect on China's market economy and future development—world multi-polarization and regional integration. In relation to these trends, they foresee the roles of China and the United States in world affairs and with one another as very important. Despite successes, China's leaders face a variety of challenges to the nation's future economic development. They have to maintain a high growth rate, deal effectively with the rural workforce, improve the financial system, and continue to reform the state-owned enterprises, foster the productive private sector, establish a social security system, improve scientific and educational development, promote better international cooperation, and change the role of the government in the economic system. Despite constraints the international market has placed on China, it nevertheless became the world's third largest trading nation after only the United States and Germany. The Fifth Plenum of the Sixteenth CCP Central Committee, in October 2005, approved the new Eleventh Five-Year Plan (2006–10), which emphasizes a shift from extensive to intensive growth in order to meet demands for improved economic returns; the conservation of resources to include a 20-% reduction in energy consumption by 2010; and an effort to raise profitability. Better coordination of urban and rural development and of development between nearby regions also is emphasized in the new plan.

Gross Domestic Product (GDP)/Purchasing Power Parity (PPP). In 2005 China had a GDP of US$2.2 trillion. China's PPP was estimated for 2005 at nearly US$8.9 trillion. PPP per capita in 2005 was estimated at US$6,800. Based on official Chinese data, the estimated GDP growth rate for 2007 was 11.3%.

Government Budget. The state budget for 2004 was US$330.6 billion in revenue and US$356.8 billion in expenditures. In the revenue column, 95.5% was from taxes and tariffs, 54.9% of which was collected by the central government and 45% by local authorities. The expenditures were for culture, education, science, and health care (18%); capital construction (12%); administration (14%); national defence (7.7%); agriculture, forestry, and water conservancy (5.9%); subsidies to compensate for price increases (2.7%); pensions and social welfare (1.9%); promotion of innovation, science, and technology (4.3%); operating expenses of industry, transport, and commerce (1.2%); geological prospecting (0.4%), and other (31.9%). The overall budget deficit in 2004 was approximately US$26 billion, an amount equivalent to about 1.5% of GDP.

Inflation. China's annual rate of inflation averaged 6% per year during the 1990–2002 period. Although consumer prices declined by 0.8% in 2002, they increased by 1.2% in 2003. China's estimated inflation rate in 2005 was 1.8%.

Special and Open Economic Zones. As part of its economic reforms and policy of opening to the world, between 1980 and 1984 China established special economic zones (SEZs) in Shantou, Shenzhen, and Zhuhai in Guangdong Province and Xiamen in Fujian Province and designated the entire island province of Hainan a special economic zone. In 1984 China opened 14 other coastal cities to overseas investment (listed north to south). Dalian, Qinhuangdao, Tianjin, Yantai, Qingdao, Lianyungang, Nantong, Shanghai, Ningbo, Wenzhou, Fuzhou, Guangzhou, Zhanjiang, and Beihai. Then, beginning in 1985, the central government expanded the coastal area by establishing the following open economic zones (listed north to south). Liaodong Peninsula, Hebei Province (which surrounds Beijing and Tianjin), Shandong Peninsula, Yangzi River Delta, Xiamen-Zhangzhou-Quanzhou Triangle in southern Fujian Province, Zhujiang (Pearl River) Delta, and Guangxi Zhuang Autonomous Region. In 1990 the Chinese government decided to open the Pudong New Zone in Shanghai to overseas investment, as well as more cities in the Yangzi River Valley. Since 1992 the State Council has opened a number of border cities and all the capital cities of inland provinces and autonomous regions. In addition, 15 free-trade zones, 32 state-level economic and technological development zones, and 53 new- and high-tech industrial development zones have been established in large and medium-sized cities. As a result, a multilevel diversified pattern of opening and integrating coastal areas with river, border, and inland areas has been formed in China.

Agriculture. China traditionally has struggled to feed its large population. Famines have periodically ravaged China's population. Great emphasis has always been put on agricultural production, but weather, wars, and politics often mitigated good intentions. Agricultural output increased to 33% of GDP by 1983. Since then, however, agriculture has decreased its share in the economy at the same time that the services sector has increased. By 2004 agriculture (including forestry and fishing) produced only 15.2% of China's GDP but still is huge by any measure. Some 46.9% of the total national workforce was engaged in agriculture, forestry, and fishing in 2004. China's cereal production is the largest in the world. (377 million tons, or 18.1% of total world production). Its plant oil crops—at 15 million tons—are a close second to those of the United States and amount to 12.6% of total world production. More specifically, China's principal crops are rice (176 million tons), corn (132 million tons), sweet potatoes (105 million tons), wheat (91 million tons), sugarcane (89 million tons), and potatoes (70 million tons). Other grains, such as barley, buckwheat, millet, oats, rye, sorghum, and tritcale (a wheat-rye hybrid), added substantially to overall grain production. Crops of peanuts, rapeseed, soybeans, and sugar beets also are significant, as is vegetable production. Among the highest levels of production were cabbages, tomatoes, cucumbers, and dry onions. In 2004 fruit production also became a significant aspect of the agricultural market. China produced large crops of watermelons, cantaloupes, and other melons that year. Other significant orchard products were apples, citrus fruits, bananas, and mangoes. China, a nation of numerous cigarette smokers, also produced 2.4 million tons of tobacco leaves. Fertilizer use was a major contributor to these abundant harvests. In 2002 China consumed 25.4 million tons of nitrogenous fertilizers, or 30% of total world consumption and more than double the consumption of other major users such as India and the United States in the same period. Among the less used fertilizers, China also was a leader. It consumed 9.9 million tons of phosphate fertilizers (29.5% of the world total) and 4.2 million tons of potash fertilizers (18.2% of the world total). With China's accession to the World Trade Organization (WTO) in 2001, food export opportunities have developed that have brought about still more efficient farming techniques. As a result, traditional areas such as grain production have decreased in favor of cash crops of vegetables and fruit for domestic and export trade.

China's livestock herds are the largest in the world, far outstripping all of Europe combined and about comparable in size to all African nations combined. For example, in 2003 China had 49.1% of the world's pigs, 22.5% of the world's goats, and 7.5% of the world's cattle. Converted into food production, China's major livestock products in 2004 were pork (47.2 million tons), poultry eggs (28.0 million tons), cow's milk (18.5 million tons), poultry meat (13.4 million tons), and beef and veal (6.4 million tons). Other meats of significant amounts were mutton, lamb, and goat. Major by-products were cattle hides (1.6 million tons), sheepskins (321,000 tons), and goatskins (375,000 tons). Honey (300,000 tons) and raw silk (95,000 tons) also were major products destined for the commercial market. Forestry products, measured in annual round wood production, also abound. In 2004 China produced an estimated 284 million cubic metres of round wood, the world's third largest supplier after the United States and India, or about 8.5% of total world production. From the round wood, some 11.3 million cubic metres of sawn wood are produced annually. China also leads the world in fish production. In 2003 it caught 16.7 million tons of fish, far out catching the second-ranked nation, the United States, with its 4.9 million tons. Aquaculture also was substantial in world terms. In the same year, China harvested 28.8 million tons of fish, an amount more than 10 times that of the second-ranked nation, India, which produced 2.2 million tons. The total fish production in 2003 was 45.6 million tons. Of this total, 63.2% was from aquaculture, an increasing sector, and 36.7% from fish caught in rivers, lakes, and the sea.

Mining and Minerals. Mineral resources include large reserves of coal and iron ore, plus adequate to abundant supplies of nearly all other industrial minerals. Besides being a major coal producer, China is the world's fifth largest producer of gold and is an important producer and exporter of rare metals needed in high-technology industries. The rare earth reserves at the Bayan Obi mine in Inner Mongolia are thought to be the largest in any single location in the world. Outdated mining and ore-processing technologies are being replaced with modern techniques, but China's rapid industrialization requires imports of minerals from abroad. In particular, iron ore imports from Australia and the United States have soared in the early 2000s as steel production rapidly outstripped domestic iron ore production. The major areas of production in 2004 were coal (nearly 2 billion tons), iron ore (310 million tons), crude petroleum (175 million tons), natural gas (41 million cubic metres), antimony ore (110,000 tons), tin concentrates (110,000 tons), nickel ore (64,000 tons), tungsten concentrates (67,000 tons), unrefined salt (37 million tons), vanadium (40,000 tons), and molybdenum ore (29,000 tons). In order of magnitude, bauxite, gypsum, barite, magnetite, talc and related minerals, manganese ore, fluorspar, and zinc also were important. In addition, China produced 2,450 tons of silver and 215 tons of gold in 2004. The mining sector accounted for less than 0.9% of total employment in 2002 but produced about 5.3% of total industrial production.

Industry and Manufacturing. Industry and construction produced 53.1% of China's GDP in 2005. Industry (including mining, manufacturing, construction, and power) contributed 52.9% of GDP in 2004 and occupied 22.5% of the workforce. The manufacturing sector produced 44.1% of GDP in 2004 and accounted for 11.3% of total employment in 2002. China is the world's leading manufacturer of chemical fertilizers, cement, and steel. Prior to 1978, most output was produced by state-owned enterprises. As a result of the economic reforms that followed, there was a significant increase in production by enterprises sponsored by local governments, especially townships and villages, and, increasingly, by private entrepreneurs and foreign investors. By 2002 the share in gross industrial output by state-owned and state-holding industries had decreased to 41%, and the state-owned companies themselves contributed only 16% of China's industrial output. An example of an emerging heavy industry is automobile manufacture, which has soared during the reform period. In 1975 only 139,800 automobiles were produced annually, but by 1985 production had reached 443,377, then jumped to nearly 1.1 million by 1992 and increased fairly evenly each year up until 2001, when it reached 2.3 million. In 2002 production rose to nearly 3.3 million and then jumped again the next year to 4.4 million. Domestic sales have kept pace with production. After respectable annual increases in the mid- and late 1990s, sales soared in the early 2000s, reaching 3 million automobiles sold in 2003. With some governmental controls in place, sales dipped to 2.4 million sold in 2004. Some forecasters expect sales to reach 6.9 million by 2015. By 2010 China's automobile production is projected to reach 9.4 million, and the country could become the number-one automaker in the world by 2020. So successful has China's automotive industry been that it began exporting car parts in 1999. China began to plan major moves into the automobile and components export business starting in 2005. A new Honda factory in Guangzhou was built in 2004 solely for the export market and is expected to ship 30,000 passenger vehicles to Europe. By 2004, 12 major foreign automotive manufacturers had joint-venture plants in China. They produced a wide range of automobiles, minivans, sport utility vehicles, buses, and trucks. In 2003 China exported US$4.7 billion worth of vehicles and components, an increase of 34.4% over 2002. By 2004 China had become the world's fourth largest automotive vehicle manufacturer. Concomitant with automotive production and other steel-consuming industries, China has been rapidly increasing its steel production. Iron ore production kept pace with steel production in the early 1990s but was soon outpaced by imported iron ore and other metals in the early 2000s. Steel production, an estimated 140 million tons in 2000, was expected to reach more than 350 million tons a year by 2010.

Energy. As with other economic categories, China is a major producer and consumer of energy resources. In 2002, the most recent year available for United Nations statistics, China produced 934.2 million tons of oil equivalent and consumed 889.6 million tons. China's energy consumption has risen dramatically since the inception of its economic reform programme. Electric power generation—mostly by coal-burning plants—has been in particular demand; China's electricity use in the 1990s increased by between 3% and 7% per year. In 2003 electricity use increased by 15% over the previous year, and supplies could not keep up with demand, thus slowing economic development. Government statistics indicate that the overall demand for electric power for 2004 was projected to be around 2 trillion kilowatt-hours, but by June of that year a 60-billion kilowatt-hour shortfall had been projected. Energy production failed to keep up with industrial demand, resulting in power cutoffs throughout most of the country. In 2005 the Chinese Communist Party expressed the determination to reduce energy consumption by 20% per capita of the GDP by 2010. China is largely self-sufficient in all energy forms. Its coal production is the highest in the world. Some 75.6% of China's energy was produced from coal in 2004. The coal reserves are among the world's largest, and mining technology has been improving since the 1990s. Coal has even been exported since the early 1970s. Petroleum fulfilled 13.5% and natural gas 3.0% of China's energy requirements in 2004. The petroleum reserves are large, of varying quality, and in disparate locations. There are oil deposit blocks in the northwest and offshore tracts believed to be among the world's largest. In December 2004, it was reported that some 20.5 billion tons of oil reserves had been discovered in North China's Bohai Bay and more than 20 billion tons in Xinjiang's Tarim Basin. There also are an estimated 28 billion cubic metres of natural gas in Xinjiang, 100 billion cubic metres in Sichuan, and 200 million cubic metres in Inner Mongolia, as well as substantial natural gas reserves offshore. Even though it has exported petroleum since the early 1970s, China, nevertheless, is a net importer of crude petroleum because the required high grades of petroleum are not available domestically. Imports of mineral fuels totaled 6.6% of the cost of total imports in 2002. In 2004 Russia agreed to expand its oil exports to China. With deliveries sent by railroad, deliveries to China reached 10 million tons in 2005 and 15 million tons in 2006. However, China's total petroleum imports have expected to exceed 100 million tons. China's hydroelectric potential is the greatest in the world and the sixth largest in capacity. However, in 2004 hydroelectric power produced only 7.9% of China's energy needs. The Three Gorges hydropower project in Hubei Province on the Yangzi River started delivering power to eastern and central provinces in July 2003 and is expected to produce 84.7 billion kilowatt-hours per year when the project is completed by 2009. The main wall of the dam was completed in 2006, two years ahead of schedule.

Construction. As might be expected in a rapidly developing nation, China's construction sector has grown substantially since the early 1980s. Investment in capital construction has experienced major annual increases.

Services. In 2005 the services sector produced 40.3% of China's gross domestic product. Prior to the onset of economic reforms in 1978, China's services sector was characterized by state-operated shops, rationing, and regulated prices. With reform came private markets and individual entrepreneurs and a comparatively free-wheeling commercial sector. Urban areas now are filled with shopping malls and dotted with Western-style retail shops and fast-food chains. Other east coast cities have followed suit, and several cities in the interior are not far behind. If anything, the retail sector "suffers from oversupply." Joint venture hotels abound in China's major cities.

Banking and Finance. Banking reform was initiated in China in 1994, and the Commercial Banking Law took effect in July 1995. The aims of these actions were to strengthen the role of the central bank—the People's Bank of China—and to allow private banks to be established. The People's Bank of China was established in 1948. It issues China's currency and implements the nation's monetary policies. China's oldest bank, founded in 1908, is the Bank of Communications Limited, a commercial enterprise located in Shanghai. China's second oldest bank was established in 1912 as the Bank of China. Since 2004 it has become a shareholding company known as the Bank of China Limited and handles foreign exchange and international financial settlements. The Agricultural Bank of China, founded in 1951, is mainly involved in rural financing and the provision of services to agricultural, industrial, commercial, and transportation enterprises in rural areas. Other major banks include the China Construction Bank; established in 1954 as the People's Construction Bank of China, it has been a state-owned commercial bank since 1994 and maintains some 15,400 business outlets inside and outside China, including six overseas branches and two overseas representative offices. The China International Trust and Investment Corporation was founded in 1979 to assist economic and technological cooperation, finance, banking, investment, and trade. The Industrial and Commercial Bank of China was founded in 1984 to handle industrial and commercial credits and international business. The Agricultural Development Bank of China, Export and Import Bank of China, and State Development Bank all were founded in 1994. China's first private commercial national bank, the China Minsheng Banking Corporation, was opened in 1996. Commercial banks are supervised by the China Banking Regulatory Commission, which was established in 2003. In 2005 the commission announced the launching of a new postal savings bank to replace the old system and its more than 36,000 outdated outlets nationwide. When first permitted in the mid-1980s, foreign banks were restricted to designated cities and could deal only with transactions by foreign companies in China. After those restrictions were loosened in 2001, some foreign banks have been allowed to provide services to local residents and businesses. In 2004 there were some 70 foreign banks with more than 150 branches in China. There are stock exchanges in Beijing, Shanghai (the third largest in the world), and Shenzhen and futures exchanges in Shanghai, Dalian, and Zhengzhou. They are regulated by the China Securities Regulatory Commission.

Tourism. China has become a major tourist destination. By 2003 China had some 9,751 tourist hotels and a burgeoning hospitality industry, much of it joint ventures with foreign partners. In 2004 China received some 109 million tourists and visitors. However, 80.7% of the total visits were made by individuals arriving via the Hong Kong and Macau special administrative regions, including those who made multiple and often same-day trips to China. Others came from Taiwan (3.3%), Japan (3.0%), South Korea (2.6%), Russia, (1.6%), and the United States (nearly 1.1%). In 2004 visitors to China spent some US$25.7 billion. At the same time, China increased its own tourism; travelers from China spent more than US$15 billion on tourism in other countries in 2002.

Labour. China's estimated employed labour force in 2005 totaled 791.4 million persons. During 2003, 49% of the labour force worked in agriculture, forestry, and fishing; 22% in mining, manufacturing, energy, and construction industries; and 29% in the services sector and other categories. In 2004 some 25 million persons were employed by 743,000 private enterprises. The All-China Federation of Trade Unions (ACFTU) is the state-sanctioned labour organization with which other official labour organizations affiliate. The ACFTU was established in 1925 to represent the interests of national and local trade unions and trade union councils. The ACFTU reported a membership of 130 million, out of an estimated 248 million urban workers, at the end of 2002. Official Chinese statistics reveal that 4.2% of the total urban workforce was unemployed in 2004, although the true figure was believed by outside observers to be 10%. As part of its newly developing social security legislation, China has an unemployment insurance system.

Foreign Economic Relations. The government traditionally has decided the composition of China's foreign trade. However, since the initiation of reforms in 1978, increasing numbers of private partnerships have developed, and trade is primarily dictated by the marketplace. After years of disagreement over trade practices with its largest export partner, the United States, China agreed to a range of economic reforms designed to open Chinese markets to private and foreign investment. Subsequently, the US Congress granted China permanent most-favored nation status in 2000.

Imports. China's imports rose by 36% in 2004, totaling US$561.4 billion. Of these imports, the major components were machinery and equipment, mineral fuels, plastics, and iron and steel. The major trading partners were Japan (16.8%), Taiwan (11.4%), South Korea (11.1%), and the United States (8%). The 2004 amount reflected the rising trend in imports during the pervious seven years. In 1996 China's imports totaled US$138.8 billion and reached US$225 billion by 2000.

Exports. China's exports rose by 35.4% in 2004, totaling US$593.4 billion and favoring machinery and equipment, textiles and clothing, footwear, toys, and mineral fuels as the major commodities. The primary trading partners were the United States (21.1%), Hong Kong (trading as a separate economy, mostly for re-export purposes, 17%), Japan (12.4%), and South Korea (4.7%). One of the burgeoning exports, toys (both unsophisticated and high-tech, of which China provides about 75% of the total worldwide), also has a growing domestic market (US$6 billion a year). The 2004 total reflected the rising trend in exports during the previous seven years, increasing from US$151 billion in 1996 and reaching US$249.2 billion by 2000.

Trade Balance. China had a favorable trade balance of US$32 billion in 2004 and US$38.7 billion in 2003. These amounts reflect the general course of a favorable trade balance during the previous eight years. In 1996 China's trade balance was US$12.2 billion, peaking at US$43.4 billion in 1998 but declining to US$24.1 billion by 2000 before starting its new increase.

Balance of Payments. China's current account balance in 2004 was nearly US$68.7 billion. Added to this total was US$54.9 billion in foreign direct investment (exceeding that invested in the United States).

External Debt. According to United Nations statistics for 2001, China's external and public, or publicly guaranteed, long-term debt had reached US$91.7 billion. China's debt had grown steadily during the 1990s, peaked at US$112.8 billion in 1997, and then declined annually thereafter. By 2004 China had US$618.5 billion in its international reserve account, 98.6% of which was from foreign exchange, not including the Bank of China's foreign exchange holdings.

Currency and Exchange Rate. China's currency is the renminbi (RMB, people's currency) or yuan. The RMB is made up of 100 fen or 10 jiao.

Infrastructure

Roads. In 2005 China had a total road network of more than 3.3 million kilometres, although approximately 1.47 million kilometres of this network are classified as "village roads." Paved roads totaled 770,265 kilometres in 2004; the remainder are gravel or merely earth tracks. Highways (totaling 130,000 kilometres) were critical to China's economic growth as it worked to mitigate a poor distribution network and authorities sought to spur economic activity directly. All major cities are expected to be linked with a 55,000-kilometre inter-province expressway system by 2020. The highway and road systems carried nearly 11.6 billion tons of freight and 769.6 trillion passenger/kilometres in 2003. The importance of highways and motor vehicles, which carry 13.5% of cargo and 49.1% of passengers, was growing rapidly in the mid-2000s. Road usage has increased significantly, as automobiles, including privately owned vehicles, rapidly replace bicycles as the popular vehicle of choice in China. In 2002, excluding military and probably internal security vehicles, there were 12 million passenger cars and buses in operation and 8.1 million other vehicles. In 2003 China reported that 23.8 million vehicles were used for business purposes, including 14.8 million passenger vehicles and 8.5 million trucks. The latest statistics from the Beijing Municipal Statistics Bureau show that Beijing had nearly 1.3 million privately owned cars at the end of 2004 or 11 for each 100 Beijing residents. Beijing currently has the highest annual rate of private car growth.

Railroads. Railroads are the major mode of transportation in China. Carrying some 24% of the world's railroad transportation volume, China's railroads are critical to its economy. Because of its limited capital, overburdened infrastructure, and need to continually modernize, the rail system, which is controlled by the Ministry of Railways through a network of regional divisions, operates on an austere budget. Foreign capital investment in the freight sector was allowed beginning in 2003. In another move to better capitalize and reform the railroad system, the Ministry of Railways established three public shareholder-owned companies in 2003. China Railways Container Transport Company, China Railway Special Cargo Service Company, and China Railways Parcel Express Company. The national rail system is modernizing and expanding rapidly and is efficient within the limits of the available track. Some 71,898 kilometres of track were operational in 2002. This total included 71, 898 kilometres of 1.435-metre gauge (18,115 kilometres of which were electrified) and 3,600 kilometres of 1.000-metre and 0.750-metre gauge local industrial lines. There were an additional 23,945 kilometres of dual-gauge track not included in the total. As of 2002, some 23,058 kilometres of the railroad routes were double tracked, representing 38.7% of the total. In 2004 China's railroad inventory included 15,456 locomotives owned by the national railroad system. National railroad freight cars numbered 520,101 and passenger coaches 39,766. In 2003 China's railroads carried 2.2 trillion tons of freight and 478.9 trillion passenger/kilometres. Only India has more passenger/kilometres and the United States more net ton/kilometres than China In October 2006, the 1,956 kilometre-long line to link the rest of China with Tibet via a hub at Xining in Qinghai Province was started. Another large-scale railroad project is the New Silk Road or Eurasian Continental Bridge project that was launched in 1992. In China the project involves the modernization and infrastructure development of a 4,131-kilometre-long railroad route starting in Lianyungang, Jiangsu Province, and traveling through central and northwestern China to Urumqi, Xinjiang Uygur Autonomous Region, to the Alataw Pass into Kazakhstan. From that point, the railroad links to some 6,800 kilometres of routes that end in Rotterdam. China also has established rail links between seaports and interior export-processing zones.

Rapid Transit. The Beijing metro system, which opened in 1969, has 113 kilometres of subway track on four lines, plus an additional 98 kilometres slated by 2010. The Guangzhou system, which opened in 1999, has 18.5 kilometres and an additional 133 kilometres planned. Shanghai metro, which opened in 1995, has 8 lines, 68 stations, and 82.8 kilometres of track, with an additional 108.4 kilometres under construction or planned. The Tianjin metro was begun in 1970 as a planned network of 153.9 kilometres on seven lines; large sections remain closed for reconstruction, but one 26.2-kilometre-long line opened for trial operations in June 2006. The Shenzhen metro opened in 2004, initially with two lines, 19 stations, and 21.8 kilometres of track. Also under construction are subway and light rail systems in Chongqing and Nanjing, and systems are planned for Chengdu and Qingdao. Metro transit in Hong Kong is covered by the privately operated Mass Transit Railway, which opened in 1979 and now has six metro lines with 50 stations. China also has the world's first commercial magnetic levitation (maglev) train service. A Sino- German joint venture, 38-kilometre-long route between downtown Shanghai and the Pudong airport opened in 2003. The project cost US$1.2 billion and has experienced an average of 8,000 passengers per day, well below capacity. In 2004 the first Chinese-made maglev train made its debut in Dalian, a major port city in Northeast China's Liaoning Province. The 10.3-metre-long train has a top speed of 110 kilometres per hour. Although the cost to build was high at US$6 million per kilometre, China's outlay was still only one-sixth of the world average.

Ports and Shipping. China has more than 2,000 ports, 130 of which are open to foreign ships. The major ports, including river ports accessible by ocean-going ships, are Beihai, Dalian, Dangdong, Fuzhou, Guangzhou,

Haikou, Hankou, Huangpu, Jiujiang, Lianyungang, Nanjing, Nantong, Ningbo, Qingdao, Qinhuangdao, Rizhao, Sanya, Shanghai, Shantou, Shenzhen, Tianjin, Weihai, Wenzhou, Xiamen, Xingang, Yangzhou, Yantai, and Zhanjiang. Additionally, Hong Kong is a major international port serving as an important trade center for China. In 2005 Shanghai Port Management Department reported that its Shanghai port became the world's largest cargo port, processing cargo topping 443 million tons and surpassing Singapore's port. As of 2004, China's merchant fleet had 3,497 ships. Of these, 1,700 ships of 1,000 gross registered tons (GRT) or more totaled 20. 4 million tons. In 2003 China's major coastal ports handled 2.1 billion tons of freight.

Inland and Coastal Waterways. China has more than 140,000 kilometres of navigable rivers, streams, lakes, and canals, and in 2003 these inland waterways carried nearly 1.6 trillion tons of freight and 6.3 trillion passenger/kilometres to more than 5,100 inland ports. The main navigable rivers are the Heilongjiang; Yangzi; Xiangjiang, a short branch of the Yangzi; and Zhujiang. Ships of up to 10,000 tons can navigate more than 1,000 kilometres on the Yangzi as far as Wuhan. Ships of 1,000 tons can navigate from Wuhan to Chongqing, another 1,286 kilometres upstream. The Grand Canal is the world's longest canal at 1,794 kilometres and serves 17 cities between Beijing and Hangzhou. It links five major rivers. the Haihe, Huaihe, Huanghe, Qiantang, and Yangzi.

Civil Aviation and Airports. As a result of the rapidly expanding civil aviation industry, by 2005 China had 489 airports of all types and sizes in operation, 389 of which had paved runways and 89 of which had runways of 3,047 metres or shorter. There also were 30 heliports, an increasingly used type of facility. With the additional airports came a proliferation of airlines. In 2002 the government merged the nine largest airlines into three regional groups based in Beijing, Shanghai, and Guangzhou, respectively. Air China, China Eastern Airlines, and China Southern Airlines, which operate most of China's external flights. By 2005 these three had been joined by six other major airlines. Hainan Airlines, Shanghai Airlines, Shandong Airlines, Xiamen Airlines, Shenzhen Airlines, and Sichuan Airlines. Together, these nine airlines have a combined fleet of some 860 aircraft, mostly Boeing from the United States and Airbus from France. To meet growing demands for passenger and cargo capacity, in 2005 these airlines significantly expanded their fleets. In June 2006, it was announced that an Airbus A320 assembly plant would be built in the Binhai New Area of Tianjin, with the first aircraft to be delivered in 2008. Major airports include the Capital International Airport, located 27 kilometres northeast of central Beijing; two in Shanghai under the control of the Shanghai Airport Authority. Hongqiao International Airport, which is located 13 kilometres west of central Shanghai, and Pudong International Airport, which is located 30 kilometres southeast of central Shanghai; and the new Baiyun International Airport, which opened in August 2004 and is located 28 kilometres from downtown Guangzhou. Other major airports are located at Chengdu, Dalian, Hangzhou, Harbin, Hohhot, Kunming, Qingdao, Shenyang, Tianjin, Urumqi, Xiamen, and Xi'an. Additionally, the Hong Kong International Airport, located at Chek Lap Kok on Lantau Island 34 kilometres northwest of Hong Kong Island. China is served both by numerous major international flights to most countries of the world and a host of domestic regional airlines. In 2003 China's civil aviation sector carried nearly 2.2 million tons of freight and 126.3 trillion passenger/kilometres.

Pipelines. As of 2004, China had 15,890 kilometres of gas pipelines, 14,478 kilometres of oil pipelines, and 3,280 kilometres for refined products. China's pipelines carried 219.9 million tons of petroleum and natural gas in 2003. As a major oil and gas consumer, China is searching for more external supplies. Construction of a 4,200-kilometre-long pipeline from Xinjiang to Shanghai was completed in 2004.

Telecommunications. China has 335 million subscribers to main telephone lines and 405 million cellular telephone subscribers, the highest numbers in both categories in the world but second per capita to the United States. Both categories showed substantial increases over the previous decade. Internet use also has soared in China from about 60,000 Internet users in 1995 to 103 million in 2005. It is second in the world. China's 2.7 million kilometres of optical fiber telecommunication cables by 2003 assisted greatly in the modernization process. China produces an increasing volume of televisions both for domestic use and export. In 2001 China produced more than 46 million televisions and claimed 317 million sets in use. At the same time, there were 417 million radios in use in China, a rate of 342 per 1,000 population.

Government and Politics

Executive Branch. The head of state of China is the president (Hu Jintao, since March 2003, when he succeeded Jiang Zemin). The vice president is Zeng Qinghong (since March 2003; he succeeded Hu). Articles 79–80 of the constitution provide for a president and vice president elected by the National People's Congress (NPC) for five-year terms and no more than two consecutive terms. The president "engages in activities involving State affairs and receives foreign diplomatic represents." In pursuance of the decisions of the NPC Standing Committee, the president appoints and recalls plenipotentiary representatives abroad and ratifies and abrogates treaties and important agreements concluded with foreign states. The vice president assists the president in his work, "may exercise such parts of the functions and powers of the President as the President may entrust to him," and succeeds to the presidency should the office of president become vacant. Should both offices become vacant, the chairman of the NPC Standing Committee becomes acting president until the NPC elects a new president and vice president. The government is led by the State Council, the equivalent of a cabinet. The State Council is headed by a premier (Wen Jiabao, since March 2003). There also are four vice premiers and five state councillors (one of whom is the secretary general of the State Council). One of the vice premiers and two of the state councillors double as ministers handling such key portfolios as national defence, public security, and public health. In 2006 there were 22 ministries and four commissions subordinate to the State Council. In addition, the People's Bank of China (China's central bank) and the National Audit Office are part of the State Council system. The five-year terms of office run concurrently with those of the National People's Congress (NPC) and are limited to no more than two consecutive terms. Executive meetings of the State Council are attended by the premier, vice premiers, state councillors, and secretary general of the State Council. The State Council reports on its work to the NPC and, when the NPC is not in session, to its Standing Committee.

Legislative Branch. According to the constitution, the National People's Congress (NPC) is "the highest organ of state power" and exercises "the legislative power of the state." Deputies to the NPC are elected from the provinces, autonomous regions, centrally administered municipalities, special administrative regions, and the armed forces. Elections are conducted by the permanent body of the NPC, the Standing Committee, and normally are held at least two months before the end of the current NPC. Deputies serve five-year terms and meet annually for two or three weeks, typically in March or April; 2,979 deputies were elected to the current 10th NPC. The NPC is empowered to amend the constitution; supervise the enforcement of the constitution; and elect the president and vice president of the People's Republic, chairman of the state Central Military Commission, president of the Supreme People's Court, and procurator general of the Supreme People's Procuratorate. It also has the authority "to decide on" the choice of the premier of the State Council upon nomination of the president and the members of the State Council upon nomination by the premier. Among the other responsibilities of the NPC is to "examine and approve" national economic and social development plans and the state budget and to "decide on questions of war and peace." The NPC also can alter or annul "inappropriate decisions" of the Standing Committee, approve the establishment of provincial-level units, and rule on the establishment of special administrative regions. The current chairman of the NPC Standing Committee since March 2003 is Wu Bangguo, a former vice premier and current member of the Standing Committee of the Chinese Communist Party (CCP) Political Bureau. When the full NPC is not in session, its Standing Committee meets and wields broad legislative powers. The NPC Standing Committee consists of a chairman, 15 vice chairmen, a secretary general, and 153 members, including the officers. Standing Committee members are not allowed to hold administrative, judicial, or procuratorial posts and, in practice, are often senior CCP and former state leaders and officials. As with the NPC membership, the chairman and vice chairmen may serve no more than two consecutive terms. Other committees, which work under the direction of the Standing Committee, include Nationalities; Law; Finance and Economic; Education, Science, Culture, and Public Health; Foreign Affairs; Overseas Chinese; and other special committees.

Another quasi-constitutional consultative body that provides an institutional framework for interaction among the CCP, state organizations, and other social and political organizations is the Chinese People's Political Consultative Conference (CPPCC). Members are distinguished scholars, educators, and intellectuals, key representatives of religious and minority nationality groups, leading members of political parties loyal to the CCP during the anti-Guomindang years, and representatives of Hong Kong, Macau, Taiwan, and Chinese overseas. The CPPCC typically meets once a year and has a standing committee that convenes when needed between sessions. The current chairman of the CPPCC is Jia Qinglin, a member of the CCP Political Bureau Standing Committee and ally of former CCP secretary general Jiang Zemin.

Judicial Branch. China has a four-level court system. At the top is the Supreme People's Court in Beijing. Lower courts are the higher people's courts in provinces, autonomous regions, and special municipalities; intermediate people's courts at the prefecture level and also in parts of provinces, autonomous regions, and special municipalities; and basic people's courts in counties, towns, and municipal districts. Special courts handle matters affecting the military, railroad transportation, water transportation, and forestry. Constitutionally, the court system exercises judicial power independently and technically is free of interference from administrative organs, public organizations, and individuals. The Supreme People's Court supervises the administration of justice by local courts and special courts, while courts at higher levels oversee the administration of courts at lower levels. At each level, the courts are "responsible to the organs of state power which created them." Judges are limited to two consecutive terms running concurrently with the National People's Congress or local people's congresses. The court system is paralleled by a hierarchy of prosecuting organs called people's procuratorates; at the apex stands the Supreme People's Procuratorate. The procurators serve as prosecutors, or district attorneys, and are limited to two consecutive terms running concurrently with the NPC or local people's congresses.

Administrative Divisions. China has 22 provinces, five autonomous regions, and four municipalities. The provinces are, in the northeast. Heilongjiang, Jilin, and Liaoning; in the north. Shandong, Hebei, Shanxi, and Shaanxi; in central China. Jiangsu, Anhui, Henan, Hubei, and Zhejiang; in the south. Hunan, Jiangxi, Fujian, Guangdong, and Hainan (an island in the South China Sea); in the southwest. Guizhou, Yunnan, and Sichuan; and in the northwest. Gansu and Qinghai. The autonomous regions—Guangxi Zhuang, Tibet (Xizang), Xinjiang Uygur, Inner Mongolia, and Ningxia Hui—are in border areas with large non-Han ethnic minority populations from which they take their names or part of their names. The four municipalities—Beijing, Tianjin, Shanghai, and Chongqing—are directly controlled by the central government. China also has two special administrative regions (SARs). Hong Kong which reverted from British control in 1997; and Macau, which reverted from Portuguese control in 1999. Beijing also claims Taiwan as a province.

Provincial and Local Government. The governors of China's provinces and autonomous regions and mayors of its centrally controlled municipalities are appointed by the central government in Beijing after receiving the nominal consent of the National People's Congress (NPC). The Hong Kong and Macau special administrative regions (SARs) have some local autonomy since they have separate governments, legal systems, and basic constitutional laws, but they come under Beijing's control in matters of foreign affairs and national security, and their chief executives are handpicked by the central government. Below the provincial level in 2004 there were 50 rural prefectures, 283 prefecture-level cities, 374 county-level cities, 852 county-level districts under the jurisdiction of nearby cities, and 1,636 counties. There also were 662 cities (including those incorporated into the four centrally controlled municipalities), 808 urban districts, and 43,258 township-level regions. Counties are divided into townships and villages. While most have appointed officials running them, some lower-level jurisdictions have direct popular elections. The organs of self-governing ethnic autonomous areas (regions, prefectures, and counties)—people's congresses and people's governments—exercise the same powers as their provincial-level counterparts but are guided additionally by the Law on Regional Ethnic Autonomy and require NPC Standing Committee approval for regulations they enact "in the exercise of autonomy" and "in light of the political, economic, and cultural characteristics of the ethnic group or ethnic groups in the areas."

Special Administrative Regions. China has two special administrative regions, Hong Kong (Xianggang in Putonghua) and Macau (Aomen in Putonghua). As a result of the First Anglo- Chinese War (1842), China ceded Hong Kong Island to the United Kingdom under the Treaty of Nanjing in 1842. In 1860 the British acquired in perpetuity the Kowloon (Jiulong) Peninsula under the Convention of Beijing. The remaining area, the New Territories, was leased for 99 years in 1898. The entire colony was returned to Chinese sovereignty in 1997 as the Hong Kong Special Administrative Region (SAR). Although originally the 1,092-square-kilometre area was part of Guangdong Province, the Hong Kong SAR reports directly to the State Council in Beijing. Hong Kong, with an estimated 6,940,432 people), has a partly popularly elected legislature and operates under the Basic Law, which embodies the principle of "one country, two systems" and states that the socialist system and policies shall not be practiced in Hong Kong; Hong Kong's previous capitalist system and lifestyle are to remain unchanged until 2047. The area that has come to be called Macau had been a maritime way station between China and India and regions farther west since the early sixteenth century. Portugal first obtained a leasehold on the area in 1557, although China retained sovereignty. In 1844, without Beijing's concurrence, Lisbon made Macau an overseas province of Portugal. Although China recognized Macau as a Portuguese colony in an 1862 treaty signed with Portugal, the treaty was never ratified by China, and Macau was never officially ceded to Portugal. A protocol dealing with relations between China and Portugal was signed in Lisbon in 1887 confirming the "perpetual occupation and government" of Macau by Portugal (with Portugal's promise "never to alienate Macau and dependencies without agreement with China"). The islands of Taipa and Coloane also were ceded to Portugal, but the border of the Macau Peninsula with the mainland was not delimited. The Treaty of Commerce and Friendship (1888) recognized Portuguese sovereignty over Macau but again was never actually ratified by China. In 1974 the new Portuguese government granted independence to all overseas colonies and recognized Macau as part of China's territory. In 1979 China and Portugal exchanged diplomatic recognition, and Beijing acknowledged Macau as "Chinese territory under Portuguese administration." Although originally the now 28.2-square-kilometre area was part of Guangdong Province, the Macau SAR reports directly to the State Council in Beijing.

Cross-Strait Relations with Taiwan. China considers Taiwan a province and an inalienable part of China, which has been separated from China since 1949 when the Guomindang (Nationalist Party) government of Jiang Jieshi (Chiang Kei-shek) fled there in the face of defeat by communist forces. Taiwan still controls one island that appertains to the mainland—Jinmen (Kinmen or Quemoy), which is part of Fujian Province. In Beijing matters dealing with Taiwan are handled by the Chinese Communist Party (CCP) Central Committee's Taiwan Work Office and the State Council's Taiwan Affairs Office. Beijing is adamantly opposed to independence or any quasi-state status for Taiwan and has alternated since the late 1970s between overtures for peaceful reunification and statements of resolution to forcefully reclaim Taiwan if necessary. Beijing has called for resuming cross-strait negotiations, formally ending the state of hostility that has persisted since 1949, and addressing cross-strait problems through timely negotiations. During the reform period, China and Taiwan began to allow economic and trade exchanges, travel, tourism, and other activities. Several breakthroughs in relations occurred in 2005. The first was the launch of two-way, round-trip, and nonstop charter flights across the Taiwan Strait starting in February 2005. This development was dampened by Taiwan's reactions to legislation adopted by China's National People's Congress (NPC) on 14 March 2005, "for the purpose of opposing and checking Taiwan's secession from China by secessionists in the name of "Taiwan independence." However, soon thereafter, further developments occurred that Beijing found more favorable to Taiwan reunification. These occurred when the leaders of three Taiwan political parties made separate trips to China between March and May 2005.

Judicial and Legal System. In 2004 the National People's Congress (NPC) amended the Constitution so that for the first time the protection of the individual was incorporated as a Constitutional requirement. Specifically, Articles 37 and 38 recognize the "freedom of the person" and the "personal dignity of citizens" as "inviolable." Although the 1997 Criminal Procedure Law allows the police to detain a person for up to 37 days before release or formal arrest, more vigorous court reviews have led to the release of thousands of unlawfully detained individuals. However, although the law stipulates that the authorities must notify a detainee's family or work unit of the detention within 24 hours, in practice timely notification is often disregarded, especially in sensitive political cases. Police sometimes hold individuals without granting access to family members or lawyers, and their trials are sometimes conducted in secret. Detained criminal suspects, defendants, their legal representatives, and close relatives are entitled to apply for bail, but, in practice, few suspects are released pending trial. The reeducation through- labour system allows non-judicial panels of police and local civil authorities to sentence individuals to up to three years in prison-like facilities. It has been reported that some detainees, usually political activists or dissidents, have been incarcerated in high-security psychiatric facilities for the criminally insane. Police and prosecutorial officials have been accused of ignoring due process provisions of the law and constitution. Citizens have a constitutional guarantee of the right to use their own spoken and written language in court proceedings. Courts and procuratorates are advised by the constitution that they "should provide translations for any party to the court proceedings who is not familiar with the spoken or written languages in common use in the locality." The constitution provides for an independent judiciary, but the courts are subjected to party and government policy guidance that influences the outcome of verdicts and sentences. Conviction rates in criminal cases in the early 2000s were approximately 90%, and trials generally were little more than sentencing hearings. Although most suspects in criminal cases are legally guaranteed the right to counsel, they often meet their appointed attorney only once before the hearing; at best, a defence attorney can obtain a reduction of the sentence. In many politically sensitive trials, rarely lasting more than several hours, the courts hand down guilty verdicts immediately following proceedings, and death sentences are often implemented within days of the rejection of an appeal.

Electoral System. Under the Organic Law of the Village Committees, all of China's approximately 1 million villages are expected to hold competitive, direct elections for sub-governmental village committees. A 1998 revision to the law called for improvements in the nominating process and enhanced transparency in village committee administration. The revised law also explicitly transferred the power to nominate candidates to villagers themselves, as opposed to village groups or Chinese Communist Party (CCP) branches. According to the Ministry of Civil Affairs, as of 2003 the majority of provinces had carried out at least four or five rounds of village elections. Deputies to local people's congresses of provinces, centrally administered municipalities, and cities divided into districts are elected by the people's congress at the next lower level. Deputies to people's congresses of counties, cities not divided into districts, municipal districts, townships, ethnic townships, and towns are elected directly by their constituencies to five-year terms. The local congresses each have corresponding standing committees that exercise legislative authority when the full congresses are not in session. Some townships and urban areas also have experimented with direct elections of local government leaders, plus local people's congresses have the constitutional authority to recall the heads and deputy heads of government at the provincial level and below. The constitution does not specify how deputies to the people's congresses of the autonomous regions, autonomous prefectures, and autonomous counties are chosen. Elected leaders, however, remain subordinate to the corresponding CCP secretary, and most are appointed by higher-level party organizations. Although China's constitution guarantees suffrage for citizens age 18 and older, the CCP maintains a close watch on electoral democracy at the grassroots levels and controls the outcome of elections at other levels.

Politics and Political Parties. After its founding in July 1921, the Chinese Communist Party (CCP) had only 57 members and little influence, but by 2005 the CCP had 70.8 million members and controlled all political, governmental, and military organs. Although political reform was not one of the Four Modernizations promulgated so earnestly after 1978, the CCP has allowed greater participation by nonparty members in economic and social developments. Within the party, the CCP practices what it calls "democratic centralism," which, in effect, means that the minority follows the decisions of the majority, each level follows the directives of the next highest level, and all follow the lead of the party's center. Constitutionally, the CCP's national congress is the party's highest body. It is convened every five years, usually prior to the National People's Congress. However, to operate, it elects a Central Committee, which in turn elects (or approves) the members of the Political Bureau and that organ's even more elite Standing Committee. The current Central Committee has 198 members and 158 alternate members. The Political Bureau has 24 members and one alternate member, and its Standing Committee has nine members, including Hu Jintao, who became CCP general secretary in November 2002, succeeding Jiang Zemin. Of its 66.4 million members, 16.6% are women, only 6.1% members of minority nationalities, and 23.1% under age 35. Unlike the largely peasant, worker, and military veteran party of the past, 29.2% are high-school graduates, 17.8% of CCP members have undergraduate degrees, and 0.5% have graduate degrees. When Mao led the party from 1935 to his death in 1976, he held the position of CCP chairman. His immediate and short-term successor Hua Guofeng also held the title of chairman, as did Hua's successor when he took office in 1981, Hu Yaobang, who held the title for a short time until the position was then abolished at the CCP Twelfth Party Congress in September 1982, endowing the general secretary as the most powerful position in the party. Deng Xiaoping, despite being the paramount leader in China in the post-Mao era, never held the top party or state positions. Instead, he allowed more junior leaders to hold these positions. When Deng's longest term successor, Jiang Zemin, retired in stages between 2002 and 2004, he appeared to have assumed a similar behind-the-throne position of influence. Day-to-day management of the CCP is carried out by a central secretariat and various functional departments. In 2004 the CCP reported more than 3.3 million party branches throughout the nation. Its main organs are the daily newspaper *Renmin Ribao* (People's Daily) and the semimonthly theoretical journal *Qiu Shi* (Seeking Truth, formerly titled *Hongqi*, or Red Flag). China also has titular "democratic" parties that were loyal to the CCP in the pre-1949 period and continue to function within the structure of the Chinese People's Political

Consultative Conference (CPPCC), namely, the China Association for Promoting Democracy, China Democratic League, China Democratic National Construction Association, China Zhigongdang (Party for Public Interest), Chinese Peasants' and Workers' Democratic Party, Jiusan (September Third—a reference to the date of the defeat of Japan in 1945) Society, Guomindang Revolutionary Committee, and Taiwan Self-Government League. An independent opposition party, the China Democracy Party, has been banned since 1998 and its leaders arrested.

Mass Media. China's electronic mass media are regulated by the State Administration of Radio, Film, and Television, a subordinate agency of the Ministry of Information Industry. The Chinese Communist Party's Propaganda Department traditionally has played a large role as arbiter of standards for appropriate broadcasts. The People's Broadcasting Station transmits radio broadcasts in standard Chinese (Putonghua) and the various dialects and minority languages throughout China. In 2004, 282 domestic radio stations and 774 short- and medium-wave radio relaying and transmitting stations operated, and many stations provided Internet access to some of their broadcasts. China National Radio, headquartered in Beijing, transmits programmes in standard Chinese, Kazakh, Korean, Mongolian, Tibetan, and Uygur. The government has been active in regulating newspapers. Although foreign investment in local news media was permissible by 2002, the government closed down 673 unprofitable state-run newspapers in 2003 and in 2004 banned subscription newspapers and periodicals. The major national newspaper, *Renmin Ribao* (People's Daily), was established in 1948 as the main organ of the Chinese Communist Party, has a print circulation of nearly 2.2 million, and offers overseas editions and Internet access in foreign languages. Other major newspapers published in Beijing are *Gongren Ribao* (Workers' Daily), *Nongmin Ribao* (Farmers' Daily), *Zhongguo Qingnian Bao* (China Youth News), *Guangming Ribao* (Bright Daily), *Jiefangjun Bao* (Liberation Army Daily), and *Zhongguo Ribao* (China Daily). There are two major newspapers published outside of Beijing. *Jiefang Ribao* (Liberation Daily), published in Shanghai, and *Nanfang Ribao* (Southern Daily), published in Guangzhou. These newspapers have circulations of between 300,000 and 2.5 million and also include Internet editions. China had more than 2,000 other newspapers in publication in 2006. Even more widely distributed were China's 9,074 magazines, which in 2003 rose to an average circulation of 199 million copies and probably more since both newspapers and magazines typically are traded among multiple readers and newspapers often are posted on community bulletin boards for passers-by. The Ministry of Information Industry regulates access to the Internet while the Ministry of Public Security and the Ministry of State Security monitor its use. A broad range of topics that authorities interpret as potentially subversive or as slanderous to the state, including the dissemination of anti-unification information or "state secrets" that may endanger national security, are prohibited by various laws and regulations. Internet service providers (ISPs) are restricted to domestic media news postings and are required to record information useful for tracking users and their viewing habits, install software capable of copying e-mails, and immediately abort transmission of material considered subversive. As a result, many ISPs practice self-censorship to avoid violations of the broadly worded regulations.

Membership in International Organizations. China holds a permanent seat, which affords it veto power, on the Security Council of the United Nations (UN).

National Security

Armed Forces Overview. The armed forces of China are officially and collectively known as the People's Liberation Army (PLA). The ground forces are referred to simply as the PLA, but the navy is called the PLA Navy and the air force is known as the PLA Air Force. The PLA's independent strategic missile forces are often referred to as the PLA Second Artillery Corps. The Chinese Communist Party (CCP) Central Military Commission sets policy for the PLA. The commission, which is chaired by China's president, has three vice chairmen, each a general in the PLA ground forces, and seven members representing various components of the PLA. Operational control is administered dually by the CCP Central Military Commission and the State Central Military Commission and the Ministry of National Defence. PLA headquarters is organized into the General Staff Department, General Political Department, General Logistics Department, and General Armaments Department. In 2005 China announced that it downsized its military by 200,000 troops in order to optimize force structures and increase combat capabilities. The active-duty troop numbers declined to 2.3 million, compared to 3.2 million in 1987. The changes included eliminating layers in the command hierarchy, reducing non-combat units, such as schools and farms, and reprogramming officer duties. The number of ground forces was reduced by the largest margin, while the navy, air force, and Second Artillery Corps were strengthened. An estimated 1.7 million military personnel are in the ground forces, 250,000 in the navy (including 26,000 naval aviation, 10,000 marines, and 28,000 coastal defence forces), an estimated 400,000 to 420,000 in the air force, and 90,000–100,000 in the strategic missile forces. Reservists number an estimated 500,000 to 600,000 and paramilitary forces in the People's Armed Police an estimated 1.5 million. The Central Military Commission of the People's Republic of China is constitutionally different from the Central Military Commission of the Chinese Communist Party. According to Article 93 of the state constitution, the state Central Military Commission directs the armed forces of the country and is composed of a chairman (currently Hu Jintao since June 2004), vice chairmen, and members whose terms run concurrently with the National People's Congress. The commission is responsible to the NPC and its Standing Committee.

Foreign Military Relations. The China North Industries Group Corporation (CNGC, often called NORINCO), China's main defence producer, has some 100 joint ventures and more than 80 overseas offices and branches in 30 countries and regions involved in military and dual-use technology production and sales. Further, China is also a major arms buyer, mostly naval and air force equipment from Russia. China is a member of the Shanghai Cooperation Organization (SCO), a joint effort with Russia, Kazakhstan, Kyrgyzstan, Tajikistan, and Uzbekistan. The SCO was established as the Shanghai Five when the partners signed agreements on strengthening mutual trust in military fields in border areas in 1996 and on mutual reduction of military forces in border areas in 1997. China also has held joint naval and counterterrorism exercises with Pakistan.

External Threat. Even while embroiled in the problems of territorial disputes with its neighbours and the dangers of periodic tensions on the Korean Peninsula and across the Taiwan Strait, China perceives the United States as its major threat. Beijing believes that the United States still maintains its Cold War policy toward China and the Asia-Pacific region and stresses ideological differences and their relationship to security issues of concern in the region. In China's view, Washington's attitude exacerbates tensions, which, in turn, lead to international turmoil. Post-Soviet Russia is now fairly benign in China's view, and relations have improved significantly from the days of border conflicts and high-level tension. Concerns about the remilitarization of Japan also resurface on occasion, often as a legacy of World War II enmity. Transnational crime, terrorism, separatism, and contradictions among nations all contribute to China's security concerns.

Defence Budget. Although China claims that the share of defence spending as a%age of the overall state budget has declined from 17.4% in 1979 to 9.5% in 1994 and 7.7% in 2004, the government has announced double-digit increases in military spending nearly every year for more than a decade. The defence budget for 2006 is expected to reach US$35.1 billion, the largest increase in four years and 16% higher than 2005 (estimated at US$29.5 billion). The report submitted in March 2006 at the Fourth Session of the 10th National People's Congress (NPC) contained a request for a budget increase to strengthen China's defensive capability and ability to respond to emergencies and to raise officer and enlisted pay levels. The NPC stated that China's military spending is still low compared to the United States, United Kingdom, France, Germany, and Japan. However, the actual defence budget is likely to be higher than expected because of the inclusion of defence-related items in non-defence budgets.

Military Service. There is selective conscription of two years for all the services starting at age 18 for males. In 2004 there were some 136,000 women in the armed forces.

Paramilitary Forces. The principal paramilitary organization is the People's Armed Police Force. There are militia forces of indeterminate strength under the control of the Chinese Communist Party (CCP). Once a critical part of Mao Zedong's "people's war" strategy, militia units are no longer an essential part of China's military and have mostly disbanded.

Police and Internal Security. The security apparatus is made up of the Ministry of State Security and the Ministry of Public Security, the People's Armed Police, the People's Liberation Army (PLA), and the state judicial, procuratorial, and penal systems. The Ministry of Public Security oversees all domestic police activity in China, including the People's Armed Police Force. The ministry is responsible for police operations and prisons and has dedicated departments for internal political, economic, and communications security. Its lowest organizational units are public security stations, which maintain close day-to-day contact with the public. The People's Armed Police Force, which sustains an estimated total strength of 1.5 million personnel, is organized into 45 divisions. internal security police, border defence personnel, guards for government buildings and embassies, and police communications specialists. The Ministry of State Security was established in 1983 to ensure "the security of the state through effective measures against enemy agents, spies, and counterrevolutionary activities designed to sabotage or overthrow China's socialist system." The ministry is guided by a series of laws enacted in 1993, 1994, and 1997 that replaced the "counterrevolutionary" crime statutes. The ministry's operations include intelligence collection, both domestic and foreign. Authorities have used arrests on charges of revealing state secrets, subversion, and common crimes to suppress political dissent and social advocacy.

Internal Threat and Terrorism. Although the government defines the outlawed Falun Gong movement as the major internal threat and the People's Armed Police Force actively pursues its members, Falun Gong is, nevertheless, not classified as a terrorist group, and it has not committed or sponsored acts of violence. Muslim separatists in Xinjiang Uygur Autonomous Region present China with its most significant terrorist threat, which emerged in the late 1980s. In 2003 Beijing published an "East Turkistan Terrorist List," which labeled organizations such as the World Uighur Youth Congress and the East Turkistan Information Center as terrorist entities. These groups openly advocate independence for "East Turkestan," and, although they have not been publicly linked to violent activity, the separatists have resorted to violence, bomb attacks, assassinations, and street fighting, which Beijing responds to with police and military action. During the summer of 2004, elite troops from China and Pakistan held joint antiterrorism exercises in Xinjiang that were aimed at the East Turkistan Islamic Movement, an organization listed as terrorist by China, the United States, and the United Nations (UN). This and other Uygur separatist groups reputedly were trained in Afghanistan to fight with the Taliban and al Qaeda. The East Turkistan Islamic Movement was established in 1990 and has links to the Islamic Movement of Uzbekistan, which operates throughout Central Asia. Premier Wen Jiabao joined leaders of other Asian and European nations in Hanoi for the October 2004 Asia-Europe Meeting (ASEM) in Hanoi, where the delegates reaffirmed their call for a war on terrorism led by the UN.

Human Rights. Article 34 of China's constitution states that the "state respects and guarantees human rights" and that "every citizen is entitled to the rights and at the same time must perform the duties prescribed by the constitution and the law." Compared to the earlier years of the Maoist regime, China's citizens enjoy a much wider range of human rights and basic exercise of their constitutional freedoms. Although tightly regulated, the mass media are relatively freer than in the past. Economic reforms have brought a new measure of individual expression and great wealth and influence for some. Reports indicate that the number and size of public protests have multiplied rapidly since the early 1990s and that such protests are now counted in the tens of thousands. Citizens cannot express opposition to the Chinese Communist Party (CCP)-led political system and do not have the right to change their national leaders or form of government. Socialism is still the theoretical basis of national politics and although Marxist economic planning gave way to pragmatism, economic decentralization has merely increased the authority of local officials. While the number of religious believers in China continues to increase, governmental respect for religious freedom has remained poor. The government, which regulates, manages, and controls the broadcast media, has censored foreign broadcasts, at times jamming radio signals from abroad. Publications are closed and otherwise disciplined for publishing material deemed objectionable by the government, and journalists, authors, academics, and researchers are reportedly harassed, detained, and arrested by the authorities. The National People's Congress has adopted amendments to the law protecting woman's rights and interests, including one outlawing sexual harassment. The government ratified International Labour Organization Convention 111 prohibiting discrimination in employment.

INDIA

The Republic of India (official Sanskrit name is *Bharat*) occupies much of the Indian subcontinent, and the mainland stretches eastward from Pakistan in the west to Bangladesh and Myanmar in the east. On the north, India borders China, Nepal, and Bhutan. The Indian Ocean to the south, the Arabian Sea to the west, and the Bay of Bengal to the east form the country's coastline. Non-contiguous to the mainland are the Lakshadweep Islands in the Arabian Sea and the Andaman and Nicobar Islands located 1,300 kilometres from the mainland in the Bay of Bengal. India has 35 cities and urban agglomerations with more than 1 million persons. The most populous cities are Mumbai (16.4 million people), Kolkata (13.2 million), New Delhi (12.8 million), Chennai (6.4 million), Bangalore (5.7 million), Hyderabad (5.5 million), and Ahmadabad (4.5 million).

India proclaimed independence from Britain on 15 August 1947. India's national flag has three horizontal bands. The upper band is saffron in color, the lower is green, and the middle is white with a 24-spoke dark blue wheel in its centre. The saffron symbolizes courage, sacrifice, and renunciation; the white represents purity and truth; and the green signifies faith and fertility. The wheel is the Dharma Chakra, an ancient Buddhist symbol used by the Indian king Ashoka to represent the "wheel of law."

Historical Background

Human settlement in India dates back to roughly 400,000 to 200,000 B.C. when extensive urbanization and trade appear to have begun in the Indus River Valley around 3000 B.C. with the Harappan civilization. From this period until the termination of British colonial rule in 1947, numerous empires ruled various portions of South Asia, often assimilating a rich array of peoples and each adding its own contribution to an increasingly rich tapestry of cultures, ideas, and technologies. Indeed, many of India's current political, cultural, and economic traits have been influenced by historical events and trends, many of which pre-date European contact.

Among the most influential early empires were the Aryans, who migrated from Persia around 2000 B.C. an early form of Sanskrit language, a tiered social system essentially based on ethnicity and occupation, and religious texts are an important part of living Hindu traditions. From 326 B.C. to around 200 B.C., the Mauryan Empire emerged as India's first imperial power and ruled its areas with a highly centralized and hierarchical administration. From 320 A.D. to 550 A.D., most of North India was ruled by the Gupta Empire, which maintained a decentralized form of government, using numerous regional and local officials to govern vast territories with an array of local political, economic, and social arrangements. Gupta authority was religiously legitimized, and this period, called the Classical Age, was when the multiple components of Hindu culture became crystallized into a more unified system of thought.

From the disintegration of the Gupta Empire to the mid-13th century, various regional kingdoms emerged, and conflicts among them often led to their defeat but rarely to their total annihilation. As a result, no highly centralized government emerged in South India, and South Indian villages and districts enjoyed much greater local autonomy than those in North India. During this period, South India engaged in flourishing trade with Arabs and Southeast Asia, which facilitated the diffusion of Indian mathematical concepts to the Middle East and Indian art, literature, and social customs to Southeast Asia.

Islamic influence in South Asia emerged around 711 A.D. as Arabs conquered part of Sindh (now in Pakistan), and by the 10th century Punjab came under the control of Turkic ruler Mahmud of Ghazni. By the 13th century, much of India had been periodically conquered, but rarely held for long, by a steady succession of Turkic rulers collectively referred to as the Delhi Sultanate or Mughal emperors. The most prominent Mughal ruler was the astute and religiously tolerant Akbar, who ruled from 1556 to 1605. Akbar oversaw substantial political and geographic consolidation by using locally established warriors and powerful *zamindar* landlords to control local populations and collect revenues. But over time, the administrative capacities of later Mughal rulers suffered from bloated and excessively corrupt bureaucracies and huge, unwieldy armies.

European economic competition in India began soon after the Portuguese arrived in 1498, and by the early 1600s it was manifested in the establishment of commercial companies, such as England's East India Company, that attempted to capture the spice trade. In order to gain competitive advantages over each other, European powers also engaged in commercial and administrative alignments with the Mughal powers. By the late 18th century, the British had defeated French and Mughal forces to become the preeminent military and economic power in India. A major turning point in the colonial occupation occurred in 1857—1858, which seriously threatened British rule and led to a marked shift in colonial attitudes and practices.

By the 1920s, various Indian groups became active in attempting to end colonial rule, and the Indian National Congress Party, which had been established in 1885, eventually became the most prominent. Led by Mohandas Gandhi and Jawaharlal Nehru, the Congress Party promoted non-violence and self-sufficiency and thus garnered respect and support among both Indians and some British. But the Congress Party generally failed to attract Muslims, who often felt culturally and physically threatened by Hindus, and in 1906 the All-India Muslim League was established. Rising civil disobedience and World War II eventually rendered India too costly and difficult to administer, and the British granted independence in 1947.

On 15August 1947, the country was partitioned into India and Pakistan, which led to massive migration of Hindus and Muslims and substantial communal conflict. Furthermore, the British had left India with a rudimentary industrial and scientific base; tremendous poverty; a large and growing population; social cleavages along caste and economic lines; and contentious territorial boundaries that have led to armed conflicts with Pakistan (1947 to 1949, 1965, 1971), China (1962), and numerous insurgent groups.

In spite of such difficulties, India can count a number of successes. India has maintained a democratic political system. Building on the British-established education system, India has developed an educational infrastructure that has trained one of the world's largest scientific and technical populations. Using Green Revolution agricultural technologies, the country has become self-sufficient in food production. A combination of socialist planning and free enterprise from the 1950s to the 1970s led to substantial industrialization with the goal of making India economically self-sufficient. In the 1980s and 1990s, socialist economic planning and import substitution industries were slowly replaced by liberalization measures, a large middle class emerged, information technology developed into an important economic sector, and economic growth has been impressive. India has also become influential in international political and economic matters and appears set to continue those trends.

Numerous problems remain, however, such as substantial poverty, large income gaps between wealthy and poor, a large mass of people who lack the skills to participate in the new economy, and numerous insurgencies that threaten the nation's territorial integrity. Some social issues remain unresolved, and the rise of Hindu nationalism has become a particularly contentious topic in both Indian society and politics. Some observers believe India is facing difficulties in the political capacity to address these problems. Intense multi-party political competition over numerous economic and social issues has resulted in often-fragile coalitions of political parties, and no single political party has held a parliamentary majority since 1989. The government changed nine times from December 1989 to the elections in May 2004 in which the Indian National Congress returned to power under Prime Minister Manmohan Singh. Thus, increasing pluralism of political parties, growing diversity in interest-group representation, and substantial ideological divisions among parties are significant obstacles in policy implementation.

Geography

India's exact size is subject to debate because some borders are disputed. The Indian government lists the total area as 3,287,260 square kilometres and the total land area as 3,060,500 square kilometres; the United Nations lists the total area as 3,287,263 square kilometres and total land area as 2,973,190 square kilometres. In either case, India is the seventh largest country in the world.

Land Boundaries. Land boundaries total 15,200 kilometres. India shares common borders with Pakistan (3,325 kilometres; the Jammu and Kashmir border is 1,085 kilometres), China (line of actual control is 3,439 kilometres), Bhutan (605 kilometres), Nepal (1,690 kilometres), Burma (1,452 kilometres), and Bangladesh (4,339 kilometres). Although India and Sri Lanka do not share a land boundary, the narrowest distance between the two countries is only 64 kilometres across the Palk Strait. Most of Jammu and Kashmir is contested with Pakistan, and the Aksai Chin area of Jammu and Kashmir is disputed with China, as is the border of Arunachal Pradesh in northeast India. Nepal claims a 75-square-kilometre area called Kalapani. Possession of recently emerged New Moore Island (South Talpatty) in the Bay of Bengal has been disputed by Bangladesh, and much of the border with Bangladesh is not demarcated.

Length of Coastline. India's total coastline is 7,516 kilometres in length, which comprises 5,422 kilometres for the mainland, 132 kilometres for the Lakshadweep Islands, and 1,962 kilometres for the Andaman and Nicobar Islands. The Indian peninsula juts 1,980 kilometres into the Indian Ocean. 50% of the Indian Ocean basin lies within a 1,500 kilometre radius of India, a reality that has strategic implications.

Maritime Claims. Under the 1982 United Nations Convention on the Law of the Sea, India has a 200 nautical mile exclusive economic zone, a 12 nautical mile territorial sea, a 24 nautical mile contiguous zone, and a legal continental shelf extending to a depth of 2,500 metres or to the end of the continental margin. India has 1,197 islands in the Indian Ocean. (572 in the Andaman and Nicobar – 38 of which are inhabited and 23 in the Lakshadweep – 10 of which are inhabited. In addition, there are 447 islands off the Western coast and 151 islands off the Eastern Coast).

Topography. There are three main geological regions, the Indo-Gangetic Plain and the Himalayas—collectively known as North India—and the Peninsula, or South India. India has diverse physiological regions that include highlands, plains, deserts, and river valleys. The country's highest elevation is 8,598 metres at Kanchenjunga, which is the third highest mountain in the world and located in the Himalayas.

Principal Rivers. India's longest rivers are the Brahmaputra and Indus, which are both 2,896 kilometres long, although neither is entirely within India. Other major rivers are the Ganga (2,525 kilometres), Godavari (1,465), Kaveri (Cauvery, 800), Krishna (1,401), Mahanandi (851), Narmada (1,312), and Yamuna (1,370).

Climate. Climate in India varies significantly from the permanently snow-capped Himalayas in the north to the tropics in the south. The country has four seasons. December to February is relatively dry and cool, March to May is dry and hot, from June to September predominating southwest maritime winds bring monsoon rains to most of the country, and in October and November there are retreating dry monsoons originating from the northeast. Average temperatures range from 12.5° C to 30° C in the northwest, 17.5° C to 30° C in the north and northeast, and 22.5° C to 30° C in the south. Average annual rainfall is around 1,000 to 1,500 millimeters for much of the country, but can be quite low in some parts of the northwest (150 to 300 millimeters annually) and very high in the northeast and along the west coast (1,500 to 2,500 millimeters annually).

Natural Resources. Commercially important natural resources include arable land, bauxite, chromite, coal (fourth-largest reserves in the world), diamonds, iron ore, limestone, manganese, mica, natural gas, petroleum, and titanium ore.

Land Use. The total arable land and land planted under permanent crops combined is about 1,697,000 square kilometres, and total irrigated land is about 548,000 square kilometres. The total of non-arable land and land not under permanent crops is about 1,276,190 square kilometres.

Environmental Factors. India is vulnerable to various natural hazards, particularly cyclones and annual monsoon floods, and various combinations of poverty, population growth, increasing individual consumption, industrialization, infrastructural development, poor agricultural practices, and resource maldistribution have led to substantial human transformation of India's natural environment. An estimated 60% of cultivated land suffers from soil erosion, water logging, and salinity. It is also estimated that between 4.7 and 12 billion tons of topsoil are lost annually from soil erosion. From 1947 to 2002, average annual per capita water availability declined by almost 70% to 1,822 cubic meters, and overexploitation of groundwater is problematic in the states of Haryana, Punjab, and Uttar Pradesh. Forest area covers 19.4% of India's geographic area (63.7 million hectares). Nearly half of the country's forest cover is found in the state of Madhya Pradesh (20.7%) and the seven states of the northeast (25.7%); the latter is experiencing net forest loss. Forest cover is declining because of harvesting for fuel wood and the expansion of agricultural land. These trends, combined with increasing industrial and motor vehicle pollution output, have led to atmospheric temperature increases, shifting precipitation patterns, and declining intervals of drought recurrence in many areas. The Indian Agricultural Research Institute has estimated that a 3° C rise in temperature will result in a 15 to 20% loss in annual wheat yields. These are substantial problems for a nation with such a large population depending on the productivity of primary resources and whose economic growth relies heavily on industrial growth.

Society

Population. The 2004 estimate of India's total population was 1,065,070,607. According to the 2001 Indian census, the total population was 1,028,610,328, a 21.3% increase from 1991 and 2% average growth rate from 1975 to 2001. India has nearly 17% of the world's population, second only to China. About 72% of the population resided in rural areas in 2001, yet the country has a population density of 324 persons per square kilometre. Major states have more than 400 persons per square kilometre, but population densities are around 150 persons or fewer per square kilometre in some border states and insular territories.

Demography. In 2001 India's birthrate was 25.4 per 1,000 population, its death rate was 8.4 per 1,000, and its infant mortality rate was 66 per 1,000 live births. In 1995 to 1997, India's total fertility rate was 3.4 children per woman (4.5 in 1980–82). According to the 2001 Indian census, 35.3% of the population was under 14 years of age, 59.9% between 15 and 64, and 4.8% 65 and older (the 2004 estimates are, respectively, 31.7%, 63.5%, and 4.8%); the sex ratio was 933 females per 1,000 males. In 2004 India's median age was estimated to be 24.4.

Ethnic Groups. The exact number of ethnic groups depends on source and method of counting, and scholars estimate that only the continent of Africa exceeds the linguistic, cultural, and genetic diversity of India. 72% of the population is Indo-Aryan, 25% Dravidian, and 3% Mongoloid and other. Each of these groups can be further subdivided into various combinations of language, religion, and caste. The Hindu caste system is technically illegal but widely practiced (generally more in rural areas) and comprises four major categories (*varnas*) that are found India-wide but are often subdivided into hundreds of sub-categories (*jatis*), many of which are often found only in specific areas. Similar hereditary and occupational social hierarchies exist within Sikh and Muslim communities but are generally far less pervasive and institutionalized. About 16% of the total population is "untouchable" (Scheduled Castes is the more formal, legal term; *Dalit* is the term preferred by "untouchables" and roughly translates to down-trodden); around 8% of the population belongs to one of 461 indigenous groups (often called Scheduled Tribes for legal purposes, although the term *adivasi* is commonly used).

Languages. The total number of languages and dialects varies by source and counting method, and many Indians speak more than one language. The Indian census lists 114 languages (22 of which are spoken by one million or more persons) that are further categorized into 216 dialects or "mother tongues" spoken by 10,000 or more speakers. An estimated 850 languages are in daily use, and the Indian Government claims there are more than 1,600 dialects. Hindi is the official language and the most commonly spoken, but not all dialects are mutually comprehensible. English also has official status and is widely used in business and politics, although knowledge of English varies widely from fluency to knowledge of just a few words. The teaching of Hindi and English is compulsory in most states and union territories. 22 languages are legally recognized by the constitution for various political, educational, and other purposes. Assamese, Bengali, Bodo, Dogri, Gujarati, Hindi, Kannada, Kashmiri, Konkani, Maithali, Malayalam, Manipuri, Marathi, Nepali, Oriya, Punjabi, Sanskrit, Santhali, Sindhi, Tamil, Telugu, and Urdu. Numerous other languages are recognized by individual states but not officially recognized by the central government, and linguistic issues related to education, employment, and politics are sometimes politically contentious. Indeed, some state borders are based on linguistic lines. The most commonly spoken languages are Hindi (40.2% of the population), Bengali (8.3%), Telugu (7.9%), Marathi (7.5%), and Tamil (6.3%).

Religion. Approximately 80.5% of the population is Hindu, 13.4% Muslim, 2.3% Christian, 1.9% Sikh, 0.8% Buddhist, and 0.4% Jain; another 0.6% belongs to other faiths, such as Zoroastrianism and numerous religions associated with Scheduled Tribes. The Indian constitution confers religious freedom for individuals and prohibits religious discrimination, but in spite of this, there have been enduring tensions among religious communities, most notably between Hindus and Muslims.

Education and Literacy. In 2000 the adult literacy rate (% aged 15 or older) was 58.5% (72.3% for males, 44.4% for females). These figures have all nearly doubled since 1961 and are higher than in most other South Asian nations. In 2001 the combined primary, secondary, and tertiary enrollment ratio was 55% of the population of official school age for the three levels. Total government expenditures on education in 2001 were 13.2% of all government expenditures and 4% of GDP. Government expenditures on education have increased steadily, as have the number of educational institutions from the primary to the university level. In most states and union territories, primary school covers standards 1 to 8 and secondary education, standards 9 and 10; all states have senior secondary education for standards 11 and 12. The majority of states and union territories have free education up to the seventh-grade level, and the majority of primary schools are government funded and managed. 34% of secondary institutions are government funded but privately managed, and 25% are privately managed without government funding.

Health. National health indicators are generally lower than in many developing countries but have shown dramatic improvement nationwide, although there are variations among states in India. An estimated 21% of the total population is malnourished, and common diseases include malaria, filariasis, leprosy, cholera, pneumonic plague, tuberculosis, trachoma, goitre, and diarrheal diseases. In November 2004, the head of the United Nations Acquired Immune Deficiency Syndrome programme (UNAIDS) claimed that India, along with China and Russia, is on the "tipping point" of having small, localized AIDS epidemics become major ones that could detrimentally affect the world's capacity to prevent and treat the disease. The above facts and figures are associated with substantial poverty and relatively low government health expenditures. In 2001 public health expenditures were 3.1% of total general government expenditures but only 17.9% of total health expenditures. By contrast, private expenditures were 82.1% of total health expenditures, all of which was out-of-pocket expense. Furthermore, total health expenditures per capita represented 5.1% of GDP in 2001, but public health expenditures were only 0.9% of GDP, and private health expenditures were 4.2% of GDP. The population's health is also a function of the relatively low number of health personnel and low level of infrastructure, which are on a par with many countries in Sub-Saharan Africa.

Welfare. Generally, central government welfare expenditures are a substantial portion of the official budget, and state and local governments play important roles in developing and implementing welfare policies. In 2000 union government expenditures on social services (includes education, health, family welfare, women and child development, and social justice and empowerment), rural development, and basic minimum services were approximately US$7.7 billion, which was 11.1% of total government expenditures and 1.7% of GDP. Furthermore, the union and state governments maintain a plethora of reserved seats in various political and education institutions for lower castes, indigenous persons, and others based on their percentage of the population. Finally, various innovative development programmes have been developed—often at state or local levels— for social development and the empowerment of women and lower castes, and the state of Kerala is internationally known for its noteworthy success in public welfare.

Economy

From 1947 to the late 1970s, the economy was characterized by central government planning and import substitution industries, and economic production was transformed from primarily agriculture, forestry, fishing, and textile manufacturing to heavy industries, transportation, and telecommunications. Agriculture still employs nearly 60% of the population, but accounts for only 22.6% of GDP. By the 1980s and 1990s, private-sector initiatives noticeably increased, and information technology emerged in importance but has proven vulnerable to changes in foreign demand, out-migration of information technology labour, and a weak but growing domestic market for information technology goods and services. In the 1980s, government liberalization measures—such as privatization of government industries and reduced tariffs on imported capital goods—have been credited for 1990s economic growth rates of around 4 to 7% annually, nearly double the 3% growth rates that characterized the previous 40 years. Furthermore, foreign direct investment has increased to an annual range of US$3 billion to US$5 billion, but remains well behind foreign direct investment in neighboring China. Furthermore, India accounts for less than 1% of world trade in spite of having 18% of the world's population, and the informal economy accounts for 23.1% of gross national income.

For most of its post-independence history, India adhered to a quasi-socialist approach with strict government control over private sector participation, foreign trade, and foreign direct investment. However, since 1991, India has gradually opened up its markets through economic reforms and reduced government controls on foreign trade and investment. Foreign exchange reserves have risen from US$5.8 billion in March 1991 to US$247 billion in September 2007, while central and state budget deficits have decreased. Privatization of publicly-owned companies and the opening of certain sectors to private and foreign participation has continued amid political debate.

Gross Domestic Product (GDP)/Power Purchasing Parity (PPP). In 2002 GDP was US$496.8 billion (Rs24.2 trillion). Since the early 1990s, GDP has grown 4 to 7% annually, which is higher than GDP growth for the European Union, the United States, or the world as a whole. In 2003 PPP per capita was US$2,880.

Government Budget. Government revenues and expenditures have grown substantially since the early 1990s. According to India's Ministry of Finance, in 2002–03 tax and non-tax revenues were US$49.7 billion (Rs2.3 trillion), total expenditures were US$88.9 billion (Rs4.1 trillion), and the fiscal deficit was US$31.1 billion (Rs1.5 trillion). Government expenditures generally have been highest in the energy, transportation, and social service sectors, which receive about two-thirds of total government expenditures. Tax revenues have grown annually around 10% or more since the early 1950s, and tax receipts have increased even more substantially since the mid-1990s with accelerated economic growth and improved government revenue collection capacities.

Agriculture. Since independence, India has changed from a food importer to a food exporter, but agriculture has declined as a percentage of GDP (from 32.8% in 1991 to 22.6% in 2001) and total exports (from 18.5% to 14.2%). Around 46% (141 million hectares) of total land is cultivated, and 16% is double cropped (49 million hectares), effectively giving India 190 million hectares of cultivated land. Another 4.8% (14.7 million hectares) is permanent pastureland or planted in tree crops or groves. Agriculture continues to employ the major, but declining, proportion of workers (from 69.4% in 1951 to 58.4% in 2001) and agricultural employment varies substantially among states (from 38.9% of workers in Punjab to 77.3% in Bihar). Most farmers cultivate plots of two hectares or less, and large landholders have only been divested in a few areas. Agricultural output—and the food security of millions—remains susceptible to often-tenuous access to arable land, credit, fertilizers, and irrigation as well as to natural conditions, particularly annual variations in rainfall. The remarkable growth in agricultural output is largely due to Green Revolution inputs such as high-yield seed varieties and fertilizers. Rice, wheat, pulses, and oilseeds dominate production, but millet, corn, and sorghum are also important crops. The main commercial crops are sugar (India is the world's second largest producer), rice (world's second largest exporter), wheat, cotton, and jute. However, the rate of output for several crops may have peaked, and problems with soil degradation, rural infrastructure, and declining per capita agricultural holdings may prevent the rate of agricultural growth from keeping pace with increasing rates of population growth and per capita food consumption.

Mining and Minerals. Since the early 1990s, mining has accounted for around 2 to 3.5% of GDP and employed less than 1% of the labour force. The majority of minerals produced by India are bauxite, copper, iron, lead, mica, rare earths, uranium ore, and zinc.

Industry and Manufacturing. For decades, Indian industries were largely import substitution industries producing textiles, steel and aluminum, fertilizers and petrochemicals, and electronics and motor vehicles. From 1950 to 2000, industrial output increased from 15 to 27% of GDP, but the sector continues to employ only about 10% of the workforce. Several industries face problems with power availability, high interest rates, customs delays, and regulatory obstacles. Domestic automobile manufacturing has increased substantially since the end of government licensing of automobile production in 1995, and car sales rose 50% by 2000. Import liberalization has also led to lowered sales for domestic industries, such as computer hardware and cement.

Energy. India is the world's sixth largest energy consumer, and the nation faces substantial challenges in meeting both present and expected demands for energy, particularly electric power. India has a growing nuclear power industry and abundant hydroelectric power (particularly in North India), and it is the world's third largest producer of coal (which provides more than half of domestic energy needs). But it is also a growing consumer and importer of petroleum and natural gas, and consumption of these products is expected to increase substantially. India also faces economic competition from China over potential oil and gas resources in the Indian Ocean that both countries need for their economic development.

Services. From 1951 to 2000, business, information technology, banking, communications, hotels, and other services increased from 27 to 48% of GDP, but most of this growth occurred in the 1990s. The percentage of the Indian workforce employed in services was 23.5% in 2000. Information technology services have emerged as an important element of the economy, but the information technology sector is believed to be vulnerable to out-migration of information technology professionals, particularly when the global economy is strong.

Banking and Finance. Under 1990s liberalization measures, restrictions on foreign direct investment have been relaxed, and foreign banks have been allowed to have greater shareholding in domestic banks (up to 49%), although foreign banks have faced some difficulties in acquiring such stakes. In 2002 government legislation enhanced banks' capacity to act against debtors, a measure that should help banks in their attempts to address the high level of bad debt held by Indian companies.

Tourism. India is one of the world's fastest growing tourism markets with an annual growth rate of approximately 8.8%. Annual tourist inflows range between 2 and 2.5 million, but tourism has proven to be susceptible to issues such as communal conflict between Hindus and Muslims and occasional spikes in tensions between India and Pakistan.

Labour. According to official figures, from 1981 to 2001 the total number of workers grew more than 50% from approximately 245 million to 402 million persons. These figures count only those who are considered to have "engaged in economically productive activity for 183 days or more." The actual number of persons in the labour force is likely to be much higher. From 1983 to 1994, the nation's unemployment rate declined from 8.3% to 6% and then increased to 7.3% by 2000. Unemployment rates have historically been higher in urban areas, but rural and urban unemployment rates became nearly equal by 2000 (7.2 and 7.7%, respectively).

Foreign Economic Relations. India's principal export and import trades are with the European Union, the United States, and Japan. Most aid is provided by the Aid-to-India Consortium, consisting of the World Bank Group, Austria, Belgium, Britain, Canada, Denmark, France, Germany, Italy, Japan, the Netherlands, Norway, Sweden, and the United States. Japan is the largest aid granter and lender. India has its own aid programmes with Bangladesh, Bhutan, Nepal, and Vietnam.

Imports. Principal imports are petroleum and petroleum products, capital goods, uncut gems, machinery, and fertilizer. Major imports are from the United States, the European Union (particularly Belgium), Singapore, the United Kingdom, and Saudi Arabia. In 2003 imports totaled US$64.5 billion, a substantial increase over 2002 imports of US$54.2 billion.

Exports. Principal exports are textile goods, finished gems and jewelry, engineered goods (including iron and steel), chemicals, and leather and leather goods. Main destinations of exports are the United States, the United Kingdom, China (particularly Hong Kong), Japan, and the European Union (particularly Germany). In 2003 total exports were valued at US$52.5 billion, a substantial increase over 2002 exports of US$47.7 billion.

Trade Balance. India's negative trade balance has grown steadily since the late 1980s. In 2003 exports were US$52.5 billion and imports were US$65.4 billion, resulting in a negative trade balance of US$12.9 billion.

Balance of Payments. Before 2002 India's surpluses in the capital account were offset by deficits in the current account, but since 2002 India has had surpluses in the current and capital accounts, leading to an accumulation of foreign reserves. The current account surplus is a small percentage of GDP (0.5% in 2003) and has been the result of non-factor services and private transfers exceeding trade deficits. Growth in foreign direct investment is largely responsible for steady growth in the capital account, and external commercial borrowings and assistance make up most net outflows.

External Debt. India's total external debt has increased from US$83.8 billion in 1991 to US$112.1 billion in 2003, but external debt declined as a percentage of gross domestic product (GDP) in the same time period (from 28.7 to 20.2%). Furthermore, in 1991 India was the world's third highest debtor nation, but it had dropped to eighth by 2002.

Foreign Investment. Foreign direct investment in India has increased from about US$97 million in 1991 to US$3.6 billion for 2003, partly because of various liberalization measures, such as reduced tariffs and relaxed restrictions on foreign ownership of domestic industries.

Currency and Exchange Rate. The rupee (Rs) has depreciated steadily against the dollar since the 1970s. Since the late 1990s, the rupee has been stable against the euro as a result of the weakening of the U.S. dollar and worldwide shift away from U.S. dollar assets.

With a GDP growth rate of 9.4% in 2006-07, the Indian economy is among the fastest growing in the world. India's GDP in terms of USD exchange-rate is US$1.103 trillion, which makes it the twelfth largest economy in the world. When measured in terms of purchasing power parity (PPP), India has the world's fourth largest GDP at US$4.156 trillion. India's per capita income (nominal) is $820, ranked 128th in the world, while it's per capita (PPP) of US$3,700 is ranked 118th.

The Indian economy has grown steadily over the last two decades; however, its growth has been uneven when comparing different social groups, economic groups, geographic regions, and rural and urban areas. Although income inequality in India is relatively small it has been increasing of late. Despite significant economic progress, a quarter of the nation's population earns less than the government-specified poverty threshold of $0.40/day. In addition, India has a higher rate of malnutrition among children under the age of three (46% in year 2007) than any other country in the world.

India has a labour force of 509.3 million, 60% of which is employed in agriculture and related industries; 28% in services and related industries; and 12% in industry. Major agricultural crops include rice, wheat, oilseed, cotton, jute, tea, sugarcane, and potatoes. The agricultural sector accounts for 28% of GDP; the service and industrial sectors make up 54% and 18% respectively. Major industries include automobiles, cement, chemicals, consumer electronics, food processing, machinery, mining, petroleum, pharmaceuticals, steel, transportation equipment, and textiles.

In 2006, estimated exports stood at US$112 billion and imports were around US$187.9 billion. Textiles, jewellery, engineering goods and software are major export commodities. Crude oil, machineries, fertilizers, and chemicals are major imports. India's most important trading partners are the United States, the European Union, China, and the United Arab Emirates. More recently, India has capitalised on its large pool of educated, English-speaking people, and trained professionals to become an important outsourcing destination for multinational corporations and a popular destination for medical tourism. India has also become a major exporter of software as well as financial, research, and technological services. Its natural resources include arable land, bauxite, chromite, coal, diamonds, iron ore, limestone, manganese, mica, natural gas, petroleum, and titanium ore.

Infrastructure

India's transportation infrastructure has undergone tremendous change since independence. While traditional, non-mechanized transport means are still quite common (elephants and camels are not an uncommon sight even in large urban areas), roads, railroads, ports, and aviation continue to expand. India now has the world's second largest road network, and its rail network is among the most used in the world for passengers and freight. Furthermore, increasing incomes and government liberalization measures have contributed to tremendous growth in the numbers of automobiles, two- and three-wheeled vehicles, private and public buses, and urban rail networks. However, there are significant, accompanying problems with pollution, increasing traffic density, unauthorized transportation providers, and high numbers of traffic fatalities.

Roads. There were about 3.3 million kilometres of roads by 2002, of which 1.4 million kilometres were surfaced and more than 1 million kilometres were covered with gravel, crushed stone, or earth. More than 150 highways are rated as national highways and carry about 40% of road traffic on a total length of 65,569 kilometres. Around 85% of all passenger traffic and 70% of all freight traffic travel by road. By 2007, highways have expanded by 13,146 kilometres, with road projects aimed at linking the country's major cities and spanning the entire country north-south and east-west. Modes of road transport are a mix of traditional and modern means. Urban transit is dominated by motor vehicles, with increasing use of automobiles, minibuses, buses, trucks, and particularly two- and three-wheeled vehicles.

Railroads. All railroads are government-owned and operated by Indian Railways. In 2002 total route length was 63,028 kilometres, and double and multiple tracks resulted in a total track length of 108,706 kilometres. Of the total track length, 86,526 kilometres were 1.676-millimeter gauge, 18,529 kilometres were 1.000-millimeter gauge, and 3,651 kilometres were 0.762- and 0.610-millimeter gauge. About 16,000 kilometres were electrified, mostly 1.676 millimeter gauge. The rail system includes 7,566 locomotives, 37,840 coaches, 222,147 freight wagons, 6,853 stations, and nearly 116,000 bridges. Both passenger and freight carriage continue to expand annually, and the rail system is the fourth most heavily used in the world, both for passengers and freight. For the financial year 2004, Indian Railways carried 557 million freight tons and more than 5 billion passengers. There are some high-speed routes and increasing use of them. Most rolling stock and other components are still domestically produced, but they are increasingly manufactured through commercial agreements with foreign companies. There have been major government investments in modernization since the early 1990s, but Indian Railways has also experienced dwindling government budgetary support and has suffered from the dual role of being both a public utility and a commercial enterprise.

Ports. India has 12 major ports and 185 minor and intermediate ports along the country's coastline. There are also 7 shipyards under the control of the central government, 2 shipyards controlled by state governments, and 19 privately owned shipyards. The major ports handled 344.6 million tons of cargo for the financial year 2004, with Chennai, Vishakhapatnam and Kandla carrying the greatest tonnage. Major ports can collectively handle 390 million tons of cargo annually, and port operations have improved since the mid-1990s. All major ports, except one (Ennore), are government administered, but private-sector participation in ports has increased. In 2000 there were 102 shipping companies operating in India, of which five were privately owned and based in India and one was owned by the government (Shipping Corporation of India). In 2000 there were 639 government-owned ships, including 91 oil tankers, 79 dry cargo bulk carriers, and 10 cellular container vessels. Indian-flagged vessels carried about 15% of overseas cargo at Indian ports for financial year 2003.

Inland and Coastal Waterways. India has approximately 14,500 kilometres of inland waterways, but the transportation potential is vastly underused. More than 3,600 kilometres are navigable by large vessels, although only about 2,000 kilometres are used. For purposes of navigational development and conservation, three inland waterways have been declared national waterways. the Allahabad-Haldia portion of the Ganga-Bhagirathi-Hooghly rivers (1,620 kilometres), the Sadiya-Dhubri section of the Brahmaputra River (891 kilometres), and a combination of western canals (205 kilometres).

Civil Aviation and Airports. The government owns two airlines (Air India and Indian Airlines) and one helicopter service (Pawan Hans), and there are twelve privately owned airlines. Private airlines account for about 45% of domestic air traffic, and the government has divested more than 50% of the equity in both government-owned airlines. Of 288 airports, 208 have permanent-surface runways, and there are two runways of more than 3,659 meters. The Airports Authority of India administers 126 airports. 11 international, 89 domestic, and 26 for defence purposes. In 2003 these airports collectively handled approximately 500,000 flights, 40 million passengers, and 900,000 tons of cargo. Major international airports are located in Kolkata, Chennai, Mumbai, New Delhi, and Thiruvananthapuram. There is also international service from Bangalore, Guwahati, Hyderabad, and Mamargao, and there are major regional airports at Ahmadabad, Allahabad, Chandigarh, Kochi, Nagpur, Pune, and Srinagar.

Pipelines. In 2003 India had an estimated 5,798 kilometres of gas pipelines, 1,195 kilometres for liquid petroleum gas, 5,613 kilometres for oil, and 5,567 kilometres for refined products. India and Iran have discussed constructing a gas pipeline, but the Indian government and oil industry analysts have expressed concerns about the pipeline's security because of its proposed route through conflict-prone areas of Pakistan.

Telecommunications. India is witnessing possibly its greatest period of change in communications, with increasing shifts from government to private providers and greater public use of various technologies. From 1995 to 2003, the number of Internet users increased from 250,000 to 18.4 million. Since the late 1990s, the number of telephones, mobile phones, and personal computers has increased substantially. In 2004 there were 40.9 million telephones and 26.2 million mobile phones, and in 2003 there were an estimated 7.5 million personal computers. Some basic telephone services were opened to private-sector competition in 1994, and portions of state-owned telecommunications services have been purchased by private entities. Government-owned radio (All India Radio) and television (Doordarshan) networks have extensive national and local coverage, but domestic and international private television networks are increasingly prolific through cable and satellite. According to government figures, there were 79.4 million television households in 2001. From 1991 to 2002, the number of radios roughly doubled to an estimated 111 million, and radio remains the main source of news for most Indians.

Government and Politics

India is a democratic republic with a system of government legally based on the often-amended 1950 constitution. The central government is also known as the union government, and its structure is much like the British parliamentary system, with distinct, but interrelated executive, legislative, and judicial branches. State governments are structured much like the central government, and district governments exist in a variety of forms. The Indian parliament is a bicameral legislature composed of a lower house (the Lok Sabha or House of the People), with 543 popularly elected members and 2 members appointed by the president, and an upper house (the Rajya Sabha or Council of States), with 12 appointed members and 233 members elected by state and union territory assemblies. Lok Sabha members serve five-year terms, and Rajya Sabha members serve six-year terms, with one-third of members up for election every two years. The legislature passes laws on constitutionally specified matters, such as central government finances and constitutional amendments. The two houses have the same powers, but the Rajya Sabha's power in the legislative process is subordinate to the Lok Sabha. India has both a prime minister and a president. Members of parliament and state legislative assemblies elect the president, currently Pratibha Patil, who was elected in 2007. Prime ministers are leaders of the majority party in parliament but are formally appointed by the president. In 2004 Manmohan Singh became prime minister. Over time, political power has become increasingly concentrated in the prime minister and Council of Ministers (cabinet), although they are responsible to the parliament. The president's duties are mostly ceremonial, although the president formally approves the prime minister and also approves the Council of Ministers based on the prime minister's advice. Furthermore, all bills require presidential approval before becoming law. The vice president is ex officio chairperson of the Rajya Sabha and acts in place of the president when the president is unable to perform his or her duties.

The Supreme Court is the top legal entity, and it is composed of a chief justice appointed by the president and 25 associate judges also appointed by the president in consultation with the chief justice. The Supreme Court has numerous legal powers, such as appellate jurisdiction over all civil and criminal proceedings, with the potential of influencing interpretation of the constitution. The parliament and Supreme Court have maintained a contentious relationship on issues related to judicial review and parliamentary sovereignty. Below the Supreme Court are high courts, followed by a hierarchy of subordinate courts, and some states also have *panchayat* (village level) courts that decide civil and criminal matters. Some high courts serve more than one state, and all are independent of state legislatures and executives. The judiciary is regarded as slow and cumbersome but is also widely respected and often takes an activist role in protecting citizens' rights.

Since independence, India has experienced a plethora of political successes and problems. Corruption, communal conflicts, and rural economic development remain difficult political issues. Furthermore, some analysts believe the government's inclusive design could undermine governing capacity and national unity as political parties and social groups press for their respective parochial interests. Yet the country maintains a democratic system of government with civil liberties that are often lacking in many poor, ethnically diverse societies. India also has an impressive record of economic development and a demonstrable commitment to correcting traditional social oppression. A wide variety of social groups have held elected office, and women, Sikhs, Muslims, and *dalits* have served as either president or prime minister. In 2004 there were 45 women elected to the Lok Sabha, and both *dalits* and indigenous groups have a certain minimum number of reserved seats in the Lok Sabha and state assemblies based on their respective percentages of the population.

Administrative Divisions. There are 28 states and 7 union territories including the national capital territory of New Delhi. State boundaries are often based on language or other social characteristics, and union territories tend to be geographically smaller and less populous than states. States and union territories contain 601 districts that are further subdivided into townships containing from 200 to 600 villages. The union government exercises greater control over union territories than over states, but the division of power between the union and state governments can appear blurred and even chaotic at times. Relationships between some state governments and the union government have been contentious, particularly when state governments are run by political parties that oppose the governing party or coalition in parliament. The tremendous variations in economic and social development among states suggest that state governments can have a greater influence on their populations than the union government. However, the union government still exercises considerable influence on states through numerous financial resources and its authority to assume control of states during times of emergency (called President's Rule), which the union government has done nearly 100 times since 1947.

Provincial and Local Government. Union territories have a council of ministers, a legislature, and a high court, but they are largely governed by the central or union government through a lieutenant governor or chief commissioner appointed by the prime minister. The structure of state governments largely mirrors that of the union government, with each state having a legislative assembly, chief minister, and high court. State government policies are largely implemented through state-level agencies, but union government agencies are also prevalent at local levels.

District and local governments are generally weak, although some states have attempted to establish traditional village councils (*panchayats*) to address local matters. State legislatures are usually unicameral with a legislative assembly composed of members elected for five-year terms. Bicameral state legislatures also have a legislative council that is largely advisory in its capacities, with members directly elected, indirectly elected, or nominated. States' chief ministers are the leaders of majority parties in state legislatures, and just as the prime minister is accountable to parliament, chief ministers are answerable to state legislatures. However, the popularity and party support of some chief ministers enable them to have some autonomy from their state legislature and a degree of influence that rivals that of the union government. States also have governors that are appointed by the president and accountable to the dominant political party in parliament. Although the position is largely honorific, governors do have important powers such as formal approval of chief ministers and their cabinets as well as the authority to recommend that the union government take control of a state government during times of emergency (President's Rule).

Judicial and Legal System. The legal system is derived from English common law and based on the 1950 constitution. Judges decide cases, and there is no trial by jury. Defendants can choose counsel independent of the government, and the government provides free legal counsel for defendants unable to afford such. The judiciary enforces the right to fair trial, and there are effective channels for appeal, but the judicial system is so overburdened with a case backlog that some courts barely function. In non-criminal matters, the government does not interfere with the personal status laws of Muslims and other communities on matters dealing with family law, inheritance, divorce, and discrimination against women. The Indian constitution contains civil liberties called Fundamental Rights that are guaranteed to all citizens and include equality before the law and freedoms of speech, expression, religion, and association. Freedom of the press is not explicitly stated but is widely interpreted as included in the freedoms of speech and expression. The Fundamental Rights were also created with the objective of addressing historical social injustices and legally prohibit bonded labour, human trafficking, and discrimination based on religion, sex, race, caste, and birthplace. Still, the government has the authority to limit civil liberties in order to preserve public order, protect national security, and for other reasons.

Electoral System. The Election Commission is the independent government body that supervises parliamentary and state elections, which are massive and sometimes marred by violence. Elections for state assemblies and the Lok Sabha are held every five years unless called earlier, such as through a no-confidence vote of the government by the Lok Sabha. Indeed, elections are often held before the five-year limits because governments have often had difficulty staying in power for the full five-year term. In the 2004 general elections, there were more than 687,000 polling stations and 671.5 million voters. Since 1952, there have been 14 general elections, with voter turnout ranging from 55 to 64% of eligible voters. The legal voting age is 18. National and state legislative elections are similar to the British House of Commons and United States House of Representatives, in which members gain office by winning a plurality of votes in their local constituency. There are 543 parliamentary constituencies. The number of constituencies for state legislatures ranges from 32 to 403, with a total of 4,120 state constituencies nationwide.

Politics and Political Parties. From 1947 until 1989, the left-of-centre Indian National Congress and its factions dominated national politics. In the 1990s, the centre-right Bharatiya Janata Party (BJP) and the centrist Janata Dal emerged as influential political parties, although Congress returned to power in May 2004. There are numerous national and state parties. Among the best known and most prominent are Akali Dal, All-India Anna DMK (AIADMK), Asom Gana Parishad, Bahujan Samaj Party (BSP), Bharatiya Janata Party (BJP), Communist Party of India (CPI), Communist Party of India-Marxist (CPI-M), Dravida Munnetra Kazhagam (DMK), Indian National Congress, Rashtriya Janata Dal (RJD), Samajwadi Party, Samata Party, Shiv Sena, and Telugu Desam. Since the late 1960s, minority parties in Parliament have often been majority parties in state legislatures. Since 1989, single political parties have generally failed to win a parliamentary majority. As a result, parliament is often run by coalitions of political parties. It is believed that the emergence of multiparty governments is caused by voters' frustration with political corruption and the fragmentation of electorate support among the growing number of political parties that represent specific parochial or local interests. Thus, those parties have strong support only in particular states. Furthermore, lower castes and other social groups have become more involved in politics as both voters and politicians.

Mass Media. India has more newspapers than any other nation, and newspaper readership annually grows by millions. There are a few state-run newspapers, but most print media are privately owned. There are more than 5,600 daily newspapers and more than 46,000 non-daily newspapers and print periodicals. In 2002 the government allowed print media to be up to 26% foreign owned, but the most powerful publishers are joint stock companies that frequently have other commercial and industrial holdings. Government authorities control most television channels, yet the growth of private FM and television stations has marked a shift away from mostly state-run electronic media such as Doordarshan (television) and All India Radio. Foreign television channels are available through cable television or Indian broadcasters. An estimated 42.3% of Indian households have a television, and 52.2% of those have cable or satellite transmission. Similarly, the number of Internet users has rapidly to an estimated 18.4 million users in 2003. India has a high degree of press and speech freedom. However, the government and police have been accused of violating journalists' civil liberties.

Foreign Relations. India's Ministry of External Affairs is the governmental body that is officially responsible for making and implementing foreign policy, although India's prime ministers have often exercised substantial influence in foreign policy decision making. India's parliament and armed forces historically have had very limited roles in the formulation of foreign policy. India's relations with all major nations traditionally have been based on principles of nonalignment and India's own economic development. The overlapping domestic and external dimensions of India's economic development continue to illustrate that many matters related to India's ongoing formation as a nation have international security implications. Attempts to promote economic growth have pushed India from its previous emphasis on domestic self-sufficiency to a major promoter of free trade and economic liberalization. Nonalignment, however, has been seriously tested as a viable basis for foreign policy with the erosion of U.S. and Soviet tensions and with India's interest in playing an influential role in regional and world politics. India's demonstration of nuclear capabilities in 1998 was driven as much by domestic desires to protect Indian influence and prestige internationally as by regional security concerns. Post-Cold War shifts in military power and concerns with terrorism have led India to create stronger bilateral relations with China, Israel, the United States, and other nations. The Ministry of External Affairs has generally been most concerned with relations with neighboring Nepal, Sri Lanka, and particularly Pakistan on issues concerning unresolved borders, natural resource distribution, immigration, and insurgent activity. India's security concerns have been most pronounced with Pakistan, as exemplified by the two countries' newfound nuclear rivalry, the 1999 Kargil War in Jammu and Kashmir, and the 2001 terrorist attack on India's parliament, which Pakistan is suspected of supporting. In spite of these difficulties, tensions between India and Pakistan have periodically thawed, and the two countries have demonstrated interest in resolving their enduring dispute over Jammu and Kashmir.

Major International Treaties. India is a signatory to numerous international treaties. India is not a party to the Treaty on the Non-Proliferation of Nuclear Weapons (NPT) or the Missile Technology Control Regime. Indian governments have argued that the NPT does not reduce nuclear weapons proliferation by states already possessing nuclear weapons and that the NPT denies non-nuclear states the right to have nuclear weapons.

National Security

The prime minister and Council of Ministers formulate national security policy. Below this level is the civilian bureaucracy, which exercises important influence, primarily through the Defence Minister's Committee of the cabinet. The third tier of defence policy making is the Chiefs of Staffs Committee. These three levels are supported by intelligence organizations, scientific and technical advisory committees, defence production, and research and development groups. There are three military services—army, navy, and air force—and a number of paramilitary and reserve forces. The army has been the dominant service in terms of both percentage of budget allotted to the armed forces and percentage of persons serving in the armed forces.

The military has undergone tremendous change since the early 1990s, and the government and military have seriously appraised the military's capabilities and organization. India's great-power aspirations have been continually hindered by its capabilities, but the situation has changed with India's emergence as a nuclear power after successful nuclear tests in May 1998 (India has since pledged a unilateral moratorium on nuclear testing). The armed services' goals of force modernization (particularly the navy and air force) through new arms acquisitions and a "Revolution in Military Affairs" via information technology are constrained by budgetary, bureaucratic, personnel, and technological obstacles. Although the military has long desired to rely on domestically produced military goods, much materiel is imported. Indeed, the Defence Research and Development Organization (DRDO), the arm of the Department of Defence responsible for providing military hardware, has been criticized by both parliament and the military for failing to provide even basic equipment, and several DRDO projects have been behind schedule. The 1984 merger of the Department of Defence Production and the Department of Defence Supplies has not yet led to reliance on domestic production of military hardware.

Service chiefs and military officers continually suggest that the military should have greater input into defence policymaking and national security, and generally such a role is not viewed as a threat to civilian control of the military. Since 2001, the government has established the Defence Intelligence Agency (DIA), the Defence Acquisitions Council (DAC, which now controls the DRDO), and the National Security Council (NSC), which suggests that India has rethought its defence policymaking structure. The government has also proposed creating a Chief of Defence Staff. However, these changes have yet to make a major impact. Indeed, the NSC issued the draft nuclear doctrine but has not otherwise played an important role in defence policymaking and is criticized as an ad hoc organization.

India has approximately 1,325,000 active-duty personnel, with 1,100,000 in the army, 55,000 in the navy (5,000 in naval aviation and 1,200 marines), and 170,000 in the air force. Reserve forces personnel totaled 535,000, and there were fourteen paramilitary forces (including the coast guard) under the control of various ministries with a total strength of 1,089,700.

Foreign Military Relations. Indian peacekeeping forces have been sent to Sri Lanka from 1987 to 1990 and to the Maldives in 1988. Since 1950 Indian military and police contingents have participated in United Nations (UN) peacekeeping forces in Angola, Bosnia and Herzegovina, Cambodia, Democratic Republic of the Congo, Costa Rica, Cyprus, Dominican Republic, El Salvador, Ethiopia and Eritrea, Gaza, Guatemala, Honduras, Iraq, Korea (during the Korean War), Kuwait, Laos, Lebanon, Liberia, Mozambique, Namibia, Nicaragua, Rwanda, Sierra Leone, Somalia, Vietnam, West New Guinea (West Irian), Yemen, and Yugoslavia. India has also provided police personnel and monitors for UN peacekeeping operations in Angola, Bosnia and Herzegovina, Cambodia, Haiti, Kosovo, Mozambique, Sierra Leone, and Western Sahara.

Foreign Military Forces. The only foreign military forces in India are with the United Nations Military Observer Group in India and Pakistan (UNMOGIP), which has 45 military observers from 9 countries stationed in Jammu and Kashmir.

External Threat. External security threats come from neighbouring countries and insurgents using foreign border areas as havens for activities in India. Countries such as Bangladesh, Bhutan, and Sri Lanka present no conventional military threat to India, but their inability to police and control areas bordering India has provided Indian insurgents with havens. Indian government and military officials have publicly expressed concern about the political instability in its neighbourhood. As far as external threats posed by other countries, popular opinion tends to regard Pakistan as the principal enemy, largely because of the Kashmir conflict and Pakistan's suspected links to numerous South Asian militant groups. However, the defence establishment generally regards China as the chief external threat, because of perceived Chinese attempts to isolate India militarily and diplomatically from the rest of Asia and perceived Chinese efforts to prevent India from becoming a permanent member of the UN Security Council. While China-India border issues remain unresolved from the Indian point of view, Sino-Indian relations have improved as China has adopted a less intimate relationship with Pakistan.

Defence Budget. India's defence budget has grown since the early 1990s, and accounts for more than two-thirds of South Asian military spending. India's defence budget was approximately US$16.6 billion in 2003, about 2.5% of GDP, and the 2004 defence budget is US$19.1 billion. By contrast, the 1994 defence budget was US$7.6 billion, which was also 2.5% of GDP in 1994. Interestingly, as a result of inefficient equipment procurement processes, defence expenditures are often less than the defence budget (around 5% less).

Major Military Units. The army has an estimated 800,000 active-duty troops and 300,000 reserves. The army is structured as 12 corps organized into 5 regional commands. The navy has an estimated 55,000 persons on active duty and an equal number of reserve troops. Navy units are structured into three area commands, and there are six naval bases with three more under construction. The air force has an estimated 170,000 active forces and 140,000 reserves. Air force units are under five regional air commands.

Military Service. The minimum age of service is 16, and the mandatory age for retirement for officers varies from 48 to 60 depending on rank. The military has expressed concern about its increasing age profile and a shortage of officers. Formal military service is completely on a volunteer basis, and India does not have—and never has had—conscription.

Paramilitary Forces. Police are under the control of state governments, and the central government can assist states by providing central paramilitary forces as deemed necessary, particularly to guard coasts, borders, and sensitive military areas and to aid local police forces against insurgencies. There are 1,089,700 active paramilitary personnel (including police) and 1,027,000 voluntary reserves.

Police. As of October 2002, there were 1,015,416 police officers in India for a national average of 1 police officer per 125 persons. Police are under the control of state governments, and, with central government permission, states are allowed to create police reserve battalions; all 13 reserve police battalions are in insurgent-prone northeastern states. State police are often assisted by—and some say depend upon—paramilitaries and the armed forces for the maintenance of internal security.

Internal Threats and Terrorism. India's top security concerns are mostly internal. Much of the national security apparatus is directed to maintaining territorial integrity as dozens of groups push for varying degrees of political or social autonomy, sometimes violently. India treats separatism with extreme concern given the possibility that successful separatism may establish a precedent that other groups might seek to follow. Internal threats can be categorized as religiously oriented conflict or ethnic violence, usually with separatist objectives. Separatist violence periodically escalates in Jammu and Kashmir. Numerous separatist insurgent groups are active in the northeast, and India has periodically expanded its military efforts in Assam against groups such as the United Liberation Front of Assam (ULFA), National Democratic Front of Bodoland (NDFB), and Bodo Security Force (BSF). Other rebel groups in Assam observe ceasefire agreements with the government. The decades-long separatist conflict in Nagaland continues with the National Socialist Council of Nagaland-Khapland (NSCN-K), although peace talks have occurred with another faction, the NSCN-IM (Isaac Muivah), after the government lifted its previous ban on the organization. In Tripura, various insurgents continue to target Bengali immigrants and Indian security forces. Religiously oriented violence has occurred, principally among Hindus and Muslims and most notably in Ayodhya (in Uttar Pradesh) and urban areas of Gujarat and Maharashtra. While less common than separatist violence, these conflicts prompt greater popular debates on Indian history, society, and politics; there are allegations that national and state-level politicians with the Bharatiya Janata Party (BJP) have facilitated such conflicts.

Human Rights. Although human rights problems exist in India, the country is generally not regarded as among the world's serious human rights violators. Human rights problems appear to be acute in areas and periods of communal violence, and security forces, insurgents, and various ethnic-based groups have all been accused of human rights violations in Jammu and Kashmir, Gujarat, Maharashtra, Uttar Pradesh, and various northeastern states. Both international human rights organizations and India's National Human Rights Commission have questioned the impartiality of police and judicial authorities in various locales. On the other hand, human rights groups have praised India's September 2004 repeal of the 2002 Prevention of Terrorism Act, which both the newly elected government and international organizations criticized as enabling human rights abuses by security forces. Indian media routinely address controversial issues, such as political corruption and discrimination against women, sexual minorities, indigenous peoples, and "untouchables." In response to cyber-crime and cyber-terrorism perpetrated by parties in both India and Pakistan, India passed the Information Technology Act of 2000, which allows cyber cafés and Internet users homes to be searched without warrants at any time as part of criminal investigations.

INDONESIA

The Republic of Indonesia (the word Indonesia was coined from the Greek *indos*—for India—and *nesos*—for island) proclaimed independence on 17August 1945, from the Netherlands. The Hague recognized Indonesian sovereignty on 27 December 1949. Indonesia is located in Southeast Asia and lies between the Indian and Pacific oceans. Estimates of the size of Indonesia's total area vary. Officially, the Indonesian government says the total land area is 1.9 million square kilometres and total sea area, 7.9 million square kilometres, including an exclusive economic zone. The Indonesian flag has two equal horizontal bands of red (top) and white.

The first formal kingdom of present day Indonesia was Srivijaya (550 – 1050 A.D.), a Buddhist trading polity in the region of present-day Palembang and reached to coastal areas on the Malaysian peninsula and Mataram, in Central Java, where magnificent Buddhist and Hindu monuments such as Borobudur and Prambanan were constructed in the 8th and 9th centuries. The greatest of the subsequent Hindu-Buddhist states, the empire of Majapahit in East Java, claimed hegemony from the late 13th to early 16th centuries stretching from Sumatra to Maluku. Islam entered the archipelago in about the 11th century, but significant conversions did not take place till the turn of the 14th century and going on to Central Java in the 17th century.

Contacts from China deepened between the 10th and 14th centuries as a result of growing trade, but Mongol attempts to control Javanese power (in the late 13th century) failed, and early Ming dynasty (1368–1644) efforts to exercise great political and economic influence were fleeting. Western visitors began appearing, with the Portuguese and Spanish, in the 16th century. They were soon followed by the Dutch (1596) and the English (1601). Europeans affected trade and politics in specific places and periods, but for most of the archipelago beyond Java and parts of Maluku, colonial rule did not set in until the mid- or late 19th century.

Dutch power in the archipelago grew very gradually, and colonial rule was not a goal of the Dutch East India Company (VOC), which dominated trade from Amsterdam and, after the early 17th century, a fortified port called Batavia (now Jakarta) in West Java. But local realities created a symbiotic Dutch-Javan relationship that survived the bankruptcy of the VOC in 1799 and soon took the shape of a colonial administration, which grew and consolidated during the late 1800s. In the first decades of the 20th century, the Dutch colonial state extended its control to most of the area we now call Indonesia. Simultaneously, some of the peoples ruled by this state discovered nationalism; the first groups date from the early 1900s, and by the 1920s and 1930s an array of modern political organizations and leaders, including the well-known nationalist figure Sukarno (1901–70), came to the fore. The struggle between the Dutch colonial government and the Indonesian nationalist movement was well under way when the Japanese occupied the Indies in 1942. They remained until the end of World War II in August 1945.

On 17 August 1945, Sukarno and Mohammad Hatta proclaimed the independent Republic of Indonesia with Sukarno as president and Hatta as vice president. Allied forces (mostly British and British Indian troops) did not arrive until six weeks later, by which time the republic had begun to establish itself and nationalist pride had burgeoned. The period October-December 1945 was filled with violent conflict in which Indonesians made it clear they would defend their independence with their lives. Forcing the Dutch to negotiate with the republic, the British withdrew in late 1946. The republic survived two Dutch "police actions" and an internal communist rebellion, and on 27 December 1949, The Hague formally recognized the sovereignty of a federated republic, which a year later was formed into a unitary Republic of Indonesia.

Despite democratic elections in 1955, the years following the struggle for independence were characterized by political and economic difficulty, regional dissidence, attempted assassinations and coups d'état, military-civilian conflict, and economic stagnation. A period of Guided Democracy was announced in 1959 by Sukarno, who in September 1963 proclaimed himself president-for-life and presided over a political system in which the civilian nationalist leadership, much of the Islamic leadership, the large Indonesian Communist Party (PKI), and the army were all at odds. This tense and hostile atmosphere was broken on 30 September 1965, with what appears to have been an attempted PKI coup against the Sukarno government. The precise circumstances remain unclear, but the immediate result was that a "New Order" coalition of students, intellectuals, Muslims, and the army brought about a military-dominated government that removed Sukarno and permitted a broad and deadly assault on communists, especially on Java, Bali, and Sumatra. In late 1965 and early 1966, an estimated 500,000 Indonesian communists and suspected communists were killed and many more arrested. On 11 March 1966, power was transferred from a seriously ill Sukarno to Suharto, an army officer. The PKI was formally banned the following day and Suharto became the acting president, and the New Order era began.

The New Order era, which lasted for more than 30 years, has a mixed record. Like Guided Democracy, it was authoritarian, but it was more successful in bringing stability to the nation. Unlike Guided Democracy, its economic achievements were enormous and the well-being of the majority of Indonesians undeniably improved, e.g. average life expectancy increased from 46 to 65.5 years. On the other hand, the state's heavy involvement in banking and industry, especially the petroleum and natural gas sectors, worked against competition and encouraged corruption on a large scale. Heavy-handed political control and propagandizing of a national ideology may have aided stability, but also did not prepare the nation for a modern political existence. An educated and better-off middle class grew, but gained little or no political clout; poverty was reduced, but some particularly severe pockets appeared to be intractable. Suharto provided strong leadership, but he did not provide for a wise transition and, in his last years, clung to power and favoured family and friends. East Timor, which had been forcibly annexed by Indonesia in 1976, saw bitter conflict between the Indonesian military and local independence movements. When the Asian financial crisis hit in 1997–98, the New Order lost the economic justification that had guaranteed much of its public support, and there was a widespread call for Suharto to step down. He resigned on 21 May 1998, little more than two months after being elected for his seventh term as president.

Suharto was succeeded by Bucharuddin Jusuf Habibie, who sought first to resolve the East Timor situation and begin a new and more open electoral process. In 1999, following Indonesia's first freely contested parliamentary elections since 1955, Abdurrahman Wahid, well-known as both a progressive intellectual and as leader of Indonesia's largest Muslim organization (Nahdlatul Ulama, NU) became president. His quirky leadership style and questions about both his competency and his health, brought increasing opposition and eventually serious threats of impeachment. He was dismissed from office in July

2001 in favor of Megawati Sukarnoputri, the vice president and head of the Indonesian Democratic Party of Struggle (PDI-P). Megawati, Sukarno's eldest daughter, was decisively defeated in the September 2004 presidential runoff election by the Democratic Party candidate, retired army general Susilo Bambang Yudhoyono. Yudhoyono was sworn in as president in October 2004.

Geography

Topography. Indonesia's land boundaries total 1,758 kilometres, including 1,107 kilometres with Malaysia, 820 kilometres with Papua New Guinea, and 288 kilometres with East Timor. Indonesia's coastline totals 54,716 kilometres on the Indian Ocean, Strait of Malacca, South China Sea, Java Sea, Sulawesi Sea, Maluku Sea, Pacific Ocean, Arafura Sea, Timor Sea, and other smaller seas. Indonesia is the largest archipelagic nation in the world. It encompasses 17,508 islands. About 6,000 of these islands are named, and about 1,000 are permanently settled. The five main islands are Java, Kalimantan, Papua (formerly called Irian Jaya), Sumatra, and Sulawesi. There are two major archipelagos, Nusa Tenggara and Maluku, and about sixty smaller archipelagos. The larger islands of Indonesia are mountainous, with some peaks reaching 3,800 metres above sea level on the western islands and as high as 5,000 metres on Papua. The highest point is Puncak Jaya (5,030 metres) on Papua. The region is tectonically unstable with some 400 volcanoes, of which 100 are active.

Principal Rivers. Indonesia's waterways total 21,579 kilometres. The principal rivers are the Musi, Batanghari, Indragiri, and Kampar rivers on Sumatra; the Kapuas, Barito, and Mahakam rivers on Kalimantan; the Memberamo and Digul rivers on Papua; and the Bengawan Solo, Citarum, and Brantas rivers on Java, which are used primarily for irrigation.

Climate. Indonesia's maritime equatorial climate typically produces high, even temperatures and heavy rainfall; temperature variations are generally due to elevation and time of day, while rainfall may vary across the archipelago as a result of many different factors, among them monsoon patterns, which themselves vary according to location. Average temperatures at or near sea level range from about 23° C to 31° C. In most of the country, rainfall is comparatively heavy throughout the year, with a pronounced rainy season roughly between December and March. East of Surabaya, however, a dry season is increasingly noticeable, especially between June and October. The high elevations of Sumatra, Kalimantan, Sulawesi, and Papua receive about 3,000 millimetres of rain annually; lower elevations, and much of Java, receive 2,000 or more millimetres; farther east rainfall ranges between 1,000 (Sumba) and 2,000 millimetres per year (Bali and Timor).

Natural Resources. Petroleum and natural gas are among Indonesia's most important natural resources. Indonesia is the world's largest exporter of liquefied natural gas. Most petroleum production is on central Sumatra, but Java also has significant production, and there are substantial proven offshore reserves. There are also large coal reserves. Other significant minerals are bauxite, copper, gold, iron, manganese, nickel, sulfur, silver, and tin. An important non-mineral resource is timber.

Land Use. 11.3% (206,753 square kilometres) of Indonesia's total land area is arable, and land planted in permanent crops, including an irrigated area of 48,150 square kilometres, represents 7.2% of the total (132,051 square kilometres). There are 1,619,687 square kilometres of non-arable land and land not under permanent crops.

Environmental Factors. Indonesia's geography leaves the nation vulnerable to severe flooding, unpredictable drought and plant pest attacks, volcanic activity, and earthquakes, which are sometimes associated with tidal waves (tsunami). The most important environmental issues associated with human activities are forest degradation (unregulated cutting, fires, smoke and haze, and erosion); water pollution from industrial wastes and sewage; air pollution from motor vehicles and industry in urban areas, and generally from smoke and haze caused by forest fires; and threats to biodiversity and rare plant and animal species.

Time Zones. Indonesia has three time zones.

Society

Population. Indonesia has the world's fourth largest population after China, India, and the United States, totaling an estimated 238,452,952 in July 2004, with a 1.5% annual growth rate. 69% of the population lives in rural areas. Java is one of the most densely populated areas in the world, with more than 120 million people, or some 945 persons per square kilometre. By contrast, the most densely populated Outer Islands have 90 persons or fewer per square kilometre. Jakarta, on the western end of Java, is the largest city, with an estimated population of 12 million.

Demography. According to estimates of Indonesia's age structure, 29.4% of Indonesians are under 14 years of age; 65.6% are between 15 and 64; and only 5.1% are 65 and older.

Ethnic Groups. Indonesia is a culturally diverse nation. Ethnic identities are not always clear, stable or agreed upon; ethnic groups may appear or profess to be more distinct socially or culturally than they actually are. There are about 350 recognized ethno-linguistic groups in Indonesia, 180 of them located in Papua; 13 languages have more than a million speakers. Javanese are 45% of the population, Sundanese 14%, Madurese 7.5%, coastal Malays 7.5%, and others 26%.

Languages. The official national language is Bahasa Indonesia, a modified form of Malay, with an estimated 17 million to 30 million mother-tongue speakers and more than 140 million second-language speakers or readers. Additionally, as many as 725 other languages and dialects are spoken. Some have large numbers of speakers. Javanese (75 million), Sundanese (27 million), Madurese (nearly 14 million), and Malay (10 million). Other languages with more than a million speakers each, in descending order, are Minangkabau, Balinese, Buginese, Acehnese, Batawi, Banjarese, Sasak, Toba Batak, Chinese of various dialects, Makasarese, Lampung, Dairi Batak, and Rejang. Since independence, and particularly since 1965, English has replaced Dutch as the main Western language spoken and is widely used in government and business circles.

Religion. Indonesia has the largest Islamic population of any nation. Most Indonesians (88%) count themselves as Muslims and observe Islamic practices to varying degrees; another 5% of Indonesians are Protestant, 3% are Roman Catholic, 2% are Hindu, 1% are Buddhist, and 1% observe other religions. In some remote areas, animism is practiced. The constitution guarantees religious freedom for the five religions (the first five mentioned) recognized by the state. In 2002 the People's Consultative Assembly rejected a proposal to introduce Islamic law as a constitutional requirement.

Education and Literacy. Indonesia has a twelve-year public and private education system (primary—grades one through six; junior high school—grades seven through nine; and senior high school—grades ten through twelve). An estimated 3.7% of government expenditures go toward education. Schooling is compulsory at the primary and, since 1993, junior high levels; senior high school education is optional. The system is supervised by the Ministry of National Education (which is responsible for nonreligious, public schools—about 92% of total enrollment at the primary level and 44% at the secondary level) and the Ministry of Religious Affairs (which is responsible for religious, private, and semiprivate schools—about 15% of total enrollment). *Pesantren* (Islamic religious boarding schools) doubled in number between 1980 and 1996 and enrolled more than twice the number of students, which in 1996 amounted to 1.9 million. Nearly 98% of students complete primary school. The adult literacy rate ranges between 88.5% and 90.2%. In public schools, emphasis on moral and civil studies under the rubric of a state philosophy known as Pancasila (Five Principles. monotheism, humanitarianism, nationalism, democracy, and social justice), was altered after the end of the New Order. Since 2000, for example, courses in "Pancasila Morality" have been known as "Civic Education" and their intensity and propagandistic qualities much reduced. Most religious schools emphasize Islamic values and thought. There are some 1,634 institutions of higher education, including the University of Indonesia in Jakarta, founded by the Dutch in the 1930s, and Gadjah Mada University in Yogyakarta, founded by Indonesians in 1946.

Health. Indonesia had a three-tiered system of community health centers in the late 1990s, with0.66 hospital beds per 1,000 population, the lowest rate among members of the Association ofSoutheast Asian Nations (ASEAN). In the mid-1990s, there were 16 physicians per 100,000 population in Indonesia, 50 nurses per 100,000, and 26 midwives per 100,000. Both traditional and modern health practices are employed. Government health expenditures are about 3.7% of the GDP. There is about a 75.25% ratio of public to private health-care expenditures. Human immuno-deficiency virus/acquired immune deficiency syndrome (HIV/AIDS) has posed a major public health threat since the early 1990s. Other health hazards are dengue fever and avian influenza.

Economy

Indonesia's estimated Gross Domestic Product (GDP) for 2007 is US$408 billion (US$1,038 bn PPP). In 2007, estimated nominal per capita GDP is US$1,812, and per capita GDP PPP was US$4,616. The services sector is the economy's largest and accounts for 45.3% of GDP (2005). This is followed by industry (40.7%) and agriculture (14.0%). However, agriculture employs more people than other sectors, accounting for 44.3% of the 95 million-strong workforce. This is followed by the services sector (36.9%) and industry (18.8%). Major industries include petroleum and natural gas, textiles, apparel, and mining. Major agricultural products include palm oil, rice, tea, coffee, spices, and rubber.

Indonesia's main export markets are Japan (22.3% of Indonesian exports in 2005), the United States (13.9%), China (9.1%), and Singapore (8.9%). The major suppliers of imports to Indonesia are Japan (18.0%), China (16.1%), and Singapore (12.8%). In 2005, Indonesia ran a trade surplus with export revenues of US$83.64 billion and import expenditure of US$62.02 billion. The country has extensive natural resources, including crude oil, natural gas, tin, copper, and gold. Indonesia's major imports include machinery and equipment, chemicals, fuels, and foodstuffs.

Indonesia is Southeast Asia's only member of OPEC, and the 1970s oil price raises provided an export revenue windfall that contributed to sustained high economic growth rates. Following further reforms in the late 1980s, foreign investment flowed into Indonesia, particularly into the rapidly developing export-orientated manufacturing sector, and from 1989 to 1997, the Indonesian economy grew by an average of over 7%.

Indonesia was the country hardest hit by the East Asian financial crisis of 1997–98. Against the US dollar, the currency dropped from about Rp. 2,000 to Rp. 18,000, and the economy shrunk by 13.7%. The rupiah has since stabilized at around Rp. 10,000, and there has been a slow but significant economic recovery. Political instability since 1998, slow economic reform, and corruption at all levels of government and business, have contributed to the patchy nature of the recovery. GDP growth, however, exceeded 5% in both 2004 and 2005, and is forecast to increase further. This growth rate, however, is not enough to make a significant impact on unemployment, and stagnant wages growth, and increases in fuel and rice prices have worsened poverty levels. As of 2006, an estimated 17.8% of the population live below the poverty line, and 49.0% of the population live on less than US$2 per day.

Government Budget. For 2003 Indonesia's government budget was Rp 334.5 trillion (US$39 billion) in revenues and Rp 368.8 (US$43 billion) in expenditures, including capital expenditures. The budget is formulated by the Ministry of Finance and approved by the legislature. Budgets are developed as part of five-year economic development plans.

Agriculture, Forestry, and Fishing. In 2004 agriculture represented a declining share (17.5% or lower; down from 20.6% in 1993) of GDP but employed a majority of workers (an estimated 45% of the total labour force) in 2004. Only about 11.3% of the total land is arable. Farming is by smallholders and on large private and government-owned commercial plantations. Rice dominates food production, but cassava, corn, fruits, sweet potatoes, and vegetables also are important subsistence crops. Green Revolution technological advances and increased use of fertilizers, pesticides, and irrigation improved rice production in the 1970s and 1980s. Cash crops include cocoa, coffee, copra, palm oil, peanuts, rubber, soybeans, sugar, tea, and tobacco. Animal husbandry (dairy and beef cattle, poultry and eggs, and pigs) and fishing are small but valuable parts of the agricultural sector. Attempts to ameliorate rural poverty by means of a transmigration programme moving families from crowded agricultural regions such as Central Java to less crowded areas in, for example, Sumatra and Kalimantan, have failed. Greatly expanding a programme begun by the Dutch early in the 20th century, at the programme's height in the 1979–84 period the Suharto government moved 500,000 people. Poor funding and preparation, local hostility, suspicions about ulterior motives, and economic growth on Java, brought about a precipitous decline; in 2000 the trans-migration programme was ended.

Mining and Minerals. Mining and mineral production represented about 11.9% of GDP and employed about 0.5% of the labour force in 2004. Crude petroleum and natural gas are predominant. About 1.2 million barrels of petroleum are produced per day, a decline from peak levels of production enjoyed in 1995, when production was at 1.6 million barrels per day. Most proven reserves (estimated at 7.1 billion barrels) are offshore. Central Sumatra is the largest oil-producing region and also has about 60% of the reserves of coal, of which a total of 114 million tons were produced nationwide in 2003. Indonesia is the world's largest exporter of liquefied natural gas. An estimated 69 billion cubic metres were produced in 2001, and Indonesia had an estimated proven reserve of 5.5 trillion cubic metres in 2002. Other minerals of significance are bauxite, copper, gold, iron sands, nickel, silver, and tin; most of these minerals are highly localized and often difficult and costly to extract.

Industry and Manufacturing. The industrial sector accounts for an increasing share of GDP—42% in 2002, up from 27% in the late 1980s and employed about 19% of the work force in 2001. Basic industries are automotive and transportation manufactures, food processing, forest products processing, metal manufactures, oil and natural gas processing, and textiles, as well as such other industries as electronic goods, footwear, furniture, garments, and paper goods. Most production is on Java and Sumatra.

Energy. Efforts are underway to decrease dependence on petroleum and to increase the use of alternative energy sources, especially natural gas and coal to generate electric power. Modernized electric power generation produced 95.78 billion kilowatts in 2001, using fossil fuels (86.9%), hydropower (10.5%), and other sources (2.6%). Indonesia has no nuclear power generation. Rural electrification projects have brought power to more than 14 million village homes since the early 1990s.

Services. Services produce between 38 and 42% of GDP and employed about 37% of the work force in 2001. Government service is one of the fastest growing sources of employment and attracts a majority of the best-educated personnel.

Banking and Finance. The country's banking and finance have exhibited both positive and negative signs. Relations with the International Monetary Fund (IMF) have been tense, and the government formally terminated its loan programme with the IMF in December 2003. In the future, Indonesia now relies on bilateral arrangements. Furthermore, the rapid growth in capital markets during the early 1990s has slowed considerably, and share indices have not yet regained their pre-1997 levels. During the financial crisis of 1997–98, many domestic banks collapsed. In 1998 the government allowed foreign ownership of banks and removed restrictions on foreign bank branches outside Jakarta. However, slow progress in bank restructuring has also made foreign investors cautious. The Indonesian Bank Restructuring Agency (IBRA) was established in 1998 to rebuild the private-sector banking industry and dismantle crony conglomerates, which involved selling the banks around which the conglomerates were structured and establishing holding companies to liquidate conglomerates' assets. Indonesia's continued efforts to deal with both domestic and international debts have hindered its attempts to attract foreign investment as well as its efforts to help business and banking recover. Limited corporate restructuring and continuing uncertainties about capital inflows have hindered banks' efforts to increase private-sector lending. Although bank loans started to rebound in 2001–02, foreign subsidiaries generally rely on foreign financial markets to raise capital, and for local services they tend to use foreign bank branches.

Tourism. The 1990s, dubbed by the government a "Visit Indonesia Decade," saw concerted efforts to increase foreign tourism. Travel agencies increased more than 600% to nearly 2,500, and rapid construction of facilities took place. Tourist arrivals reached about 5 million in 1996, earning in excess of US$6 billion. The upheaval and violence associated with the end of the New Order brought declines.

Labour. The New Order period saw the rapid growth of an industrial work force and increasing labour unrest. There were about 350 strikes in 1996, nearly twenty times the number only seven years earlier. Government policy attempted to repress labour activism, but at the same time adopted a policy of raising the minimum wage annually; by 1997 it was three times what it had been six years earlier. The fall of Suharto lifted many pressures on unions and raised minimum wages even more quickly, Jakarta's rising nearly 40% in 2001 alone and steadily after that, to about US$80 a month in 2004. In 2002 Indonesia's the labour force numbered 100.5 million, of which an estimated 10.5 million were unemployed. Another 32 million individuals fell into the category of "disguised unemployment."

Foreign Economic Relations. The principal export trade is with, in descending order of importance, Japan, the European Union, the United States, Singapore,

South Korea, China, and Taiwan. The most important export commodities are crude petroleum and petroleum products; electrical and telecommunications equipment, natural gas (mostly to Japan), natural rubber, plywood, and textiles also are important. Key import partners are Japan, the European Union, the United States, Singapore, South Korea, China, Australia, and Taiwan. The principal imports are machinery and equipment, chemicals, fuels, and foodstuffs.

Foreign Aid. Indonesia received US$43 billion in IMF aid in 2003, and this assistance has traditionally been an important part of the central government's budget. From 1967 to 1991, most aid was coordinated through the Inter-Governmental Group on Indonesia (IGGI) founded and chaired by the Netherlands; since 1992, without the Netherlands, the organization has been known as the Consultative Group on Indonesia (CGI). Although Indonesia terminated its IMF aid programme in December 2003, it still receives bilateral aid through the CGI, which pledged US$2.8 billion in grants and loans for 2004. Japan and the Asian Development Bank also have been key donors.

Currency. Indonesia's currency is the rupiah.

Infrastructure

Roads. Based on 1999 estimates, Indonesia had a total of 342,700 kilometres of roads, mostly (about 60%) located on Java, Madura, Bali, and Sumatra; 158,670 kilometres (46%) were paved, of which 27,358 kilometres were classified as main roads and 40,490 kilometres as secondary roads. Another 184,030 kilometres (54% of the total) were unpaved. About 32% of the roads were classified as highways. There are smaller networks of roads on Sulawesi and Kalimantan, while smaller islands often have limited roads within or connecting major settlements. Urban transit is dominated by motor vehicles; the use of automobiles (there were 3.4 million in use in 2002), buses, minibuses, and motorcycles is widespread, even in seemingly remote areas.

Railroads. Track length totaled 6,458 kilometres in 2002, of which 125 kilometres were electrified. All rail facilities were government-owned and -operated until 1991, when government liberalization created a public corporation, now called PT Kereta Api, which operates Indonesian Railways. The corporation possesses almost total commercial freedom, with the exception of some passenger fares that remain fixed by the government, but it continues to face financial problems as the rising demand for its services is coupled with shortfalls in investment and revenues. However, some of this demand has been met by private passenger and freight service operators that have entered the market since 1995. All railroads are narrow gauge, with 5,931 kilometres 1.067 meter gauge, and 497 kilometres 0.750 meter gauge in 2002. Some 211 kilometres of roadbed are double tracked, and 125 kilometres of 1.067 gauge electrified, all on Java. Other railroads are located on Madura and Sumatra. Most were used for passenger transportation as of 2002, but there was increasing use for freight from the early 1980s onward. A 15-kilometer-long mass rapid transit system, partly underground, was planned for Jakarta, but as of 2004 (it was initially expected to be completed in 2001) construction had not begun because of a lack of funds.

Ports. Indonesia has 379 ports and harbors controlled by the Ministry of Communications for international and inter-island trade. The four main ports—all designated gateways to handle Indonesia's exports—are at Tanjung Priok (near Jakarta), Tanjung Perak (near Surabaya), Belawan (Medan), and Makassar (South Sulawesi). Other major ports are at Cilacap, Cirebon, and Semarang (all on Java), Kupang (Timor), and Palembang (Sumatra). Some 127 ports are classified as capable of handling international shipping. As a result of port improvements begun in the mid-1980s, container handling capacity has doubled at both Makassar and Tanjung Perak, and there are future plans to provide much-needed improvements to Tanjung Priok and Belawan.

Inland and Coastal Waterways. Inter-island transportation is critical to domestic commerce. Traditional sailing craft are widely used, but they increasingly are motorized. The merchant fleet is composed of 718 ships of 1,000 gross registered tons or more. These ships include, by type, the following. cargo (398), refrigerated cargo (2), container (57), bulk carrier (47), roll on/roll off (15), petroleum tanker (128), chemical tanker (13), specialized tanker (12), liquefied natural gas (6), passenger (10), passenger/cargo (13), short-sea passenger (9), vehicle carrier (7), and livestock carrier (1). There also are 35 oceangoing vessels, 259 inter-island vessels, more than 1,000 modernized local-use vessels, almost 4,000 traditional vessels, and 1,900 special bulk carriers. River transport plays a major role in eastern Sumatra, Kalimantan, and Papua. Most of Indonesia's major rivers are at least partly navigable, but those on Java are used primarily for irrigation.

Civil Aviation and Airports. The government owns one airline, Garuda Indonesia, and one smaller subsidiary, Merpati Nusantara Airlines. Civil aviation as a private-sector venture has greatly increased from one private airline in 1993 to 27 private domestic airlines by 2004. The major air facility is Sukarno-Hatta International Airport, which opened outside Jakarta in 1985, and in 1991 an additional terminal greatly increased airport capacity. There are other major airports in Denpasar, Medan, Surabaya, and Batam Island. In 2003 there were an estimated 661 airports in Indonesia, of which 154 had paved runways (four with more than 3,000-metre runways) and 507 had unpaved runways. Six of the larger airports can accommodate wide-bodied aircraft. Additionally, there were 22 heliports in 2003. Indonesia had a fledgling domestic turbo-prop airliner industry under development under the government-owned Indonesia Aerospace in the late 1990s, but it reached only a prototype-level of production.

Pipelines. In 2003 Indonesia had 672 kilometres of condensate, 125 kilometres of condensate/gas, 8,183 kilometres of gas, 7,429 kilometres of oil, 66 kilometres of oil/gas/water, 1,329 kilometres of refined products, and 72 kilometres of water pipelines.

Telecommunications. Indonesia has been a pioneer in national satellite communications since 1975. A third generation of satellites, known as Palapa C1 and C2, was launched in 1996; these satellites provide a number of interisland and international telecommunications services. In 2002 there were some 7.8 million telephones and 11.7 million mobile cellular telephones in use, producing a ratio of some 91 units per 1,000 people. International telephone service was widely available. Radio and television were long dominated by government networks, but private stations have been on the rise since the early 1990s. As of 1998, there were 678 AM, 43 FM, and 82 shortwave radio stations and more than 31 million radios. In 2000 more than 31.7 million television receivers were in use. Estimates vary as to the number of Internet users in Indonesia—between nearly 4 million and 8 million. By 2002 there were more than 2.3 million personal computers, producing a ratio of 11.9 units per 1,000 people.

Government and Politics

Indonesia is a republic based on limited separation of powers among the executive, legislative, and judicial branches. The constitution of 1945 is in force, but, based on a constitutional amendment of August 2002, beginning with the 2004 presidential elections, the once powerful, party-centered presidency is subject to popular election and limited to two five-year terms. Prior to the 2004 elections, the People's Consultative Assembly (Majelis Permusyawaratan Rakyat—MPR) chose the president and vice president, who were not necessarily from the same political party. Under the new law, the president and vice president are elected on a single ticket and the winning ticket must win more than 50% of the popular vote and at least 20% of the vote in half of the provinces. If these percentages are not met, a second-round runoff election is held. The president is both chief of state and head of government.

The MPR, the highest authority of the state, has both elected and appointed members. Under the amendment that surrendered its presidential election powers, the MPR also replaced its 200 non-elected members (representatives of provinces and various social groups) with elected members of a new legislative body, the 200-seat House of Regional Representatives (Dewan Perwakilan Daerah—DPD), which was established by constitutional amendment in 2001. The DPD joins the existing 500-seat House of People's Representatives (Dewan Perwakilan Rakyat— DPR) in a bicameral, all-elected legislature. The members of both houses make up the MPR. The highest court of the land is the Supreme Court (Mahkamah Agung), composed of justices appointed by the president from a list of candidates approved by the legislature. In 2004 the Supreme Court was preparing to assume administrative responsibility for the lower-court system, currently run by the Ministry of Justice and Human Rights. Under the Supreme Court is a quadripartite judiciary of general, religious, military, and administrative courts. Appeals can be made, sequentially, from a district court to a high court to the Supreme Court. A separate Constitutional Court was established in 2003. The Supreme Audit Board (Badan Permeriksa Keuangan) oversees accountability of public finance and is independent of the chief executive, but its members are chosen by the president.

The judicial branch is theoretically equal to the executive and legislative branches and has the right of judicial review over laws passed by the DPR, as well as government regulations and presidential, ministerial, and gubernatorial decrees. In practice, however, the judiciary is less influential than the executive and legislative branches, and it has often been heavily influenced by the executive branch. Indonesia has not accepted compulsory International Court of Justice jurisdiction.

Administrative Divisions. Indonesia has 30 provincial-level units. 27 provinces (*propinsi*), two special regions (*daerah istimewa*; Aceh and Yogyakarta), and one special capital city region (*daerah khusus*; Jakarta). Since January 1, 2001, when central control over local affairs was lessened, the 357 districts (*kabupaten*) and municipalities (*kotamadya*)—the first-level provincial subdivisions—became the administrative units responsible for providing most government services. Following a 1999 referendum agreed to by the legislature, and a period of United Nations stewardship, the province of Timor Timur became the independent nation of the Democratic Republic of Timor-L'este (East Timor) on 20 May 2002.

Provincial and Local Government. Provinces (*propinsi*) are divided into districts or regencies (*kabupaten*), which are further divided into subdistricts (*kecamatan*). There also are some municipalities or city governments (*kotamudya*) that are on the same administrative level as the districts and others that are on the sub district level. The lowest level of the administrative hierarchy is the village (*desa*). The chief executives are provincial governors, district or regency heads, mayors of cities, and village heads. Legislation is handled by provincial and district parliaments. Under the revised election laws, governors, mayors, and district heads (regents) were to be directly elected for the first time in 2004.

Judicial and Legal System. The legal system is based on Roman-Dutch law, modified by indigenous concepts and by new criminal procedures and election codes. There are 2,418 district courts, each of which has a panel of judges that conducts trials by posing questions, hearing evidence, deciding on guilt or innocence, and assessing punishment. Both the defence and prosecution can appeal verdicts. Arbitrary arrest and detention are prohibited, but the government lacks adequate enforcement mechanisms, and authorities have routinely violated the Criminal Procedures Code. The code provides prisoners with the right to notify their families promptly, and specifies that warrants must be produced during an arrest. Exceptions are allowed if, for example, a suspect is caught in the act of committing a crime. The law allows investigators to issue warrants; at times, however, authorities make arrests without warrants.

Electoral System. Indonesia has direct, popular election of its parliamentary representatives. All citizens 17 years of age and older are eligible to vote.

Politics and Political Parties. The old emphasis on consensus, unity, and controlled political development came to an end in the post-Suharto era, starting in 1998. Whereas the official government party, Golkar, once held an absolute majority, there are now numerous parties vying for power, and none enjoys national majority support. These parties include the Crescent Moon and Star Party (PBB), Democratic Party (PD), Indonesia Democratic Party-Struggle (PDI-P), National Awakening Party (PKB), National Mandate Party (PAN), Prosperous Justice Party (PKS), and United Development Party (PPP).

Mass Media. The constitution provides for freedom of speech and freedom of the press; however, the government has a history of restricting these rights in practice. In August 1990, the government formally announced that it would refrain from censoring domestic and foreign media and from revoking the publishing licenses of newspapers that violated regulations governing the press. Private press in current operation includes nearly 50 daily newspapers, dozens of magazines, 10 foreign press bureaus, and five private commercial television stations. There are also 10 foreign press bureaus, two government radio stations (Radio Republik Indonesia and Voice of Indonesia), one government news agency (Antara), and one independent national news agency (Kantorberita Nasional Indonesia). The government does not restrict Internet usage or content.

Foreign Relations. Indonesia is a charter member of the Nonaligned Movement, which was established in September 1961. The April 1955 Asian-African Conference—held in Bandung, Indonesia—was an important milestone in the development of the Nonaligned Movement's goal of independence from the Cold War superpowers (the United States and the Soviet Union) and the former colonialist powers and put Indonesia on the international stage for a time. As the Sukarno era progressed, however, Indonesia's government was at odds with the Dutch over West New Guinea (now called Papua) and increasingly hostile toward neighboring Malaysia to the point that Sukarno withdrew Indonesia from the United Nations when Malaysia was appointed a non-permanent member of the Security Council in 1964. In 1967 Indonesia participated in establishing a new officially nonaligned grouping of neighbors, the Association of Southeast Asian Nations (ASEAN), which was friendly toward the Western powers. Its secretariat was placed in Jakarta, and its first secretary general was an Indonesian. The commemoration of the 30th anniversary of the Bandung Conference in 1985 saw

Indonesia's full reemergence on the world stage, allowing Jakarta to project itself as a leading voice in the Nonaligned Movement and providing it with an extra-regional platform for claiming proper international standing. Indonesia's diplomatic relations with China had been reinstituted in 1990. Indonesia continues to play an important role in ASEAN affairs. Indonesia's most contentious regional relations are those with Australia, mostly over the situation in East Timor.

National Security

Armed Forces Overview. The Indonesia Armed Forces (Tentara Nasional Indonesia—TNI) totaled some 346,000 active-duty personnel in 2004. The component services are the Army (TNI—Angkatan Darat), 265,000; Navy (TNI—Angkatan Laut), an estimated 57,000, of which 15,000 are marines and 1,000 are part of Naval Aviation; and Air Force (TNI—Angkatan Udara), 24,000, of which 4,000 are "quick-action" paratroopers. There is a reserve force of 400,000. With the transition to democratic rule beginning in 1998, the government endeavored to undertake steps to reform the TNI in order to improve public opinion about the military and to bring the military under civilian control. Among such steps were the devolution of the national police from the armed forces to the Office of the President and official transfer of responsibility for internal security from the TNI to the police in April 1999, focusing the military's attention on national defence rather than domestic policing. Another important reform was a provision that military personnel had to retire or resign before occupying an elected or appointed civilian government position. However, the TNI successfully resisted transformation of its territorial command structure because of threats of terrorism and separatism, and because it needs this structure to support its huge business empire, from which it obtains an estimated two-thirds of its funding (the government budget provides only one-third of the funds needed to operate and equip the military and national police). After several years in disrepute because of revelations of extensive human rights abuses, the TNI has regained much of its lost prestige. Many Indonesians appear to favor military firmness as the country is facing terrorist, separatist, and ethnic conflict as well as a moribund economy.

Foreign Military Relations. Indonesia enjoys cordial military-to-military relations with a wide range of nations. Its closest ties are with fellow members of ASEAN. Formerly close ties to the United States, Australia, and some European countries became strained in the 1990s over human rights issues; many countries cut back their military relations with the TNI after the rampage of army and army-supported militia forces in East Timor in 1999. Because of arms sales embargoes imposed by its primary sources in the United States, Indonesia has turned to Russia and other nations of the former Soviet Union, South Korea, and Poland, among others, for major arms purchases.

External Threat. Indonesia has no conventional external threat to its security. The primary outside threat is that of international terrorism. Terrorists belonging to the regional terrorist group Jemaah Islamiyah (Community of Islam) have conducted a number of recent bomb attacks, including the bombing of two night clubs on Bali in October 2002 that killed 202 people and injured more than 300, while a bombing at the Marriott Hotel in Jakarta in August 2003 killed 12 people and injured 150. Prompt police investigative actions and international cooperation resulted in the arrests of dozens of suspects and revealed an extensive network of affiliations among al-Qaeda, Jemaah Islamiyah, and Islamic extremist groups inside Indonesia. More than 30 men were convicted in the Bali bombing case and several more in the Jakarta attack. Many of them were also involved in other terrorist attacks across Indonesia dating back to 2000. Another terrorist bombing, that of the Australian Embassy in Jakarta in September 2004, killed ten people and injured 160 and led to a new round of investigations and tightened security. Other threats to Indonesian security include piracy, particularly in the Strait of Malacca, smuggling, and maritime poaching.

Defence Budget. Indonesia's defence budget officially totaled approximately Rp1.26 trillion (US$1.4 billion using an exchange rate of Rp9,000 to US$1), or 1.06% of the GDP in 2004. However, most analysts believe that approximately two-thirds of military spending is derived from sources other than the official defence budget (diversions from other budgetary entities and from the military's huge business empire).

Major Military Units. The army includes 30 battalions under the centrally controlled Army Strategic Reserve Command (Kostrad), 100 battalions under 12 Military Regional Commands (Kodams), 3 operational groups in the Army Special Forces Command (Kopassus), and a 2-squadron Aviation Command. The navy has two fleets (Armadas), and the air force has two operational commands (Ko-Ops).

Military Service. The earliest age of service is 18, and two years of selective conscription of males are authorized.

Military Forces Abroad. Indonesian forces abroad are currently involved in several United Nations peacekeeping operations.

Police. The strength of the Indonesian National Police stood at approximately 285,000 in 2004. The national police force was formally separated as a branch of the armed forces and placed under the President in 1999. It also includes 12,000 marine police and an estimated 40,000 People's Security trainees who serve as a police auxiliary and report for three weeks of basic training each year. There has been occasional friction between police and the military, with several instances of armed combat between them, usually caused by disputes over shady business enterprises.

Internal Threats and Terrorism. There are two general threats to Indonesian domestic security, terrorism and ethnic and religious conflict. The terrorists causing the greatest problems in Indonesia are members of the regional group, Jemaah Islamiyah (Community of Islam). Although Jemaah Islamiyah operates primarily in Indonesia, it has operational units in peninsular Malaysia, Singapore, Australia, and Papua New Guinea. Jemaah Islamiyah has perpetrated significant terrorist acts and is believed to have strong links with al-Qaeda. The government announced at the time of the October 2002 Bali bombings that terrorism was "a real and potential threat to national security" and has called upon the public to confront domestically based terrorists.

Centre-region relations have been perennially problematic, with the government continuing to experience difficulties in maintaining order and the rule of law in outlying regions. The most pressing threats are separatists in Aceh and Papua (formerly Irian Jaya). The major insurgent groups are Gerakan Aceh Merdeka (GAM—Free Aceh Movement), which wants an independent Islamic state in Aceh and has an estimated strength of 2,000 armed activists; and Organisasi Papua Merdeka (OPM—Free West Papua Movement), which seeks independence for Papua and has an estimated 150 activists.

Human Rights. The Indonesian government's human rights record is rated as poor. Murders, torture, rape, beatings, and arbitrarily detaining civilians and members of separatist movements were all documented as abuses by security force members. The government also was accused of having frequently failed to protect adequately the fundamental rights of children, women, peaceful protesters, journalists, disabled persons, religious minorities, and indigenous people, among others. Aceh and Papua provinces were seen as the scenes of the most apparent human rights abuses.

MALAYSIA

Malaysia is a federation of thirteen states in Southeast Asia. The country consists of two geographical regions divided by the South China Sea. Peninsular Malaysia (or West Malaysia) on the Malay Peninsula shares a land border on the north with Thailand and is connected by the Johore-Singapore Causeway and the Malaysia-Singapore Second Link to the south with Singapore. It consists of nine sultanates (Johor, Kedah, Kelantan, Negeri Sembilan, Pahang, Perak, Perlis, Selangor and Terengganu), two states headed by governors (Malacca and Penang), and two federal territories (Putrajaya and Kuala Lumpur). Malaysian Borneo (or East Malaysia) occupies the northern part of the island of Borneo, bordering Indonesia and surrounding the Sultanate of Brunei. It consists of the states of Sabah and Sarawak and the federal territory of Labuan.

Its total area is 329,750 square kilometres (land—328,550 square kilometres and water—1,200 square kilometres). Its land boundaries total 2,669 kilometres with Brunei (381 kilometres), Indonesia (1,782 kilometres) and Thailand (506 kilometres). Its coastline extends 4,675 kilometres. Putrajaya is the newly created administrative capital for the federal government of Malaysia, aimed in part to ease growing congestion within Malaysia's capital city, Kuala Lumpur. Kuala Lumpur remains the seat of parliament, as well as the commercial and financial capital of the country.

Malaysia gained independence from Britain on 31 August 1957. The Malaysian flag has 14 equal horizontal stripes of red (top) alternating with white (bottom); there is a blue rectangle in the upper hoist-side corner bearing a yellow crescent and a yellow 14-pointed star (the crescent and the star are traditional symbols of Islam). Malaysia adopted its Constitution on 31 August 1957 (amended on 16 September 1963)

History

The earliest inhabitants of the Malay peninsula were the orang asli or indigenous people who migrated from Siam around 2500 BC. Proto-Malays originating from Java began arriving between 1500 BC and 500 BC. From the mid to the late first millennium, much of the Peninsula as well as the Malay Archipelago were under the influence of Srivijaya. Originally these were Hindu or Buddhist nations.

There were numerous Malay kingdoms in the 2nd and 3rd century. Kedah—known as Kedaram or Kataha, in ancient Pallava or Sanskrit—was in the direct route of invasions of Indian traders and kings. Rajendra Chola, and his successor, Vir Rajendra Chola, ruled over the region. The coming of the Chola reduced the majesty of Srivijaya which had exerted influence over the peninsula till then.

The Buddhist kingdom of Ligor took control of Kedah shortly after, and its King Chandrabhanu used it as a base to attack Sri Lanka in the 11th century, an event noted in a stone inscription in Nagapattinum in Tamil Nadu and in the Sri Lankan chronicles, Mahavamsa. During the first millennium, the people of the Malay peninsula adopted Hinduism and Buddhism and the use of the Sanskrit language until they eventually converted to Islam, but not before Hinduism, Buddhism and Sanskrit became embedded into the Malay worldview. Traces of the influences in political ideas, social structure, rituals, language, arts and cultural practices exist to this day.

In the early 15th century, the Sultanate of Malacca was established under a dynasty founded by Parameswara, a prince from Palembang with bloodline related to the royal home of Srivijaya, who fled from the island Temasek (now Singapore). At its height, the sultanate controlled the areas which are now Peninsula Malaysia, southern Thailand (Patani), and the eastern coast of Sumatra. It existed for more than a century, and within that time period Islam spread to most of the Malay Archipelago.

The first evidence of Islam in the Malay Peninsula dates from the 14th century in Terengganu. In 1511, Malacca was conquered by Portugal, which established a colony there. The sons of the last Sultan of Malacca established two sultanates elsewhere in the peninsula—the Sultanate of Perak to the north, and the Sultanate of Johore to the south. After the fall of Malacca, three nations struggled for the control of Malacca Strait: the Portuguese (in Malacca), the Sultanate of Johor, and the Sultanate of Aceh. This conflict went on till 1641, when the Dutch gained control of Malacca.

Britain established its first colony in the Malay peninsula in 1786, with the lease of the island of Penang to the British East India Company by the Sultan of Kedah. In 1824, the British took control of Malacca following the Anglo-Dutch Treaty of 1824 which divided the Malay archipelago between Britain and the Netherlands, with Malaya in the British zone. In 1826, Britain established the crown colony of the Straits Settlements, uniting its three possessions in Malaya: Penang, Malacca and Singapore. The Straits Settlements were administered under the East India Company in Calcutta until 1867, when they were transferred to the Colonial Office in London.

During the late 19th century, many Malay states decided to obtain British help in settling their internal conflicts. The commercial importance of tin mining in the Malay states to merchants in the Straits Settlements led to British government intervention in the tin-producing states in the Malay Peninsula. British gunboat diplomacy was employed to bring about a peaceful resolution to civil disturbances caused by Chinese gangsters, and the Pangkor Treaty of 1874 paved the way for the expansion of British influence in Malaya. By the turn of the 20th century, the states of Pahang, Selangor, Perak, and Negeri Sembilan, known together as the Federated Malay States were under the de facto control of British Residents appointed to advise the Malay rulers. The British were "advisers" in name, but in reality they exercised substantial influence over the Malay rulers.

The remaining five states in the peninsula, known as the Unfederated Malay States, while not directly under rule from London, also accepted British advisors around the turn of the 20th century. Of these, the four northern states of Perlis, Kedah, Kelantan and Terengganu had previously been under Siamese control. On the island of Borneo, Sabah was governed as the crown colony of British North Borneo, while Sarawak was acquired from Brunei as the personal kingdom of the Brooke family, who ruled as White Rajahs.

Following the Japanese occupation of Malaya during World War II, popular support for independence grew. Post-war British plans to unite the administration of Malaya under a single crown colony called the Malayan Union foundered on strong opposition from the Malays, who opposed the emasculation of the Malay rulers and the granting of citizenship to the ethnic Chinese. The Malayan Union, established in 1946 and consisting of all the British possessions in Malaya with the exception of Singapore, was dissolved in 1948 and replaced by the Federation of Malaya, which restored the autonomy of the rulers of the Malay states under British protection.

During this time, rebels under the leadership of the Communist Party of Malaya launched guerrilla operations designed to force the British out of Malaya. The Malayan Emergency, as it was known, lasted from 1948 to 1960, and involved a long anti-insurgency campaign by Commonwealth troops in Malaya.

Against this backdrop, independence for the Federation within the Commonwealth was granted on 31 August 1957.

In 1963 Malaya along with the then-British crown colonies of Singapore, Sabah (British North Borneo) and Sarawak formed Malaysia. The Sultanate of Brunei, though initially expressing interest in joining the Federation, withdrew from the planned merger due to opposition from certain segments of the population as well as arguments over the payment of oil royalties and the status of the Sultan in the planned merger.

Independence was marred by conflict with Indonesia (Konfrontasi) over the formation of Malaysia, Singapore's eventual exit in 1965, and racial riots in 1969. The Philippines also made an active claim on Sabah in that period based upon the Sultanate of Brunei's cession of its north-east territories to the Sultanate of Sulu in 1704. The claim is still ongoing. After the racial riots of 1969, the controversial New Economic Policy—intended to increase the share of the economic pie owned by the bhumiputras ("indigenous people", which includes the majority Malays, but not always the indigenous population) as opposed to other ethnic groups—was launched by Prime Minister Tun Abdul Razak. Malaysia has since maintained a delicate ethno-political balance, with a system of government that has attempted to combine overall economic development with political and economic policies that favour Bhumiputras.

Between the 1980s and the mid 1990s, Malaysia experienced significant economic growth under the premiership of Tun Dr Mahathir bin Mohammad. The period saw a shift from an agriculture-based economy to one based on manufacturing and industry in areas such as computers and consumer electronics. It was during this period, too, that the physical landscape of Malaysia has changed with the emergence of numerous mega-projects. The most notable of these projects are the Petronas Twin Towers (at the time the tallest building in the world), KL International Airport (KLIA), North-South Expressway, the Sepang F1 Circuit, the Multimedia Super Corridor (MSC), the Bakun hydroelectric dam and Putrajaya, the new federal administrative capital.

In the late 1990s, Malaysia was shaken by the Asian financial crisis as well as political unrest caused by the sacking of the deputy prime minister Dato' Seri Anwar Ibrahim. In 2003, Dr Mahathir, Malaysia's longest serving prime minister, retired in favour of his deputy, Abdullah Badawi.

Geography

The two distinct parts of Malaysia, separated from each other by the South China Sea, share a largely similar landscape in that both West and East Malaysia feature coastal plains rising to often densely forested hills and mountains, the highest of which is Mount Kinabalu at 4,095.2 metres on the island of Borneo. The local climate is equatorial and characterised by the annual southwest (April to October) and northeast (October to February) monsoons.

The Strait of Malacca, lying between Sumatra and Peninsular Malaysia, is arguably the most important shipping lane in the world. Malaysia's natural resources include tin, petroleum, timber, copper, iron ore, natural gas, and bauxite. Malaysia is the world's primary exporter of natural rubber and palm oil, which together with sawn logs and sawn timber, cocoa, pepper, pineapple and tobacco dominate the growth of the sector. Palm oil is also a major generator of foreign exchange.

The country has 5.46% of arable land of which 17.54% is under permanent crops. Irrigated land covers an area of 3,650 square kilometres. Natural hazards include flooding, landslides, forest fires. Environmental issues include air pollution from industrial and vehicular emissions; water pollution from raw sewage; deforestation and smoke/haze from Indonesian forest fires.

Tin and petroleum are the two main mineral resources that are of major significance in the Malaysian economy. Malaysia was once the world's largest producer of tin until the collapse of the tin market in the early 1980s. In the 19th and 20th century, tin played a predominant role in the Malaysian economy. It was only in 1972 that petroleum and natural gas took over from tin as the mainstay of the mining sector.

Meanwhile, the contribution by tin has declined. Petroleum and natural gas which were discovered in oilfields offshore Sabah, Sarawak and Terengganu have contributed much to the Malaysian economy particularly in those three states. Other minerals of some importance or significance include copper, gold, bauxite, iron-ore and coal together with industrial minerals like clay, kaolin, silica, limestone, barite, phosphates and dimension stones such as granite as well as marble blocks and slabs. Small quantities of gold are produced.

In 2004, Minister in the Prime Minister's Department, Datuk Mustapa Mohamed, revealed that Malaysia's oil reserves stood at 4.84 billion barrels while natural gas reserves increased to 89 trillion cubic feet. The government estimates that at current production rates Malaysia will be able to produce oil up to 18 years and gas for 35 years.

Society

Malaysia is a multi-ethnic, multi-cultural and multilingual society. The population as of February 2007 is 26.6 million consisting of 62% Malays, 24% Chinese, 8% Indians, with other minorities and indigenous peoples. Malay is the national language of the country. In the past, Malays wrote in Sanskrit or using Sanskrit-based alphabets. After the 15th century, Jawi (a script based on Arabic) became popular. Over time, romanized script overtook Sanskrit and Jawi as the dominant script. This was largely due to the influence of the colonial education system, which taught children in romanised writing rather than in Arabic script.

By constitutional definition, all Malays are Muslim. About 30% of the population are Malaysians of Chinese descent. Malaysians of Indian descent comprise about 8% of the population. About 90% of the Indian community is Tamils but various other groups are also present, including Malayalis, Punjabis and Gujaratis. There are also various non-Malay peoples who are designated as indigenous, mostly in East Malaysia. These make up about 7% of the population.

Non-Malay indigenous groups make up more than half of the state of Sarawak's population—constitute about 66% of Sabah's population—and also exist in much smaller numbers on the Peninsula, where they are collectively known as Orang Asli. The non-Malay indigenous population is divided into dozens of ethnic groups, but they share some general cultural similarities. Population distribution is uneven, with some 20 million residents concentrated on the Malay Peninsula, while East Malaysia is relatively less populated.

Due to the rise in labour intensive industries, Malaysia has 10 to 20% foreign workers with the uncertainty due in part to the large number of illegal workers, mostly Indonesian. There are a million legal foreign workers and perhaps another million unauthorized foreigners. The state of Sabah alone has nearly 25% of its 2.7 million population listed as illegal foreign workers.

Although the Malaysian constitution theoretically guarantees religious freedom, in practice the situation is not so simple. All ethnic Malays are Muslim as defined in the Malaysian constitution. Additionally, all non-Muslims who marry a Muslim must renounce their religion and convert to Islam. Meanwhile, Non-Muslims experience restrictions in activities such as construction of religious buildings and the celebration of certain religious events in some states. Malaysians tend to personally respect one another's religious beliefs, with inter-religious problems arising mainly from the political sphere. However, there is a growing divide because many Chinese and Indians feel oppressed by recent religiously-related political sentiments that threaten freedom of religion.

Education

Education in Malaysia is monitored by the federal government Ministry of Education. Most Malaysian children start schooling between the ages of three to six, in kindergarten. Most kindergartens are run privately, but there are a few government-operated kindergartens.

Children begin primary schooling at the age of seven for a period of six years. There are two major types of government-operated or government-assisted primary schools. They are the national schools (Sekolah Kebangsaan) which use Malay as the medium of instruction, and the national-type schools (Sekolah Jenis Kebangsaan) which use either Chinese or Tamil as the medium of instruction. Before progressing to the secondary level of education, students in Year 6 are required to sit for the Ujian Pencapaian Sekolah Rendah (UPSR), or Primary School Assessment Examination.

Secondary education in government secondary schools last for five years. Government secondary schools use Malay as the main medium of instruction. The only exceptions are the Maths and Science subjects as well as languages other than Malay. At the end of the third year or Form Three, students sit for the Penilaian Menengah Rendah (PMR), Lower Secondary Assessment. The combination of subjects available to Form 4 students vary from one school to another. In the last year (Form 5), students sit for Sijil Pelajaran Malaysia (SPM), Malaysian Certificate of Education. Mathematics and Science subjects in government primary and secondary schools such as Biology, Physics, and Chemistry are taught in English. The reasoning was that students would no longer be hindered by the language barrier during their tertiary education in fields such as medicine and engineering.

Students who wish to enter public universities must complete one and a half more years of secondary schooling in Form Six and sit for the Sijil Tinggi Persekolahan Malaysia (STPM), Malaysian Higher School Certificate. As for tertiary education, there are public universities such as University of Malaya, Universiti Sains Malaysia and Universiti Kebangsaan Malaysia. In addition, five international reputable universities have set up their branch campuses in Malaysia since 1998. Students also have the option of enrolling in private colleges after secondary studies. Most colleges have educational links with overseas universities especially in the United States, the United Kingdom and Australia. Malaysian students abroad study mostly in the UK, United States, Australia, New Zealand, Canada, Singapore, and Japan.

Healthcare

Malaysian society places importance on the expansion and development of healthcare, putting 5% of the government social sector development budget into public healthcare—an increase of more than 47% over the previous figure. This has meant an overall increase of more than RM 2 billion. With a rising and aging population, the Government wishes to improve in many areas including the refurbishment of existing hospitals, building and equipping new hospitals, expansion of the number of polyclinics, and improvements in training and expansion of telehealth. Over the last couple of years they have increased their efforts to overhaul the systems and attract more foreign investment.

The Malaysian healthcare system requires doctors to perform a compulsory three years service with public hospitals to ensure the manpower of these hospitals is maintained. Recently foreign doctors have also been encouraged to take up employment here. There is still, however, a compound shortage of medical workforce, especially that of highly trained specialists resulting in certain medical care and treatment only available in large cities. Recent efforts to bring many facilities to other towns have been hampered by lack of expertise to run the available equipment made ready by investments.

The majority of private hospitals are in urban areas and, unlike many of the public hospitals, are equipped with the latest diagnostic and imaging facilities. Private hospitals have not generally been seen as an ideal investment—it has often taken up to ten years before companies have seen any profits. However, the situation has now changed and companies are now looking into this area again, particularly in view of the increasing interest by foreigners in coming to Malaysia for medical care and the recent government focus to develop the health tourism industry.

Government and Politics

Malaysia is a federal constitutional elective monarchy. The federal head of state of Malaysia is the Yang di-Pertuan Agong, commonly referred to as the King of Malaysia. The Yang di-Pertuan Agong is elected to a five-year term among the nine hereditary Sultans of the Malay states; the other four states, which have titular Governors, do not participate in the selection.

The system of government in Malaysia is closely modeled on that of Westminster parliamentary system, a legacy of British colonial rule. In practice however, more power is vested in the executive branch of government than in the legislative, and the judiciary has been weakened by sustained attacks by the government during the Mahathir era. Since independence in 1957, Malaysia has been governed by a multi-party coalition known as the Barisan Nasional (formerly known as the Alliance).

Legislative power is divided between federal and state legislatures. The bicameral parliament consists of the lower house, the House of Representatives or Dewan

Rakyat (literally the "Chamber of the People") and the upper house, the Senate or Dewan Negara (literally the "Chamber of the Nation"). The 219-member House of Representatives are elected from single-member constituencies that are drawn based on population for a maximum term of 5 years. All 70 Senators sit for 3-year terms; 26 are elected by the 13 state assemblies, 2 representing the federal territory of Kuala Lumpur, 1 each from federal territories of Labuan and Putrajaya, and 40 are appointed by the king. Besides the Parliament at the federal level, each state has a unicameral state legislative chamber (Malay:Dewan Undangan Negeri) whose members are elected from single-member constituencies. Parliamentary elections are held at least once every five years, with the last general election being in March 2004. The cabinet is chosen from among members of both houses of Parliament and is responsible to that body.

State governments are led by chief ministers (Menteri Besar in Malay states or Ketua Menteri in states without hereditary rulers), who is a state assembly member from a majority party in the state assemblies (Dewan Undangan Negeri).

Administrative divisions. Putrajaya is the administrative capital of Malaysia. The country has 13 states (Johor, Kedah, Kelantan, Melaka, Negeri Sembilan, Pahang, Perak, Perlis, Pulau Pinang, Sabah, Sarawak, Selangor, and Terengganu) and one federal territory with three components (city of Kuala Lumpur, Labuan, and Putrajaya)

Judiciary. The legal system is based on English common law. Judicial review of legislative acts in the Supreme Court is at the request of the supreme head of the federation. Malaysia has not accepted jurisdiction of the International Court of Justice. Islamic law is applied to Muslims in matters of family law. Judges to the Federal Court are appointed by the paramount ruler on the advice of the prime minister)

Economy

The Malay Peninsula and indeed Southeast Asia has been a centre of trade for centuries. Various items such as porcelain and spice were actively traded even before Malacca and Singapore rose to prominence. Over time, Malaya has become the world's largest major producer of tin, rubber, and palm oil. These three commodities, along with other raw materials, firmly set Malaysia's economic tempo well into the mid-20th century.

As Malaya moved towards independence, the government began implementing economic five-year plans, beginning with the First Malayan Five Year Plan in 1955. Upon the establishment of Malaysia, the plans were re-titled and renumbered, beginning with the First Malaysia Plan in 1965.

In 1970s, Malaysia began to imitate Asian Tigers and committed itself to a transition from being reliant on mining and agriculture to an economy that depends more on manufacturing. With Japanese investment, heavy industries flourished and in a matter of years, Malaysian exports became the country's primary growth engine. Malaysia consistently achieved more than 7% GDP growth along with low inflation in the 1980s and the 1990s.

During the same period, the government tried to eradicate poverty with the controversial New Economic Policy (NEP). Its main objective was the elimination of the association of race with economic function, and the first five-year plan to begin implementing the NEP was the Second Malaysia Plan. The success or failure of the NEP is the subject of debate, although it was officially retired in 1990 and replaced by the National Development Policy (NDP).

The rapid economic boom led to a variety of supply problems, however. Labour shortages soon resulted in an influx of millions of foreign workers, many illegal. Cash-rich PLCs and consortia of banks eager to benefit from increased and rapid development began large infrastructure projects. This all ended when the Asian Financial Crisis hit in the fall of 1997, delivering a massive shock to Malaysia's economy.

As with other countries affected by the crisis, there was speculative short-selling of the Malaysian currency, the ringgit. Foreign direct investment fell at an alarming rate and, as capital flowed out of the country, the value of the ringgit dropped from MYR 2.50 per USD to, at one point, MYR 4.80 per USD. The Kuala Lumpur Stock Exchange's composite index plummeted from approximately 1300 points to around 400 points in a matter of weeks. After the controversial sacking of finance minister Anwar Ibrahim, a National Economic Action Council was formed to deal with the monetary crisis. Bank Negara imposed capital controls and pegged the Malaysian ringgit at 3.80 to the US dollar. Malaysia refused economic aid packages from the International Monetary Fund (IMF) and the World Bank surprising many analysts. However, the post Y2K slump of 2001 did not affect Malaysia as much as other countries.

While the pace of development today is not as rapid, it is seen to be more sustainable. Although the controls and economic housekeeping may not have been the principal reason for recovery, there is no doubt that the banking sector has become more resilient to external shocks. The current account has also settled into a structural surplus, providing a cushion to capital flight. Asset prices are now a fraction of their pre-crisis heights. Currently, Malaysia is considered a newly industrialized country.

Malaysia is a net exporter of electricity with a production of 79.28 billion kWh (2003). Its oil – production is 770,000 bbl/day (2005 estimate) and it's an oil-exporting country, with proved reserves of 3.1 billion bbl (2005 estimate). Its natural gas production is estimated at 53.5 billion cu m, nearly half of which it exports. It's proved natural gas reserves stand at 2.124 trillion cu m (2005 estimate).

Infrastructure

Malaysia has extensive roads that connect all major cities and towns on the western coast of Peninsular Malaysia. The total length of the Malaysian expressway network is 1,192 kilometres. The network connects all major cities and conurbations such as Klang Valley, Johor Bahru and Penang to each other. The major expressway, the North-South Expressway spans from the northern and the southern tips of Peninsular Malaysia at Bukit Kayu Hitam and Johor Bahru respectively. It is a part of the Asian Highway Network, which also connects into Thailand and Singapore.

Roads in the East Malaysia and the eastern coast of Peninsular Malaysia are still relatively undeveloped. Those are highly curved roads passing through mountainous regions and many are still unsealed, gravel roads. This has resulted in the continued use of rivers and the necessary use of airplanes as the main or alternative mode of transportation for the interior residents.

Train service in West Malaysia is operated by the Keretapi Tanah Melayu (Malayan Railways) and has extensive railroads that connect all major cities and towns on the peninsular, including Singapore. There is also a short railway in Sabah operated by Sabah State Railway that mainly carries freight.

There are seaports throughout the country. The major ports are Port Klang and Port of Tanjung Pelepas in Johor. Other important ports can be found in Tanjong Kidurong, Kota Kinabalu, Kuching, Kuantan, Pasir Gudang, Penang, Sandakan and Tawau.

Airports are also found throughout the country. Kuala Lumpur International Airport (KLIA) is the main airport of the country. Other important airports include Kota Kinabalu International Airport, Penang International Airport, Kuching International Airport, Langkawi International Airport, and Senai International Airport. There are also airports in smaller towns, as well as small domestic airstrips in rural Sabah and Sarawak. There are daily flight services between West and East Malaysia, which is the only convenient option for passengers travelling between the two parts of the country. Malaysia is the home of the first low-cost carrier in the region, Air Asia.

The intercity telecommunication service is provided on Peninsular Malaysia mainly by microwave radio relay. International telecommunications are provided through submarine cables and satellite. One of the largest and most significant telecommunication companies in Malaysia is Telekom Malaysia Berhad (TM), providing products and services from fixed line, mobile as well as dial-up and broadband Internet access service. It has the near-monopoly of fixed line phone service in the country.

The merchant marine of Malaysia comprises 312 ships (1000 GRT or over) 5,360,403 GRT/7,353,105 DWT (bulk carrier 18, cargo 105, chemical tanker 38, container 45, liquefied gas 26, livestock carrier 1, passenger 1, passenger/cargo 6, petroleum tanker 62, roll on/roll off 5, vehicle carrier 50 of which 74 are foreign-owned (China 1, Germany 2, Hong Kong 14, Japan 1, Singapore 56). 66 ships registered in other countries(The Bahamas 12, Belize 1, Cayman Islands 1, Panama 13, Philippines 1, Singapore 35, US 3) Shipping ports and terminals include Bintulu, Johor, Labuan, Lahad Datu, Lumut, Miri, George Town (Penang), Port Kelang, and Tanjung Pelepas.

National Security

Malaysia has asserted sovereignty over the Spratly Islands together with China, Philippines, Taiwan, Vietnam, and Brunei. While the 2002 "Declaration on the Conduct of Parties in the South China Sea" has eased tensions over the Spratly Islands, it is not the legally binding "code of conduct" sought by some parties. Malaysia was not party to the March 2005 joint accord among the national oil companies of China, the Philippines, and Vietnam on conducting marine seismic activities in the Spratly Islands.

Disputes continue over deliveries of fresh water to Singapore, bridge construction Singapore's land reclamation, maritime boundaries, and Pedra Branca Island/Pulau Batu Putih. Both parties agreed to arbitration on the island dispute within three years. The ICJ awarded Ligitan and Sipadan islands, also claimed by Indonesia and Philippines, to Malaysia but left the maritime boundary in the hydrocarbon-rich Celebes Sea in dispute, resulting in confrontations in March 2005 over concessions to the Ambalat oil block.

Separatist violence in Thailand's predominantly Muslim southern provinces prompted measures to close and monitor its border with Malaysia to stem terrorist activities. Philippines retains a claim to Malaysia's Sabah State in northern Borneo. In 2003, Brunei and Malaysia ceased gas and oil exploration in their disputed offshore and deepwater sea beds and negotiations have stalemated prompting consideration of international adjudication. Malaysia's land boundary with Brunei around Limbang is in dispute.

Piracy remains a problem in the Malacca Strait besides the issue of refugees (15,181 from Indonesia and 9,601 from Burma in 2005). Malaysia is a regional transit point for some illicit drugs, though drug trafficking is prosecuted vigorously and carries severe penalties.

Armed Forces

The military of Malaysia is known officially as the Malaysian Armed Forces (MAF, Malay: Angkatan Tentera Malaysia-ATM). It consists of three branches; the Royal Malaysian Navy (RMN, Malay: Tentera Laut Diraja Malaysia-TLDM), the Malaysian Army (Malay: Tentera Darat Malaysia-TD) and the Royal Malaysian Air Force (RMAF, Malay: Tentera Udara Diraja Malaysia-TUDM). General (Jen) Tan Sri Dato' Sri Abdul Aziz bin Hj Zainal, is the Chief of Armed Forces Staff, Malaysia.

In the early 1990s, Malaysia undertook a major programme to expand and modernize its armed forces. The role of the MAF is to defend the sovereignty and strategic interests of Malaysia from all forms of threat. It is responsible to assist the civilian authorities to overcome all international threats, preserve public order, assist in natural disasters and participate in national development programs.

The main theatres of operations were within Malaysian borders, primarily to fight an insurgency led by the Communist Party of Malaya (CPM) in what was known as the Emergency. Operations on foreign soil have mainly been peacekeeping operations under the auspices of the United Nations.

The conflicts in which the military have been involved are:

Sarawak Communist Insurgency (1963-1990). An insurrection and guerilla war of the Sarawak Communist Organisation (from 1971, the North Kalimantan Communist Party or NKCP) against the British and Malaysian governments to establish an independent nation comprising the states of Sabah, Sarawak and Brunei. The insurgency ended when the NKCP signed a peace treaty with the Malaysian government in 1990.

Indonesia-Malaysia confrontation (1963-1966). An intermittent armed conflict between Malaysia and Indonesia with skirmishes mainly occurring in Sarawak and Sabah in the island of Borneo. In 1964, armed raids were made on Peninsular Malaysia. Combat eased with the deposing of Indonesia's President Sukarno in 1965 by the Indonesian army and the conflict was declared over by both sides in 1966.

Communist Insurgency War (1967-1989). A low level resurgence of insurgent activity by the armed elements of the CPM from sanctuaries in the Malaysian-Thai border. The insurgency was only ended after the CPM signed a peace treaty with the Governments of Malaysia and Thailand on 2 December 1989.

In early 2004, the Ministry of Defense initiated a compulsory National Service programme for 17 years old Malaysians. Participants of the Malaysian National Service are chosen randomly. Currently, only 20% of those eligible are inducted but plans call for this programme to eventually cover all 17 year olds.

In light of the increasing crude oil price worldwide, the military had volunteered in a pioneering programme to use biodiesel. All diesel-type vehicle in the Malaysian Armed Forces use biodiesel consist of 95% diesel and 5% oil palm diesel.

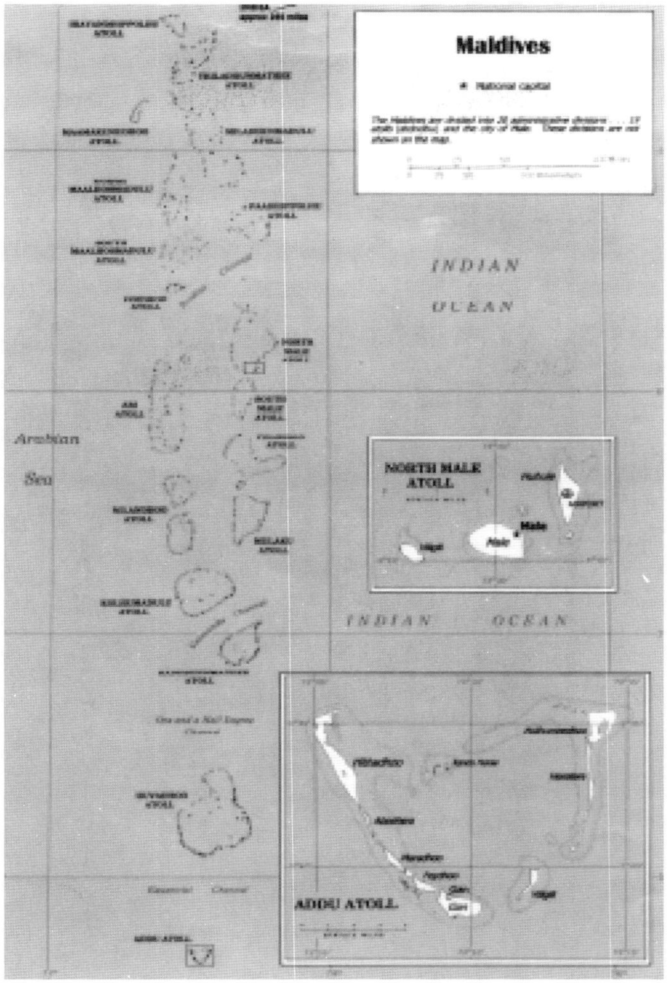

REPUBLIC OF MALDIVES

The Maldives, officially the Republic of Maldives, is an island nation consisting of a group of atolls in the Indian Ocean. The Maldives is located south of India's Lakshadweep islands, and about seven hundred kilometres south-west of Sri Lanka. The Maldives' twenty-six atolls encompass a territory featuring 1,192 islets, roughly two hundred of which are inhabited by local communities. The Maldives is the smallest Asian country in terms of population. It is also the smallest predominantly Muslim nation in the world.

The name "Maldives" derives from the Sanskrit maladvipa, meaning "garland of islands". Originally the inhabitants were Buddhist, but Islam was introduced in 1153. It later became a Portuguese (1558), Dutch (1654), and British (1887) colonial possession. In 1965, the Maldives obtained independence from Britain, and in 1968 the Sultanate was replaced by a Republic. However, in thirty-eight years, the Maldives have seen only two Presidents. Historically, Maldives had a strategic importance because of its location on the major maritime routes of the Indian Ocean. Sri Lanka and India have had cultural and economic ties with it for centuries.

History

Maldivian tradition suggests that the first settlers were Dravidian people, probably fishermen from the southwest coast of the Indian Subcontinent and the western shores of Sri Lanka. Buddhism came to the Maldives at the time of Emperor Ashoka's expansion and became the dominant religion until the 12th century AD. According to a legend, a prince named Koimala from India entered the Maldives from the North (Ihavandhu) and became the first king from the House of Theemuge. The ancient Maldivian Kings promoted Buddhism and the first Maldive writings and artistic achievements in the form of highly developed sculpture and architecture are from that period. The conversion to Islam began from the end of the 12th century AD. Over the centuries, the islands have been visited and their development influenced by sailors and traders from countries on the Arabian Sea and the Bay of Bengal.

From 1887 to 1965, Maldives was ruled by a succession of sultans. They were hereditary until 1932. Maldives remained a British crown protectorate until

1953 when the sultanate was suspended and the First Republic was declared under the short-lived presidency of Muhammad Amin Didi. Muslim conservatives in Male ousted his government, and during a riot over food shortages, Didi was beaten by a mob and died on a nearby island. In 1956 Britain obtained permission to reestablish its wartime airfield on Gan in the southernmost Addu Atoll on a 100-year lease and a payment of £2,000 a year, as well as some 44 hectares on Hitaddu for radio installations. In 1960 Maldives allowed Britain to continue at Gan and the Hitaddu for a thirty-year period, with the payment of £750,000 over the period of 1960 to 1965 for the purpose of Maldives' economic development.

In 1959 the inhabitants of the three southernmost atolls protested against the government. They formed the United Suvadive Republic and elected, Abdullah Afeef as president and Hithadhoo as capital of this republic. On 26 July 1965, Maldives gained independence from Britain, who retained the use of the Gan and Hitaddu facilities. After independence from Britain in 1965, the sultanate continued to operate for another three years under King Muhammad Fareed. On 11 November 1968, the monarchy was abolished and replaced by a republic, although this was a cosmetic change without any significant alteration in the structures of government. The official name of the country was changed from Maldive Islands to the Maldives in a progressive manner. Tourism began to be developed on the archipelago about five years later.

Elected to replace Nasir for a five-year presidential term in 1978 was Maumoon Abdul Gayoom, a former university lecturer and Maldivian ambassador to the United Nations. The peaceful election ushered in a period of political stability and economic development. The local populace benefited from increased tourism and the corresponding increase in foreign contacts involving various development projects. Gayoom's popularity remained strong, allowing him to win three more presidential terms, receiving more than 95 percent of the vote as the government did not allow any legal opposition.

During the 1970s, the economic situation in Maldives suffered a setback when the Sri Lankan market for Maldives' main export of dried fish collapsed. Adding to the problems was the British decision in 1975 to close its airfield on Gan in line with its policy of abandoning defence commitments east of the Suez Canal. A steep commercial decline followed. As a result, the popularity of Nasir's government suffered and the twenty-year period of authoritarian rule under Nasir abruptly ended in 1978 when he fled to Singapore. A subsequent investigation revealed that he had absconded with millions of dollars from the state treasury.

In November 1988, a group of Maldivians headed by Mr. Lutfee a small time businessman used Tamil mercenaries from Sri Lanka to stage a coup against President Gayyoom. After an appeal by the Maldivian government for help, the Indian military intervened against the mercenaries in order to reinstate Gayyoom in power. On the night of 3 November 1988, the Indian Air Force airlifted a parachute battalion group from Agra and flew them non-stop over 2,000 kilometres to the Maldives. The Indian paratroopers landed at Hulule and secured the airfield and restored the Government rule at Malé within hours. The brief, bloodless operation, labelled Operation Cactus, also involved the Indian Navy.

On 26 December 2004, the Maldives were devastated by a tsunami following the 2004 Indian Ocean earthquake. Only nine islands were reported to have escaped any flooding, while fifty-seven islands faced serious damage to critical infrastructure, fourteen islands had to be totally evacuated, and six islands were decimated. A further twenty-one resort islands were forced to shut down due to serious damage. The total damage was estimated at over 400 million dollars or some 62% of the GDP. A total of 108 people, including six foreigners, reportedly died in the tsunami. The destructive impact of the waves on the low-lying islands was mitigated by the fact there was no continental shelf or land mass upon which the waves could gain height. The tallest waves were reported 14 feet high.

Geography

The Maldives holds the record for being the flattest country in the world, with a maximum natural ground level of only 2.3 metres, though in areas where construction exists this has been increased to several metres. Over the last century, sea levels have risen about 20 centimetres. The ocean is likely to continue rising and this threatens the existence of Maldives. The Indian ocean is particularly important for its diverse sea life and coral reefs, and the Maldives are among the richest of the Indian ocean locations in this regard.

The first accurate maritime charts of this complex Indian Ocean atoll group were the British Admiralty Charts. In 1834-36 Capt. Robert Moresby, assisted by Lieutenants Christopher and Young, undertook the difficult cartography of the Maldive Islands. The resulting charts were printed as three separate large maps by the Hydrographic Service of the Royal Navy. A tsunami in the Indian Ocean caused by the 2004 Indian Ocean earthquake caused parts of the Maldives to be covered by sea water and left many people homeless. After the disaster, cartographers are planning to redraw the maps of the islands due to alterations by the tsunami.

Demographics

The Maldivian ethnic identity is a blend of the cultures reflecting the peoples who settled on the islands, reinforced by religion and language. Some social stratification exists on the islands. It is not rigid, since rank is based on varied factors, including occupation, wealth, Islamic virtue, and family ties. Traditionally, instead of a complex caste system, like the Vedic one, there was merely a distinction between noble (befulhu) and common people in the Maldives. Members of the social elite are concentrated in Malé. Outside of the service industry, this is the only location where the foreign and domestic populations are likely to interact. The tourist resorts are not on islands where the natives live, and casual contacts between the two groups are discouraged.

A census has been recorded since 1905, which shows that the population of the country remained around 100,000 for the first seventy years of the last century. Following independence in 1965, the health status of the population improved so much that the population doubled by 1978, and the population growth rate peaked at 3.4% in 1985. By 2005, the population had reached 300,000, although the census in 2000 showed that the population growth rate had declined to 1.9%. Life expectancy at birth stood at 46 years in 1978, while it has now risen to 72 years. Infant mortality has declined from 127 per thousand in 1977 to 12 today, and adult literacy stands at 99%. Combined school enrolment stands in the high 90s.

The Maldives has one of the highest birth rates in the world. The result is that many islands have become overpopulated and are completely covered by homesteads. As of July 2006, more than 50,000 foreign employees live in the country. They comprise mainly of people from the neighbouring South Asian countries of India, Sri Lanka, Bangladesh and Nepal.

Language and Culture

Maldivian culture is derived from a number of sources, the most important of which are its proximity to the shores of Sri Lanka and southern India. Thus the population is mainly a mix of Indo-Aryan, Dravidian and Semitic from the anthropological point of view. The official and common language is Dhivehi, an Indo-European language having some similarities with Elu, the ancient Sinhalese language. The present-day written script is called Thaana and is written from right to left. English is used widely in commerce and increasingly as the medium of instruction in government schools.

The language is from Indo-Iranian Sanskritic origin, which points at a later influence from the north of the subcontinent. According to the legends, the kingly dynasty that ruled the country in the past has its origin there. Possibly these ancient kings brought Buddhism from the subcontinent, but the Maldivian legends don't make it clear. After the long Buddhist period of their history, Maldivians converted to Sunni Islam in the mid-12th century. Islam is the official religion of the entire population, as adherence to it is required for citizenship.

In the island culture there are a few elements of African origin as well from slaves brought to the court by the royal family and nobles from their hajj journeys to Arabia in the past. There are islands like Feridhu and Maalhos in Northern Ari Atoll, and Goidhu in Southern Maalhosmadulhu Atoll where many of the inhabitants trace their ancestry to released African slaves.

Economy

In ancient times the Maldives were renowned for the cowries, coir rope, dried tuna fish (Maldive Fish), ambergris (Maavaharu) and coco de mer (Tavakkaashi). Local and foreign trading ships used to load these products in the Maldives and transport them to other harbours in the Indian Ocean.

Today tourism and fisheries form the two key components of the Maldivian economy. The country's shipping, banking and manufacturing sectors are growing at a considerable pace. Among the South Asian nations, the Maldives has the second highest per-capita GDP at 3,900 USD (2002 figure). Major trading partners include India, Sri Lanka, Thailand, Malaysia and Singapore. The development of tourism has fostered the overall growth of the country's economy. It has created direct and indirect employment and income generation opportunities in other related industries. Today, tourism is the country's biggest foreign exchange earner, contributing to twenty percent of the GDP. With eighty-seven tourist resorts in operation. The year 2006 recorded 467,154 tourist arrivals.

The mechanization of the traditional fishing boat called "Dhoni" in 1974 was a major milestone in the development of the fisheries industry and the country's economy in general. A fish canning plant was installed in the island of Felivaru in 1977, as a joint venture with a Japanese firm. In 1979, a Fisheries Advisory Board was set up with the mandate of advising the government on policy guidelines for the overall development of the fisheries sector. Manpower development programs were begun in the early 1980s, and fisheries education was incorporated into the school curriculum. Fish aggregating devices and navigational aids were located at various strategic points. Moreover, the opening up of the Exclusive Economic Zone (EEZ) of the Maldives for fisheries has further enhanced the growth of the fisheries sector. Today, fisheries contribute over fifteen percent of the GDP and engage about thirty percent of the country's work force. It is also the second-largest foreign exchange earner after tourism.

Airports with two permanent-surface runways exist at Male and Gan. Air Maldives is national airline. Maldives has minimal domestic and international facilities with one television station; and one Indian Ocean International Telecommunications Satellite Corporation (Intelsat) earth station.

The major daily newspaper is Haveeru (North Side) in Male. Aafathis, is another daily in Dhivehi and English. Maldives also has a number of weekly and monthly publications as well as several news agencies and publishers. Hindi-language films, newspapers, and magazines from India are popular. The government radio station Voice of Maldives, established in 1962, broadcasts to the entire country in Dhivehi and English.

Administrative Divisions

The Maldives have been divided into 21 administrative divisions (20 administrative atolls and Malé city). In addition to a name, every administrative division is identified by the Maldivian code letters, such as "Haa Alif" for Thiladhunmati Uthuruburi (Thiladhunmathi North); and by a Latin code letter. The first corresponds to the geographical Maldivian name of the atoll. The second is a code adopted for convenience. It began in order to facilitate radio communication between the atolls and the central administration. As there are certain islands in different atolls that have the same name, for administrative purposes this code is quoted before the name of the island, for example: Baa Funadhoo, Kaafu Funadhoo, Gaafu-Alifu Funadhoo. Since most Atolls have very long geographical names it is also used whenever the name of the atoll has to be quoted short, for example in the atoll website names.

Each atoll is administered by an Atoll Chief (Atholhu Veriyaa) appointed by the President. The Ministry of Atoll Administration and its Northern and Southern Regional Offices, Atoll Offices and Island Offices are collectively responsible to the President for Atolls Administration. The administrative head of each island is the Island Chief (Katheeb), appointed by the President. The Island Chief's immediate superior is the Atoll Chief.

Politics

Politics in the Maldives takes place in the framework of a presidential republic, whereby the President is the head of government. The President heads the executive branch and appoints the cabinet. The President is nominated to a five-year term by a secret ballot of the Majlis (parliament), a nomination which is confirmed by national referendum.

The unicameral Majlis of the Maldives is composed of fifty members serving five-year terms. Two members from each atoll are elected directly by universal suffrage. Eight are appointed by the president, which is the main route through which women enter parliament. The country introduced political parties for the first time in its history in July 2005, six months after the last elections for the parliament. Nearly thirty-six members of the existing parliament joined the Dhivehi Raiyyathunge Party (the Maldivian People's Party) and elected President Gayoom as its leader. Twelve members of parliament became the Opposition and joined the Maldivian

Democratic Party. Two members remained independent. In March 2006, President Gayoom published a detailed Roadmap for the Reform Agenda, providing time-bound measures to write a new Constitution, and modernise the legal framework. Under the Roadmap, the government has submitted to the Parliament a raft of reform measures. The Roadmap provides the deadline of 31 May 2007 for the Assembly to conclude its work and to pave the way for the first multi-party elections in the country by October 2008.

On 19 June 2006, the Assembly voted to hold a public referendum to decide the form of government under the new constitutional settlement. The political structure of the Maldives has remained practically unchanged for centuries. Despite the passage from monarchy to republic, the contemporary political structure shows a clear continuity with the feudal past in which power was shared among a few families at the top of the social structure. In some islands, the offices have remained within the same family for generations.

National Security

The National Security Service of about 2,000 members performs army, police, and maritime duties. The Republic of Maldives has no armed forces, faces no internal or external threat and is not involved in any international dispute. Threat perceptions include global factors like the threat to the environment, ozone depletion and global warming. Military expenditure was $34.5 million in 2001 (8.6% of the GDP). Maldives has a Coast Guard Force with 400 Personnel. There are 4 Tracker II Class, 1 Cheverton Class and 1 Dagger Class Patrol Craft. They also have a Hamilton Jet powered Landing Craft built by Colombo Dockyards, Sri Lanka

As a result of the coup attempt in November 1988, the Maldives undertook a review of its defence requirements by overhauling and modernizing its NSS. It added six British vessels to its existing force, doubled the infantry to 2,000 men under arms, acquired four armored cars and tried to improve its airborne surveillance. It also decided to create the Defence Intelligence Services to monitor external and internal developments.

Maldives has traditionally sought to maintain an independent status, while preserving cordial relations with all members of the world community. The purpose is to keep the Indian Ocean area at peace. It joined the UN in 1965 and the World Bank and the IMF in 1978. In connection with its concern over the security of the Indian Ocean area, Maldives became a founder of the South Asian Association for Regional Co-operation in 1985.

Maldives' first-ever terror strike occurred on 29 September 2007, when an Islamist cell triggered an explosive device in Male's Sultan Park. Investigators discovered that the cell had connections with Lashkar-e-Taiba operatives at the Jamia Salafiyya in Faisalabad —a seminary that has produced key Lashkar commanders.

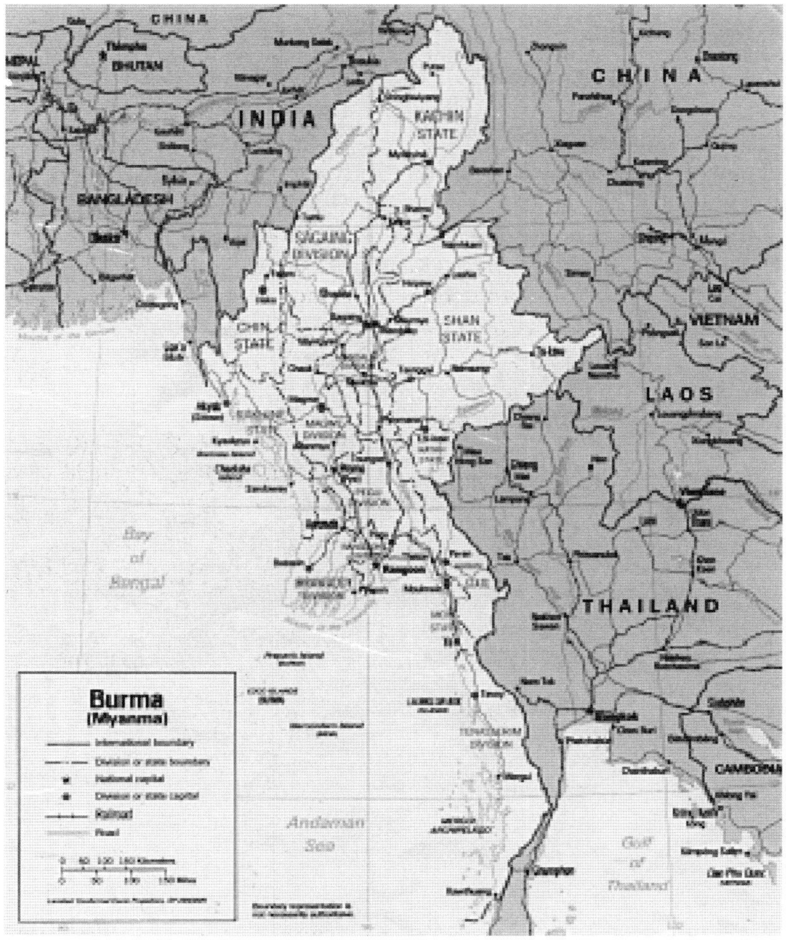

MYANMAR

Burma, officially the Union of Myanmar, is the largest country by geographical area in mainland Southeast Asia. Myanmar achieved independence from Britain on 4 January 1948, as the "Union of Burma." It became the "Socialist Republic of the Union of Burma" on 4 January 1974, before reverting to the "Union of Burma" on 23 September 1988. On 18 June 1989, the State Law and Order Restoration Council adopted the name "Union of Myanmar." This was recognised by the United Nations, but not by the US Government as this decision was not approved by any sitting legislature. Its capital is Rangoon (Yangon).

The flag of Myanmar is red with a blue rectangle in the upper hoist-side corner bearing, 14 white five-pointed stars encircling a cogwheel containing a stalk of rice; the 14 stars represent the seven administrative divisions and seven states. It is bordered by China on the north, Laos on the east, Thailand on the southeast, Bangladesh on the west, and India on the northwest, with the Bay of Bengal to the southwest. One-third of Myanmar's total perimeter, 1,930 kilometres, forms an uninterrupted coastline.

Myanmar's diverse population has played a major role in defining its politics, history and demographics in modern times. Its political system remains under the tight control of the State Peace and Development Council, the military government led, since 1992, by Senior General Than Shwe. The Burmese military has dominated government since General Ne Win led a coup in 1962 that toppled the civilian government of U Nu. The country's culture, heavily influenced by neighbours, is based on Theravada Buddhism intertwined with local elements.

History

The Mon people are thought to be the earliest group to migrate into the lower Ayeyarwady valley and, by the mid-900s BC, were dominant in southern Burma. The Mons became one of the first in South East Asia to embrace Theravada Buddhism. The Tibeto-Burman speaking Pyu arrived later in the 1st century BC, and established several city states—of which Sri Ksetra was the most powerful—in central Ayeyarwady valley. The Mon and Pyu kingdoms were an active overland trade route between India and China. The Pyu kingdoms entered a period of rapid decline in early 9th century AD when the powerful kingdom of Nanzhao (in present-day Yunnan) invaded Ayeyarwady valley several times. In 835, Nanzhao decimated the Pyu by carrying off many captives to be used as conscripts.

Tibeto-Burman speaking Burmans, or the Bamar, began migrating to the Ayeyarwady valley from present-day Yunnan's Nanzhao kingdom starting in 7th century AD. Filling the power vacuum left by the Pyu, the Burmans established a small kingdom in Bagan in 849. But it was not until the reign of King Anawrahta (1044–1077) that Bagan's influence expanded throughout much of present-day Burma.

After Anawrahta's capture of the Mon capital of Thaton in 1057, the Burmans adopted Theravada Buddhism from the Mons. The Burmese script was created, based on the Mon script, during the reign of King Kyanzittha (1084–1112). Prosperous from trade, Bagan kings built many magnificent temples and pagodas throughout the country – many of which can still be seen today. Bagan's power slowly waned in 13th century. Kublai Khan's Mongol forces invaded northern Burma starting in 1277, and sacked Bagan city itself in 1287. Bagan's over two century reign of Ayeyarwady valley and its periphery was over.

The Mongols could not stay for long in the searing Ayeyarwady valley. But the Tai-Shan people from Yunnan who came down with the Mongols fanned out to the Ayeyarwady valley, Shan states, Laos, Siam and Assam, and became powerful players in South East Asia. The Bagan empire was irreparably broken up into several small kingdoms:

- The Burman kingdom of Ava or Innwa (1364–1555), the successor state to three smaller kingdoms founded by Burmanized Shan kings, controlling Upper Burma.
- The Mon kingdom of Hanthawady Pegu or Bago (1287–1540), founded by a Mon-ized Shan King Wareru (1287–1306), controlling Lower Burma.
- The Rakhine kingdom of Mrauk U (1434–1784), in the west.
- Several Shan states in the Shan hills in the east and the Kachin hills in the north.

By the late 15th century, constant warfare had left Ava greatly weakened. Its peripheral areas became either independent or autonomous. In 1486, King Minkyinyo (1486–531) of Taungoo broke away from Ava and established a small independent kingdom. In 1527, Mohnyin (Shan: Mong Yang) Shans finally captured Ava, upsetting the delicate power balance that had existed for nearly two centuries. The Shans would rule Upper Burma until 1555.

Reinforced by fleeing Burmans from Ava, the minor Burman kingdom of Taungoo under its young, ambitious king Tabinshwehti (1531–1551) defeated the more powerful Mon kingdom at Bago, reunifying all of Lower Burma by 1540. Tabinshwehti's successor King Bayinnaung (1551–1581) would go on to conquer Upper Burma (1555), Manipur (1556), Shan states (1557), Chiang Mai (1557), Ayutthaya (1564, 1569) and Lan Xang (1574), bringing most of western South East Asia under his rule. Bayinnaung died in 1581, preparing to invade Rakhine, a maritime power controlling the entire coastline west of Rakhine Yoma, up to Chittagong province in Bengal. Bayinnaung's massive empire unraveled soon after his death in 1581. Ayutthaya Siamese had driven out the Burmese by 1593 and went on to take Tanintharyi. The country was in chaos.

The Burmese under King Anaukpetlun (1605–1628) regrouped and re-established a smaller reconstituted kingdom based in Ava covering Upper Burma, Lower Burma and Shan states (but without Rakhine or Taninthayi). After the reign of King Thalun (1629–1648), who rebuilt the war-torn country, the kingdom experienced a slow and steady decline for the next 100 years. The Mons successfully rebelled starting in 1740 with French help and Siamese encouragement, broke away Lower Burma by 1747, and finally put an end to the House of Taungoo in 1752 when they took Ava.

King Alaungpaya (1752–1760), established the Konbaung Dynasty in Shwebo in 1752. He founded Yangon in 1755. By his death in 1760, Alaungpaya had reunified the country. In 1767, King Hsinbyushin (1763–1777) sacked Ayutthya. The Qing Dynasty of China invaded four times from 1765 to 1769 without success. The Chinese invasions allowed the new Siamese kingdom based in Bangkok to repel the Burmese out of Siam by the late 1770s.

King Bodawpaya (1782–1819) failed repeatedly to reconquer Siam in 1780s and 1790s. Bodawpaya did manage to capture the western kingdom of Rakhine, which had been largely independent since the fall of Bagan, in 1784. Bodawpaya also formally annexed Manipur, a rebellion-prone protectorate, in 1813.

King Bagyidaw's (1819–1837) general Maha Bandula put down a rebellion in Manipur in 1819 and captured then independent kingdom of Assam in 1819 (again in 1821). The new conquests brought the Burmese adjacent to the British India. The British defeated the Burmese in the First Anglo-Burmese War (1824–1826). Burma had to cede Assam, Manipur, Rakhine (Arakan) and Tanintharyi (Tenessarim).

In 1852, the British attacked a much weakened Burma during a Burmese palace power struggle. After the Second Anglo-Burmese War, which lasted 3 months, the British had captured the remaining coastal provinces: Ayeyarwady, Yangon and Bago, naming the territories as Lower Burma.

King Mindon (1853–1878) founded Mandalay in 1859 and made it his capital. He skillfully navigated the growing threats posed by the competing interests of Britain and France. In the process, Mindon had to renounce Kayah (Karenni) states in 1875. His successor, King Thibaw (1878–1885), was largely ineffectual. In 1885, the British, alarmed by the French conquest of neighboring Laos, grabbed Upper Burma. The Third Anglo-Burmese War (1885) lasted a mere one month insofar as capturing the capital Mandalay was concerned. The Burmese royal family was exiled to Ratnagiri, India. British forces spent at least another four years pacifying the country – not only in the Burman heartland but also in the Shan, Chin and Kachin hill areas. By some accounts, minor insurrections did not end until 1896.

Upper Burma and Lower Burma were reunited, and Burma was administered as a single province within British India despite Burma's independent history and traditions. To stimulate trade and facilitate changes, the British brought in Indians and Chinese who quickly displaced the Burmese in urban areas. To this day Yangon and Mandalay have large ethnic Indian populations. Railroads and schools were built, as well as a large number of prisons including the infamous Insein Jail, then as now used for political prisoners. Burmese resentment was strong and was vented in violent riots that paralyzed Yangon on occasion all the way until the 1930s. Much of the discontent was caused by a perceived disrespect for Burman culture and traditions, for example, what the British termed the Shoe Question: the colonisers' refusal to remove their shoes upon entering Buddhist temples or other holy places.

In October 1919, Eindawya Pagoda in Mandalay was the scene of violence when tempers flared after scandalized Buddhist monks attempted to physically expel a group of shoe-wearing British visitors. The leader of the monks was later sentenced to life imprisonment for attempted murder. Such incidents inspired the Burmese resistance to use Buddhism as a rallying point for their cause. Buddhist monks became the vanguards of the independence movement, and many died while protesting. One monk-turned-martyr was U Wisara, who died in prison after a 166-day hunger strike to protest a rule that forbade him from wearing his Buddhist robes while imprisoned

On 1 April 1937, Burma became a separately administered territory, independent of the Indian administration. The vote for keeping Burma in India, or as a separate colony divided the populace, and laid the ground work for the insurgencies to come after independence. In the 1940s, the Thirty Comrades, commanded by Aung San, founded the Burma Independence Army. The Thirty Comrades received training in Japan.

During World War II, Burma became a major frontline in the Southeast Asian Theatre. The British administration collapsed ahead of the advancing Japanese troops, jails and asylums were opened and Rangoon was deserted except for the many Anglo-Burmese and Indians who remained at their posts. A stream of some 300,000 refugees fled across the jungles into India; known as 'The Trek', all but 30,000 of those 300,000 arrived in India. Initially the Japanese-led Burma Campaign succeeded and the British were expelled from most of Burma, but the British counter-attacked using primarily troops of the British Indian Army. By July 1945, the British had retaken the country. Although many Burmese fought initially for the Japanese, some Burmese also served in the British Burma Army. In 1943, the Chin Levies and Kachin Levies were formed in the border districts of Burma still under British administration. The Burma Rifles fought as part of the Chindits under General Orde Wingate from 1943–1945. Later in the war, the Americans created American-Kachin Rangers who also fought for the occupiers. Many other Burmese fought with the British Special Operations Executive. The Burma Independence Army under the command of Aung San and the Arakan National Army fought with the Japanese from 1942–1944, but switched allegiance to the Allied side in 1945.

In 1947, Aung San became Deputy Chairman of the Executive Council of Burma, a transitional government. But in July 1947, political rivals assassinated Aung San and several cabinet members. On 4 January 1948, the nation became an independent republic, named the Union of Burma, with Sao Shwe Thaik as its first President and U Nu as its first Prime

Minister. Unlike most other former British colonies and overseas territories, it did not become a member of the Commonwealth. A bicameral parliament was formed, consisting of a Chamber of Deputies and a Chamber of Nationalities.

The geographical area Burma encompasses today can be traced to the Panglong Agreement, which combined Burma Proper, which consisted of Lower Burma and Upper Burma, and the Frontier Areas, which had been administered separately by the British. In 1961, U Thant, then Burma's Permanent Representative to the United Nations and former Secretary to the Prime Minister, was elected Secretary-General of the United Nations; he was the first non-Westerner to head any international organization and would serve as UN Secretary-General for ten years.] Among the Burmese to work at the UN when he was Secretary-General was a young Aung San Suu Kyi.

Democratic rule ended in 1962 when General Ne Win led a military coup d'état. He ruled for nearly 26 years and pursued policies under the rubric of the Burmese Way to Socialism. In 1974, the military violently suppressed anti-government protests at the funeral of U Thant. In 1988, unrest over economic mismanagement and political oppression by the government led to widespread pro-democracy demonstrations throughout the country known as the 8888 Uprising. Security forces committed the massacre of hundreds of demonstrators, and General Saw Maung staged a coup d'état and formed the State Law and Order Restoration Council (SLORC). In 1989, SLORC declared martial law after widespread protests. The military government finalized plans for People's Assembly elections on 31 May 1989.

In May 1990, the government held free elections for the first time in almost 30 years. The National League for Democracy (NLD), the party of Aung San Suu Kyi, won 392 out of a total 489 seats, but the election results were annulled by SLORC, which refused to step down. Led by Than Shwe since 1992, the military regime has made cease-fire agreements with most ethnic guerrilla groups. In 1992, SLORC unveiled plans to create a new constitution through the National Convention, which began 9 January 1993. To date, this military-organized National Convention has not produced a new constitution despite well over ten years of operation. In 1997, the State Law and Order Restoration Council was renamed the State Peace and Development Council (SPDC).

On 23 June 1997, Myanmar was admitted into the Association of Southeast Asian Nations (ASEAN). The National Convention continues to convene and adjourn. Many major political parties, particularly the NLD, have been absent or excluded, and little progress has been made. On 27 March 2006, the military junta, which had moved the national capital from Yangon to a site near Pyinmana, officially named it Naypyidaw, meaning "city of the kings".

In November of 2006, the International Labour Organization announced it will be seeking "to prosecute members of the ruling Myanmar junta for crimes against humanity" over the continuous forced labour of its citizens by the military at the International Court of Justice.

Mass public demonstrations reappeared on 18 August 2007, when the government raised the price of gas and diesel oil by 500% in order to cover a budget deficit that resulted from a salary hike for civil servants. The junta's move of the Burmese capital to Pyinmana, now called Naypyidaw (King's Royal City), may also have contributed to the budget deficit. The military government usually covers these deficits by printing new money or by declaring some denominations void. Its privatizations since 1988 have enriched a new class of well-connected business people or oligarchs at the expense of the impoverished majority.

The August 2007 demonstrations were led by well-known dissidents, such as Min Ko Naing (with the nom de guerre Conqueror of Kings), Su Su Nway (now in hiding) and others. The military quickly cracked down and still has not allowed the International Red Cross to visit Min Ko Naing and others who are reportedly in Insein Prison after being severely tortured. Reports have surfaced of at least one death, of activist Win Shwe, under interrogation. Following the August protests, the monks of Myanmar, coordinated by an underground organization, stepped into the foreground and added new life to the movement. Under Suu Kyi's leadership, passive resistance, with Suu herself worshiping with leading monks, has been the norm since 1988.

On 19 September 2007, several hundred (possibly 2000 or more) monks staged a protest march in the city of Sittwe. Larger protests in Rangoon and elsewhere ensued over the following days. Security became increasingly heavy handed, resulting in a number of deaths and injuries. By 28 September, internet access had been cut and journalists reputedly warned not to report on protests. Internet access was restored on 5 October.

World governments remain divided on how to deal with the military junta, countries calling for further sanctions include United Kingdom, USA and France, but neighbouring countries including China claim that sanctions will not help solve the issue.

Geography

Myanmar has an area of 678,500 square kilometres (land: 657,740 square kilometres and water: 20,760 square kilometres). Its land boundaries total 5,876 kilometres with Bangladesh (193 kilometres), China (2,185 kilometres), India (1,463 kilometres), Laos (235 kilometres) and Thailand (1,800 kilometres). It has a coastline of 1,930 kilometres. It has a strategic location near major Indian Ocean shipping lanes.

The climate of Myanmar is characterized as tropical monsoon with cloudy, rainy, hot, humid summers (southwest monsoon, June to September) and less cloudy, scant rainfall, mild temperatures, lower humidity during winter (northeast monsoon, December to April).

The terrain comprises central lowlands ringed by steep, rugged highlands. The highest point is Hkakabo Razi (5,881 metres). Myanmar's natural resources include petroleum, timber, tin, antimony, zinc, copper, tungsten, lead, coal, some marble, limestone, precious stones, natural gas and hydropower. 14.92% of the land is arable with only 1.31% under permanent crops. Irrigated land comprises 18,700 square kilometres. Myanmar is prone to natural hazards like destructive earthquakes and cyclones. Flooding and landslides are common during rainy season (June to September). The country also experiences periodic droughts. Current environmental issues include deforestation and industrial pollution of air, soil, and water. Inadequate sanitation and water treatment also contribute to disease

The Ayeyarwady delta, which is approximately 50,400 square kilometres in area, is largely used for rice cultivation. In the north, the Hengduan Shan mountains form the border with China. Three mountain ranges, namely the Rakhine Yoma, the Bago Yoma, and the Shan Plateau exist within Myanmar, all of which run north-to-south from the Himalayas. The mountain chains divide Myanmar's three river systems, which are the Ayeyarwady, Thanlwin, and the Sittang rivers. The Ayeyarwady River, Myanmar's longest river, nearly 2,170 kilometres long, flows into the Gulf of Martaban. Fertile plains exist in the valleys between the mountain chains. The majority of Myanmar's population lives in the Ayeyarwady valley, which is situated between the Rakhine Yoma and the Shan Plateau.

Myanmar's slow economic growth has contributed to the preservation of much of its environment and ecosystems. Forests, including dense tropical growth and valuable teak in lower Myanmar, cover over 49% of the country. Other trees indigenous to the region include rubber, acacia, bamboo, ironwood, mangrove, coconut and betel palm. In the highlands of the north, oak, pine and various rhododendrons cover much of the land. The lands along the coast support all varieties of tropical fruits. In the Dry Zone, vegetation is sparse and stunted.

Typical jungle animals, particularly tigers and leopards are common in Myanmar. In upper Myanmar, there are rhinoceros, wild buffaloes, wild boars, deer antelopes and elephants, which are also tamed or bred in captivity for use as work animals, particularly in the lumber industry. Smaller mammals are also numerous, ranging from gibbons and monkeys to flying foxes and tapirs. The abundance of birds is notable with over 800 species, including parrots, peafowl, pheasants, crows, herons and paddy birds. Among reptile species there are crocodiles, geckos, cobras, pythons and turtles. Hundreds of species of freshwater fish are wide-ranging, plentiful and are very important food sources.

People

The major Burmese ethnic groups are Burman 68%, Shan 9%, Karen 7%, Rakhine 4%, Chinese 3%, Indian 2%, Mon 2%, other 5%. The religions are Buddhist 89%, Christian 4% (Baptist 3%, Roman Catholic 1%), Muslim 4%, animist 1%, other 2%. Burmese is the major languages, though minority ethnic groups have their own languages. Myanmar has an estimated population of 47,382,633. The median age is 27 years with a population growth rate of 0.81%.

Myanmar has a population of about 55 million. Current population figures are rough estimates because the last partial census, conducted by the Ministry of Home and Religious Affairs under the control of the military junta, was taken in 1983. No trustworthy nationwide census has been taken in Myanmar since 1931. There are over 600,000 registered migrant workers from Myanmar in Thailand, and millions more work illegally. Burmese migrant workers account for 80% of Thailand's migrant workers. Myanmar has a population density of 75 persons per km², one of the lowest in Southeast Asia. Refugee camps exist along Indian-Burmese, Bangladeshi-Burmese and Burmese-Thai borders while several thousand are in Malaysia. Conservative estimates state that there are over 295,800 refugees from Myanmar, with the majority being Rohingya, Kayin, and Karenni.

Myanmar is home to four major linguistic families: Sino-Tibetan, Austronesian, Tai-Kadai, and Indo-European. Sino-Tibetan languages are most widely spoken. They include Burmese, Karen, Kachin, Chin, and Chinese. The primary Tai-Kadai language is Shan. Mon, Palaung, and Wa are the major Austroasiatic languages spoken in Myanmar. The two major Indo-European languages are Pali, the liturgical language of Theravada Buddhism, and English. According to the UNESCO Institute of Statistics, Myanmar's official literacy rate as of 2000 was 89.9%. Historically, Myanmar has had high literacy rates. To qualify for least developed country status by the UN in order to receive debt relief, Myanmar lowered its official literacy rate from 78.6% to 18.7% in 1987.

Myanmar is ethnically diverse. The government recognizes 135 distinct ethnic groups. While it is extremely difficult to verify this statement, there are at least 108 different ethno-linguistic groups in Myanmar, consisting mainly of distinct Tibeto-Burman peoples, but with sizable populations of Daic, Hmong-Mien, and Austroasiatic (Mon-Khmer) peoples. The Bamar form an estimated 68% of the population.[10] 10% of the population are Shan. The Kayin make up 7% of the population. The Rakhine people constitute 4% of the population. Overseas Chinese form approximately 3% of the population. Mon, who form 2% of the population, are ethno-linguistically related to the Khmer. Overseas Indians comprise 2%. The remainder are Kachin, Chin, Anglo-Indians and other ethnic minorities. Included in this group are the Anglo-Burmese. Once forming a large and influential community, the Anglo-Burmese left the country in steady streams from 1958 onwards, principally to Australia and the U.K. Today, it is estimated that only 52,000 Anglo-Burmese remain in Myanmar.

Culture

A diverse range of indigenous cultures exist in Myanmar, the majority culture is primarily Buddhist and Bamar. Bamar culture has been influenced by the cultures of neighbouring countries. This is manifested in its language, cuisine, music, dance and theatre. The arts, particularly literature, have historically been influenced by the Burmese form of Theravada Buddhism. Considered the national epic of Myanmar, the Yama Zatdaw, an adaptation of Ramayana, has been influenced greatly by Thai, Mon, and Indian versions of the play. Buddhism is practiced along with nat worship which involves elaborate rituals to propitiate one from a pantheon of 37 nats.

In a traditional Burmese village, the monastery is the centre of cultural life. Monks are venerated and supported by the lay people. A novitiation ceremony called shinbyu is the most important coming of age events for a boy when he enters the monastery for a short period of time. All boys of Buddhist family need to be a novice (beginner for Buddhism) before the age of twenty and to be a monk after the age of twenty. It is compulsory for all boys of Buddhism. The duration can be at least one week. Girls have ear-piercing ceremonies at the same time. Burmese culture is most evident in villages where local festivals are held throughout the year, the most important being the pagoda festival. Many villages have a guardian nat, and superstition and taboos are commonplace in Burmese life.

British colonial rule also introduced Western elements of culture to Myanmar. Myanmar's educational system is modelled after that of the United Kingdom. Colonial architectural influences are most evident in major cities such as Yangon. Many ethnic minorities, particularly the Karen in the southeast, and the Kachin and Chin who populate the north and northwest, practice

Christianity. Members of the Buddhist monk hood are venerated throughout Myanmar, which is one of the most predominantly Theravada Buddhist countries in the world.

Government and Politics

Executive branch. The Chief of State and Chairman of the State Peace and Development Council (SPDC) is Senior General Than Shwe (since 23 April 1992). The head of government is Prime Minister, General Soe Win (since 19 October 2004). The cabinet is overseen by the SPDC (military junta), so named on 15 November 1997. It assumed power on 18 September 1988 under the name State Law and Order Restoration Council (SLORC).

Legislative branch. Myanmar has a unicameral People's Assembly or Pyithu Hluttaw (485 seats; members elected by popular vote to serve four-year terms). Elections were last held on 27 May 1990, but the Assembly was never allowed by the military junta to convene. In the elections the number of seats won (party-wise) were—NLD 392 (opposition), SNLD 23 (opposition), NUP 10 (pro-government), others 60.

Judicial branch. Remnants of the British-era legal system are in place, but there is no guarantee of a fair public trial; the judiciary is not independent of the executive.

Myanmar is governed by a strict military regime. The current head of state is Senior General Than Shwe, who holds the posts of "Chairman of the State Peace and Development Council" and "Commander in Chief of the Defense Services". General Khin Nyunt was prime minister until 19 October 2004, when he was replaced by General Soe Win, after the purge of Military Intelligence sections within the Myanmar armed forces. The majority of ministry and cabinet posts are held by military officers, with the exceptions being the Ministry of Health, the Ministry of Education, the Ministry of Labour, and the Ministry of National Planning and Economic Development, posts which are held by civilians.

Elected delegates in the 1990 People's Assembly election formed the National Coalition Government of the Union of Myanmar (NCGUB), a government-in-exile since December 1990, with the mission of restoring democracy. Dr. Sein Win, a first cousin of Aung San Suu Kyi, has held the position of prime minister of the NCGUB since its inception. The NCGUB has been outlawed by the military government.

Major political parties in Myanmar are the National League for Democracy and the Shan Nationalities League for Democracy, although their activities are heavily regulated and suppressed by the military government. Many other parties, often representing ethnic minorities, exist. The military government allows little room for political organizations and has outlawed many political parties and underground student organizations. The military supported the National Unity Party in the 1990 elections and, more recently, an organization named the Union Solidarity and Development Association.

Several human rights organizations have reported on human rights abuses by the military government. They have claimed that there is no independent judiciary in Myanmar. The military government restricts Internet access through software-based censorship that limits the material citizens can access on-line. Forced labour, human trafficking, and child labour are common. The military is also notorious for rampant use of sexual violence as an instrument of control, including systematic rapes and taking of sex slaves as porters for the military. A strong women's pro-democracy movement has formed in exile, largely along the Thai border and in Chang Mai. The Women's League of Myanmar is the leading women's civil society organization, working for democracy and women's human rights in Myanmar.

ASEAN has also stated its frustration with Myanmar's government. It has formed the ASEAN Inter-Parliamentary Myanmar Caucus to address the lack of democratisation in Myanmar. Dramatic change in the country's political situation remains unlikely, due to support from major regional powers such as India, Russia, and, in particular, China.

Administrative Divisions

Myanmar is divided into seven states and seven divisions. Divisions are predominantly Bamar. States, in essence, are divisions which are home to particular ethnic minorities. The administrative divisions are further subdivided into townships, wards, and villages. Major cities are divided into districts called townships.

The Divisions are:

- Ayeyarwady Division
- Bago Division
- Magway Division
- Mandalay Division
- Sagaing Division
- Tanintharyi Division
- Yangon Division

The States are:

- Chin State
- Kachin State
- Kayin (Karen) State
- Kayah (Karenni) State
- Mon State
- Rakhine (Arakan) State
- Shan State

Constitution

Myanmar adopted its Constitution on 3 January 1974. It has been suspended since 18 September 1988. A national convention was convened in 1993 to draft a new constitution but collapsed in 1996. It was reconvened in 2004 but does not include participation of any democratic opposition. Myanmar has not accepted compulsory International Court of Justice jurisdiction.

Economy

Under British administration, Myanmar was one of the wealthiest countries in Southeast Asia. It was once the world's largest exporter of rice. During British administration, Myanmar supplied oil through the Myanmarh Oil Company. Myanmar also had a wealth of natural and labor resources. It produced 75% of the world's teak and had a highly literate population. The country was believed to be on the fast track to development.

Myanmar is a resource-rich country, which suffers from pervasive government controls, inefficient economic policies and rural poverty. Steps in the early 1990s to liberalize the economy after decades of failure under the "Burmese Way to Socialism" stalled, and liberalization measures were rescinded. Myanmar does not have monetary or fiscal stability. The economy suffers from serious macro-economic imbalances, inflation, multiple official exchange rates overvaluing the Burmese kyat, and a distorted interest rate regime.

Most overseas development assistance ceased after the suppression of the democracy movement in 1988 and refusal of the junta to honour the results of the 1990 legislative elections. In response to the government of Myanmar's attack in May 2003 on Aung San Suu Kyi and her convoy, the US imposed new economic sanctions against Myanmar, including a ban on imports of Burmese products and a ban on provision of financial services by US persons. A poor investment climate further slowed the inflow of foreign exchange. The most productive sectors are in extractive industries, especially oil and gas, mining, and timber. Other areas, such as manufacturing and services, are struggling with inadequate infrastructure, unpredictable import/export policies, deteriorating health and education systems, and corruption. The inflation rate is assessed to be 20.2% (in 2005)

A major banking crisis in 2003 shuttered the country's 20 private banks and disrupted the economy. The largest private banks operate under tight restrictions limiting the private sector's access to formal credit. Official statistics are inaccurate. Published statistics on foreign trade are greatly understated due to the size of the black market and unofficial border trade, estimated to be as large as the official economy. Myanmar's trade with India Thailand and China is rising. The Burmese government has good economic relations with its neighbours but better investment and business climates and an improved political situation are needed to promote foreign investment, exports, and tourism.

The GDP (purchasing power parity) in 2005 was estimated at $78.74 billion. At the official exchange rate the GDP was $7.464 billion with a growth rate of 2.9%. The GDP per capita (PPP) was estimated at $1,700. The composition of the GDP by sector is agriculture—56.4%, industry—8.2%, and services—35.3%. The labour force is about 27.75 million in agriculture—70%, industry—7%, and services: 23%. The unemployment rate is estimated at 5%, with 25% of the population assessed to be below the poverty line.

Oil production in Myanmar is estimated at 18,500 barrels per day. It has proven reserves of about 1 billion barrels. Myanmar is a net exporter of natural gas, with a production of 9.98 billion cubic metres. It has proven reserves of 283.2 billion cubic metres. The official export figures are grossly underestimated due to the value of timber, gems, narcotics, rice, and other products smuggled to Thailand, China, and Bangladesh. The general commodities officially exported are clothing, gas, wood products, pulses, beans, fish, and rice to Thailand 44.5%, India 11.9%, China 6.8%, and Japan 5.1% (2005). The commodities imported are fabric, petroleum products, plastics, machinery, transport equipment, construction materials, crude oil; and food products from China 28.4%, Thailand 21.5%, Singapore 18.1%, South Korea 5.9%, and Malaysia 5.4% (2005).

Myanmar is estimated to have reserves of foreign exchange and gold of $763 million. The country has an external debt of $6.99 billion (2005 estimate). Its currency is the kyat, with an exchange rate of kyats per US dollar—5.761 (2005) at the official exchange rates. The unofficial exchange rate by year-end 2005 was 1,075 kyat per US dollar.

Today, Myanmar lacks adequate infrastructure. Goods travel primarily across the Burmese-Thai border, where most illegal drugs are exported, and along the Irrawaddy River. Railroads are old and rudimentary, with few repairs since their construction in the late nineteenth century. Highways are normally unpaved, except in the major cities. Energy shortages are common throughout the country including in Yangon. Myanmar is also the world's second largest producer of opium, accounting for 8% of entire world production and is a major source of illegal drugs, including amphetamines. Other industries include agricultural goods, textiles, wood products, construction materials, gems, metals, oil and natural gas.

The major agricultural product is rice which covers about 60% of the country's total cultivated land area. Rice accounts for 97% of total food grain production by weight. Through collaboration with the International Rice Research Institute (IRRI), 52 modern rice varieties were released in Myanmar between 1966 and 1997, helping increase national rice production to 14 million tons in 1987 and to 19 million tons in 1996. By 1988, modern varieties were planted on half of the country's rice lands, including 98 percent of the irrigated areas.

The lack of an educated workforce skilled in modern technology contributes to the growing problems of the Burmese economy. Inflation is also a serious problem for the Burmese economy.

Transportation

Myanmar has 85 airports, with 21 having paved runways. The country has 2,056 kilometres of gas pipelines and 558 kilometres of oil pipelines. The railways extend over 3,955 kilometres (most of it narrow gauge). The roadways extend 27,000 kilometres (paved—3,200 kilometres; unpaved—23,800 kilometres. Its waterways extend 12,800 kilometres.

The merchant marine of Myanmar has 34 ships (1000 GRT or over) 402,724 GRT/620,642 DWT, that include bulk carriers—8, cargo—18, passenger—2, passenger/cargo—3, roll on/roll off – 2 and specialized tanker – 1. (9 are foreign-owned: Germany 5, Japan 4). The major ports and terminals are Moulmein, Rangoon and Sittwe.

Armed Forces

Myanmar's armed forces are known as the Tatmadaw, which numbers 488,000. The Tatmadaw comprises the Army, the Navy, and the Air Force. The military is very influential in the country, with top cabinet and ministry posts held by military officers. Although official figures for Burmese military spending are not available, the Stockholm International Peace Research Institute, in its annual rankings, ranked Myanmar in the top 15 military spenders in the world. The country imports most of its weapons from Russia, Ukraine, China and India.

National Security

Over half of Myanmar's population consists of diverse ethnic groups with substantial numbers of kin beyond its borders. Despite continuing border committee talks, significant differences remain with Thailand over boundary alignment and the handling of ethnic rebels, refugees, and illegal cross-border activities. Ethnic Karens flee into Thailand to escape fighting between Karen rebels and Burmese troops. In 2005 Thailand sheltered about 121,000 Burmese refugees. Karens also protest Thai support for a Burmese hydroelectric dam on the Salween River near the border. Environmentalists in Myanmar and Thailand continue to voice concern over China's construction of hydroelectric dams upstream on the Nujiang/Salween River in Yunnan Province.

India seeks cooperation from Myanmar to keep Indian Nagaland separatists from hiding in remote Burmese uplands. Myanmar has about 550,000-1,000,000 refugees and internally displaced persons due to government offensives against ethnic insurgent groups near its borders. Most of them are ethnic Karen, Karenni, Shan, Tavoyan, and Mons.

Myanmar is the world's second largest producer of illicit opium (estimated production 292 metric tons). The cultivation is estimated to be over 30,900 hectares. Lack of government will to take on major narco-trafficking groups and lack of serious commitment against money laundering continues to hinder the overall anti-drug effort. Myanmar is the major source of methamphetamine and heroin for regional consumption. The country is currently under Financial Action Task Force countermeasures due to continued failure to address its inadequate money-laundering controls.

Myanmar is building a research nuclear reactor near May Myo (Pyin Oo Lwin) with help from Russia. Myanmar is one of the signatories of the nuclear non-proliferation pact since 1992 and a member of the IAEA since 1957. The military junta had informed the IAEA in September 2000 of its intention to construct the reactor. The research reactor outbuilding frame was built by ELE steel industries limited of Yangon and water from Anisakhan/BE water fall will be used for the reactor cavity cooling system.

ASEAN will not defend Myanmar in any international forum following the military regime's refusal to restore democracy. In April 2007, the Malaysian Foreign Ministry parliamentary secretary Ahmad Shabery Cheek said Malaysia and other ASEAN members had decided not to defend Myanmar if the country's issue was raised for discussion at any international conference.

NEPAL

Nepal is officially known, according to its Interim Constitution, as the State of Nepal (previously known as Kingdom of Nepal). It is a landlocked nation in South Asia, bordering the People's Republic of China to the north and India to the south, east and west. Its capital is at Kathmandu. Nepal previously had the distinction of being the world's only Hindu state, with over 80% of the people following this faith. However, on 18 May 2006 Nepal was declared a secular state.

The national flag consists of two vertically stacked crimson red triangles with blue borders. The upper portion has an eight-pointed disc rising out of a white crescent moon, and the bottom portion has a white sun. The moon and sun symbolize the eternal eyes of god, the red color represents energy in action, and the blue border signifies Nepal's peaceful nature.

History

Founded in 1559, Gorkha was one among the hill states until the rule of Prithvi Narayan Shah (1743–75), when the Nepalese state was established. An astute military strategist, Shah obtained financial assistance and armaments from India and then created alliances with neighbouring states or purchased their neutrality. In fact, his forces even managed to repel British troops. On 29 September 1768, Gorkha troops entered Kathmandu during religious celebrations and took it without a fight. Intrigue and infighting among the royalty continued until 1846, when Jang Bahadur Kunwar, a military commander, established a dynasty of prime ministers that ruled until 1951. The Rana dynasty was a parallel monarchy in which the pre-eminent authority was the prime minister, a hereditary position. The monarchy was reduced to a ceremonial position that legitimized Rana rule and monarchs were either exiled or kept under house arrest. Rampant nepotism and inefficient administration handicapped political development. The Ranas provided some positive development, such as eliminating slavery, establishing schools and factories. On 8 January 1951, the last Rana oligarch, Mohan Shamsher, agreed to restore the king to power and hold elections. In February 1951, King Tribhuvan (r. 1911–55) returned to power.

From February 1951 numerous short-lived governments ruled either under an interim constitution or under King Tribhuvan and his successor, Mahendra (r. 1955–72). The kings regularly dismissed uncooperative or poorly functioning ministries and continually postponed elections. After popular protests, the king allowed the first national elections in February 1959. The Nepali Congress won. But the king dismissed this government in 1960, and instituted a *panchayat* (village council) government, a four-tiered system of representative government with traditional village-level councils at the local level and the National Panchayat at the national level. King Mahendra died in January 1972, and his successor, Birendra (r. 1972–2001), adopted a more liberal approach to government.

In May 1980, King Birendra held a national referendum on the *panchayat* system. He interpreted the narrow margin of support (54.7 percent voted in favour) as a need for political change. He allowed direct elections to the National Panchayat and Nepal once again underwent tumultuous change. Nepal's improving relations with China placed stress on its relations with India, and for this and other reasons India terminated trade and transit treaties in March 1989. After a long and rich history, during which the country splintered and coalesced under a variety of absolute rulers, Nepal became a constitutional monarchy in 1990. A new constitution was promulgated on 9 November 1990, with provisions for basic human rights, adult franchise, and a multiparty democracy with the king as a constitutional monarch. Elections were held in May 1991, and the Nepali Congress came to power.

This arrangement caused increasing instability, both in the parliament and, since 1996, throughout large swathes of the country that have been fought over by Maoist insurgents. The civil conflict has continued for nearly a decade, in which the Communist Party of Nepal (Maoist) killed, expelled, and threatened government officials, landlords, and others it charged with economic and political oppression. Initially, the government largely ignored the conflict, but by 2000 the conflict expanded to nearly two-thirds of the country. Unstable political institutions and worsening civil conflict weakened the government's capacity to address economic, social, and other problems. Factional fighting within and among political parties led to rapid changes in government and prompted parties to spend time and resources on maintaining or acquiring power. In 1994 the Nepali Congress was defeated in midterm elections, and the Communist Party of Nepal (Unified Marxist-Leninist) formed a minority government that lasted nine months. A coalition government led by the Nepali Congress came into power in September 1995 with Sher Bahadur Deuba as prime minister. This coalition remained in power until 2002, but contentious relations with opposition parties and within the coalition undermined the coalition's stability.

In one of the most remarkable events in Nepal's history, Crown Prince Dipendra killed the king, queen, and other royal family members on 1 June 2001, reportedly over his choice of a bride. The crown passed to Gyanendra, Dipendra's uncle, who adopted a firm approach to political issues. When cease-fire talks with the Maoists ended in November 2001, King Gyanendra declared a state of emergency and sent the army into the conflict. This action intensified the conflict. The king dissolved parliament in May 2002 and later unconstitutionally released Deuba's government and assumed executive powers. In the face of unstable governments and a Maoist siege on the Kathmandu Valley in August 2004, popular support for the monarchy began to wane. A seven-party alliance government was installed, whose primary task is to change the constitution.

Following the 2006 democracy movement, the king agreed to relinquish the sovereign power back to the people and reinstated the dissolved House of Representatives on 24 April 2006. Using its newly acquired sovereign authority, on 18 May 2006, the newly resumed House of Representatives unanimously passed a motion to curtail the power of the king and declared Nepal a secular state.

The seven political parties have arrived at a consensus to proclaim a republic from parliament but difference still persists on the date of enforcement.

Geography

Nepal is a landlocked country in the Himalaya Mountains, with India to the east, south, and west and China to the north. Its total land area is 147,181 square kilometres. Its boundary with China is 1,236 kilometres and with India is 1,690 kilometres. Nepal and China have no territorial disputes, but Nepal and India have several: possession of a 75-square-kilometre area called Kalapani, further complicated by its proximity to the Chinese border; the boundary of the Maha Kali River (Sarda River in India), with ramifications for development and distribution of hydropower and water resources; possession of 209 hectares of land after changes in the course of the Mechi River; and sovereignty over several areas comprising nearly 600 square kilometres along the border.

Mountains and rugged hills cover nearly 75 percent of Nepal. It has three main physiographic regions that run laterally across the country. In the south, the plains of the Terai Region cover about 23 percent of Nepal's total area and are the main agricultural and most densely populated region. The Hill Region covers about 42 percent of the total area and consists of hills, flat lands, and valleys. Farther north, the Himalayan Region covers nearly 35 percent of the total area with 200 peaks more than 6,000 metres in elevation and 13 peaks more than 8,000 metres high, including Sagarmatha (Mount Everest), the world's highest mountain (8,850 metres). Eight out of ten world's highest mountains are in Nepal. Nepal's major river systems are—from east to west—the Kosi (513 kilometres), Narayani (332 kilometres), and Karnali (507 kilometres) are major tributaries of the Ganges in India. Nepal lies within a subtropical monsoon climate zone. Climatic conditions and precipitation vary with elevation, ranging from tropical in the Terai plains to alpine and tundra in the northern mountain areas. Nepal's natural resource base is insufficient for its economic needs, and "scenic beauty" is seen as one of the most commercially important resources. Fuel resources are especially scarce. Permanent crop cultivation has reduced the proportion of land used for forest harvesting. Nepal has numerous environmental problems.

Society

Nepal has a total population of 27,676,547 as of July 2005, with a growth rate of 2.2%. 39% of the population is up to 14 years old, 57.3% are aged between 15 and 64, and 3.7% above 65. The median age is 20.07 (19.91 for males and 20.24 for females). There are 1,060 males for every 1,000 females. Life expectancy is 59.8 years (60.9 for males and 59.5 for females). Nepal is the only country in the world where males outlive females. Total literacy rate is 53.74% (68.51% for males and 42.49% for females). Nepal also has approximately 102,892 refugees from Bhutan most of whom are from Nepalese ethnic groups. Population size, density, and growth rates are highest in areas bordering India and around Kathmandu. 84.1 percent of the population lives in rural areas.

No anthropological or linguistic survey of the population has ever been conducted. The names of ethnic groups are derived from the language they speak, and ethnic identity is based on various combinations of national origin, region, language, religion, and caste. The demographic composition is Hindus (59 percent), indigenous Janajatis (31 percent), Newars (5.5 percent), Muslims (4.3 percent), and others—Sikhs, Bengalis, Marwaris, and Jains (0.2 percent). Nepal has 92 languages spoken as mother tongues. Many languages are rarely spoken outside of specific areas, but knowledge of more than one language is common. Nepali is the national language and the most common mother tongue (spoken by 48.6 percent of the population), as well as the most common second language. Maithili is the second most common mother tongue (12.3 percent), and English is increasingly prominent as well as compulsory in public schools and universities.

Groups are the Brahman-Hill 12.5%, Magar 7%, Tharu 6.6%, Tamang 5.5%, Newar 5.4%, Kami 3.9%, Yadav 3.9%, other 32.7%, unspecified 2.8%. Nepali is the national language with 47.8% of the population speaking it as their first language. Other languages include Maithili 12.1%, Bhojpuri 7.4%, Tharu (Dagaura/Rana) 5.8%, Tamang 5.1%, Nepal Bhasa 3.6%, Magar 3.3%, Awadhi 2.4%, other 10%, White 2.6% unspecified 2.5%. Differences between Hindus and Buddhists have been in general very subtle and academic in nature due to the intermingling of Hindu and Buddhist beliefs. Both share common temples and worship common deities and many of Nepal's Hindus could also be regarded as Buddhists and vice versa. Gurkhas are from Nepal. Buddhism was relatively more common among the Newar. Among the other natives of Nepal, those most influenced by Hinduism were the Magar, Sunwar, Limbu and Rai. Hindu influence is less prominent among the Gurung, Bhutia, and Thakali groups, who employ Buddhist monks for their religious ceremonies.

Health indicators are poor by international standards, especially in rural areas. Disease prevalence is higher than in other South Asian countries. Nepal's Human Development Index (HDI) was 0.504 in 2002, ranking Nepal 140 out of 177 countries. Health-care facilities, hygiene, nutrition, and sanitation generally are poor and beyond the means of most, particularly in rural areas. Provision of health services is constrained by low government spending, rugged terrain, and lack of health education (which lowers the demand for health services).

Economy

Prior to 1990 economic relations were in the form of cross-border trade with India and China. Since 1990, the government has adopted market-oriented policies with greater liberalization of the domestic economy and trade focusing on privatizing state industries and creating joint-venture projects, particularly in financial institutions. The economy is characterized by dependence on agriculture, a poor export base, unbalanced regional development, dependence on foreign aid, excessive government control and regulation, and inefficient public enterprises and administration. The GDP is US$6.2 billion, with 3.6 percent annual growth. Inflation stands around 5 percent. The consumer price index averaged 4.5 percent for fiscal year 2005.

Agriculture sustains 76% of the population and accounts for about 39% of the GDP; services comprise 41%, and industry 22%. Hilly and mountainous terrain in the northern two-thirds of the country has made the building of roads and other infrastructure difficult and expensive. There were just over 8,500 km of paved roads, and one 59 km railway line in the south in 2003. Aviation is in a better state, with 48 airports, ten of them with paved runways. There is less than one telephone per 19 people; landline services are not adequate nationwide but concentrated in cities and district headquarters; mobile telephony is in a reasonable state in most parts of the country with increased accessibility and affordability. There were around 175,000 Internet connections in 2005, but after the imposition of the "state of emergency", intermittent losses of service were reported.

Its landlocked location and technological backwardness and the long-running civil war have also prevented Nepal from fully developing its economy. The country receives foreign aid from India, Japan, United Kingdom, United States, European Union, China, Switzerland, and Scandinavian Countries. The government's budget is about US$1.153 billion, with expenditures of $1.789bn (FY05/06). The inflation rate has dropped to 2.9% after a period of higher inflation during the 1990s. The Nepali Rupee has been tied to the Indian Rupee at an exchange rate of 1.6 for many years. Since the loosening of exchange rate controls in the early 1990s, the black market for foreign exchange has all but disappeared. A long-standing economic agreement underpins a close relationship with India.

The distribution of wealth among the Nepali is consistent with that in many developed and developing countries: the highest 10% of households control 39.1% of the national wealth and the lowest 10% control only 2.6%.

Agriculture provides nearly half of the gross domestic product (GDP) and employs most of the population. However, its contribution to the economy has declined. As a result, Nepal has not been self-sufficient in food grain production since the 1980s. Industry and manufacturing have grown but lag behind. Most energy is derived from traditional sources, particularly fuel wood. Nepal relies heavily on hydropower, but its tremendous potential for increasing hydroelectric output is limited by difficult terrain, lack of infrastructure, and insufficient capital investment.

Services are 36.7 percent of the GDP, divided among finance and real estate (27 percent); trade, restaurants, and hotels (25.8 percent); community and social services (24.3 percent); and transportation, communication, and storage (22.8 percent). The government's strong influence over many major financial institutions is a major reason for the sector's poor performance. Foreign investment is low. The government has major shareholdings in the two largest commercial banks, which possess 50 percent of total banking assets and thus provide the state a near monopoly on credit. These banks have operated at a loss for years.

Tourism is an important component of the economy, but the security situation has hurt the industry. Since the early 1990s, the government has abolished travel restrictions in some remote areas, constructed numerous tourist centres, and allowed access to 263 mountains. Most goods come either from or through India. Trade disputes with India have exacerbated a perpetual trade deficit and reduced Nepalese exports to India. Nepal's imports of goods and services grew to US$1.8 billion in 2004. Increases in oil costs have been a major contributor to growth in imports. Imports of goods and services have averaged 20.7 percent between 1965–2004. Major imports include petroleum products, textiles, vehicles, fertilizer, crude palm oil, and machinery. More than 50 percent of imports come from India. Other important sources of imports are Singapore, China, Malaysia, and Indonesia.

Exports of goods and services stood at US$712 million in 2004. Major exports include garments, carpets, grain, vegetable oil (*ghee*), pashmina wool, jute goods, and leather goods. Approximately 50 percent of exports go to India. Nepal has had a trade deficit every year since 1965. It now stands at about US$1.1 billion—nearly 18 percent of GDP. Nepal's external debt was US$3.5 billion in 2004. Foreign direct investment is mainly from India, with 37 percent of total fixed capital investment. Nepal relies heavily on foreign aid and official development assistance was US$177 million in 2004. The official currency is the Nepalese rupee. For domestic usage, the Nepalese rupee has a fixed exchange rate with the Indian rupee. The two currencies are freely convertible in Nepal but have different international exchange rates.

Although Nepal shares no boundaries with Bangladesh, the two countries are separated by a narrow strip of land about 21 kilometres wide, called the Chicken's Neck. Efforts are underway to make this area a free-trade zone.

Nepal's workforce of about 10 million suffers from a severe shortage of skilled labour. Agriculture employs 81% of the workforce, services 16% and manufacturing/craft-based industry 3%. Agricultural produce—mostly grown in the Terai region bordering India—includes rice, corn, wheat, sugarcane, root crops, milk, and water buffalo meat. Industry mainly involves the processing of agricultural produce, including jute, sugarcane, tobacco, and grain. The spectacular landscape and deep, exotic culture of Nepal represents considerable potential for tourism, but growth in this export industry has been stifled by recent political events. The rate of unemployment and underemployment approaches half of the working-age population. Thus many Nepali citizens move to India in search of work, the Gulf countries and Malaysia being new sources of work. Poverty is acute. Nepal receives US$50 million a year through the Gurkha soldiers who serve in the Indian and British armies and are highly esteemed for their skill and bravery. The total remittance value is worth around 1 billion USD, including money sent from Persian Gulf and Malaysia, who combined employ around 700,000 Nepali citizens.

Nepal's GDP for the year 2005 was estimated at just over US$39 billion (adjusted to Purchasing Power Parity). Per-capita income is less than US$ 300. Nepal's exports of mainly carpets, clothing, leather goods, jute goods and grain total $822 million. Import commodities of mainly gold, machinery and equipment, petroleum products and fertilizer total US$2 bn. India (53.7%), the US (17.4%), and Germany (7.1%) are its main export partners. Nepal's import partners include India (47.5%), the United Arab Emirates (11.2%), China (10.7%), Saudi Arabia (4.9%), and Singapore (4%).

Infrastructure

Nepal's transportation system is poor. The mountainous terrain physically constrains development of the transportation network, and the government has lacked funds to maintain, improve and expand the transportation infrastructure, which has thus relied heavily on foreign funding. The transportation infrastructure is concentrated in the central and eastern parts of the Terai. Roads are Nepal's principal transportation mode. The total road length is 17,217 kilometres, including 4,781 kilometres paved, 4,703 kilometre gravel-covered, and 7,643 kilometres classified as fair weather roads.

Nepal's railroad system is small, outdated, and declining in use and quality. Two rail lines link to railheads in India. The passenger traffic is about 1.7 million per year and freight traffic, 21 tons. The railroad has lost money for years because of low fares, overstaffing, and political intervention. Civil aviation has been slow to develop. In 2005 Nepal had 44 airports of varying standards and only one international airport, Tribhuvan, near Kathmandu. The number of international tourists arriving by air was 288,356 in 2004.

Telecommunications are generally poor in quality and available mostly in Kathmandu. The Nepal Telecommunications Authority (NTA) established in 1998 regulates and promotes competition. By 2005 there were 144 licensed telecommunications providers, and the number of fixed telephone lines increased to 448,639. The waiting list for a telephone line is lengthy, only 3.1 of every 100 citizens had access to any type of telephone and nearly 50 percent of village development areas did not have a single public phone. In July 2005, Nepal had 248,820 mobile telephone subscribers and approximately 225,000 Internet users.

Government and Politics

The movement in April 2006 brought about a change in the nation. The autocratic King was forced to give up power. The dissolved House of Representatives was restored. The House of Representatives formed a government which had successful peace talks with the Maoist Rebels. An interim constitution was promulgated and an interim House of Representatives was formed with Maoist members. The number of seats were also increased to 330. The peace process in Nepal made a giant leap in April 2007, when the Communist Party of Nepal (Maoist) joined the interim government of Nepal. The peace process seems to be in jeopardy after Maoists decided to leave coalition government on 18 September 2007, demanding the declaration of a republic before the scheduled constituent assembly.

Executive Branch: Executive power is held by the Council of Ministers, which is headed by the prime minister. The Council of Ministers is responsible for the general administration of the country. The Council of Ministers has a central secretariat consisting of 22 ministries and the secretariat of the National Planning Commission.

Legislative Branch: Nepal's legislature consists of a bicameral parliament. The lower house of parliament, the House of Representatives (Pratinidhi Sabha), has authority over the Council of Ministers and is regarded as the more powerful of the two houses. It has 205 members directly elected for five-year terms. The prime minister is the leader of the majority party and the country's chief executive. The upper house, the National Council (Rashtriya Sabha), has 60 members, appointed or indirectly elected to six-year terms.

Judicial Branch: The 1990 constitution is the fundamental law of the land and establishes a three-tier court system consisting of 75 district courts, 16 appellate courts, and the Supreme Court. Village and municipal bodies may exercise quasi-judicial functions for minor offenses. The Supreme Court has a chief justice appointed by the king on the recommendation of the Constitutional Council and 14 judges appointed by the king on the recommendation of the Judicial Council, which also appoints appellate and district court judges. The judiciary is widely regarded as becoming more autonomous, but it suffers from large case backlogs, insufficient finances and personnel, political intervention, poor demarcation of jurisdiction between courts, and biases based on caste and economic status.

Administrative Divisions: Nepal is divided into 14 zones and 75 districts, grouped into 5 development regions. Each district is headed by a fixed chief district officer responsible for maintaining law and order and coordinating the work of field agencies of the various government ministries. The 14 zones are:

Bagmati	Lumbini
Bheri	Mahakali
Dhawalagiri	Mechi
Gandaki	Narayani
Janakpur	Rapti
Karnali	Sagarmatha
Koshi	Seti

Provincial and Local Government: Government below the national level is complex, evolving, and a highly debated political topic. All administrative divisions have one or more governing bodies, and members are directly elected, indirectly elected, or appointed by the central government.

Foreign Relations: Nepal's foreign policy has been directed toward preserving autonomy and addressing domestic economic and security issues. Nepal's most substantive international relations are with international economic institutions, such as the Asian Development Bank, the International Monetary Fund, the World Bank, and the South Asian Association for Regional Cooperation. The country also maintains strong political relations with India and China, usually attempting to balance one against the other. Relations with India are fraught with trade and border disputes and Indian suspicions that Nepalese and Pakistani rebels use Nepal as a haven to attack India. Relations with Bhutan have been strained since 1992 over the nationality and possible repatriation of refugees from Bhutan.

Culture

Nepalese culture has been largely shaped by Indian culture to the south and Tibetan to the north. Similarities can be observed in the clothing, way of life, language and food. A typical Nepalese meal is dal-bhat, a kind of a lentil soup served with rice and vegetables. This is consumed twice daily, usually in the morning and shortly after sunset. Between these main meals, snacks such as chura (beaten rice) and tea are consumed. Meat, eggs, and fish are also consumed, particularly in the mountainous regions, where the diet tends to be richer in protein. Rakshi, a millet-based alcoholic drink, is a popular traditional drink.

Folklore is an integral part of Nepalese society. Traditional stories are rooted in the reality of day-to-day life—tales of love, affection, battles, and demons and ghosts; they reflect and explain local lifestyles, cultures and belief systems. Many Nepalese folktales are enacted in dance and music. The Newar people are well-known for masked dances that tell stories of the gods and heroes. Music is percussion-based, sometimes with flutes or shawm accompanying the intense, nasal vocal lines. Musical styles are a variety of pop, religious and folk music, among other styles. Musical genres from Tibet and India have had a strong influence on traditional Nepalese music. Women, even of the musician castes, are less likely than men to play music, except in specific situations such as traditional all-female wedding parties.

Houses in rural parts of Nepal are made up of bamboo cowdung and earth. The sarangi, a four-stringed, hand-carved instrument is usually played by wandering minstrels. In recent times, Nepali rock or rock music, sung to Nepali lyrics, has become popular among youth. Soccer is the most popular sport, followed by cricket and kabaddi. The Martyrs Soccer League is the national soccer championship.

Armed Forces

Nepal's military consists of the Royal Nepalese Army which includes the Royal Nepalese Army Air Service, (the air force unit under it), and the Nepalese Police Force. Service is voluntary and the minimum age for enlistment is 18 years. Nepal spends $99.2 million (2004) on its military—1.5% of its GDP. Most of the equipment and arms are supplied by the India.

Nepal has close ties with both of its neighbours, India and China. In accordance with a long standing treaty, Indian and Nepalese citizens may travel to each others' countries without a passport or visa. Nepalese citizens may work in India without legal restriction. Although Nepal and India typically have close ties, from time to time Nepal becomes caught up in the problematic Sino-Indian relationship. India considers Nepal as part of its realm of influence, and views Chinese aid with concern. Some Indians consider Nepal to be part of a greater pan-Indian state, an attitude that has caused Nepalese antagonism towards India. In 2005, after King Gyanendra took over, Nepalese relations with India, the US, and the UK have worsened. These three foreign countries have been vociferous opponents to the crackdown on civil liberties in Nepal.

National Security

Nepal has only one military service, the Royal Nepalese Army (RNA). The army's stated purpose is to protect Nepal from external threats, but because its capabilities are far smaller than those of neighboring China and India, the government historically has used diplomacy rather than force to maintain territorial integrity. The RNA has been mostly involved in ceremonial functions, international peacekeeping, and supporting the monarchy against domestic opposition. The army also is engaged in domestic non-combat activities, such as infrastructure development, nature conservation, and disaster relief. The RNA's limited resources have constrained its ability to protect infrastructure from the Maoists, and the defense budget has increased substantially since 2000. Nepalese serve in both the British and Indian armies. Nepal faces no threats from another country's regular military forces.

The Ministry of Defense budgeted approximately US$149.8 million for FY2006, but its expenditures exceeded this amount. The prestigious reputation of Nepalese soldiers is due in no small part to their foreign service. The Indian army has 40,000 Nepalese, and approximately 3,300 Nepalese serve in the British Army's Brigade of Gurkhas.

There are allegations that Nepalese territory is used as a haven by Islamic militants either from or supported by Pakistan and al Qaeda. It is unclear whether they militants pose a threat to Nepalese security or are primarily a threat to India. Unquestionably, the civil conflict has been the gravest threat to Nepal's internal security and tourism, banking, social services, and physical infrastructure have suffered considerably. The Communist Party of Nepal (Maoist)—CPN(M)— led by Pushpakamal Dahal, alias Prachanda, and Babu Ram Bhattarai have stated goals that include establishment of a constituent assembly to draft a new constitution, land reform, establishment of Nepal as a secular nation, termination of several treaties with India, and abolition of untouchability.

PAKISTAN

The Islamic Republic of Pakistan is located in the Indian sub-continent. Pakistan borders Iran to the southwest, Afghanistan to the west and north, China to the northeast, and India to the east. The Arabian Sea marks Pakistan's southern boundary. Pakistan's exact size is debated because of its disputed border with India. According to the United Nations, the country has a total area of 796,095 square kilometres. This figure, however, does not include the Pakistan-administered portions of Jammu and Kashmir and the Northern Areas, with areas of 11,639 square kilometres and 72,520 square kilometres, respectively.

Pakistan proclaimed independence on 14 August 1947, from Britain. Pakistan's flag is green with a narrow vertical white band on its left side. A white crescent and star are in the center of the green band. Green signifies the Muslim majority, white denotes minorities, the crescent represents progress, and the star symbolizes light and knowledge.

Pakistan shares borders with Afghanistan (2,430 kilometres), China (523 kilometres), India (2,912 kilometres), and Iran (909 kilometres). Afghanistan disputes the legitimacy of its border with Pakistan, and at times Afghanistan's governments have argued that all Pashtun (Pakhtun) territory in Afghanistan and Pakistan should be under Afghan control. Pakistan and India have disputed possession of Jammu and Kashmir since 1947, and the issue remains unresolved despite numerous cease-fire agreements. Jammu and Kashmir is split between the two countries by a border called the Line of Control. Pakistan's coastline totals 1,064 kilometres along the Arabian Sea.

Pakistan has seven cities with a population of 1 million or more. Karachi (9,339,023), Lahore (5,143,495), Faisalabad (2,008,861), Rawalpindi (1,409,768), Multan (1,197,384), Hyderabad (1,166,894), and Gujranwala (1,132,509).

History

Existing archaeological evidence suggests that humans lived in what became Pakistan around 2.2 million years ago, and the first civilization in South Asia, the Harappan Civilization, is believed to have started around 3000 B.C. in the Indus River valley. Indus civilizations endured until around 1750 B.C., when nomadic tribes from Central Asia called Aryans conquered much of the Indus Valley. The Aryans maintained a system of social stratification based on inherited occupation and physical separation of themselves from native peoples, and this system was justified religiously in scripts called Vedas that form the basis of Hinduism. By 326 B.C., Chandra Gupta Maurya established the first empire in South Asia, but it was his grandson, Ashoka, who led the Mauryan Empire to political prominence around 200 B.C. In the following centuries, various powers exercised control in the subcontinent, although most only temporarily maintained dominance over particular regions.

Around 711 A.D. the Arab general Muhammad bin Qasim introduced Islam into Sindh, and by the 10th century, Islam was further promoted by the Turkish sultan Mahmud of Ghazni, who controlled Punjab. By the 13th century, a succession of Turkic rulers known as the Mughals ruled most of India, and their influence on architecture, cuisine, and language endures. However, Mughal rule eventually suffered from numerous difficulties in controlling a large land area with distinct economies and cultures. One notable challenge to Mughal rule came from Sikh rulers who took control of the Punjabi capital Lahore in 1761. The Sikh ruler, Ranjit Singh, eventually controlled vast areas of Punjab by 1818 and Kashmir by 1819 but, after his death in 1840, the British took advantage of the dissipation of Sikh power and ended Sikh rule by 1849.

The British East India Company initially administered most of the Indian subcontinent, but the Indian-led Sepoy Rebellion of 1857 seriously challenged British occupation and caused the British government to administer India directly. This near defeat for the British prompted changes in their administration of the subcontinent and in their attitudes toward Indians, particularly Muslims. Prior to 1857, Muslims were prominent in economics and administration, and Muslim leaders are believed to have led the Sepoy Rebellion to regain the political and economic advantages enjoyed under Mughal rule. The British responded by dropping Urdu and Persian as official languages and replacing them with English, thus rendering many Muslims functionally illiterate and unemployable. The British also placed Hindus in many positions previously occupied by Muslims. As a result, Muslims perceived Hindus as accomplices to the British oppression of Muslims, and this impression has endured.

Muhammad Iqbal conceived the concept of a Muslim homeland called Pakistan ("Land of the Pure") in the 1920s, but the establishment of Pakistan was most advanced by Mohammad Ali Jinnah, a Bombay lawyer who proved to be a shrewd leader of the Muslim League political party. Jinnah claimed that India contained two nations, one Hindu and one Muslim, and that Muslims could not safely exist in a Hindu-dominated India. The degree to which Jinnah's objectives were motivated by religion is still debated, but his ideas resonated with Muslims who felt politically, economically, and socially discriminated against and with Muslims having theological interests in an Islamic state.

World War II and widespread resistance to British rule in India created burdens that the British found too costly to bear, and in July 1947 the British announced their intention to withdraw from India. Pakistan was born as a bifurcated state in August 1947, divided by 1,600 kilometres of Indian soil and by economic and social divisions between a largely Bengali East Wing and a heavily Punjabi and Sindhi West Wing. The country also faced problems with absorbing millions of Muslim refugees from India, addressing substantial poverty, and establishing both a functioning government and a sense of national unity over a geographically and ethnically divided state.

The founding fathers, Mohammad Ali Jinnah and Liaquat Ali Khan, passed away by 1951, and their deaths were precursors to the subsequent series of short-lived governments that changed just as often by military coup as by election. Pakistan was initially governed by a Constituent Assembly responsible for drafting a constitution and issuing legislation until the constitution went into force. However, the constitution's drafting was delayed by disagreements over how different regions would be represented and how the state would embody Islamic principles. Legislative paralysis prompted Governor General Ghulam Mohammad to dismiss the Constituent Assembly in 1954. This action is now seen as the beginning of "viceregal" politics in Pakistan, in which the military and civil bureaucracy, not elected officials, govern the country and maintain substantial influence over society and the provinces. A new Constituent Assembly wrote the first constitution in 1956 and reconstituted itself as the Legislative Assembly. However, regional rivalries between East and West Pakistan and ethnic and religious tensions threatened political stability, and on 7 October 1958, President Iskander Mirza disbanded the Legislative Assembly. Later that month, Mirza himself was overthrown by General Mohammad Ayub Khan.

Ayub Khan saw himself as a reformer who would bring much-needed stability to the country, and he started by establishing a system of local governments called Basic Democracies for communities to have meaningful input into politics. But Ayub quickly lost interest and turned toward the civil bureaucracy for policy advice and formation. A new constitution was promulgated in 1962, and it established a weak legislature (the National Assembly) and a president with substantial legislative, executive, and financial powers. Possibly the most notable event of Ayub's tenure was a 17-day war with India in 1965 over the Kashmir dispute. The 1965 war had the unintended consequences of interrupting impressive economic growth and deflating the military's confidence in its own abilities. Amid worsening societal and political problems, substantial popular opposition, and his own declining health, Ayub Khan resigned in 1969.

Subsequently, General Agha Mohammad Yahya Khan became president and chief martial law administrator, and he attempted to reinstitute parliamentary democracy. However, festering tensions over representation in the National Assembly led to civil war between East and West Pakistan in 1971. With Indian assistance, East Pakistan seceded and became the independent nation of Bangladesh. At the same time, India and West Pakistan fought a 14-day war which ended in a cease-fire agreement. Largely as a result of Pakistan's military losses, Yahya resigned in 1971, and Zulfiqar Ali Bhutto was appointed president, becoming the first civilian head of government in nearly two decades.

Bhutto lifted martial law, and a new constitution came into effect in August 1973. The constitution was heavily concerned with the role of Islam, the distribution of power between the federal and provincial governments, and the division of responsibilities between the president and prime minister, the latter assuming greater authority than before. Bhutto nationalized numerous industries, and the government's heavy involvement in the economy would have enduring economic repercussions. The country appeared to be democratizing, but political opposition grew against Bhutto's repression of political opponents and alleged voting irregularities. In July 1977, Bhutto was overthrown, and General Mohammad Zia ul-Haq became chief martial law administrator. Bhutto eventually was sentenced to death on charges of conspiring to murder a political opponent and was executed in 1979.

Zia adapted the structure of Ayub Khan's Basic Democracies to a new system of local governments and also adopted various measures to create an Islamic state. When the Soviet Union invaded Afghanistan in 1979, Pakistan became the recipient of numerous Afghan refugees and large-scale foreign aid from the United States, China, Saudi Arabia, and others. The refugees and financial assistance continued until the war's end in 1989. Zia officially terminated martial law in 1985 by assuming the presidency and reinstating the 1973 constitution. However, he also added the Eighth Amendment, which empowered the president to appoint and dismiss the prime minister and provincial governors and to dissolve the national and provincial legislatures. When Zia died in an airplane crash in August 1988, Benazir Bhutto—head of the Pakistan People's Party (PPP) and daughter of Zulfiqar Ali Bhutto became prime minister. Pakistan thus became the first Muslim country with a female head of government.

Bhutto's government was plagued by ethnic conflict, severe economic problems, and a lack of legislative support. In October 1990, Mian Nawaz Sharif, leader of the Islamic Democratic Alliance (IDA), became prime minister and faced the same problems that troubled Bhutto. In 1993 Bhutto's PPP won the National Assembly, and she once again became prime minister. However, in 1996 President Farooq Leghari dismissed Bhutto on charges of corruption, and in 1997 Nawaz Sharif replaced her. In 1998 India conducted nuclear tests, and two weeks later Pakistan reacted by detonating five nuclear devices. Many countries responded with condemnation and sanctions, but Pakistan felt that it finally possessed sufficient deterrent force against its perennial rival, India. Deterrence failed to hold, however, and in October 1999 India and Pakistan engaged in a limited conflict (the Kargil War), which Pakistan was widely seen as precipitating because of its suspected support of militants who entered Indian-held Kashmir from Pakistani-held Kashmir. The conflict proved to be embarrassing for the government, and, with the economy suffering tremendously, General Pervez Musharraf overthrew Nawaz Sharif in late October 1999.

Musharraf became both president and chief of army staff, and he further consolidated his power through various legal measures. After the 11 September 2001 terrorist attacks in the United States, Musharraf's government benefited from an infusion of economic and military aid, because Pakistan is seen as an important ally in the war on terrorism. However,

Pakistan was widely suspected of complicity in a terrorist attack on India's parliament in December 2001. In an April 2002 national referendum, Musharraf's tenure as president was extended to 2007. In late 2004, Musharraf reneged on a previous commitment to relinquish his position as chief of army staff, much to the chagrin of many secular and religious political parties, who demanded that elections be held in early 2005. Pakistan continues to face many of the same problems that have plagued the country since its inception—government instability, tense relations with India, ethnic tensions, political divisions among provinces, economic dependence on international aid, and weak prospects for democracy. However, Pakistan continues to survive and its society to endure in spite of such difficulties, occasionally exhibiting remarkable flexibility and resilience. Indeed, it is often difficult to tell if Pakistan is on the precipice of disintegration or on the verge of renewal.

Geography

Topography. Pakistan has a diverse array of landscapes spread among nine major ecological zones. Its territory encompasses portions of the Himalayas, Hindu Kush and Karakoram mountain ranges, making it home to some of the world's highest mountains, including K2, which at 8,611 metres above sea level is the world's second highest peak. Inter-mountain valleys make up much of the North-West Frontier Province, and rugged plateaus cover much of Balochistan Province in the west. In the east, expansive, irrigated plains along the Indus River cover much of Punjab and Sindh provinces, which have deserts as well (Cholistan in Punjab, Thar in Sindh).

Principal Rivers. The main rivers are the Indus (2,749 kilometres within Pakistan) and its tributaries. the Chenab (730 kilometres), Ravi (680 kilometres), Jhelum (611 kilometres), and Sutlej (531 kilometres). The navigable portions of these rivers are generally small and unconnected as a result of seasonal variations in water flows and the presence of substantial irrigation structures.

Climate. Most of Pakistan has a generally dry climate and receives less than 250 millimetres of rain per year, although northern and southern areas have noticeable climatic differences. The average annual temperature is around 27°C, but temperatures vary with elevation from –30°C to –10°C during the coldest months in mountainous and northern areas of Pakistan-administered Kashmir to 50°C in the warmest months in parts of Punjab, Sindh, and the Balochistan Plateau. Mid-December to March is dry and cool; April to June is hot, with 25 to 50% relative humidity; July to September is the wet monsoon season; and October-November is the dry post-monsoon season, with hot temperatures nationwide.

Natural Resources. Economically important natural resources include arable land, chromite, coal, copper, fireclay, gypsum, iron, limestone, oil, natural gas, rock salt, and silica sand.

Land Use. More than 40% of the working population is employed in agriculture, yet the per capita amount of agricultural land is declining, and there are significant natural limitations to increasing the quantity of arable land. According to official statistics for 2004, the country's total land area is 79.6 million hectares, but only 59.3 million hectares have been surveyed. Out of the surveyed land area, 24.6 million hectares are classified as not available for cultivation, 3.6 million hectares are forest area, and 9.2 million hectares are unused but believed to be cultivable. Approximately 22 million hectares are used for cultivation, of which nearly 16 million hectares are actually sown, with the remainder left fallow. About 13.5 million hectares of the sown area are irrigated, and 6.5 million hectares are sown more than once per year. Most cultivable and irrigated land is located in the eastern provinces of Punjab and Sindh around the Indus River and its tributaries. Pakistan has an extensive but inefficient canal system for irrigation, and much of the crop area is rain fed, but precipitation tends to be unevenly distributed throughout the year.

Environmental Factors. Numerous environmental problems threaten the economy and the population's health, and there is little indication of their abatement. A 1997 World Bank study estimated the annual cost of Pakistan's environmental problems at US$1.8 billion in health expenditures, reduced labour productivity, and other costs. The availability of natural resources is limited by the dry climate and mountainous terrain, substantial population growth is increasing pressure on the resource base, and resource management has suffered from the emphasis on rapid economic growth and often-unregulated forms of economic productivity. As a result, human transformation of the environment is manifest in several problems. Population growth and poor water infrastructure have reduced per capita water availability from 53,000 cubic metres to 1,200 cubic metres, and heavy reliance on firewood has contributed to the world's second highest rate of deforestation. Poor agricultural practices have led to soil erosion, groundwater degradation, and other problems that have hindered crop output and contributed to health problems for rural communities. Solid waste burning, low-quality fuels, and the growing use of fuel-inefficient motor vehicles have contributed to air pollution that in some cities—such as Islamabad, Lahore, and Rawalpindi—has exceeded levels deemed safe by the World Health Organization. The government has expressed concern about environmental threats to economic growth and social development and, since the early 1990s, has addressed environmental concerns with new legislation and institutions such as the Pakistan Environment Protection Council. Only 0.04% of the government's development budget goes to environmental protection.

Society

Population. Pakistan has a large, mostly rural population with a high rate of growth. The government estimated the population at 152.8 million in December 2004, not including 1.2 million refugees from Afghanistan. The population growth rate expects it to double approximately every 26 years. The population is clustered in the eastern provinces of Punjab and Sindh, which contain 78.6% of the total population.

Demography. Pakistan's fast-growing population has a substantial proportion of youths. In 2004, 40.2% of the population was aged 14 or younger, 55.7% was 15–64 years of age, and only 4.1% of the population was 65 and older. According to Pakistan government statistics, 52% of the population is male.

Ethnic Groups. Ethnic groups in Pakistan generally are categorized according to various combinations of religion, language, and sometimes tribe. Punjabis are the largest linguistic group (44.2% of the population) and often are divided into three occupational castes. Rajputs, Jats, and Arains. Pakhtuns (15.4%) are the dominant ethnic group in the North-West Frontier Province, but Pakhtuns belong to different tribes or kinship groups and have no central governing authority. Sindhis (14.1%) are dominant in Sindh and are divided into occupational and caste groupings. Balochis (3.6%) are dominant in Balochistan and are divided into various eastern and western tribes. Other ethno-linguistic groups include the Siraikis, who live mostly in Punjab; Urdu-speaking Muhajirs, refugees from India and their descendants who migrated to Pakistan during the 1947 partition and are concentrated in Sindh; and Brahuis, a Dravidian language group in Sindh and Balochistan.

Languages. Urdu is the national language and the language of most print media. English has official status and often is regarded as the language of the elite and upwardly mobile. Urdu and English often are used in government and business. Punjabi is the most common language, spoken by 44.2% of the population, followed by Pakhtu (15.2%), Sindhi (14.1%), Siraiki (10.5%), Urdu (7.8%), and Balochi (3.8%). Smaller linguistic groups include the Hindko in the North-West Frontier Province, the Farsi-speaking Hazaras of Balochistan, and the Brahuis in Sindh and Balochistan. Language often articulates ethnic identity, and provincial boundaries are linguistically based. Urdu has been promoted as a means of unifying ethnic groups, but it is the mother tongue of only the Muhajirs. Furthermore, many groups perceive the establishment of Urdu as the national language as threatening to their employment potential, political participation, and ethnic identity.

Religion. The overwhelming majority of the population (96.3%) is Muslim, of whom approximately 95% are Sunni and 5% Shia. Sunnis and Shias are subdivided into numerous sects. Approximately 1.6% of the population is Hindu, 1.6% is Christian, and 0.3% belongs to other religions, such as Bahaism and Sikhism. Some 0.2% of the population is Ahmadiyya (also known as Qadiani), a small but influential sect that maintains some Islamic beliefs but is considered heretical by orthodox Muslims and is not recognized as Muslim by Pakistani law. The country was founded to promote religious freedom, and the constitution guarantees freedom of religion. However, Islam is the state religion, and the constitution states that religious practice is "subject to law, public order, and morality." The government also has Islamic institutions such as the Federal Shariat Court and the Council of Islamic Ideology, which advise politicians on the congruence of legislation with Islamic injunctions. It is debatable whether the government has established such institutions for religious or political reasons, but the government has promoted Islam as a means of unifying numerous ethnic groups. Nevertheless, political, economic, and religious differences have been manifested in occasionally violent conflicts between religious communities, particularly between Sunni and Shia militias.

Education and Literacy. Pakistan has low indicators of educational attainment, and education has been under-funded for decades. In 2001 the government announced plans to institute universal primary education by 2010 and 78% literacy by 2011. However, more than 50% of the funds for this initiative are expected to come from international donors. During the 1980s and most of the 1990s, public expenditures on education averaged 2.5% of GDP, but have fallen to less than 2% of GDP since 1998. Free primary education is a constitutional right and is compulsory in every province except Balochistan. The education system is designed for 12 years of schooling, with five years in primary school, three in middle school, and four in high school. According to 2001 government figures, the system included 147,736 primary schools, 25,472 middle-level schools, 15,416 high schools and vocational institutions, 352 professional colleges, and 26 universities. In addition to public and private schools, an indeterminate number of mosque-administered madrassas provide free room, board, and theological education, which makes them an attractive option for poor families. Some madrassas are suspected of having links to religious militants, prompting the government to announce its intention of establishing greater regulation over these institutions.

Health. Pakistan's health indicators, health funding, and health and sanitation infrastructure are generally poor, particularly in rural areas. About 19% of the population is malnourished – a higher rate than the 17% average for developing countries—and 30% of children under age five are malnourished. Leading causes of sickness and death include gastroenteritis, respiratory infections, congenital abnormalities, tuberculosis, malaria, and typhoid fever. AIDS is a major health concern, and both the government and religious community are engaging in efforts to reduce its spread. In 2003 there were 68 physicians for every 100,000 persons in Pakistan. According to 2002 government statistics, there were 12,501 health institutions nationwide, including 4,590 dispensaries, 906 hospitals with a total of 80,665 hospital beds, and 550 rural health centers with a total of 8,840 beds. According to the World Health Organization, Pakistan's total health expenditures amounted to 3.9% of GDP in 2001, and per capita health expenditures were US$16. The government provided 24.4% of total health expenditures, with the remainder being entirely private, out-of-pocket expenses.

Welfare. Indicators for education, health, and some other aspects of human development have improved since the early 1990s. Nevertheless, poverty has increased and the country's population growth reduced income growth. The proportion of the population living below the poverty line increased from 34% in 1991 to 44% by 2002, reversing decades of decline. Social service funding and institutions are inadequate to address the development problems faced by much of the Pakistani population. Provincial governments are responsible for providing social services but often lack the financial and institutional resources to do so. Most social services funding comes from the federal government and international aid, but corruption and institutional inefficiencies have hindered programmes designed to alleviate unemployment, poverty, and other social ills. Furthermore, the economic, political, and educational opportunities of women and religious minorities have been limited by persistent discrimination in both government and society.

Economy

Throughout the 1990s, Pakistan's economy suffered for a number of reasons, but from 2002 to 2004 the economy has recovered as a result of changes in government policies and the resumption of international lending. Economic statistics do not reflect the reality of the economy, because official economic data omit the informal economy, which is estimated to equal about 30% of the formal economy. Agriculture employs the greatest proportion of the working population but accounts for less than 25% of GDP. This discrepancy is the result of rapid growth in services and industry since the 1980s, although major industries, such as textiles and sugar, are heavily reliant on agriculture. Since independence, economic growth rates have been impressive but also have fluctuated widely. These fluctuations have occurred largely because successive governments have emphasized different sectors through changes in subsidies, regulations, and state ownership of industry. Furthermore, shifts in international aid and foreign capital flows have influenced economic growth through changes in government spending and budget deficits. Still, from 2002 to 2004 there were surpluses in the current account, inflation was low, and export growth was the highest in almost a decade. Economic liberalization and deregulation began in the early

1980s, and is continuing. The government has shifted from state ownership of many industries and heavy regulation of the private economy to privatization of some state industries, deregulation, facilitation of capital flows, and reforms of the financial system and monetary policy. Still, lax fiscal and monetary policies, infrastructural deficiencies, a poorly developed human resource base, and persistent market distortions that benefit a small elite of landowners, industrialists, and others undercut economic potential.

Agriculture, Forestry, and Fishing. According to official sources, agriculture, livestock, fishing, and forestry produced an estimated 23.3% of GDP for 2004. Employment in this sector has declined as other economic sectors have grown. Approximately 43.1% of the working population was employed in agriculture, forestry, and fishing in 2002, down from 48.3% in 1992, but still the largest proportion of the workforce among all economic sectors. The major crops are wheat, rice, sugarcane, and cotton. Because of the generally arid climate and low soil moisture, agricultural production relies heavily on irrigation, nearly all of which is found in the east, around the Indus River and its tributaries. Agricultural growth has averaged around 4% annually since independence, and from 1947 to 2003 total food crop production increased from 4.7 million tons to 25.9 million tons.

Mining and Minerals. Mining and minerals historically have been a weak economic sector. Since 2000 mining and quarrying have accounted annually for around 1.4% of GDP and employed an estimated 0.1% of the working population. Chromite is the only metallic ore that has been exploited on a commercial scale, but the country has substantial deposits of copper and iron ores as well. Pakistan also has significant deposits of non-metallic ores such as anhydrite, dolomite, gypsum, limestone, marble, and rock salt.

Industry and Manufacturing. Since the mid-1960s, the industrial sector has produced 19 to 25% of GDP, accounting for 24.5% of GDP in 2004. Manufacturing and construction dominate the industrial sector, accounting for around 19% of GDP. Since the 1980s, approximately 17 to 20% of the working population has been employed in the industrial sector (25% in 2004), mostly in manufacturing and construction. Although the industrial base has diversified since independence, the production base depends heavily on textiles and sugar. Manufacturing output is therefore vulnerable to adverse weather conditions and fluctuations in international prices for cotton and sugar. Various liberalization reforms have been pursued since the early 1980s but have been hindered by substantial corruption, frequent raw material shortages, the government's tendency to provide generous concessions to particular sectors (such as sugar refining and yarn spinning), and a burdensome tax structure that has helped promote the development of the informal economy.

Energy. Economic growth, population growth, and rising urbanization have increased energy demand, much of which is met by imported energy sources because of the country's limited domestic energy resources. Traditional resources, such as firewood and dung, are commonly used, particularly in rural areas, and the government plans to reduce firewood consumption by introducing solar power to rural areas. Coal has provided around 5% of total domestic energy supply for decades, but most is of poor quality and generally is used in brick kilns. With regard to nontraditional sources, oil and natural gas have provided around 37 to 43% of total energy supplies each since the late 1970s, and the country is attempting to expand hydropower production. For decades, Pakistan has depended heavily on oil imports, and in 2003 imported oil provided 31.6% of total energy supplies—at a cost of US$3.1 billion. Domestic oil provided 6.7% of total energy supplies, and domestic recoverable petroleum reserves have fallen to less than 50% of their estimated original amount. However, natural gas production nearly doubled to 2.7 million cubic feet per day in FY 2003, providing 43.8% of the total energy supply. The government has considered pipelines that could import around 1.5 billion cubic feet of gas per day, but as of early 2005 these plans were still under review. Hydropower has declined from 17.7% of total energy supply in 1979 to 11.3% in 2003. The government is interested in reversing this trend, but the area with the greatest potential for hydropower expansion (the mountainous north) is difficult to access and would have high transmission costs. Finally, nuclear power production was meagre until the2001 inauguration of the country's second nuclear power facility, and nuclear energy production increased to 1.2% of total energy supply in 2003.

Services. The services sector accounts for about 50% of Pakistan's annual GDP. From 2000 to 2004, transportation, wholesale and retail trade, finance, public administration, defence, and services collectively provided about 52% of GDP. Services alone were about 9 to 10% of GDP. The services sector has suffered from many of the same problems as the industrial sector, such as political corruption and crippling tax rates, and sectoral growth has been limited by a dearth of educational resources and skilled labour.

Tourism. The number of foreign tourists declined throughout the 1990s, as did earnings from foreign tourism. The number of foreign tourists ranged from 80,000 to 180,000 from the mid-1980s to the mid-1990s but dropped to around 70,000 annually thereafter. Pakistan receives about 6% of the foreign tourists who visit South Asia. The decline in foreign tourists is believed to be due to security concerns and lack of government effort to attract tourists.

Labour. Labour figures are difficult to assess, partly because of the large number of workers in the informal economy. According to government statistics for 2004, 30.4% of the total population is in the official, civilian labour force, with 28.1% classified as employed and 2.3% categorized as unemployed. Other figures put the unemployment rate at around 19.7%. A much greater percentage of men (83.1%) than women (16.9%) are active in the official civilian labour force. Agriculture, forestry, and fishing employ the greatest proportion of the civilian labour force (43.1%), followed by "community, social, and personal services" (15%), wholesale and retail trade (14.8%), and manufacturing (13.7%). These percentages have changed little since the 1960s. However, the informal economy employs the majority of workers—about 70% according to government data from 1974 to 2004—with most employed in wholesale and retail trade, manufacturing, or "community, social, and personal services." Child labour is regarded as a prevalent problem. Although the exact number of child labourers is not known, official data indicate that 12.8% of those 10 to 14 years of age are active in the official labour force.

Foreign Economic Relations. Historically, political issues have affected Pakistan's foreign trade and aid. In 1998 the United States and international donors imposed sanctions because of Pakistan's successful nuclear tests. Those sanctions were dropped after the 11 September 2001, terrorist attacks because the United States regarded Pakistan as an important ally against transnational terrorists operating out of Afghanistan.

Balance of Payments. Data varies by source, and from 1993 to 2004 government institutions did not report relevant statistics according to International Monetary Fund guidelines for member states. Pakistan has had balance of payments difficulties for decades, largely as a result of current account deficits due to trade deficits. However, from 2002 to 2004 current account surpluses ranged from US$1.9 billion to US$4.2 billion as trade deficits declined and private transfers increased—particularly remittances from Pakistanis working outside the country. As a result of balance of payments problems, the official currency has declined in value, and the government frequently has had to reschedule debt payments and resort to high-interest emergency borrowing.

External Debt. Estimates of the size of Pakistan's external debt vary by source. However, observers generally believe that the combination of poor tax administration, high government expenditures, and heavy dependence on external funds has resulted in massive fiscal deficits that, at times, have nearly crippled the economy and rendered Pakistan one of the world's most indebted countries. When the United States and international lending agencies imposed sanctions after Pakistan's 1998 nuclear tests, the country was close to defaulting on external obligations. According to the World Bank and the State Bank of Pakistan, Pakistan's total external debt was approximately US$3.4 billion in 1970, US$9.9 billion in 1980, US$20.6 billion in 1990, and US$36.1 billion in 2003 (about 52.6% of the gross domestic product).

Foreign Investment. Since the 1980s, the government has introduced reforms to attract foreign investment. Foreign investment has increased over time, but corruption, civil disorder, and occasional international economic sanctions have acted as major disincentives to investment. According to World Bank figures, foreign direct investment (FDI) in Pakistan increased from US$23 million in 1970 to US$612 million in 2003 (approximately 1% of the 2003 FDI in China). From 2000 to 2003, FDI increased in finance, transport, communications, mining, quarrying, oil, and gas, with the principal sources being Switzerland, the United States, the United Arab Emirates, and the United Kingdom.

Foreign Aid. The economy is heavily dependent on bilateral and multilateral aid, which substantially influences economic growth. Aid flows have been reduced as a result of international sanctions for Pakistan's suspected support of insurgents in Kashmir and for the country's 1998 nuclear tests. However, after 11 September 2001, the United States and other countries dropped economic sanctions against Pakistan because of its potential role in the war on terrorism. Prior to 2000, Pakistan had never completed an International Monetary Fund (IMF) lending programme because of government unwillingness to comply with loan package conditions and political issues such as nuclear weapons tests or difficulties in Kashmir. However, from 2004 Pakistan's relations with the IMF showed marked improvement.

Recently, wide-ranging economic reforms have resulted in a stronger economic outlook and accelerated growth especially in the manufacturing and financial services sectors. There has been great improvement in the foreign exchange position and rapid growth in hard currency reserves in recent years. The 2005 estimate of foreign debt was close to US$40 billion. However, this has decreased in recent years with assistance from the International Monetary Fund (IMF) and significant debt-relief from the United States. Pakistan's gross domestic product, as measured by purchasing power parity (PPP), is estimated to be US$475.4 billion while its per capita income stands at $2,976. Pakistan's GDP growth rates have seen a steady increase over the last 5 years. However, inflationary pressures and a low savings rate, among other economic factors, could make it difficult to sustain a high growth rate, according to some analysts.

The growth of non-agricultural sectors has changed the structure of the economy, and agriculture now only accounts for roughly 20% of the GDP. The service sector accounts for 53% of the country's GDP with wholesale and retail trade forming 30% of this sector. In recent times, the Karachi Stock Exchange has soared, along with most of the world's emerging markets. Large amounts of foreign investments have been made into several industries. The top industries in Pakistan are telecom, software, automotives, textiles, cement, fertilizer, steel, ship building, and more recently, aerospace.

Pakistan has accomplished many engineering feats such as construction of the world's largest earth filled dam Tarbela, the world's twelfth largest dam Mangla, as well as, with collaboration with China, the world's highest international road: the Karakoram Highway. There are also half a dozen additional dams planned such as Kalabagh Dam, Diamer-Bhasha Dam, Munda, Akhori and Skardu Katzara.

In November of 2006 China and Pakistan signed a Free Trade Agreement hoping to triple bilateral trade from $4.2 billion (USD) to $15 billion (USD) within the next five years; Pakistan's annual exports amounted to $20 billion (USD) last year. Pakistan is also home to a thriving arms industry which exports $200 million (USD) annually, mostly defence equipment and arms to countries in the Middle East and South Asia, and its defence officials are hopeful that these exports will surpass $500 million (USD) a year within the next five years.

In keeping with its rapid economic development in recent years, Pakistan registered an economic growth rate of 7 percent in the financial year 2006–07, the fourth consecutive year of seven percent growth.

Infrastructure

Roads. Roads, road traffic, and motor vehicles all have increased substantially since the early 1990s. According to government statistics, from 1994 to 2003 total road length increased from 196,877 to 251,845 kilometres, and highways increased, from 104,001 to 151,028 kilometres. The total number of registered motor vehicles also increased from 3.5 million to 5.2 million, including 2.5 million motorcycles, 1.3 million automobiles, and 178,000 trucks. In the early 1990s, the government announced plans to shift passenger and freight traffic from roads to rail, but by 2004 the declining quality and quantity of rail service continued to prompt increases in private and commercial use of roads.

Railroads. The railroad system is publicly owned, but government funding has been insufficient to maintain the system. Government figures indicate that operating revenues exceeded operating expenses from 1994 to 2003, but the deterioration in the quantity and quality of service suggests that major problems persist. From 1994 to 2003, the quantity of track kilometres fell from 8,775 to 7,791 kilometres, and route kilometres dropped from 12,625 to 11,515 kilometres. Of the track kilometres, 7,346 kilometres were 1.676-millimeter gauge, and 445 kilometres were 1.000-millimeter gauge. Passenger journeys peaked at 85 million in 1989 and declined until 1999, after which they increased to 72.4 million in 2003. Freight tonnage fell from 8 million tons in 1994 to 6.2 million tons in 2003. In the same period, the number of locomotives decreased from 676 to 577, and the quantity of coaches fell from 2,831 to 1,843. Since 1992, various privatization ventures have been terminated and placed back on the market, and the federal government has attempted to transfer responsibility for some rail services to local and provincial authorities. Urban and suburban passenger rail service is often irregular and slower than road transport, but the government plans to build passenger rail systems in Karachi, Lahore, Islamabad, and Rawalpindi. A proposed rail line connecting Pakistan with Iran has been stalled because of a lack of funding.

Ports. According to government statistics, the tonnage handled by ports increased from 30 million tons in 1994 to 41.2 million tons in 2003. In the same period, the number of twenty-foot-equivalent-units (TEUs) increased from 409,670 to 615,826. In 2004 Pakistan had two ports, Karachi and Port Qasim, both of which were upgraded in the 1990s. Karachi handles approximately 60% of import and export cargo and is linked by a daily container train to an inland terminal at Lahore. Port Qasim handles about 40% of import and export cargo. The first phase of a multipurpose port located at Gwadar on the Balochistan coast is operational, with a second phase still under construction. A deepwater port at Keti Bandar, 100 kilometres southeast of Karachi, is planned as part of a private power project.

Civil Aviation and Airports. Since the 1980s, the air network has expanded. Pakistan has 50 airports with permanently surfaced runways. Karachi, Lahore, Peshawar, Quetta, and Rawalpindi handle both international passenger and cargo flights, and Multan and Turbat handle international cargo. The airports in Karachi and Lahore have expanded their facilities since 1994. From 1994 to 2003, international passengers increased from 4.1 million to 5.1 million, and international cargo increased slightly from 1.1 million tons to 1.2 million tons. In the same time period, however, domestic passengers declined from 9.1 million to 5.5 million, and domestic cargo fell from 243,000 tons to 187,000 tons. The major international airline is government-owned Pakistan International Airlines, and four other private airlines offer international passenger and cargo services. Pakistan International Airlines flights to New Delhi beginning in January 2004 have been viewed as a sign of improved relations between India and Pakistan.

Pipelines. The government currently is considering several proposed gas pipelines linking Pakistan with Afghanistan, India, Iran, Turkmenistan, and others. These proposals are still under consideration, partly because the proposed routes would go through areas of periodic civil unrest. Pakistan has a gas pipeline network with coverage of 56,400 km in 1050 towns. It has nearly 1600 CNG stations and the gas throughput in Pakistan is 38 MMSCMD per day. The number of gas customers in Pakistan is estimated at 19 lakh, and Pakistan runs vehicles on CNG whose number is estimated at 15.60 lakh.

Telecommunications. From 1991 to 2002, the estimated number of radios increased only slightly from 10 to 10.2 million, and the estimated number of televisions was unchanged at 2.1 million. The government runs both Azad Kashmir Radio, with three stations, and Pakistan Broadcasting Corporation, with 35 stations. Three private radio stations also are in operation. Government-run Pakistan Television Corporation maintains four domestic television channels, and there are three private television broadcasters. Foreign channels are available by satellite and cable. Domestic phone service is poor. In the early 2000s, Pakistan had approximately 3.7 million telephones, 8 million cellular telephones, 600,000 personal computers, and 500,000 Internet users.

Government and Politics

Overview. The government is based on the much-amended constitution of 1973, which was suspended twice (in 1977 and 1999) and reinstated twice (in 1985 and 2002). According to the constitution, Pakistan is a federal parliamentary system with a president as head of state and a prime minister as head of government. The legislature, or parliament, is the Majlisi- Shoora (Council of Advisers), consisting of the Lower House, which is often called the National Assembly, and the Upper House, or Senate. National Assembly members are directly elected for five-year terms. Senate members are elected by provincial assemblies, with equal representation from each of the four provinces as well as representatives from the Federally Administered Tribal Areas and Islamabad Capital Territory. Both the Senate and National Assembly may initiate and pass legislation, but only the National Assembly can approve federal budgets and finance bills. However, parliament often has had little real political power. For example, in 2003 the only bill passed by the National Assembly was the national budget. Executive power lies with the prime minister and president. The prime minister is an elected member of the National Assembly and is the leader of the National Assembly's dominant party or coalition.

However, the prime minister also is appointed formally by the president. The prime minister is assisted by a cabinet of ministers who are appointed by the president on the prime minister's advice. An electoral college composed of members of the national and provincial legislatures elects the president for a five-year term, and no individual may hold the office for more than two consecutive terms. By law the president must be a Muslim. The president acts on the advice of the prime minister but has the power to prevent passage of non-finance bills and may dissolve the National Assembly if he concludes that the government cannot operate according to the constitution. The Senate, however, cannot be suspended.

Politics in Pakistan often have not operated according to the constitution. The military and Civil Service of Pakistan (CSP) frequently have been the pre-eminent actors in the country's power structure. Moreover, there has been some concern that Pakistan could become a "failed state" because of the apparent inability of any single entity to control the country, the weakened productivity of a population beset by years of economic difficulties, and continuing problems of communal conflict and terrorism. Ethnic and provincial tensions often are manifested in rivalries between political parties, and several governments have been ended by assassination or military coup rather than by formal, electoral change.

Religion has played an important role in politics, and religious differences have been very salient in Pakistani government and civil society. The government has consistently been faced with tensions of whether and how to synthesize Islamic principles into an essentially secular and Western form of government. Religious differences among politically influential actors have become increasingly prominent since the early 1980s, when politics became more religiously oriented under the rule of General Zia ul-Haq (1977–88). As religious groups' access to government resources increased, groups competed for political resources and the capacity to promote their approach to Islam, and sectarian divisions often became violent.

Administrative Divisions. Pakistan has four provinces—Balochistan, North-West Frontier Province, Punjab, and Sindh—and numerous federally administered areas. Provincial boundaries correspond with areas of numerically dominant linguistic groups, and provinces are divided into a total of 26 divisions that are further subdivided into 101 districts. Federally administered areas include the capital (Islamabad) and 13 Federally Administered Tribal Areas (FATAs).

Provincial and Local Government. Each province has a governor appointed by the president, and provinces also have an elected legislative assembly and a chief minister who is the leader of the legislative assembly's majority party or coalition. The chief minister is assisted by a council of ministers chosen by the chief minister and formally approved by the governor. Federally administered areas also have their own legislative entities, which have had less autonomy from the federal government than provincial legislatures. However, tribal areas in the west have traditional legal systems that operate independently of the federal government. Various regimes have promoted local-level Basic Democracies so that communities can have input into federal policy, but these entities have suffered from inconsistent federal government support. Although provinces and federally administered areas have their own political and administrative institutions, federal government agencies are heavily involved in the affairs of these areas. There are some matters over which both federal and provincial governments can make laws and establish departments for their execution. For example, provincial governments administer agricultural and social services, but the federal government legislates on these matters, and federal agencies also are involved in their administration. Moreover, the federal government has the power to dismiss provincial chief ministers and legislatures.

Judicial and Legal System. The legal system is derived from English common law and is based on the much-amended 1973 constitution and Islamic law (sharia). The Supreme Court, provincial high courts, and other courts have jurisdiction over criminal and civil issues. The president appoints the Supreme Court's chief justice and formally approves other Supreme Court justices as well as provincial high court judges on the advice of the chief justice. The Supreme Court has original, appellate, and advisory jurisdiction, and high courts have original and appellate jurisdiction. The Federal Shariat Court determines whether laws are consistent with Islamic injunctions. Special courts and tribunals hear particular types of cases, such as drugs, commerce, and terrorism. Pakistan's penal code has limited jurisdiction in tribal areas, where law is largely derived from tribal customs.

The 1973 constitution guarantees freedom of speech, press, and religion as well as the right to bail, counsel, habeas corpus, representation, appeal, and numerous other protections. However, the government has constitutional authority to limit civil liberties in accordance with Islamic doctrine, national security, and other circumstances. Pakistani courts can impose the death penalty, and some crimes are punishable by stoning, lashing, or amputation, although these punishments rarely occur outside of tribal areas. The judiciary has limited independence from the executive branch, and the legislative and executive branches often attempt to remove themselves from judicial oversight. The judiciary also suffers from low public credibility, large case backlogs, corruption, and a lack of resources.

Electoral System. Pakistan has universal adult suffrage, and those 18 years of age and older are eligible to vote. As of 2005, there were 72 million registered voters. The minimum age of candidates is 25 years of age for national and provincial assemblies, 30 for the Senate, and 45 for president. The president sets election dates, and the Election Commission (EC) conducts national and provincial assembly elections, but the EC's chair, the chief election commissioner, oversees elections for local governments, the Senate, and the presidency. The EC is an independent, financially autonomous body, but it has been criticized as having little power to enforce codes of conduct on political parties and candidates. Constituencies are demarcated by population, administrative boundaries, and other factors. In 2002 there were 357 constituencies for the National Assembly and 728 constituencies for provincial assemblies. Sixty seats in the National Assembly and 128 in the provincial assemblies are reserved for women. In addition, 10 seats in the National Assembly and 23 in the provincial assemblies are reserved for non-Muslims. Domestic and international observers have criticized recent elections as flawed.

Politics and Political Parties. Political parties have increased in number but declined in political power, particularly in relation to the military. Since the late 1990s, numerous parties have splintered into factions, dividing electoral support and leading to the formation of coalitions that often also dissolve into factions. The three parties with the greatest electoral support since 1988 all have become shadows of their former selves. The Pakistan People's Party (PPP) and Pakistan Muslim League-Nawaz Sharif (PML-N) have splintered into numerous parties, and the Muttahida Quami Movement (MQM) has lost substantial legitimacy as a result of involvement in violence. Officially, 73 parties contested the 2002 National Assembly elections, but only 3% of voters were registered as members of a political party. As a result of elections in 2002, a coalition led by the Pakistan Muslim League-Quaid-e-Azam (PML-Q) assumed control of provincial assemblies in Punjab and Sindh and the National Assembly. This party has been closely associated with the government of General Musharraf. Parties often have no constitutions, membership lists, or documentation of funding sources. Furthermore, electoral support is rarely nationwide and most often is drawn from particular religious, ethnic, or regional bases. The military has given financial support to religious parties as a counterweight to secular parties, but electoral support for religious parties has been well below 10% nationwide. Many parties have separate wings for women and youth, and many are accused of having militias that collect funds and intimidate opponents.

Mass Media. In the early 21st century, the amount of print media in Pakistan declined precipitously while total circulation increased. From 1994 to 1997, the total number of daily, monthly, and other publications increased from 3,242 to 4,455 but had dropped to just 945 by 2003 with most of the decline occurring in Punjab Province. However, from 1994 to 2003 total print circulation increased substantially, particularly for dailies (3 million to 6.2 million). Print media are published in 11 languages, but most are published in Urdu and Sindhi, and English language publications are numerous. The press generally publishes free from censorship and has played an active role in national elections, but journalists often exercise self-censorship as a result of arrests and intimidation by government and societal actors. Most print media are privately owned, but the government controls the National Press Trust, a major newspaper publisher, and the Associated Press of Pakistan, one of the two major news agencies. The constitution guarantees the rights of free speech and press but also allows for government restrictions in cases of offenses against Islam, public morality, national security, and other circumstances. In fact, the government can fine and imprison those who broadcast material that is deemed inconsistent with "national and social values."

Foreign Relations. Pakistan's primary foreign policy objectives are protection from external threats and the preservation of territorial integrity. Foreign alliances often have been based on mutual—and sometimes ephemeral—strategic interests. Contentious relations with India dominate foreign relations and are largely due to perennial tensions over Kashmir, which was the basis of wars in 1948, 1965, 1971, and 1999. Various talks have eased tensions but not mutual suspicions. China has perhaps been Pakistan's most consistent ally because of shared antipathies of other countries, such as India and Russia, but in the 1990s

China assumed a more distant relationship as a result of India's growing military prowess, Russia's military decline, and other factors. However, China is alleged to have supplied Pakistan with nuclear weapons material, ostensibly to counter India's nuclear weapons. Relations with Afghanistan have been harmonious and tense, often simultaneously. The two countries have a disputed border, but Pakistan supported insurgents in Afghanistan against Soviet occupation in the 1980s and was a key ally of the Taliban in the 1990s. Since their 1971 war, Pakistan and Bangladesh typically have had close ties based largely on shared opposition to India. Relations with Islamic Middle Eastern countries generally have been close, but ties with largely Shia Iran have been strained. For countries outside South Asia and the Middle East, relations generally are based on Pakistan's perceived strategic value in the international system. Pakistan's successful nuclear tests in 1998 initially led to international sanctions that were later eased as a result of concerns that an economically weakened Pakistan might provide nuclear material to other nations. After 11September 2001, the United States and other countries saw Pakistan as an important ally in fighting international terrorists operating in Afghanistan, and international aid increased substantially. Pakistan's relations with the United States have resumed the closeness of the 1980s. However, Pakistan's improved relations with the United States have had important ramifications for the government's domestic support, particularly among some religious parties who perceive the government as acting against Islamic injunctions.

Membership in International Organizations. Pakistan is an active participant in international organizations, although its membership in the British Commonwealth of Nations was suspended from 1999 to 2004 because of the military coup. Pakistan views international organizations as a means of addressing the actions of relatively stronger countries and often appeals to international organizations such as the United Nations (UN) on matters such as Kashmir.

Major International Treaties. Pakistan has signed but not ratified the Convention on Fishing and Conservation of Living Resources of the High Seas. It is not a party to either the Treaty on the Non-Proliferation of Nuclear Weapons (NPT) or the Missile Technology Control Regime (MTCR). Pakistan has argued that the NPT and MTCR are not relevant to the country's security concerns because they do not reduce nuclear weapons proliferation by states already possessing nuclear weapons, and they deny non-nuclear states the right to have nuclear weapons.

Armed Forces. The Pakistan Armed Forces consists of approximately 619,000 active personnel in the army (550,000), air force (45,000), and navy (24,000), as well as 513,000 reserves. Under the 1973 constitution, the federal government controls the armed forces, and the president is the commander in chief. The Ministry of Defence has a permanent staff of civil servants headed by the defence secretary general, and the minister of defence is a civilian member of the prime minister's cabinet. The Joint Chiefs of Staff Committee deals with problems concerning military aspects of state security and is charged with integrating and coordinating the army, navy, and air force. The committee's secretariat acts as the principal link between the service headquarters and the Ministry of Defence.

The Directorate for Inter-Services Intelligence (ISI) is of particular importance at the joint services level because it manages covert operations outside of Pakistan and because it has been involved in domestic politics, usually to keep track of the incumbent regime's opponents. The chief of the army staff (COAS) is the key power holder in the armed forces and is also one of the triumvirate that runs the country, along with the prime minister and president. The COAS usually operates from army headquarters in Rawalpindi. The military is forbidden constitutionally from acting independently of the elected political leadership in domestic matters. However, from 1947 to 2004 military generals have acted as head of state for nearly 30 years, and in times of civilian government the armed forces have routinely intervened on domestic and foreign policy issues. The military justifies its consistent involvement in politics as protection from malign foreign interests and corrupt and incompetent politicians. Although public opinion surveys are rare, it appears that the public dislikes military rule, yet consistently has a more favourable view of the military than of elected officials.

Because the military conducts its affairs with carefully defended secrecy, the degree to which army officers and personnel are religiously motivated is debated. However, Western analysts tend to conclude that whereas the military increasingly sees itself as serving Islam, the institution's decision making is still largely secular. Military intervention in politics is designed to limit civilian involvement in sensitive matters, such as Kashmir, nuclear disarmament, internal military personnel decisions, and defence spending. The military also is extensively involved in the economy, and military enterprises produce approximately 3% of the gross national product. Military enterprises include the Army Welfare Trust (AWT), whose assets include the Askari Bank, one of the country's largest financial institutions, and the Fauji Foundation, which is the country's biggest conglomerate. These and other military financial institutions often are exempt from taxes and regulations covering the manufacturing sector and asset disclosure.

With regard to military strategy, the military's budget and personnel have reduced strategy to largely defensive objectives, such as limited offensive tactics in bordering areas (particularly Kashmir), use of irregular forces, and deterring and countering possible attacks from foreign powers (particularly India). The military's history of far lower military expenditures and capabilities than India has prompted the military to attempt to impose high costs on India to force its withdrawal from Kashmir. Furthermore, the military hopes that its nuclear capabilities can reduce the disadvantages of its conventional forces. However, the theoretical deterrence between nuclear powers has not limited military engagement between India and Pakistan—as exemplified by the 1999 Kargil War—and analysts believe that Pakistan's military strategy historically has suffered from overly optimistic assessments of potential success and underestimations of diplomatic and military losses, as well as a lack of contingency planning.

Foreign Military Relations. Pakistan has sought to become an important actor in international politics, but its foreign military alliances often are intended to address matters with bordering countries. Other countries have established alliances with Pakistan to address their own strategic interests in South and Central Asia, and these alliances have tended to be ephemeral. Pakistan's military relationship with China started in the 1970s as a way of countering India, but China has softened its relations since India's military strength has increased. Still, Pakistan and China maintain a military relationship, including periodic joint military exercises. United States aid in the 1980s was significantly reduced after the Soviet Union pulled out of Afghanistan in 1989 but resumed after the 11 September 2001, terrorist attacks. Moreover, in March 2004 the United States granted Pakistan status as a major non-North Atlantic Treaty Organization ally, which provides access to U.S. military equipment and cooperation. In fact, the United States is one of the largest suppliers of military equipment to Pakistan along with China and Russia. Pakistan's military relations with India have been contentious, and the two countries fought a limited conflict in Kashmir in 1999. However, under the 1999 Lahore Agreement the two countries provide each other with advance notification of missile tests, and in 2003 and 2004 they engaged in several high-level discussions that have eased tensions.

External Threat. The military and public generally view India as the nation's primary security threat, and opposition to India is often a greater source of social cohesion than either Islam or Urdu. India's far greater military capabilities have been a source of both fear and frustration, and many suspect that this imbalance has prompted Pakistan to engage Indian forces indirectly through supporting insurgents morally, financially, or otherwise. India is not the country's only security concern, as Pakhtun and Balochi irredentist movements in Pakistan's western provinces have contributed to sometimes-tense relations with neighbouring Afghanistan.

Defence Budget. According to World Bank figures for 1988 to 2005, Pakistan's military expenditures represented 25–29% of central government expenditures and 6–7% of gross national income. Historically, Pakistan's governments have used defence spending to stimulate economic growth.

Major Military Units. The army, with 550,000 active personnel and 500,000 reserves, is organized into nine corps located at Bahawalpur, Gujranwala, Karachi, Lahore, Mangla, Multan, Peshawar, Quetta, and Rawalpindi. The Northern Area Command is headquartered at Gilgit and is directly responsible to army general headquarters. The army has 2 armoured divisions, 19 infantry divisions including 1 area command, 9 corps artillery brigades, 26 independent brigades (7 armoured, 1 mechanized, 6 infantry, 5 artillery, and 7 engineer), 3 armored reconnaissance regiments, 1 special forces group, and 1 air defence command. The navy has 24,000 active personnel—including 1,400 marines and 2,000 in the Maritime Security Agency—and 5,000 reserves. The navy has four commands. fleet, logistics, naval installations in the north of Pakistan, and fleet headquarters at Karachi, the nation's only major naval base. Two bases are under construction at Gwadar and Ormara. The air force has 45,000 active personnel and 8,000 reserves. Air force headquarters in Rawalpindi has directorates for operations, electronics, administration, and maintenance. The air force has three regional air commands. Northern (in Peshawar), Central (Sargodha), and Southern (Faisal).

Military Service. Military service is voluntary, and active-service personnel are liable for duty eight years after active service ends. Officers are obligated to serve until 50 years of age, other ranks until 45 years of age. Women serve in the military but are a numerical minority.

Paramilitary Forces. The central government (specifically the Ministry of Interior) controls the coast guard, paramilitary forces, and numerous specialized police agencies, such as the Federal Investigative Agency and railroad and airport police forces. However, provincial governments organize paramilitary forces, which often act as an extension of the army to assist provincial police in internal security matters. In addition, senior government officials often have strong control over security forces and have at times established personal security forces. The largest paramilitary organization is the 185,000-member National Guard, which comprises the National Cadet Corps, the Women Guards, and the Janbaz Force. The Frontier Corps reportedly has 65,000 members and is responsible for Balochistan and the North-West Frontier Province. The Pakistan Rangers has 35,000 to 40,000 members and deals with unrest in Punjab. The Northern Light Infantry has an estimated 12,000 members, and the Maritime Security Agency, which is under the navy's direction, has an estimated 2,000 personnel.

Foreign Military Forces. Pakistan hosts 45 military observers from nine countries stationed in Jammu and Kashmir under the United Nations Military Observer Group in India and Pakistan. U.S. military forces work with Pakistan's military against insurgents supporting the Taliban and al Qaeda in areas of Pakistan bordering Afghanistan.

Police. Provincial governments are charged with police administration in their respective jurisdictions, and provincial police forces operate independently. The federal government is largely uninvolved in provincial police administration but controls police in federally administered and tribal areas. The federal minister of interior supervises police nationwide, and the Police Service of Pakistan (PSP) selects, trains, and assigns senior officers to provincial or central government agencies. Although service in the PSP is competitive and well paid, lower ranking police personnel often have accused of routine extortion, violating civil liberties, and acting to preserve the tenure of government officials rather than the rule of law. The quantity of overall crime and various types of crime (such as murder and banditry) have increased steadily over the years, and the extensive availability and use of automatic weapons in Pakistani society is often referred to as the "Kalashnikov Culture." The population generally does not perceive the police to be effective against crime or publicly accountable.

Internal Security and Terrorism. Pakistan has numerous categories of terrorism and internal threats, with most insurgent groups identifying themselves as religious or ethnic separatists. Some political parties represent distinct religious and ethnic communities, and rivalries among these parties have been violent. Violence between religiously identified groups is rarely based solely on differing religious doctrines but rather the different social, political, and economic statuses that correlate with religion. Some Islamic militias have connections to the Taliban and al Qaeda, which was linked to two assassination attempts on President Musharraf in December 2003. Militant organizations have some influence on Pakistan's foreign policy, and militants in Pakistan (such as Harkat-ul-Ansar) have assisted militant organizations in countries whose governments are perceived as oppressing Muslims. There are also concerns that Pakistan's nuclear arsenal could be seized by insurgents in an event such as a coup or assassination of the nation's president. However, the government claims that it has enacted security measures to prevent such a threat and that the numerical and political superiority of religious moderates over religious extremists is a substantial obstacle to the latter's access to Pakistan's nuclear weapons.

The most significant violence between religious groups is between Islamic militias, the Shia militia Sipah-e-Mohammed Pakistan (SMP, "Army of Mohammed") and the Sunni militias Sipah-e-Sahaba Pakistan (SSP, "Army of the Friends of the Prophet") and Lashkar-e-Jhangvi (LeJ, "Army of Jhangvi"). The violence has, at times, disrupted both civil order and the economies in areas of Sindh and Punjab provinces. The violence has resulted in large part from the influx of weapons and returning mujahideen from Afghanistan, as well as financial support from large landowners, drug lords, and some political parties. Tensions between ethnic groups often stem from perceptions that other ethnic groups dominate politics and economics to the detriment of minority ethnicities. The Muhajir Quami Movement (MQM) was involved in substantial conflict in the 1980s and early 1990s but has since been far more quiescent as a result of internal factionalism and an apparent lack of motivating doctrine. The only other significant ethnic violence involves secessionists in Balochistan, who contend that the government is appropriating the province's mineral wealth while providing little economic benefit in return. There are also long-suspected connections of foreign-sponsored subversion, such as Indian support of Sindhi dissidents and Iranian ties to Shia and Balochi militants.

Human Rights. The government's human rights record is generally regarded as poor by domestic and international observers, although there have been some improvements since 2000. Security forces use excessive and sometimes lethal force and are complicit in extrajudicial killings of civilians and suspected militants. The police and military have been accused of engaging in physical abuse, rape, and arbitrary arrest and detention, particularly in areas of acute conflict. Although the government has enacted measures to counter these problems, abuses continue. Furthermore, courts suffer from lack of funds, outside intervention, and deep case backlogs that lead to long trial delays and lengthy pretrial detentions. Many observers contend that Pakistan's legal code is largely concerned with crime, national security, and domestic tranquility and less with the protection of individual rights. Provincial and local governments have arrested journalists and closed newspapers that report on matters perceived as socially offensive or critical of the government. Journalists also have been victims of violence and intimidation by various groups and individuals. In spite of these difficulties, the press publishes freely, although journalists often exercise self-restraint in their writing. In 2002 citizens participated in elections for the National Assembly, but those elections were criticized as deeply flawed by domestic and international observers.

Societal actors also are responsible for human rights abuses. Violence by drug lords and sectarian militias claims numerous innocent lives, discrimination and violence against women are widespread, human trafficking is problematic, and debt slavery and bonded labour persist. The government often ignores abuses against children and religious minorities, and government institutions and some Muslim groups have persecuted non-Muslims and used some laws as the legal basis for doing so. The Blasphemy Law, for example, allows life imprisonment or the death penalty for contravening Islamic principles, but legislation was passed in October 2004 to eliminate misuse of the law. Furthermore, the social acceptance of many these problems hinders their eradication. One prominent example is honor killings ("karo kari"), which are believed to have accounted for more than 5,000 deaths from 1998 to 2006. Many view this practice as indicative of a feudal mentality and as an anathema to Islam, but others defend the practice as a means of punishing violators of cultural norms and view attempts to stop it to as an assault on cultural heritage.

SINGAPORE

The Republic of Singapore is a city-state located on the south-central coast of the island of Singapore, but urbanization has taken over most of the territory of the island.

Singapore attained independence from Britain on 31 August 1963 and on 9 August 1965 from the Federation of Malaysia. The Singaporean flag has two equal horizontal bands of red (top) and white; a vertical white crescent (closed portion toward the hoist side), partially enclosing five white-point stars arranged in a circle, positioned near the hoist side of the red band. The red band symbolizes universal brotherhood and the equality of men; the white band, purity and virtue. The crescent moon represents a young nation on the rise, while the five stars stand for the ideals of democracy, peace, progress, justice, and equality.

History

The island of Singapore was known to mariners for centuries. When a succession of maritime states arose throughout the Malay Archipelago, Singapore probably was one of the many trading outposts serving as an entrepôt and supply point for Malay, Thai, Javanese, Chinese, Indian and Arab traders. A 14th century Javanese chronicle referred to the island as Temasek, and a 17th century Malay annal noted the 1299 founding of the city of Singapura ("lion city") after a strange, lion-like beast that had been sighted there. Singapura was controlled by a succession of regional empires and Malayan sultanates.

Portuguese explorers captured the port of Melaka (Malacca) in 1511, forcing the reigning sultan to flee south, where he established a new regime, the Johore Sultanate that incorporated Singapura. The Portuguese burned down a trading post at the mouth of the Temasek (Singapore) River in 1613; after that, the island was largely abandoned and trading and planting activities moved south to the Riau Islands and Sumatra. However, planting activities had returned to Temasek by the early 19th century. In 1818 Temasek was settled by a Malay official of the Johore Sultanate and his followers, who shared the island with several hundred indigenous tribal people and Chinese planters.

In 1819 Sir Thomas Stamford Raffles arrived as the lieutenant governor of the British enclave of Bencoolen (Bengkulu on the west coast of Sumatra) and an agent of the British East India Company. He obtained permission from the local Malay official to establish a trading post. He called it Singapore, after its ancient name, and opened the port to free trade and free immigration on the south coast of the island at the mouth of the Singapore River. At the time, Singapore had about 1,000 inhabitants. By 1827 Chinese had become the most numerous of Singapore's various ethnic groups.

During the 50 years following Raffles's establishment of his free-trade port, Singapore grew in size, population, and prosperity. In 1824 the Dutch formally recognized British control of Singapore, and London acquired full sovereignty over the island. From 1826 to 1867, Singapore, along with two other trading ports on the Malay Peninsula—Penang and Malacca—and several smaller enclaves were ruled together as the Straits Settlements from the British East India Company headquarters in India. In 1867 the British needed a better location than fever-ridden Hong Kong to station their troops in Asia, so the Straits Settlements were made a crown colony and its capital Penang, ruled directly from London. The British installed a governor and executive and legislative councils. By that time, Singapore had surpassed the other Straits Settlements in importance, as it had grown to become a bustling seaport with 86,000 inhabitants. Singapore also dominated the Straits Settlements Legislative Council. After the Suez Canal opened in 1869 and steamships became the major form of ocean transport, British influence increased in the region, bringing still greater maritime activity to Singapore.

In the 20th century, Singapore became a major point of disembarkation for hundreds of thousands of laborers brought in from China, India, the Dutch East Indies, and the Malay Archipelago, bound for tin mines and rubber plantations to the north. Singapore prospered as financial institutions, transportation, communications and government infrastructure expanded rapidly to support the booming trade and industry of the British Empire. Although Singapore was largely unaffected by World War I it experienced the postwar boom and depression as the rest of the world. Along with the influx of Chinese migrants over the previous decades came secret societies and kinship and place-name associations that grew to have great influence on society.

Japan attacked Malaya in December 1941, and by February 1942 the Japanese had taken control of both Malaya and Singapore. They renamed Singapore *Sh Çnan* ("Light of the South") and set about dismantling the British establishment. Singapore suffered greatly during the war, first from the Japanese attack and then from Allied bombings of its harbor facilities. By the war's end, the colony was in poor shape, with a high death rate, rampant crime and corruption, and severe infrastructure damage. During the 1942–45 occupation period, a favorable view of the colonial relationship had lapsed among the local population, as it had in other British colonies, and upon the return of the British, resulted in demands for self-rule. In 1946 Singapore became a separate crown colony with a civil administration.

When the Federation of Malaya was established in 1948 as a move toward self-rule, Singapore continued as a separate crown colony. The same year, the Malay Communist Party launched an insurrection in Malaya and Singapore, and the British declared a State of Emergency that was to continue until 1960. The worldwide demand for tin and rubber had brought economic recovery to Singapore by this time, and the Korean War (1950–53) brought even further economic prosperity to the colony.

In 1953 a British commission recommended partial internal self-government for Singapore. In this milieu, other political parties began to form in 1954. One was the Labour Front led by David Marshall, who called for immediate independence and merger with Malaya. The same year, the People's Action Party (PAP) was established under the leadership of Lee Kuan Yew, a Cambridge-educated lawyer. The PAP also campaigned for an end to colonialism and a merger with Malaya. Following Legislative Assembly elections in 1955, a coalition government was formed with Marshall as chief minister.

In 1957 Malaya was granted independence, and the next year the British Parliament elevated the status of Singapore from colony to state and provided for new local elections. The PAP swept the elections held in May 1959, and Lee Kuan Yew was installed as the first prime minister. The PAP's strongest opponents were communists operating in both legal and illegal organizations. There also were fears that communists within the PAP would seize control of the government, but moderates led by Lee held sway. In 1962 Singaporean voters approved the PAP's merger plan with Malaya, and on 16 September 1963, Singapore joined Malaya and the former British territories on the island of Borneo—Sabah and Sarawak—to form the independent Federation of Malaysia. Only Brunei opted out of the federation.

Between 1963 and 1965, Singapore was an integral part of the Federation of Malaysia. Lee declared Singapore's independence from Britain on 31 August

1963; dissolved the Legislative Assembly; and called for an election to obtain a new mandate for the PAP pro-merger government. Many political opponents of the merger were jailed, and the PAP won a majority of seats in the assembly. Despite threats of military confrontation from Indonesia and actual raids on Sabah and Sarawak by Indonesian commandos, the merger took place. The new federation was based on an uneasy alliance between Malays and ethnic Chinese. Communal rioting ensued in various parts of the new nation, including usually well controlled Singapore. In the end, the merger failed. As a state, Singapore did not achieve the economic progress it had hoped for, and political tensions escalated between Chinese-dominated Singapore and Malay-dominated Kuala Lumpur, the capital of Malaysia. Fearing greater Singaporean dominance of the federation and further violence between the Muslim and Chinese communities, the government of Malaysia decided to separate Singapore from the fledgling federation.

After separation from Malaysia on 9 August 1965, Singapore was forced to accept the challenge of forging a viable nation—the Republic of Singapore—on a small island with few resources beyond the determination and talent of its people. Under the leadership of Lee Kuan Yew and the PAP, the new nation met the challenge. Trade with Japan and the United States increased substantially since Singapore became a supply centre for the increasing U.S. involvement in Vietnam.

In 1967, Singapore joined Brunei, Indonesia, Malaysia, the Philippines, and Thailand in forming the Association of Southeast Asian Nations (ASEAN) for the purpose of promoting regional stability, economic development, and cultural exchange. In 1968 Britain announced its decision to withdraw from its military bases in Singapore within three years. Because of defence implications and the amount of British spending (accounting for about 25% of the gross national product [GNP] of Singapore), the government called for new elections, seeking a new mandate to proceed. Because the PAP won all 58 parliamentary seats, the government was able to pass stricter labour legislation and thus overcome the nation's reputation for frequent labour disputes and strikes. Former British naval base workers were retrained to work in what became the Sembawang Shipyard, and eventually a major shipbuilding and ship repair centre. By the 1970s, Singapore had achieved status as a world leader in shipping, air transport, and oil refining. Singapore was no longer dependent on peninsular Malaysia for its economic prosperity.

In the 1970s through the 1990s, Singapore experienced sustained economic growth. Along with Hong Kong, South Korea, and Taiwan, it was called one of the "Four Tigers" of Asian economic prosperity. Labor-intensive industries were relocated to other ASEAN nations and were replaced by high-technology industries and services. The PAP developed a stable and corruption-free government, marked by strong central development planning and social policies. Despite authoritarian governmental practices and one-party dominance, the PAP maintained its large popular mandate. A Singaporean identity, distinct from that of the Malay and Chinese, emerged as the nation increasingly integrated itself into the global economy. In 1990 Lee Kuan Yew stepped down as prime minister, and Goh Chok Tong, the first deputy prime minister and first minister of defence, took over as part of the succession to a new generation of leaders. The Asian economic crisis of 1997–98 was not the major setback for Singapore that it was for other Southeast Asian nations; the regional economic downturn did bring fluctuating growth rates to Singapore but no serious problems. Except for oil-rich Brunei, Singapore remained the most prosperous nation in the region. After 14 years in office, in 2004 Goh stepped down in favor of Lee Hsien Loong, the minister of finance and son of Lee Kuan Yew. The elder Lee agreed to stay on as minister mentor and Goh as senior minister in order to oversee the transition of the new generation of leaders. Lee Hsien Loong was confirmed in office in a democratic election held on 6 May 2006.

Geography

Singapore is located in Southeast Asia between Malaysia and Indonesia at the narrowest point of the Strait of Malacca, one of the world's strategic sea routes connecting the Indian Ocean with the South

China Sea. Lying off the southern tip of the Malay Peninsula, Singapore is connected to Malaysia by a causeway. The land area is 699 square kilometres; and water area is 10 square kilometres, for a total national area of 709 square kilometres. The area has increased through land reclamation and landfill projects along the coast. Since 1988 the total land area has increased by some 63 square kilometres.

Singapore is an island nation with no land boundaries. Malaysia lies to the north across the Johore Strait and Indonesia to the south across the Strait of Malacca. Singapore comprises one main island and 58 islets. The total coastline is 193 kilometres. Since 1988, the coastline has increased by 55 kilometres as a result of extensive land reclamation and landfill projects.

Singapore is mainly low-lying, with rounded granite hills, especially in the island's centre. At 166 metres above sea level, the highest point is Bukit Timah Peak. Low but steep ridges are found in the west and southwest. To the east is a large region of generally flat alluvial soils, where streams have cut steep-sided valleys and gullies. Singapore was once covered with tropical rain forest and surrounded by mangrove swamps, but as the island urbanized, hills were leveled and swamps drained. The forest cover is only about 4,000 hectares, or 6.6% of the land area. The gently undulating central plateau contains a water catchment area and a nature preserve.

The Singapore River is only 4.1 kilometres in length but historically was an important resource for early settlers and traders. It has five tributaries: the Geylang, Kallang, Pelton, Rochor, and Whampoa rivers. Also there are other small streams, some of which flow directly into the sea through mangrove swamps, lagoons, or broad estuaries. Several of the large streams have been dammed at their mouths to form freshwater reservoirs. Singapore has 10 major reservoirs, both coastal and inland.

Only two degrees north of the equator, Singapore has a tropical climate; elevated temperatures are moderated by sea breezes and high humidity. There are two monsoon seasons, the northeastern (dry) monsoon from December to March and the southwestern (wet) monsoon from June to September. Even between the monsoon seasons, afternoon and early evening thunderstorms frequently occur.

Only 1.6% of the land is arable. In 1967, 25% of the land was in agricultural use, but by 1988, despite increases through land reclamation, that had decreased to 8.5% and is predicted to shrink to 3.2% by 2030. Singapore has no irrigated land, and none of the land is planted to permanent crops. More than 60% of the land is devoted to residential, industrial, commercial, institutional, and infrastructure spaces. The major environmental issues are industrial pollution, limited freshwater resources, waste disposal, and seasonal smoke and haze resulting from forest fires in Indonesia.

Society

Population. Singapore's population was reported at 4,351,400 in July 2005, an increase of some 333,660 since the 2000 census. Of this total, 3,553,500 were citizens or permanent residents. Foreign estimates for July 2006 put the total population at 4,492,150. In 2005 the annual population growth rate, based on total residents, was 1.9%, and population density was estimated at 6,222 persons per square kilometer.

According to the 2000 census, ethnic Chinese make up 76.8% of the population. The largest groups are descendants of Hokkien-speaking migrants from southern Fujian Province in China. The second largest groups are descendants of Teochiu speakers from northeastern Guangdong Province in China. The third largest groups are those whose Yue-dialect ancestors came from the Guangzhou area of Guangdong Province. The Chinese population also includes Hakka (guest family) from upland areas of both Guangdong and Fujian and other groups from coastal areas of Fujian. The remainder of Singapore's population is Malay (13.9%), Indian (mostly Tamil, 7.9%), or other (1.4%).

Languages. Singaporeans speak many different languages, and the majority speak at least two languages. Malay is the national language and one of the four official languages, along with Chinese, Tamil, and English. Chinese is the majority language, spoken by about 76% of the population. The major Chinese dialect is Minnan, followed by Yue (Cantonese), Mandarin, Hakka, Mindong, Puxian, and Minbei. Although the post independence generation and most Chinese migrants to Singapore over the centuries spoke southern Chinese dialects, since 1979 the government has promoted fluency in Mandarin Chinese. Other languages, in order of use, are Malay (about 15%), English (about 9%), and Tamil (about 4%). Less frequently spoken languages, in order of use, include Malayalam, Baba Malay (a Malay-Chinese creole), Punjabi, Madurese, Sinhala, Gujarati, and Javanese.

Religion. According to the 2000 census, 2.9 million Singaporeans professed adherence to a religious faith. Of these, Buddhists and Daoists made up 51.0% of the total, or 64.4% of the Chinese population and 13.9% of the "other" ethnic composition. Islam had the second largest following at 14.9%, or 99.6% of the Malay population. Christians represented 14.6% of religious believers and 53.3% of the "other" ethnic category. Hindus made up 4.0% of believers, or about 55.5% of the Indian population. Other religions made up only 0.4% of the total, and 14.8% professed no religious affiliation.

Education and Literacy: The British-inspired education system includes six years of compulsory primary school, four years of secondary school, and two years of junior college for those aspiring to higher education. All children between age six and 14 are required to attend school, and school attendance in 2005 was almost universal at both primary and secondary levels. English is the primary medium of instruction. In 2003 Singapore claimed 175 schools, 299,993 students, and 12,025 teachers at the primary level and 162 schools, 206,426 students, and 10,830 teachers at the secondary level. At the postsecondary level, Singapore maintained two centralized institutes with 851 students and 103 teachers and 16 junior colleges with 23,708 students and 1,956 faculty members. Postsecondary education also includes Singapore Polytechnic, which in 2004–5 had 13,738 full-time students; the Institute of Technical Education with 21,796 students; and the National Institute of Education with 5,092 students. Singapore has two public universities: the National University of Singapore, founded in 1905, with 31,735 undergraduate and graduate students in academic year 2005–6; and Nanyang Technical University, founded in 1955, with 25,715 undergraduate and graduate students in academic year 2005–6. A third, government-funded, privately managed institution, the Singapore Management University, was established in 2000 and has grown to more than 3,800 undergraduate and graduate students in 2005–6. Together, these three universities enroll in excess of 61,250 students. Public expenditures on education totaled 2.7% of the gross domestic product for school year 2004–5. Literacy is estimated at 95% overall, and 57.8% of Singaporeans have secondary school diplomas or even higher qualifications.

Health: The state of health in Singapore is good by international standards. According to the Ministry of Health, rising standards of living, high levels of education, good housing, safe water supply and sanitation, quality medical services, and the active promotion of preventive medicine all have helped to significantly boost the health of Singaporeans. Two health care delivery "cluster" systems are available to Singaporeans. The western cluster, the National Healthcare Group, provides comprehensive public health care through a network of four hospitals, one national centre, nine polyclinics, three specialty institutes, nine business divisions, and more than 11,000 staff members. The eastern cluster, Singapore Health Services, offers three hospitals, five national specialist centres, a network of primary health care clinics, and more than 12,000 staff members. Medical insurance is available via Medisave for hospitalization and some outpatient services, Medifund for those unable to pay for their medical expenses, Medishield for catastrophic illness, and Eldershield for senior citizens with severe disabilities. In 2005 Singapore had 29 hospitals with 11,830 hospital beds, as well as 6,748 physicians (1.6 physicians per 1,000 population or one physician for every 640 persons) and 20,167 nurses and midwives (4.6 nurses per 1,000 population or one nurse for every 220 persons). Traditional Chinese medicine also is widely practiced. In fiscal year (FY) 2005, 6.3% of total government expenditures was spent on health care.

Welfare: The Central Provident Fund is Singapore's compulsory national social security savings plan. It was established in 1955 to ensure the financial security of all workers either retired or no longer able to work. Citizens and permanent residents are eligible to participate. Since the early 1990s, contributions of 40% of the gross wages of employees under 55 have been mandated, but employee and employer share the burden equally. Singaporeans can use these funds to invest in approved securities, to purchase homes in government housing projects, or to pay for hospitalization and retirement. The government makes major expenditures—43% of total government spending in 2005—for "social development." Some 93% of Singapore residents (citizens and permanent residents) own their own homes. Of these, 72.3% reside in high-density buildings in four-room or larger apartments.

Economy

Along with Hong Kong, South Korea and Taiwan, Singapore is one of the Four Asian Tigers. The economy depends heavily on exports refining imported goods, especially in manufacturing. Manufacturing constituted 26% of Singapore's GDP in 2005.The manufacturing industry is well-diversified into electronics, petroleum refining, chemicals, mechanical engineering and biomedical sciences manufacturing. In 2006, Singapore produced about 10% of the world's foundry wafer output. Singapore is the busiest port in the world in terms of tonnage shipped. Singapore is the world's fourth largest foreign exchange trading centre after London, New York City and Tokyo.

Singapore has been rated as the most business-friendly economy in the world, with thousands of foreign expatriates working in multi-national corporations. The city-state also employs tens of thousands of foreign blue-collared workers from around the world.

In 2001, a global recession and slump in the technology sector caused the GDP to contract by 2.2%. The Economic Review Committee (ERC), set up in December 2001, recommended several policy changes with a view to revitalising the economy. Singapore has since recovered from the recession, largely due to improvements in the world economy; the Singaporean economy itself grew by 8.3% in 2004, 6.4% in 2005 and 7.9% in 2006. In the first half of Year 2007, the economy grew by 7.6%. The growth forecast for the whole year is expected to be between 7% to 8%, up from the original estimation of 5% to 7%.Singapore's economy is expected to grow by at least 4-6% annually over the next 5-10 years.

The per capita GDP in 2005 was US$26,833 and the unemployment rate was 2.4% as of 31 July 2007, a record six year low. In 2006, there were 173,000 new jobs being created, a record high. In the first half of Year 2007, 111,000 new jobs were created, reaching another breaking record.

Singapore is a popular travel destination, making tourism one of its largest industries. About 9.7 million tourists visited Singapore in 2006 The Orchard Road district is the centre of shopping hub in Singapore. To attract more tourists, the government decided in 2005 to legalize gambling and to allow two Integrated Resorts to be developed at Marina South and Sentosa. To compete with its many rivals such as Hong Kong, Tokyo and Shanghai, the government has announced that the city area would be transformed into a more vibrant and exciting place with more buzz by lighting up the city completely. Other than the Integrated Resort, about 15 new developments are coming up, which include the Singapore Flyer, which would be the largest Ferris wheel in the world, the Gardens by the Bay and a 280-metre Double Helix Bridge. Cuisine has been heavily promoted as an attraction for tourists, with the Singapore Food Festival in July organized annually to celebrate Singapore's cuisine.

Singapore is also growing its medical tourism sector. 230,000 foreigners sought medical care in the country in 2003 and Singapore Medical services are aiming to serve one million foreign patients annually by 2012. In doing so it is hoped to generate $3 billion in revenue and create at least 13,000 new jobs within the health industries. Singapore hospitals are actively engaged in international healthcare accreditation, at least partly as a by-product of this desire to grow the income from medical tourism.

Agriculture, Forestry, and Fishing: As an economic category, agriculture, forestry, and fishing are not large enough to be reported as a part of the GDP but are instead subsumed under industrial production. In 1960 Singapore had 20,000 small farms on 14,000 hectares of land. By 1995 farmland had been severely reduced and was concentrated on 1,500 hectares of agro-technology parks that housed modern intensive farms. By 2004 Singapore had only 266 farms on 803 hectares of land. In 2000 the government established the Agri-Food and Veterinary Authority of Singapore to oversee the agro-technology parks (including the current 67 vegetable farms and five egg-laying farms), the development of agro-technology and agri-biotechnology (knowledge of agriculture and molecular biology applied to large-scale, intensive farming), and the promotion of investments in the agri-industry. Singapore's agricultural products include, in order of value, rubber, copra, fruit, orchids (15% of the world market), vegetables, poultry, eggs, and ornamental fish (30% of the world market). In 2004 Singapore produced about US$143 million in agricultural products, including livestock and fish, for both domestic consumption and export. Since the 1980s, the government has made a concerted effort to conserve the surviving forest areas of Singapore. The last reported timber harvests were in 1992, when 25,000 cubic metres of sawn wood were produced. Around this time, a mere 100 hectares of forest and 600 hectares of mangrove swamps had survived. Fishing is by capture (36%) and aquaculture (64%). The total catch in 2004 was 7,579 tons of fish and shellfish.

Industry and Manufacturing: Industry accounted for 33.6% of the gross domestic product (GDP) in 2005. Singapore's primary industries in order of value are electronics, chemicals, oil drilling equipment, petroleum refining, rubber processing and rubber products, processed food and beverages, ship repair, and offshore platform construction. Manufacturing output grew by 12.8% in 2005 and employed 20.5% of the workforce.

Energy: In 2004 Singapore produced nearly 36.8 billion and consumed nearly 33.2 billion kilowatt-hours of electricity. Singapore produced no oil or natural gas but consumed an estimated 749,000 barrels per day in 2004 and 5.3 billion cubic metres in 2003, respectively. Although Singapore is 100% dependent on imports of oil and natural gas, it ranks as one of the world's top three crude oil refining and trading hubs. Singapore's crude oil refining capacity is estimated at 1.3 million barrels per day. However, India, Malaysia, and Thailand are challenging Singapore's regional petroleum refining dominance. In keeping with government policy, natural gas usage is rising rapidly. By 2003 this relatively environmentally clean source of energy, carried by pipeline from neighboring Malaysia, accounted for 60% of electricity generation.

Services: Services produced 66.4% of the gross domestic product and occupied 68.7% of the labor force in 2005. Major services include financial services, life sciences, and entrepôt trade.

Banking and Finance: The Monetary Authority of Singapore is responsible for regulating the country's banking and investment sector. In May 2006, Singapore had about 500 local and foreign financial services companies, including 108 commercial banks and 154 insurance companies. Singapore's stock exchange, the Singapore Exchange (SGX), has separate divisions for the trading of securities and derivatives.

Labour: Of 2.3 million Singaporeans employed at the end of 2005, 68.7% worked in services, 20.5% were employed in manufacturing, 10.1% were employed in construction, and 0.7% were employed in other sectors. According to the Ministry of Manpower, the annual average unemployment rate for 2005 was 3.1%.

Foreign Economic Relations: Located on the strategic Strait of Malacca, Singapore is a major trading hub and home to the world's busiest port. The nation's prosperity has been built on a free trade policy. In May 2006, the director general of the World Trade Organization observed that Singapore, with its strong tradition of open markets, benefits from bilateral as well as global trade agreements, unlike most small countries that relinquish their interests in bilateral negotiations with larger and more powerful trading partners.

Imports: Singapore's imports totaled around US$210.7 billion in 2005. Machinery and equipment, mineral fuels, chemicals, and foodstuffs are Singapore's major import commodities. The major import partners in 2005 were Malaysia (13.7%), the European Union (11.6%), the United States (11.6%), China (10.3%), Japan (9.6%), Taiwan (5.9%), Indonesia (5.2%), Saudi Arabia (4.5%), South Korea (4.3%), and Thailand (3.8%).

Exports: Singapore's exports totaled US$241.9 billion in 2005. The major exports are machinery and equipment (especially electronic components and parts), consumer goods, chemicals, and mineral fuels and petroleum products (processed for re-export). The major export partners in 2005 were Malaysia (13.2%), the European Union (12.0%), the United States (10.2%), Hong Kong (9.4%), China (8.6%), Japan (5.5%), Thailand (4.1%), Taiwan (3.9%), and South Korea (3.5%).

Trade Balance: Singapore maintains a favorable balance of trade. In 2005 exports totaled US$241.9 billion, exceeding imports of US$210.7 billion.

Balance of Payments: Singapore's current account balance was US$35.1 billion for 2005.

External Debt: The U.S. government estimated that Singapore had US$24.7 billion of external debt in 2005.

Foreign Investment: Foreign direct investment (FDI) in Singapore totaled US$15.36 billion in 2005. The cumulative value of FDI was US$155 billion at the end of 2003. Most investment is concentrated in manufacturing, financial services, and commerce and comes primarily from the United Kingdom (16.1%), the United States (15.4%), and Japan (13.5%).

Currency: Singapore's currency is the Singapore dollar (S$).

Infrastructure

Singapore has a sophisticated urban transit network of light rail, metro rail, and buses to move commuters throughout the urbanized nation. As the home of the world's busiest port, Singapore provides free-trade zones and shipping services at a strategic juncture of shipping lanes and water, air, and land trade routes.

Roads: Singapore has 3,188 kilometres of roads. Of this total, 150 kilometres are expressways. A causeway links the Singapore road system to Malaysia's road system across the Johore Strait. The Ministry of Transport reported that at the end of 2004 Singapore had 419,470 mostly private automobiles, 20,407 taxis, 13,173 buses, and more than 137,316 commercial and other vehicles plus 137,029 motorcycles and scooters.

Railroads: Singapore has only 23 kilometres of railroad track, all operated by Malaysian Railways and technically located on Malaysian territory per an agreement brokered in 1965. The line provides passenger service three times daily from Singapore's Keppel Station across a 1.2- kilometer causeway that spans the Johore Strait to the Malaysian mainland and Kuala Lumpur. Weekly luxury train service also is available from Keppel Station to Chang Mai and Bangkok, Thailand, with connections to Kuala Lumpur.

Rapid Transit: Singapore's principal public mass transit system is operated by Singapore Mass Rapid Transit (SMRT) Corporation, which also runs light rail, bus, and taxi services. In fiscal year (FY) 2005, SMRT trains conveyed 402.59 million passengers on the system's 89.4 kilometres of above- and underground track. The system has 16 underground stations, 34 elevated stations, and one station at grade and operates on two lines, the North-South and East- West lines. The Bukit Panjang Light Rail Transit system is a fully automated service that carried 37,800 passengers per day in FY 2005, using some 7.8 kilometres of elevated guide ways and serving 14 stations. More than 1 billion passengers rode on SMRT and SBS Transit buses in FY 2004. SBS Transit, which started as a bus company (Singapore Bus Services) in 1973, began light rail and its mass rapid transit operations in 2003. By 2005 SBS was operating two minimetro light-rail feeder lines and one full metro line—the North East Line—with 14 operational underground stations and 20 kilometres of track. SBS and SMRT metro lines intersect at key interchange points.

Ports: The Port of Singapore, with a deep harbor and a strategic location, is the busiest in the world. More than 130,000 ships arrived with about 1.15 billion gross registered tons (GRT) in 2005. In the same year, the port handled 423.3 million tons of general and bulk cargo and 23 million twenty-foot equivalent units of containers. The port has three major anchorages—the Eastern, Western, and Johore sectors—which offer specialized locations for various types of cargo and ships of various sizes and purposes, including foreign warships. There are five port terminals, each specializing in different types of cargo, and some 15 kilometres of wharves. The port has seven free-trade zones, six for seaborne trade and one for air cargo. Goods are stored in these zones for processing and re-exportation with minimum customs formalities. Singapore also offers extensive technology-driven warehouse and oil storage facilities. More than 3,000 ships are registered in Singapore, which itself has the fifteenth largest merchant fleet in the world, numbering 900 ships of 1,000 GRT or more for a total of 23.1 million GRT. The major ships include 136 bulk carriers, 84 cargo ships, 96 chemical tankers, 4 combination bulk carriers, 8 combination ore and oil carriers, 186 container ships, 41 liquefied natural gas carriers, 10 specialized tankers, 3 livestock carriers, 2 multifunctional large-load carriers, 5 roll-on/roll-off carriers, 1 short-sea passenger ship, and 32 vehicle carriers.

Civil Aviation and Airports: Singapore has 10 airports, mostly for military use, two of which have paved runways of more than 3,047 metres. The main international airport is Singapore Changi Airport, whose major passenger and air cargo facilities are located on the northeast side of Singapore, about 20 kilometres from the city centre. Seletar Airport, 13 kilometres from downtown Singapore, also handles some commercial traffic. Singapore's main airline is Singapore Airlines (SIA), a scheduled international carrier serving 90 destinations in 37 countries throughout the world. SIA provides both passenger and cargo service, using 117 relatively new Airbus and Boeing aircraft. Originally SIA was 100% state-owned, but the government's stockholding in SIA has decreased to 56%. Silkair, with a fleet of 11 Airbus aircraft, provides service to numerous Southeast Asian cities plus selected destinations in China and India. Two other Singapore private airlines, Tiger Airways and ValuAir, provide short-trip regional service. Singapore handled some 1.8 million tons of air cargo in 2005.

Pipelines: Singapore had 139 kilometres of natural gas pipelines in 2004.

Telecommunications: Telecommunications policy, regulation, and promotion are the responsibility of a government agency, Infocomm Development Authority of Singapore. Postal and telecommunications services are provided by Singapore Telecommunications (SingTel), which is 68% owned by Temasek Holdings, a government holding company that is 32% privately owned. Seventeen FM stations and two shortwave stations broadcast to some 2.6 million radios as of 2003. Seven television broadcast stations also were in operation in 2003, and more than 1.3 million televisions were in use. Singapore had 1.85 million landline telephones and 4.2 million cellular phones (equivalent to some 978 subscribers per 1,000 population) in use in 2005. The highly touted telephone system uses submarine cables to Malaysia (both Peninsular Malaysia and Sabah), Indonesia, and the Philippines, as well as two earth satellite stations relaying to Intelsat satellites (one each) positioned over the Indian and Pacific oceans. Singapore had 2.4 million Internet users and some 440 Internet subscribers per 1,000 population in 2005.

Government and Politics

Singapore is a parliamentary republic. The constitution for the State of Singapore, based on that promulgated on June 3, 1959, was amended in 1965 at independence. The presidency is largely ceremonial, and the prime minister is the most powerful political figure. The current prime minister, Lee Hsien Loong, however, has been in office only since August 12, 2004, and serves under the advice of his father, long-time prime minister and now minister mentor, Lee Kuan Yew. The younger Lee assumed the office of prime minister when the incumbent Goh Chok Tung, who succeeded Lee Kuan Yew in 1990, stepped down, but Lee's mandate was democratically confirmed in an election held on May 6, 2006. Goh Chok Tong serves as senior minister. The People's Action Party (PAP), founded in 1954, has governed without serious opposition since 1959.

Constitution: The constitution of the Republic of Singapore, promulgated in 1965, has undergone two major revisions, once in 1985 and again in 1999. Based on English common law, it has 14 parts and 153 articles. Although it provides all the mechanics for a liberal democracy, Singapore's one-party rule for more than 45 years has not offered the opposition a meaningful chance to develop.

Executive Branch: The president is S.R. Nathan, who ran unopposed and was elected to a six-year term by direct popular vote on August 18, 1999. He was sworn in for his first term on September 1, 1999, and on September 1, 2005, was sworn in for a second term without even being required to stand for election after the government declared his opponent ineligible to run. The largely ceremonial president and head of state is assisted by the Council of Presidential Advisers (CPA), a body established by constitutional amendment in 1991. The president is required to consult the CPA before he vetoes the government budget or appoints government nominees to key posts. In other matters, such as withholding assent to certain bills passed by parliament, appointments to statutory boards, and withholding concurrence in regard to detention of persons in times of national emergency, the president may use his discretion on consulting the CPA. The CPA has six members: two appointed by the president at his discretion, two nominated by the prime minister, one put forward by the chief justice of the Supreme Court, and another suggested by the chairman of the Public Service Commission. CPA members are appointed to initial six-year terms and can be reappointed for additional four-year terms. The current chairman of the CPA is Sim Kee Boon.

The head of government is the prime minister. The current incumbent, Lee Hsien Loong, has held office since August 12, 2004, and concurrently serves as minister of finance. The prime minister is assisted by a senior minister (since August 12, 2004, Goh Chok Tong, the former prime minister), a minister mentor (since August 12, 2004, Lee Kuan Yew, the prime minister's father), two deputy prime ministers, and 14 other ministers. The president appoints as prime minister a member of Parliament believed likely to command the confidence of the majority of the members of Parliament. There is no set tenure for the office of prime minister. On the advice of the prime minister, the president appoints the other members of the cabinet. The cabinet, responsible collectively to the Parliament, oversees government policies and day-to-day administration of the affairs of state.

Legislative Branch: The unicameral 84-seat Singapore Parliament is modeled after the Westminster system of parliamentary democracy where members are voted in at regular general elections and the leader of the majority party is invited by the president to assume the post of prime minister. The prime minister then selects ministers from elected members of Parliament to form the cabinet, which in turn runs the executive branch of government. When the new

Parliament first convenes, a speaker is elected. Each Parliament sits for five years from the date of its first session after a general election, and general elections are to be held within three months of the dissolution of Parliament. Members are elected by universal suffrage. The president appoints a maximum of nine "nominated members" from among persons who have rendered distinguished public service, brought honor to the republic, or made notable contributions in the fields of arts and letters, culture, the sciences, business, industry, the professions, social or community service, or the labor movement. Parliament also can seat up to six "non-constituency members" to represent a political party or several parties not a part of the government, although nominated and non-constituency members are prohibited from voting on amendments to the constitution, money and supply bills, no-confidence measures, and removal of the president from office. The constitution further provides for group representation in Parliament of the Malay, Indian, and minority communities.

Judicial Branch: The judicial branch is headed by a Supreme Court, whose chief justice is appointed by the president on the advice of the prime minister. Other Supreme Court judges then are appointed by the president on the advice of the chief justice. The Supreme Court consists of the Court of Appeals and the High Court. Supreme Court judges or former Supreme Court judges can sit as judges on the Court of Appeals and the High Court, as designated by the president after consultation with the prime minister. Judges normally serve until age 65. Subordinate courts include criminal courts, criminal mentions courts (at which charges are first placed), and traffic, night, coroners', civil, and family courts, plus various other tribunals and services that support the subordinate court system. The Shariah Court, established in 1955, adjudicates Muslim marriages, divorces, property dispositions, and other matters relating to Muslim inheritance, betrothal, marriage, and divorce.

Administrative Divisions: Singapore is a unitary state with no second-order administrative divisions. It has no provincial or local government although there are some advisory bodies based on the 23 electoral divisions.

Judicial and Legal System: The legal system is based on English common law. According to Article 2 of the constitution, the laws of Singapore include written laws and any legislation of the United Kingdom or other enactments or instruments in operation in Singapore. Common law and any custom or usage having the force of law in Singapore also are in effect according to Article 2. Representation by legal counsel is provided by law, but the right to trial by jury was abolished in 1959 for all except capital offenses, and all jury trials were abolished in 1969.

Electoral System: Suffrage begins at 21 years of age and is universal and compulsory. Singapore has 23 electoral divisions or constituencies. Nine single-member constituencies and 14 group representation constituencies, each with between three and six individuals, are represented by 75 members of Parliament. Singapore has only two kinds of elections, presidential and parliamentary. According to the constitution, the president is elected by popular vote for a six year term, but the current president, Sellapan Rama Nathan, was nominated unopposed and was elected to the presidency on August 18, 1999. He was sworn in for a second term on September 1, 2005, after the government had declared potential opponents ineligible to run. The leader of the majority party in Parliament or—although this has never happened—the leader of a majority coalition is normally appointed prime minister by the president. The People's Action Party (PAP) dominated the most recent parliamentary elections held on May 6, 2006, as it has every election since 1959. The PAP, headed by Lee Hsien Loong, won 66.6% of the vote and 82 of the 84 seats in Parliament, including 37 seats that the opposition declined to contest. A third "non-constituent" seat was awarded to the opposition. The Workers' Party of Singapore gained one regular and one non-constituent seat. The Singapore Democratic Alliance won a regular seat.

Politics and Political Parties: The majority party, which has been in power since 1959, is the People's Action Party (PAP). Of the opposition parties, only the Workers' Party of Singapore (WP) and the Singapore Democratic Alliance (SDA), an umbrella group, hold seats in Parliament. The SDA consists of the Singapore National Malay Organization (Pertuhan Kebangsaan Melayu Singapura—PKMS), National Solidarity Party (NSP), Singapore's People's Party (SPP), and Singapore Justice Party (SJP). Two opposition parties not holding seats in Parliament are the Democratic Progressive Party (DPP) and Singapore Democratic Party (SDP). In the May 2006 parliamentary elections, the Singapore government continued its customary tradition of intimidation against opposition candidates, which consisted mainly of costly defamation lawsuits. Following the 2006 elections, the Asian Network for Free Elections, a watchdog group based in Bangkok, recommended that

Singapore establish an independent election commission, which now reports to the prime minister.

Mass Media: The media industry is regulated by the government's Media Development Authority. All newspapers in Singapore are required by law to be public companies and are regulated by the government. Major daily newspapers are published in various languages. English-language publications include the venerable *Straits Times*, founded in 1845; *Business Times*; and three tabloids, *The New Paper*, *Straits*, and *Today*. Chinese-language newspapers include *Lianhe Wanbao*, *Lianhe Zaobao*, *Shin Min Daily News*, and *Toh Lam Hhat*. Two other dailies are the Malay *Berita Harian* and Tamil *Murasu*. Weekly newspapers are offered in English and Malay, and most newspapers can be accessed on the Internet. There also is a lively magazine circulation with 17 domestic English, one Malay, and nine Chinese titles. Most broadcasting is produced by radio and television companies owned by the Media Corporation of Singapore and Radio Corporation of Singapore. Other radio stations include Radio Heart, Rediffusion, and SAFRA (Singapore Armed Forces Reservists' Association) Radio. Cable, satellite, and traditional television broadcasters include CNBC (formerly stood for Consumer News Business Channel) Asia Pacific, Singapore CableVision, Singapore Television 12; SPH (Singapore Press Holdings) MediaWorks, and Television Corporation of Singapore. Broadcasts are in Chinese, English, Malay, and Tamil, but primarily in Chinese and English.

Foreign Relations: Singapore maintains diplomatic relations with 165 nations. Overseas, it has seven high commissions, 17 embassies, two permanent representations to the United Nations (UN), and 14 consulates general and consulates. Singapore hosts embassies or high commissions of 55 nations, 37 foreign consular posts, and offices of eight international organizations. In addition, more than 60 nonresident foreign ambassadors are accredited to Singapore. Singapore seeks to maintain a credible defensive military to under gird its foreign policy. It promotes good relations with its neighbors and any nation wishing to establish friendly relations. As a founding member of the Association of Southeast Asian Nations (ASEAN), Singapore is committed to maintaining a secure peaceful environment in and around Southeast Asia and in the Asia-Pacific region. After breaking off a long-term diplomatic relationship with the Republic of China on Taiwan in 1990, Singapore established relations with the People's Republic of China. Since this change, numerous high-level delegations have traded visits and have developed a wide range of political, economic, cultural, and scientific and technical exchanges. Tensions over Singapore's relations with Taiwan—emanating from both Beijing and Taipei—continue. Continued good relations with the United States are based on bilateral free trade and close military ties.

National Security

The Singapore Armed Forces (SAF) had 72,500 personnel on active duty in 2005, 35,000 of whom were conscripts. The service components are the army, numbering 50,000, with 35,000 conscripts; navy, 9,000, with 1,800 conscripts; and air force, 13,500, with 3,000 conscripts. There are an estimated 312,500 personnel in reserve status (army, abou300,000; navy, about 5,000; and air force, about 7,500). The SAF is led by a chief (a major general) supported by army, navy, and air force chiefs of staff. As of 2006, the Ministry of Defence was headed by Teo Chee Hean, who also oversees the administration of the Defence Policy Group, Defence Administration Group, Singapore Armed Forces, and Defence Science and Technology Agency.

Foreign Military Relations: The British Far East Command and the British naval presence in Singapore formally ended in 1971. At that time, Singapore became a participant in the Five- Power Defence Arrangement with Australia, Malaysia, New Zealand, and the United Kingdom, and a joint military force was in place until 1975. Singapore continues to provide facilities for servicing foreign naval vessels, but its official policy disallows the establishment of a naval base on the island by another country. Under the five-power arrangement, joint military and naval manoeuvres are held annually. Singapore supports a strong U.S. military presence in the Asia- Pacific region. In 1990 the United States and Singapore signed a memorandum of understanding (MOU) that allows U.S. access to Singapore facilities at the Paya Lebar Airbase and the Sembawang wharves. In accordance with the MOU, the U.S. Navy established a logistics unit in Singapore in 1992. Furthermore, U.S. fighter aircraft are deployed periodically to Singapore for exercises, and U.S. Navy vessels visit Singapore. The MOU was amended in 1999 to permit U.S. naval vessels to berth at the Changi Naval Base, which was completed in 2001. In October 2003, Singapore and the United States announced their intention to expand cooperation in the area of defence and security and to negotiate a Framework Agreement for a Strategic Cooperation Partnership. Areas of cooperation include counterterrorism, counter proliferation of weapons of mass destruction, joint military exercises and training, policy dialogue, and technology exchange. Singapore has conducted joint naval exercises with the United States and has joined the United States-led Proliferation Security Initiative. Joint naval and air force exercises are held annually with Australia. Singapore maintains relationships with the armed forces of Australia, Brunei, France, Thailand, and the United States, primarily for the purpose of training. Although it does not have diplomatic relations with Taiwan, Singapore maintains training facilities there. Most of Singapore's major military imports since 1998 have been purchased from the United States. It also has acquired submarines from Sweden and has a frigate on order from France.

External Threat: Singapore faces a potential military threat from Malaysia if historical tensions were to reemerge. In particular, Singapore fears that the Malaysian state of Johor could cut off its water supply, an act that would be regarded as a casus belli. Singapore also is concerned about the possibility of a terrorist strike sponsored by the Indonesia-based Jemaah Islamiah (Community of Islam) or the Moro Islamic Liberation Front, a Philippines-based separatist group.

Defence Budget: Military expenditures in fiscal year (FY) 2005 were estimated at US$5.87 billion, or about US$1,349 per capita, representing about 5% of the gross domestic product (GDP). The projected defence budget for FY 2006 is US$6.37 billion, an 8.5% increase over the previous year. Projected defence spending for 2006 represents 22.5% of the total federal budget.

Major Military Units: The army has three combined arms divisions, a rapid deployment division, and a mechanized division. Included in these organizations are nine infantry brigades with both active-duty and reserve personnel. The navy has a fleet with two flotillas and a submarine squadron and coastal, naval logistics, and training commands. The air force is organized into 20 combat, reconnaissance, transportation, support, and helicopter squadrons. It also has one squadron of unmanned aerial vehicles and an air defence division with four field defence squadrons.

Military Service: Singapore has compulsory military service for males reaching the age of 18 and voluntary service for those reaching 16 years of age. The conscription term of service is 24 months. Reservists attend annual training until age 40 for enlisted ranks and age 50 for officers.

Paramilitary Forces: Singapore's paramilitary consists of 93,800 active-duty personnel and 44,000 reserves. The active-duty paramilitary encompasses the Civil Defence Force, the Singapore Police Force, and the Singapore Gurkha Contingent.

Foreign Military Forces: In 2005 the United States had 89 liaison personnel assigned to Singapore (39 air force and 50 navy). New Zealand had an 11-person liaison support unit stationed in Singapore.

Police and Internal Security: The Singapore Police Force has an estimated strength of 12,000, including 3,500 conscripts. There also are 21,000 reserve police officers. The Singapore Police Force includes the Police Coast Guard, which has inshore patrol craft and about 60 other boats.

Terrorism: Singapore perceives a threat from international terrorist organizations. As a consequence, the Five-Power Defence Arrangement, to which Singapore belongs along with Australia, Malaysia, New Zealand, and the United Kingdom, was expanded after 2001 to include counterterrorism. The Indonesia-based Jemaah Islamiah (Community of Islam), an affiliate of al Qaeda, has operational units in peninsular Malaysia, Singapore, Australia, and Papua New Guinea. Another terrorist group of concern is the Moro Islamic Liberation Front, a Philippines based separatist group. Singapore maintains a high level of readiness and cooperation in the area of counterterrorism, especially in the wake of terrorist bombings in neighboring Indonesia, in Bali in 2002, and Jakarta in 2003. Singapore is believed to hold in indefinite detention between 36 and 40 individuals who are suspected of links to terrorist organizations. In February 2006, Mas Selamat Kastari, who was accused of plotting to crash an airplane into Changi Airport in retaliation for Singapore's imprisonment of fellow Jemaah Islamiah members, joined the detainees when he was deported to Singapore after spending four years in custody in Indonesia. Particular emphasis has been placed on protective and preventive actions against attacks on critical infrastructure, cyber terrorism, and chemical and biological attacks. Maritime piracy, long a problem in the immediate area, is of special concern to Singapore. The threat of a terrorist ship hijacking, possibly with the placement of conventional or nuclear explosives onboard, has led Singapore to increase maritime security on its own and with its neighbors.

Human Rights: The Ministry of Home Affair's Internal Security Department enforces the Internal Security Act as a counter to potential espionage, international terrorism, threats to racial and religious harmony, and subversion. According to the U.S. Department of State's 2005 *Country Reports on Human Rights Practices*, the government maintains effective control over all security activities, but there were some reports of human rights abuses of detainees by security forces during the year. The government generally respects the human rights of its citizens, but, nevertheless, retains broad powers to limit citizen rights and to handicap the political opposition. Caning, in addition to imprisonment, has been a routine punishment for numerous offenses. Preventive detention has been used to deal with espionage, terrorism, organized crime, and narcotics. Citizens' privacy rights occasionally have been infringed, and the government has restricted freedom of speech and freedom of the press and limited other civil and political rights. Government pressure to conform has resulted in the practice of self-censorship by journalists. The government has instigated court proceedings and defamation suits against political opponents and critics. Such suits have consistently been decided in favor of the government, a phenomenon that inhibits political speech and action and leads observers to believe that the ruling party uses the judicial system for political purposes. During 2005 a moderate level of debate occurred in the media on various public issues. However, the government has continued to prohibit discussion of sensitive ethnic or religious issues and has restricted freedom of assembly and freedom of association, and some religious groups, such as the Jehovah's Witnesses and the Unification Church, have been banned.

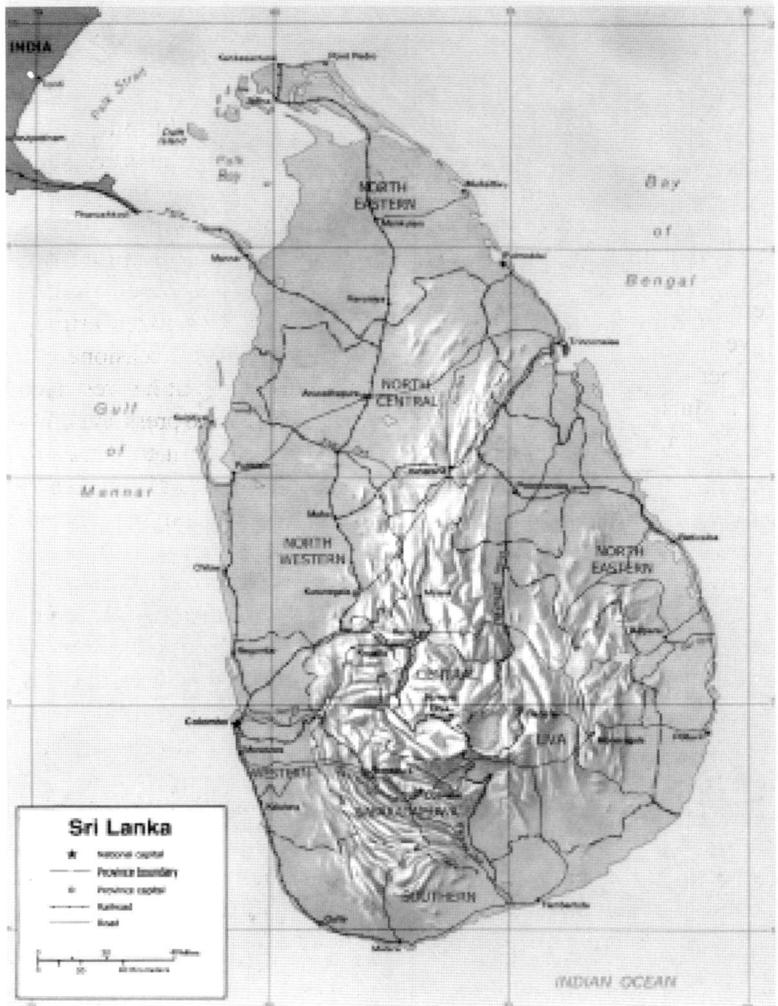

SRI LANKA

Sri Lanka, officially the Democratic Socialist Republic of Sri Lanka, (known as Ceylon before 1972) is an island nation in South Asia, located about 31 kilometres off the southern coast of India. It is popularly referred to as the Pearl of the Indian Ocean. Its capital is at Sri Jayawardenapura-Kotte. It declared its Independence from the United Kingdom on 4 February 1948 and became a Republic on 22 May 1972. Its largest city is Colombo.

Due to its location in the path of major sea routes, Sri Lanka is a strategic naval link between West Asia and South East Asia, and has been a centre of Buddhist religion and culture from ancient times. Today, the country is a multi-religious and multi-ethnic nation, with nearly a third of the population following faiths other than Buddhism, notably Hinduism, Christianity and Islam. The Sinhalese community forms the majority of the population, with Tamils, who are concentrated in the north and east of the island, forming the largest ethnic minority. Other communities include the Muslim Moors and Malays and the Burghers.

Famous for the production and export of tea, coffee, rubber and coconuts, Sri Lanka boasts a progressive and modern industrial economy and the highest per capita income in South Asia. The natural beauty of Sri Lanka's tropical forests, beaches and landscape, as well as its rich cultural heritage, make it a world famous tourist destination.

After over two thousand years of rule by local kingdoms, parts of Sri Lanka were colonized by Portugal and the Netherlands beginning in the 16th century, before the control of the entire country was ceded to the British Empire in 1815. During World War II, Sri Lanka served as an important base for Allied forces in the fight against the Japanese Empire. A nationalist political movement arose in the country in the early 20th century with the aim of obtaining political independence, which was eventually granted by the British after peaceful negotiations in 1948. Since then, Sri Lanka has enjoyed a stable democracy and continuous economic progress, despite the ongoing conflict with a separatist militant group known as the Tamil Tigers in northeastern parts of the country.

The total land area of Sri Lanka is 65,610 square kilometres. Its population, according to a 2005 estimate, is 19,668,000, with a density of 310 per square kilometre.

History

One of the first written references to the island is found in the Indian epic Ramayana, which described the emperor Ravana as monarch of the powerful kingdom of Lanka, which was created by the divine sculptor Vishwakarma for Kubera, the treasurer of the Gods. The main written accounts of the country's history are the Buddhist chronicles of Mahavansa and Dipavamsa. The earliest-known inhabitants of the island were probably the ancestors of the Wanniyala-Aetto people, also known as Veddahs and numbering roughly 3,000. Linguistic analysis has found a correlation of the Sinhalese language with the languages of the Sindh and Gujarat, although most historians believe that the Sinhala community emerged well after the assimilation of various ethnic groups. From the ancient period date some remarkable archaeological sites including the ruins of Sigiriya, the so-called "Fortress in the Sky", and huge public works. Ancient Sri Lanka was also the first in the world to have established a dedicated hospital in Mihintale in the 4th century BCE.

Since ancient times Sri Lanka was ruled by monarchs, most notably of the Sinha royal dynasty that lasted over 2000 years. The island was also infrequently invaded by South Indian kingdoms and parts of the island were ruled intermittently by the Chola dynasty, the Pandya dynasty, the Chera dynasty and the Pallava dynasty. The island was also invaded by the kingdoms of Kalinga (modern Orissa) and those from the Malay Peninsula. Buddhism arrived from India in the 3rd century BCE, brought by Bhikkhu Mahinda, who is believed to have been the son of Mauryan emperor Ashoka. Mahinda's mission won over the Sinhalese monarch Devanampiyatissa of Mihintale, who embraced the faith and propagated it throughout the Sinhalese population. The Buddhist kingdoms of Sri Lanka would maintain a large number of Buddhist schools and monasteries, and support the propagation of Buddhism into Southeast Asia.

Sri Lanka had always been an important port and trading post in the ancient world, and was increasingly frequented by merchant ships from the Middle East, Persia, Burma, Thailand, Malaysia, Indonesia and other parts of Southeast Asia. The islands were known to the first European explorers of South Asia and settled by many groups of Arab and Malay merchants. A Portuguese colonial mission arrived on the island in 1505 headed by the Lourenço de Almeida the son of Francisco de Almeida. At that point the island consisted of three kingdoms, namely Kandy in the central hills, Kotte at the Western coast, and Yarlpanam (Anglicised Jaffna) in the north. The Dutch arrived in the 17th century. Although much of the island came under the domain of European powers, the interior, hilly region of the island remained independent, with its capital in Kandy. The British East India Company established control of the island in 1796, declaring it a crown colony in 1802, although the island would not be officially connected with British India. The fall of the kingdom of Kandy in 1815 unified the island under British rule.

European colonists established a series of tea, cinnamon, rubber, sugar, coffee and indigo plantations. The British also brought a large number of indentured workers from Tamil Nadu to work in the plantation economy. The city of Colombo was established as the administrative centre, and the British established modern schools, colleges, roads and churches that brought Western-style education and culture to the native people. Increasing grievances over the denial of civil rights, mistreatment and abuse of natives by colonial authorities gave rise to a struggle for independence in the 1930s, when the Youth Leagues opposed the "Ministers' Memorandum," which asked the colonial authority to increase the powers of the board of ministers without granting popular representation or civil freedoms. During World War II, the island served as an important Allied military base. A large segment of the British and American fleet were deployed on the island, as were tens of thousands of soldiers committed to the war against Japan in Southeast Asia.

Following the war, popular pressure for independence intensified. On 4 February 1948 the country won its independence as the Commonwealth of Ceylon. Don

Stephen Senanayake became the first Prime Minister of Sri Lanka. In 1972, the country became a republic within the Commonwealth, and the name was changed to Sri Lanka. On 21 July 1960 Sirimavo Bandaranaike took office as prime minister, and became the first female head of government in post-colonial Asia and the first female prime minister in the world.

Since 1983, there has been on-and-off civil war, predominantly between the government and the Liberation Tigers of Tamil Eelam (LTTE, also known as the Tamil Tigers), a separatist militant organization who fight to create an independent state named Tamil Eelam in the North and East of the island.

Geography

The island of Sri Lanka lies in the Indian Ocean, to the southwest of the Bay of Bengal and to the southeast of the Arabian Sea. It is separated from the Indian subcontinent by the Gulf of Mannar and the Palk Strait. According to Hindu mythology, a land bridge to the Indian mainland, known as Rama's Bridge, was constructed during the time of Rama by the vanara architect Nala. Often referred to as Adam's Bridge, it now amounts to only a chain of limestone shoals remaining above sea level. According to geological surveys, this is a natural causeway which was formerly complete, but was breached by a violent storm in 1480. The tear drop shaped island consists mostly of flat-to-rolling coastal plains, with mountains rising only in the south-central part. Amongst these are Sri Pada (Adams Peak) and the highest point Pidurutalagala, at 2,524 meters (8,281 ft). The Mahaweli Ganga (Mahaweli River) and other major rivers provide fresh water to the population.

Sri Lanka's climate can be described as tropical, and quite hot. Its position between 5 and 10 north latitude endows the country with a warm climate, moderated by ocean winds and considerable moisture. The mean temperature ranges from a low of 16 °C in Nuwara Eliya in the Central Highlands (where frost may occur for several days in the winter) to a high of 32 °C in Trincomalee on the northeast coast (where temperatures may reach 38 °C. The average yearly temperature for the country, as a whole, ranges from 28° to 30 °C. Day and night temperatures may vary by 4 to 7 °C. In January, the coolest month, many people wear coats and sweaters in the highlands and elsewhere. May, the hottest period, precedes the summer monsoon rains. The rainfall pattern is influenced by the monsoon winds of the Indian Ocean and Bay of Bengal, which encounter the slopes of the Central Highlands; they unload heavy rains on the mountain slopes and the southwestern sector of the island. Some of the windward slopes receive up to 2,500 millimetres (98 in) of rain per month, but the leeward slopes in the east and northeast receive little rain. Periodic squalls occur and sometimes tropical cyclones bring overcast skies and rains to the southwest, northeast, and eastern parts of the island. Between December to March, monsoon winds come from the northeast, bringing moisture from the Bay of Bengal. Humidity is typically higher in the southwest and mountainous areas and depends on the seasonal patterns of rainfall. At Colombo, for example, daytime humidity stays above 70% all year, rising to almost 90 percent during the monsoon season in June. Anuradhapura experiences a daytime low of 60% during the monsoon month of March, but a high of 79% during the November and December rains. In the highlands, Kandy's daytime humidity usually ranges between 70 and 79%.

Government and Politics

The Constitution of Sri Lanka establishes a democratic, socialist republic in Sri Lanka, which is also a unitary state. The government is a mixture of the presidential system and the parliamentary system. The President of Sri Lanka is the head of state, the commander in chief of the armed forces, as well as head of government, and is popularly elected for a six-year term. In the exercise of duties, the President is responsible to the Parliament of Sri Lanka, which is a unicameral 225-member legislature. The President appoints and heads a cabinet of ministers composed of elected members of parliament. The President's deputy is the Prime Minister, who leads the ruling party in parliament and shares many executive responsibilities, mainly in domestic affairs.

Members of parliament are elected by universal (adult) suffrage based on a modified proportional representation system by district to a six-year term. The primary modification is that, the party that receives the largest number of valid votes in each constituency gains a unique "bonus seat." The president may summon, suspend, or end a legislative session and dissolve Parliament any time after it has served for one year. The parliament reserves the power to make all laws. On July 1, 1960 the people of Sri Lanka elected the first-ever female head of government in Prime Minister Sirimavo Bandaranaike. Her daughter Chandrika Kumaratunga served multiple terms as prime minister and as president from 1999 to 2005. The current president and prime minister, both of whom took office on 21 November 2005, are Mahinda Rajapaksa and Ratnasiri Wickremanayake respectively.

Sri Lanka has enjoyed the longest period of continuous multi-party democracy with universal suffrage in a non-western country (since 1931). Politics in Sri Lanka are controlled by rival coalitions led by the left-wing Sri Lanka Freedom Party, headed by President Rajapaksa, the comparatively right-wing United National Party led by former prime minister Ranil Wickramesinghe and Marxist JVP. There are also many smaller Buddhist, socialist and Tamil nationalist political parties that oppose the separatism of the LTTE but demand regional autonomy and increased civil rights. Since 1948, Sri Lanka has been a member of the Commonwealth of Nations and the United Nations. It is also a member of the Non-Aligned Movement, the Colombo Plan, Asia-Pacific Economic Cooperation and the South Asian Association for Regional Cooperation. Through the Cold War-era, Sri Lanka followed a foreign policy of non-alignment but has remained closer to the United States and Western Europe. The military of Sri Lanka comprises the Sri Lankan Army, the Sri Lankan Navy and the Sri Lankan Air Force. These are administered by the Ministry of Defence. Since the 1980s, the army has led the government response against the Marxist militants of the JVP and now the LTTE militant forces. Sri Lanka receives considerable military assistance from Pakistan and China].

Administrative Divisions

Sri Lanka is divided into 9 provinces and 25 districts. Each province is administered by a directly-elected provincial council, as under:

Province	Capital	Districts
Central	Kandy	Kandy, Matale, Nuwara Eliya
North Central	Anuradhapura	Anuradhapura, Polonnaruwa
Northern	Jaffna	Jaffna, Kilinochchi, Mannar, Vavuniya, Mullativu
Eastern	Trincomalee	Ampara, Batticaloa, Trincomalee
North Western	Kurunegala	Kurunagala, Puttalam
Southern	Galle	Galle, Hambanthota, Mathara
Uva	Badulla	Badulla, Monaragala
Sabaragamuwa	Ratnapura	Kegalle, Rathnapura
Western	Colombo	Colombo, Gampaha, Kaluthara

The districts are further subdivided into Divisional Secretariats, and these in turn to Grama Sevaka divisions.

Economy

In the 19th and 20th centuries, Sri Lanka became a plantation economy, famous for its production and export of cinnamon, rubber and Ceylon tea, which remains a trademark national export. The development of modern ports under British rule raised the strategic importance of the island as a centre of trade. During World War II, the island hosted important military installations and Allied forces. However, the plantation economy aggravated poverty and economic inequality. From 1948 to 1977 socialism strongly influenced the government's economic policies. Colonial plantations were dismantled, industries were nationalised and a welfare state established. While the standard of living and literacy improved significantly, the nation's economy suffered from inefficiency, slow growth and lack of foreign investment.

From 1977 the UNP government began incorporating privatisation, deregulation and promotion of private enterprise. While the production and export of tea, rubber, coffee, sugar and other agricultural commodities remains important, the nation has moved steadily towards an industrialised economy with the development of food processing, textiles, telecommunications and finance. By 1996 plantation crops made up only 20% of export, and further declined to 16.8% in 2005 (compared with 93% in 1970), while textiles and garments have reached 63%. The GDP grew at an average annual rate of 5.5% during the early 1990s, until a drought and a deteriorating security situation lowered growth to 3.8% in 1996. The economy rebounded in 1997-2000, with average growth of 5.3%. The year of 2001 saw the first recession in the country's history, as a result of power shortages, budgetary problems, the global slowdown, and continuing civil strife. Signs of recovery appeared after the 2002 ceasefire. The Colombo Stock Exchange reported the highest growth in the world for 2003, and today Sri Lanka has the highest per capita income in South Asia.

In April 2004, there was a sharp reversal in economic policy after the government headed by Ranil Wickramesinghe of the United National Party was defeated by a coalition made up of Sri Lanka Freedom Party and the leftist-nationalist Janatha Vimukthi Peramuna called the United People's Freedom Alliance. The new government stopped the privatization of state enterprises and reforms of state utilities such as power and petroleum, and embarked on a subsidy program called the Rata Perata economic program. Its main theme to support the rural and suburban SMEs and protect the domestic economy from external influences, such as oil prices, the World Bank and the International Monetary Fund.

The GDP (PPP) of Sri Lanka according to a 2005 estimate is $86.72 billion with a per capita income of $4,600.

Demographics

Sri Lanka is the 53rd most populated nation in the world, with an annual population growth rate of 0.79%. Sri Lanka has a birth rate of 15.63 births per 1,000 people and a death rate of 6.49 deaths per 1,000 people. Population density is the greatest in western Sri Lanka, especially in and around Colombo. There is a small population on the island of the Wanniyala-Aetto people, also known as Veddahs. These are believed to be the oldest and indigenous ethnic group to inhabit the island. The Sinhalese people form the largest ethnic group in the nation, composing approximately 81.9% of the total population. Tamils are concentrated in the North, East, Central and Western provinces of the country. Tamils who were brought as indentured labourers from India by British colonists to work on estate plantations, nearly 50% of whom were repatriated following independence in 1948, are called "Indian Origin" Tamils. They are distinguished from the native Tamil population that has resided in Sri Lanka since ancient times. According to 2001 census data, Indian Tamils are 5.1% of the Sri Lankan population and, Sri Lankan Tamils 4.3%. Though this figure only accounted for Sri Lankan Tamils in government-controlled areas, not accounting for those in rebel-held territories. There is a significant population (8.0%) of Moors, who trace their lineage to Arab traders and immigrants from the Middle East. Their presence is concentrated in the cities and the central and eastern provinces. There are also small ethnic groups such as the Burghers (of mixed European descent) and Malays from Southeast Asia.

Sinhalese and Tamil are the two official languages of Sri Lanka. English is spoken by approximately 10% of the population, and is widely used for education, scientific and commercial purposes. Members of the Burgher community speak variant forms of Portuguese Creole and Dutch with varying proficiency, while members of the Malay community speak a form of creole Malay that is unique to the island. Sri Lanka also enjoys significant religious diversity. Approximately 69% of Sri Lankans are adherents of Buddhism. Theravada Buddhism is the predominant school, with distinctive sects such as Ramanna Nikaya, Amarapura Nikaya and Siam Nikaya being widely followed. Buddhism in Sri Lanka has been deeply influenced by indigenous faiths and traditions, as well as the influences of prevailing Buddhist schools in South East Asia. The ancient and famous Sri Dalada Maligawa or "Temple of the Tooth" is the principal Buddhist Temple in Sri Lanka, and by tradition houses the Tooth of Buddha. It is visited every year by millions of pilgrims. There are many other famous religious institutions in Sri Lanka that attract many visitors daily. Hinduism is practiced by 7.9% of the population, mainly from the Tamil community. Christianity is practiced by 7% of the population, especially by Burgher people though most Christians are Sinhalese or Tamils. While most Sri Lankan Christians are Catholics, there are also significant numbers who adhere to Dutch Reformed Church and the Anglican Communion. Islam in Sri Lanka is practiced by 8.5% of the population and its adherents are almost entirely Moors and Malays.

Transportation

The railroads are government owned; about 1,944 kilometres of track; network extends radially from Colombo to northern, eastern, and southern coastal cities; services to northern and eastern areas are erratic because of domestic unrest.

Deep water ports are at Colombo, Trincomalee and Galle. Sri Lanka has 14 airfields, 11having permanent surface runways.

International telecommunications services are provided by satellite earth stations and submarine cable;

international telephone, telex, and direct dialing in operation; about 106,500 telephones nationwide; about 29 radio stations, 24 of which are AM, at least 5 are FM) in operation, with more than 2 million registered receivers in use; 2 television networks broadcast over 4 channels; 350,000 television sets nationwide.

Culture and Arts

The island is the home of two main traditional cultures: the Sinhalese (centered in the ancient cities of Kandy and Anuradhapura) and the Tamil (centered in the city of Jaffna). In more recent times a British colonial culture was added, and lately Sri Lanka, particularly in the urban areas, has experienced a dramatic makeover in the western mold. Until recently, for example, most Sri Lankans, certainly those in the villages, have eaten traditional food, engaged in traditional crafts and expressed themselves through traditional arts. But economic growth and intense economic competition in developed countries has spilled over to most of Sri Lanka, producing changes that might variously be identified as progress, westernization or a loss of identity and assimilation.

Education

With a literacy rate of 92%, and 83% of the total population having had Secondary Education, Sri Lanka has one of the most literate populations amongst developing nations. An education system which dictates 9 years of Compulsory Schooling for every child is in place, with 99% of the children entering the first grade. A free education system initiated in 1945 by Dr. C. W. W. Kannangara, a former minister of education, has greatly contributed to this. Mr. Kannangara led the establishment of the Madhya Maha Vidyalayas (Great Central Schools) in different parts of the country in order to provide education to Sri Lanka's rural population. In 1942 a special education committee proposed extensive reforms to establish an efficient and quality education system for the people. In recent decades, a large number of private and international schools have been established across the nation. The International Baccalaureate and General Certificate of Secondary Education are popular education programmes.

Most secondary schools in Sri Lanka provide education from grades 1 to 13 in the same institution. Students sit for the GCE Ordinary Level Examination (O/ Levels) in grade 11 and the GCE Advanced Level Examination (A/levels) in grade 13. These schools are modelled on British colleges and universities. A majority of them are public, but a number of elite private schools do exist. While most reputed schools centered on large cities are usually single-sex institutions, rural schools tend to be coeducational.

Sri Lanka has a number of large public universities. They include the University of Colombo, the University of Kelaniya, the University of Sri Jayewardenepura, the University of Moratuwa, the University of Peradeniya, the University of Jaffna, the University of Ruhuna, the Eastern University of Sri Lanka, the Rajarata University of Sri Lanka, the Sabaragamuwa University of Sri Lanka, the Wayamba University of Sri Lanka and the Uva Wellassa University of Sri Lanka. However, the lack of space in these institutions and the unwillingness to establish private universities has led to a large number of students been denied entry into formal universities. As a result, a number of private institutions have emerged, which provide specialized education in a variety of fields, such as computer science, business administration and arts. These include the government owned Sri Lanka Institute of Information Technology and the Institute of Technological Studies.

Armed Forces

The Sri Lanka Army has three divisions headquarters, an armoured brigade, an air mobile brigade, 33 infantry brigades, a Special Forces brigade, a commando brigade, four artillery regiments, and several support regiments. The infantry and artillery brigades have both regular and active volunteer battalions. The army has about 120,000 soldiers. It is impossible to determine the exact strength due to large number of desertions. Recruitment is extremely difficult. Retention is poor and the army periodically offers amnesty for the deserters (the army has offered nearly 20 amnesty's since 1990). Most soldiers desert with their weapons. In September 2004, the SLA attempted to recruit more soldiers with a promise of higher pay, but the recruitment goal of 4,000 soldiers was not met.

The Sri Lanka Navy has four regional headquarters; Colombo (NAV WEST), Boossa (NAV SOUTH), Trincomalee (NAV EAST), and Karanger (NAV NORTH). Due to the limited naval role in fighting the LTTE, the SLN recently set up OM NOR CEN, a headquarters to command naval units performing defence measures on land; especially in areas recaptured from rebels. The Sri Lanka Navy's primary mission is to support the government's counter-terrorism efforts against the Tamil insurgents by guarding the coastline, particularly in the island's north and east. A secondary mission is to support of the Sri Lanka Army by transporting troops and supplies to their cut-off bases on the Jaffna Peninsula. The navy still needs smaller, well-armed craft capable of stopping the LTTE's small ships

Sri Lanka's armed forces are designed to fight counter-insurgency – not defend the country from an external threat. The three services remain focussed on defeating the Tamil insurgency. Though the army is prepared to fight the LTTE and is increasing its firepower, desertions are rampant in infantry units. The emergence of a more heavily armed LTTE has caught the SLA by surprise (once again) and it is likely that the LTTE is continuing with its training and equipping while the SLA remains in their garrison locations.

The Sri Lanka Air Force is deployed in four zones. The northern zone has the No. 1 Flying Training Wing based at Anuradhapura and the No. 6 Helicopter Squadron at Vavuniya. The Palaly airbase is also in the northern zone but no aircraft are permanently based there. The western zone has the No. 4 VIP Helicopter Squadron, No. 5 Jet Squadron, and the No. 10 Jet Squadron at Katunayake. Airbases at Colombo and Ekala are also in the zone but without any permanently based aircraft. The southern zone has the No. 2 Heavy Helicopter Squadron and the No. 8 Light Helicopter Squadron at Ratmalana. The Katukurunda, Koggola, Wirawila, and Diyatalawa airbases are also part of the southern zone but without any aircraft based on them. The eastern zone has the No. 9 Attack Squadron and the No. 7 Helicopter Squadron at Hingurakgoda. The airbases at Chinabay, Batticaloa, and Ampara are in the eastern zone but are not permanent bases. The air force has increased its attack helicopters to conduct better close air support.

Sri Lanka's military forces are incapable of defending the country from an external attack. The three services have spent the last two decades fighting the LTTE and configured their forces with the organization, manning, and equipment required to defeat the insurgents.

Security Issues

The strategic importance of Sri Lanka emanates from its geo-strategic location in the Indian Ocean. Trincomalee, on the eastern coast of Sri Lanka, is one of the best natural harbours in the world. Adequate support facilities in terms of port and other infrastructure also exist in Sri Lanka to meet medium scale repairs and refits. Incumbent on the creation of facilities at Trincomalle, Sri Lanka has the potential to emerge as the maritime hub in the region for shipping traffic. Sri Lanka is in fact better placed to provide bunkering and other facilities to ships than Singapore, which has emerged as a maritime hub.

India has been extremely sensitive about the role of extra-regional players in Sri Lanka, which is separated from it by the narrow 24-kilometre wide Palk Strait. Given its geographical proximity, Sri Lanka is within the Indian security orbit. The common Tamil ethnicity in the two countries exerts a gravitational pull. Happenings in Sri Lanka, therefore, have direct bearing on India. The insurgency in Sri Lanka has its ramifications on the internal politics and security in the state of Tamil Nadu in India. India cannot afford to have any sort of military rivalry in its backyard. Though Indian has a policy of non-interference in Sri Lankan affairs, the geographical and cultural linkages make it an indispensable factor in the peace process. The bottom line for Indian security planners is that Indian can acquiesce to a divided Sri Lanka only at its own peril. The conflict in Sri Lanka has already created a sympathetic constituency amongst certain political groups in the state of Tamil Nadu towards the LTTE and its political goal.

The threats to Sri Lankan national security are internal rather than external. The Tamil insurgency is the most severe of these, involving attacks on military and civilian targets throughout the island. A second source of instability is from leftist nationalist Sinhalese groups opposed to Tamil autonomy. The problem of a restless, unemployed youth, although separate from the ethnic difficulties, is instrumental in providing a fertile recruiting ground for extremists in search of a following. Political and economic conflict between the Sinhalese and Tamil communities is a problem of growing urgency.

THAILAND

The Kingdom of Thailand, with its capital at Bangkok, is located in the centre of peninsular Southeast Asia. Burma is to the west, Laos to the north and east, Cambodia to the southeast, and Malaysia to the south. The south coast of Thailand faces the Gulf of Thailand, while the Isthmus of Kra is bordered on the west by the Andaman Sea (part of the Indian Ocean) and on the east by the Gulf of Thailand. Thailand also has coastal islands in the Andaman Sea and the Gulf of Thailand. The largest, with provincial status, is Phuket, off the west coast; on the gulf side, the largest islands are Samui and Pangan.

Thailand has a total of 511,770 square kilometres of land area and 2,230 square kilometres of water area for a total of 514,000 square kilometres. The total land boundary is 4,863 kilometres in length, including borders with Burma (1,800 kilometres), Laos (1,754 kilometres), Cambodia (803 kilometres), and Malaysia (506 kilometres). A dispute between Thailand and Laos over Mekong River islands continues to delay completion of an agreement on the demarcation of their boundary. Thailand has significant differences with Burma over the alignment of their boundary. There are disputed sections of the Thai—Cambodia border where border markers are missing. Land mines, the remnants of former conflicts are still to be found—sometimes with lethal consequences—along Thailand's borders with Cambodia and Laos. Although Thailand has no actual border dispute with Malaysia, terrorist and insurgent activities in the frontier area lead to frequent border closures and tight security.

The coastline is 3,219 kilometres long: 750 kilometres on the Andaman Sea and 2,469 kilometres on the Gulf of Thailand.

The traditional founding date of Thailand is 1238. Unlike other nations in Southeast Asia, Thailand was never colonized. Its flag consists of five horizontal bands of red (on top), white, blue (double width), white, and red. The red stripes represent unity of the nation, the white strips represent purity of religion, and the blue stripe in the centre represents the king.

History

In the 9th century B.C., Mon and Khmer people established kingdoms that included large areas of what is now Thailand. Much of what these people absorbed from contacts with South Asian peoples—religious, social, political, and cultural ideas and institutions—later influenced the development of Thailand's culture and national identity. In the 2nd century B.C., the Hindu-led state of Funan in present-day Cambodia and central Thailand had close commercial contact with India and was a base for Hindu merchant-missionaries. In the southern Isthmus of Kra, Malay city-states controlled routes used by traders and travelers journeying between India and Indochina (present-day Cambodia, Laos, and Vietnam).

In 1238 a Tai chieftain, Sri Intraditya, declared his independence from Khmer overlords and established a kingdom at Sukhothai in the Chao Phraya Valley in central Thailand. The people of the central plain took the name *Thai*, which means "free," to distinguish themselves from other Tai people still under foreign rule. The Kingdom of Sukhothai conquered the Isthmus of Kra in the thirteenth century and financed itself with war booty and tribute from vassal states in Burma, Laos, and the Malay Peninsula. During the reign of Ramkhamhaeng (Rama the Great, r. 1279–98), Sukhothai established diplomatic relations with the Yuan Dynasty (1279–1368) in China and acknowledged China's emperor as its nominal overlord. After Ramkhamhaeng's death, the vassal states gradually broke away; a politically weakened Sukhothai was forced to submit in 1378 to the rising new Thai Kingdom of Ayutthaya and was completely absorbed by 1438.

The city-state of Ayutthaya was founded in 1350 and established its capital in 1351 on the Chao Phraya River in central Thailand, calling it Ayutthaya, after Ayodhaya, the Indian city of the hero Rama in the Hindu epic *Ramayana*. In 1360 Ramathibodi (r. 1351–69) declared Theravada Buddhism as the official religion and compiled a legal code based on Hindu legal texts and Thai custom that remained in effect until the late nineteenth century. Ayutthaya became the region's most powerful kingdom, eventually capturing Angkor and forcing the Khmer to submit to Thai suzerainty. Rather than a unified kingdom, Ayutthaya was a patchwork of self-governing principalities and tributary provinces ruled by members of the royal family who owed allegiance to the king. The king, however, was an absolute monarch who took on god-like aspects. This belief in a divine kingship continued until the 18th century. The kingdom became increasingly sophisticated as new social, political, and economic developments took place.

After a bloody dynastic struggle in the 1690s, Ayutthaya entered what some historians have called its golden age—a relatively peaceful period in the second quarter of the 18th century when art, literature, and learning flourished. The rising power of Burma led to a Burmese invasion of Ayutthaya and the destruction of its capital and culture in 1767. Only a Chinese attack on Burma kept the chaotic Thai polity from Burmese subjugation.

Another general, Chakri, assumed the throne and took the name Yot Fa (Rama I, r. 1782–1809). Yot Fa established the ruling house that continues to the present. The court moved across the river to the village of Bangkok, the kingdom's economy revived, and what remained of the artistic heritage of Ayutthaya was restored. The Kingdom of Bangkok consolidated claims to territory in Cambodia and the Malayan state of Kedah while Britain annexed territory in an area that had been contested by the Thai and the Burmese for centuries. Subsequent treaties—in 1826 with Britain and in 1833 with the United States— granted foreign trade concessions in Bangkok. The kingdom's expansion was halted in all directions by 1851. The reign of King Mongkut (Rama IV, r. 1851–68) marked a new opening to the Western nations. To avoid the humiliations suffered by China and Burma in their wars with Britain and the resulting unequal treaties, Bangkok negotiated and signed treaties with Britain, the United States, France, and other European countries between 1855 and 1870. As a result, commerce with the West increased and, in turn, revolutionized the Thai economy and connected it to the world monetary system. Foreign demands for extraterritoriality convinced Mongkut that legal and administrative reforms were needed if Siam (as the Thai kingdom was officially known from 1855 to 1939 and from 1946 to 1949; prior to then, the Thai traditionally named their country after the capital city) were to be treated as an equal by the Western powers. Monkut's death in 1868 postponed further reforms, however.

Real reform occurred during the reign of Chulalongkorn (Rama V, r. 1868–1910). After his formal enthronement in 1873, he announced reforms of the judiciary, state finance, and the political structure. An antireform revolt was suppressed in 1874, after which Chulalongkorn embarked on less radical approaches. In time, he ordered the gradual elimination of slavery. He introduced currency based taxes and a conscription-based regular army. In 1893 a centralized state administration replaced the semi-feudal provincial administration. The regime established European-style schools for children of the royal family and sent government officials, promising civil servants, and military officers to Europe for further education. The first railroad line was opened between Bangkok and Ayutthaya in 1897 and extended farther north in 1901 and 1909. To the south, rail connections were made in 1903, linking with British rail lines in Malaya. During this time, British and French colonial advances in Southeast Asia posed serious threats to Siam's independence and forced Siam to relinquish its claims in Cambodia, Laos, and the northern Malay states. Although much diminished in territory by the 1910s, Siam preserved its independence, and the kingdom served as a buffer state between the British and French colonies.

Siam joined the Allies in declaring war against Germany during World War I (1914–18) and sent a small expeditionary force to the European western front. These actions won Siam favorable amendments to its treaties with France and Britain at the end of the war. Siam also gained, as spoils of war, impounded German ships for use in its merchant marine. Siam took part in the Versailles peace conference in 1919 and was a founding member of the League of Nations.

A bloodless coup d'état in 1932, engineered by a group of Western-oriented and nationalist-minded government officials and army officers, ended the absolute monarchy and ushered in a constitutional regime. The first parliamentary elections were held in November 1933. After World War II broke out in Europe (1939–45), Japan used its influence with the Vichy regime in France to obtain territorial concessions for Thailand in Laos and Cambodia. The war for Thailand began in earnest on December 8, 1941, when Thai and Japanese troops clashed on the Isthmus of Kra. Bangkok acceded to Japan's demands that its troops be permitted to cross the isthmus to invade Burma and Malaya. In January 1942, Thailand signed a mutual defence pact with Japan and declared war against Britain and the United States. However, the anti-Japanese Thai ambassador to Washington, refused his government's orders to deliver the declaration of war, and the United States refrained from declaring war on Thailand.

In May 1946, a new constitution was promulgated. It called for a bicameral legislature with a popularly elected lower house and an upper house elected by the lower house. The name Siam was officially restored. The civilian government's failure eventually led to the restoration of the military faction in a coup in November 1947. In 1955 SEATO's headquarters was established in Bangkok, and Thailand offered the United States the use of Thai military bases. Military-controlled government continued between 1957 and 1967. There was talk under Prime Minister Sarit Thanarat of a "restoration" of the king, and a strong popular affection for the monarchy arose. The regime emphasized the kingdom's Buddhist heritage in an effort to gain support from monks for government programmes.

Anticommunism continued to influence Thailand's foreign affairs, and in 1961 Thailand, the Philippines, and newly independent Malaya (since 1963, Malaysia) formed the Association of Southeast Asia (ASA). In 1967 Thailand became a founding member of the Association of Southeast Asian Nations (ASEAN), a broader regional cooperative organization that replaced the ASA. At the same time, Prime Minister Thanom Kittikachorn decided to shorten the timetable for the country's transition from the military-dominated leadership structure to a popularly elected government In June 1968, a new constitution was proclaimed, but martial law, which had been imposed in 1958, remained in effect. Party politics resumed in 1968, and Thanom's United Thai People's Party carried the February 1969 National Assembly elections. The new government, however, had to respond to numerous issues: a Muslim insurgency in southern Thailand, communist guerrillas operating in jungle areas north of the Thai-Malaysian border, the successes of communist forces in Vietnam and Laos, and other regional unrest and protests against the government. In November 1971, Thanom carried out a coup against his own government, thereby ending the three-year experiment in parliamentary democracy. The constitution was suspended, political parties were banned, and the military took full charge in suppressing opposition.

The stern moves by the Thanom regime led to popular dissatisfaction among university students and organized labour, accompanied by growing anti-U.S. sentiments. Some feared Thanom would even overthrow the monarchy and establish a republic. In a demonstration on 13 October 1973, some 250,000 people pressed their grievances against the government. The following day, troops fired on the demonstrators, killing 75 of them. King Bhumibol took a rare direct role, forcing the cabinet's resignation; Thanom and his close colleagues were allowed to leave the country secretly. A new constitution went into effect in October 1974, providing for a popularly elected House of Representatives. The elections were inconclusive, and in October 1976, when violent student demonstrations were suppressed by security forces, a military junta took control of the government, declared martial law, annulled the constitution, banned political parties, and strictly censored the media.

The period from 1976 till 1992 saw military rule and limited Parliamentary government. Strict censorship continued, and the regime tightly controlled labour unions and purged suspected communists from the civil service and educational institutions. As a result, many students joined the communist insurgency.

Coups and elections continued periodically till 2006. In mid-1997 a major financial crisis ensued, the baht—Thailand's currency, was devalued, the Central Bank governor resigned, and widespread protests took place. The government announced austerity measures, and the International Monetary Fund (IMF) intervened, but the economy continued to deteriorate. Despite a new constitution promulgated in October 1997, confidence continued to slide, and elections saw transfer of power without military intervention, from one elected leader to another. This represented a major breakthrough in the development of democratic processes in Thailand. The baht continued to devalue, however, and social unrest recurred. By the summer of 1998, the economy had become more stable, although investigations into banking practices continued to uncover mismanagement and irregularities. With assistance from the IMF, Thailand gradually regained macroeconomic stability.

The first-ever elections to the Senate were held in 2000, and, in January 2001 one party—the Phak Thai Rak Thai (Thai Loves Thai Party)—won an absolute majority in the House of Representatives. Because of widespread allegations of illegal election practices, new polling took place in February in some constituencies. The Thai Rak Thai, having merged with another party since the January election, still won the absolute majority of seats, but a coalition government with the New Aspiration Party and Chat Thai was established. Police Lieutenant Colonel Thaksin Chinnawat became prime minister. The Thai Rak Thai was further strengthened in 2002 when it absorbed many members of the New Aspiration Party.

Thaksin set out to stabilize several problematic areas. One was to launch a major anti-drug campaign. Some 2,275 people were killed in a three-month period ending in April 2003, and the government claimed to have eradicated 90% of Thailand's drug problem. In October 2004, the government launched a second anti-drug campaign. Another problem confronting the kingdom was terrorist violence, primarily in the south. In 2002 several police officers were killed when the minister of interior toured the violence-prone area, and five schools suffered damage from arsonists. The Thai military attributed these actions to a group thought to be an al Qaeda affiliate and arrested suspected members of Jemaah Islamiah (Community of Islam) in June 2003. They confessed to plotting attacks on embassies in Bangkok and tourist sites. Further arsons and bombings occurred, and attacks on police and army bases in 2004 heightened the terrorist threat. In 2004 alone, more than 500 people died as a result of insurgent and terrorist violence in the south. This loss of life was exacerbated when a massive tsunami hit the Andaman coast on December 26, 2004, killing more than 5,300 Thai and foreigners and leaving another 2,900 reported missing.

In February 2005, the Thai Rak Thai won a 75% majority in the House of Representatives elections, and, for the first time, a single-party government was formed. The following year, however, there were mass protests calling for Thaksin's resignation over corruption issues. He called for early parliamentary elections in April 2006 that were boycotted by the major opposition parties and declared unconstitutional in May. Amidst growing protests, Thaksin continued as prime minister until 19 September 2006, when military forces staged a successful coup and set up a military-controlled regime.

Geography

Topography: Topography and drainage define four main regions: north, northeast, central, and south. In the north, the chief topographic features are high mountains along the borders with Burma and Laos and extending down the Isthmus of Kra to the southern border with Malaysia. The central plain, which extends to the Gulf of Thailand, is a lowland area drained by the Chao Phraya and its tributary rivers. The narrow, tropical Isthmus of Kra runs from mainland Thailand to the border with peninsular Malaysia. It has a low-lying range of hills at the narrowest part, about 600 metres in elevation. The highest point is Doi Inthanon, in Chiang Mai Province in northwestern Thailand, at 2,565 metres above sea level. The lowest point is along the Gulf of Thailand at zero metres above sea level.

Principal Rivers: The principal river is the Chao Phraya, which, with its tributaries, drains about 33% of the national territory and flows south into a delta at Bangkok. The Mun and many other smaller upland rivers are tributaries of the Mekong, which forms the border between Thailand and Laos before flowing into Cambodia and Vietnam and into the South China Sea. Together, the Chao Phraya and Mekong systems sustain Thailand's agricultural economy and provide waterways for inland navigation.

Climate: A tropical country, Thailand has three distinct seasons. The first is a hot and dry season from February to May, with an average temperature of 34E C and 75% relative humidity. This season is followed by a rainy, cooler season brought by the southwest monsoon from June to September, with an average daily temperature of 29E C and 87% relative humidity. A cooler, dry season, caused by the northeast monsoon, lasts from November to January, with temperatures ranging from 32E C to less than 20E C and lower relative humidity. The Isthmus of Kra is always hot and humid and has the heaviest rainfall. The lightest rainfall is in the northeast. Temperatures in Bangkok range between 20E C and 35E C.

Natural Resources: Thailand's major natural resources are fluorite, gypsum, lead, lignite, natural gas, rubber, tantalum, tin, and tungsten. Renewable resources include fish and timber.

Land Use: Roughly 20% of Thailand is covered by mountains and hills, the steepness of which generally precludes agriculture. As of 2005, rich arable land accounted for nearly 27.5% of the total area. About 6.9% was planted to permanent crops. Some 49,860 square kilometres of land were irrigated according to 2003 estimates.

Environmental Factors: The depletion of the water table around Bangkok has led to land subsidence. Despite the annual southwest monsoon, Thailand is subject to drought. Other environmental issues include air pollution from vehicle emissions, water pollution from organic and factory wastes, deforestation, soil erosion, and wildlife population depletion from illegal hunting. Thailand is also vulnerable to devastating tsunamis, such as the one that struck the Andaman Sea coast on December 26, 2004. It killed more than 5,300 people, including foreign visitors, and left another 2,900 missing.

Society

Population: Thailand's population was estimated at 64,631,595 in July 2006, making it the nineteenth most populous country in the world. The population growth rate was estimated in 2006 at 0.68%. The net migration rate, also based on a 2006 estimate, is 0%. In 2005 about 68% of the population lived in rural areas and 32% in urban areas. The largest population, according to 2000 census data, was in the northeast, with 20.7 million inhabitants and a population density of 122.9 persons per square kilometre. The central region, excluding Bangkok, had the next largest population in 2000, with 14 million inhabitants and a density of 137.8 persons per square kilometre. Bangkok itself had a population of 6.3 million inhabitants and a population density of 4,038 persons per square kilometre. The mountainous north had nearly 11.4 million people, with a density of 67 persons per square kilometre, while the south had 8 million people and a density of 113.9 persons per square kilometre.

Demography: According to estimates of Thailand's age structure for 2006, 22% of inhabitants are less than 15 years of age, 70% are 15–64 years of age, and 8% are 65 and older. Estimates made in 2006 indicate a birthrate of 13.8 births per 1,000 population and a death rate of 7 deaths per 1,000. In 2006 life expectancy was estimated at 74.6 years for women and 69.9 years for men, or nearly 72.2 years total. The infant mortality rate was estimated at nearly 19.4 per 1,000 live births in 2006. The total fertility rate for 2006 has been estimated at nearly 1.6 children per woman.

Ethnic Groups: Official government estimates indicate that people of Thai ethnicity make up 75% of the population. Another 14% are ethnic Chinese, and 4% are Malay, leaving 7% as uncategorized. An estimated 1 million members of hill tribes, collectively called "highlanders," live in the northwest. Remnants of 1940s Chinese Nationalist military forces and their descendants and children of Vietnamese immigrants live in northeastern Thailand.

Languages: Nearly 94% of the people speak Tai-Kadai (Daic) languages, with Thai (in various dialects) being predominant and the national and official language. Another 2% speak Austro-Asiatic languages, 2% speak Austronesian languages, 1% speaks Tibeto-Burman languages, and 0.2% speaks Hmong-Mien languages. Standard Thai is based on the dialect spoken in the Chao Phraya Valley. The Thai alphabet, with 44 consonants and 32 vowels, originated during the reign of King Ramkhamhaeng (Rama the Great, r. 1279–98) and is an adaptation of Mon and Khmer scripts derived from Indian Devanagari. Some 74 languages are spoken in Thailand, including numerous Thai dialects plus English, which is the secondary language among the well educated and is widely understood, especially in Bangkok and other large urban areas, where it is a major language of business. Ethnic and regional dialects also are spoken, as are various dialects of Chinese.

Religion: The predominant religion is Theravada Buddhism, representing about 94% of the practicing population and about 90% of all Thai people. Muslims represent 4.6%; Christians, 0.7%; Hindus, 0.1%; and Sikhs, Baha'i Faith, and others, 0.6%. Section 73 of the constitution states that the state shall patronize and protect Buddhism and other religions, promote harmony among the followers of all religions, and encourage the application of religious principles "to create virtue and develop the quality of life." Religious instruction is required in public schools at both the primary and secondary education levels.

Education and Literacy: The Ministry of Education supervises public and private education. Starting in October 2002, the education system offered 12 years of free basic education to students nationwide: six years of primary education beginning at age six or seven, followed by three years of middle school and three years of high school, ending at age 18. Education has been compulsory through the ninth grade (from age seven to 16) since January 2003. With the addition of two years of preprimary schooling, the length of education was extended to 14 years in May 2004. In 2006 an estimated 96% of students completed grade six, 80% completed grade nine, and 79% completed grade 12. In 2004 more than 8.8 million students were enrolled in 32,413 primary, middle, and high schools; 631,000 students were enrolled in 612 vocational education institutions. Thailand also has 20 state universities, 12 of which are in Bangkok, plus 26 private universities and colleges and some 120 other institutions of higher education. Some 1.9 million students were enrolled in postsecondary education in 2003–4. About half of all university graduates were women in 2004. The literacy rate in Thailand is 92.6%.

Health: Data on health care are out of date, but in 1995 Thailand had 0.3 physicians and 1.9 hospital beds per 1,000 population. In 2002 annual spending on health care amounted to US$321 per person in purchasing power parity (PPP). Total expenditures represented about 4.4% of the gross domestic product (GDP); of this amount, 57.1% came from public sources and 42.9% from private sources. Some 85% of the population had access to potable water in 2002, and 99% had access to sanitation. Human immunodeficiency virus/acquired immune deficiency syndrome (HIV/AIDS) is a serious problem in Thailand. The United Nations Programme on HIV/AIDS (UNAIDS) reported in November 2004 that the Thai government had launched a well-funded, politically supported, and pragmatic response to the epidemic. As a result, national adult HIV prevalence has decreased to an estimated 1.5% of all persons aged 15 to 49 years (or about 1.8% of the total population). It was also reported that 58,000 adults and children had died from AIDS since the first case was reported in 1984. The government has begun to improve its support to persons with HIV/AIDS and has provided funds to HIV/AIDS support groups. Public programmes have begun to alter unsafe behavior, but discrimination against those infected continues. The government has funded an antiretroviral drug programme and, as of September 2006, more than 80,000 HIV/AIDS patients had received such drugs. Highly pathogenic H5N1 avian influenza (bird flu) has been found among birds in Thailand as well as surrounding areas. The government has pledged financial support for the prevention effort, which mainly focuses on changing poultry farming methods. Major infectious diseases in Thailand also include bacterial diarrhea, hepatitis, dengue fever, malaria, Japanese encephalitis, rabies, and leptospirosis.

Welfare: Thailand has social welfare and social insurance systems. Social welfare involves welfare services aimed at the poor, persons with disabilities, children, the elderly, women, minority hill tribes, and other disadvantaged individuals. The social insurance system provides sickness, maternity, disability, death, dependent child, old age, and unemployment benefits. There also is a social security system for private-sector employees and medical security and pension systems for public-service employees, employees of national enterprises, and military personnel.

Economy

Thailand's developing, free-enterprise economy has recovered from the Asian financial crisis triggered by speculation against the Thai baht in 1997–98. By 2002 Thailand's standard of living had returned to the level prevailing before the financial crisis. The recovery reflected the benefit of reform measures tied to assistance by the International Monetary Fund, direct investment from Japan, the United States, Singapore, and other nations, and surging exports. During 2001–4 the economy grew at a moderate rate, but the rate of growth was slower than in the booming 1980s and the first half of the 1990s. A long-term shift from agriculture to manufacturing and services continues, but about 39% of the workforce is still employed in agriculture, forestry, and fishing, although this sector is responsible for only 10% of gross domestic product (GDP). The economy is heavily dependent on exports, such as textiles and computer components, which account for 60% of GDP. Between 2002 and 2005, the number of poor declined by around 2 million. In% terms, the poverty rate declined from 15.6% in 2002 to 12% in 2004 and to 9.8% in 2005, according to the World Bank.

The military coup that took place on September 19, 2006, has not had a serious impact on the economy. The baht and financial markets experienced brief declines but soon stabilized when investment experts speculated that the coup would help resolve a political standoff that was hurting the economy. Thailand's bond ratings are unchanged; however, credit rating agencies have reported that they may be downgraded depending on future developments. According to investment experts, the economy is strong enough to overcome the temporary disruption caused by the coup.

Gross Domestic Product (GDP): In 2006 Thailand's GDP was US$196.6 billion, reflecting a growth rate of 4.4% over 2005. Per capita GDP was US$9,100 using purchasing power parity. In 2006 services constituted 45.2% of GDP, followed closely by industry with a 44.9% share. Agriculture accounted for the remaining 10%.

Government Budget: In 2005 Thailand's central government budget was estimated at US$35.2 billion. The budget was essentially in balance, with a small surplus of around US$467 million.

Inflation: Consumer prices increased by 4.5% in 2005, up from 1.8% the previous year, partly as a result of global demand for crude oil.

Agriculture, Forestry, and Fishing: In 2006 agriculture, forestry, and fishing contributed less than 10% of gross domestic product (GDP) but employed about 39% of the workforce. Thailand is the world's leading exporter of rice and a major exporter of shrimp. Other agricultural products include coconuts, corn, rubber, soybeans, sugarcane, and tapioca. In 1985 Thailand officially designated 25% of the nation's land area for protected forests and 15% for timber production. Protected forests have been set aside for conservation and recreation, while production forests are available for the forestry industry. Between 1992 and 2001, exports of logs and sawn timber increased from 50,000 cubic metres to 2 million cubic metres per year. The regional avian flu outbreak led to a contraction of Thailand's agricultural sector during 2004, and the tsunami disaster of December 26, 2004, devastated the west coast fisheries industry. In 2006 agricultural GDP was estimated to have contracted by 10%.

Mining and Minerals: Thailand's major minerals include fluorite, gypsum, lead, lignite, natural gas, rubber, tantalum, tin, and tungsten. The tin mining industry has declined sharply since 1985, and Thailand has gradually become a net importer of tin. As of 2003, the main mineral export was gypsum. Thailand is the world's second largest exporter of gypsum after Canada, even though government policy limits gypsum exports to prevent price cutting. In 2003 Thailand produced more than 40 types of minerals with an annual value of about US$740 million. However, more than 80% of these minerals were consumed domestically. In September 2003, in order to encourage foreign investment in the mining industry, the government relaxed severe restrictions on mining by foreign companies and reduced mineral royalties payable to the state.

Industry and Manufacturing: In 2006 industry contributed 44.9% of gross domestic product (GDP) but employed only 23% of the workforce. This relationship is the opposite of the one applying to agriculture. Industry expanded at an average annual rate of 3.4% during the 1995–2004 period. The most important sub sector of industry is manufacturing, which accounted for 34.5% of GDP in 2004. Thailand is becoming a centre of automobile manufacturing for the Association of Southeast Asian Nations (ASEAN) market. By 2004 automobile production had reached 930,000 units, more than twice as much as in 2001. Two automakers active in Thailand are Toyota and Ford. The expansion of the automotive industry has been a boon for domestic steel production. Thailand's electronics industry faces competition from Malaysia and Singapore, while its textile industry faces competition from China and Vietnam.

Energy: In 2004 Thailand's total energy consumption was estimated at 3.4 quadrillion British thermal units, representing about 0.7% of total world energy consumption. Thailand is a net importer of oil and natural gas, but the government is promoting the use of ethanol to reduce imports of petroleum and the gasoline additive methyl tertiary butyl ether. Thailand's four oil refineries have a combined capacity of 703,100 barrels per day. Thailand's government is considering establishing a regional oil processing and transportation hub, serving the needs of south-central China. Also in 2004, estimated coal consumption of 30.4 million short tons exceeded coal production of 22.1 million short tons. As of January 2007, proven oil reserves totaled 290 million barrels, and proven natural gas reserves were 14.8 trillion cubic feet. In 2003 recoverable coal reserves totaled 1,492.5 million short tons. In 2005 Thailand consumed about 127 billion kilowatt-hours of electricity. Electricity consumption rose by 4.7% in 2006 to 133 billion kilowatt-hours. According to the state electricity utility, the Electricity Generating Authority of Thailand, power consumption by residential consumers has been increasing because of more favorable rates given to residential customers over the industry and business sectors. Thailand's state-controlled electric utility and petroleum monopolies are undergoing restructuring.

Services: In 2006 the services sector, which ranges from tourism to banking and finance, contributed 45.2% of gross domestic product (GDP) and employed 38% of the workforce.

Banking and Finance: Dangerous levels of nonperforming assets at Thai banks helped trigger the attack on the Thai baht by currency speculators that led to the Asian financial crisis in 1997–98. By 2003 nonperforming assets had been cut in half to about 30%. Despite a return to profitability, however, Thailand's banks continue to struggle with the legacy of the financial crisis in the form of unrealized losses and inadequate capital. Therefore, the government is considering various reforms, including establishing an integrated financial regulatory agency that would free up the Bank of Thailand to focus on monetary policy. In addition, the Thai government is attempting to strengthen the financial sector through the consolidation of commercial, state-owned, and foreign-owned institutions. Specifically, the government's Financial Sector Reform Master Plan, which was first introduced in early 2004, provides tax breaks to financial institutions that engage in mergers and acquisitions. The reform programme has been deemed successful by outside experts. As of 2007, there were three state-owned commercial banks and five state-owned specialized banks, 15 Thai commercial banks, and 17 foreign banks in Thailand. The Bank of Thailand sought to stem the flow of foreign funds into the country in December 2006. This led within one day to the largest drop in stock prices on the Stock Exchange of Thailand since the 1997 Asian financial crisis. The massive selling by foreign investors amounted more than US$708 million.

Tourism: Tourism makes a larger contribution to Thailand's economy (typically about 6% of gross domestic product) than that of any other Asian nation. In 2004 some 11 million tourists visited Thailand. However, terrorism in southern Thailand and in Indonesia and natural disasters, most notably the December 2004 tsunami, has taken their toll on tourism. One of the negative side effects of Thailand's tourism industry is a burgeoning sex tourism industry and a related threat from human immunodeficiency virus/acquired immune deficiency syndrome (HIV/AIDS).

Labour: Thailand's labour force was estimated at 35.5 million in 2006. About 39% were employed in agriculture, 38% in services, and 23% in industry. In 2005 women constituted 48% of the labour force and held an increasing share of professional jobs. Less than 4% of the workforce is unionized, but 11% of industrial workers and 50% of state enterprise employees are unionized. Although laws applying to private-sector workers' rights to form and join trade unions were unaffected by the September 19, 2006, military coup and its aftermath, workers who participate in union activities continue to have inadequate legal protection. According to the U.S. Department of State, union workers are inadequately protected. In 2006 Thailand's unemployment rate was 2.1% of the labour force.

Foreign Economic Relations: Thailand seeks expanded trade through free-trade agreements and multilateral cooperation within such organizations as the Asian Development Bank, Asia-Pacific Economic Cooperation, Association of Southeast Asian Nations, and World Trade Organization. Under the auspices of the Asian Development Bank, Thailand joined the Greater Mekong Sub region's development programme in 1992. Japan and the United States are Thailand's top two trading partners and sources of direct investment. Thailand grants the United States preferential treatment for investment under the Thai-U.S. Treaty of Amity and Economic Relations of 1966.

Despite close economic ties between Thailand and the United States, the relationship suffers from disputes over agricultural trade, intellectual property rights, and customs procedures. In July 2005, Thailand reached bilateral free-trade agreements with key trading partners, such as Australia, New Zealand, China, India, and Bahrain. However, the trade deals were unpopular with domestic political opponents of the Thaksin Chinnawat government (2001–6) who claimed that the agreements failed to sufficiently protect Thai interests. China is gaining importance as a trading partner and competitor for foreign direct investment and export markets, particularly in the areas of agriculture, computer hardware, and textiles.

Imports: In 2006 Thailand imported US$125.9 billion of goods, including raw materials and intermediates (US$51.9 billion), capital goods (US$33.1 billion), fuel and lubricants (US$25.4 billion), consumer goods (US$9.5 billion), and consumer durables, such as electrical appliances (US$6 billion). Thailand's principal import partners in 2006 were Japan (20.4%), China(10.6%), the United States (6.7%), Malaysia (6.6%), and the United Arab Emirates (4.8%).

Exports: In 2005 Thailand exported US$109.2 billion of goods. Most exports related to manufacturing, including machinery and mechanical appliances (US$16.1 billion), electrical apparatus for circuits (US$8.9 billion), integrated circuits and parts (US$5.5 billion), and textiles (US$5.5 billion). Thailand's principal export partners in 2005 were the United States (15.4%), Japan (13.7%), China (8.3%), Singapore (6.8%), and Hong Kong (5.6%).

Trade Balance: In 2006 Thailand posted a merchandise trade surplus of US$2.3 billion.

Balance of Payments: In 2005 Thailand had a negative current account balance of US$3.7 billion. This deficit reflected the deterioration in the merchandise trade account, mainly because of a sharp rise in the import bill. According to an International Monetary Fund report, the current account deficit stood at US$3.7 billion in 2005.

External Debt: As of June 2006, total external debt was US$57.83 billion, or about 34% of gross domestic product (GDP). Foreign exchange reserves, once depleted during the financial crisis of 1997–98, increased steadily to US$41 billion in 2003, US$51 billion in 2004, US$52 billion in 2005, and US$59 billion in 2006.

Foreign Investment: In 2005 foreign direct investment was inbound US$3.3 billion. The largest foreign investors were the United States, Japan, Singapore, and the European Union.

Foreign Aid: On July 31, 2003, Thailand repaid its outstanding obligations under a standby arrangement from the International Monetary Fund designed to help it recover from the 1997–98 Asian financial crisis. Payment was made one year ahead of schedule, reflecting the achievement of macroeconomic and balance-of-payments stability. In 2005 the World Bank was funding eight development projects in Thailand. These projects encompassed the areas of social investment (US$300 million), education (US$225 million), land titling (US$118 million), technical assistance (US$30 million), and energy (US$245 million). Despite the devastating tsunami of 26 December 2004, the Thai government announced it did not need any international financial assistance in response.

Currency: Thailand's currency is the baht.

Infrastructure

Overview: Where topography allows it, Thailand has an extensive network of roads and railroads. Rapid transit is burgeoning in an otherwise gridlocked

Bangkok. Tourism and improved economic development led Bangkok to become a major regional air hub. New technology development has brought some improvements to the nation's telecommunications network.

Roads: Estimates vary on the length of roads in Thailand. According to a U.S. government estimate in 2000, Thailand had 57,403 kilometres of roads, 56,542 kilometres of which were paved and 861 kilometres, unpaved. Other sources indicate a lower total of fewer than 45,000 kilometres. Streets in Bangkok are frequently gridlocked, with an overabundance of motor vehicles flowing into the central city via expressways.

Railroads: Railroads are operated under the auspices of the State Railway of Thailand. In 2005 the system totaled an estimated 4,071 kilometres of narrow-gauge (1.000-meter gauge) track. The system currently has some 270 diesel locomotives and nearly 250 diesel railcars or multiple unit cars. According to figures provided for 2002, 55.7 million passenger journeys occurred, and the rail system hauled 9.9 million tons of freight. Freight traffic is considered an important part of Thailand's domestic container transport to and from seaport and inland terminals.

Rapid Transit: The Mass Rapid Transit Authority of Thailand operates a full metro service on a 21-kilometre-long, 18-station line that opened in Bangkok in 2004. The inaugural line will be extended in phases totaling 27 kilometres, and two future lines, totaling 67 kilometres, are planned.

Ports: Thailand's ports in order of size are Bangkok, Laem Chabang, Pattani, Phuket, Sattahip, Si Racha, and Songkhla. The Thai merchant fleet comprises 400 ships of 1,000 gross registered tons or more, including 145 cargo carriers, 91 petroleum tankers, 60 bulk carriers, 32 refrigerated cargo ships, 29 liquefied gas ships, 21 container ships, 14 chemical tankers, 6 passenger/cargo ships, 1 passenger ship, and 1 specialized tanker.

Inland and Coastal Waterways: Thailand has some 4,000 kilometres of navigable inland waterways, 92% of which, or 3,701 kilometres, are navigable by boats with drafts up to 0.9 metres. Thailand's long coastlines lend themselves to intercoastal trade.

Civil Aviation and Airports: In 2006 Thailand had an estimated 108 airports and three heliports. Sixty-six of the airports had paved runways, including eight of more than 3,047 metres in length. Bangkok International Airport at Don Muang, 24 kilometres north of the capital, is an important regional hub for pass-through flights and as a destination. About 80 airlines provide service to the Bangkok International Airport and carry a reported 25 million passengers and 700,000 tons of cargo a year. Ground was broken for a new Bangkok international airport at Suwannabhumi, 30 kilometres east of Bangkok, in January 2002, with a new projected opening in 2006. When Suwannabhumi opens, Don Muang will be used for domestic flights only. Other major airports are at Chiangmai, Hat Yai, and Pattani. There are two Thai flag carriers. Thai Airways International, founded in 1960, offers domestic and worldwide coverage with a fleet of 81 passenger and cargo aircraft. Since 1977, Thai Airways has been fully owned by the Thai government. Bangkok Airways is a privately owned company founded in 1968 as an air taxi company; since 1986, it has served primarily as a domestic carrier. It also flies to Phnom Penh, Cambodia, and offers charter flights to Burma; it has a fleet of 11 aircraft.

Pipelines: In 2006 Thailand had 3,760 kilometres of gas pipelines and 379 kilometres of refined products pipelines.

Telecommunications: In 2002 the Thai government formed a new Ministry of Information and Communications to oversee all aspects of telecommunications. By 2006 the ministry was to have liberalized the provision of telecommunications services under World Trade Organization guidelines. However, the proposed privatization of the state-owned Telephone Organization of Thailand and Communications Authority of Thailand remains controversial. The ministry also is responsible for implementing the country's information technology policy, called IT 2010, which is designed to strengthen Thailand's telecommunications infrastructure as a means of promoting overall economic development. Thailand's telecommunications network suffers from delays and other shortfalls in the provision of telephone services as a result of inadequate investment. The quality and availability of telephone service are much better in Bangkok and other cities than in rural areas. Mobile telephones (27.3 million in 2005) are much more prevalent than landline phones (6.7 million in 2004). In 2005 Thailand had 8.4 million Internet users, representing less than 11% of the population. State entities, including the police and military, and government allies own almost all television and radio stations and play an important role in determining programming content. The government's Public Relations Department requires that all Thai radio stations carry 30 minutes of official news prepared by Radio Thailand, the government's national radio network, twice daily. Radio Thailand has seven networks that specialize in such areas as news and information, public affairs, social issues, education, and foreign-language broadcasts. Thailand has five television channels, two of which are run by the central government, two by the army, and one by a private enterprise. Altogether, Thailand has 204 AM radio stations, 334 FM radio stations, 6 shortwave stations, and 111 television broadcast stations. Additionally, there are between 2,000 and 3,000 community radio stations, many of which operate outside the law by using frequencies restricted to government entities. Those that register are allowed to continue broadcasting but others, including those critical of the government, have been shut down. Thailand has about 14 million radios and 15 million television sets.

Government and Politics

Thailand is a constitutional monarchy with, until September 19, 2006, a democratically elected bicameral legislature. On September 19, a military junta led by the commander in chief of the Thai army, Lieutenant General Sonthi Bunyaratklin, ousted the elected government of Prime Minister Thaksin Shinawatra. When the coup was staged in Bangkok, Thaksin himself was in New York City to address the opening session of the United Nations General Assembly. He attempted to issue a martial law decree and demanded Sonthi's arrest. The response was the establishment of the Council for Democratic Reform under Sonthi's chairmanship, suspension of the 1997 constitution, a crackdown on the open media, and detention of cabinet members and political opponents of the military regime. On the day of the coup, King Bhumibol Adulyadej and Queen Sirikit met with coup leaders, and on September 21 the king officially appointed Sonthi as chairman of the military authorities, known as the Council for National Security (CNS).

An interim 39-article constitution drafted by the council was endorsed by King Bhumibol and promulgated on October 1, 2006. It is to remain in place until a permanent constitution is proclaimed, prior to legislative elections scheduled for October 2007. The interim constitution gives overwhelming power to the executive branch and the CNS, with the CNS chairman having the power to appoint and remove the prime minister. Although the details of the permanent constitution are not yet known, internal observers predicted that it will restrict the economic and political authority of the prime minister and more closely delineate the powers of the monarchy, military, and parliament.

Whereas previous governments had relied on fragile coalitions, since becoming prime minister in 2001, Thaksin Shinawatra had steadily increased his parliamentary power by forging alliances with other parties and attracting members of other parties to his Thai Rak Thai Party (Thai Loves Thai Party). The Thai Rak Thai's continuous success in national elections allowed it to assume a more dominant position in government and to dictate policy much more easily. Opposition parties, such as the Phak Prachathipat Party (Democratic Party), were greatly weakened, while coalition parties, such as the Phak Chat Thai Party (Thai Nation Party) and Pak Khwam Wang Mei (New Aspiration Party), were merged with the Thai Rak Thai. In the elections of February 2005, the Thai Rak Thai won 377 out of 500 seats, and for the first time in its history Thailand formed a democratically elected one-party government. The Thai Rak Thai's growing domination engendered deep concerns over Thaksin's overwhelming power and influence. In particular, objections frequently were raised about his tendency to reorganize the government and to reshuffle the cabinet with his personal friends and family members. After coming to power, Thaksin instituted 12 cabinet shuffles, the most recent in August 2005. Public and parliamentary criticism of Thaksin's regime eventually led to mass demonstrations in the latter months of 2005 and early 2006 and dissolution of parliament by Thaksin on February 24, 2006. Consequently, new elections were held on April 2, 2006. However, Thailand's Constitutional Court invalidated the results after the opposition parties refused to compete against Thaksin's Thai Rak Thai.

On 24 August 2006, police intercepted an explosives-laden automobile, operated by a former driver in the Internal Security Operations Command, near Thaksin's residence in Thonburi. Although critics accused Thaksin of fabricating the plot to boost his popularity in the upcoming October general elections, five army officers were arrested for their role in the plot. Three of them were released after the military overthrew the Thaksin government in September. According to a white paper issued by the CNS in November 2006, causes of the coup were corruption, abuse of power, lack of integrity, interference in the checks and balances system, human rights violations, and destroying the unity of the people during the leadership of the Thaksin government.

Political opposition leaders and pro-democracy advocates initially embraced the September 19 coup. However, the CNS's popularity declined following an escalation of violence with Islamic separatists in the south, a series of bombings in Bangkok, slow progress on a new constitution, and the adoption of populist economic measures and capital controls that have alarmed foreign investors. On January 31, 2007, General Sonthi made a public announcement that he would hold democratic elections before the end of the year. He also promised that the army would immediately hand over control to a civilian government following the inauguration of a new prime minister.

Executive Branch: The constitutional monarch and head of state, since June 9, 1946, is King Bhumibol Adulyadej (Rama IX of the Chakri Dynasty). The Privy Council, which is still provided for in the interim constitution, is an 18-member constitutional body that advises the king on matters of legislation, government affairs, clemency, awards, and other matters requiring the king's signature. The Privy Council, whose members are appointed by and serve at the pleasure of the king, also recommends the name of a suitable person to hold the position of regent when the king is absent from Thailand or unable to perform his duties. Under the interim constitution, executive governmental power is exercised through a cabinet headed by a prime minister appointed by the king (with the concurrence of the Council for National Security (CNS) chairman) and the 19 members of the Council of Ministers who head major ministries. However, the military coup in September 2006 abolished the cabinet and installed the Council for Democratic Reform. The first appointments to the council were the supreme commander of the armed forces, Boonsrang Naimpradit, the three military service chiefs of staff, the police commissioner, and the secretary general of the CNS. The interim prime minister (since October 1, 2006) is Surayut Chulanon, a retired general and privy councilor to King Bhumibol.

Legislative Branch: Prior to the September 2006 military coup, legislative power was exercised through a bicameral National Assembly composed of the House of Representatives (Saphaputhan Ratsadon) and Senate (Wuthisapha). All legislative matters of national policy received the approval of the National Assembly and the signature of the king before becoming law. Members of both houses served four-year terms. The number of representatives was determined by the size of the population. At the time of the coup, House membership stood at 500; 100 members were elected from a party list and 400 on a constituency basis. According to the 1997 constitution, the Senate was an appointed body until members were elected in single seat constituencies for the first time in March 2000. The 200 members of the Senate had to have attained the minimum age of 40 and not belong to any political party in any capacity. The constitution also stated that the number of senators should not exceed 75% of the total number of representatives. Upon assuming control in September 2006, the Council for National Security (CNS) dissolved both chambers of the National Assembly and subsequently arranged for the king to appoint a new 242-member (250 are authorized by the interim constitution) legislature, a significant proportion of which was composed of retired government officials and members of the military. In accordance with Article 7 of the interim constitution, the CNS chairman countersigns the king's appointments to the National Assembly. The new National Assembly, which serves as both the House of Representatives and the Senate, was charged with governing the country in the period leading up to the general elections scheduled for October 2007.

Judicial Branch: Following the September 19, 2006, military coup and the repeal of the 1997 constitution, the Council for National Security issued a decree announcing that all courts with the exception of the Constitutional Court (which was dissolved) would continue to operate as before. The interim constitution, promulgated on October 1, 2006, guarantees the independence of the judiciary. Thailand has a three-level court system collectively known as the Courts of Justice. At the top is the Supreme Court of Justice. Below it is the Court of Appeal and, at the third level, the Courts of First Instance, over which the Supreme Administrative Court, which was established in 1999, presides. The Courts of First Instance include the Central Administrative Court and 16 regional administrative courts. A new Constitutional Tribunal, composed of justices from the Supreme Court of Justice and the Supreme Administrative Court, was established on October 1, 2006, to replace the functions of the Constitutional Court. Judges of the Supreme Court of Justice and the Supreme Administrative Court are subject to Senate approval. Other judges are members of the career civil service and are not subject to parliamentary review. Separate administrative courts adjudicate disputes involving state agencies, state enterprises, and local government organizations or between state officials and private individuals. Administrative appellate and supreme administrative courts operate at higher levels. A separate Military Court deals with military personnel and persons arrested during periods of martial law. Islamic sharia courts hear civil cases involving members of the Muslim minority.

Administrative Divisions: Thailand has 76 provinces (*changwat*), including Bangkok Municipality. The provinces are divided into 795 districts (*amphoe*), 81 subdistricts (*king amphoe*), 7,255 rural administrative subdistricts (*tambon*), and 69,866 villages (*muban*).

Provincial and Local Government: Local government is based on the principles of decentralization and self-government when certain legal conditions are met. Under the 1997 constitution, elected local assemblies and elected or appointed local administrative committees were allowed four-year terms. Central government officials could not serve as local officials. Bangkok is a provincial-level entity with an elected governor and the legislative Metropolitan Administration Council. Supervision of provincial and local government takes place through the Department of Local Administration of the Ministry of Interior. However, as a result of the September 2006 military coup, Bangkok and the provinces came under the direct control of the supreme commander of the armed forces and the national police.

Judicial and Legal System: The interim constitution of October 1, 2006, had been criticized by many internal observers for granting legal authority to the junta's post coup announcements and orders, including bans against demonstrations and political activities. Until the coup, the Thai legal system had been based on an amalgam of traditional and modern laws and customs, including Islamic law, where applicable. Most of the modern legal system is based on criminal, civil, and commercial codes adopted from the British and other European legal systems, along with borrowings from India, China, Japan, and the United States. Traditional civil rights were protected under the old constitution, but even under the old constitution there was no trial by jury. A single judge decided trials for misdemeanors; two or more judges were required for more serious cases. The 1997 constitution also provided for the presumption of innocence, and criminal detainees were guaranteed access to legal counsel; however, local police have been accused of ignoring this procedure and conducting interrogations of suspects without providing access to an attorney. Regulations outlined in the Criminal Code require public prosecutors to rely exclusively on the recommendations of the police when determining whether to bring a case forward for criminal prosecution. Police are required to bring criminal cases to prosecutors for the filing of court charges within 48 hours of arrest. Extensions of up to three days are permitted, and police, with court permission, may hold suspects for up to 82 days for serious offenses while investigations are being conducted.

Electoral System: There are no elections for the heads of state and government. The monarchy is hereditary and based on the Palace Law of Succession enacted in 1924, which allows the king to appoint his heir. If he has failed to do so, the Privy Council nominates an heir for National Assembly consideration. The heir suggested by the Privy Council may be a prince or princess. Under the 1997 constitution, the prime minister was selected from among the members of the House of Representatives following elections. Officially, the king appoints the prime minister, who, before the September 2006 coup, was normally the leader of the party that had an outright majority or organized a majority coalition in the House of Representatives. The Senate also was elected by popular vote for nonparty candidates.

Politics and Political Parties: Active political parties include the Phak Prachathipat Party (Democratic Party); Phak Mahachon Party (Great People's Party); Phak Chat Thai Party (Thai Nation Party); and Thai Rak Thai Party (Thai Loves Thai Party). After the September 2006 military coup, new elections were scheduled for October 2007.

Mass Media: The Thai media are generally free but even before the September 19, 2006, military coup had acted with restraint because of fear of lawsuits and, from time to time, government censorship. In the aftermath of the September coup, the military quickly clamped down on the media and banned political gatherings of more than five people, but it subsequently lifted its restrictions. Since then the Thai press has routinely published critical commentary on the military and covered Thaksin Chinnawat's travel movements in exile. However, the government ordered the Thai broadcast media to cease reporting statements by Thaksin and to stop airing views defending the former prime minister. There are 18 major Thai-language daily newspapers, 3 major English-language dailies, and 4 major Chinese-language dailies. Thailand also has 204 AM radio stations, 334 FM radio stations, 6 shortwave stations, and 111 television broadcast stations.

Foreign Relations: According to the foreign policy statement issued by the interim government in November 2006, Thailand's foreign policy includes support for the Association of Southeast Asian Nations (ASEAN) in the interest of regional stability and emphasis on a close and longstanding security relationship with the United States. Since the 1990s, Thailand has taken an increasingly active role on the international stage. When East Timor gained independence from Indonesia, Thailand, for the first time in its history, contributed troops to the international peacekeeping effort. As part of its effort to improve international ties, Thailand has sought observer status in such regional organizations as the Organization of American States (OAS) and the Organization for Security and Co-operation in Europe (OSCE). Despite the widespread international condemnation of the September 19, 2006, military-led coup, Thailand's relations with its allies have not been seriously affected. The U.S. ambassador to Thailand met with coup leader General Surayud Chulanont on October 2, 2006, and reported that he had been assured that the military-installed civilian government would protect civil liberties and move toward a quick return to a democratically elected administration. However, foreign observers also predicted that if there are delays in the restoration of civilian government, relations between the United States and Thailand could take a turn for the worse. This would also likely be the case with the European Union and Australia, which expressed concerns about the coup and called for a speedy return to democratic rule.

It has signed but not ratified the United Nations Law of the Sea Treaty.

National Security

Armed Forces Overview: The military includes three branches: the Royal Thai Army (123,000), the Royal Thai Navy (77,000, including 2,000 naval aviation personnel and 27,000 members of the Royal Thai Marine Corps), and the Royal Thai Air Force (estimated at 47,500). Reserve forces total 200,000 personnel. Under normal operating circumstances, the minister of defence and the supreme commander of the armed forces are at the top of the chain of command and maintain control; however, real power is held by the three service chiefs. Since the September 19, 2006, coup, the army commander in chief has been dominant, and it is unclear what the chain of command is and how it might change in the future.

Foreign Military Relations: A long-standing ally of the United States, Thailand signed numerous bilateral defence and mutual security agreements between 1950 and 2003. In 2002 Thailand received Foreign Military Assistance from the United States in the amount of US$3 million; in 2003 it received US$3.7 million; in 2004, US$3.4 million; and in 2005, US$1.4 million. Most Thai military equipment is from the United States, the United Kingdom, and China.

External Threat: Thailand faces a number of external threats from cross-border activities. Those on the border with Burma involve the handling of ethnic rebels, refugees, and illegal crossings, often related to drugs and arms trafficking. There have been periodic armed border clashes between Thai and Burmese border guards. Some 98,000 Karen refugees live in camps on the Thai side of the Burma–Thailand border, and rebel members of this group have skirmished with Thai troops. In 2001 and 2002, Thai and pro-Rangoon forces clashed in Thai territory, leading to strained relations between the two nations. Similarly, separatist insurgents in predominantly Muslim southern Thailand allegedly have operated from neighboring Malaysia, leading to cooperation between the two governments and Malaysian arrests of separatist ringleaders. Thailand has periodically closed border areas where communist Cambodian insurgents at odds with the Phnom Penh government control neighboring territory. The Cambodian government has accused Thailand of complicity with the insurgents.

Defence Budget: Defence expenditures in fiscal year (FY) 2006 were estimated at US$2 billion, representing 1.09% of the gross domestic product (GDP). The military-backed administration that came to power following the September 2006 coup endorsed an almost 35% increase in the defence budget for FY 2007. A Ministry of Defence spokesperson said additional funding was needed to make up for shortfalls accumulated during Thaksin Shinawatra's five-year rule, expand the counterinsurgency campaign in the southern provinces, replace or refurbish equipment, and replenish ammunition, stores, and fuel stocks. The projected defence budget for FY 2007 was US$3.2 billion.

Major Military Units: The army has four regional armies, two corps, three armored infantry divisions, two cavalry divisions, two mechanized infantry divisions, two special forces divisions, one artillery division, one air defence artillery division, one engineer division, one economic development division, one independent cavalry regiment, eight independent infantry battalions, four reconnaissance companies, and one armored air cavalry regiment. Four rapid-reaction force battalions are being formed, and there are four reserve infantry divisions. The navy has three fleets (North Gulf, South Gulf, and Andaman Sea), one naval air division, and five naval bases (including one supporting its Mekong River Operating Unit). The marines are organized into one division with two infantry regiments, one artillery regiment, one amphibious assault battalion, and one reconnaissance battalion. The air force is organized into four air divisions.

Military Service: Men reaching 21 years of age are subject to two years of compulsory military service. Volunteers may join at the minimum age of 18. Women may also join the military, but they are not accepted in the police or military academies. They do serve, however, as military academy instructors.

Paramilitary Forces: Thailand has about 113,700 active-duty paramilitary personnel. These forces include about 20,000 members of a light infantry force called the Thahan Phran (Hunter Soldiers or Royal Thai Rangers), which was organized in 1978 to fight communist guerrillas and is now deployed in active trouble spots along the border. The 45,000-strong Volunteer Defence Corps provides the border patrol police with law and order support during military emergencies and natural disasters.

Foreign Military Forces: The United States has 30 air force, 10 navy, and 29 marine corps personnel station in Thailand.

Police and Internal Security: The Royal Thai Police have approximately 213,000 officers organized in 10 geographic regions. These forces include provincial police, marine police, police aviation, and border patrol police. The national police are under the command of the police commissioner general, who reports directly to the prime minister—a member of the military junta—and the 20-member Police Commission. The police commissioner general is appointed by the prime minister, subject to cabinet and royal approval. The Border Patrol Police have special authority and responsibility in border areas to combat insurgent and Thailand also has a Central Police Academy and provincial police training schools.

Terrorism: Since the September 11, 2001, terrorist attacks on the United States, Thailand has pledged itself as a strong ally in the United States–led war on terrorism. Thailand itself has been confronted with terrorist violence, primarily in the predominantly Muslim southern provinces of Narathiwat, Pattani, and Yala, which border Malaysia. In 2002 Thai police officers were killed and bombs were detonated when the minister of interior toured the violence-prone area; five schools suffered damage from arsonists. The Thai military attributed these actions to Guragan Mujahideen Islam Pattani (Pattani Islamic Mujahideen Movement), thought to be an al Qaeda affiliate, which was established in 1995 as a constituent group of Bersatu (United Front for the Independence of Pattani). Bersatu was established in 1989, and both organizations have the goal of establishing a Muslim state in southern Thailand. In 2003 suspected members of Jemaah Islamiah (Community of Islam, a regional group affiliated with al Qaeda, established in 1993 or 1994), who were arrested in June 2003, confessed to plotting attacks on embassies in Bangkok and tourist sites. Further arsons and bombings and attacks on police and army bases in 2004 heightened the terrorist threat. When seven Muslim protesters were shot and 78 others died in police custody in October 2004, 30 Buddhists were killed in November in retaliation. In 2004 alone, more than 500 people died as a result of insurgent and terrorist violence in the south. This separatist violence has led to border closures and security tightening with neighboring Malaysia to inhibit terrorist activities. During 2006 violence in the southern provinces, and particularly violence aimed at public school teachers, sporadically forced the temporary closure of public schools and disrupted the educational process in those areas. Fears of terrorism against Thailand's own tourist resorts emanated from the terrorist bombings in Bali, Indonesia, in October 2002. There were allegations that the Bali bombers, members of Jemaah Islamiah, may have planned their attack while living in southern Thailand.

On December 31, 2006, and January 1, 2007, four bombs exploded in Bangkok, followed by several more explosions in various parts of the city, killing at least three people and injuring more than 38. Prime Minister Surayut Chulanon said that the bombs were designed to resemble those used by the southern insurgents. However, it was announced later that closer inspection confirmed that there was no link. On January 20, 2007, police announced that 15 military officers and civilians had been arrested related to the bombing incident. General Sonthi, head of the junta, strongly criticized the chief of police for seeking scapegoats within the military, claiming that the 15 suspects had no connection to the incident.

Human Rights: Following the September 19, 2006, military coup, the Council for National Security—the junta's ruling body—imposed some limits on freedom of speech, freedom of the press, and freedom of assembly. Prior to the coup, the government under the now-abrogated 1997 constitution, generally respected the human rights of its citizens. Some significant problems, however, continued under the interim government. During 2006, according to the U.S. Department of State's *Country Reports on Human Rights Practices*, "security forces continued to use excessive force against criminal suspects and committed or were connected to dozens of extrajudicial, arbitrary, and unlawful killings." There also were reports that disappearances continued in the southern provinces, particularly after the missing allegedly had been questioned by security officials. There also were reports that police tortured, beat, and otherwise abused detainees and prisoners, generally with impunity. Authorities used defamation suits and, in some cases, charges of sedition against critics, which led to self-censorship by the media and non-governmental organizations. Human rights workers, particularly those focusing on disappearances and the violence in the south, experienced government harassment. Thailand continued to be a source, transit point, and destination for trafficking in women and children for a variety of purposes, including indentured servitude, forced labour, and prostitution. Members of hill tribes without proper documentation continued to face restrictions on their movement, could not own land, and were not protected by labour laws.

Trafficking in women and children and forced prostitution and labour are serious problems in Thailand. It is conservatively estimated that between 200,000 and 300,000 men, women, and children—but particularly women and young girls—are engaged in prostitution as part of Thailand's illegal sex tourism industry. Of these, between 30,000 and 40,000 prostitutes are under the age of 18 years; this figure does not include foreign migrants, many of whom come from Burma, Cambodia, China, and Laos. Thai and migrant women also are trafficked to Japan, Malaysia, Singapore, Bahrain, Australia, South Africa, Europe, and the United States for prostitution and sweatshop labour. Men, women, and children from China and Southeast Asian neighbors also are trafficked for sweatshop, fishery, construction, farm, and industrial labour.

MILITARY BALANCE

AFGHANISTAN

Army 34,000

The Afghan National Army (ANA), HQ in Kabul, currently comprises some 34,000 troops trained out of a projected force of 70,000 (encompassing all ethnic and tribal groups). *Operation Enduring Freedom* (US and NATO International Security Assistance Force) strength is expected to increase.

Forces

Army

201 Corps (Kabul); 2 brigades in Kabul and 1 in Kunar
203 Corps (Gardez); 1 brigade each at Gardez, Khost and Paktika
205 Corps (Kandahar); 1 brigade each at Kandahar, Helmand and Zabul
207 Corps (Herat); 1 brigade plus 1 battalion each at Shindin and Farah
209 Corps ((Mazar); 1 brigade with battalions at Kunduz, Mazar and Faryab

Equipment

Tanks	**MBT**: some T-62; some T-54/T-55
Reconnaissance	**BRDM:** some BRDM-1/BRDM-2; **AIFV: BMP**: some BMP-1/BMP-2; **APC: APC (W); BTR**: some BTR-152/BTR-40/BTR-60/BTR-70/BTR-80
Artillery	**Towed: 76mm**: some M-1938/IS-3 *M-1942;* **100mm**: some M-1944; **122mm**: some D-30/M-30 *M-1938;* **130mm**: some M-46; **152mm**: some D-1-20/M-1937; **MRL: 122mm**: some BM-21; **140mm**: some BM-14; **220mm**: some 9P140 *Uragan;* **Mortars: 82mm**: some M-37; **107mm** some **120mm**: some M-43
Anti-tank	**RCL: 73mm**: some SPG-9; **82mm**: some B-10; **Guns: 85mm**: some D-48
Air Defence	**SAM**: some SA-13 *Gopher* SP/SA-7 *Grail* MANPAD; **Guns 100mm; Towed**: some KS-19; **14.5mm** some **23mm; Self-Propelled**: some ZSU-23-4; **Towed**: some ZU-23; **37mm Towed**: some M-1939; **57mm Towed**: some S-60; **85mm Towed**: some M-1939 *KS-12:* **Missiles Tactical**: some FROG-7; some *Scud*

Air Force 3,600

Forces

Fighter Ground Attack	5 FGA
Transport	An-24 *Coke*
Training	2 L-39 *Albatross*
Helicopters	5 Mi-24 *Hind*; 8 Mi-8 *Hip*/Mi-8MT *Hip H*

Equipment

Aircraft	up to 5 combat capable; **FGA**: up to 5; **Transport**: some An-24 *Coke;* **Training** 2: 2 L-39 *Albatross*
Helicopters	**Anti-tank** 5: 5 Mi-24 *Hind*; **Support: MI-8** 8: 8 Mi-8 *Hip*/Mi-8MT *Hip*

Afghan National Police (ANP); 64,000

BANGLADESH

Army: 220,000

Forces

Armour	1 brigade (2 armoured regiments); 2 regiments
Infantry	7 division headquarters; 17 brigades (*total:* 26+ infantry battalions)
Commando	1 battalion
Artillery	1 division (6 artillery regiments)
Engineers	1 brigade
Aviation	2 squadrons
Air Defence	1 brigade

Equipment

Tanks	220+; **Main Battle tanks** 180: 80 Type-59/Type-69; 100 T-54/T-55; **Light tanks** 40+: 40+ Type-62
Armoured Personnel Carriers	180+; APC (T) 50+: some MT-LB; 50 Type-63; APC (W); BTR 130: 60 BTR-70; 70 BTR-80
Artillery	190+, **Towed** 140+; 105 mm 80: 50 M-101; 30 Model 56 pack howitzer; 122 mm 20: 20 Type-54 (M-30) *M-1938*: 130 mm 40+: 40+ Type-59 (M-46); Mortars 50+: some 81 mm; 82 mm: some Type-53 (M-937); 120 mm 50: 50 Type-53 (M-1943)
Anti-Tank	**Recoilless** 106 mm60: M-40 30: 30 M-40A1; **Guns** 68; 57 mm 18: 18 6-pdr; 76 mm 50: 50 Type-54 (ZIS-3)
Aircraft	6; 4 Cessna 152; Cessna 337 2: 2 Cessna 337F *Skymaster*
Air Defence	**Surface-to-Air Missiles** Man-portable HN-5: some HN-5A; **Guns** 37 mm Towed 16: 16 Type-55 (M-1939); 57 mm Towed: some Type-59 (S-60)

Navy: 25,950

Forces

Headquarters located at Chittagong

Equipment by Type

Frigates	5; **FFG** 2: 1 *Bangabandhu* in refit (ROK *Ulsan*) with 2 B515 *ILAS-3* triple 324 mm each with A244 LWT 4 single each and 1Otomat tactical SSM, 1 76 mm gun, 1 helicopter landing platform (hangar for operation of *Lynx* sized helicopter); *Osman* (PRC *Jianghu* I) with 2 twin (4 eff.) each with 1 HY-2 (CSS-N-2) *Silkworm* tactical SSM, 2 RBU 1200 (10 eff.), 4 100 mm gun; **FF** 3: 2 *Abu Bakr* (UK *Leopard*) each with 2 115 mm twin gun (4 eff.); 1 *Umar Farooq* training (UK *Salisbury*) with 3 *Squid*, 2 115 mm twin gun (4 eff)
Patrol and Coast Combatants	33; **PCC** 4: 2 *Karnaphuli*; 2 *Meghna* (fishery protection) **PCI** 4: 2 *Akshay* less than 100 tonnes; 1 *Bakarat* less than 100 tonnes; 1 *Bishkali* less than 100 tonnes; **PCR** 5: 5 *Pabna* less than 100 tonnes; **PFC** 4: 4 *Shahead Daulat*; **PFM** 10: *Durbar* less than 100 tonnes (PRC *Hegu*) each with 2 single with 2 SY-1 tactical SSM; 5 *Durdarsha* (PRC *Huangfeng*) each with 4 single each with 1 HY-2 (CSS-N-2)

	Silkworm tactical SSM; **PHT** 4: 4 *Huchuan* less than 100 tonnes (PRC) each with 2 single 533 mm TT each with 2 YU 1 Type 53 HWT; **PCO** 2: 1 *Durjoy* (PRC *Hainan*) with 4 RBU 1200 (20 eff.); 1 *Madhumati* (*Sea Dragon*) with 1 76 mm gun
Mine Countermeasures	4; **MSI** 3: 3 *Shapla* (UK *River*); **MSO** 1: 1 *Sagar*
Amphibious Craft	14: 7 LCU; 3 LCVP; 4 LCM
Logistics and Support	8; **AGHS** (Survey) 2: 2 *Yuch'in*; **AGOR** 1: 1 *Shaibal* (UK *River*, MCM capable); **AOT** (coastal)**AR** 1,**AT** 1, **ATF** 1,
Training	1: 1 *Shaheed Ruhul Amin*
Facilities	Bases - Chittagong, Dhaka, Kaptai, Khulna and Mongla

Air Force: 16,500

Forces	
Fighter/FGA	4 squadrons with 6 MiG-29 *Fulcrum*; 23 F-7M *Airguard*/J-7II *Fishbed*; 18 A-5C (Q-5III) *Fantan*; 16 F-6 (MiG-19S) *Farmer B*; 2 MiG-29UB *Fulcrum* (*total:* 1 OCU squadrons with 8 L-39ZA *Albatross*; 10 FT-6 (MiG-19UTI) *Farmer*)
Transport	3 An-32 *Cline*
Helicopters	3 squadrons with 1 Mi-8 *Hip*; 15 MI-17 (Mi-8MT) *Hip H*; 3 Mi-171; 11 Bell 212
Training	20 PT-6 (CJ-6); 8 CM-170 *Magister*; 31 T-37B *Tweet*; 2 Bell 206L *LongRanger*
Equipment	
Aircraft	83 combat capable; **FTR** 29: 6 MiG-29 *Fulcrum*; 23 F-7M *Airguard*/ J-7II *Fishbed*; **FGA** 34: 18 A-5C (Q-5III) *Fantan*; **MiG-19** 16: 16 F-6 (MiG-19S) *Farmer B*; **TPT** 3: 3 An-32 *Cline*; **TRG** 79: 8 CM-170 *Magister*; 10 FT-6 (MiG-19UTI) *Farmer;* **L-39** 8: 8 L-39ZA *Albatross;* **MiG-29U** 2: 2 MiG-29UB *Fulcrum* **PT-6 (CJ-6)** 20 **T-37** 31: 31 T-37B *Tweet*
Helicopters	**Support** 16: **MI-8** 16: 1; 15 MI-17 (Mi-8MT) *Hip H* **Utility** 13; **BELL 206** 2: 2 Bell 206L *LongRanger*; **Bell 212** 11
Tactical Missiles	**AAM**: some AA-2 *Atoll*

Paramilitary 63,200

Ansars	20,000+ Security Guards (180,000 unembodied)
Armed Police	5,000 rapid action force
Bangladesh Rifles	40,000; Border Guard; Paramilitary 41 battalions
Coast Guard	
Patrol and Coastal Combatants	PCI 1: 1 *Bishkali* less than 100 tonnes

BHUTAN

Royal Bhutan Army 10,000

Forces

Royal Bhutan Army	No.1 Wing	-	Tendu
	No.2 Wing	-	Damthang
	No.3 Wing	-	Goinichawa
	No.4 Wing	-	Yonphula
	No. 5 Wing	-	Samchi
	No. 6 Wing	-	Wangdi
	No. 7 Wing	-	Paro
	No. 8 Wing	-	Samchi
	No. 9 Wing	-	Geylephug
	No. 10 Wing	-	Deothang
	No. 11 Wing	-	Rimte
	No. 12 Wing	-	Wangdi
	No. 13 Wing	-	Deothang
	No. 14 Wing	-	Nanglam
	No. 15 Wing	-	Thimpu (Rbg)
	No. 16 Wing	-	Gelegphug
	Training Wing	-	Tenchholing

Independent Companies — 9 (Ha, Damthang, Gumchawa, Punakha, Kalikhola, Thimphu (2), Khakthang and Deothang)

Special Forces — (six companies)

Wangchuk Lo Dzong Military Training School — Ha

Royal Bodyguards — Three companies - Royal Palace (Thimpu)

Forest Guards

Army Aviation — Dornier DO-28 1; Mil Mi-28 helicopters - 7

Royal Bhutan Police

Police Training Centres — 3 (Jigmiling, Geylephug and Zilnon Namgyeling)

CHINA

***Armed Forces* 2,255,000**	**Army 1,600,000; Navy 255,000; Air Force 400,000 Paramilitary 3,969,000** *Selective Conscription - All services 2 years* **Reserves 800,000**
<u>Strategic Forces</u>	
Strategic Missile Forces	(100,000+)
Offensive	20 launch brigades within 6 missile armies; organisation varies by missile type; one testing and one training base
Missiles	**Strategic** 806; **ICBM** 46: 6 DF-31 (CSS-9) (1 brigade); 20 DF-4 (CSS-3) (2 brigade); 20 DF-5A (CSS-4 Mod 2) (4 brigades); **IRBM** 35: 33 DF-21 (CSS-5) (4 Brigade); 2 DF-3A (CSS-2 Mod) (1 brigade); **SRBM** 725 **DF-11/M-11 (CSS-7)** 500: 500 DF-11A/M-11A (CSS-7 Mod 2) (4 brigades); **DF-15/M-9 (CSS-6)** 225 (2 brigades)
Navy	**Submarines Strategic; SSBN** 1 Xia (capacity 12 JL-1 (CSS-N-3) strategic SLBM);
Defensive *Radar*	**Strategic**: some phased array radar; some detection and tracking radars (covering Central Asia and Shanxi (northern border)) located at Xinjiang

***People's Liberation Army* 800,000**

<u>Forces</u>	
Group Army	Strength from 30–65000, organisation varies, normally with 2–3 mechanized/motorized infantry division/brigade, 1 armoured division/brigade, 1 artillery division /brigade, 1 SAM/AAA or AAA brigade, combat readiness category varies with 10 GA at Category A and 8 at Category B (reorganisation to brigade structure in progress)
Army	**18** (Group) Armies (total: 1 mechanized infantry brigade, 1 anti-tank brigade, 12 armoured brigades, 12 air defence artillery brigades, 14 artillery brigades, 15 infantry divisions, 2 amphibious assault divisions, 22 motorized infantry brigades, 24 motorized infantry divisions, 3 mechanized infantry divisions, 4 anti-tank regiments, 7 artillery divisions, 9 armoured divisions, 9 (SAM/AAA) air defence brigades)
Artillery / Air Defence	Coastal defence air forces
Military Regions	**7: *North East–Shenyang Military Region*** *250,000* Army; 3 groups ((Heilongjiang, Jilin, Liaoning Military District): 2 armoured, 1 mechanized, 4 motorized, 1 artillery division; 2 armoured, 5 motorized, 3 artillery, 1 SAM/ AAA, 3 AAA, 1 anti-tank brigade) **North–Beijing Military Region** 300,000; Army; 3 groups ((Beijing, Tianjin Garrison, Inner Mongolia, Hebei, Shanxi Military District): 2 armoured, 1 mechanized, 5 motorized, 1 artillery division; 3 armoured, 7 motorized infantry, 4 artillery, 2 SAM/AAA, 3 AAA brigade; 1 anti-tank regiment) **West–Lanzhou Military Region** 220,000: Army; 2 groups ((incl Ningxia, Shaanxi, Gansu, Qing-hai, Xinjiang, South Xinjiang Military District): 1 armoured, 2 motorized infantry, 1 artillery division; 1 armoured, 2 motorized infantry, 1 artillery, 1 AAA brigade; 1 anti-tank regiment)

South-West–Chengdu–Military Region 180,000:Army; 2 groups ((incl Chongqing Garrison, Sichuan, Guizhou, Yunnan, Tibet Military District): 4 motorized infantry, 1 artillery division; 2 armoured, 1artillery, 2 AAA brigade)

South–Guangzhou Military Region 180,000: Army; 2 groups ((Hubei, Hunan, Guangdong, Guangxi, Hainan Military District): 1 mechanized, 3 motorized infantry, 1 artillery division; 2 armoured, 1 artillery, 1 SAM/AAA, 1 AAA brigade. Hong Kong: 7, 000 with 1 infantry brigade (3 infantry, 1 mechanized infantry, 1 artillery regiment, 1 engineer battalion), 1 helicopter unit)

Centre–Jinan Military Region *190,000* Army; 3 groups ((Shandong, Henan Military District): 2 armoured, 1 mechanized infantry, 3 motorized infantry, 1 artillery division; 1 armoured, 1 mechanized infantry, 4 motorized infantry, 2 artillery, 2 SAM/AAA, 1 AAA brigade, 1 anti-tank regiment)

East–Nanjing Military Region *250,000:* Army; 3 groups ((Shanghai Garrison, Jiangsu, Zhejiang, Fujian, Jiangxi, Anhui Military District): 2 armoured, 1 mechanized infantry, 3 motorized infantry, 1 artillery division; 1 armoured, 4 motorized infantry, 2 artillery, 2 SAM/AAA, 1 AAA brigade; 1 anti-tank regiment)

Provincial Military	**28** districts
Infantry	**5** (border) independent regiments
Motorized infantry	**1** independent brigade; 1 independent regiment
Mountain infantry	**2** (independent) brigades
Airborne	**1** (manned by Air Force) corps (3 airborne divisions, 35,000)
Artillery	**1** independent regiment
SSM	**1** independent brigade; 9 (coastal defence) regiments
Air Defence Artillery	**1** independent regiment
Engineers	**1** independent brigade; 50 regiments
Signals	**50** regiments
Aviation	**2** (independent) regiments (training); 8 independent regiments
Guards	**4** (garrison) commands (with 1 mountain infantry brigade, 12 infantry divisions, 4 infantry brigades, 87 (battalion) infantry regiments)
Air Defence	**8** (coastal defence) regiments
Reserves	some 30 infantry divisions (each 3 infantry, 1 artillery regiment); 12 AD divisions; 7 logistic support brigades

Equipment

Tanks	**8,780+: MBT** 7,580+: 1,200 Type-96; 1,000 Type-88A/Type-88B; 80 Type-98A; 300 Type-79; 5,000+ Type-59-II/Type-59-I; **Light tanks** 1,200: **Type-62** 400: 400 Type-62 Lt Tk Tk/Type-62-I; **Type-63** 600: 200 **Type-63A** 400
AIFV	1,000: 1,000 **Type-86A** WZ-501
Armoured Personnel Carriers	5,000+; **APC (T)** 2,600; **Type-63** 2,300: 2,300 **Type-63-II/Type-63-I/Type-63A/Type-63C; Type-89-I** 300; **APC (W)** 900+; **TYPE-77** 200: 200 Type-77-II; **Type-92** 600+; **WZ-523** 100
Artillery	**17,700+: Towed** 14,000: 13,850 Type-54 (D-1) 152mm/Type-54-1 (M-30) M-1938 122mm/Type-59 (M-1944) 100mm/Type-59 (M-46) 130mm/Type-59-I 130mm/Type-60 (D-74) 122mm/Type-66 (D-20) 152mm/Type-83 122mm; 150 Type 88 WAC-21 155mm **Self-propelled** 1,700: **122mm** 700: e200 Type-70-I; 500 Type-89; **152mm** 500: e500 Type-83; **Gun/Mor 120mm** 100: 100 2S23 NONA-SVK; **MRL** 2,400+: 2,400+ Type-70 SP 130mm/Type-81 122mm/

	Type-82 130mm/Type-83 273mm/Type-89 SP 122mm/Type-96 (WS-1) 320mm; **Mor 81mm**: some Type-W87 **82mm**: some Type-53 (M-37)/Type-67/Type-82 SP/Type-82 **100mm**: some Type-71; **120mm**: some Type-55 (including self-propelled); some Type-56 (M-160)
Anti-tank	**Missiles** 7200: 7,176 HJ-73A/HJ-73B/HJ-73C/HJ-8A/HJ-8C/HJ-8E; 24 HJ-9 Red Arrow 9; **Recoilless 105mm**: some Type-75; **75mm**: some Type-56 **82mm**: some Type-65 (B-10)/Type-78; **Rocket Launchers • 62mm**: some Type-70-1; **Guns** 300+: **100mm**: some Type-73 (T-12)/Type-86 **120mm** 300+: 300+ Type-89 SP
Helicopters	**SAR 7:** 7 SA-321 Super Frelon; **Anti-Tank**31: 31 WZ-9 **Assault** 8: 8 SA-342 Gazelle (with HOT); **SPT** 260: **AS-350 Ecureuil** 53; **Mi-171** 95: 45; 50 Mi-171V5; **Mi-6 Hook** 3; **S-70** 19: 19 S-70C2 (S-70C) Black Hawk **Mi-8** 90: 40 MI-17 (Mi-8MT) Hip H; 50 Mi-8T Hip **Utility** 69+: **AS-365** 61: 61 AS-365 Dauphin 2 utilty helicopter/Z-9 (AS-365N) Dauphin 2; **SA-316 Alouette III** 8; **Z-10** some
Unarmed Aerial Vehicles	some ASN-104/ASN-105/ASN-206/W-50
Air Defence	**SAM** 284+: **HQ-61 (CSA-N-2)** 24: 24 HQ-61A Red Leader **SP** 260; **HQ-7** 200: 200 HQ-7A; **SA-15 Gauntlet** 60 (Tor-M1); **MANPAD: HN-5**: some HN-5A/HN-5B Hong Nu **FN-6/QW-1/QW-2** some; **Guns** 7,700+: 50+ Type-90 (GDF-002) towed 35mm; 7,650 Type-55 (M-1939) towed 37mm/Type-56 (M-1939) **KS-12** towed 85mm/Type-59 (KS-19) towed 100mm/Type-59 (S-60) towed 57mm/Type-65 towed 37mm/Type-74 towed 37mm/Type-80 (ZU-23-2) towed 23mm/Type-80 SP SP 57mm/Type-85 towed 25mm/Type-88 SP SP 37mm
Radar	**Land**: some Cheetah (artillery); some RASIT (vehicle, artillery); some Type-378 (vehicle); **Missiles Tactical SSM**: some HY-2 (CSS-C-3) Seerseeker; some HY-4 (CSS-C-7) Sadsack

Navy 215,000; 40,000 conscript (total 255,000)

North Sea Fleet	HQ located at Qingdao; Responsible for coastal defence from DPRK border (Yalu River) to south of Lianyungang (approx 35°10´N); equates to Shenyang, Beijing and Jinan Military Region, and to seaward **9** coastal defence districts **Support bases:** Qingdao(HQ), Lushun
East Sea Fleet	HQ located at Dongqian Lake (Ninsbo); Responsible for coastal defence from south of Lianyungang to Dongshan (approx 35°10´N to 23°30´N); equates to Nanjing Military Region, and to seaward **7** coastal defence districts **Support Bases:** Fujian, Zhousnan, Dongqian Lake (Ninsbo)
South Sea Fleet	HQ located at Guangzhou; Responsible for coastal defence from Dongshan (approx 23°30´N) to Vietnam border; equates to Guangzhou Military Region, and to seaward (including Paracel and Spratly Islands) **Support Bases:** Yulin, Guangzhou, Zuanjiang
Submarines	69: **Strategic SSBN** 1: 1 Xia (capacity 12 JL-1 (CSS-N-3) strategic SLBM); **Tactical** 68: **SSN** 5: 5 Han (Type 091) each with YJ-82 tactical SSM, 6 single 533mm TT; **SSG** 1: 1 modified Romeo (Type S5G) with 6 YJ-1 (CSS-N-4) Sardine tactical SSM, 8 single 533mm TT (test platform); **SSK** 61: 2 Kilo (RF Type EKM 636) each with 6 single 533mm TT 2 Kilo (RF Type EKM 877) each with 6 single 533mm TT

3 Ming (Type ES5C/D) each with single 533mm TT 35 Romeo† (Type ES3B) each with 8 533mm TT; 3 Song each with YJ-2 (CSS-N-8) Saccade tactical SSM, 6 single 533mm TT; 16 Ming (imported, Type ES5E) each with 8 single 533mm TT; **SS** 1: 1 Golf (SLBM trials)

Principal Surface Combatants 63

Destroyers

DDG 21: 2 Hangzhou (capacity either 1 Z-9C (AS-565SA) Panther ASW helicopter or 1 KA-28 ASW helicopter) (RF Sovremeny) each with 2 SA-N-7 SAM, 2 Twin 533mm ASTT (4 effective), 2 quad (8 effective) each with SS-N-22 Sunburn tactical SSM, 2 RBU 1000 Smerch 3, 2 twin 130mm gun (4 effective)

1 Luda III with 2 triple 324mm ASTT (6 effective), 4 Twin (8 effective) each with 2 YJ-1 (CSS-N-4) Sardine tactical SSM, 2 twin 130mm gun (4 effective); 11 Luda Type-051 each with 2 triple 324mm ASTT (6 effective), 2 triple (6 effective) each with HY-2 (CSS-N-2) Silkworm/ YJ-1 (CSS-N-4) Sardine, 2 FQF 2500 (24 effective), 2 twin 130mm gun (4 effective); 1 Luhai (capacity either 2 Z-9C (AS-565SA) Panther ASW helicopter or 2 KA-28 ASW helicopter) with 2 triple 324mm ASTT (6 effective), 1 octuple (8 effective) with 8 Crotale SAM, 4 quad (16 effective) each with YJ-1 (CSS-N-4) Sardine tactical SSM, 1 twin 100mm gun (2 effective); 2 Luhu (capacity 2 Z-9C (AS-565SA) Panther ASW helicopter) (Type 052A) each with 2 triple 324mm ASTT (6 effective), 1 octuple (8 effective) with Crotale SAM, 4 quad (16 effective) each with YJ-1 (CSS-N-4) Sardine tactical SSM, 2 FQF 2500 (24 effective), 1 twin 100mm gun (2 effective); 2 modified Luda (capacity 2 Z-9C (AS-565SA) Panther ASW helicopter) each with 2 triple 324mm ASTT (6 effective), 2 triple (6 effective) each with HY-2 (CSS-N-2) Silkworm tactical SSM, 1 twin 130mm gun (2 effective), mine (capability); 2 modified Luda Type-051DT each with 1 octuple (8 effective) with Crotale SAM, 2 quad (8 effective) each with YJ-1 (CSS-N-4) Sardine tactical SSM, 2 FQF 2500 (24 effective), 2 twin 130mm gun (4 effective), mine (capability)

Frigates

FFG 42: 26 Jianghu Type I each with 2 Twin (4 effective) each with 2 SY-1 (CSS-N-1) Scrubbrush tactical SSM, 4 RBU 1200 (20 effective), 2 100mm gun; 1 Jianghu Type II (capacity 1 Z-9C (AS-565SA) Panther ASW helicopter) with 1 twin (2 effective) with SY-1 (CSS-N-1) Scrubbrush tactical SSM, e2 RBU 1200 (10 effective), 1 twin 100mm gun (2 effective) 3 Jianghu Type III each with 8 YJ-1 (CSS-N-4) Sardine tactical SSM, 4 RBU 1200 (20 effective), 2 twin 100mm gun (4 effective); 4 Jiangwei I (capacity 2 Z-9C (AS-565SA) Panther ASW helicopter) each with 1 HQ-61 (CSA-N-2) SAM, 2 triple (6 effective) each with 3 YJ-1 (CSS-N-4) Sardine tactical SSM, 2 RBU 1200 (10 effective), 1 twin 100mm gun (2 effective) 8 Jiangwei II (capacity 2 Z-9C (AS-565SA) Panther ASW helicopter) each with YJ-1 (CSS-N-4) Sardine tactical SSM, 1 octuple (8 effective) with 1 Crotale SAM, 2 RBU 1200 (10 effective), 2 100mm gun

Patrol and Coastal Combatants

368: **PCC** 21:2 Haijui each with 4 RBU 1200 (20 effective)19 Haiqing each with 2 Type-87 (12 effective); **PCI** 87: 8 Haizui less than 100 tonnes; 79 Shanghai less than 100 tonnes; **PCR** å30 less than 100 tonnes; **PFC** 88: 88 Hainan each with e4 RBU 1200 (20 effective); **PFM** 96: 31 Houku (Komar-Type) each with 2 SY-1 (CSS-N-1) Scrubbrush tactical SSM 22 Houxin each with 4 YJ-1 (CSS-N-4) Sardine tactical SSM 5 Huang each with 6 YJ-1 (CSS-N-4) Sardine tactical SSM 38 Huangfeng/Hola (FSU Osa I-Type) each with 4 SY-1 (CSS-N-1) Scrubbrush tactical SSM; **PHT** 9: 9 Huchuan;

Mine Warfare 130: **Mine Countermeasures** 129: **MSC** 55: 50 Lienyun aux; 5 Wosao; **MSD Inshore** 46: 4 drone; 42 in reserve; **MSI** 4:1Shanghai II; 3 Wochang; **MSO** 24: 24 T-43; **Minelayers: ML** 1: 1 Wolei

Amphibious **LS** 50: **LSM** 31: 1 Yudao; 1 Yudeng (capacity 9 tanks; 500 troops); 12 Yuhai (capacity 2 tanks; 250 troops); 17 Yuliang (capacity 3 tanks; 100 troops); **LST** 19: 3 Shan (capacity 16 tanks; 165 troops) (US LST-1); 7 Yukan (capacity 10 tanks; 200 troops); 9 Yuting (capacity 10 tanks; 250 troops) each with 2 helicopters; **Craft** 285+: 45 LCU; 230+ in reserve; 10 ACV utility

Logistics and Support 163: **AF** 14; **AGB** 4; **AGOR** 33; **AH (MED)** 6: 6 Qiongsha **AO** 3: 2 Fuqing; 1 Nanchang; **AOT** 33; **AR** 2; **AS** 10; **ASR** 1; **ATF** 25; **Transport** 30; **Training** 2 (one helicopter training)

Merchant Fleet **Logistics and Support** 1957: 913 (other) **AOT** 298 **Containers** 191 **Dry bulk** 555

Naval Aviation *26,000: **Aircraft** 436 combat capable; **BBR** 68: 50 H-5,F-5,F-5B (Il-28) Beagle (torpedo-carrying light bomber); 18 H-6D each with YJ-6 (CAS-1) Kraken ALCM ASM; **Fighter** 74; **J-8** 36: 24 J-8 Finback fighter aircraft/J-8A Finback; 6 J-8B Finback; 6 J-8D Finback; **J-8IIA Finback** 12; **MiG-21** 26: 26 J-7 (MiG-21F) Fishbed C; **FGA** 274: 20 JH-7; e30 Q-5 Fantan; 24 Su-30Mk2; e200 J-6 (MiG-19S) Farmer B; **ASW** 4: 4 PS-5 (SH-5); **RECCE** 7: 7 HZ-5 (Il-28R) Beagle; **MP** 4: 4 Y-8X; **TKR** 3: 3 HY-6; **Transport** 66; **An-12** 4: 4 Y-8 (An-12BP) Cub A; **Y-5 (An-2) Colt** 50; **Y-7 (An-24) Coke** 4; **Y-7H (An-26) Curl** 6; **Yak-42** 2; **TRG** 73: 16 JJ-6 (MiG-19UTI) Farmer*; 4 JJ-7 Mongol A*; 53 PT-6 (CJ-6); **Helicopters SAR** 27: 15 SA-321; 12 Z-8,Z-8A (SA-321Ja) Super Frelon; **ASW • KA-27** 8: 8 Ka-28 (Ka-27PL) Helix A*

Assault 8: 8 AS-565; **SPT** 8: 8 Mi-8 Hip; **Missile Tactical ASM ALCM**:**YJ-6 (CAS-1)**: some; some YJ-61 (CAS-1 (improved)) Kraken; **YJ-8K (CSS-N-4) Sardine**

Marines 10,000

Forces

Army 3 (also have amphibious role) divisions

Marine Infantry 2 brigades (each: 1 infantry battalion, 1 AD battalion, 1 (armoured) mechanized infantry battalion, 2 amphibious reconnaissance battalions, 2 artillery battalions, 2 tank battalions)

Equipment

Tanks **Light tanks** Type-63 150: 150 Type-63A

APC **APC (T)** 60: 60 Type-63; **APC (W)**: some Type-92

Artillery **Towed: 122mm**: some Type-83; **MRL 107mm**: some Type-63

Anti-tank **Missiles**: some HJ-73; some HJ-8

Air Defence **SAM MANPAD**: some HN-5 Hong Nu/Red Cherry

Air Force 210,000; 40,000 (strategic forces); 150,000 conscript (total 400,000)

Forces

Bomber 5 regiments with up to 50 H-6E/H-6F/H-6H; 8 regiments with 94 H-5,F-5,F-5B (Il-28) Beagle; 1 (nuclear ready) regiment with up to 20 H-6 (Tu-16) Badger; 3 regiments with 46 H-6H (possibly with YJ-63 cruise missile)

Fighter — **3** regiments with 28 J-8 IIB Finback; 3 regiments with 62 J-8D Finback; 16 regiments with 400 J-7II Fishbed/J-7IIA; 1 regiment with 11 J-8F Finback; 9 regiments with 116 J-11 (Su-27SK) Flanker; 12 regiments with 296 J-7E Fishbed; 5 regiments with 32 Su-27UBK Flanker; 2 regiments with 36 J-7C Fishbed; 1 regiment with 24 J-7G Fishbed; 4 regiments with 80 J-8 Finback; 1 regiment with 24 J-8 IID Finback; 2 regiments with 40 J-8III Finback

Fighter Ground Attack — **12** regiments with 408 Q-5C Fantan/Q-5D Fantan; 2 regiments each with 31 J-10; 25 regiments with 722 MiG-19 Farmer; 4 regiments with 73 Su-30MKK Flanker; 2 regiments each with 13 JH-7A

ELINT / Reconnaissance — **2** regiments with 45 JZ-6 (MiG-19R); some regiments with e126 Aircraft; JZ-7 (MiG-21R) Fishbed H; 1 Tu-154M Careless; 1 regiment with 8+ JZ-8 Finback

AEW / AWACS — some regiments with A-50 Mainstay; 4 Y-8

Transport — **1** regiment with 16+ Tu-154M Careless; 3 regiment with 13 Il-76MD Candid B; 3 regiment with 4 transport; 1 An-12 Cub; 170 Y-5 (An-2) Colt; 41 Y-7 (An-24) Coke/Y-7H (An-26) Curl; 15 B-737-200 (VIP); 5 CL-601 Challenger; 2 Il-18 Coot; 20 Y-11; 8 Y-12

Tanker — **1** regiment with 10 HY-6

ADA / SAM — **1** division located at North

ADA — **1** brigade located at Centre; 1 brigade located at East; 1 brigade located at North-East

Training — **1** regiment with 12 H-6H; some regiments with 142 PT-6 (CJ-6); 179+ JJ-7 Mongol A; 140+ JL-8 (K-8); JJ-6 (MiG-19UTI) Farmer

Helicopter*s* — some regiments with e30–40 helicopters; 6 AS-332 Super Puma (VIP); 50 Mi-8 Hip; 20 Z-9 (AS-365N) Dauphin 2; 4 Bell 214

SAM — **3** divisions located at North; 2 brigades located at South; 1 brigade located at North-East; 2 brigades located at East; 1 brigade located at South West; 100+ unit with 60+ HQ-7; 24 HQ-9; 144 S-300PMU2 (SA-10C) Grumble/SA-10D Grumble; 500+ HQ-2 (SA-2) Guideline/HQ-2A/HQ-2B(A); 160 (Strategic Air Defence) units with 850 S-300PMU1 (SA-10B) Grumble/S-300PMU2 (SA-10C) Grumble

Equipment

Aircraft — 2,643 combat capable

Bombers — **222**: 94 H-5,F-5,F-5B (Il-28) Beagle; up to 20 H-6 (Tu-16) Badger; up to 50 H-6E/H-6F/H-6H; 12 H-6H; 46 (possibly with YJ-63 cruise missile)

Fighters — **1,252:** J-7II 400: 400 J-7II Fishbed Fighter Aircraft/J-7IIA J-7C Fishbed 36; J-7E Fishbed 296; J-7G Fishbed 24; J-8 153: 80; 62 J-8D Finback; 11 J-8F Finback; J-8IIA 52: 28 J-8 IIB Finback; 24 J-8 IID Finback; J-8III Finback 40; J-10 62; Su-30 73: 73 Su-30MKK Flanker; Su-27 116: 116 J-11 (Su-27SK) Flanker;

FGA — **1,169:** JH-7 39: 13; 26 JH-7A; Q-5 408: 408 Q-5C Fantan/Q-5D Fantan; MiG-19 Farmer 722

Reconnaissance — **53+:** 45 JZ-6 (MiG-19R); some JZ-7 (MiG-21R) Fishbed H; 8+ JZ-8 Finback

AEW — **4+:** some A-50 Mainstay; 4 Y-8

Tanker — **10**: 10 HY-6

Transport — 296+: 4 An-12 Cub 1; B-737 15: 15 B-737-200 (VIP) CL-601 Challenger 5 Il-18 Coot 2; Il-76 13: 13 Il-76MD Candid B; Tu-154 17+: 17+ Tu-154M Careless; Y-11 20 Y-12 8 Y-5 (An-2) Colt 170 Y-7 (An-24) Coke/Y-7H (An-26) Curl 41

Training	493+: 142 JJ-6 (MiG-19UTI) Farmer some JJ-7 Mongol A 179+ JL-8 (K-8) 140+ PT-6 (CJ-6) some Su-27UB 32: 32 Su-27UBK Flanker
Helicopters	**SPT** 56: 6 AS-332 Super Puma (VIP); 50 Mi-8 Hip **UTL** 24; AS-365 20: 20 Z-9 (AS-365N) Dauphin 2; Bell 214 4
UAV	some Chang Hong 1
Air Defence	**SAM** 1,578+: SP 1,078+: 60+ HQ-7; 24 HQ-9 S-300PMU (SA-10) 994: 850 S-300PMU1 (SA-10B) Grumble/S-300PMU2 (SA-10C) Grumble; 144 S-300PMU2 (SA-10C) Grumble/SA-10D Grumble; HQ-2 (SA-2) Guideline Towed/HQ-2A/HQ-2B(A) 500+; **Guns 16,000:** 16,000 100mm/85mm; **Missile Tactical** 4,500+
ASM	some AS-14 Kedge; some AS-17 Krypton; some AS-18 Kazoo; some YJ-63 (expected)
AAM	**4,500+:** 100 AA-12 Adder; 1,200 P-27 (AA-10) Alamo; 3,200 P37 (AA-11) Archer; some PL-12; some PL-2B; some PL-5B; some PL-8

Paramilitary 1,500,000 active
People's Armed Police 1,500,000

Ministry of Public Security

Police	45 divisions (14 each with 4 regiments, remainder no standard organisation; 1–2 divisions per province)
Border Defence	100,000+
Commissars	69,000+
Internal Security	800,000

INDIA

Organisations	
Strategic Forces Command	In charge of all nuclear assets
Forces	
Missiles	Three regiments each with 15 SS-150 *Prithvi*/SS-250 *Prithvi*/SS-350 *Prithvi*; one group with 8-12 *Agni*-3; one group with 8-12 *Agni*-2
Equipment	
Strategic Missiles	69; **IRBM Agni** 24: 8-12 *Agni*-2; 8-12 *Agni*-3 **SRBM Prithvi** 45: 45 SS-150 *Prithvi*/SS-250 *Prithvi*/SS-350 *Prithvi*

Army 1,100,000

Forces	
Regional Commands	Northern (Udhampur) Western (Chandimandir) Central (Lucknow) Southern (Pune) Eastern (Kolkata) South Western (Jaipur)
Training Command	ARTRAC (Shimla)
Corps HQ	14; (three strike corps, 11 'holding' corps – including 1 desert corps)
Armoured	Three divisions (*each:* one SP artillery brigade (1 medium regiment, 2 SP artillery regiments) and 2-3 armoured brigades); 8 independent brigades; 59 armoured regiments 11 regiments each with 55 T-55 40 regiments each with 55 T-72M1 8 regiments each with 55 T-90S
Mechanised infantry	25 battalions
Infantry	4 RAPID (Reorganised Army Plains Infantry Divisions divisions (*each:* one mechanised infantry brigade) 18 infantry divisions (*each:* one artillery brigade, 3-5 infantry brigades) 8 independent brigades 360 battalions 10 mountain divisions (*each:* 1+ artillery brigade, 3-4 mountain infantry brigades) 2 independent mountain brigades
Special Forces / Airborne	1 independent brigade; 5 special forces Battalions; 7 airborne battalions
Artillery	2 divisions (*each:* 3 artillery brigade); 44 regiments 15 independent artillery brigades
Medium artillery	84 regiments
Self-Propelled medium artillery	11 regiments
Field artillery	185 regiments
Self-Propelled field artillery	3 regiments
Mountain artillery	39 regiments
MRL	9 regiments
SSM	2 regiments; 2 (*Prithvi*) regiments
Air Defence Artillery	45 regiments

Engineers	4 brigades
Helicopters	12 squadrons
Anti-tank helicopters	5 squadrons
Air Defence	6 brigades; 5 regiments with 320 ZU-23-2 (some Self-Propelled); 30 'flak' regiments with 1,920 L40/70 (*each:* 4 Air Defence batteries); 12+ regiments SAM 12 regiments; 2 groups (*each:* 2-5 SAM batteries)

Reserve organisations

Reserves	300,000 reservists (1st line reserve within 5 years full time service); 500,000 reservists (commitment until age of 50) **(total 800,000)**
Territorial Army	160,000 reservists (only 40,000 regular establishment) 4 Ecological battalions; 29 Departmental unit (from government ministries) Infantry 25 battalions Air Defence 20 'flak' regiments with 1,280 L40/60

Equipment

Tanks	**MBT** 3,996 **T-90** 562, ***Arjun*** 124, **T-72M:** 2400, **T-55 Light Tanks:** 850
Reconnaissance	**BRDM** 110: 110 BRDM-2 each with AT-4 *Spigot*/AT-5 S*pandrel*, some ***Ferret***
AIFV	**BMP** 1700+ (700 BMP-1; 1,000+ BMP-2), **APC** 817+: 500+ in reserve in store (Czech and Soviet types)
Mine Protection	Mine protection vehicle **Aditya 250**
Artillery	Up to 12,675+; **Towed** up to 5,625+; **75 mm** 1,115: 900 75/24 mountain; 215 M-48 Tito Gun, **105 mm** up to 1,350+, **IFG** 600+, **LFG** up to 700 **M-56** 50 **122 mm** 550: 550 D-30, **130 mm** 2,200: 1,200 M-46; 500 (upgrading to 155 mm); 500 in reserve **155 mm FH-77** 410: 410 FH-77B, **Self-Propelled** 150+ **105 mm** 80: 80 *Abbot* in store, **130 mm** 70: 70 M-46 *Catapult* in store, **152 mm**: some 2S19 *Farm*, **MRL** 218 **122 mm** 150: 150 BM-21/LRAR, **214 mm** 30: 30 *Pinaka,* 38 *Smerch9K58;* **Mortars** 6720+; **81 mm** 5000+: 5,000+ E1; **120 mm** 1500+: some (Self-Propelled) **AM-50/E1** 1,500 (some E1 Self-Propelled) **160 mm** 220: 20 M-58 Tampella; 200 in store
Anti-Tank	**Missiles** some AT-3 *Sagger* (being phased out); some AT-4 *Spigot* (some Self-Propelled); some AT-5 *Spandrel* (some Self-Propelled); some *Milan* **Recoilless 106 mm M-40** 3,000+: M-40A1 **84 mm** some *Carl Gustav*
Helicopters	**Assault** 12: 12 *Lance,* **Utility SA-315** 48: 48 HAL *Cheetah* (SA-315B) *Lama* **SA-316** 100:100 HAL *Chetak* (SA-316B) *Alouette III*, *Dhruv* 32
UAV	*Nishant* 12; *Searcher II* 100; *Heron II* 50 **Reconnaissance Tactical**
Air Defence	**SAM** 3,500+, **Self-Propelled** 880+: 250 SA-13 *Gopher*; 180 SA-6 *Gainful,* **SA-8** 50+: 50+ SA-8B, **SA-9 *Gaskin*** 400, *Tungushka* 108 **MANPAD** 2,620+: 2,000+ SA-16 *Gimlet*; **Guns** 2,339+; **20 mm Towed**: some Oerlikon **23 mm** 395, **Self-Propelled** 75: 75 ZSU-23-4

	Towed 320: 320 ZU-23-2 (some Self-Propelled) **30 mm Self-Propelled** 84: 84 2S6 **40 mm Towed** 1,920: 1,920 L40/70 **RADAR Land** 12+: 12 AN/TPQ-37 *Firefinder*; some BSR Mk.2; some *Cymbeline*; some EL/M-2140; some M-113 A1GE *Green Archer* (mortar); some MUFAR; some *Stentor*
Amphibious	**Craft** 2: 2 LCVP

Navy 55,000 (including 7,000 Naval Aviation and 2,000 Marine Commandos)

Forces	
Fleets	MumbaiVishakhapatnam Kochi
Equipment	
Submarines	**Tactical SSK** 19; 2 *Kursura*† (FSU *Foxtrot*) each with 10 single 533 mm TT (6 forward, 4 aft), 3 *Kursura* in reserve (FSU *Foxtrot*) each with 10 single 533 mm TT (6 forward 4 aft), 4 *Shishumar* (Ge T-209/1500) each with 1 single 533 mm TT (+ 2 Type 1500 ordered locally), 9 *Sindhughosh* (FSU *Kilo*) each with 6 single 533 mm TT (all *Kilos* to be fitted with SS-N-27) 1 *Sindhughosh* (FSU Type 636 *Kilo*) with 6 single 533 mm TT each with SS-NX-27 *Club-S* tactical SSM
Principal Surface Combatants	54
Aircraft Carrier	**CV** 1; 1 *Viraat* (UK *Hermes*) (capacity 30 *Sea Harrier* FRS MK51 (*Sea Harrier* FRS MKI) FGA aircraft each with *Sea Eagle* tactical ASM;7Ka-27; 7 Ka-27 *Helix* ASW helicopter/*Sea King* MK42B ASW helicopter)
Destroyers	**DDG** 8: 3 *Delhi* (capacity either 2 *Sea King* MK42A ASW helicopter or 2 ALH utility helicopter) each with 5 x1 533 mm ASTT, 4 quad (16 effective.) each with 4 SS-N-25 *Switchblade* tactical SSM, 2 single with 24 SA-N-7 SAM, 1 100 mm gun, 5 *Rajput* (FSU *Kashin*) each with 1 Ka-25 *Hormone*/KA-28, 5 x1 533 mm ASTT, 2 Twin (4 effective) each with 1 SS-N-2C *Styx* tactical SSM, 2 (4 effective) each with 16 SA-N-1 *Goa* SAM, 2 RBU 6000 *Smerch 2* (24 effective), 2 76 mm gun
Frigates	17; **FFG** 9: 3 *Brahmaputra* (capacity either 2 HAL *Chetak* (SA-316B) *Alouette III* SA-316 Utility/*Sea King* MK42 ASW helicopter or 2 *Sea King* MK42 ASW helicopter) each with 20 SA-N-4 *Gecko* SAM, 2 triple 324 mm ASTT (6 effective.), 4 quad (16 effective.) each with 4 SS-N-25 *Switchblade* tactical SSM, 1 76 mm gun 3 *Godavari* (capacity either 2 *Sea King* MK42 ASW helicopter or 2 HAL *Chetak* (SA-316B) *Alouette III* SA- 316 Utility/*Sea King* MK42 ASW helicopter) each with 2 triple 324 mm ASTT (6 effective.), 4 single each with 1 SS-N-2D *Styx* tactical SSM, 1 twin (2 effective.) with 20 SA-N-4 *Gecko* SAM, 3 *Talwar* (capacity either 1 KA-31 *Helicopterix B* AEW helicopter/KA-28 ASW helicopter or 1 ALH utility helicopter) each with SS-N-27 *Club* tactical SSM **FF** 8: 1 *Arnala* (FSU *Petya*) with 3 x1 533 mm ASTT, 4 RBU 2500 *Smerch 1* (64 effective.), 4 76 mm gun 1 *Krishna* in reserve (UK *Leander*; training role) 4 *Nilgiri* (UK *Leander*) each with 1 *Limbo* ASW Mor (triple), 1 HAL *Chetak* (SA-316B) *Alouette III* SA-316 Utility, 2 triple 533 mm ASTT

(6 effective), 2 114 mm guns, 2 *Nilgiri* in reserve (UK *Leander*) each with 1 *Limbo* ASW mor (triple), 1 HAL *Chetak* (SA-316B) *Alouette III* SA-316 utility, 2 triple 533 mm ASTT (6 effective), 2 114 mm gun

Corvettes 28; **FSG** 24; 4 *Khukri* each with 1 76 mm gun, 2 twin (4 effective) each with 2 SS-N-2C *Styx* tactical SSM, 1 helicopter landing platform (For ALH/*Chetak*)

4 *Kora* each with 1 quad (4 effective) with SA-N-5 *Grail* SAM, 4 (16 effective) each with 4 SS-N-25 *Switchblade* tactical SSM, 1 76 mm gun, 1 helicopter landing platform (For ALH/*Chetak*), 6 *Veer* (FSU *Tarantul*) each with 2 quad (8 effective) (quad manual aiming) each with SA-N-5 *Grail* SAM, 4 single each with 1 SS-N-2D *Styx* tactical SSM, 1 76 mm gun 6 *Vibhuti* (modified *Veer*) each with 1 quad (4 effective) (quad manual aiming) with SA-N-5 *Grail* SAM, 4 (16 effective) with 16 SS-N-25 *Switchblade* tactical SSM, 1 76 mm gun

2 *Vibhuti* (advanced version) each with 4 quad (16 effective) each with SA-N-5 *Grail* SAM, 16 SS-N-25 *Switchblade* tactical SSM, 1 (4 effective) (quad manual aiming) with SA-N-5 *Grail* SAM, 16 SS-N-25 *Switchblade* tactical SSM, 1 76 mm gun with SA-N-5 *Grail* SAM, 16 SS-N-25 *Switchblade* tactical SSM

1 *Vijay Durg* (FSU *Nanuchka* II) with 1 twin (2 effective) (twin) with 20 SA-N-4 *Gecko* SAM, 2 (4 effective) each with 1 SS-N-2C *Styx* tactical SSM

FS 4; 4 *Abhay* (FSU *Pauk* II) each with 2 x1 533 mm ASTT (twin), 1 quad (4 effective) SA-N-5 *Grail* SAM, 2 RBU 1200 (10 effective), 1 76 mm gun

Patrol and Coastal Combatants 41; **Miscellaneous Boats/Craft** 17: 17 boats, **PCI** 6: 6 SDB Mk 3, **PFI** 5: 5 *Super Dvora* less than 100 tonnes

PFM 8: 8 *Osa* II, **PCO** 6: 6 *Sukanya*

Mine Warfare Mine Countermeasures 18; **MSI** 6: 6 *Mahe* less than 100 tonnes (FSU *Yevgenya*) **MSO** 12: 12 *Pondicherry* (FSU *Natya*)

Amphibious **LS** 7, **LSM** 5: 5 *Ghorpad* (FSU *Polnocny* C), **LST** 2: 2 *Magar*

Craft **LCU** 10: 10 *Vasco da Gama*

Logistics and Support 32; **AGHS (SVY)** 12: 4 *Makar*; 8 *Sandhayak*

AGOR 1: 1 *Sagardhwani*, **AH (medium)** 1, **AO** 3: 1 *Aditya* (mod *Deepak*); 1 *Deepak*; 1 *Jyoti*, **AOT** 6 (small) **AWT** 2 **Diving tender/support** 3 **TRV** 3, **Training** 1: 1 Tir

Facilities

Bases Mumbai , Vishakhapatnam, Kochi (Cochin)

Karwar (under construction) Chennai (under construction) Kolkata (under construction)

Port Blair (Andaman Islands)

Naval airbases at Arakonam and Goa

Naval aviation 7,000

Forces

Air HQ (Arakonam)

FGA 1 squadron with 15 *Sea Harrier* FRS MK51 (*Sea Harrier* FRS MKI); 2 T-60

ASW 6 squadrons with 9 Ka-31 *Helix B*; 7 Ka-25 *Hormone*; 18 Ka-28 (Ka-27PL) *Helix A*; 35 *Sea King* MK42A/*Sea King* MK42B; 26 HAL *Chetak* (SA-316B) *Alouette III*

Maritime Reconaissance 3 squadrons with 6 Il-38 *May*; 11 Tu-142M *Bear F*; up to 20 Do-228-201; 15 B-2 *Defender*

Search and Rescue 1 squadron with 6 *Sea King* MK42C; HAL *Chetak* (SA-316B) *Alouette III* (several in SAR role)

Transport 1 squadron with 10 HAL-784M (HS-748M)

Communications 1 squadron with 10 Do-228

Training 2 squadrons with 6 HJT-16 MKI *Kiran*; 6 HJT-16 MKII *Kiran II*; 8 HPT-32 *Deepak*

Equipment

Aircraft 34 combat capable; **FGA** 15: 15 *Sea Harrier* FRS MK51 (*Sea Harrier* FRS MKI, **ASW** 17: 6 Il-38 *May*, **Tu-142** 11: 11 Tu-142M *Bear F* , **MP** up to 20: up to 20 Do-228-201, **Transport** 35: 15 B-2 *Defender*; 10 Do-228
HS-748 10: 10 HAL-784M (HS-748M), **Training** 22:
HJT-16 MKI 12: 6; 6 HJT-16 MKII *Kiran II*
HPT-32 *Deepak* 8 **T-60** 2

Helicopters **AEW** 9: 9 KA-31 *Helix B,* **SAR** 6: 6 *Sea King* MK42C
ASW 25: 7 Ka-25 *Hormone,* **KA-27** 18: 18 Ka-28 (Ka-27PL) *Helix A, Sea King* **MK42A ASW/***Sea King* **Mk42B ASW/ASUW** 35, **Utility** 51+; **SA-316** 26+: 26 HAL *Chetak* (SA-316B) *Alouette III*; some (several in SAR role) **SA-319 *Alouette III*** 25

Missiles **Tactical ASM**: some *Sea Eagle*; some KH-35/*Sea Skua*
AAM R-550: some R-550 *Magic 2*/R-550 *Magic* tactical AAM

Marines 2,000; Amphibious 1 brigade; Commando 1 (marine) force

Command Headquarters

Western	- Mumbai
Southern	- Kochi
Eastern	- Vishakhapatnam
Andaman and Nicobar	- Port Blair

Air Force 170,000

Forces

Fighter 3 squadrons with 74 MiG-29B *Fulcrum*
1 squadron with 45 MiG-23MF *Flogger E*/MiG-23UM; 1 squadron with 18 MiG-21FL *Fishbed E*

FGA 3 squadrons with 48 M-2000H (M-2000E) *Mirage*/M-2000TH (M-2000ED) *Mirage* (secondary ECM role);
10 squadrons with 165 MiG-21bis *Fishbed L & N*
4 squadrons with 55 MiG-21MF *Fishbed J*/MiG-21PFMA *Fishbed*;
4 squadrons with 100 *Jaguar* S International
2 squadrons with 42 Su-30 MKI; 8 Su-30K *Flanker*
7 squadrons with 120 MiG-27M *Flogger J2*
3 squadrons with 72 MiG-23bis *Flogger H*

Maritime attack 1 squadron with 16 *Jaguar* S (I) each with *Sea Eagle* tactical ASM

Elint some squadrons with 2 B-707; 2 B-737; 5 HS-748

MR /Survey some squadrons (all operated by Aviation Research Centre - Intelligence Wing) with 2 Gulfstream IV SRA-4; 3 An-32 *Cline*; 2 B-707; 2 *Learjet* 29

ECM 1 squadron with 24 MiG-23 bis *Flogger H*;
1 squadron with 24 MiG-21M *Fishbed J*;
1 squadron with 3 B(I) MK 58 *Canberra*; 2 PR-57 *Canberra*; 2 PR-67 *Canberra*; 2 T-54 *Canberra*; 3 TT-18 *Canberra* (target towing)

Transport	3 squadrons with 3 ALH; 60 HAL *Cheetah* (SA-315B) *Lama*/HAL *Chetak* (SA-316B) *Alouette III*; 6 squadrons with 119 An-32 *Cline*; 2 squadrons with 43 Do-228; 16 squadrons with 43 Mi-8 *Hip*; 100 MI-17 *Hip H*; 1 squadron with 10 Mi-26 *Halo* (heavy transport); 2 squadrons with 30 Il-76 *Candid*; 2 squadrons with 40 HS-748
Tankers	some squadrons with 6 Il-78 *Midas*
VIP	1 squadron HQ with 2 B-707; 4 B-737; 7 HS-748
Anti-tank helicopters	3 squadrons with 40-60 Mi-25 *Hind D*/Mi-35 *Hind*
Training	some squadrons with 27 BAe-748 (training/transport); 120 HJT-16 MKI *Kiran*; 56 HJT-16 MKII *Kiran II*; 88 HPT-32 *Deepak*; 40 MiG-21U *Mongol A*; 9 MiG-29UB *Fulcrum*; 15 MiG-27UM; 44 PZL TS-11 *Iskra*; 14 *Jaguar* B(I) (SEPECAT *Jaguar* International B); 20 HAL *Chetak* (SA-316B) *Alouette III; 24 Hawk Mk 132 Advanced Jet Trainer*
UAV	some squadrons with *Searcher* MK II
SAM	30 squadrons with S-125 (SA-3B) *Goa*; 8 squadrons with SA-8B; 4 flt with SA-16 *Gimlet*

<u>Equipment</u>

Aircraft	1,430 combat aircraft **Fighter** 386; **Su-30** 80: 72 Su-30 MKI *Flanker*; 8 Su-30K *Flanker*, **MiG-29** 74: 74 MiG-29B *Fulcrum* **MiG-23MF *Flogger E* Fighter/MiG-23UM *Flogger* Training** 45, **MiG-21** 262: 18 MiG-21FL *Fishbed E* **MiG-21M** 24: 24, **MiG-21MF *Fishbed J*/MiG-21PFMA *Fishbed*** 55, **MiG-21bis *Fishbed L & N*** 165 **Strike/FGA** 3: 3 B(I) MK 58 *Canberra* **FGA** 380, **M-2000** 48: 48 M-2000H (M-2000E) *Mirage*/M-2000TH (M-2000ED) *Mirage* (secondary ECM role), **MiG-27** 120: 120 MiG-27M *Flogger J2* ***Jaguar* S(I) (*Jaguar* S International)** 16 each with *Sea Eagle* tactical ASM; 100 more **MiG-23B** 96: 96 MiG-23 *Flogger H* **Reconnaissance** 9; **MR** 2: 2 Gulfstream IV SRA-4 ***Canberra*** 2 **PR-67 *Canberra*** 2 **Tankers** 6: 6 Il-78 *Midas* **Transport** 288: 122 An-32 *Cline*; 6 B-707; 6 B-737; 27 BAe-748 (training/transport); 43 Do-228; 52 HS-748; 30 Il-76 *Candid*; 2 *Learjet* 29 **Training** 378; **HJT-16 MKI** 176: 120; 56 HJT-16 MKII *Kiran II* , **HPT-32 *Deepak*** 88 *Jaguar* **B(I) (Sepecat** *Jaguar* **International B)** 14, **MiG-21U *Mongol A*** 40, **MiG-25U *Foxbat*** 2 15 **MiG-27UM MiG-29U** 9: 9 MiG-29UB ***Fulcrum* PZL TS-11 *Iskra*** 44 **T-54;** 24 ***Hawk Mk 132*** *Advanced Jet Trainer*; ***Canberra*** 2 **TT-18 *Canberra*** 3 (target towing)
Helicopters	**Anti-tank** 60: 40-60 Mi-25 *Hind D*/Mi-35 *Hind* **Support** 153: 10 Mi-26 *Halo* (heavy transport) **MI-8** 143: 43; 100 MI-17 (Mi-8MT) *Hip H* **Utility** 83: 3 ALH; 60 HAL *Cheetah* (SA-315B) *Lama* SA-315/HAL *Chetak* (SA-316B) *Alouette III* SA-316 **SA-316** 20: 20 HAL *Chetak* (SA-316B) *Alouette III*
UAV	some *Searcher* MK II .

Air Defence	**Surface-to-Air Missiles SA-3**: some **S-125** (SA-3B) *Goa* Self-Propelled • **SA-8**: some SA-8B **MANPAD**: some SA-16 *Gimlet* **Missiles Tactical**, **ASM**: some AM-39 *Exocet* **AS-11**: some AS-11B (ATGW) **AS-12** ***Kegler*** some **AS-17** ***Krypton*** some **AS-30** some **AS-7** ***Kerry*** some ***Sea Eagle*** some **SSM**: some *Prithvi* MK II **AAM**: some AA-10 *Alamo*; some AA-11 *Archer*; some AA-12 *Adder*; some AA-7 *Apex*; some AA-8 *Aphid*; some R-550 *Magic* **R530 Super 530**: some Super 530D

Paramilitary 1,295,000

Assam Rifles	64,000; Ministry of Home Affairs; 7 HQ; 31 battalions
Artillery , **Mortars**	240: 240 81 mm
Border Security Force	208,000; Ministry of Home Affairs. Paramilitary 157+ battalions Small arms, light artillery, some anti-tank weapons
Artillery: Mortars	942: 942 81 mm
Aircraft:	Some transport (air support)
Central Industrial Security Force	94,000 (lightly armed security guards only) Ministry of Home Affairs; Guards public-sector locations
Central Reserve Police Force	230,000 Ministry of Home Affairs Paramilitary 2 Mahila (women) battalions; 125 battalions; 13 rapid action force battalions

Coast Guard *8,000+*

Forces	
Air	3 squadrons
Equipment	
Patrol and Coastal Combatants	50: 17 **PB**, **PCC** 21: 7 *Jija Bai*; 14 *Jija Bai* Mod 1 **PCO** 12: 3 *Samar*; 9 *Vikram*
Aircraft	**Transport** 24: 24 Do-228
Helicopters	**Utility SA-316** 17: 17 HAL *Chetak* (SA-316B) *Alouette*
Defence Security Corps	***31,000;*** provides security at Defence Ministry sites
Indo-Tibetan Border Police	***36,324;*** Ministry of Home Affairs.
National Security Guards	***7,357;*** Anti-terrorism contingency deployment force, **comprising elements of the armed forces, CRPF and Border Security Force**
Railway Protection Force	***70,000***
Rashtriya Rifles	67,000; Ministry of Defence; 60 battalions

Shastra Seema Bal	***31,554***
Special Frontier Force	10,000
Special Protection Group	***3,000***
State Armed Police	***450,00;*** For duty primarily in home state only, but can be moved to other states.

Reserve organisations

Civil Defence	500,000 reservists; Fully trained in 225 categorised towns in 32 states. Some units for NBC defence
Home Guards	487,821 reservists (actual) (515,000 authorised) In all states except Arunachal Pradesh and Kerala. Not usually armed in peacetime -weapons held in state armouries. Used for civil defence, rescue and fire-fighting teams in wartime.

INDONESIA

Armed Forces 302,000	Army 233,000; Navy 45,000 Air Force 24,000 Paramilitary 280,000 (Terms of service 2 years; Selective conscription authorized) Reserves 400,000

Organisations

Army 233, 000

Military Area Commands	**12** Provincial (*KOREM*) and District (*KODIM*) Commands **Kodam Iskandar Muda**, Aceh **Kodam I/Bukit Barisan**, North Sumatra, West Sumatra, Riau and Riau Islands. **Kodam II/Sriwijaya**, South Sumatra, Jambi, Bengkulu, Bangka Belitung and Lampung. **Kodam Jaya**, Jakarta, Bekasi and Tangerang. **Kodam III/Siliwangi**, West Java and Banten. **Kodam IV/Diponegoro**, Central Java and Yogyakarta. **Kodam V/Brawijaya**, East Java. **Kodam VI/Tanjungpura**, Kalimantan island (Borneo). **Kodam VII/Wirabuana**, Gorontalo, and Sulawesi. **Kodam IX/Udayana**, Bali, East Nusa Tenggara and West Nusa Tenggara. **Kodam XVI/Pattimura**, Maluku and North Maluku. **Kodam XVII/Trikora**, West Irian Jaya and Papua.
Aviation / Composite	1 squadron
Cavalry	8 battalions
Infantry	2 brigades (6 battalions); 60 battalions
Airborne	5 battalions
Field Artillery	10 battalions
Engineers	7 battalions
Helicopters	1 squadron
Air Defence	7 battalions
Special Forces Command	(*KOPASSUS*) 5, 300
Special Forces:	3 groups (total: 1 training unit, 1 (intelligence) SF unit, 2 commando/ parachute unit, 8 counter-terrorist units)
Strategic Reserve Command	(*KOSTRAD*) 35,000
Armoured	2 battalions
Infantry	2 div HQ; 3 brigades (9 battalions)
Airborne	2 brigades
Field Artillery	2 regiments (6 battalions)
Air Defence	1 regiments (2 battalions)
Engineers	2 battalions

Equipment

Tanks	Light tanks 350: 275 AMX-13 (being upgraded); 15 PT-76; 60 Scorpion 90

Reconnaissance	**142:** 55 Ferret (13 upgraded); 69 Saladin (16 upgraded); 18 VBL
Armoured Fighting Vehicles	**BMP 11**: 11 BMP-2; **APC** 356; **APC (T)** 115: 75 **AMX-VCI**; 40 FV4333 Stormer; **APC (W)** 241; **BTR** 114: 80 **BTR-40**; 34 **BTR-50PK; Commando Ranger** 22; FV603 Saracen 45 (14 upgraded) LAV 60: 60 LAV-150 Commando
Artillery	**1060**: **Towed** 185; 76mm 50: 50 M-48 M-1948; 105mm 130: 120 M-101; 10 M-56; 155mm 5: 5 FH-2000; **Mortars** 875: 81mm 800; 120mm 75: 75 Brandt
Anti-Tank	**Recoilless** 135: 106mm M-40 45: 45 M-40A1; 90mm 90: M-67 **Rocket launcher** 89mm 700: 700 LRAC
Aircraft	**Transport** 11: 3 DHC-5 Buffalo; 6 NC-212 (CASA 212) Aviocar; 2 Rockwell Turbo Commander 680
Helicopters	**Anti-tank** 2: 2 Mi-35 Hind; **Utility** 37: BELL 205/A 8: 8 NB-412 (Bell 412) Twin Huey 12; NBO-105 (BO-105) 17; **Training** HUGHES 300 12: 12 Hughes 300C
Air Defence	**Missiles** 68: 51 Rapier; 17 RBS-70; **Guns Towed** 413: 20mm 121: 121 Rh 202; 40mm 36: 36 L/70; 57mm 256: 256 S-60

Navy 69,000

Eastern Command	HQ located at Surabaya
Facilities:	13 Minor bases
Western Command	HQ located at Teluk Ratai (Jakarta)
Facilities:	10 Minor bases
Equipment	
Submarines	**Tactical** SSK 2: 2 Cakra each with 8 single 533mm TT with 14 SUT HWT
Principal Surface Combatants	**29**
Frigates	**13: FFG 10:** 6 Ahmad Yani (capacity either 1 HAS-1 Wasp ASW helicopter or 1 NBO-105 (BO-105) utility helicopter) each with 2 triple 324mm ASTT (6 effective) each with Mk 46 LWT, 2 SIMBAD x2 manual each with Mistral SAM, 2 Mk 141 Harpoon quad (8 effective) each with 1 RGM-84A Harpoon tactical SSM, 1 76mm gun 3 Fatahillah each with 2 B515 ILAS-3/triple 324mm ASTT (2-6 effective) (not on Nala) with 12 A244/Mk 46, 2 twin (4 effective) each with 1 MM-38 Exocet tactical SSM, 1 2 tube Bofors 375mm (2 effective), 1 120mm gun 1 Hajar Dewantara (capacity 1 NBO-105 (BO-105) utility helicopter) (training) with 2 x1 533mm ASTT each with SUT HWT, 2 twin (4 effective) each with 1 MM-38 Exocet tactical SSM, 1 single; **FF 3**: 3 Samadikun each with 2 triple 324mm ASTT (6 effective) each with Mk 46 LWT, 1 76mm gun
Corvettes	**FS 16:** 16 Kapitan Patimura each with 4 x1 400mm ASTT, Twin each with SA-N-5 Grail SAM, 2 RBU 6000 Smerch 2 (24 effective), 1 57mm gun
Patrol and Coastal Combatants	**23: PCC 11:** 3 KAL-35 each with 2 20mm gun 8 Sibarau; **PFM 4:** 4 Mandau each with 4 MM-38 Exocet tactical SSM; **PCT 4:** 4 Singa each with 2 Single 533mm TT; **PCO 4:** 4 Kakap
Mine Warfare	**Mine Countermeasures** 11: **MCC 3:** 1 Pulau Rani; 2 Pulau Rengat; **MSC 8:** 8 Palau Rote

Amphibious	**LS • LST 26:** 1 Teluk Amboina (capacity 16 tanks; 200 troops); 12 Teluk Gilimanuk; 7 Teluk Langsa (capacity 16 tanks; 200 troops); 6 Teluk Semangka (capacity 17 tanks; 200 troops); **Craft** 65: 65 **LCM/ LCVP**
Logistics and Support	**15:** AGOR 6; AO 2: 1 Arun; 1 Sorong; AOT 2: 2 Khobi; AR 1 ATF 2; RY 1 (Presidential Yacht); Support 1

Marines 15,000

Forces	
Special Forces	1 battalion
Marine	2 (corps) groups (each: 1 independent marine infantry brigade (3 marine infantry battalions), 3 marine infantry battalion)
Combat Support	1 regiment (artillery, Air Defence)
Equipment	
Tanks	**Light tanks 55**: 55 PT-76†
Reconnaissance	**21**: 21 BRDM; **AIFV 34:** 24 AMX-10P; 10 AMX-10 PAC 90 APC APC (W), BTR, BTR-50 100: 100 BTR-50P
Artillery	**62+: Towed 50+** 105mm LG1 22: 22 LG1 MK II 122mm 28+: 28+ M-38 M-1938; **MRL** 140mm 12: 12 BM-14; **Mortars:** some 81mm
Air Defence	150+ guns incl. 5 L/60/L/70 40mm, S-60 towed 57mm
Naval Aviation	1,000
Aircraft	MP 27: 2 CASA 235 MPA; 15 GAF N-22B Searchmaster B; 10 GAF N-22SL Searchmaster L; **Transport** 15; CN-235 1: 1 CN-235M; DHC-5 Buffalo 2, NC-212 (CASA 212) 4: 4 CASA 212-200 Aviocar; PA-34 Seneca 4; Rockwell Commander 100 4; **Training** 6: 6 PA-38 Tomahawk
Helicopters	**ASW 9**: 9 HAS-1 Wasp; **Support** • AS-332 6: 6 NAS-322L (AS-332L) Super Puma; **Utility 28;** EC-120 9: 9 EC-120B Colibri; NB-412 (Bell 412) Twin Huey 2 NBO-105 (BO-105) 17
Facilities	**Bases** at Belawan, Vayapura and Ujung Pandang

Air Force 28,000

Operational Commands	2: East and West plus Training Command. (only 45% of aircraft operational)
Forces	
Fighter	1 squadron with 8 F-5E Tiger II; 4 F-5F Tiger II
FGA	1 squadron with 2 Su-30 MKI Flanker (multi-role); 2 Su-27SK Flanker (AD); 1 squadron with 7 F-16A Fighting Falcon; 3 F-16B Fighting Falcon; 1 squadron with 11 A-4E Skyhawk; 1 TA-4H Skyhawk; 2 TA-4J Skyhawk; 2 squadron with 7 Hawk MK109; 28 Hawk MK209 (FGA/fighter)
Reconaissance	1 flight with 12 OV-10F Bronco
Maritime Reconaissance	1 squadron with 3 B-737-200

Transport	5 squadrons with 1 B-707; 8 C-130B Hercules; 4 C-130H Hercules; 6 C-130H-30 Hercules; 10 NC-212 (CASA 212) Aviocar; 10 CN-235-110; 5 Cessna 401; 2 Cessna 402; 6 F-27-400M Troopship; 1 F-28-1000; 2 F-28-3000; 3 L-100-30; 1 SC.7 3M Skyvan (survey); 4 Cessna 207 Stationair
Tanker	some squadrons with 2 KC-130B Hercules
Training	3 squadrons with 2 Cessna 172; 39 AS-202 Bravo; 7 Hawk MK53*; 7 KT-1B; 19 SF-260M/SF-260W Warrior; 20 T-34C Turbo Mentor; 6 T-41D Mescalero
Helicopter	3 squadrons with 10 S-58T; 5 NAS-322L (AS-332L) Super Puma (VIP/CSAR); 11 NAS-330 (SA-330) Puma (1 NAS-330SM VIP); 12 EC-120B Colibri

Equipment

Aircraft	**94** combat capable
Fighter	26: F-5 12: 8 F-5E Tiger II; 4 F-5F Tiger II; Su-30 2: 2 Su-30 MKI Flanker (multirole) F-16 10: 7 F-16A Fighting Falcon; 3 F-16B Fighting Falcon Su-27 2: 2 Su-27SK Flanker (AD)
Fighter Ground Attack	**18:** A-4 11: 11 A-4E Skyhawk; Hawk MK109 7; Hawk MK209 (FGA/fighter) 28; FAC OV-10 12: 12 OV-10F Bronco
Tanker	KC-130 2: 2 KC-130B Hercules
Transport	**62:** B-707 1; B-737 3: 3 B-737-200; C-130 18: 8 C-130B Hercules; 4 C-130H Hercules; 6 C-130H-30 Hercules; CN-235 10: 10 CN-235-110: Cessna 401 5; Cessna 402 2; F-27 6: 6 F-27-400M Troopship; F-28 3: 1 F-28-1000; 2 F-28-3000; L-100 3: 3 L-100-30; NC-212 (CASA 212) Aviocar: 10; SC.7 3M Skyvan: 1 (survey): **Utility 6:** 2 Cessna 172; 4 Cessna 207 Stationair; **Training 129:** AS-202 Bravo 39; Hawk MK53* 7 KT-1 7: 7 KT-1B SF-260 19: 19 SF-260M/SF-260W Warrior T-34 20: 20 T-34C Turbo Mentor T-41 6: 6 T-41D Mescalero TA-4 3: 1 TA-4H Skyhawk*; 2 TA-4J Skyhawk
Helicopters	SAR 10: 10 S-58T; SUPPORT 16; AS-332 5: 5 NAS-322L (AS-332L) Super Puma (VIP/CSAR) NAS-330 (SA-330) Puma 11 (1 NAS-330SM VIP) UTILITY • EC-120 12: 12 EC-120B Colibri
Missiles	**Tactical ASM**; AGM-65: some AGM-65G Maverick AAM • AIM-9: some AIM-9P Sidewinder

Special Forces (Paskhasan)

Special Operations	3 (*PASKHASAN*) Wings (total: 6 Special Operations squadrons); 4 independent companies; Reserves some 6,000 (to age 45)

Organisations

Army	3,200 (including 300 recalled reserves)

Forces

Infantry	7 battalion
Special Operations	1 company
Artillery	1 battery
Engineers	1 battalion

Equipment	
Artillery	**16: Towed** 85mm 4: 4 25-pdr (ceremonial); **Mortar** 12: 12 81mm
Helicopters	**Support** 1: 1 AS-355 Ecureuil; **Utility** 1: 1 AS-365 Dauphin 2
Navy	**300**
Equipment	
Patrol and Coastal Combatants	**9:** PCC 3: 3 Kula; PCI 6: 2 Levuka; 4 Vai
Logistics and Support	**2:** AGHS (SVY) 1: 1 Tovutu; **Training** 1: 1 Cagi Donu (Presidential Yacht)
Facilities	Bases located at Walu Bay and Viti 1 (Training)

Paramilitary 280,000 active

Customs	
Patrol and Coastal Combatants	**72**: 72 PFI
Marine Police	
Patrol and Coastal Combatants	**25:** 10 PCC; 6 PCI (small); 9 more

MALAYSIA

Armed Forces 110,000	(Army 80,000; Navy 15,000; Air Force15,000) Paramilitary 20,100 Reserves 51,600 (Army 50,000, 1,000 Air Force 600) Paramilitary 244,700
***Army** 80,000*	
<u>Forces</u>	2 Military Regions 1 HQ Field Command 4 Area Commands (divisions)
Armoured	6 regiments
Mechanised infantry	1 brigade; 3 battalions
Infantry	11 brigades; 28 battalions
Special Forces	1 regiment (3 Special Forces battalions)
Airborne	1 (Rapid Deployment Force) brigade (1 light tank squadron, 1 light artillery regiment, 3 airborne battalions)
Artillery	2 (medium) regiments
Field Artillery	7 regiments
MRL	1 regiments
Air Defence	3 regiments
Engineers	5 regiments
Helicopters	1 squadrons
Artillery locating	1 regiment
Reserves	
Territorial Army	Police 5 (highway safety) battalions Infantry 16 regiments
<u>Equipment</u>	
Tanks	*48 Twardy PT-91;* **Light Tanks** 26 Scorpion 90
Reconnaissance	418: **AML** 140: 140 AML-60/AML-90; **Ferret**92 (60 mod) **SIBMAS** 186
APC	1020: **APC (T)** 347: 211 Adnan (including variants); 25 FV4333 Stormer; 111 KIFV (including variants) **APC (W)** 673: 452 Condor (150 upgraded); 37 M-3 Panhard; 184 LAV-150 Commando/V-100 Commando
Artillery	414: **Towed** 164 **105mm** 130: 130 Model 56 pack howitzer **155mm** 34: 12 FH-70; 22 G-5; **MRL** 18: 18 ASTROS II (equipped with 127mm SS-30); **Mortar** 232: 232 81mm
Anti-tank	**Missiles** 60: 18 AT-7 Saxhorn; 24 Eryx; 18 HJ-8; **RCL** 260 **106mm** 24: 24 M-40; **84mm** 236: 236 Carl Gustav **RL • 73mm** 584: 584 RPG-7 Knout
Amphibious Craft	**LCA** 165: 165 Damen assault craft 540 (capacity 10 troops)
Helicopters	**Utility SA-316** 9: 9 SA-316B Alouette III
Air Defence	**SAM MANPAD** 48+: some Anza; some SA-18 Grouse (Igla); 48 Starburst **Guns** 60: **35mm**: 24 GDF-005 towed **40mm**: 36 L40/70 towed

Navy 15,000

Equipment

Principal Surface Combatants	10
Frigates	4: **FFG** 2: 2 Lekiu (capacity 1 Super Lynx utl helicpters) each with 2 B515 ILAS-3 triple 324mm each with 1 Sting Ray LWT, 2 quad (8 effective) each with 1 MM-40 Exocet tactical SSM, 1 Sea Wolf VLS with 16 Sea Wolf SAM **FF** 2: 1 Hang Tuah Training with 3 Limbo non-operational, 1 57mm gun, 1 helicopters landing platform (for Wasp or Super Lynx) 1 Rahmat with 3 Limbo, 1 114mm gun, 1 helicopters landing platform
Corvettes	6: **FSG** 4: 4 Laksamana each with 2 B515 ILAS-3 triple 324mm each with A244 LWT, 1 quad (4 effective) with 12 Aspide SAM, 3 twin (6 effective) each with 1 Mk 2 Otomat SSM, 1 76mm gun **FS** 2: 2 Kasturi each with 2 twin (4 effective) each with 1 MM-38 Exocet tactical SSM, 1 Mle 54 Creusot-Loire 375mm Bofors (6 effective), 1 100mm gun, 1 helicpters landing platform (For 1 Westland Wasp HAS Mk 1
Patrol and Coastal Combatants	35: **PCC** 18: 14 Kris; 4 Sabah **PCI** 1: 1 Kedah **PFC** 6: 6 Jerong **PFM** 8: 4 Handalan each with 2 twin (4 effective) each with 1 MM-38 Exocet tactical SSM, 1 57mm gun 4 Perdana each with 2 single each with 1 MM-38 Exocet tactical SSM, 1 57mm gun **PCO** 2: 2 Musytari each with 1 100mm gun, 1 helicpters landing platform
Mine Warfare	**MCO** 4: 4 Mahamiru
Amphibious	**LS LST** 1: 1 Sri Inderapura (capacity 10 tanks; 400 troops)
AGHS (Survey) /AGOS	2 **Amphibious Craft** 115: 115 LCM/LCU
Logistics and Support	3: 1 diving tender/support; 2 Support
Naval Aviation	160
Helicopters	**ASW** 6: 6 Wasp
Special Forces	
Naval commandos	1 unit

Air Force 15,000

Air Operational HQ	2 Air Divisions Training and Logistics Command Integrated Area Defence Systems HQ

Forces

Fighter	2 squadrons with 15 MiG-29N (MiG-29) Fulcrum; 2 MiG-29U Fulcrum
FGA	1 squadron with 8 F/A-18D Hornet; 2 squadron with 8 Hawk MK108; 17 Hawk MK208
FGA / Reconnaissance	1 squadron with 13 F-5E Tiger II/F-5F Tiger II; 2 RF-5E Tigereye
Maritime	1 squadron with 4 Beech 200T Maritime Patrol
Special Forces	1 (Air Force Commando) unit (air field defence)
Transport	2 squadrons with 4 KC-130H Hercules (tanker); 4 C-130H Hercules; 8 C-130H-30 Hercules; 9 Cessna 402B (2 modified for aerial survey); 1 (VIP) squadron with 1 B-737-700 BBJ; 1 BD700 Global Express; 1 F-28 Fellowship; 1 Falcon 900; 2 S-61N; 2 S-70A Black Hawk; 1 A-109; 1 squadron with 6 CN-235

Training	some squadrons with 8 MB-339A; 20 MD3-160; 45 PC-7 MK II Turbo Trainer; 13 SA-316 Alouette III
Helicopters	4 (Transport/SAR) squadrons with 31 S-61A-4 Nuri; 2 S-61N; 2 S-70A Black Hawk *8 Aermacchi MB-339CM*
SAM	1 squadron with Starburst
Equipment	
Aircraft	63 combat capable
Fighter	46: **F-5** 13: 13 F-5E Tiger II/F-5F Tiger II; **MiG-29N (MiG-29) Fulcrum** 15; *18 Su-30MKM*
FGA	16: **F/A-18** 8: 8 F/A-18D Hornet Hawk **MK108** 8
Reconnaissance	2: 2 RF-5E Tigereye
Maritime	4: 4 Beech 200T Maritime Patrol
Tanker	**KC-130** 4: 4 KC-130H Hercules (tanker)
Transport	31; **B-737** 1: 1 B-737-700 BBJ **BD700 Global Express** 1 **C-130** 12: 4 C-130H Hercules; 8 C-130H-30 Hercules **CN-235** 6 **CESSNA 402** 9: 9 Cessna 402B (2 modified for aerial survey) **F-28 Fellowship** 1 Falcon **900** 1
Training	92: Hawk **MK208** 17 **MB-339** 8: 8 MB-339AB **MD3-160** 20 **MiG-29U Fulcrum** 2* **PC-7** 45: 45 PC-7 MK II Turbo Trainer
Helicopters	**ASW S-61/S-61A** 31: 31 S-61A-4 Nuri **Support** 8: 4 S-61N; 4 S-70A Black Hawk **Utility** 14: 1 A-109; 13 SA-316 Alouette III; *8 Aermacchi MB-339CM*
UAV	**Tactical** 3: 3 Eagle 150
Air Defence	**SAM • MANPAD**: some Starburst **MISSILE • TACTICAL ASM**: AGM-65 Maverick; AGM-84D Harpoon **AAM**: some AA-10 Alamo; AA-11 Archer; some AIM-7 Sparrow; some AIM-9 Sidewinder

Paramilitary 20, 100

***Police-General Ops Force** 18,000*

Forces	
	Police 5 Engineers HQ; 2 (Aboriginal) battalions; 19 battalions; 4 independent companies
Special Operations	1 battalion
Equipment	
Reconnaissance	100:100 S52 Shorland **APC (W)** 170: 140 AT105 Saxon; e30 SB-301

Marine Police

Equipment	
Patrol and Coastal Combatants	150: 120 PBI **PFI** 30: 9 Imp PX; 15 Lang Hitam; 6 Sangitan
Logistics and Support	8: 2 AT; 6 Transport
Facilities	Bases at Kuala Kemaman, Penang, Tampoi and Sandakan

Police Air Unit

Aircraft	**Transport** 7: 7 PC-6 Turbo-Porter **Utility** 10: 4 Cessna 206; 6 Cessna 208 Caravan I
Helicopters	**Support AS-355** 2: 2 AS-355F Ecureuil II **Utility BELL 206** 1: 1 Bell 206L Long Ranger

***Area Security Units (R)** 3,500*

Auxiliary General Operations Force	
Paramilitary	89 units

MYANMAR

Total Armed Forces: 581,000 (Tatmadaw)

Army: 428,250

Organization	
Bureau of Special Operations	4
Regional Commands	12 (Myitkina, Lashio, Mandalay, Taunggyi, Monywa, Sittwe, Kengtung, Toungoo, Hainggyi, Yangon, Mawlamyine, Myeik)
Light Infantry	11 division headquarters
	Military Operations Command 1 (Kyaukme, Shan State)
	Military Operations Command 2 (Loilem, Shan State)
	Military Operations Command 3 (Mogaung, Kachin State)
	Military Operations Command 4 (Phugyi, Yangon)
	Military Operations Command 5 (Ann, Rakhine State)
	Military Operations Command 6 (Pyinmana, Mandalay)
	Military Operations Command 7 (Phekon, Shan State)
	Military Operations Command 8 (Dawei, Tanintharyi)
	Military Operations Command 9 (Kyauktaw, Rakhine)
	Military Operations Command 10 (Kyeekone, Mandalay)
	Military Operations Command 11
	Military Operations Command 12 (Kawkareik, Kayin)
	Military Operations Command 13 (Bokpyin, Tanintharyi)
	Military Operations Command 14 (Mongsat, Shan State)
	Military Operations Command 15 (Buthidaung, Rakhine)
	Military Operations Command 16 (Theinni, Shan State)
	Military Operations Command 17 (Mongpan, Shan State)
	Military Operations Command 18 (Hehalsai, Shan State)
	Military Operations Command 19 (Ye, Mon State)
	Military Operations Command 20 (Kawthaung)
	Military Operations Command 21 (Bhamo, Kachin State)
	Military Operations Command 22
	Military Operations Command 23
	Military Operations Command 24
Armour	2 divisions
Artillery	10 divisions (brigades)

Forces	
Armour	7 armoured regiments
Airborne	1 brigade
Infantry	412 light infantry regiments (battalions)
Artillery	22 artillery regiments; 27 artillery companies
Engineers	1 brigade

Equipment	
Tanks	280+; **Main Battle tanks** 280: Type-63/Type-69
Armoured Fighting Vehicles	250+; Type-85; 240+Type 90; 50 BMP-1; 140 EE9 *Escavel*
Armoured Personnel Carriers	80 Universal T-16 Bren Gun Carriers; 40 Humber APC
	6 Ferret Scout Cars; 50 Daimler Scout Cars

Artillery	640+, 30 Nora B-52 self-propelled; 16 M-845P 155mm Howitzers; 100+ KH-179 155mm Howitzers; 16 Soltam 155mm Howitzers; some140mm 5.5-inch Medium Guns; 16 Type 59 M-46 130mm Field Guns; 340+105mm Howitzers (US M-101, M-56/M101 Howitzer,105-mm; 50 88mm 25-Pounder Field Guns; 80 75mm Field Guns; 100 M-48 B1 Mountain Guns **MLRS:** 30 240 mm truck mounted MLRS; 120 Type 90 122mm MLRS; some BM-21 MLRS; 30 Type 63 107mm Towed MLRS; some BA-84 81mm Towed MLRs **Mortars** 400+ × 120mm; Ka Pa Sa BA-97; *Hotchkiss-Brandt* MO-120-60; MA-6; *Soltam* K-6; *Tampella* Mk 2; Type 53; UBM-52; 120mm *Soltam* M-65/*Tampella M-65*
Anti-Tank	**Recoilless** 106 mm60: M-40 30: 30 M-40A1; **Guns** 68; 57 mm 18: 18 6-pdr; 76 mm 50: 50 Type-54 (ZIS-3)
Air Defence	**Missiles** TOR M1 / SA-15; 24 BUK-M1-2 / SA-17; 24 Tunguska M1 SA-19; 24 SA-6 *Gainful*; 24 *Pechora-2M*; 48 *Volga M SA-2 Guideline*; 2 BAe Dynamics *Bloodhound Mk II*; 400 SA-18 *Grouse;* **MANPADS** 200 CPMIEC HN5; 100 *Igla-1E* / SA-16 *Gimlet*; some FIM-92 *Stinger*; **Guns** 200 14.5mm KPV in quadruple AAA mounts; 200 37mm/40mm/57mm Anti-Aircraft Guns (various models)

Navy: 17,500

Forces

Headquarters located at Yangon

Organization

Regional Operations Commands	5 (Sittwe, Hainggyi Island, Yangon, Mawlamyine, Katan Island) **Irrawaddy Regional Command** (Yangon) Thanhklyet Soon Naval Base Bassein Naval Base Coco Island Base (Naval Radar Unit) **Danyawaddy Regional Command** (Sittwe) Kyaukpyu Naval Base Thandwe (Sandoway) Naval Base **Panmawaddy Regional Command** (Hainggyi Island) **Mawyawaddy Regional Command** (Moulmein) **Tanintharyi Regional Command** (Mergui) Zadetkyi Island Naval Base Mali (Tavoy) Naval Base Palai Island Naval Base Kadan Naval Base Sakanthit Naval Base Lambi Naval Base Pearl Island Naval Base Zadetkale Naval Base (Radar Unit)

Equipment

Corvettes	4; Ex-US *PCE-827 class*; Ex-US *Admirable class*
Offshore Patrol Vessels	3; *Osprey class*
Coastal Patrol Craft	30+; 10: Type-037 *Chinese Hainan class*; 6 PGM-Type-401; 6 Ex-US *PGM Type-412*; 3 *Type-PB Yugoslav*; 3 *Swift Type*; 2 *FAC (G) Nawarat class*

River Gun Boats	36; 2 *Improved Y-301*; 10 *Y-301*; 2 *Ex-US CGC*; 2 *Yugoslav*
Amphibious Craft	20: 1 LCU; 19 LCM

Air Force: 16,000

Organization	
Operational Commands	4 (Nampong, Mandalay, Hanthawady, Myike)
Training Command	1
Airbases	Pathein, Mingaladon, Myitkyinar, Myike, Namsang, Taungoo, Meikhtila, Shante (training and operations), Homemalin
Equipment	
Fighter/FGAAircraft	124; 48 *F-7*; 39 *A-5-II*; 6 *G-4 Super Galeb*; 10 *FT-7*; 22 *Mig-29*
Transport	16: 3 *F-27*; 4 *FH-227*; 5 *PC-6A/6B*; 4 *Y-8*
Helicopters	72; 20 *Mi-2*; 23 *Bell-205/206/212*; 12 *Mi-17*, 5 *Aloeutte; Dhruv*
Training	45: 30 *PT-6*; 14 *K-8*

NEPAL

Army 69,000

Forces by Role

Army	3 Division HQ; 1 (valley) command
Infantry	7 brigades (*total:* 16 infantry battalions); 44 independent companies
Special Forces	1 brigade (1 AB battalion, 1 (*Ferret*) cavalry squadron, 2 independent Special Forces companies)
Rangers	1 battalion
Artillery	1 brigade (1 artillery regiment, 1 AD regiment)
Engineers	1 brigade (4 engineer battalions)
Royal Guards	1 brigade (1 MP battalion)

Equipment

Reconnaissance	40: 40 *Ferret*
Armoured Personnel Carriers	**APC (W)** 40: 40 *Casspir*
Artillery	95+; **Towed** 25, **75 mm** 6: 6 pack **94 mm** 5: 5 3.7 inch Mountain (training), **105 mm** 14: 8 L-118 Light Gun; pack howitzer non-operational; **Mortars** 70+: 81 mm, **120 mm** 70: 70 M-43
Air Defence	**Guns** 32+; **14.5 mm Towed** , **ZPU** 30: 30 Type-56 (ZPU-4) **37 mm** some (PRC) **40 mm Towed** 2: 2 L/60

Air Wing 320

Aircraft	**Transport** 2: 1 BAe-748; 1 SC.7 3M *Skyvan*
Helicopters	**Support** 7, **AS-332** 3: **AS-332L** 3: 1; 2 AS-322L1 Super Puma **AS-350 Ecureuil** 1,**MI-8** 3: 3 MI-17 (Mi-8MT) *Hip H* **Utility** 5; **BELL 206** 2: 2 Bell 206L *LongRanger* **SA-315** 1: 1 HAS-315B (SA-315B) *Lama* **SA-316** 2: 2 SA-316B *Alouette III*

Paramilitary 62,000

Armed Police Force 15,000

Ministry of Home Affairs

Police Force 47,000

PAKISTAN

Army: 550,000 (Reserves: 513,000)

Strategic Assets	**National Command Authority** (for control of nuclear weapons)
<u>**Equipment**</u>	
Strategic Missiles	*Hatf-I/IA* 100+; some *Abdali Hatf-II*; *Ghaznavi Hatf-III* 100+; *Shaheen-I Hatf-IV* 75-150; *Ghauri-I Hatf-V* 100+; *Ghauri-II Hatf-VA* 100+; *Shaheen-II Hatf-VI* 2 200+; *Babur Hatf-VII* Cruise Missile 400; some *Ghauri-III Hatf-VIII*; some M-11 some *Shaheen-III*
<u>**Forces by Role**</u>	
Army	**9 corps headquarters** (Mangla, Multan, Lahore, Karachi, Rawalpindi, Peshawar, Quetta, Gujranwala, Bahawalpur) Northern Areas Command (Gilgit)
Armoured	2 divisions; 7 (independent) brigades; 3 reconnaissance regiments
Mechanised	8 (independent) brigade
Infantry	18 divisions;1 (area) command; 6 (independent) brigades
Special Forces	2 groups (3 Special Forces battalions)
Artillery	2 divisions; 9 (corps) brigades
Engineers	8 brigades
Aviation	1 (VIP) squadron; 5 (composite) squadrons
Helicopters	13 squadrons
Air Defence	1 command; 3 Air Defence groups (*total:* 8 Air Defence brigades)
<u>**Equipment**</u>	
Tanks	**2,461;** T-80UD MBT 320; *Al Khalid* 600;Type 85IIAP 500;*Al-Zarar* 320;Type 69IIAP (Chinese T-59 Upgrade) 250 Being phased out by *Al Khalid*; T-63 & 60 Light Tank 100; Type 59 1200
Armoured Personnel Carriers	1,266; some *Hamza* Infantry fighting Vehicle; *Al-Fahd* Infantry fighting vehicle 140; Talha 400+; some *Saad* Armoured Personnel M113 1500+; BTR-70; some *Mohafiz* Light; Scorpion Light jeep 260
Artillery	4,291+; **Self-Propelled** M109A5 155 mm 115 with 150 A5 upgrade kits; M109A2 155 mm 150; M110A2 203 mm 40; M-7 105 mm 50; **Towed** T-56 85 mm 200; M-56 105 mm 80; M-101 105 mm 300; T-60 122 mm 200; T-54 122 mm 400; T-59I 130 mm 200; M-59 155 mm 30; M-114 155 mm 60;M-198 155 mm 120; M-115 203 mm 40; Panter T-155 mm 12;
Mortars	2,350+: **81 mm**; **120 mm** AM-50, M-61
Anti Tank	10,500; **Missiles**: 1,829 HJ-8/TOW (TOW M-901 SP) **Recoilless** 3,700: **75 mm** Type-52/**106 mm** M-40A1 **Rocket Launchers 3 mm**: some RPG-7 *Knout*; **89 mm**: some M-20 **Guns**; **85 mm** 200: 200 Type-56 (D-44)
Aircraft	**Reconaissance / Observation** 80: 30 Cessna O-1E *Bird Dog*; **Transport** 4: 1 Cessna 421; **Y-12** 3: 3 Y-12(II) **Utility** 95: 95 SAAB 91 *Safari* (50 observation, 45 liaison); **Survey** 2
Helicopters	**Anti-tank** 22, **AH-1** 21: 21 AH-1F *Cobra* (TOW) **Mi-24** *Hind* 1; **Support** 54: 31 SA-330 *Puma*; **MI-8** 23: 10; 13 MI-17

	(Mi-8MT) *Hip H*; **Utility** 55; **Bell 205 Bell 205A** 5: 5 AB-205A-1 (Bell 205A-1); **Bell 206** 13: 13 Bell 206B *JetRanger II*; **SA-315** 12: 12 SA-315B *Lama*; **SA-319** *Alouette III* 20; **UH-1** 5: 5 UH-1H *Iroquois*; **Training** 22: 12 Bell 47G; 10 Hughes 300C
UAV	some *Bravo*; some *Jasoos*; some *Vector*
Air Defence	**Surface-to-Air Missiles MANPAD** 2,990+; ANZA 2500: 2,500 Mk1/ Mk2; FIM-92A *Stinger* 60; HN-5: some HN-5A; Mistral 230 RBS-70 200 **Guns**1,900: **14.5 mm** 981; **35 mm Towed GDF** 215: 215 GDF-002/ GDF-005; **37 mm Towed** 310: 310 Type-55 (M-1939)/Type-65; **40 mm Towed** 50: 50 L/60; **57 mm Towed** 144: 144 Type-59 (S-60); **85 mm Towed** 200: 200 Type-72 (M-1939) *KS-12* **Radar Land**: some AN/TPQ-36 *Firefinder* (artillery, mortar); some RASIT (vehicle, artillery)
Missiles	**Tactical SSM** 165: 95 *Hatf* 1; 50 *Hatf* 3 (PRC M-11); 15 *Hatf* 5 *Ghauri* (upto 20); 6 *Shaheen* 1 *Hatf-4*

Navy 24,000 (including 1,400 Marines and 2,000 Maritime Security Agency; and 5,000 Reserves)

Forces

Commands	**4;** Fleet, Logistics; Naval installations in the North of Pakistan; and Fleet Headquarters.

Equipment By Type

Submarines	**Tactical** 11; **SSK** 8: 4 *Hangor* (French *Daphne*) each with up to 12 x1 533 mm ASTT (8 bow, 4 stern) with 12 L5 HWT/UGM-84A *Harpoon* tactical USGW; 2 *Hashmat* (French *Agosta* 70) each with 4 x1 533 mm ASTT each with 20+ F17P HWT/UGM- 84 *Harpoon* tactical USGW; 2 *Khalid* (French *Agosta* 90B) each with some 1x533 mm ASTT each with SM-39 *Exocet* tactical USGW; **SSI** 3: 3 MG110 (SF delivery)
Principal Surface Combatants Frigates	7; **FFG** 6: 4 *Tariq* (UK *Amazon*) (capacity 1 *Lynx* Utility Helicopter) each with 2 single each with TP 45 LWT, 2 Mk-141 *Harpoon* twin each with 1 RGM-84D *Harpoon* tactical SSM, 1 114 mm gun; 2 *Tariq* (capacity 1 *Lynx* Utility Helicopter) (D184, D186) each with 2 triple 324 mm ASTT (6 effective) each with Mk 46 LWT, 1 sextuple (6 effective) with LY-60 (Aspide) SAM, 1 114 mm gun; **FF** 1: *Zalfiquar* (UK *Leander*) (capacity 1 SA-319 *Alouette III* utlility helicopter) with 3 Mk 10 *Limbo*, 2 114 mm gun
Patrol and Coastal Combatants	10; **PCC** 3: 1 *Larkana*; 2 *Quetta* (PRC *Shanghai*, operated by the Maritime Security Agency); **PCI** 1: 1 *Rajshahi* less than 100 tonnes **PFM** 6: 3 *Jalalat* II each with 2 twin (4 effective) each with 1 C-802 (CSS-N-8) *Saccade* tactical SSM; 3 *Sabqat* (PRC *Huangfeng*) each with 2 twin (4 effective) each with 1 HY-2 (CSS-N-3) *Seersucker* tactical SSM
Mine Warfare Mine Countermeasures	**Mhc** 3: 3 *Munsif* (French *Eridan*)
Logistics and Support	9; AGHS (Survey) 1: 1 *Behr Paima*; **AO** 2: 1 *Fuqing* with 1 SA-319 *Alouette III* Utility Helicopter; 1 *Moawin* (capacity 5 *Lynx* Utility Helicopter) with 1 *Sea King* MK45 ASW helicopters; **AOT** 3: 1 *Attock*; 2 *Gwadar*; **AT** 3

Facilities

Bases	Karachi; Ormara (under construction) Gwadar (under construction)
Marines	**1,400**
Commando	1 group
Naval aviation	**Aircraft 9** combat capable**;** MP 9: 3 *Atlantic* (also ASW); 4 F-27 MK 200MPA; P-3 2: 2 P-3C *Orion* (operated by Air Force); Transport F-27 1: 1 F-27-400M Troopship (ASW/MR)
Helicopters	**ASW** 12: 6 *Lynx* MK3; **Sea King MK45** 6: 6 *Sea King* MK45 ASW helicopter/*Sea King* MK45C; **Utility** 14: 7 SA-319 *Alouette III*; 7 (SAR)
Missiles; Tactical: Anti-ship	some AM-39 *Exocet*

Air Force 45,000 (Reserves 10,000)

Forces

Regional Commands	Northern (Peshawar) Central (Sargodha) Southern (Faisalabad)
Fighter	2 squadrons with 43 *Mirage* IIIEP (*Mirage* IIIE); 7 *Mirage* IIIOD (*Mirage* IIID); 1 squadron with F-16A *Fighting Falcon*/F-16B *Fighting Falcon*; 5 squadrons with F-7P *Skybolt*/FT-7 (JJ-7) *Mongol A*; 2 squadrons with F-7PG (F-7MG) *Airguard*
Fighter Ground Attack	1 squadron with 13 *Mirage* IIIEP (*Mirage* IIIE) each with AM-39 *Exocet* tactical ASM; 3 *Mirage* IIIB (training); 2 squadrons with 41 A-5C (Q-5III) *Fantan*; 2 squadrons with *Mirage* 5PA3; *Mirage* 5PA2/*Mirage* 5PA; *Mirage* 5DPA (*Mirage* 5D)/*Mirage* 5DPA2
ELINT / ECM	some squadrons with 2 Da-20 *Falcon*
Reconaissance	1 squadrons with 15 *Mirage* IIIRP (*Mirage* IIIR) *
SAR	7 squadrons with SA-316 *Alouette III*
Transport	some squadrons with 1 An-26 *Curl*; 3 B-707; 1 Beech 200 *Super King Air*; 2 C-130 *Hercules*; 11 C-130B *Hercules*/C-130E *Hercules*; 4 CN-235; 2 F-27-200 *Friendship* (1 with navy); 1 *Falcon* 20; 1 L-100 *Hercules*; 1 Y-12; 1 Beech F-33 *Bonanza*
OCU	1 squadron with F-7PG (F-7MG) *Airguard*; 1 squadron with F-7P *Skybolt*/FT-7 (JJ-7) *Mongol A*; 1 squadron with F-16A/F-16B *Fighting Falcon*; 1 squadron with *Mirage* 5PA3; *Mirage* 5PA2/*Mirage* 5PA; *Mirage* 5DPA (*Mirage* 5D)/*Mirage* 5DPA2
Training	some squadrons with 12 K-8; 80 MFI-17B *Mushshak* *; 25 FT-5 (MiG-17U) *Fresco*; 15 FT-6 (MiG-19UTI) *Farmer*; 20 T-37C *Tweet*
Surface to Air Missiles	1 battery with 6 CSA-1 (SA-2) *Guideline*; SA-16 *Gimlet*; 6 batteries each with 24 *Crotale*

Equipment

Aircraft	415 combat capable; **JF-17 Thunder** 4 Multi-Role (246 more planned); **Chengdu J-10** Multi-Role 36; **F-16A** 24 Multi-Role; **F-16B** 11 Training & Multi-Role; **F-16 C/D** Multi-Role 18; **Chengdu F-7PG** 46 Interceptor; **Chengdu F-7MP Skybolt** 90 Interceptor & Ground-Support; **Chengdu FT-7P Skybolt** 15 Training; **Chengdu FT-7PG** 9

	Training; **Dassault Mirage ROSE-I (Mirage-IIIEA)** (Refurbished: Ex-Australian) 28 Interceptor; **Dassault Mirage ROSE-I (Mirage-IIIDP)** 4 Training & Interceptor; **Dassault Mirage ROSE-II (Mirage-VEF)** (Refurbished: Ex-French) 16 Strike & Ground-Support; **Dassault Mirage ROSE-II (Mirage-VDF)** (Refurbished: Ex-French) 6 Training & Strike & Ground-Support; **Dassault Mirage ROSE-III (Mirage-VEF)** (Refurbished: Ex-French) 14 Precision Strike; **Dassault Mirage-IIIEP**16 Interceptor & Ground-Support; **Dassault Mirage-IIIEL** (Refurbished: Ex-Lebanese)11 Interceptor & Ground-Support; **Dassault Mirage-IIIDA** (Refurbished: Ex-Australian) 7 Training; **Dassault Mirage-IIIRP10** Reconnaissance; **Dassault Mirage-VPA3** 9 Naval Support; **Dassault Mirage-VPA2** 35 Ground Support; **Dassault Mirage-VPA** 28 Ground Support; **Dassault Mirage-VDPA2** 2 Training; Dassault Mirage-V (Refurbished: Ex-Libyan) 10 Interceptor & Ground-Support; **Nanchang Q-5/A-5C** 40 Ground-Support & Tactical Strike (Currently being phased out); **Chengdu FT-5** 20 Fighter Conversion (Advanced Jet Training); **Karakoram K-8** 80 Basic & Intermediate Jet Training; **Cessna 172** 6; **Cessna T-37** 20 Basic Jet Training; **Super Mushak MFI-395** 20 Primary Training; **Mushak MFI-17** 80 Primary Training; **Dassault Falcon** 2 ELINT/ECM; **Lockheed Martin C-130B/E** 30 Medium-Lift Transport; **Antonov An-26 '*Curl*'** 1 Medium-Lift Transport; **CN-235** 4 V.I.P & Light-Lift Transport; **HAMC Y-12(II)** 1 Light-Lift Transport; **Boeing 707** 3 VIP Transport **Fokker F-27** 2 Light Transport; **Dassault Falcon** 1 VIP Transport; **Super King Air** 1 Light Transport; **Lockheed L-100** 1 Tactical Transport; **Airbus A310** 1 VIP Transport; **Saab 2000** 6 Airborne Early Warning
Helicopters (Utility)	some SA-316 *Alouette III*
Air Defence	**Surface-to-Air Missiles** 150+: 144 *Crotale*; **Towed** 6: 6 CSA-1 (SA-2) *Guideline*; **MANPAD**: some SA-16 *Gimlet*
Radar - Land	51+: 6 **AR-1** (AD radar low level); some *Condor* (AD radar high level); some FPS-89/100 (AD radar high level); **MPDR** 45: 45 MPDR 45/ MPDR 60/MPDR 90 (AD radar low level);**TPS-43G** some (AD radar high level)**Type 514** some (AD radar high level)
Missiles tactical	**Anti-Ship Missiles**: some AGM-65 *Maverick*; some AM-39 *Exocet*; **Air-to-Air Missiles**: some AIM-9L *Sidewinder*/AIM-9P *Sidewinder*; **R530**: Super 530
Unmanned Aerial Vehicle	**MQ-1** Predator; some ***Baaz***; some ***Ababeel***

Facilities

Radar air control sectors 4; Radar control and reporting station 7

Paramilitary up to 302,000 active

Coast Guard

Patrol and Coastal Combatants up to 23

Miscellaneous Boats/Craft

Frontier Corps upto 65,000 (reported) Ministry of Interior (Balochistan and NWFP)

Forces By Role	
Armoured reconnaissance	1 independent squadrons
Paramilitary	11 regiments (*total:* 40 paramilitary battalions)
Equipment	
APC	**APC (W)** 45: 45 UR-416
Maritime Security Agency	2,000
Principal Surface Combatants	
Destroyers	**DD** 1: 1 *Alamgir* (US *Gearing*, no ASROC or TT)
Patrol and Coast Combatants	6: 2 PCC (PRC Shanghai); **PCO** 4: 4 *Barkat*

National Guard 185,000

Janbaz Force

Mujahid Force

National Cadet Corps

Women Guards

Northern Light Infantry	12,000
Paramilitary	3 battalions
Pakistan Rangers	upto 40,000 (Ministry of Interior)

SINGAPORE

***Armed Forces** 72,500*	(Army 50,000; Navy 9,000; Air Force 13,500) Paramilitary 93,800 Reserves 312,500 (Army 300,000 5,000 Air 7,500) Paramilitary 44,000

***Army** 15,000; 35,000 conscripts (total 50,000)*

1 Rapid Deployment division (1 infantry brigade, 1 amphibious brigade (3 amphibious battalions),
1 air mobile brigade);
3 (mixed active/reserve formations) combined arms division (each: 2 infantry brigade (each: 3 infantry battalions), 1 armoured brigade, 1 reconnaissance battalion, 2 artillery battalions, 1 AD battalion, 1 engineer battalion)

Forces

Reconnaissance	4 battalions
Mechanised	1 brigade
Infantry	9 battalions
Commando	1 battalions
Artillery	4 battalions
Engineer	4 battalions
Reserves	9 infantry brigades included in mixed active/inactive reserve formations listed above; 1 operational reserve division with an additional infantry brigade; 2 People's Defence Force Commands with 12 infantry battalions Reconnaissance / light armoured 8 battalions Infantry 60 battalions Commando 1 battalion Artillery 12 battalions Engineer 8 battalions

Equipment

Tanks	**450**: **MBT** 100: 80-100 Centurion **Light tanks AMX-13** 350: e350 AMX-13 SM1
AIFV	**294: AMX-10P** 44: 22; 22 AMX-10 PAC 90 (reconnaissance); **IFV-25** 250; **APC** 1,280+ **APC (T)** 1,000+: some ATTC Bronco; 250 IFV-40/50; **M-113** 750+: 750+ M-113A1/M-113A2 (some with 40mm AGL, some with 25mm gun); **APC (W)** 280: 250 LAV-150 Commando/V-200 Commando; 30 V-100 Commando
Artillery	**286+**: **Towed** 206 **105mm** 37: 37 LG1 **155mm** 169: 18 FH-2000; 52 FH-88; 16 M-114A1 some in store; 45 M-68 some in store; 38 M-71S **SP • 155mm** 18: 18 SSPH-1 Primus Mor 62+: **81mm**: some, some SP **120mm**: 50, some SP in M-113 **160mm** 12: 12 M-58 Tampella
Anti-tank	**MSL** 30+: 30+ Gil/Spike Spike/Milan **RCL** 290; **106mm M-40** 90: 90 M-40A1 in store **84mm** 200: 200 Carl Gustav **RL 67mm**: some Armbrust **89mm**: some M-20
Air Defence	**SAM • MANPAD** 75+: 75+ Mistral/RBS-70/SA-18 Grouse (Igla) (some self-propelled as V-200; air force; **Guns 20mm Towed** 30: 30 GAI-C01 (some self-propelled)

Radar — **Land**: some AN/TPQ-36 Firefinder/AN/TPQ-37 Firefinder (Artillery, mortar)

<u>**Facilities**</u>

Training camps — 3 (including infantry, artillery and armoured) located in Taiwan (Republic of China), 1 (artillery, combat engineers) located in Thailand

Navy *2,200; 1,800 conscript; 5,000 active reservists (total 9,000)*

<u>**Equipment**</u>

Submarines — **Tactical SSK** 3: 3 Challenger each with 4 single 533mm TT

Principal Surface Combatants

Corvettes — **FSG** 6: 6 Victory each with 2 triple ASTT (6 effective), 2 octuple (16 effective) each with 1 Barak SAM, 2+ Mk 140 Harpoon quad (8 effective) each with 1 RGM-84C Harpoon tactical SSM, 1 76mm gun

Patrol and Coastal Combatants — 17 **PFM** 6: 6 Sea Wolf each with 2 Mk 140 Harpoon quad (8 effective) each with RGM-84C Harpoon tactical SSM, 1 twin (2 effective) (manually operated) with Mistral SAM, 4 (8 effective) each with GI Gabriel I tactical SSM, 1 57mm gun **PCO** 11: 6 Fearless each with 2 Sadral sextuple each with Mistral SAM 5 Fearless each with 2 Sadral sextuple each with Mistral SAM, 1 76mm gun

Mine Warfare — **MHC** 4: 4 Bedok

Amphibious — **LS LST** 4: 4 Endurance (capacity 350 troops; 18 MBTs; 4 LCVP; 2 hel) (with hel deck) each with 2 Twin (4 effective) each with Mistral SAM, 1 76mm gun; **Craft** 36: 30 LCU; 6 LCM

Logistics and Support — 2: **AS** 1: 1 Kendrick

Training — 1 **Launcher TT 324mm** 6: 6 x1 **Gun**1 76mm

<u>**Facilities**</u> — **Bases** located at Changi and Tuas (Jurong)

Air Force *10,500; 3,000 conscript; 7,500 reservists (total 21,000)*

<u>**Forces**</u>

Fighter Ground Attack — 2 squadrons with 28 F-5S Tiger II; 9 F-5T Tiger II (secondary GA role); 2 (in US) squadron each with 24 F-16C Fighting Falcon/F-16D Fighting Falcon; 3 squadron with 6 F-16A Fighting Falcon/F-16B Fighting Falcon; 38 F-16C Fighting Falcon/F-16D Fighting Falcon

Reconnaissance — 1 squadron with 8 RF-5S Tiger

Reconnaissance /transport — 1 squadron with 4 KC-130B Hercules (tanker/transport); 1 KC-130H Hercules; 5 C-130H Hercules (2 Elint); 1 squadron with 9 F-50 Maritime Enforcer (4 transport, 5 MR)

Airborne Early Warning — 1 squadron with 4 E-2C Hawkeye

Tanker — 1 squadron with 4 KC-135R Stratotanker

Training — detachment with 12 F-16C Fighting Falcon/F-16D Fighting Falcon on lease located at Cannon AFB, (NM), US; 12 on lease located at Luke Air Force Base, (Arizona), US; AH-64D Apache located at Marana, (Arizona), US; 6+ CH-47D Chinook located at Grand Prairie, (Texas), US; 1 squadron with 12 AS-550 Fennec; 1 squadron with 4 A-4SU Super Skyhawk; 10 TA-4SU Super Skyhawk; 1 squadron with 27 S-211

Helicopters	1 squadron with 6 AB-205A (Bell 205A); 19 UH-1H Iroquois; 1 squadron with 10 CH-47SD Super D Chinook; 2 squadron with 18 AS-332M Super Puma (including 5 SAR); 12 AS-532UL Cougar; 2 squadron with 8 AH-64D Apache; 20 AS-550A2 Fennec/AS-550C2 Fennec
Unarmed Aerial Vehicles	1 squadron Blue Horizon; 24 Chukar III; 40 Searcher MK II.

Equipment

Aircraft	111 combat capable
Fighter	43: **F-5** 37: 28 F-5S Tiger II; 9 F-5T Tiger II (GA role) **F-16** 6: 6 F-16A Fighting Falcon/F-16B Fighting Falcon
Fighter Ground Attack	44; **A-4** 6: 6 A-4SU Super Skyhawk **F-16C Fighting Falcon/F-16D Fighting Falcon** 38
Reconnaissance	8: 8 RF-5S Tiger
Maritime Reconnaissance	9: 9 F-50 Maritime Enforcer (4 transport, 5 MR)
Airborne Early Warning	**E-2** 4: 4 E-2C Hawkeye
Tanker	9; **KC-130** 5: 4 KC-130B Hercules (trk/transport); 1 KC-130H Hercules **KC-135** 4: 4 KC-135R Stratotanker
Transport	**C-130** 5: 5 C-130H Hercules (2 Elint)
Training	47: 27 S-211 **TA-4** 10: 10 TA-4SU Super Skyhawk
Helicopters	**Anti-tank** 28 **AH-64** 8: 8 AH-64D Apache **AS-550A2 Fennec/AS-550C2 Fennec** 20 **SPT** 28 **AS-332** 18: 18 AS-332M Super Puma (including 5 SAR) **CH-47** 10: 10 CH-47SD Super D Chinook **UTL** 54 **AS-532** 12: 12 AS-532UL Cougar **AS-550 Fennec** 12 **Bell 205** 6: 6 AB-205A (Bell 205A) **UH-1** 24: 24 UH-1H Iroquois
UAV	64+: some Blue Horizon; 24 Chukar III; 40 Searcher MK II.

Facilities	School 1 (training) located in Brunei, 1 with 27 S-211 (flying training) located at Pearce, Aus, 1 with 12 AS-332 Super Puma Spt/AS-532 Cougar Utility (training) located at Oakey, Australia

Air Defence Systems Divison

Forces

Air	4 (field defence) squadrons

Equipment

Missiles	**Tactical ASM**: some AGM-45 Shrike **AGM-65**: some AGM-65B Maverick; some AGM-65G Maverick **AGM-84 Harpoon** some **AAM AIM-120**: some AIM-120C AMRAAM in store (US) **AIM-7**: some AIM-7P Sparrow **AIM-9**: some AIM-9N Sidewinder/AIM-9P Sidewinder

Air Defence Brigade

Forces

Air	some brigades (total: 1 AD squadron with Oerlikon, 1 AD squadron with 18+ MIM-23 HAWK, 1 AD squadron with Rapier-Blindfire)
Equipment	**Radar Land**: some Blindfire

Air Force Systems Brigade

Air	some brigades (total: 1 AD squadron with radar (mobile), 1 AD squadron with LORADS)

Divisional Air Defence Artillery Brigade *attached to Army divisions*

<u>**Forces**</u>

Air Defence	some brigades (total: 1 AD battalion with 36 Mistral, 1 AD battalion with SA-18 Grouse (Igla), 3 AD battalions with RBS-70)

<u>**Equipment**</u>

SAM	36+: 36 Mistral; some RBS-70
MANPAD	some SA-18 Grouse (Igla)

***Paramilitary** 93,800 active*

Civil Defence Force	81,800 incl. 1,600 regulars, 3,200 conscripts, 23,000 reservists; 54,000+ volunteers; 1 construction brigade (2,500 conscripts)

***Singapore Police Force** 8,500; 3,500 conscript; 21,000 reservists (total 33,000)*

***Singapore Gurkha contingent** 1,500 (6 companies)*

<u>**Deployment Overseas**</u>

Australia	**Air Force:** *230 personnel* ***Aircraft: Training** 27: 27 S-211* ***Helicopters**: 12 AS-332* Super Puma *Spt/AS-532* Cougar *Utility* **Facilities:** *School - 1 with 12 AS-332* Super Puma *Spt/AS-532* Cougar *utility (flying training) located at Oakey, 1 with 27 S-211 training aircraft (flying training) located at Pearce*
Brunei	**Air Force:** *500 personnel; 1 helicopter detachment with 5 UH-1H* Iroquois **Facilities:** *School - 1 (training)*
France	**Air Force:** *200 personnel; some training squadron with 6 A-4SU* Super Skyhawk*; 10 TA-4SU* Super Skyhawk
Taiwan (Republic of China)	**Army:** *Training camp - 3 (including infantry, artillery and armoured)*
Thailand	**Army:** *Training camp - 1 (Artillery, combat engineers)*
United States	**Air Force: *Aircraft* • *FGA*** *24: 12 F-16C* Fighting Falcon*/F-16D* Fighting Falcon *on lease located at Cannon AFB, (NM), US; 12 on lease located at Luke AFB, (AZ), US* ***Helicopters: Anti-tank AH-64**: some AH-64D* Apache *located at Marana, (AZ); **Support: CH-47** 6+: 6+ CH-47D* Chinook *located at Grand Prairie, (TX)*
United States Navy	**Support facility located at Singapore USPACOM:** 1 logistic support squadron located at Singapore

SRI LANKA

Army 120,000; including 15,000 National Guardsmen

Forces	
Divisional HQ	9
Armoured	3 regiments
Armoured reconaissance	3 regiments (battalions)
Air mobile	1 brigade
Infantry	33 brigades
Special Forces	1 independent brigade
Commando	1 brigade
Field Artillery	3 (1 light and 2 medium regiments)
Field Engineers	3 regiments

Equipment	
Tanks	**MBT T-55** 62: 62 T-55AM2/T-55A
Reconnaissance	15: 15 *Saladin* **AIFV BMP** 62: 13 BMP-1; 49 BMP-2 **APC** 192; **APC (T)** 35: 35 Type-85; **BTR-80 APC (W)/BTR-80A AIFV** 25; **APC (W)** 157: 31 *Buffel*; 21 FV603 *Saracen*; 105 *Unicorn*
Artillery	963; **Towed** 157; **88 mm** 3: 3 25-pdr; **122 mm** 74; **130 mm** 40: 40 Type-59-I; **152 mm** 40: 40 Type-66 (D- 20) **MRL 122 mm** 22: 22 RM-70 *Dana*, **Mortars** 784: 520 81 mm; 209 82 mm; **120 mm** 55: 55 M-43
Anti-tank	**RCL** 40; **105 mm** 10: 10 M-65; **106 mm** 30: 30 M-40
Guns	**85 mm** 8: 8 Type-56 (D-44)
UAV	1: 1 *Seeker*
Air Defence	**Guns** 27;**40 mm Towed** 24: 24 L/40; **94 mm • Towed** 3: 3 3.7in
Radar	**LAND** 2: 2 AN/TPQ-36 *Firefinder* (arty)

Navy 15,000 (including 2400 recalled reservists)

Forces	
Commands	5; Eastern Naval Area; North Central Naval Area; Northern Naval Area; Southern Naval Area; Western Naval Area

Equipment	
Patrol and Coastal Combatants	up to 113
Miscellaneous Boats/Craft	up to 52: up to 52 boats; **PCC** 10: 3 *Abeetha* (PRC modified *Shanghai*); 2 *Prathapa* (PRC modified *Haizhui*); 2 *Ranajaya* (PRC *Haizhui*); 1 *Ranarisi* (PRC *Shanghai* II); 2 *Weeraya* (PRC *Shanghai*); **PFI** 46: 19 *Colombo* less than 100 tonnes; 3 *Dvora* less than 100 tonnes; 3 *Killer* less than 100 tonnes (ROK); 7 *Shaldag* less than 100 tonnes; 5 *Trinity Marine* less than 100 tonnes; 9 *Super Dvora* less than 100 tonnes; **PFM** 2: 2 *Nandimithra* (Il Saar 4) each with 3 single each with 1 GII *Gabriel II* tactical SSM, 1 76 mm gun; **PCO** 3: 1 *Jayesagara*; 1 *Parakrambahu*; 1 *Sayura* (In Sukanya)
Amphibious:	4 Fast Personnel Carrier; **LS • LSM** 1: 1 *Yuhai* (capacity 2 tanks; 250 troops); **CFT** 5; **LCU** 2: 2 *Yunnan*; **LCM** 2; **ACV** 1: 1 M 10 (capacity 56 troops)

Facilities

Bases	Northern Command located at Kankesanthurai Southern Command located at Galle North Central Command located at Medawachiya HQ and Western Command located at Colombo Main base and Eastern Command located at Trincomalee

Air Force 18,000

Forces

Fighter Ground Attack	1 squadron with 4 MiG-27M *Flogger J2*; 1 FT-7 (JJ-7) *Mongol A*, 3F-7M; 2 FT-5 (MiG-17U) *Fresco*; 1 MiG-23UB *Flogger C* (conversion trg); 1 squadron with 7 *Kfir* C-2; 2 *Kfir* C-7; 1 *Kfir* TC-2
Transport	1 squadron with 7 An-32B *Cline*; 2 BAe-748; 1 Beech 200 *Super King Air*; 2 C-130K *Hercules*; 1 Cessna 421C *Golden Eagle*; 3 Y-12; 5 Cessna 150; 6 Bell 412 *Twin Huey* (VIP)
Anti-tank Helicopters	some squadrons with 1 Mi-24V *Hind E*; 13 Mi-35P *Hind*; 10 Bell 212
Training	some squadrons with 10 PT-6 (CJ-6); 3 K-8; 5 SF-260TP; 6 Bell 206 *JetRanger*
Utility Helicopters	some squadrons with 3 MI-17 (Mi-8MT) *Hip H*; 6 Bell 206 *JetRanger*
Reserves	Air Force Regiment, 3 squadrons; airfield construction, 1 squadron

Equipment

Aircraft	21 combat capable; **FGA** 13: 7 *Kfir* C-2; 2 *Kfir* C-7; **MiG-27** 4: 4 MiG-27M *Flogger J2*, 3 F-7M; **Transport** 16; **An-32** 7: 7 An-32B *Cline*; **BAe-748** 2 **Beech 200** *Super King Air* 1; **C-130** 2: 2 C-130K *Hercules;* **CESSNA 421** 1: 1 Cessna 421C *Golden Eagle*; **Y-12** 3; **Training** 28: 5 Cessna 150; 2 FT-5 (MiG-17U *Fresco*); 1 FT-7 (JJ-7) *Mongol A*; 3 K-8; 1 *Kfir* TC-2; **MiG-23U** 1: 1 MiG-23UB *Flogger C*; **PT-6 (CJ-6)** 10; **SF-260** 5: 5 SF-260TP
Helicopters	**Anti-tank** 14; **MI-24** 1: 1 Mi-24V *Hind E*; **MI-35** 13: 13 Mi-35P *Hind;* **Support MI-8** 7: 3 MI-17 (Mi-8MT) *Hip H*; 4 in store; **Utility** 28: 12 Bell 206 *JetRanger*; 10 Bell 212; 6 Bell 412 *Twin Huey* (VIP)
UAV	3 **Reconnaissance • *Tactical*** 2: 2 *Searcher*; ***Scout*** 1

Paramilitary 88,600

Home Guard	13,000
National Guard	15,000
Police Force	30,200; 1,000 (women); 30,400 reservists (total 61,600)

Ministry of Defence Special Task Force 3,000 (anti-guerrilla unit)

THAILAND

Armed Forces, 306,600	**(Army 190,000; Navy 70,600; Air Force 46,000)** **Paramilitary 113,700** **Reserves 200,000; Paramilitary 45,000**

Organisations by Service

Army *120,000; 70,000 conscript (total 190,000)*

	4 Regional Army HQ, 2 Corps HQ
Forces	
Armoured Air Cavalry	1 regiment (3 air mob companies)
Rapid Reaction	1 force (1 battalion per region)
Cavalry	2 divisions; 1 independent regiment
Reconnaissance	4 companies
Mechanised Infantry	2 divisions
Armoured Infantry	3 divisions
Infantry	8 independent battalions
Special Forces	2 divisions
Light Infantry	1 division
Artillery	1 division
Air Defence Artillery	1 division (6 Air Defence Artillery battalions)
Engineers	1 division
Helicopters	some flights
Economic development	4 divisions
Reserves	
Infantry	4 division HQ
Equipment	
Tanks	745: **MBT** 330; **M-60** 178: 53 M-60A1; 125 M-60A3 **Type-69** 50 training in store; **M-48** 105: 105 M-48A5; **Light Tanks** 415: 155 M-41; 104 Scorpion; 50 in store; 106 Stingray
Reconnaissance	32+: some M1114 HMMWV; **S52** 32: 32 S52 Mk 3
Armoured Personnel Carriers	950: **APC (T)** 790; **M-113** 340: 340 M-113A1/M-113A3 **Type-85** 450; **APC (W)** 160: 18 Condor; **LAV** 142: 142 LAV-150 Commando
Artillery	2470+: **Towed** 550; **105mm** 353; **LG1** 24: 24 LG1 MK II **M-101** 285: 285 M-101 -Mod/M-101 105mm Towed; **M-102** 12; **M-618A2** 32; **130mm** 15: 15 Type-59-I; **155mm** 185; **GHN-45** 42: 42 GHN-45 A1; **M-114** 50; **M-198** 61; **M-71** 32; **SP • 155mm • M-109** 20: 20 M-109A2; **MRL • 130mm**: some Type-85 (reported); **Mortars** 1,900: 1,867 81mm/M-106A1 107mm; **81mm • M-125** 21: 21 M-125A3 (SP); **120mm** 12: 12 M-1064A3 (SP)
Anti-tank	**Missiles** 318+: 300 M47 Dragon; **TOW** 18+: some **M-901** 18: 18 M-901A5; **Recoilless** 180; **106mm** 150: 150 M-40; **75mm** 30: 30 M-20; **Rocket Launcher: 66mm**: some M-72 LAW
Aircraft	**Reconnaissance • OBS** 40: 40 Cessna O-1A Bird Dog **TRANSPORT** 10 **BEECH 1900** 2: 2 Beech 1900C **Beech 200 Super King Air** 2 **CASA 212 Aviocar** 2 **Jetstream 41** 2 **Short 330UTT** 2 **Utility: U-17** 10: 10 U-17B **TRG** 33 **MX-7** 18: 18 MX-7-235 Star Rocket **T-41** 15: 15 T-41B Mescalero
Helicopters	**Anti-tank AH-1** 5: 5 AH-1F Cobra **Support • CH-47** 6: 6 CH-47D Chinook **Utility** 159: 65 AB-212 (Bell 212)/Bell 206 JetRanger/Bell 214/Bell 412 Twin Huey; 92 UH-1H Iroquois; 2 UH-60L Black Hawk **Training: Hughes 300** 42: 42 Hughes 300C

Unarmed Aerial Vehicles — **Reconnaissance: Tactical**: some Searcher

Air Defence — **SAM • Static**: some Aspide **MANPAD**: some FIM-43 Redeye **HN-5**: some HN-5A **Guns** 202 **20mm** 48 **SP** 24: 24 M-163 Vulcan **Towed** 24: 24 M-167 Vulcan
37mm 52: 52 Type-74 towed **40mm** 78: 30 M-1 towed/M-42 SP; 48 L/70 towed **57mm** 24+: 6 Type-59 (S-60) towed; 18+ non-operational towed

Radar — **Land**: some AN/TPQ-36 Firefinder (Artillery, mortar); some RASIT (vehicle, artillery)

Navy 44,750 (including Naval Aviation, Marines, Coastal Defence); 25,850 conscript (total 70,600)

Forces

Air wing — 1 division

Navy — Fleet HQ located at Sattahip
Mekong River Operating Unit HQ at Nakhon Phanom

Equipment

Principal Surface Combatants 18

Aircraft Carrier — **CVH** 1: 1 Chakri Naruebet (capacity 9 AV-8A Harrier FGA aircraft; 6 S-70B Seahawk ASW helicopters)

Frigates — 12: **FFG** 8: 2 Chao Phraya each with 4 twin (8 effective) each with 1 CSS-N-4 Sardine tactical SSM, 2 (4 effective) non-operational each with 1 HQ-61 (CSA-N-2) SAM non-operational, 2 RBU 1200 (10 effective), 2 twin 100mm gun (4 effective), 2 twin 37mm gun (4 effective), 1 helicopters landing platform 2 Kraburi (capacity 1 AB-212 (Bell 212) utility helicopters) each with 2 twin (4 effective) each with 1 HQ-61 (CSA-N-2) SAM, 4 (8 effective) each with 1 CSS-N-4 Sardine tactical SSM, 2 RBU 1200 (10 effective), 1 twin 100mm gun (2 effective), 2 twin 37mm gun (4 effective) 2 Naresuan (capacity either 1 S-70B-2 Seahawk ASW helicopters or 1 Super Lynx utility helicopters) each with 2 Mk 141 Harpoon quad (8 effective) each with 1 RGM-84A Harpoon tactical SSM, 2 triple 324mm TT (6 effective), 1 8 cell Mk 41 VLS with 1 RIM-7M Sea Sparrow SAM, 1 127mm gun 2 Phuttha Yotfa Chulalok (capacity 1 AB-212 (Bell 212) utility helicopters) (leased from US) each with 2 Twin ASTT (4 effective) with 22 Mk 46 LWT, 1 Mk16 Mk 112 octuple with 1 RGM-84C Harpoon tactical SSM, tactical ASROC, 1 127mm gun **FF** 4: 1 Makut Rajakumarn with 2 triple ASTT (6 effective), 2 114mm gun 1 Pin Klao with 6 x1 324mm ASTT, 3 76mm gun 2 Tapi each with 6 x1 324mm ASTT each with Mk 46 LWT, 1 76mm gun

Corvettes — 5: **FSG** 2: 2 Rattanakosin each with 2 triple ASTT (6 effective), 1 Albatros octuple with 1 Aspide SAM, 2 Mk 140 Harpoon quad (8 effective) each with 1 RGM-84A Harpoon tactical SSM, 1 76mm gun **FS** 3: 3 Khamronsin each with 2 triple ASTT (6 effective), 1 76mm gun

Patrol and Coastal Combatants — 110: **PBR** 35 **PC** 6: 6 Sattahip each with 1 40mm gun, 1 76mm gun **PCC** 3 each with 1 40mm gun, 1 76mm gun **PCI** 49: 12 Swift; 10 T-11; 15 T-213; 3 T-81; 9 T-91 **PCR** 6 **PFC** 3: 3 Chon Buri each with 2 76mm gun **PFM** 6: 3 Prabparapak each with 2 single each with 1 GI Gabriel I tactical SSM, 1 triple (3 effective) with 1 GI Gabriel I tactical SSM, 1 40mm gun, 1 57mm gun 3 Ratcharit each with 2 twin (4 effective) each with 1 MM-38 Exocet tactical SSM, 1 76mm gun **PCO** 2: 2 Hua Hin each with 2 20mm gun, 1 76mm gun

Mine Warfare	**Mine Countermeasures** 20; **MCC** 2: 2 Bang Rachan **MCM Support** 1: 1 Thalang **MCMV** 2: 2 Lat Ya **MS** å12 **MSC** 3: 3 Bangkeo
Amphibious	**LS** 9: 2 **LSM** 1: 1 Kut (capacity 4 tanks) **LST** 6: 4 Angthong (capacity 16 tanks; 200 troops) each with 6 40mm gun 2 Srichang (capacity 14 tanks; 300 troops) training each with 2 40mm gun, 1 helicopters landing platform **CRAFT** 53: 1; e13 LCU; 12 LCVP; 24 LCM; 3 ACV
Logistics and Support	18: **AG** 5 **AOR** 2: 1 Chula; 1 Similan (1 helicopters)**AOT** 5: 4 Prong; 1 Samui **YTL** 2 **YTM** 4
Facilities	Bases at Bangkok, Sattahip, Songkhla, Phang Nga, Nakhon and Phanom

Naval Aviation 1,940

Aircraft	18 combat capable
Fighter Ground Attack	**AV-8** 7: 7 AV-8A Harrier
Reconnaissance	**Observation** 9: 9 Sentry 02-337 **MP** 9: 5 DO-228-212*; 2 F-27 MK 200MPA*; 2 P-3T (P-3A) Orion*
Transport	**F-27** 2: 2 F-27-400M Troopship **Utility** 7: 2 CL-215-III; 4 GAF N-24A Search Master; 1 UP-3T (UP-3A) Orion
Training	20: **TA-7** 18: 14; 4 TA-7C Corsair II **TAV-8** 2: 2 TAV-8A Harrier
Helicopters	**ASW** 6: 6 S-70B Seahawk **Utility** 17: **AB-212 (Bell 212)** 5 **Bell 214** 5: 5 AB-214ST **S-76** 5: 5 S-76B **Super Lynx** 2
Missiles	**Tactical ASM**: some AGM-84 Harpoon

Marines 23,000

Forces

Reconnaissance	1 battalion
Amphibious assault	1 battalion
Infantry	2 regiments
Artillery	1 regiment (1 Air Defence Artillery battalion, 3 Field artillery battalions)
Marine	1 division HQ

Equipment

APC	**APC (W) LAV** 24: 24 LAV-150 Commando **AAV** 33: 33 LVTP-7
Artillery	**Towed** 48: 36 105mm (reported); 12 GC-45 155mm
Anti-tank	**Missiles** 24+: some M47 Dragon **TOW** 24+: some; 24 HMMWV
Air Defence	**Guns** 14: 14 12.7mm

Air Force 46,000

4 air divisions, 1 Flying Training school

Forces

FTR/FGA	2 squadrons with 34 L-39ZA/MP Albatros; 1 squadron with 20 Alpha Jet; 3 (1 aggressor) squadron with 35 F-5E Tiger II/F-5F Tiger II (32 being upgraded), 2 F-5B; 3 squadrons with 41 F-16A Fighting Falcon; 9 F-16B Fighting Falcon
Reconnaissance/ELINT	1 squadron with 3 IAI-201 Arava, 2 Learjet 35A
Transport	1 squadron with 9 Basler Turbo-67; 15 GAF N-22B Nomad; 1 squadron with 4 BAe-748; 3 G-222; 1 squadron with 7 C-130H Hercules; 5 C-130H-30 Hercules

VIP	1 (Royal Flight) squadron with 1 A-310-324; 1 Airbus A319CJ; 1 B-737-200; 2 BAe-748; 2 737-400; 2 Beech 200 Super King Air; 3 SA-226AT Merlin IV/IVA; 3 AS-532A2 Cougar MKII; 3 AS-332L Super Puma; 2 Bell 412 Twin Huey
Utility	1 squadron with 22 AU-23A Peacemaker*, 1 squadron with 12 L-392A, 1 with 10 Alpha Jet
Liaison	some squadrons with 2 Beech 65 Queen Air; 1 Beech E90 King Air; 3 Rockwell Commander 500; 3 Cessna 150; 12 T-41D Mescalero
Survey	some squadrons with 3 SA-226AT Merlin IV/IVA; 3 GAF N-22B Nomad
Training	some squadrons with 29 CT-4B/E Airtrainer; 23 PC-9; 6 Bell 206B JetRanger II
Helicopters	1 squadron 20 UH-1H Iroquois; 1 squadron 13 Bell 412

Equipment

Aircraft	165 combat capable
FTR/FGA	87: **F-5** 49: 35 F-5E Tiger II/F-5F Tiger II (32 being upgraded), 2 F-5B **F-16** 50: 41 F-16A Fighting Falcon; 9 F-16B Fighting Falcon
Transport	47: **A-310** 1: 1 A-310-324 **A-319CJ** 1**B-737** 3: 1 B-737-200; 2 B737-400 **BAe-748** 6 **Basler Turbo-67** 9 **Beech 200 Super King Air** 2 **Beech 65 Queen Air** 2 **Beech 90** 1: 1 Beech E90 King Air **C-130** 12: 7 C-130H Hercules; 5 C-130H-30 Hercules **G-222** 3 **IAI-201 Arava** 3 **LEARJET 35** 2: 2 Learjet 35A **Rockwell Commander 500** 3 **SA-226** 6: 6 SA-226AT Merlin IV/IVA
Utility	37: 22 AU-23A Peacemaker; 15 GAF N-22B Nomad
Training	123: 10 Alpha Jet; 29 CT-4B/E Airtrainer; 3 Cessna 150 **L-39** 46: 46 L-39ZA/MP Albatros **PC-9** 23 **T-41** 12: 12 T-41D Mescalero
Helicopters	**Support** 19: 3 AS-332L Super Puma; 3 AS-532A2 Cougar MKII; 13 Bell 212 **Utility** 28 **Bell 206** 6: 6 Bell 206B JetRanger II **Bell 412 Twin Huey** 2 **UH-1** 20: 20 UH-1H Iroquois
Missiles	**Tactical AAM**: some AIM-120 AMRAAM **AIM-9**: some AIM-9B Sidewinder/AIM-9J Sidewinder **Python III** some **ASM:** some AGM-65 Maverick

***Paramilitary** 113,700 active*

Border Patrol Police 41,000

Marine Police 2,200
Patrol and Coastal Combatants 124+: 3 PCC; 110+ PCI; 8 PFI; 3 PCO

National Security Volunteer Corps 45,000

Police Aviation 500

Aircraft	**Transport** 16: 2 CN-235; 1 Fokker 50; 8 PC-6 Turbo-Porter; 3 SC.7 3M Skyvan; 2 Short 330UTT **Utility** 6: 6 AU-23A Peacemaker
Helicopters	**Utility** 67 **AB-212 (Bell 212)** 20 **Bell 205** 27: 27 Bell 205A **Bell 206 Jet Ranger** 14 **Bell 412 Twin Huey** 6

Provincial Police 50,000 (including 500 Special Action Force)

Thahan Phran (Hunter Soldiers) 20,000

Volunteer Irregular Force

Paramilitary 13 regiments

INDIAN SPACE RESEARCH PROGRAMME

INDIAN SPACE RESEARCH PROGRAMME

Introduction

Space research is an inter-disciplinary venture with several innovations in science and technology. It is almost a 'green' technology which enhances the quality of life on earth in various fields – communications, information and utilization of the earth's resources. Many medical developments, especially in the cardiac field, are by-products of space research.

Despite its limited resources, India has developed a broad-based space programme with indigenous launch vehicles, satellites, control facilities, and data processing. Since its first satellite was orbited by the USSR in 1975 and its first domestic space launch in 1980, India has become a true space-faring nation and an example to other countries wishing to move into the space age. Indian remote sensing, communications, and meteorological satellites are comparable to many similar space systems operated by more affluent countries, and is one of only a half dozen countries/ organizations with a geostationary launch capability. Today, India can launch any type of satellite and launch vehicle. It is self-sufficient in building satellite technology, with a large scientific, technical and support staff along with nearly 500 support industries and academic institutions.

The Indian Space Programme may be divided in two major categories. One is the Satellite Programme and the other is the Launcher Programme. The Satellite programme involves putting the satellites in space and managing them. The satellites may be lifted by Indian-made launchers or it may involve commercial launch vehicles. The satellites are also of two different categories, communication satellites and remote sensing satellites. The launcher programme involves the designing, fabrication and launching of launch vehicles. India has developed a series of launch vehicles, after a long research and development through its successes and failures.

Rakesh Sharma is the first Indian to reach space aboard the Soyuz T-11 capsule on 2 April 1984, as part of an Indo-Soviet manned space mission, the Soviet Inter-cosmos programme.

Organizations

The Indian Space Research Organization (ISRO) was established in 1969 and functions under the Department of Space. The Chairman of ISRO, since 1994, is Krishnaswamy Kasturirangan. The headquarters of ISRO is located in Bangalore and it has a workforce of approximately 20,000. Activities related to satellites, launch vehicles, and applications are carried out at numerous centres throughout the country. These are:

- **Vikram Sarabhai Space Centre (VSSC).** ISRO's single largest facility, near Thiruvananthapuram providing the technology base for launcher & propulsion development.
- **Liquid Propulsion Systems Centre (LPSC).** Development branches in Bangalore and Thiruvananthapuram are supported by major test facilities at Mahendragiri for wide spectrum of liquid motors, from reaction control system thrusters to the 720kN Vikas and cryogenic engines.
- **ISRO Satellite Centre (ISAC).** ISRO's lead centre for the design, fabrication & testing of science, technology and applications satellites.
- **ISRO Inertial Systems Unit (IISU).** Provides inertial systems & components for satellites and launchers.
- **SHAR Centre.** The ISRO's orbital launch site and largest solid motor production and test facility.
- **ISRO Telemetry, Tracking & Command Network (ISTRAC).** Headquartered in Bangalore, ISTRAC operates a network of ground station to provide TTC support for launcher & satellite operations.
- **Space Applications Centre (SAC).** Located at Ahmedabad, SAC is ISRO's applications R&D centre, including communications, remote sensing and geodesy.
- **Development & Educational Communications Unit (DECU)** at Ahmedabad.
- **INSAT Master Control Facility (MCF)** at Hassan, 180km from Bangalore.

Brief History

Dr. Vikram Sarabhai is the founding father of the Indian space programme. After the launch of Sputnik in 1957, he recognized the potential that satellites provided. India's first Prime Minister, Jawaharlal Nehru, who saw scientific development as an essential part of India's future, placed space research under the jurisdiction of the Department of Atomic Energy in 1961. Its director, Homi Bhabha - who started India's atomic programme, established the Indian National Committee for Space Research with Dr. Sarabhai as Chairman in 1962.

Unlike every other major space programme with the exception of Japan and Europe, India's capabilities were not born out of an existing military ballistic missile programme, but out of the practical goal of eventually having satellite launch capabilities. From its establishment in 1962, the Indian space programme began with the launch of sounding rockets, which was complemented by India's geographical proximity to the equator. These were launched from the newly-established Thumba Equatorial Rocket Launching Station (TERLS), built near Thiruvananthapuram in Kerala. Initially, American sounding rockets like the Nike-Apache, and French sounding rockets like the Centaure, were fired and used for studying the upper atmospheric electrojet, which until then had only been studied from ship-based sounding rocket launches in the Pacific Ocean. These were soon followed by British and Russian rockets. India soon began developing its own sounding rockets, using solid propellants - these were called the Rohini family of sounding rockets.

Recognizing the need for indigenous technology, and the possibility of future instability in the supply of parts and technology, the Indian space programme endeavoured to indigenize every material supply route, mechanism and technology. As the Indian Rohini programme continued to launch sounding rockets of greater size and complexity, the space programme was expanded and eventually given its own government department, separate from the Department of Atomic Energy. In 1969 the Indian Space Research Organisation (ISRO) was created.

Meanwhile, India also began developing satellite technology, anticipating the remote sensing and communication needs of the future. India's first foray into space began with the launch of its satellite Aryabhata in 1975 by a Soviet booster. By 1979, the SLV was ready to be launched from the newly-established second launch site, the Sriharikota Rocket Launching Station (SRLS). The first launch in 1979 was a failure, attributed to a control failure in the second stage. By 1980 this problem had been worked out. The first indigenous satellite launched by India was called Rohini-1.

Following the success of the SLV, ISRO began construction of a satellite launch vehicle that would be able to put truly useful satellites into polar orbits. The Polar Satellite Launch Vehicle (PSLV) was designed as India's workhorse launch system, taking advantage of both old technology with large reliable solid-stages, and new liquid engines. At the same time, it was decided that it would be prudent to develop a smaller rocket, based on the SLV, which would serve as a test bed for many of the new technologies that would be used on the PSLV. The Augmented Satellite Launch Vehicle (ASLV) would test technologies like strap-on boosters and new guidance systems so that experience could be gained before the PSLV went into full production. This was in line with advice that Wernher von Braun had given when paying a visit to ISRO: "If you have to do anything in rocketry do it yourself. SLV-3 is a genuine Indian design and you may have your own troubles. But you should always remember that you do not just build on success, you also build on failure".

Rather than indigenously develop liquid engines for the PSLV, the ISRO made a deal which would cut a couple of years from the development of a new engine. In exchange for a modest sum of money, and some Indian help with minor aspects of the production of the engine, France agreed to transfer technology for the Viking liquid engine to India. The deal was probably motivated by the fact that the French were, at the time, receiving little interest from the European community in the development of the Ariane launcher, forcing them to look elsewhere for support. The Indian version of this engine is called Vikas.

Eventually, the ASLV was flight tested in 1987, but this launch was a failure. After minor corrections, another launch was attempted in 1988. This launch again failed, and this time a full investigation was launched into the cause, providing valuable experience, specifically because the ASLV's failure had been one of control - the vehicle could not be adequately controlled on removal of the stabilizing fins that were present on the SLV, so extra measures like improved manoeuvring thrusters and flight control system upgrades were added. The ASLV development had also proven useful in the development of strap-on motor technology.

It was not until 1992 that the first successful launch of the ASLV took place. At this point the launch vehicle, which could only put very small payloads into orbit, had achieved its objective. In 1993, the time had come for the maiden flight of the PSLV. The first launch was a failure. The first successful launch took place in 1994, and since then, the PSLV has become the workhorse launch vehicle - placing both remote sensing and communications satellites into orbit, creating the largest cluster in the world, and providing unique data to Indian industry and agriculture. Continual performance upgrades have increased the payload capacity of the rocket significantly.

Work then started on the next class of launch vehicles, intended to place larger satellites into geostationary transfer orbit (GTO), and thus a launcher partly derived from the PSLV design, but featuring large liquid strap-on motors and a cryogenic upper-stage motor, was devised - the Geostationary Satellite Launch Vehicle. Following the success of the Viking engine acquisition, ISRO had planned to acquire booster technology from the Russian space organization Glavkosmos. The United States, which had begun imposing restrictions on the Indian Space programme when India moved closer to the Soviet Union in the 1970s, opposed the technology transfer on non-proliferation grounds and imposed sanctions against ISRO in May 1992. It is debatable as to whether this action by the US was relevant in terms of preventing proliferation, as cryogenic engines are never used in the construction of ballistic missiles, and India had the technical capability to construct rockets anyway.

Under pressure, Glavkomos halted the transfer of the associated manufacturing and design technology to India. Until then, ISRO had not been affected by technology transfer restrictions due to its foresight in indigenizing technology. When ISRO was considering cancellation of indigenous cryogenic projects Russia agreed to provide fully built engines. India began developing an indigenous cryogenic engine to replace them, in the GSLV-II. There is still some controversy over the issue of the cryogenic engine acquisition, with many pointing to the decision to cancel indigenous projects as being a grave mistake - India would have likely had a fully indigenous engine operating by the time the GSLV launched if indigenous development had started from day one.

In 2001, the first development flight of the GSLV took place. Despite this, the GSLV has had to suffer payload cutbacks, and was delayed. The indigenous cryogenic engine for the GSLV's upper stage was flown in 2007. It is currently the most powerful Indian launch vehicle in operation. Due to the questionable effectiveness of the GSLV for the needs of the current decade, ISRO began development of a new launch vehicle, the GSLV Mark III, which despite its name, is not at all related to the GSLV-I/II, but is in fact a new heavy launch vehicle, that will incorporate larger versions of proven technology, and be indigenously built. Based around the proven format of liquid main stages and two solid strap-on boosters, the GSLV Mark III will resemble the Ariane-5 and several other modern launchers. The first flight is scheduled for 2008. Although India has stated that it can fulfil space interests without the need for manned missions, the GSLV-M3 would provide more than enough payload capacity for manned spaceflight.

India is also developing a project to send an unmanned probe to the moon in 2008, as a first attempt at exploration of the solar system. This project, called CHANDRAYAAN, will use a modified PSLV rocket to send a small probe into lunar orbit, from where it will survey the surface of the moon in greater detail than ever before, in an attempt to locate resources. Other countries, including the US, have expressed interest in attaching their own payloads to the mission. ISRO and NASA have entered into an agreement for carrying two NASA probes as a payload.

Another more long-term project that is underway is the effort to develop a reusable launch vehicle (RLV) called AVATAR, similar to many other countries, but only for the launch of satellites. Theoretically such a vehicle, designed on the basis of scramjet technology, would be able to launch small satellites into orbit for a fraction of the cost of current launches, opening up many potential commercial avenues, and making certain satellite technologies feasible for the first time. A scaled-down technology demonstrator is scheduled to fly in 2008. ISRO has also successfully tested a scramjet air breathing engine which produced Mach 6 for seven seconds. ISRO is continuing research related to using scramjets in RLVs after 2010.

ISRO has also entered the lucrative market of launching payloads of other nations upon its rockets from Indian soil, as illustrated by the launches of the Israel Space Agency Ofeq-7 spy satellite and the Israeli Tauvex-II satellite module. The CARTOSAT-II, launched in July 2006, carries a small Indonesian payload of 56 kg.

Since its formation, ISRO has launched numerous satellites; they include the IRS (Indian Remote Sensing) satellite series, the INSAT (Indian National Satellite) series (in Geo-Stationary orbit), the GSAT series (launched using GSLV) and METSAT 1 (launched by PSLV). As of 2007, the total number of satellites of all varieties built by ISRO is 45. The IRS system is the world's largest constellation of remote sensing satellites and ISRO offers the cheapest commercial access to space.

A brief chronology of events, in the space research programme, is tabulated on the next page.

Event	Date	Description and Status
Aryabhata	19 April 1975	Launched by SL-8 rocket, made by Russia, from Kapustin Yar. Weight was 360 kg and the Perigee/Apogee was 563 x 619 km.
Bhaskara -1	7 June 1979	Launched by SL-8 rocket, made by Russia, from Kapustin Yar. Weight was 360 kg and the Perigee/Apogee was 563 x 619 km. Telemetry was received until reentry on 17 February 1989.
Rohini-1A	10 August 1979	Launching tried by SLV-3 rocket, made by India, from Sriharikota. Rocket failed.
Rohini-1B	18 July 1980	Launched by SLV-3 rocket, made by India, from Sriharikota. Weight was 35 kg and the Perigee/Apogee was 305x 919 km. India's first successful launch. Re-entry on 20 May 1981
APPLE	19 June 1981	APPLE was launched by Ariane rocket, made by France and launched from Kourou in French Guyana. Weight was 670 kg and it is India's first Geo Stationary rocket. Deactivated in September 1983.
Bhaskara-2	20 Nov 1981	Launched by SL-8 rocket, made by Russia, from Kapustin Yar. Weight was 444 kg. and the Perigee/Apogee was 541 x 557km. Telemetry was received until re-entry on 30 November 1991.
INSAT-1A	10 April 1982	Launched by Delta rocket, made by USA, from Canaveral. Weight was 1152 kg Abandoned on 4 September 1982.
Rohini-3	17 April 1983	Launched by Indian launcher, SLV-3, from Sriharikota. Weight 41.5 kg and orbit 371X861 km. Reentered its orbit on 19 April 1990.
INSAT-1B	30 August 1983	Launched by STS-8, made by USA and from Cape Canaveral. Weight was 1152 kg. It worked till 17 July 1990 and then was kept stand-by. Removed from orbit in August 1993.
SROSS-1	24 March, 1987	Launched by ASLV rocket. Failed due to rocket failure.
IRS-1A	17 March 1988	Launched by SL-3 rocket, by Russia from Tyuratam.Weight 950 kg. India's first remote sensing satellite.
SROSS-2	13 July 1988	Launched by ASLV rocket, by India. Failed due to second ASLV rocket failure.
INSAT-1C	21 July 1988	INSAT-1C was launched by Ariane rocket, made by France and launched from Kourou in French Guyana. Weight was 700 kg. Abandoned on 22 November 1989.
INSAT-1D	12 June 1990	Launched by Delta rocket, made by USA, from Cape Canaveral. Weight was 1152 kg. The last of the first generation INSAT.
IRS-1B	29 August 1991	Launched by SLV-3, Indian rocket. Identical to IRS-1A
SROSS-C3	20 May 1992	Launched by Indian rocket ASLV-D3 from Sriharikota. 106 kg. Reentered on 14 July 1992
INSAT-2A	9 July 1992	INSAT-2A was launched by Ariane-4 rocket, made by France and launched from Kourou in French Guyana. Weight was 1906 kg.
INSAT-2B	22 July 1993	INSAT-2B was launched by Ariane rocket, made by France and launched from Kourou in French Guyana. Transponder failed in April 1999.
IRS-1E	20 Sept 1993	Launched by Indian made PSLV-D1 from Sriharikota. Weight 106 kg. However, it could not attain orbit.
SROSS-C2	4 May 1994	Launched by Indian made PSLV-D2 from Sriharikota. Weight 113 kg.
IRS-P2	15 October 1994	Launched by Indian made PSLV-D2 from Sriharikota.
INSAT-2C	6 December 1995	INSAT-2C was launched by Ariane 4 rocket, made by France and launched from Kourou in French Guyana.
IRS-1C	28 December 1995	Launched by Russian rocket Molniya-M from Baikanour in Sun-synchronous orbit.
IRS-P3	21 March 1996	Launched by Indian rocket PSLV-D3 from Sriharikota.
INSAT-2D	4 June 1997	Launched by French rocket, Ariane-4, from Kourou. It was abandoned in October 1997 after a major power failure.
IRS-1D	29 September 1997	Launched by Indian rocket PSLV-C1. Placed in elliptical orbit instead of circular orbit due to a technical snag. It was partly corrected.
INSAT-2E	3 April 1999	Launched by French rocket, Ariane-4, from Kourou. Last second generation INSAT.
IRS-P4	26 May 1999	Launched by Indian rocket, PSLV-C2. Also known as Oceansat-1
INSAT-3A	22 March 2000	Launched by French rocket, Ariane-5, from Kourou.
GSLV	18 April 2001	Successful flight test of Geo-Synchronous Launch vehicle (GSLV)

(Contd.)

Event	Date	Description and Status
TES	22 October 2001	
INSAT-3C	24 January 2002	
KALPANA-1	12 September 2002	PSLV-C4 launches KALPANA-1
GSAT-2	8 May 2003	GSLV-D2, the second developmental launch of GSLV with GSAT-2 successful
INSAT-3B	10 April 2003	
INSAT-3E	28 September 2003	
RESOURCESAT-117	October 2003	
EDUSAT	20 September 2004	First operational flight of GSLV (F01). Successfully launched EDUSAT.
CARTOSAT-1	5 May 2005	Launch of CARTOSAT and HAMSAT by PSLV-C6 from the second launch pad (Universal Launch Pad)
HAMSAT	5 May 2005	
CARTOSAT-2	10 January 2007	Successful launch of SRE-1, LAPAN-TUBSAT and PEHUENSAT-1 on PSLV C7. SRE-1 splashed down in the Bay of Bengal on 22 January 2007 and was successfully recovered by the Indian Coast Guard and Indian Navy, making India one of the few countries to have re-entry technology.
INSAT-4A	12 March 2007	INSAT-4B successfully launched by Arianespace
AGILE	23 April 2007	PSLV-C8 successfully places an Italian satellite, AGILE, into its orbit.
INSAT-4CR	2 September 2007	INSAT-4CR was successfully placed in orbit, on a GSLV-F04 rocket. It is the first INSAT satellite successfully launched from India.

Space Transportation Systems

All Indian space launches are conducted from the Sriharikota High Altitude Range (SHAR) on Sriharikota Island off the east coast of India in the Bay of Bengal. The original SLV-3 launch complex was converted to support the ASLV. Two new complexes with one pad each to the south were selected to support the PSLV and GSLV. The Vikram Sarabhai Space Center at the southern tip of India is the site of most launch vehicle stage development.

ISRO operates 3 launch stations:

- Thumba (TERLS - Thumba Equatorial Rocket Launching Station/Vikram Sarabhai Space Center, Kerala),
- Sriharikota (SRLS - Sriharikota Rocket Launching Station/Satish Dhawan Space Center, Andhra Pradesh).
- Balasore (BRLS - Balasore Rocket Launching Station, Orissa).

The Sriharikota range is used for launch of satellites and multi-stage rockets. The launch station has two launch pads including the newest Universal Launch Pad. The two launch pads allow the station to hold up to 6 launches per year. The other two launch facilities are capable of launching sounding rockets, and other small rockets that don't produce spent stages.

Indian Remote Sensing Satellite System

Following the successful demonstration flights of Bhaskara 1 and Bhaskara 2 satellites launched in 1979 and 1981, respectively, India began to develop indigenous IRS (Indian Remote Sensing Satellite) program to support the national economy in the areas of agriculture, water resources, forestry and ecology, geology, water sheds, marine fisheries and coastal management. Later India established the National Natural Resources Management System (NNRMS) for which the Department of Space (DOS) is the nodal agency, providing operational remote sensing data services. Data from the IRS satellites is received and disseminated by several countries all over the world. With the advent of high resolution satellites, new applications in the areas of urban sprawl, infrastructure planning and other large scale applications for mapping have been initiated.

The Indian Remote Sensing Satellite system is the largest constellation of remote sensing satellites in operation today in the world. With the launch of CARTOSAT-2 [3], the constellation now has six satellites in operation – IRS-1D, OCEANSAT-1, Technology Experiment Satellite (TES), RESOURCESAT-1, CARTOSAT-1 and the latest CARTOSAT-2. All these are placed in polar sun-synchronous orbit and provide data in a variety of spatial, spectral and temporal resolutions to enable several applications to be undertaken relevant to the national development.

Data from Indian Remote Sensing satellites are used for various applications of resources survey and management under the National Natural Resources Management System (NNRMS). The applications include:

- Pre-harvest crop area and production estimation of major crops.
- Drought monitoring and assessment based on vegetation condition.
- Flood risk zone mapping and flood damage assessment.
- Hydro-geomorphologic maps to locate underground water resources for drilling wells.
- Irrigation command area status monitoring
- Snow-melt run-off estimates for planning water use in down stream projects
- Land use and land cover mapping
- Urban planning
- Forest survey
- Wetland mapping
- Environmental impact analysis
- Mineral Prospecting
- Coastal studies
- Integrated Mission for Sustainable Development (initiated in 1992) for generating locale-specific prescriptions for integrated land and water resources development in 174 districts.

The initial versions of the satellites are composed of the 1 (A, B, C, D). The later versions are named based on their area of application including OceanSat, CartoSat, ResourceSat. Some of the satellites have alternate designations based on the launch number and vehicle (P series for PSLV). The Indian Remote Sensing Satellite launch log is as follows:

Satellite	Date of Launch	Launch Vehicle	Status
IRS 1A	17 March 1988	Vostok, USSR	Mission Completed
IRS 1B	29 August 1991	Vostok, USSR	Mission Completed
IRS P1 (also IE)	20 September 1993	PSLV-D1	Crashed, due to launch failure of PSLV
IRS P2	15 October 1994	PSLV-D2	Mission Completed
IRS 1C	28 December 1995	Molniya, Russia	Mission Completed
IRS P3	21 March 1996	PSLV-D3	Mission Completed
IRS 1D	29 September 1997	PSLV-C1	In service
IRS P4 (Oceansat-1)	27 May 1999	PSLV-C2	In service
Technology Experiment Satellite (TES)	22 October 2001	PSLV-C3	In service
IRS P6 (Resourcesat 1)	17 October 2003	PSLV-C5	In service
IRS P5 (Cartosat 1)	5 May 2005	PSLV-C6	In service
Cartosat 2 (IRS P7)	10 January 2007	PSLV-C7	In service

Future launches are planned for strengthening the fleet of IRS satellites and widening their applications. They include:

RISAT (Radar Imaging Satellite)	A microwave remote sensing mission with Synthetic Aperture Radar (SAR) operating in C-band and having a 6 x 2 meter planar active array antenna based on trans-receiver module architecture. SAR is an all weather-imaging sensor capable of taking images in cloudy and snow covered regions and also both during day and night. RISAT weighs 1,750 kg. It is slated to be launched in 2007-2008.
Oceansat-2	It is envisaged to continue the service of OCEANSAT-1. It will carry an Ocean Colour Monitor (OCM) and a Ku-band pencil beam scatterometer. It is slated to be launched in 2007-2008.
Resourcesat-2	It will have imaging sensors similar to RESOURCESAT-1. Payload electronics have been miniaturized to reduce the overall weight. RESOURCESAT-2 is planned for launch by PSLV in 2009-10.
TWSAT (Third World Satellite)	TWSAT is the first satellite in the micro satellite series envisaged to provide 100 kg class satellite platform for carrying payloads for earth imaging, space science, atmospheric and ocean studies. TWSAT will carry a multi-spectral camera providing images with about 36 m. spatial resolution and swath of 151 km. The data generated will be transmitted to user terminals. The user terminals will be PC based systems along with RF downlink and antenna systems. The software will be capable of providing data products to standard product level with radiometric and geometric corrections.

Satellite Data Acquisition and Processing

The National Remote Sensing Agency (NRSA) at Hyderabad is the nodal agency for reception, archival, processing and dissemination of remote sensing data in the country. NRSA acquires and processes data from all Indian remote sensing satellites like CARTOSAT-1, CARTOSAT-2, RESOURCESAT-1, IRS-1D, OCEANSAT-1 and TES as well as foreign satellites like Terra, NOAA and ERS. As per the Remote Sensing Data Policy, NRSA is the national acquisition/ distribution agency for all satellite data within India.

Future Plans

ISRO has begun the development of a mission to the Moon, named Chandrayaan-1. It will be India's first step towards exploration of deep space. In 2005, the Indian government approved Rs.364 crore rupees for the planned moon mission expected to be launched by 2008. Apart from ISRO made instruments, Chandrayaan will carry science instruments from NASA and ESA as opportunity payloads free of cost and with the understanding of sharing the data from the instruments. If the mission goes as planned, ISRO would be the sixth space agency in the world, after the Soviet Union, NASA, Japan, European Space Agency and China, to have sent an unmanned mission to the Moon.

ISRO also plans to undertake a totally indigenous manned space exploration in the next decade by planning to send a person to space. The name gaganaut, derived from *gagana* (the heavens), has become popular amongst the Indian space community as a term for Indian astronauts. The term *antariksha yaatri* has also been suggested as a more proper name (*antariksha* signifies space beyond our Earth and *yaatri* means 'traveller'), and this is the name used in official documents, as well as the Indian media. The question of having a manned space programme in future was first substantially raised in November 2006 in the form a proposal. It outlined a goal which would be to design, develop and launch an Indian human spacecraft, a two-seat space capsule, which would be used to send an Indian into space by 2015. The vehicle would be launched by India's Geosynchronous Satellite Launch Vehicle (GSLV-Mk II)]. The Government of India has approved the project and allocated 50 crores for pre-project initiatives for 2007-08. A manned mission into space would require about Rs. 10,000 crore ($3 billion) over an eight-year period. The first signs of having a manned space programme were the 600-kg Space Capsule Recovery Experiment (SRE), launched using the Polar Satellite Launch Vehicle (PSLV) rocket, and safely returned to earth 12 days later. This demonstrates India's capability to develop heat resistant materials necessary for re-entry technology.

ISRO has started the development of the next launch vehicle version, known as the GSLV Mark-III, with an indigenous cryogenic engine capable of launching satellites weighing up to 6 tons in the final configuration. ISRO will be launching various satellites for European and Russian space programs including Agile and the GLONASS series of navigation satellites. In December 2005, during the annual Indo-Russian summit in Moscow, the two states agreed on joint development of the GLONASS-K series, which will be launched by Indian launchers. ISRO also plans to launch payloads SRE-1, RISAT-1, ASTROSAT, OCEANSAT series, INSAT series, CARTOSAT series, and GSAT series over the next couple of years. The RLV-TD, a technology demonstrator of possible scramjet launch technology, will fly around 2008.

India is also of the view that the time is now for the international community to start laying in place the foundation stones of future space security architecture that will promote continued peaceful exploitation of space and dampen the drivers of conflict that already have emerged. However, no nation is going to sign a treaty or international agreement that it does not feel serves its interests, particularly in the area of national security.

CLIMATE CHANGE:
A SECURITY THREAT IN SOUTH ASIA

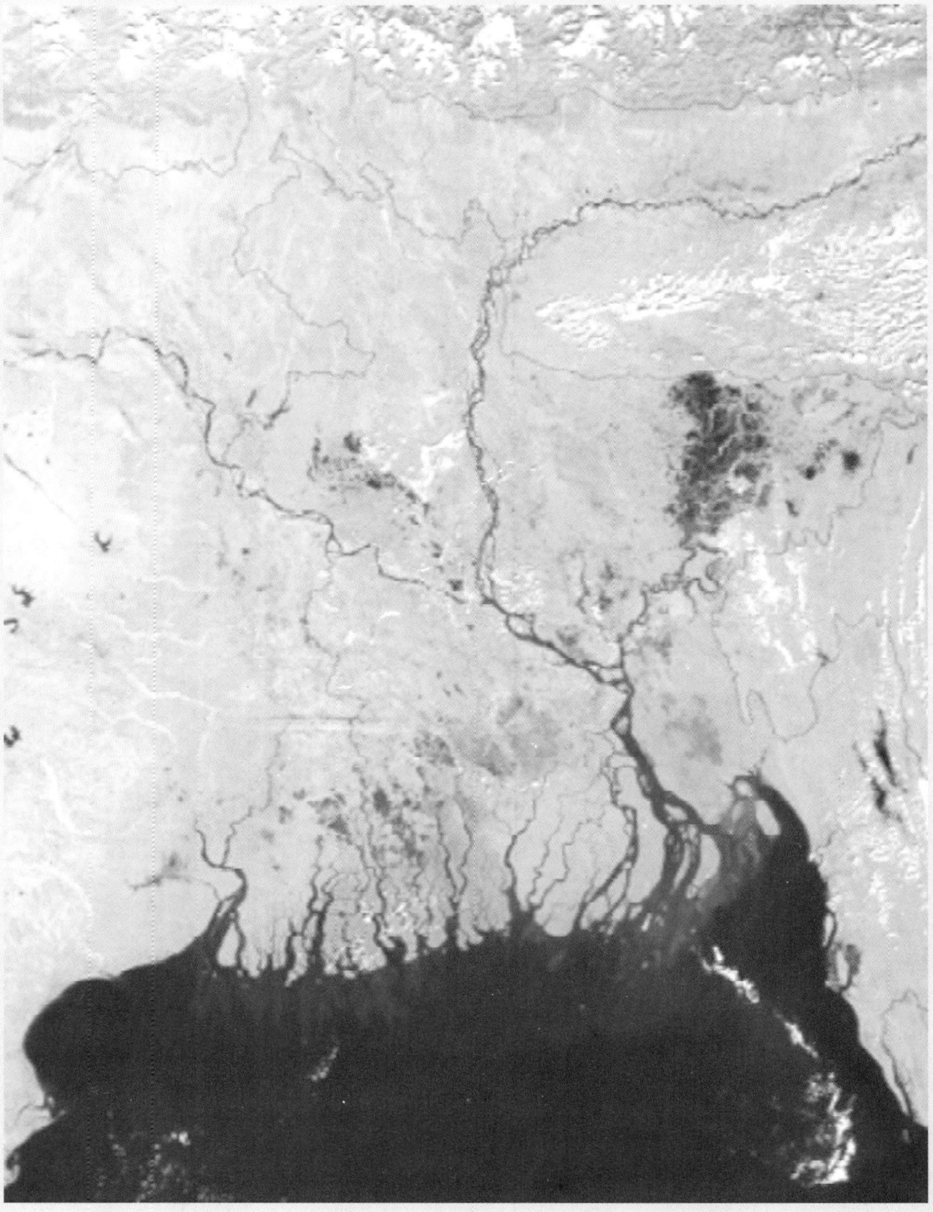

CLIMATE CHANGE: A SECURITY THREAT IN SOUTH ASIA

The world is today at a crossroads in many areas. Global warming, rising demands of energy, the availability of oil and gas, depletion of the ozone layer, rapidly growing population levels, rising sea levels, the availability of water and changing weather patterns are some of the pressing issues facing mankind, besides war and other forms of conflict. The global environmental situation facing the entire international community in the foreseeable future is fraught with danger. There is a growing realization that achieving energy and climate security is at the core of future security challenges, with implications that go well beyond traditional policy spheres. The situation is even more volatile in South Asia where climate change amplifies mechanisms which could lead to insecurity and violence, political instability and even conflicts. The earth's atmosphere is a common resource for all of humankind. The problem lies not in accessing this resource but in its excessive usage.

In the larger picture, the politics surrounding climate change in the coming months and years will run on two parallel tracks. One level is the near term, which focusses on a political resolution of the current climate change policy. Another level focusses on how people live their lives and view their relationships to major environmental issues. The latter, driven by advocacy of sustainable consumption, is more important. It will determine the long-term future of energy and global energy policy, but the first is important, too, as it will set the ground rules for the policies that follow in the coming decades.

The Inter-governmental Panel on Climate Change (IPCC) in their Fourth Assessment Report 2007 have emphasized the linkages between global environmental issues and the challenge of meeting key human needs such as adequate food, clean water, clean air and adequate and affordable energy services. The Report states that it is 90% certain that mankind is responsible for rising global temperatures.

Some of the effects that may be forthcoming, according to the IPCC, are:

- At continental, regional, and ocean basin scales, numerous long-term changes in climate have been observed. These include changes in Arctic temperatures and ice, widespread changes in precipitation amounts, ocean salinity, wind patterns and aspects of extreme weather including droughts, heavy precipitation, heat waves and the intensity of tropical cyclones.
- Average Arctic temperatures increased at almost twice the global average rate in the past 100 years. Arctic temperatures have high decadal variability, and a warm period was also observed from 1925 to 1945.
- Satellite data since 1978 show that annual average Arctic sea ice extent has shrunk by 2.7% per decade, with larger decreases in summer of 7.4% per decade.
- Temperatures at the top of the permafrost layer have generally increased since the 1980s in the Arctic (by up to 3°C). The maximum area covered by seasonally frozen ground has decreased by about 7% in the Northern Hemisphere since 1900, with a decrease in spring of up to 15%.

The key conclusions are:

- Warming of the climate system is unequivocal.
- Most of (>50% of) the observed increase in globally averaged temperatures since the mid-20th century is very likely (confidence level >90%) due to the observed increase in anthropogenic (human) greenhouse gas concentrations.
- Hotter temperatures and rises in sea level "would continue for centuries" even if greenhouse gas levels are stabilized, although the likely amount of temperature and sea level rise varies greatly depending on the fossil intensity of human activity.
- The probability that this is caused by natural climatic processes alone is less than 5%.
- World temperatures could rise by between 1.1 and 6.4°C during the 21st century and:
  - Sea levels will probably rise by 18 to 59 centimetres.
  - There is a confidence level >90% that there will be more frequent warm spells, heat waves and heavy rainfall.
  - There is a confidence level >66% that there will be an increase in droughts, tropical cyclones and extreme high tides.
  - Both past and future anthropogenic carbon dioxide emissions will continue to contribute to warming and sea level rise for more than a millennium.

- Global atmospheric concentrations of carbon dioxide, methane, and nitrous oxide have increased markedly as a result of human activities since 1750 and now far exceed pre-industrial values over the past 650,000 years.

There is now incontrovertible evidence that the atmospheric concentration of greenhouse gases, like carbon dioxide, methane and nitrous oxide, has by far exceeded the usual range of the last 6,50,000 years. The carbon dioxide concentration has, in fact, touched the highest levels in recorded history. How will this impact South Asia? Climate change will affect all countries, putting them under additional pressure to adapt their societies to the problem.

Weak governance structures and conflicts. Violent conflicts are a very frequent feature of weak and fragile states, and which are characterized by the permanent weakening or even the dissolution of their state structures. The impacts of climate change will particularly affect those regions in which states with weak steering and problem-solving capacities already predominate. Climate change could thus lead to the further proliferation of weak and fragile statehood and increase the probability of violent conflicts occurring.

Economic performance and tendency to violence. Empirical studies show that poor countries are far more prone to conflict than affluent societies. Climate change will result in tangible economic costs for developing countries in particular: a drop in agricultural yields, extreme weather events and migratory movements can all impede economic development. Climate change can thus reinforce obstacles to development and heighten poverty, thereby increasing the risk of conflicts.

Demographics and conflict. Wherever high population growth and density, resource scarcity (farmland, water) and a low level of economic development occur in tandem, there is an increased risk of conflict. In countries and regions which are already affected by high population growth and density as well as poverty, climate change will exacerbate resource scarcity and thus heighten the risk of conflict.

Spillover risk in conflict regions. Conflicts which are initially limited to local or national level often destabilize neighbouring countries, e.g. through refugee flows, arms trafficking or combatant withdrawal. Conflicts thus have a spillover effect. The social impacts of climate change can transcend borders, expanding the geographical extent of crisis and conflict regions.

Study of the long-term climate record has shown that even a minor shock to the system can cause an enormous change in outcome, a non-linear response that has come to be called "abrupt climate change." Less well recognized is that social and economic systems are also highly sensitive to climate perturbations. Seemingly modest fluctuations in rainfall, temperature and other meteorological factors can create havoc in vulnerable societies.

Recent years have shown that shifts in rainfall can bring down governments and even set off wars. The African Sahel, just south of the Sahara, is an example. The deadly carnage in Darfur, Sudan, which is almost always discussed in political and military terms, has roots in an ecological crisis directly arising from climate shocks. Darfur is an arid zone with overlapping, growing populations of impoverished pastoralists (tending goats, cattle and camels) and sedentary farmers. Both groups depend on rainfall for their livelihoods. The average rainfall declined, leaving Darfur prone to drought and violence ensued. Communities fought to survive by raiding others and attempting to seize or protect scarce water and food supplies.

A drought-induced famine is much more likely to trigger conflict in a place that is already impoverished and bereft of any cushion of physical or financial resources. Darfur was also pushed over the edge by ethnic and political conflict, with ambitious, violent and unscrupulous leaders preying on the ethnic divisions. These vulnerabilities, of course, are not unique to Darfur. Several studies have shown that a temporary decline in rainfall has generally been associated throughout sub-Saharan Africa with a marked rise in the likelihood of violent conflict in the following months.

Climate sceptics who ask why we should care about "a degree or two" increase in the global mean temperature understand neither the climate nor the social and economic systems in which we live. Both climate and society are subject to great instability, nonlinear responses and high unpredictability. Climate changes may influence storms, droughts, floods, crop yields, disease vectors and much more, well beyond what the current "average" forecasts suggest.

The Intergovernmental Panel on Climate Change Fourth Assessment report provided specific information for South Asia region concerning the nature of future impacts. They include:

- Glacier melting in the Himalayas is projected to increase flooding and will affect water resources within the next two to three decades. If current warming rates persist, glaciers on the Tibetan plateau will shrink rapidly from 500,000 square kilometers to 100, 000 square kilometers by 2030. The glacial meltdown will first result in rivers being flooded and then drying up. The Ganges delta would turn infertile.

- Climate change will compound the pressures on natural resources and the environment due to rapid urbanization, industrialization, and economic development.
- Crop yields could decrease up to 30% in South Asia by the mid-21st century. The gross per capita availability of water in India is expected to decline from the current 1,820 cubic metre a year to as low as 1,140 cubic metre a year by 2050 – a 30% drop. (1,000 cubic meters is classified by the UN as a water scarcity zone).
- Mortality due to diarrhea primarily associated with floods and droughts will rise in South Asia.
- Sea-level rise will exacerbate inundation, storm surge, erosion and other coastal hazards. Island countries like the Maldives and low-lying coastal countries like Bangladesh would experience severe flooding and erosion of land. Vast stretches of mangroves and salt marshes would be destroyed.
- 25% of the flora and fauna in South Asia would become extinct by 2030.

The resulting ecological effects, especially on societies already facing hunger or financial and political fragility, can be enormous and dire. Public debates tend to neglect these powerful effects because they focus on politics and only rarely on the underlying environmental pressures. Ecological risks to economic well-being and national security need to be recognized. Countries need to look much harder for practical approaches to mitigating the pressures that society is now placing on the earth's ecosystems. In the face of the lack of a coherent grassroots movement in support of action on climate change, small changes in climate can cause wars, topple governments and crush economies already strained by poverty, corruption and ethnic conflict.

Some of the dire predictions are that The Maldives will disappear along with many island nations; one third of Bangladesh will be under water and, likewise, low lying belts of many coastal states would also be inundated. Consequently, there would be other disastrous effects. For example, there would be frequent incidents of extreme weather conditions like floods, heat waves, droughts and hurricanes that would trigger natural calamities, making human life more difficult than ever.

The SAARC region will suffer the most. The melting of glaciers in the Himalayas would adversely affect the entire SAARC region and its weather pattern, causing abnormal drought and floods, which will contribute to the scourge of famine upon one billion people, inviting extraordinary problems of human survival in the entire South Asian region.

Numerous problems not yet identified would emerge, leaving no space for easy resolution. SAARC nations are already witnessing huge problems for their economic development, and tackling the issues of poverty will have to confront additional formidable problems. Eventually, it would invite inconceivable conflicts amongst communities, states and nations making it extremely difficult to find a point of resolution. An abrupt climate change scenario could potentially de-stabilize geo-political environments, leading to skirmishes, battles, and even war due to resource constraints.

Other relevant climate change inputs are:

- Significantly increased precipitation has been observed in parts of southern Asia.
- Changes in precipitation and evaporation over the oceans are suggested by freshening of mid and high latitude waters together with increased salinity in low latitude waters.
- Mid-latitude westerly winds have strengthened since the 1960s.
- More intense and longer droughts have been observed over wider areas since the 1970s, particularly in the tropics. Increased drying linked with higher temperatures and decreased precipitation has contributed to changes in drought.
- Changes in sea surface temperatures, wind patterns, and decreased snow pack and snow cover have also been linked to droughts.
- The frequency of heavy precipitation events has increased over most land areas, consistent with warming and observed increases of atmospheric water vapour.
- Widespread changes in extreme temperatures have been observed over the last 50 years. Cold days, cold nights and frost have become less frequent, while hot days, hot nights, and heat waves have become more frequent.

Given the possibilities for conflict created by the above changes in the global climate, whether it is over petroleum, refugee flows, fresh water or food, it rapidly becomes apparent that in South Asia, given its high population levels and endemic poverty, that the possibilities for conflict are overwhelming. Glaciers in the Himalayas from which much of South Asia obtains its water supplies are retreating; the Gangotri Glacier is retreating at 23 metres per year. The Khumbu Glacier on Mount Everest has retreated more than five kilometres in the past 60 years. Himalayan glaciers supply water to the Ganges, Indus, Brahmaputra, Mekong, Salween, Yangtze and Yellow rivers. Any disruption of the water supply in these rivers could have widespread consequences for the region. The predicted increase in extreme weather including higher temperatures, changing patterns of precipitation coupled with increasing domestic and agricultural use of water is a recipe for disaster.

If to the scenario above one adds "Peak Oil" it becomes even more disturbing. The Peak Oil theory states "it is widely accepted that oil is a finite resource; there are basic laws which describe the depletion of any finite resource:

- Production starts at zero;
- Production then rises to a peak which can never be surpassed;
- Once the peak has been passed, production declines until the resource is depleted.

These simple rules apply to any relevant system, including the depletion of petroleum resources. The rate of production of a natural resource can be plotted on a graph against time. This gives a picture of the lifetime of that resource. It is important to note that the point of maximum production (known as the Hubbert Peak) tends to coincide with the midpoint of depletion of the resource under consideration. In the case of oil, this means that when we reach the Hubbert Peak, we will have used half of all the recoverable oil that ever existed on our planet". The overwhelming problems facing South Asia today, from climate change and rising populations to peak oil and the need for alternative sources of energy, and the potential for conflict triggered by resource shortages signals that the South Asian community cannot afford to let peace continue to elude it.

It is necessary for all states to drastically reduce their carbon output. This can be accomplished through carbon sequestration, adaptation of alternative sources of energy and energy conservation. In the agricultural sector modern forms of irrigation should be adopted in order to conserve water and provide a measure food security. In arid areas new techniques of dry land farming should be promoted. Steps need to be taken to combat soil erosion, degradation, and the decline in soil fertility. A national energy security plan is a vital planning tool for all states and should be undertaken as a matter of urgency.

What would be the effect when glacial retreat and melting of the Himalayan peaks occur at the same time? There are huge human settlements near the banks of rivers, and most of the fertile lands in the hills lie on the banks of rivers. When such catastrophes occur, it will wash away people and inundate and fill up adjoining agricultural lands with sand.

No one can even predict the magnitude of its implication for India and Bangladesh, where huge devastations and disasters will wash away millions of people and waste millions of hectares of agricultural land. Towns and cities will be transformed into graveyards.

Clean hydropower should be developed and used by adopting an equitable sharing of the benefits of the immense water resources of the region. This is, perhaps the best time for resolving outstanding issues on sharing and utilising the huge water resources in the SAARC region by addressing past grievances and also accommodating future needs of all nations on an equal and equitable basis.

Hundreds of millions of people, including many of the poorest farm households, live in river valleys where irrigation is fed by glacier melt and snowmelt. The glaciers are disappearing, and the annual snowmelt is coming earlier each year, synchronizing it less and less well with the summer season. The vast numbers of farmers in the Indo-Gangetic Plain will most likely face severe disruptions in water availability. This region is already experiencing profound water stress due to unsustainable rates of groundwater pumping performed to irrigate large expanses of Northern India. Surface water bodies in these regions are already over-appropriated and degraded.

Climate change is no longer an issue for the distant future. It is already taking place, and the South Asian countries, particularly the poorest people, are most at risk. The impacts of higher temperatures, more variable precipitation, more extreme weather events, and sea level rise are felt in South Asia and will continue to intensify.

The consequences of such environmental changes include:

- decreased water availability and water quality in many arid and semiarid regions
- an increased risk of floods and droughts in many regions
- reduction in water regulation in mountain habitats
- decreases in reliability of hydropower and biomass production
- increased incidence of waterborne diseases such as malaria, dengue, and cholera
- increased damages and deaths caused by extreme weather events
- decreased agricultural productivity
- adverse impacts on fisheries
- adverse effects on many ecological systems

Much of this damage would come in the form of severe economic shocks. In addition, the impacts of climate change will exacerbate existing social and environmental problems and lead to migration within and across national borders. In sum, climate change is clearly not just an environmental issue but one with severe socio-economic implications in South Asia.

South Asia must adopt the principle of common but differentiated responsibilities. Adaptation is the key for developing countries and that it needs to be adequately resourced without diverting funds meant for development. India is challenged constantly by climate variability. It spends every year over 2% of its GDP in development measures like cyclone warning and protection, coastal protection, flood control, drought relief, and food security.

In 2006, the Government of India adopted a National Environment Policy. A special committee has been appointed to look into the impact of climate change. It will study the impact of anthropogenic climate change on India and identify the measures to be taken. Measures for sustainability and clean development include the use of CNG for public transport; introduction of metro rail in many cities; and a major bio-diesel programme including mandatory blending of ethanol in petrol. A Green India project has also been started that will be the world's largest afforestation project covering six million hectares of degraded forest land. Energy efficiency has been raised in all the major energy intensive sectors—steel, aluminium, fertilizer, paper and cement.

ENERGY: A REGIONAL OVERVIEW

ENERGY: A REGIONAL OVERVIEW

Overview

The South Asia region (Bangladesh, Bhutan, India, the Maldives, Nepal, Pakistan and Sri Lanka) is important to world energy markets for its large and rapidly growing population of over 1.4 billion people - more than one-fifth of the world total and is experiencing rapid energy demand growth. South Asia is also a major and growing contributor to global emissions of carbon dioxide. Despite recent rapid economic growth, the nations in the region have among the lowest per capita incomes in the world. India is by far the largest South Asian country in terms of population, Gross Domestic Product (GDP), and land area, followed by Pakistan and Bangladesh. The Indian economy continues to show impressive economic growth. The country's real gross domestic product (GDP) grew at an impressive rate of 9.1 percent during the first half of fiscal 2006 (April – September 2006), after growing by 8.7 percent in fiscal 2005. Together with the country's impressive growth, India has also become a significant consumer of energy resources. India was the fifth largest consumer of oil in the world during 2006.

The fuel structure amongst the countries of the region varies significantly. A significant change in the fuel structure in recent years has been the increase in the share of natural gas, because of important gas discoveries made in India, Pakistan, and Bangladesh and the environmental considerations arising from the large quantities of coal consumed in the region. At present, gas accounts for only about 8% of the total energy consumption in India, whereas it is the main source of energy in Bangladesh.

Economic and population growth in South Asia have resulted in rapid increases in energy consumption in recent years. South Asia's primary energy consumption has shown an increase of nearly 64% between 1992 and 2002 (only "commercial" energy sources and not animal waste, wood, or other biomass, which accounts for more than half of South Asia's total energy consumption). South Asia accounts for approximately 4.5% of world commercial energy consumption, up from 2.8% in 1991. Despite this growth in energy demand, South Asia continues to have the lowest levels of per capita energy consumption in the world, but among the highest levels of energy consumption per unit of GDP.

Discounting "non-commercial" sources of energy including animal waste, wood, and other biomass, South Asia's commercial energy mix is 46% coal, 34% petroleum, 12% natural gas, 6% hydroelectricity, 1% nuclear and 0.3% "other". There are significant variations within the region. Bangladesh's energy mix, for example, is dominated by natural gas (66.4%), while India relies heavily on coal (54.5%). Sri Lanka and the Maldives are overwhelmingly dependent on petroleum (82% and 100%, respectively); Pakistan is diversified among petroleum (42.7%), natural gas (42.2%, and hydroelectricity (10%). Bhutan and Nepal have the highest shares of hydroelectric power in their energy consumption mix at 80% and 31%, respectively.

Most of South Asia is grappling with energy shortfalls, typically in the form of recurrent, costly, and widespread electricity outages. Because of the economic and political ramifications arising from such shortfalls, improving the supply of energy, particularly the supply of electricity is an important priority of national and local governments. The countries of South Asia are looking to diversify their traditional energy supplies, promote additional foreign investment for energy infrastructure development, improve energy efficiency, reform and privatize energy sectors, and promote and expand regional energy trade and investment.

Another important implication of rising energy demand in South Asia is its impact on the region's level of carbon emissions. South Asia presently accounts for 4.8% of global carbon emissions. With the demand for coal in India projected to increase rapidly in the coming decade (from 359 million tons in 2000 to 430 million tons by 2010) and the recent introduction of coal into the fuel mix of other countries in the region, significant increase in emissions is certain. Carbon dioxide is the most abundant anthropogenic (human-caused) greenhouse gas in the atmosphere. In recent years, atmospheric concentrations of carbon dioxide have been rising at a rate of about 0.5% per year, and because anthropogenic emissions of carbon dioxide result primarily from the combustion of fossil fuels for energy, world energy use has emerged at the centre of the climate change debate. World carbon dioxide emissions are projected to rise from 26.9 billion metric tons in 2004 to 33.9 billion metric tons in 2015 and 42.9 billion metric tons in 2030.

Oil

South Asia contains reserves of only 5.7 billion barrels of oil, around 0.5% of world reserves. In 2002, the region consumed around 2.72 million barrels per day (bbl/d) of oil, and produced approximately 0.70 million bbl/d, making, South Asia a net oil importer of around 2.0 million bbl/d. The vast majority (around 819,000 bbl/d in 2003) of South Asia's oil production comes from India, whose offshore Bombay High field accounts for approximately one-third of total Indian oil output. Most of the remainder of South Asia's oil production comes from Pakistan (around 62,000 bbl/d in 2003). South Asia's oil imports are projected to more than double by 2020. The Middle East has been and is expected to remain the primary source of South Asian oil imports. In an effort to reduce oil import dependence, a number of South Asian countries have sought to expand domestic petroleum exploration by attracting private and foreign investors. In July 2003, the Sri Lankan government approved the Petroleum Resources Act to allow for private and foreign investment in its offshore oil and gas fields. Similarly, Pakistan has executed Production Sharing Agreements (PSA) with exploration companies based in France, Malaysia and Austria. India is implementing its 1997 New Exploration Licensing Policy (NELP) to increase foreign involvement in exploration, by awarding exploration blocks.

Growing demand for transportation fuels and industrial power has been a major factor behind the growth in South Asian oil consumption. Between 1990 and 2000, South Asian oil consumption – led by India – grew by about 75%. India's oil consumption is forecast to grow another 33% by 2010, reaching 2.8million bbl/d (up from 2.2 million bbl/d in 2002). In Sri Lanka, where oil is the dominant source of energy, oil consumption roughly doubled between 1991 and 2000. (In 2002, Sri Lanka's oil consumption was 75,000 bbl/d). Sri Lanka imports all of its crude oil and uses it largely for electricity generation and transportation. The country has a refining capacity of 50,000 bbl/d. In recent years, Sri Lanka has further increased oil imports to avoid over reliance on hydroelectricity. Several recent oil finds in India may reduce import dependence in South Asia.

In the face of growing oil demand, several South Asian countries have plans to expand their refining and transportation capacities. Since 1998, India's total refining capacity increased by 86% to 2.1 million bbl/d in 2004. The Reliance Industries refinery at Jamnagar, the only privately owned refinery in India, began operation in 1999 and has a capacity of 5,40,000 bbl/d. In August 2003, Bharat Petroleum Corp. Ltd. (BPCL), the second largest refinery in India, expanded its Mumbai refinery from 1,80,000 bbl/d to 2,40, 000 bbl/d in 2004. Petronet India is in the process of building pipelines that will add approximately 5,00,000 bbl/d to the existing 3,25,000 bbl/d of pipeline capacity, thereby displacing rail as the main mode of transportation for petroleum products.

In Pakistan, the 1,00,000-bbl/d "Pak-Arab" refinery, has helped to alleviate the country's dependence on refined product imports. Two additional planned refinery projects include a private venture near Karachi and an "Iran-Pak" partnership project near the border with Iran. The "Iran-Pak" project envisages two refineries that will add an estimated 1,60,000 bbl/d to Pakistan's refining capacity.

Natural Gas

In 2004, South Asia's proven natural gas reserves were estimated at 67.5 trillion cubic feet (tcf), approximately 1% of the world total, with potentially larger resources suspected but unproven. India's and Pakistan's reserves are roughly equal in size at 30.14 tcf and 26.83 tcf, respectively, while the only other South Asian country with reserves, Bangladesh, has approximately 10.6 tcf. Foreign energy companies including Shell and Unocal believe that Bangladeshi reserves may be higher at 32.1 tcf in "undiscovered reserves." If the estimates are correct, Bangladesh could become a major gas producer and supplier to the potential market in India.

At present, all natural gas production in South Asia is consumed domestically. Natural gas is seen as playing an important part in supplying new power plants in the region and diversifying from expensive oil imports. As a result, natural gas usage has increased rapidly in South Asia over the last decade, growing about 59% between 1992 and 2002. In 2002, the region produced and consumed around 2.1 tcf of natural gas. Around 42% was consumed by India, 39% by Pakistan, and the remaining 19% by Bangladesh.

Indian consumption of natural gas has risen faster than that of any other fuel in recent years and accounts for approximately 6.5% of the country's energy demand. At nearly 0.9 tcf in 2002, Indian gas demand is estimated to reach 2.5 tcf in 2025. Increased use of natural gas in power generation will account for much of the change. Like India, Pakistan plans to increase the use of natural gas for future electric power generation projects, a move that will necessitate a sharp rise in production and/or imports of natural gas. Because natural gas is already Bangladesh's primary source of commercial energy, gas exports are a controversial topic within Bangladesh, as many people feel that Bangladeshi gas resources should be used for domestic purposes before exporting.

If long-term projections of rapidly increasing gas demand for South Asia are correct, the region will require significant increases in production and/or imports. Even with expanded production, however, increased consumption of natural gas in South Asia is constrained by the region's inadequate domestic infrastructure. Gas imports would require construction of infrastructure – either cross-border pipelines or liquefied natural gas (LNG) facilities – and their success would hinge on the construction of domestic gas pipeline infrastructure. A number of such infrastructure projects have been proposed in India and Pakistan.

Although India's Foreign Investment Promotion Board (FIPB) approved 12 prospective LNG import terminal projects, several were delayed or cancelled following the government's decision not to extend payment guarantees to power projects which were to have been the largest LNG consumers. An import terminal at Dahej received India's first cargo of LNG in January 2004. LNG projects in Gujarat and Kerala are also under construction. Shell has commissioned an LNG import terminal in India, and several other LNG terminals are in planning stages. Myanmar is a potential source of supply for India.

Natural gas consumption in South Asia is projected to expand by 4.6% per year on average from 2004 to 2030. In India, natural gas currently is a minor fuel in the overall energy mix, representing only 8% of total primary energy consumption in 2004; however, India is rapidly expanding infrastructure to serve demand. India increased its spot and short-term LNG purchases in 2006, reportedly paying more than $9 per million Btu for one cargo (a year earlier, Royal Dutch/Shell could not find customers for LNG from its Hazira regasification terminal at a price of about $8 per million Btu). Natural gas shortages in India have reportedly left natural-gas-fired electric power plants and fertilizer plants underutilized in the past few years. India's natural gas consumption is projected to rise rapidly in the mid-term, growing by 6.2% per year on average from 2004 to 2015. As international natural gas prices gain acceptance in India, and as supplies from the Krishna-Godavari basin come on line around 2010, domestic natural gas supply is expected to catch up with currently underserved demand and also expand to serve new demand.

Pakistan expects recent discoveries to add about 1 billion cubic feet per day (bcfd) to its natural gas production. In 2001, Pakistan's government stated that it would permit a gas pipeline linking Iranian gas reserves to India to cross its territory. Pakistan would earn transit fees for Iranian gas supplied to India and be able to purchase gas from the pipeline itself. While Iran and Pakistan have shown great interest in the project, India has been reluctant to move forward due to political and military tensions with Pakistan.

Pakistan may also be linked into the Dolphin Project, a scheme to supply gas from Qatar's North Dome gas field to the United Arab Emirates and Oman via a sea link. Although Pakistan has signed an agreement to eventually purchase gas from Qatar, it seems unlikely that Pakistan will be included in the project in the near-term due to financial weakness and uncertainty about sufficient demand growth. A third possible gas pipeline would link gas-rich Turkmenistan with Daulatabad in central Pakistan via Afghanistan and continue into India. Although the governments of Pakistan, Afghanistan, and Turkmenistan have reached an agreement to develop the pipeline, financial and security challenges are likely to prevent its development.

Bhutan, the Maldives, Nepal, and Sri Lanka do not produce or consume any natural gas.

Coal

Although coal deposits are widely distributed, 67% of the world's recoverable reserves are located in four countries: the United States (27%), Russia (17%), China (13%), and India (10%). In 2004, these four countries, taken together, accounted for 66% of total world coal production. By rank, anthracite and bituminous coal account for 53% of the world's estimated recoverable coal reserves (on a tonnage basis), sub bituminous coal accounts for 30%, and lignite accounts for 17%.

Nearly 70% of the growth in India's coal consumption is expected to be in the electric power sector and most of the remainder in the industrial sector. In 2004, India's coal-fired power plants consumed 5.6 quadrillion Btu of coal, representing 69% of the country's total coal demand. Coal use for electricity generation in India is projected to grow by 2.4% per year, to 10.5 quadrillion Btu in 2030, as an additional 104 gigawatts of coal-fired capacity (net of retirements) is brought on line. As a result, India's coal-fired generating capacity more than doubles in the IEO2007 projections, from 82 gigawatts in 2004 to 186 gigawatts in 2030.

India has planned 11 gigawatt of new coal-fired generating capacity to be completed during its tenth power plan period (ending March 2007), and it is planning to complete more than 50 gigawatts of new coal-fired capacity during its eleventh plan period (ending in March 2012) [14]. In addition, India's government is also pursuing the development of between five and seven large coal fired power projects that would have between 20 and 28 gigawatts of combined generating capability. In India, demand for coal imports in 2030 is projected to be almost double the demand in 2005, as the country continues to encounter problems with coal production and transportation within its borders.

South Asia contains coal reserves of 95.5 billion tons or approximately 9% of the world total. Although coal accounts for 43% of South Asia's energy consumption, nearly all of the coal in this region is produced and consumed by India, the only South Asian country with significant coal reserves (93 billion tons) and the world's third largest coal producer after the Untied States and China. Pakistan has limited coal reserves of 2.5 billion tons. Power generation accounts for about 70% of India's total coal consumption, followed by steel and other industries. Despite the fact that Indian coal is generally of poor quality —i.e. low in calorific content and high in ash – and primarily located far from major consuming centres, Indian coal consumption is expected to increase to 510 million short tons (Mmst) by 2020, up 42% from 393 Mmst in 2002. South Asia's carbon emissions are expected to increase sharply in the coming years due to increased coal consumption.

Coal currently plays a relatively minor role in Pakistan's energy mix (5% in 2002), but the discovery of large volumes of low ash, low sulphur lignite in the Tharparkar Desert in the Sindh province is expected to have a positive impact on consumption levels by fuelling large electric power plants. Bangladesh and Sri Lanka have small coal reserves but currently consume almost no coal. Bangladesh began commercial coal production in April 2003 with the opening of the Barapukuria Coal Mine, in part to fuel a proposed coal-fired power plant to be developed with Chinese assistance. The project is to produce one million short tons of coal per year, principally for electricity generation. Another Coal mining project at Kalashpir is under consideration. Sri Lanka has also approved the development of its first coal-fired plant (300 MW) on its northern coast but plans to use imported coal for fuel.

Biomass (Non-Commercial Fuels)

South Asia continues to rely heavily on biomass (i.e. animal waste, wood, etc.) for residential energy consumption, particularly in rural areas. According to the International Energy Agency (IEA), biomass accounted for about 80% of residential energy consumption in 2000 and will account for 70% of total residential energy consumption by 2020. Because the primary end uses of biomass are cooking and heating, the expansion of electricity access, used primarily for lighting, is not expected to have a significant affect on biomass use in the near future.

Electricity

In 2002, South Asia generated 642 billion kilowatt hours (Bkwh) of electricity. Of this, around 81% was from conventional thermal power plants, 16% from hydroelectric plants, 3% from nuclear, and less than 1% from "other renewables" (like wind and solar). India accounts for the vast majority (85%) of the region's electricity generation, followed by Pakistan (11%), Bangladesh (3%), Sri Lanka (1%), Nepal, Bhutan and the Maldives (1% total). Regional electricity generation is expected to increase significantly in coming years. Natural gas is expected to displace some coal-fired generation in India, although have been delays in importing natural gas. The net level of coal-fired generation in South Asia is expected to rise. Non-hydroelectric "renewable" capacity (i.e., wind, solar, ocean, biomass, geothermal) is small at present, but it is increasing, with solar and wind power considered most promising.

Electricity demand in most of South Asia is currently outstripping supply, and the region is characterized by chronic shortages. The reasons for this situation include: shortfalls in generating capacity; low plant load factors due to aging generators and poor maintenance of equipment at existing plants; and losses of power due to poor-quality transmission lines and theft. South Asia's rapidly rising electricity demand has heightened the need for additional investment by independent power producers (IPPs). However, bureaucratic obstacles and regulatory policies have led to construction delays and foreign investor disillusionment. As a result, many large IPP projects in the region have been delayed or cancelled. Electricity rates are widely subsidized in South Asia, and state electricity boards are faced with the challenge of paying IPPs their asking price for power while providing lower rates to their customers. Electricity companies also lose a substantial percentage to theft. The IMF and the World Bank have encouraged liberalization of South Asian power sectors, including the reduction of subsides. Discussions have been underway for some time among South Asian nations to develop a regional electricity grid connecting India, Bhutan, Nepal and Bangladesh. Such a grid would lead to increased efficiencies and reduced power generation and transmission costs. Nepal and Bhutan have substantial untapped hydroelectricity potential that could be consumed domestically or exported to India, Pakistan, and Bangladesh.

India accounts for about four-fifths of the electricity generated in South Asia. In 2002, total generating capacity in India was 120 gigawatts (GW). India generates approximately 84% of its electricity from conventional thermal power plants, around 12% from hydroelectric plants (located mainly in the north and northeast of the country), and 3% from nuclear plants. India is facing serious power supply problems, with current generation being 30% below demand. Although 80% of India's population has access to electricity, power outages and brownouts are common. The International Energy Outlook projects more than a doubling of Indian power demand from 554 BkWh in 2001 to 1,216 BkWh in 2025.

The majority of power generated in India (approximately 55% in 2002) is fuelled by coal. Much of India's new generation is fuelled by natural gas, however, and the government has taken a long-term interest in expanding the country's hydropower capacity. The Indian government has a target of capacity additions of 1, 00,000 MW over the next 10 years. In June 2003, the government approved an electricity bill to eliminate controls on generation, transmission and distribution and reduce two major problems plaguing the sector: cross-subsidies and high accounts receivable. Many improvements occurring in the electricity sector are as a result of assistance from international organizations including the Asian Development Bank. The Indian government is committed to power sector reform. India has about 12,020 megawatts of hydroelectric capacity under construction, and letters of award have been issued for the 1,000-megawatt Tehri Pass project (scheduled for completion by 2012) and the 1,200-megawatt Kotlibhel-IA project.

In 2002, Pakistan had 18 GW of installed electric generating capacity. Thermal plants (oil, gas and coal) make up 70% of this capacity, with hydroelectricity constituting 28% and nuclear plants 2%. Pakistan currently maintains excess generation capacity, but because few of Pakistan's rural areas have access to electricity and less than half of the population is connected to the national grid, significant demand growth is expected in the long term. Rotating blackouts ("load shedding") are necessary in some areas, and transmission losses are approximately 30% due to poor infrastructure and significant power theft. Pakistan's total power generating capacity has increased in recent years, due largely to foreign investment in the mid-1990s, but payment problems have discouraged significant new investment. Recent power project developments include the 1,450-MW Ghazi Barotha hydropower project and an agreement with China to develop two 600-MW coal plants in the Sindh province by exploiting coal reserves in Tharparkar. A new hydro plant, the Kalabagh project, will supply 2,400 to 3,600 MW.

Bangladesh maintains 3.6 GW of electricity generation capacity. As a result, only around 18% of the population (25% in urban areas and 10% in rural areas) has access to electricity, and per capita commercial energy consumption is among the lowest in the world (4.0 million Btu). Power demand grew over 60% from 1991 to 2000. Bangladesh generates its electricity mainly at thermal power plants (93%), and some hydroelectric dams (7%).

Net electricity consumption in Sri Lanka doubled between 1992 and 2002. To satisfy the growing demand for electricity, the government secured a loan from the Asian Development Bank in 2002 to expand its electricity infrastructure. The government aims to provide electricity to 80% of the population by 2010. Sri Lanka relies on hydropower for most of its electricity, making it vulnerable to fluctuations in rainfall. In an effort to diversify, the Sri Lankan government is working to attract foreign investors to build independent thermal power plants. A 168-MW combined-cycle power project has been completed in the southern part of the nation.

Nepal relies almost exclusively on hydroelectricity to meet its power requirements, and at the end of 2002, its installed capacity was 400 MW. Nepal has large untapped hydroelectric potential (estimated at 43,000 MW), which could be developed to provide for the 60% of the population without electricity, as well as for export. In March 2002, the 144-MW Kaligandaki "A" hydroelectric dam began generating electricity. Australia's Snowy Mountains Hydro (SMEC) has assisted in the development of the 750-MW West Seti hydroelectric dam and will export power primarily to India. Renewable power sources are increasing in Nepal through rural electrification programs which aim to lessen the disparity in electricity access between rural (30%) and urban (90%) areas. The overall quality of Nepal's electricity infrastructure, however, is low.

Bhutan's hydropower potential is estimated at 30,000 MW. Hydropower is the dominant source of commercial energy for the country and sales of hydroelectricity exports to India provided 45% of the government's revenues and constituted an 11.6% share of GDP in 2001. India's Tata Power Company and the Power Grid Corporation of India Ltd. have constructed the 1, 20-MW Tala hydropower project in Bhutan and a 750-mile transmission line to export power produced by the Tala project to New Delhi and surrounding areas of India.

Energy Consumption and Carbon Dioxide Emissions in South Asian Countries

Commercial Energy Consumption #								
Country	**Total (Quadrillion Btu)**	**Petroleum**	**Natural Gas**	**Coal**	**Nuclear**	**Hydro-electric**	**Other@**	**Carbon Dioxide Emissions $ (Million metric tons of carbon)**
Bangladesh	0.57	31%	66%	1%	0%	2%	0%	8.8
Bhutan	0.02	13%	0%	7%	0%	80%	0%	0.08
India	13.99	32%	7%	55%	2%	5%	0%	279.9
Maldives	0.01	100%	0%	0%	0%	0%	0%	0.2
Nepal	0.06	55%	0%	15%	0%	31%	1%	0.8
Pakistan	1.83	43%	41%	5%	1%	10%	0%	29.6
Sri Lanka	0.19	82%	0%	0%	0%	17%	0%	3.1
Total	16.67	34%	12%	46%	1%	6%	0.3%	322.5

: Does NOT include such "non-commercial" energy sources as animal waster, wood, and other biomass, which account for more than half of South Asia's total final energy consumption.

@ : Other includes consumption of wind electric power for India and net imports of electricity for India and Nepal. Other does NOT include biomass or other "non-commercial" sources of energy.

$: Includes carbon dioxide emissions from the consumption of petroleum, natural gas, and coal, and from the flaring of natural gas. Tons of carbon can be converted to tons of carbon dioxide gas by multiplying by 3.667.

Note : percentages may not add to 100% because of independent rounding.

Source: Energy Information Administration, International Energy Database, October 2004.

Energy Supply Indicators – South Asia

	Fossil Fuel Proved Reserves			**Fossile Fuel Production**				
	Crude Oil (Million barrels)	**Dry Natural Gas, 1/1/04 (Trillion cubic feet)**	**Coal (Billion short tons)**	**Petroleum, (Thousand barrels per day)**	**Dry Natural Gas (Trillion cubic feet)**	**Coal (Million short tons)**	**Electric Generating Capacity (Million kilowatts)**	**Crude oil Refining capacity, (Thousand barrels per day)**
Bangladesh	56.0	10.6	0	5.0	.38	0	3.6	33
Bhutan	0	0	0	0	0	0.06	0.4	0
India	5,371.2	30.1	93.0	661.8	.88	392.6	120.3	2,135
Maldives	0	0	0	0	0	0.01	0.03	0
Nepal	0	0	0	0	0	0.01	0.4	0
Pakistan	288.7	26.8	2.5	60.9	.81	3.7	18.0	269
Sri Lanka	0	0	0	0	0	0	2.1	48
Total	5,715.9	67.5	95.5	727.7	2.07	396.4	144.8	2,485

Sources: Crude Oil and Natural Gas Reserves : Penn Well Publishing Co., Oil & Gas Journal, 12/22/03; Crude Oil Refining Capacity : Penn Well Publishing Co., Oil & Gas Journal, 12/22/03; All Other Data : Energy Information Administration, International Energy Database, October 2004.

Afghanistan

Afghanistan is an energy-deprived country. Almost half of the energy used in Afghanistan comes from firewood. Most of the rest comes from gas, oil, and hydroelectricity. There are dams and hydroelectric stations on the Kondoz, Kabul, Arghandab, and Helmand rivers. Three hydroelectric power dams provide base load power to Kabul: the 100-MW Naghlu dam, the 66-MW MahiPar dam, and the 22-MW Sarobi dam. Due to a lack of water flow on the Kabul River, only the Naghlu Dam, which has a sizable reservoir capacity, is operational all-year round to meet the needs of Kabul. The dams are located about 50 miles from Kabul and are linked by a 110-kV, double-circuit transmission line.

The energy sector of Afghanistan was poorly developed before its political problems began in 1980. Only 6% of the country's territory was electrified and only 9% of country's population could use electricity. Annual production of electric power per capita was less than 70 kW/h. In view of the absence of a strong energy sector, fuel resources, and also because of the scarcity of power engineering hydro resources, the focus at present is on power supply from the Central Asian republics to Afghanistan.

Turkmenistan supplies electricity to much of northwestern Afghanistan, including Mazar-i-Sharif and Herat. Uzbekistan also supplies electricity to the northern area around Mazar-i-Sharif, supplementing a small local gas-fired power plant. Tajikistan supplies electricity to the northern Afghanistan province of Kunduz. Iran also supplies electricity to Afghanistan, in some areas directly adjacent to the Afghan-Iranian border in Herat, Farah, and Nimroz provinces.

The estimated consumption of petroleum in Afghanistan is 5, 000 bbl/day. Petroleum products such as diesel, gasoline, and jet fuel are imported, mainly from Pakistan and Uzbekistan, with limited volumes from Turkmenistan and Iran serving regional markets. Turkmenistan also has a petroleum product storage and distribution facility at Tagtabazar (Kushka – on the Turkmen side) near the Afghan border, which supplies northwestern Afghanistan.

According to some studies, Afghanistan may be possessing up to 36 trillion cubic feet of natural gas, 3.6 billion barrels of petroleum and up to 1,325 million barrels of natural gas liquids. Northern Afghanistan has possible natural gas reserves of about 5 Tcf. This area, which is a southward extension of the highly prolific, natural gas-prone Amu Darya Basin, has the potential to hold a sizable undiscovered gas resource base. Afghanistan's crude oil potential is more modest, with perhaps up to 100 million barrels of medium-gravity recoverable from Angot and other fields that are undeveloped.

Besides oil and natural gas, Afghanistan also is estimated to have 73 million tons of coal reserves, most of which is located in the region between Herat and Badashkan in the northern part of the country. Although Afghanistan produced over 100,000 short tons of coal annually as late as the early 1990s, the country is producing only around 1,000 short tons.

In addition to commercial energy, Afghanistan utilizes such traditional, "non-commercial" energy sources as wood. According to a study, more than 85 percent of Afghanistan's energy needs are met by such traditional fuels, but this has led to serious deforestation in the country.

Afghanistan could become an important pipeline transit route. Due to its location between the oil and natural gas reserves of the Caspian Basin and the Indian Ocean, Afghanistan has long been considered a potential pipeline route. However, in the near term, there are several obstacles to building a pipeline across Afghanistan. Today, there are two pipeline projects that would connect Central Asian exporters and South Asian markets. One is a projected Iran-Pakistan-India line (IPI) and the other is a Turkmenistan-Afghanistan-Pakistan-India line (TAP).

The Afghan government has tried to revive the Trans-Afghan Pipeline (TAP) plan, with periodic talks held between the governments of Afghanistan, Pakistan, and Turkmenistan on the issue. The project could generate \$100-\$300 million per year in transit fees for Afghanistan, while creating thousands of jobs in the country. However, so far no major Western companies have expressed interest in building the project. The security situation in Afghanistan remains an obvious problem, while the difficulty in getting an agreement between India and Pakistan makes it hard to extend the pipeline into India and its large (and growing) gas market. The pipeline's \$2.5-\$3.5 billion estimated cost could be an obstacle to its construction. The TAP project, however, is promising. It envisions a 56-inch diameter pipeline, with a design capacity of 1.16 Tcf per year. The pipeline would start in Turkmenistan and run 1,043 miles through Afghanistan and Pakistan, terminating at Fazilka, in India. The feasibility study estimated a cost of \$3.3 billion. At this point, the TAP needs sponsors, if it is to move forward.

Analysis

India is expected to experience the fastest expansion in transportation sector energy use in the world. India's transportation energy use is projected to grow at an average rate of 3.3% per year compared with the world average of 1.7% per year. In comparison with other countries in the South Asia region, India's transportation infrastructure is well developed and used effectively by a large section of the population. Its railways are particularly established. India will continue to expand its public transportation networks, allowing robust increases in both road and rail transport and resulting in a more than doubling of transportation energy use between 2004 and 2030.

China and India account for the worlds largest projected increases in national electric power demand over the 2004 to 2030 period. China already is the world's largest coal consumer, and India is the third largest (after the United States). A sizable portion of the coal consumed in India is used for power generation. However, coal's share is projected to decline to 69% of the country's total power generation in 2030.

In India, consumption of petroleum liquids for electricity generation will remain modest, as relatively high world oil prices make other fuels economically more attractive. Some increases in oil use for electricity generation are projected for other countries in the region, because many rural areas that currently do not have access to transmission lines are expected to replace noncommercial energy sources with electricity from diesel-fired generators until transmission infrastructure can be put into place. Nevertheless, the liquids share of electricity generation in South Asia is projected to fall from 4% in 2004 to 2% in 2030.

South Asia is expected to lead the world in the installation of new nuclear capacity over the projection period, accounting for 51% of the projected net increment in nuclear capacity worldwide. India is projected to add 17 gigawatts of nuclear capacity by 2030. Strong growth in nuclear capacity in India will help improve fuel diversification in the power sector, although thermal generation will continue to dominate. In India, the nuclear share of total electricity generation is projected to rise from 2% in 2004 to 8% in 2030.

Although electricity generation from renewable energy sources is projected to grow at an average annual rate of 2.0%, the renewable share of total generation will decline if fossil fuels and nuclear power grow more strongly in the region. Much of the growth in South Asia's renewable energy consumption is projected to come from mid- to large-scale hydroelectric facilities. In India, for instance, about 12,020 megawatts of hydroelectric capacity is under construction, and letters of award have been issued for the 1,000-megawatt Tehri Pass project (scheduled for completion by 2012) and the 1,200-megawatt Kotlibhel-IA project.

As South Asia struggles to get out of low-growth equilibrium and achieves above 6% GDP growth rate, it is faced with one of the biggest challenges of meeting a higher demand for energy. As compared to the last two decades, when the energy consumption was 5.8% against low energy production of 2.3%, the demand for energy is growing at a rate of 9% annually, whereas the deficit in energy production has almost doubled in the last decade. Even though South Asia has the lowest per capita consumption of energy in the world (0.45 toe), it is going to have the highest rate of energy consumption by 2010 and beyond. While 60% (775.3 million) of its population remains without electricity and is dependent on biomass, the energy intensity (total energy divided by per unit of GDP) is 0.65 toe, as compared to the world average of 0.29 toe.

Higher rates of growth of economy, population and urbanisation in the South Asian region are resulting in higher consumption of energy well above the world average. Therefore, South Asia is faced with the multiple challenges of sustainable development: increasing energy demand, harnessing vast local natural resources, import substitution, making available cleaner and cheaper energy, developing an inter and intra-regional market and an energy grid while exploiting the economy of scale, reforming an inefficient power sector and attracting private investment, conserving natural resources and protecting environment. If South Asian economies are to grow at a higher rate and overcome poverty and backwardness, they will have to grapple with the energy crisis not only at their respective national levels, but also collectively at inter and intra-regional levels.

The South Asian countries have a great potential of energy and have complementary endowments on a contiguous landmass, which is a prerequisite to developing an integrated power infrastructure like power grids and gas pipelines. High levels of complementarities in energy sectors among the countries of the region allow varying comparative advantages: If India has an edge in producing coal-based energy; Pakistan and Bangladesh have the benefit of gas-based power generation, while Nepal and Bhutan are hydro-based. As opposed to trade, where compatibilities are few, these complementarities can be exploited to the mutual benefit of each other. The SAARC Summit envisaged an 'energy ring' and formed a working group to explore the possibilities of cooperation in the energy sector. A network of gas pipelines and power grid will enhance energy security in the region, reduce cost of fuel transportation and help in an optimal and efficient harnessing of energy resources. Although India is much ahead in the energy sector, it will still be depending heavily on external energy sources, especially from and through Nepal and Bangladesh, and Pakistan.

Located in close proximity to the Persian Gulf and Central Asia, South Asia can tremendously benefit from their immense resources of oil and gas. The natural gas supplied via pipelines by these countries would cost 35% less than the cost of liquid natural gas (LNG) in India and Pakistan. By 2010, according to estimates, the demand for gas in India and Pakistan would be 8 billion cubic feet per day and only a quarter of it could be met locally while the rest would have to be imported. Pakistan, besides meeting its own needs, can serve as the gateway for supplying natural gas from Iran, Persian Gulf and Central Asia to India and beyond.

Bangladesh has substantial reserves of gas, 22.9 trillion cubic feet, according to latest estimates, of which 16 tcf has been proven, whose greater utilisation would require huge investment in infrastructure for installations and transportation. Bangladesh can choose to export it to India — whose unmet demand would reach 60 bcm by 2010 - and Nepal. Besides developing gas-based domestic industries, Bangladesh can export 200 mcf gas to India and earn revenues worth US$ 400 million annually while substantially reducing its trade deficit with India.

While there is a huge potential for hydroelectricity in the Hindukush-Himalayan region, only 11% of it has so far been exploited; of this less than 1% in Nepal, 1.5% in Bhutan, 29% in India, and 13% in Pakistan could be tapped. Bhutan has the hydroelectric potential of 30,000 MW and Nepal has sites to produce 43,000 MW, mostly for export to India and Bangladesh. India will have to upgrade its transmission lines to reach West Bengal, Bihar and Uttar Pradesh and require a corridor through Bangladesh for such lines ensuring smooth and easy supply of Bhutanese power. The Indo-Bhutan collaboration in hydro-power is a successful model for others to emulate.

Collaboration in hydro-power seems difficult between India and Pakistan, although a large potential for joint projects exists, given the sharp differences over various dams being built by the upper riparian India in Jammu and Kashmir and Pakistan's serious objections on them under the Indus Water Treaty. Thermal power is the dominant source of energy in most of South Asia. It accounts for about 92% of the installed capacity in Bangladesh, 73% in India and 69% in Pakistan. India, Pakistan and Bangladesh can cooperate in thermal-based power generation.

India is experiencing accelerated economic growth. Annual growth rates of between 8% & 9% are driving the nation's increasing demand for energy. India is, therefore, concerned about existing and potential sources of supply for meeting its requirements on a sustained basis for which it faces formidable challenges. According to the Integrated Energy Policy document of the Government of India, the country would need to expand its current primary energy supply levels by 3-4 times and electricity generation by 5-6 times in the next 25 years in order to sustain the high growth levels required to attain our developmental goals and to eradicate poverty. Owing to the limited availability of oil and gas within India, 70% of its energy requirements are dependent on hydrocarbon imports and this import dependence is going to accentuate further in the coming years.

India is adopting proactive approaches for ensuring its energy security, particularly with reference to hydrocarbons, which account for nearly half of India's total energy needs. The task of investing in overseas energy assets for the country has, therefore, become an important aspect of India's economic diplomacy. Indian oil companies have concluded arrangements, including investment agreements, with many countries for the supply of oil and its derivatives to India and in most of the cases, delivery has begun. In addition, the possibility of bilateral cooperation in the downstream sectors, petrochemicals, non-conventional energy and joint ventures are also being constantly explored with various resource-rich countries.

The newly created Energy Security Unit in the Ministry of External Affairs shows the government's resolve to treat this as a matter of urgent national importance. India is keen to secure long term, cost effective and reliable modes of resource supply, as well as to explore the prospects of sourcing energy from the neighborhood and beyond. India is presently looking at an all-round effort wherein domestic exploration exercises are being intensified, coupled with greater emphasis on 'equity oil' from overseas. Indian companies are collaborating with international companies for greater sharing of technology and know-how leading to higher efficiency in operations, including adoption of advanced technology and professional management, as well as forays into tapping emerging areas like coal gasification, Coal Bed Methane (CBM), gas hydrates and other sources of energy. Greater consideration is also being given to efficient utilization of energy resources.

Exploration activity has been intensified and positive results have been forthcoming with important discoveries in the Krishna-Godavari Basin and the on-shore blocks in Rajasthan. India has re-doubled its efforts to attract investments to develop its energy sector, including power generation and oil refining, which are now open to private and foreign investment. Possibilities of cooperation on the non-conventional energy front are also being explored. An Agreement has been signed with Brazil for cooperation in bio-fuels and ethanol.

Like many developing countries, India is an energy deficient country. In 2006-07, India produced 662 billion units of electricity from all sources for a population of over a billion people. The per capita consumption of energy is 530 kgoe of primary energy compared to a world average of 1770 kgoe. India's per capita emission of CO_2 is among the lowest in the world: it is approximately 1 tonne per annum as against a world average of 4 tonnes per annum. Currently, developing countries bear an inordinate share of the burden of Climate Change, though this is due to the high-level of emissions of developed countries. Developing countries are, therefore, obliged to significantly augment their capacity to cope with and adapt to climate change.

World Oil Reserves by Country as of 1 January 2007 (Billion Barrels)

Country	Oil Reserves
Saudi Arabia	262.3
Canada	179.2
Iran	136.3
Iraq	115.0
Kuwait	101.5
United Arab Emirates	97.8
Venezuela	80.0
Russia	60.0
Libya	41.5
Nigeria	36.2
Kazakhstan	30.0
United States	21.8
China	16.0
Qatar	15.2
Mexico	12.4
Algeria	12.3
Brazil	11.8
Angola	8.0
Norway	7.8
Azerbaijan	7.0
Rest of World	65.5
World Total	1,317.4

Source: "Worldwide Look at Reserves and Production," Oil & Gas Journal, Vol. 104, No. 47 (December 18, 2006), pp. 24-25.

Energy cooperation in South Asia presents tremendous potential for the development of regional resources in an integrated manner by exploiting the comple-mentarities and optimal utilisation of available resources. Much will depend on how South Asia benefits from its proximity with south western and central Asia to meet its gas and oil needs. But the real issues are of political economy, both at inter- and intra-regional levels, further liberalisation and deregulation of an inefficient energy sector, attracting foreign investment and developing an integrated infrastructure of production, transmission and gas pipelines at a regional scale.

It may be relevant to mention the state of energy resources of the world to see South Asia, in comparison:

> Asia—led by China and India—is projected to be the region with the fastest growth in electric power generation worldwide, averaging 4.2% per year from 2004 to 2030. South Asia is expected to see continued robust economic growth, with corresponding increases in demand for electricity to power lighting, heating and cooling, household appliances.

World Natural Gas Reserves by Country as of January 1, 2007

Country	Reserves (Trillion Cubic Feet)	% of World Total
World	6,183	100.0
Top 20 Countries	5,602	90.6
Russia	1,680	27.2
Iran	974	15.8
Qatar	911	14.7
Saudi Arabia	240	3.9
United Arab Emirates	214	3.5
United States	204	3.3
Nigeria	182	2.9
Algeria	162	2.6
Venezuela	152	2.5
Iraq	112	1.8
Turkmenistan	100	1.6
Kazakhstan	100	1.6
Indonesia	98	1.6
Norway	82	1.3
China	80	1.3
Malaysia	75	1.2
Uzbekistan	65	1.1
Egypt	59	0.9
Canada	58	0.9
Kuwait	55	0.9
Rest of World	581	9.4

Source: "Worldwide Look at Reserves and Production," Oil & Gas Journal, Vol. 104, No. 47 (December 18, 2006), pp. 22-23.

FOURTEENTH SAARC SUMMIT

DECLARATION OF THE FOURTEENTH SAARC SUMMIT

The President of the Islamic Republic of Afghanistan, His Excellency Mr. Hamid Karzai; the Chief Adviser of the Government of the People's Republic of Bangladesh, His Excellency Dr. Fakhruddin Ahmed; the Prime Minister of the Kingdom of Bhutan, His Excellency Lyonpo Khandu Wangchuk; the Prime Minister of the Republic of India, His Excellency Dr. Manmohan Singh; the President of the Republic of Maldives, His Excellency Mr. Maumoon Abdul Gayoom; the Prime Minister of Nepal, Rt. Hon'ble Mr. Girija Prasad Koirala; the Prime Minister of the Islamic Republic of Pakistan, His Excellency Mr. Shaukat Aziz; and the President of the Democratic Socialist Republic of Sri Lanka, His Excellency Mr. Mahinda Rajapaksa, met at the Fourteenth Summit meeting of the South Asian Association for Regional Cooperation (SAARC) held in New Delhi, India on April 3-4, 2007.

2. The Heads of State or Government welcomed the entry of the Islamic Republic of Afghanistan into SAARC. This was a historic moment as Afghanistan assumed its rightful place as a valued member of the SAARC fraternity.

3. The Heads of State or Government reiterated their commitment to the principles and objectives enshrined in the SAARC Charter. With the welfare of the peoples of South Asia uppermost in their mind, they agreed to build a Partnership for Prosperity and work towards shared economic cooperation, regional prosperity, a better life for the people of South Asia, and equitable distribution of benefits and opportunities of integration among the peoples and the nations.

4. The Heads of State or Government recognised the importance of connectivity in fulfilling these objectives. It was vital to first have better connectivity within South Asia and then with the rest of the world. They agreed to improve intra-regional connectivity, particularly physical, economic and people-to-people connectivity. They agreed to the vision of a South Asian community, where there was smooth flow of goods, services, peoples, technologies, knowledge, capital, culture and ideas in the region. The SAARC Car Rally, in the run-up to the Fourteenth SAARC Summit, had vividly symbolized this connectivity.

5. The Heads of State or Government recognised that the remarkable growth of the economies of SAARC countries has opened new opportunities to pursue the fight against poverty with firm resolve. They called for deepening of pro-poor orientation of growth process, including through enhancing investment in human capital and infrastructure, increasing budgetary allocations for relevant sectors and improved delivery of services. They reiterated their commitment towards project-based cooperation to strengthen collective efforts in the region.

6. The Heads of State or Government acknowledged that there is a wide range of homegrown best practices and innovative solutions for transforming the lives of peoples in South Asia. They decided to earmark one rural community as SAARC Village in each Member State to showcase these innovative models of development in order to further replicate these across the region.

7. The Heads of State or Government recognised that the implementation of the Social Charter needs focused attention and directed the National Coordination Committees (NCCs) to formulate concrete programmes and projects to complement national implementation efforts. They underscored that civil society organizations have a vital role to play in driving forward the implementation of the Social Charter and directed the NCCs to mobilize civil society organizations to achieve this end.

8. The Heads of State or Government appreciated the Independent South Asian Commission on Poverty Alleviation (ISACPA) for its elaboration of the SAARC Development Goals (SDGs), which reflect the regional determination to make faster progress towards attaining the Millennium Development Goals (MDGs). They agreed that the national plans for poverty alleviation should appropriately mirror the regional consensus reached in the form of the SDGs and the Plan of Action on Poverty Alleviation. Deciding that resource mobilization for achieving the SDGs would remain a high priority in the Decade of Poverty Alleviation, the Leaders directed translation of the highest regional level political commitment into action for creating opportunities for productive employment and greater access to resources for the poor that are essential for them to enhance their livelihood and realize their potentials. They entrusted the Two-tier Mechanism on Poverty Alleviation to monitor the progress and fine-tune the approaches towards pro-poor growth process.

9. The Heads of State or Government recognized the full benefits of an integrated multimodal transport system in the region. They emphasized that this would not be realized unless physical infrastructure and matters relating to customs clearance and other facilitation measures, including multimodal transport operations, were addressed comprehensively. They called for an extension of the SAARC Regional Multimodal Transport Study (SRMTS) to include Afghanistan as well. They also called for early implementation of the recommendations contained in the Study in a phased manner. In this context, the Heads of State or Government directed the Inter-Governmental Group on Transport to identify and develop sub-regional and regional projects based on the prioritised recommendations of the SAARC Regional Multimodal Transport Study (SRMTS) and to develop appropriate regional agreements. They noted the offer of India to hold the Meeting of SAARC Ministers of Transport in New Delhi in 2007. They also directed that pilot projects for improving connectivity be identified and implemented through mutual consultations among the Member States.

10. The Heads of State or Government emphasized that in its third decade of existence, there was an urgent need to move SAARC from declaratory to implementation phase. They directed that the focus of SAARC should be on implementing collaborative projects that are concrete and effective. The SAARC Development Fund (SDF) is an important pillar that would bring concrete benefits to the people of the region. They directed that the SDF be made operational at the earliest. They agreed that the resources for SDF would be mobilised both from within and outside the region. They stressed the importance of decision making and working of the SDF being consistent with the SAARC Charter. They called for early identification and implementation of regional and sub-regional projects under the SDF.

11. The Heads of States or Governments recognized the region's rapidly increasing energy demands for meeting the developmental needs of SAARC countries. They also acknowledged the need of expediting development of conventional sources of energy in a sustainable manner and for strengthening renewable energy development such as in hydro-power, bio-fuel, solar and wind. They welcomed the organizing of the first ever South Asia Energy Dialogue in March 2007 in Delhi. They called for early implementation of the recommendations of the Second SAARC Energy Ministers' Meeting to enhance regional cooperation.

12. The Heads of State or Government reiterated their deep concern at the continued degradation of environment and reaffirmed the need to further strengthen cooperation towards protection and conservation of the environment as a priority area. In this regard, while noting the progress in the implementation of the SAARC Plan of Action on Environment, they called for concerted efforts to implement various initiatives under the Plan in a timely manner.

13. The Heads of State or Government expressed satisfaction at the launching of 2007 as the 'Year of Green South Asia'. They reiterated that collaboration in addressing the problem of arsenic contamination of groundwater, desertification and melting of glaciers and assistance to affected peoples should be deepened. They expressed deep concern over global climate change and the consequent rise in sea level and its impact on the lives and livelihoods in the region. They emphasised the need for assessing and managing its risks and impacts. They called for adaptation of initiatives and programmes; cooperation in early forecasting, warning and monitoring; and sharing of knowledge on consequences of climate change for pursuing a climate resilient development in South Asia. They agreed to commission a team of regional experts to identify collective actions in this regard.

14. The Heads of State or Government stressed the need for closer regional cooperation in the field of information and communication technology. They noted with appreciation the establishment of a collaborative health care project involving a regional telemedicine-network. They directed that steps be taken to extend it to other ICT enabled fields such as education. They agreed to take steps to facilitate rationalization of telecom tariff on a reciprocal basis. They also agreed that national and regional telecom infrastructure should be upgraded to boost people-to-people connectivity in the region.

15. The Heads of State or Government noted with satisfaction timely ratification of SAFTA Agreement by all member countries. They stressed the need for ensuring effective market access through smooth implementation of trade liberalization programme and directed the SAFTA bodies to review the progress on a regular basis. They emphasized that SAFTA should be implemented in letter and spirit. Successful implementation of SAFTA will catalyse other areas of regional economic cooperation. They stressed that to realize its full potential, SAFTA should integrate trade in services. They called for a finalisation of an

Agreement in the services sector at the earliest. They also directed that the Agreement on Investment Promotion and Protection be finalized.

16. The Heads of State or Government underlined the importance of implementing trade facilitation measures, especially standardization of basic customs nomenclature, documentation and clearing procedures. They directed that a comprehensive agreement on harmonizing customs procedures be finalised. They also noted that harmonization of technical and phyto-sanitary standards and their implementation in a trade-friendly manner is important in boosting intra-regional trade. They appreciated the establishment of the SAARC Standards Coordination Board that would function as a precursor to the SAARC Regional Standards Body.

17. The Heads of State or Government complimented the SAARC Finance Ministers for finalising the framework of cooperation on financial issues in the region. They expressed satisfaction at the work of the Inter-Governmental Expert Group on Financial Issues.

18. The Heads of State or Government emphasized the need to develop, at an early date, a roadmap for a South Asian Customs Union and a South Asian Economic Union in a planned and phased manner.

19. The Heads of State or Government noted the cultural and social ties among the SAARC countries, based on common history and geography, and reiterated that the future of peoples of South Asia is interlinked. They stressed the importance of people-to-people contact as a key constituent in regional connectivity. They acknowledged the importance of intra-regional tourism and increased exchanges, particularly among the youth, civil society, and parliamentarians. They launched the SAARC Agenda for Culture and directed that annual SAARC Festivals for cultural exchange be institutionalized. They agreed to take measures to charge nationals of SAARC Member States fees for entry into archeological and heritage sites as applicable to their own nationals. They also directed that an enlarged SAARC Scholarship Scheme in ICT and related areas be instituted. They welcomed the offer of Bangladesh to host the First SAARC Youth Camp in 2007.

20. The Heads of State or Government decided to establish the South Asian University in India. They welcomed the signing of the Intergovernmental Agreement establishing the University. They further directed that the Intergovernmental Steering Committee be set up at the earliest to complete its tasks relating to the Charter, bye laws, rules and regulations, curriculum development, business plans and other issues. They also decided to strengthen cooperation and dialogue on educational matters through development of exchanges between academics, experts, policymakers, students and teachers. They called for inter-institutional cooperation, partnerships, and other regional initiatives in the field of education.

21. The Heads of State or Government acknowledged that women's full participation in all spheres of society, including participation in the decision-making process are fundamental for the achievement of equality and development. They noted that many sections of women and children continue to be in disadvantaged positions and lack equal opportunities for economic and social development. They emphasized that women's empowerment should be a major objective of regional cooperation. Regional projects should focus on addressing issues relating to women and children.

22. The Heads of State or Government stressed the need to collectively overcome the challenges of poverty, disease, natural disasters and terrorism. They confirmed that countries of South Asia must work together to deal with these challenges in order to secure the region's collective prosperity.

23. The Heads of State or Government acknowledged that countries of South Asia face challenges of food insecurity and malnutrition. In order to manage emergencies caused by natural and manmade calamities and food shortages, they welcomed the signing of the Intergovernmental Agreement establishing the SAARC Food Bank with the participation of all the SAARC countries. The Food Bank will supplement national efforts to provide food security to the people of the region.

24. The Heads of State or Government noted the challenges confronted by the countries of South Asia in ensuring food and nutritional security as well as in maintaining vibrant rural economy for agricultural development. They underscored the need for enhancing productivity and real wage in rural sectors, and for creating adequate non-farm employment to sustain the progress made in reducing poverty. Noting the constant decline in land availability and biodiversity, depleting soil and natural resources, lowering ground water levels, shrinking farm holdings as well as low and stagnating productivity, they recognized the imperative of reducing the wide gap between yields at the research and the farm level. They stressed, in particular, that

South Asian agriculture must benefit from collaborative efforts within and among SAARC countries in developing an effective agriculture research, extension and farmers' linkages, and exchange of farm technology.

25. The Heads of State or Government underlined that terrorism is a threat to peace and security in the region. They condemned the targeted killing of civilians and terrorist violence, in all its forms and manifestations, wherever and against whomsoever committed. The Heads of States or Government affirmed that terrorism violates the principles of the Charters of the United Nations and SAARC and is a clear and present threat to international peace and security. They reaffirmed their commitment to implement all international conventions relating to combating terrorism, to which SAARC Member States were respectively parties, as well as the SAARC Regional Convention on Suppression of Terrorism and the Additional Protocol to the SAARC Regional Convention dealing with the prevention and suppression of financing of terrorism. While urging continued efforts to combat terrorism, the Heads of State or Government also called for urgent conclusion of a Comprehensive Convention on International Terrorism.

26. The Heads of State or Government agreed to work on the modalities to implement the provisions of the existing SAARC Conventions to combat terrorism, narcotics and psychotropic substances, trafficking in women and children and other trans-national crimes. They expressed their commitment to take every possible measure to prevent and suppress, in particular, financing of terrorist acts by criminalizing the provision, acquisition and collection of funds for such acts, including through front organizations and also to counter illicit trafficking of narcotic drugs, trafficking in persons and illicit arms. They reiterated the need for law enforcement authorities of Member States to enhance cooperation in the prevention, suppression and prosecution of offences under these Instruments. They noted the initiative of India to prepare a draft of SAARC Convention on Mutual Assistance in Criminal Matters and welcomed the offer of Sri Lanka to hold a meeting of Legal Advisers to examine the idea of a draft convention, before the Second Meeting of SAARC Interior/Home Ministers scheduled to be held in October 2007 in India. They also directed them to ensure regular follow-up and implementation of the decisions taken.

27. The Heads of State or Government recognised that corruption was an issue of serious concern and agreed to exchange information on national experience in combating corruption to effectively address this problem.

28. The Heads of State or Government reaffirmed their commitment to a rule-based multilateral trading system. They recalled that the Doha Round was premised on the centrality of development. They directed the Commerce Ministers to work closely to co-ordinate their positions to ensure that the centrality of the development dimension in all areas of negotiations for creating new opportunities and economic growth for developing countries was fully realized. They called upon all members of WTO to show commitment for a successful conclusion of the Doha Round.

29. The Heads of State or Government welcomed the People's Republic of China, Japan, European Union, Republic of Korea and the United States of America, to be associated as Observers to SAARC. The region would benefit from these external linkages and help its economic integration with the international community. The Heads of State or Government also welcomed the Islamic Republic of Iran to be associated as Observer to SAARC.

30. The Heads of State or Government welcomed with appreciation the offer of the Maldives to host the 15th Summit Meeting of the Heads of States or Governments of the South Asian Association for the Regional Cooperation (SAARC).

SOUTH ASIA TERRORISM REPORT

SOUTH ASIA TERRORISM REPORT

Terrorism is premeditated, politically motivated violence perpetrated against noncombatant targets by sub national groups or clandestine agents, usually intended to influence an audience. (*US definition*). This overview outlines the status of terrorist-related activity in South Asia during the year 2007, with special emphasis on Pakistan.

Afghanistan

Afghanistan continues its attempt at building a stable and democratic government, despite a strong Taliban offensive and an increase in suicide bombings and attacks on soft targets throughout the country. Coalition Forces continue to conduct counterinsurgency operations, focusing on the south and east and carrying out reconstruction and development.

The Afghan National Army (ANA), with more than 31,000 personnel trained and equipped, and to a lesser extent the Afghan National Police (ANP), with 61,500 trained and equipped, are functional, mainly in and around Kabul.

The Taliban-led insurgency is a threat to stability, particularly in the Pashtun south and east. It's fighting ability, funding and recruitment into its ranks from its core base of rural Pashtuns is a dangerous factor. Taliban financing from various sources, including collusion with narco-traffickers responsible for 92% of the world's opium supply, as well as safe haven in the Federally Administered Tribal Areas (FATA) across the border in Pakistan, have allowed the insurgency to strengthen its capabilities.

The past year has witnessed an increasing number of violent incidents. More than 1,400 civilians were killed in terrorist attacks during the year. The use of IEDs and suicide bombings has increased. Insurgents have increasingly targeted politicians, NGOs, women's affairs officials, and ministry buildings and officials. The frequency of attacks on coalition forces in southern and eastern Afghanistan increased and resurgent Taliban and Al Qaeda forces present a serious threat to Afghan reconstruction efforts. A major spike in Afghan opium production has spurred acute concern that Afghanistan may soon become a "narco-state," and that terrorist groups and their supporters in both Afghanistan and Pakistan may reap huge profits from the processing and trafficking of heroin.

Pakistan

Pakistan remains a major source of Islamic extremism and a safe haven for terrorist leaders. It has experienced attacks from Al Qaeda and its supporters, as well as violence stemming from Sunni-Shia sectarian strife and militant sub-nationalists. Frequent attacks have occurred in the regions bordering Afghanistan: Balochistan, the North West Frontier Province (NWFP), and the adjacent FATA. Despite having approximately 80,000 troops in the FATA, including Army and Frontier Corps (FC) units, the Government of Pakistan has been unable to exert control over vast swathes of its territory.

Recognizing that military operations alone would not restore security and stability to the FATA, the government tried to put in place plans to accelerate economic and social development, strengthen political administration and enhance security in the region. This venture has not made any headway.

Armed conflict between the national government and militant Baloch nationalists escalated. They have continued, even after the 26 August 2006 death of Nawab Akbar Khan Bugti during a raid by security forces on his mountain hideout. The "Balochistan Liberation Army" (BLA) has carried out dozens of terror attacks on government offices and economic infrastructure in the province, as well as in neighbouring Sindh and Punjab.

Sectarian violence, a scourge in Pakistan for more than two decades, claimed hundreds of lives during the past year. The government's crackdown on banned organizations, hate material, and incitement by religious leaders continued unevenly. Madrassa registration, foreign student enrollment in madrassas, and financial disclosure requirements remained a source of friction between government and religious leaders.

Al Qaeda forces remain active on Pakistani territory, and have links with indigenous Pakistani terrorist groups that support separatist militancy in Indian Kashmir. Pakistan's ethnic Pashtun population largely sympathizes with the Taliban and Al Qaeda. Osama bin Laden, Egyptian Islamic radical leader Ayman al-Zawahiri, and Taliban chief Mohammed Omar are suspected to be in FATA.

Pakistan experienced its first Islamist terrorist suicide attack on 22 March 2002. Till the end of 2006, there were a total of 22 suicide attacks in the country. In 2007 (till 10 November) there have already been 44 suicide attacks. The fidayeen have ceaselessly targeted Army convoys and check-posts, police stations and training units, government officials, restaurants and mosques.

Militant violence across the country has assumed staggering proportions. At least 2,467 people, including 949 civilians, 467 security force personnel and 1,051 terrorists, have been killed in 2007 (till November 10). This adds to the 1,471 persons, including 608 civilians and 325 security force personnel, who died in terrorism/insurgency-related violence in Pakistan during year 2006. Crucially, the 2006 level already reflected well over a doubling in fatalities since 2005, when a total of 648 persons (including 430 civilians and 81 SF personnel) were killed in insurgent and terrorist conflicts.

The Army's failure to dominate the Federally Administered Tribal Areas (FATA), and particularly Waziristan, is now well known. But as President Pervez Musharraf struggles to contain the consequences of his ill-advised 'second coup', events in the North West Frontier Province (NWFP) show signs of hurtling entirely out of control, providing disturbing indices of the magnitude of Pakistan's slide into anarchy. The NWFP is spread over an area of 74,521 square kilometres, with 24 districts and a population of 17.7 million.

The appellation of 'failed' or 'failing state' has been repeated about Pakistan frequently. It has been reinforced after General Pervez Musharraf's 'second coup' on 3 November 2007, when the Supreme Court was overrun by troops and its Chief Justice dismissed forthright. It is significant that the US Central Command Chief, Admiral William Fallon, was in Islamabad at the time of the declaration of the Emergency. It suggests that there was clear prior or subsequent US approval of Musharraf's initiative. Generals enforcing a coup normally suspend the Constitution to remove from power unpopular rulers, usually weakened civilians. This is the first time an unpopular military ruler has suspended the Constitution to save his own position.

Al Qaeda, the Taliban, and Pakistani Extremism. Al Qaeda members are identified as Arabs or other non-Afghans who are fighting an international jihad. Taliban members are ethnic Pashtun Afghans who are fighting for Islamic rule in Kabul. Since the Taliban's ouster from power in Kabul and their retreat to the rugged mountainous region near the Afghanistan-Pakistan border, they have been able to regroup and conduct limited military operations. There are increasing links between Al Qaeda and Pakistani intelligence agents, weapons experts, and militant leaders. Since the time that Islamabad was actively supporting the Afghan Taliban regime it had helped to create, Pakistan's powerful Inter-Services Intelligence (ISI) agency has provided shelter to Al Qaeda members in both Pakistan and Kashmir and known Islamic extremists remain active on Pakistani territory.

Local Taliban are in effective control of most of Waziristan. Islamabad has been trying since 2002 to evict or neutralise the foreign militants there. Despite the deployment of an estimated 80,000 troops along the Afghan border in the FATA, the situation is far from stable in the region. The pro-Taliban militants have ensured the closure of girls' schools, bombed shops selling video cassettes and music CDs and prohibited barbers from shaving beards. They have established kangaroo courts for settling disputes and are arresting 'criminals' and parading and punishing them in the streets. While there is a considerable spill-over of militancy from the tribal areas to the settled areas of NWFP, the fact is that the state has itself ceded space for radical Islam. The 'peace deal' signed in Waziristan between the militants and the military regime further emboldened Islamist radicals and militants now operate openly and without fear. The NWFP has emerged as a safe haven for militants from Waziristan, which they already dominate, as well as extremist elements from other parts of Pakistan and Afghanistan.

Indigenous Pakistani Terrorist Groups. In a landmark speech, in January 2002 President Musharraf vowed to end Pakistan's use as a base for terrorism, and he criticized religious extremism and intolerance in the country. However, Pakistan continues to be a base for numerous indigenous terrorist organizations. Despite a ban on Lashkar-e-Taiba (LeT), Jaish-e-Mohammed (JeM), and Sipah-e-Sahaba Pakistan (SSP), they continue to operate under new names: LeT became Jamaat al-Dawat; JeM became Khudam-ul Islam. These groups have links to individuals and organizations actively fighting in Afghanistan and Pakistan, as well as with groups that pursue a violent separatist campaign in Kashmir.

Following Al Qaeda's relocation of its elements in Pakistani cities such as Karachi and Peshawar, some

Al Qaeda activists have joined forces with indigenous Pakistani Sunni militant groups, including LeT, JeM, SSP, and Lashkar-i-Jhangvi (LJ), an offshoot of the SSP. A November 2003 cease-fire agreement between Pakistan and India holds and appears to have contributed to a decrease in the number of terrorist infiltrations into Kashmir. However, separatist militants have vowed to continue their struggle regardless of the status of the Pakistan-India dialogue.

Musharraf's efforts to crack down on outlawed groups, along with a perceived softening of Kashmir policies, has fueled outrage among radical Islamists already angered by Pakistan's September 2001 policy reversal, when Musharraf cut ties with the Afghan Taliban regime and facilitated US-led anti-terrorism operations in the region. A 14 December 2003 remote-controlled bombing attempt on Musharraf's motorcade and dual suicide car bomb attacks on his convoy 11 days later were blamed mainly on JeM operatives. It is considered likely that future assassination attempts will occur.

Madrassas and Pakistan Islamists. The Taliban movement began among students attending Pakistani religious schools. Among the 10,000-20,000 madrassas in Pakistan, with an approximate enrolment of 1.5 million students, are some that are implicated in teaching militant anti-Western and anti-Hindu values. Many of them are financed and operated by Pakistani Islamist political parties such as Jamaat-e-Ulema Islam (JUI, closely linked to the Taliban), as well as by foreign entities. There is little evidence of any crack down on the more extremist madrassas. There are doubts about Islamabad's commitment to concerns in the vast "lawless zones" of the Afghan-Pakistani border region where Islamic extremists find shelter. In August 2003, at least three Pakistani army officers, including a lieutenant colonel, were arrested on suspicion of having ties to Islamic extremists.

The Muttahida Majlis-e-Amal (MMA), a coalition of six Islamist opposition parties, holds about 20% of Pakistan's National Assembly seats, while also controlling the provincial assembly in the NWFP and leading a coalition in the provincial assembly of Balochistan. Pakistan's Islamists denounce military operations in tribal areas, resist governmental attempts to reform religious schools that teach militancy, and harshly criticize any cooperation with the US and any move toward rapprochement with India. The leadership of the MMA's two main constituents — the Jamaat-i-Islami and the Jamiat-Ulema-Islami-Fazlur, have called for "jihad" against what they view as the existential threat to Pakistani sovereignty. The networks and support structures of Islamist extremism in Pakistan, painstakingly constructed through the Pakistan-Afghanistan arc, have little interest in engaging with Musharraf's 'enlightened moderation'.

Military Operations. Since 15 July 2007, when the Pakistani Taliban unilaterally terminated the 10-month old truce with the military regime, there has been a welter of violence in the tribal areas. In North Waziristan, military convoys are being attacked on a regular basis with sophisticated explosive devices. There are widespread reports of demoralisation, desertions and the refusal by 'outside' (particularly Punjabi) regiments of the Army to serve in Waziristan and the NWFP, and a number of surrenders by Government forces – Army, Police and Paramilitary – to small Taliban contingents, that indicate a growing unwillingness, ideological conflict and ethnic polarisation within the Pakistan Army. On 1 November 2007, the Taliban paraded 50 'captured' paramilitary troops in the Swat Valley. On 3 November, the militants confirmed another 100 military personnel had been 'captured' in the same area. These 'captures' were, in fact, desertions or willing surrenders, with not a shot exchanged. On 4 November, the militants in South Waziristan freed 211 soldiers, including a Lieutenant Colonel and a Major – who had been 'captured' without firing a shot on August 30 – in an exchange deal against the release of 28 militants from Government custody.

There have been reports of 160 cases of desertion by soldiers in the NWFP and FATA between 11-16 October. Military operations against the Taliban-al Qaeda forces in NWFP and FATA have inflicted high costs on the Government troops, with a low kill ratio of 1:1.37. The Pakistan Army's capabilities are being challenged by jihadis seeking a wider space in the country's disordered political structure. Any intensification of the military operations against the Islamists in Pakistan will push the Army to the knife-edge, pitting traditional loyalties and religious fervour against an ebbing professionalism, with potentially catastrophic consequences for the power structure in the country. Pakistan's future remains wedded to chaos. Support for the 'there is no alternative' theory, being extended to the military regime will become progressively unsustainable. Large tracts of Pakistan are now clearly violence-afflicted with a wide array of anti-state actors engaging in varying degrees of armed activity and subversion.

Balochistan. The Balochistan province accounts for approximately 44% of Pakistan's landmass. It is afflicted by insurgency alongwith parts of North and South Waziristan in FATA, another 3% of the country's total land area. Gilgit-Baltistan has long been simmering, and it is only the repeated cycles of repression and state-backed Sunni violence that have kept the restive population in check in a region that accounts for another 8% of the country. Thus, at least 55% of Pakistani territory is outside the realm of civil governance. Most of the violence in Balochistan is, however, 'nationalist' and there is no co-operation between Islamist terrorists in pockets in the North and the Baloch insurgents. While the violence level in Balochistan has decreased after the assassination of Nawab Akbar Khan Bugti, the insurgency continues to simmer and there have been bomb and rocket attacks on gas pipelines, railway tracks, power transmission lines, bridges, and communications infrastructure, military establishments and governmental facilities. Currently, all 27 districts of Balochistan are affected either by a sub-nationalist tribal insurgency or, separately, by Islamist extremism.

Major Terrorist Incidents. Some of the major terrorism/militancy related incidents of 2007 in Pakistan include:

January 16:	Pakistan Army helicopter gun-ships attacked a suspected militant hideout at Salamat village in South Waziristan, killing at least 20 militants.
January 22:	A suicide bomber rammed his explosives-laden car into a military convoy near Mirali in North Waziristan, killing four SF personnel and a woman, and injuring 23 persons.
January 26:	A suicide bomber blew himself up outside Hotel Marriott in Islamabad, killing a guard and wounding five persons. The suicide bombing occurred hours before a Republic Day function at the hotel hosted by India's High Commission.
January 27:	Fifteen people, including six police officials, were killed and 60 others injured in a suicide attack targeting a Muharram procession near Qasim Ali Khan Mosque in Peshawar. The Peshawar police commissioner, a Deputy Superintendent of Police, three other police personnel and a Nazim (local official) were among those killed.
January 29:	A suicide bomber killed two people at Dera Ismail Khan in NWFP. The suicide bomber, wearing a black shawl, blew himself up as the police was searching him.
February 3:	A suicide bomber drove his explosives-laden jeep into a military convoy, killing two soldiers and injuring seven others in the Barakhel area of Tank district in NWFP.
February 6:	A suicide attacker blew himself up in the car park of Islamabad airport, killing himself and injuring 10 people.
February 17:	Seventeen people, including a senior civil judge, were killed and 30 others injured in a suicide bombing in the District Courts of Quetta, capital of Balochistan.
February 20:	An Islamist 'fanatic' shot dead the Social Welfare Minister of Punjab province, Zile Huma Usman, in an open court in her hometown of Gujranwala.
March 6-7:	19 people died and several others were wounded during a clash between the Wazir Zalikhel sub-tribe and foreign militants near Azam Warsak in South Waziristan.
March 19-22:	160 people, including 130 foreign militants, were killed in four days of fighting between al Qaeda-linked militants and pro-Government tribesmen in South Waziristan.
March 21:	Five Frontier Corps personnel were killed and four injured when insurgents ambushed their vehicle in the Bramcha area of the Chagai District in Balochistan.
March 26:	A police officer and two attackers were killed; and13 persons injured when suspected militants attacked a police station, an Armoured Personnel Carrier and Frontier Corps fort with hand grenades in Tank city.
March 28:	25 Taliban militants and a soldier were killed in a gun-battle that continued for six-hours at Tank in the NWFP, when more than 200 Taliban cadres attacked the city from all sides. Two police stations, a paramilitary fort and several banks were looted in the attack. Curfew was imposed in the city and the civil administration asked the Army for help in preventing the Taliban from taking control of the city.
March 30:	Pro-government tribesmen exchanged heavy rocket and mortar fire with foreign militants linked to the al Qaeda in South Waziristan, leaving 56 people dead. Interior Minister Aftab Sherpao claimed that the dead included 45 foreigners.
April 4:	Approximately 50 persons were killed during clashes between pro-government tribesmen and foreign militants in South Waziristan. A tribal army led by Maulana Nazir, a pro-government Taliban commander, captured the strategic Sheen Warsak after an encounter in which 19 Uzbeks, five tribesmen and three paramilitary soldiers were killed. In a separate encounter in Zaghunday, north of Sheen Warsak, the tribal army killed 25 Uzbeks.

April 6: Pro-government tribesmen overran strategic bunkers occupied by the Uzbek-led foreign al Qaeda militants in South Waziristan, killing at least 20 people.

April 6-11: 113 people died in sectarian clashes between Sunni and Shia combatants in the Kurram Agency of FATA.

April 28: 31 people, including five police personnel, were killed and Federal Interior Minister Sherpao and his son Sikandar Sherpao Khan were among several people wounded in a suicide attack, moments after the minister finished a speech at a public rally in his hometown Charsadda in NWFP.

May 15: 25 people were killed and at least 35 others were injured when a suicide bomber blew himself up on the ground floor of the Marhaba Hotel in Peshawar, capital of the NWFP. A majority of those dead were Afghans.

May 30: Militants from South Waziristan attacked the house the Khyber Tribal Region's Political Agent, with rocket-propelled grenades, hand grenades and assault rifles, after midnight and shot dead 13 people, including two women.

June 14: 8 soldiers, a police constable and a passer-by were killed when some unidentified armed men attacked a van on the Zarghoon road in Quetta, capital of Balochistan. The victims were going to the Quetta Staff College from the railway station in a hired vehicle after arriving in the city by Chiltan Express.

June 19: 34 people were killed when a missile hit a cluster of compounds in the Datakhel area of North Waziristan.

July 3: The Lal Masjid – Jamia Hafsa crisis, which had been six months in the making, finally erupted, when militant students tried to grab property near the mosque and were confronted by the Security Forces. An armed engagement followed, and subsequent Army operations resulted. Abdul Rashid Ghazi, deputy chief cleric of the Lal Masjid died when Pakistan Army commandos stormed the mosque compound after a weeklong standoff. 91 civilians and 11 soldiers lost their lives in the operation, including a Lieutenant Colonel of the Special Services Group. 248 people sustained injuries in the operation.

July 6: President Pervez Musharraf's plane was shot at when it was taking off from the military airfield at Chaklala in Rawalpindi. A machine gun and two artillery weapons were subsequently recovered from the roof of a house nearby, though officials initially denied there had been an assassination attempt.

July 8: Three Chinese men were shot dead and a fourth critically wounded , in Peshawar where the victims had set up a small unit to manufacture three-wheel auto rickshaws.

July 15: In apparent revenge attacks by militants for the Lal Masjid operation at least 13 SF personnel and six civilians, including three children, were killed and more than 50 people sustained injuries at Matta in the Swat district when two suicide bombers rammed two cars packed with explosives into an army convoy. A suicide bomber blew himself up at the Dera Ismail Khan Police Lines as candidates took the Police entrance exams and 26 people were killed, including 12 police personnel and the suicide bomber, and 61 others were wounded.

July 15: Tribal militants in North Waziristan unilaterally scrapped their 10-month-old peace accord with the Government and threatened to launch attacks against the security forces in the area.

July 17: A suicide bomber struck outside the venue of a lawyers rally in Islamabad on, 2007, killing 16 people and wounding at least 63.

July 19: 15 persons were killed and several people sustained injuries when a suicide bomber blew himself up at a mosque in the Kohat Cantonment area of NWFP. Most of the victims were reportedly Army personnel. Separately, five civilians and two policemen were killed and 35 others injured when a suicide bomber set off his explosives-packed car at the Hangu Police Training College.

July 19: 22 civilians and seven police officers were killed and around 50 people wounded in a suicide car bomb attack at the Gadani Bus Stop in the industrial town of Hub in Balochistan

July 23: A military statement mentioned heavy fighting killed at least 35 militants and two soldiers in North Waziristan.

July 24: Abdullah Mehsud blew himself up to avoid arrest after he was surrounded by security forces in a house at Zhob in Balochistan.

July 27: 15 people, including eight police personnel, were killed and 53 others wounded, when a suicide bomber struck a group of police personnel in a restaurant following a clash between the Lal Masjid (Red Mosque) activists and the police after Friday prayers in Islamabad.

August 4: Nine persons were killed and 43 others wounded when a suicide car bomber triggered an explosion at a busy bus stop of Parachinar city in the Kurram Agency of FATA.

August 9: At least 15 people were reported to have died after the Army's helicopter gun-ships attacked the Degan village in North Waziristan in the evening of, following a roadside bomb blast which left four soldiers injured.

August 17-18: 32 persons, including 19 militants and 12 soldiers, were killed in clashes in the Chagmalai, Spla Toi, Tanga, Berwand, Maulvi Khan Sarai and Zawar areas of South Waziristan.

August 19: 15 militants were killed during military operations that targeted militant hideouts near Mir Ali town in North Waziristan.

August 20: Six soldiers died and 18 persons were injured on, when a suicide bomber rammed an explosives-laden car into a checkpoint on Kurram Road in the Hangu District.

August 24: Seven soldiers were killed and 12 others wounded in North Waziristan in two suicide bombings targeting the same Pakistan Army convoy at two different places.

August 26: Four police personnel were killed and two others wounded in a suicide attack on a police van in the mountainous Shangla District NWFP.

August 30: Militants in South Waziristan abducted around 150 Pakistan Army personnel and shifted them to their hideouts in the mountains. They reportedly laid siege to two Pakistan Army convoys which were on their way from Wana and Shakai to Ladha subdivision. Both the convoys comprised 16 vehicles in which around 150 soldiers were traveling. The militants accused the soldiers of violating the peace accord signed between the Government and Taliban on 9 February 2005, under which security forces were to have withdrawn from the areas inhabited by the Mahsud tribesmen.

September 4: 30 people were killed and 70 others wounded in two suicide attacks at Qasim Market and RA Bazaar in the garrison city of Rawalpindi. The first suicide bomber targeted a bus that was carrying about 35 defence employees to their office near the Qasim Market, killing at least 20 people. Soon after, another blast occurred near the RA Bazaar police station, killing 10 more people.

September 10: Prime Minister Nawaz Sharif was arrested and deported to Saudi Arabia, four-and-a-half hours after he arrived in Islamabad

September 11: 19 people were killed and 15 wounded when a teenage suicide bomber blew himself up near a thickly-populated area of Bannu Choongi in the Dera Ismail Khan district of NWFP.

September 13: 20 persons killed in a bomb blast in a high-security military area in Tarbela Ghazi near Islamabad. The bomb exploded in the mess of Karar Company of the Special Services Group.

September 13: Taliban militants attacked a military base near the Afghan border leading to an encounter with the security forces in which at least 50 militants and two soldiers were killed.

October 1: A suicide bomber disguised in a woman's burqa (veil) blew himself up at a busy police check-post in Bannu in the North West Frontier Province (NWFP) killing 16 people, including four police personnel.

October 7-9: At least 150 militants and 45 soldiers are reported to have died during clashes in North Waziristan.

October 7: Security forces with heavy artillery and helicopter gun-ships killed 65 militants but lost 20 soldiers in two encounters at Mirali and Miranshah in North Waziristan.

October 18: Suicide bombings in a crowd welcoming former Prime Minister Benazir Bhutto killed 143 persons and injured approximately 550 others at night in Karachi.

October 25: 18 soldiers and two civilians died and 35 persons, including nine civilians, were injured in a bomb blast aimed at a vehicle carrying Frontier Constabulary (FC) personnel in the Swat district of NWFP.

October 28: 29 people were killed and 55 others wounded in clashes between Taliban militants and security forces. The dead included 15 militants, 11 SF personnel and three civilians.

October 31: Fierce clashes between militants and the security forces at Khwazakhela town in the Swat District of NWFP, with conflicting reports about casualties. The NWFP Home Secretary, Badshah Gul Wazir, put the number of casualties at 60-70, all militants.

November 3: President Pervez Musharraf imposed a state of Emergency in the country and promulgated a Provisional Constitutional Order (PCO) holding the Constitution in abeyance.

November 7: Pro-Taliban militants captured a Police Station, paramilitary forces' camp and other government buildings at Kalam, extending their hold over the Swat Valley. Militants loyal to the rebel cleric Maulana Fazlullah are reportedly in control of most of Swat District.

November 10: Musharraf issued an Ordinance enabling the military to try civilians on charges of terrorism, anti-national activities, sedition, attacks on Army personnel and assault on the President, with the intent of disrupting the exercise of his powers. Military courts can also try civilians accused of waging war against the state, abetment to any of these offences, rioting while armed with deadly weapons, and making statements conducive to public mischief.

November 13: Around 500 local Taliban militants took over control of the Shangla District headquarters, in Swat, occupying the District Police Office, District Coordination Office and Police lines, without facing any resistance from the Government.

November 21: Baloch leader Nawabzada Balach Marri was killed along with his bodyguards in a clash triggering widespread violence in Quetta and other parts of Balochistan.

November 24: Two suicide bombers simultaneously targeted military personnel and installations at two different places in Rawalpindi, claiming over 32 lives and wounding 55 others. In the first attack, the suicide bomber hit the Inter-Services Intelligence (ISI), Agency's staff bus. The blast killed over 30 personnel on the bus and the guards standing at the main gate. Another suicide bomber blew up his car after hitting an Army check-post, killing two Army personnel.

December 17: 12 Army recruits were killed and two wounded in a suicide attack near the Army Public College in the heart of the Kohat Cantonment area in the NWFP.

December 21: 60 persons were killed and more than 100 others injured when a suicide bomber blew himself up in the midst of worshippers offering Id-ul-Adha prayers at the Markazi Jamia Masjid Sherpao in Charsadda, 20 kilometres from capital Peshawar in the NWFP. The target was Aftab Ahmed Khan Sherpao, former Federal Interior Minister, who was among the worshippers. He escaped unhurt in the attack, though his son was among the wounded.

December 23: Nine civilians and four Security Force personnel were killed, and more than 25 wounded, in a suicide attack on a military convoy in Mingora in the Swat District of NWFP.

December 27: Benazir Bhutto, leader of the Pakistan People's Party, and former Prime Minister was assassinated after addressing an election rally in Rawalpindi. 20 others were also killed in the accompanying bomb blast, which injured several others.

In more ways than one, the real fight in Pakistan has only just begun. Musharraf's brinkmanship and manipulations have brought Pakistan's inherent contradictions to the fore, and the prospect of a failed or disintegrating state are now a more proximate reality than ever before.

India

Separatist violence in India's Jammu and Kashmir state has continued unabated since 1989. India holds Pakistan responsible for providing material support and training facilities to Kashmiri militants. Several anti-India militant groups fighting in Kashmir are based in Pakistan and are closely linked to Islamist groups there. They include:

- Harakat ul-Mujahideen, based in Muzaffarabad and Rawalpindi, is aligned with the Jamiat-i Ulemai Islam Fazlur Rehman party (JUI-F), itself a main constituent of the MMA Islamist coalition in Pakistan's National Assembly.
- Hizbul Mujahideen, which has bases in Pakistan, is the militant wing of Pakistan's largest Islamic political party and leading MMA member, the Jamaat-i-Islami.
- Jaish-e-Mohammed, based in Peshawar and Muzaffarabad, also is aligned with JUI-F.
- Lashkar-e-Taiba based in Muzaffarabad and near Lahore, is the armed wing of a Pakistan-based, anti-U.S. Sunni religious organization formed in 1989.

Pakistan's powerful and largely autonomous ISI is widely believed to provide significant support for militant Kashmiri separatists in what is perceived as a proxy war against India. India estimates that there are about 3,000 "terrorists" being trained in camps on the Pakistani side of the LOC. Pakistan-based terrorist groups, particularly the Lashkar-e-Toiba (LeT) and Jaish-e-Mohammed (JeM), are increasingly depending on "surrogate bases" in Bangladesh, Nepal and the Middle East for movement of trained cadres and finances for their operations and cross-border terrorism is no longer Jammu and Kashmir-centric. The current strategy of Pakistan-based terrorist groups is to:

- Maintain a continuous flow of finances to sustain the terrorist networks in India.
- Target vital installations and economic infrastructure in India.
- Recruit and train local modules.
- Attack soft targets like market places, public transport system, places of worship and congregation, etc.

- Provoke communal tensions to create a wedge between communities.
- Supply hardware through land and sea routes.

India has also identified crime figure Dawood Ibrahim as a "global terrorist" with links to both Al Qaeda and Lashkar-e-Taiba. Ibrahim, wanted by the Indian government for 1993 Bombay bombings that killed and injured thousands, is believed to be in Pakistan.

Major terrorist incidents in India, during the year, have been:

February 18:	66 persons, including some Pakistani nationals, were killed and 13 others injured in explosions in two coaches of the Delhi-Attari special train at Diwana near Panipat in Haryana. Two improvised explosive device (IED)-laden suitcases, one from the rail track and another from the train, were also recovered subsequent to the explosions.
May 18:	11 people were killed and over 64 wounded in a powerful bomb blast at the Mecca Masjid (Mecca Mosque) near Charminar in Hyderabad. Over 10,000 people were offering prayers at the 400-year-old mosque at 1.15 p.m. when the bomb exploded. The explosive device was triggered with a cellular phone and was hidden underneath a thick marble platform.
August 25:	44 persons were killed and another 54 were injured in twin blasts at a laser show at the Lumbini Park, and at the Gokul Chat eatery in the Kothi locality in Hyderabad.
September 7:	The former Andhra Pradesh Chief Minister, N. Janardhan Reddy, and his wife, N. Rajyalakshmi, who is also Minister for Women's Development and Child Welfare in the Andhra Pradesh Cabinet, escaped unhurt while three Congress party workers were killed and five others wounded in a Communist Party of India-Maoist (CPI-Maoist)-triggered landmine blast near Chitwedu village in the Nellore District.
October 11:	Three persons were killed and 16 others injured when a bomb exploded in the shrine of the Sufi saint Khwaja Moinuddin Chishti in Ajmer in Rajasthan.
October 14:	Seven persons, including a 10-year old child, were killed and 40 others injured in a bomb blast inside a cinema hall in Ludhiana. The victims were identified as migrants from other States who were watching a Bhojpuri language film at the Shringaar Cinema.

In the ongoing campaign against the separatist United Liberation Front of Asom (ULFA) in Assam State, the Government seems to have gained a distinct advantage. Between 24 September 2006 — when a temporary truce between the authorities and the ULFA ended — and 31 October 2007, a total of 655 ULFA militants have surrendered to the authorities across the State. In addition to the surrenders, quite a large number of ULFA militants have either been killed by security forces or arrested. Among the dozens of insurgent groups active in the northeast are the National Democratic Front of Bodoland (NDFB); National Liberation Front of Tripura; and United National Liberation Front (seeking an independent Manipur). The territory of Bangladesh, Myanmar, Nepal, and Bhutan has been used as "shelter" for anti-India insurgent groups. In addition, Pakistan's intelligence agency has been known to provide them with training and material support. Fencing along the 4,097 kilometre-long border with Bangladesh, suggested as a remedy to the problem, has not been completed, leaving ample scope for easy entry and exit by insurgents.

With 4,383 militancy-related fatalities between 1992 and 2006, Manipur remains the third most violent theatre of conflict in the country, behind Jammu & Kashmir (J&K) and Assam. Apart from the overall insecurity resulting from the threat to and loss of life, Manipur has one of the most comprehensive networks of terrorist extortion in the country, affecting almost every earning citizen in the State. Manipur is assessed to be affected by over 20 insurgent groups.

Naxalite (a Maoist agrarian peasant movement) terrorism, which covers a broad region of eastern, central, and southern India, has grown in sophistication and lethality. Naxalites launched several high-level attacks, raising the insurgency's profile, and expanded the rural territory under their control. Most notable are the People's War Group (PWG), mainly active in Andhra Pradesh state, and the Maoist Communist Centre of West Bengal and Bihar. Both are designated as terrorist groups; each is believed to have about 2,000 cadres. The Maoist threat has now overtaken all other insurgencies in the country – at least from the perspective of geographical spread, currently afflicting at least 165 districts in 14 states.

Bangladesh

There is increasing concern among analysts that Bangladesh might serve as a base from which both South and Southeast Asian terrorists could regroup. There have been reports that up to 150 Taliban and Al Qaeda fighters fled to Bangladesh from Afghanistan in December 2001 aboard the *MV Mecca,* which reportedly sailed from Karachi to Chittagong. This was evidently not the beginning of Al Qaeda connections with Bangladesh. Al Qaeda had reportedly recruited Burmese Muslims, known as the Rohingya, from refugee camps in southeastern Bangladesh to fight in Afghanistan, Kashmir and Chechnya.

An Al Qaeda affiliate, Harkat-ul-Jihad-al- Islami (HuJI) was founded by Osama bin Laden associate Fazlul Rahman. It has the objective of establishing Islamic rule in Bangladesh. HuJI has recruited its members, thought to number 15,000, from the tens of thousands of madrassas in Bangladesh, many of which are led by veterans of the "jihad" against the Soviets in Afghanistan. The Bangladesh National Party coalition government included the small Islamic Oikya Jote party which has connections to HuJI.

The Rohingya Solidarity Organization (RSO) is the largest organization representing the over 120,000 Rohingyas in Bangladesh. The number of Rohingyas varies depending on the level of pressure they are under in their homelands in Myanmar. The Rohingya also speak the same language as Bangladeshis from the Chittagong area. These "destitute and stateless people" have proved to be a "fertile ground" for recruitment to various militant Islamist groups. The RSO has reportedly received support from the Jamaat-e-Islami in Bangladesh.

Nepal

The Maoists have manoeuvred themselves to the centre of the democratic and political stage in Nepal, paralysed the Army, and neutralized the King without diluting their own capacity for violence, and with a significant expansion – including a dominant presence in the Kathmandu Valley – in their ability for mass mobilization. It is increasingly clear that the Maoist objective in Nepal is not the sharing of power, but the seizure of power.

After the Maoist withdrawal from the Interim Government on 18 September 2007, the alliance of seven political parties decided to suspend the Constituent Assembly elections slated for November 22. The parties failed to break the deadlock that emerged after the CPN-Maoist stuck to their demands for declaring a republic through the parliament and proportional representation formula for the polls. The CPN-Maoist chairman, Pushpa Kamal Dahal aka 'Prachanda', has proposed a referendum to be held before the Constituent Assembly elections to gauge support for a full proportional representation system and a republic. The security situation in Nepal has deteriorated as a result.

This year also saw the beginning of a disturbing new trend with the activation of the separatist Maoist-splinter terrorist group called the Janatantrik Terai Mukti Morcha (JTMM), which aims to bring about the secession of the southern Terai plains from the rest of Nepal. According to the 2001 Census, 48.4% of the over 23 million Nepalese in the country reside in the "Madhesh, also known as Terai region (the flat southern region of Nepal, extending from east to west. It occupies about 17% of the country's landmass).

Sri Lanka

The Liberation Tigers of Tamil Eelam (LTTE) of Sri Lanka have been recognized as a terrorist organization the world over. More than 64,000 people have died in Sri Lanka's unresolved civil war over the past 20 years. The LTTE is reportedly responsible for more suicide attacks than any other terrorist organization worldwide. Many LTTE innovations, such as explosive belts, vests, and bras, using female suicide bombers, and waterborne suicide attacks against ships, have been copied by other terrorist groups. The Norwegian government has played an active role in trying to broker a lasting peace between the LTTE and the Sri Lankan government.

The 2002 cease-fire between the Sri Lankan government and the LTTE continued to erode amidst numerous violations and escalating military engagement between the LTTE and government security forces. The Sri Lankan Army remains deployed across the country to fight the insurgency.

There has been a continuous escalation of violence between the Security Forces and the LTTE since the election of Mahinda Rajapakse as President in November 2005. The military offensive in July 2006 inflicted heavy losses on the LTTE, forcing the rebels out from their erstwhile Eastern strongholds, and wreaking considerable damages in rebel capacities in the Jaffna and Wanni sectors.

A new facet of LTTE operations seen during 2007 was the introduction of an air arm. On 26 March, two locally converted Czech-made Zlin-143 bombers flew over hundreds of kilometres of government-held territory from Iranamadu, in the Wanni jungles, and dropped two bombs on an engineering facility of the Sri Lankan Air Force at Katunayake, 30 kilometres north of Colombo, and flew back without being detected. Further attacks were carried out at Palali airfield on 24 April and at the oil storage tanks near Colombo on 28 August (at Night). On 22 October, they attacked the Sri Lanka Air Force base at Anuradhapura, destroying aircraft on the ground.

With the killing of S.P. Thamilchelvan, the leader of the political wing of the LTTE and the de facto number two of the organisation, on 2 November 2007, Colombo has clearly declared its intent to increase confrontation with the rebels after their successes in the Eastern province through July 2007. LTTE chief, Velupillai Prabhakaran, while mourning Thamilchelvan's demise, reaffirmed that the rebels would "continue to travel on our path towards the goal with renewed determination."

The Army chief Sarath Fonseka stated on 26 September 2007, that the LTTE have lost 60 percent of the territory they controlled in the Northern and Eastern provinces during the last two years. Colombo is clearly readying for a final showdown, and the LTTE has limited capacities to resist the state's armed forces in positional warfare. Inevitably, its stealth and terrorist strikes against state and civilian targets in the Sinhala heartland will escalate, and this will bring extraordinary economic pressures to bear on the Government.

All conflicts have one quality in common: they all contribute to reshaping international relations, sometimes in dramatic ways. The global war on terror started out to destroy al Qaeda and other terrorist organizations with global reach. It may end up reshaping the world.

TRENDS IN MILITARY TECHNOLOGY

LETHALITY AND ARMAMENT

Metal Storm

The concept of stacked projectiles predates Metal Storm. Roman Candles, a traditional firework design, employ the same basic concept. However, in the case of Roman Candles the residual propellant will burn in a manner that all projectiles in the barrel are discharged following from the single ignition. Over the years, various methods of separately firing each propellant package behind stacked projectiles have been proposed. The difficulty with the proposed methods was that they did not eliminate the problem of unintended propellant ignition caused by hot gases leaking back up the barrel.

In the original Metal Storm patents the propellant immediately behind the projectile closest to the muzzle of the gun barrel was ignited by an electronically fired primer, the projectile was set in motion, and at the same time a reactive force acted on the remaining stacked projectiles in the barrel, pushing them backwards. By design, the remaining projectiles would distort under this load, expanding radially and sealing against the gun barrel wall. This created a seal, which prevented the blow back gases from prematurely igniting the remaining propellant charges in the barrel. As each of these propellant charges was selectively ignited, the force unlocked the projectile in front and propelled it down the gun barrel, and reinforced the radial expansion (and hence the seal) between the projectiles remaining in the barrel and the barrel wall.

Subsequent designs discarded this 'distorting shell sealing against the barrel' concept in favour of containing the propellant in skirts that form the rear part of each projectile. These skirts are part of the projectile, and are open-ended at the rear. The nose of the following projectile in the barrel provides the rearward seal to the skirt. The firing of projectile results in a rearward impulse on the remaining projectiles stacked in the barrel. This effectively creates a seal that prevents hot gases in the barrel triggering unintended ignition of the subsequent projectiles. Metal Storm uses inductive electronic ignition of the propellant, effectively from outside the barrel. This overcame technical issues in maintaining physical contact with the propellant charges, which move slightly backwards within the barrel during firing.

The skirt-to-nose joint has allowed for the incorporation of an easy-release arrangement which allows the shells to be clipped together to form robust ammunition tubes which can be inserted directly into the barrels. The tubes can be pulled apart and reconstructed in the field to make combinations of ammunition, and facilitate the replenishment of a partly discharged tube that is still in the barrel. In the absence of ammunition feed and casing ejection systems, barrels can be clustered into a barrel array or pod; or for their attachment as single units mounted on existing weapons mounts, including infantry weapons. The absence of a mechanical feed mechanism and the inherently compact lightweight nature of Metal Storm systems also make them suitable for attachment to platforms such as robotic ground and aerial vehicles.

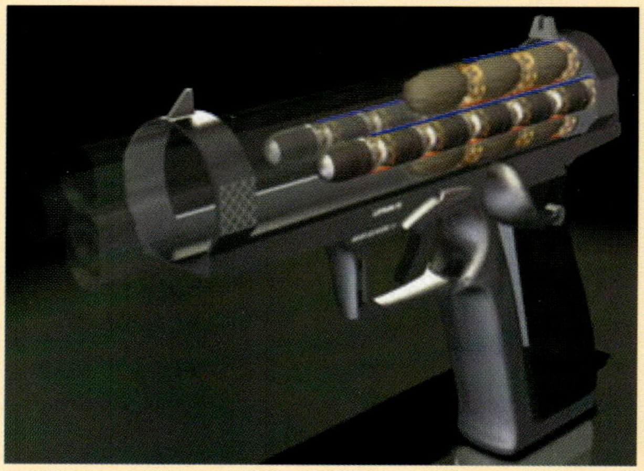

The electronic firing also creates the potential for tighter integration with electronic targeting systems, with electronically programmable fuses in airburst ammunition, and with electronic grip recognition technology. The clustered barrel array has been further developed to allow selective firing from any barrel in a cluster and within each barrel the ability to control the rate of fire.

The ability to deploy a range of munitions from effectively 'one' weapon systems, and to selectively escalate responses from the non-lethal to lethal without reloading is an advantage in urban warfare and insurgency situations where a range of responses may be quickly required in close quarter fighting and crowd control.

There is also a design where the gun tubes at the edges of the array are angled outwards from the main axis so that a gun tube array mounted on a tracking platform would have the potential to engage a target before the bulk of the centrally located gun tubes reached the optimal aiming position. The always loaded nature of the technology and the potential to rapidly produce a very high projectile density makes it ideal for this technology in close-in weapons support roles.

Corner shot

Designed by retired officers of the Israeli army the CornerShot is a special-purpose weapon that can fire around corners. It was designed in the early 2000's for SWAT teams and special forces in hostile situations usually involving terrorists and hostages.

The weapon is mounted in the front end of the Cornershot. The Cornershot bends horizontally at a mid-gun sixty-degree hinge. There is a digital camera and a flashlight attached to the barrel in the bayonet position. On the butt side of the hinge are the trigger, camera and controls for the camera and light. The observation screen is fixed on a horizontal hinge of the left of the weapon and slides out to allow the user to view images from the camera fixed at the front end of the weapon.

The high-resolution digital cameras allow the weapon to double up as a surveillance tool. The images from the camera can also be transmitted wirelessly to other devices.

The flashlight and camera let it operate by day or night. A variety of optional interchangeable cameras, as well as a folding stock, is available, and a universal accessory rail is standard. The versatile Corner Shot is available in several variations. The standard weapon mounts a normal semi-automatic pistol in the front part of the weapon, with a remote linkage to the trigger mechanism in the rear part. The trigger pull of the weapon is 21 newtons. In its standard form it is 820 millimetres long, with a weight of 3.86 kilograms.

The 40 mm breech-loading Grenade Launcher is a single shot weapon system. Operated manually, it fires grenades, less-lethal and non-lethal ammunition, and tear/irritant gas projectiles; spent cartridges are ejected for easier reloading. The same system is available in 37 mm size for law enforcement agencies. The 40 mm model has a rifling of 1:1.224, is 900 mm long, and weighs 4.4 kg (9.5 lb). Its range for precision fire, single target is 150 metres; and for area coverage, with fragmentation munitions, is 350 metres. The CornerShot Panzerfaust debuted at the Eurosatory 2004 military trade show in Paris. It is a derivative of the system for use against armoured vehicles and is designed to fire Panzerfaust anti-tank rockets. Further improvements include a 90 degrees swivel instead of the standard 60 degrees.

XM307 Advanced Crew Served Weapon

The XM307 Advanced Crew Served Weapon (ACSW) is a developmental 25 mm belt-fed autocannon with smart shell capability. A lightweight weapon the XM307 is designed to be two-man portable, as well as vehicle mounted. The XM307 can incapacitate or suppress enemy soldiers out to 2,000 metres or 2,200 yards, and destroy lightly armoured vehicles, watercraft, and helicopters at 1,000 metres or 1,100 yards.

The weapon has dual hand grips which allow the gun to be raised or lowered and moved laterally with a touch of a button. This means the gunner never has to take his hands off from the weapon. The XM307 has a full-solution fire control system that includes a laser range finder and a day/night sight. The weapon delivers highly lethal and suppressive fire out to 2,000 metres against personnel and lightly armoured vehicles. Highly portable within small soldier units, the XM307 provides overwhelming lethality compared to existing systems. The XM307 provides devastating firepower against visible and hidden targets, such as those in foxholes, behind rocks and walls, and inside buildings with windows.

General Dynamics Ordnance and Tactical Systems are developing the airburst 25mm ammunition. Kaman Dayron, Inc. is developing the fuze and Raytheon is developing the full-solution fire control. But by far one of the most revolutionary features of the XM307 ACSW is that the M307 system can be quickly and easily converted to a 12.7mm / .50-calibre machine gun. The XM312 can be converted from a .50-calibre machine gun to the M307 firing 25mm airburst ammunition in two minutes by changing four parts. Being able to convert the 312 to 307 while in field will give the front-line soldier flexibility in choosing weapons to meet the mission.

MARITIME TECHNOLOGY

Underwater Express Program

The United States Defense Advanced Research Projects Agency's (DARPA) Advanced Technology Office (ATO) is soliciting proposals for the Underwater Express Programme to demonstrate stable and controllable high-speed underwater transport through supercavitation. The intent is to determine the feasibility for supercavitation technology to enable a new class of high-speed underwater craft for future operational requirements.

Through this programme, DARPA is seeking to facilitate new operational opportunities in the underwater battle space. Also relevant are the current limitations for small high-speed surface craft, which suffer performance degradation in waves and are subject to exposure, while underwater alternatives today are very slow.

The military advantage of very high-speed underwater craft has yet to be exploited to its full potential because significant technological breakthroughs are needed for operational viability of such a craft. The ability to attain substantial underwater speeds for this class of vehicle is severely constrained by the power required to overcome the large drag forces on an underwater body. Without a radical means to solve this problem, strides that could be made in underwater propulsion are limited, as are breakthroughs needed in underwater sensing, navigation, and communications, all critical to taking strategic advantage of the underwater space.

Supercavitation offers 60-70% reduction in total drag on an underwater body. It can be attained by going fast enough to develop a full vaporous cavity, or it can be induced at lower speeds by injecting gas into a partially developed cavity. Although the technology has been applied to weapons with minimal control capability, its application to larger vessels with transport missions will require thorough development.

PACSCAT

The United Kingdom's Ministry of Defence has awarded a contract for the design, construction and evaluation trials on a technology demonstrator vessel, which will be a contender for the next generation of fast landing craft. The high speed Partial Air Cushion Supported CATamaran vessel (PACSCAT), if selected, will be used to support future amphibious operations.

The increased speed / payload balance possesed by the PASCAT will allow task force commanders to effectively conduct 'over the horizon' amphibious operations. The PASCAT will allow task forces to remain at safe distances and yet give them the abilty to come close to recover the beached troops at short notice

The PACSCAT craft will be capable of a variety of roles where high speed and high payload capacity are required and its low and variable draught will give it exceptional beaching qualities. Trials already conducted with a 1/3 scale manned model have proved it to be capable of beaching on a 1:120 gradient beach in scaled operational conditions.

Ballistic Missile Submarines - Ohio Class

Ohio class submarines, in service in the United States (US) Navy for a while have recently seen a technology upgrade to accommodate Intercontinental ballistic missiles or ICBMs in their arsenal. This is not a particularly new technology but advances and upgrades are being made to this technology every day. The US and British navies have incredible military technology at their disposal and this upgrade adds to the list. One of the best strategic military technologies that the US and their allies have developed is the ability to fire ballistic missiles from a submarine. The addition of supersonic and hypersonic cruise missiles to these submarines is in the pipeline. Vessels such as the Ohio class submarine carry **Trident-II** *intercontinental ballistic missiles*. The **Trident II** has 8 independently targeted re-entry vehicles or a MIRV setup as it is called, all of which can carry warheads to different targets. The Ohio class submarine is what makes up a lot of the US nuclear weapons threat. The United States has 18 Ohio Class submarines currently in service serving as a friendly reminder to any hostile nations.

AEROSPACE

Fire Scout - UAV Helicopter

The awe-inspiring Fire Scout Unarmed Aerial Vehicle (UAV) helicopter, developed and manufactured by Northrop Grumman is a remote control helicopter capable of autonomous take-off, landing, and flight. Its performance and technical features are rated as one of the best in stealth technology. Armed with lethal weaponry the release of this UAV helicopter coincided with an upgrade to the Hydra 70 rockets typically fired from the rocket pods mounted on AH-64 Apache helicopters. These are integrated with the helicopter and the upgrade includes laser guidance. The latest Metal Storm gun capable of firing at an extremely high rate of fire has also been mounted to the weapons pylons of some of the helicopter UAVs.

The UAV has already been procured by the US Army, whose interest, in turn, spurred a purchase by the US Navy. The Fire Scout actually landed on a moving ship on auto-pilot, during its testing phase. The Fire Scout is intended to be deployed in the field with units and formations, where it will form part of the reconnaissance and surveillance assets. Its firepower will also provide the commanders with added flexibility of destroying targets. It is thus an ideal platform for seek and destroy missions. The Fire Scout, in addition to adding to the already impressive arsenal, has one more futuristic advantage. It comes equipped with the latest electronics and communication equipment which will ensure its ready acceptance as an important piece of equipment as part of the network-centric warfare concept.

Boeing Pelican Concept

It would most certainly be the largest transport vehicle in the history of aviation.

At almost twice the external dimensions of the world's current largest aircraft, the Russian AN-225, the Pelican could transport five times its payload, a whooping 1,400 tons of cargo. Dwarfing all previous flying giants, the Pelican, a high-capacity cargo plane concept currently being studied by Boeing Phantom Works, would stretch more than the length of a US football field and have a wingspan of 500 feet and a wing area of more than one acre. Designed primarily for long-range, transoceanic transport, the Pelican would fly as low as 20 feet above the sea, taking advantage of the aerodynamic phenomenon called ground effect. Over land, it would fly at altitudes of 20,000 feet or higher. Operating only from ordinary paved runways, the aircraft would use 38 fuselage-mounted landing gears with a total of 76 tyres to distribute its weight.

It is much faster than ships at a fraction of the operational cost of current airplanes. This will be attractive to commercial and military operators who desire speed, worldwide range and high throughput. The Pelican can multiply the aircraft's 1-percent share in a commercial market now dominated by container ships. The aircraft's size and efficiency would allow it to carry types of cargo equivalent to those carried by container ships, at more than 10 times the speed. Powered by four turboprop engines, the **Pelican** is intended as a large-capacity transport craft for military and civilian use.

Selex Unmanned Air Vehicle

Selex Sensors and Airborne Systems unveiled three new mini unmanned air vehicle systems as part of the company's plans to significantly expand its autonomous technologies footprint to include all classes including the advanced tactical and lower end medium-altitude, long-endurance categories.

The three new systems exhibited at IDEX 2007 included an electric-powered ducted fan, a hand-launched mini electric fixed-wing system and a small catapult-launched tactical flying wing UAV. All are intended to operate using common ground-control and data link systems.

The ducted fan UAV designated **Asio** made its debut flight in early 2006. The air vehicle duct is 0.6m (1.9ft) across with veined fins used to provide steering. Forward flight is achieved by positioning the aircraft at a 45° angle. The development programme is focusing on close-range operations up to 10-15km (5-8nm) and **Selex** does not intend to develop a full 90° transition capability. However, two air vehicles could be operated in tandem, with one to provide data relay to extend the surveillance horizon to 25km. Maximum speed is 25kt (46km/h), with an endurance of around 50 minutes.

The hand-launched **Otus** system has a 1.5m span and a length of 0.9m. The aircraft has a typical operational weight of 2.3kg (5lb), including a 1kg payload, and endurance of up to one hour. Rapid prototyping work and a demonstrator flew in mid-December. The flying wing **Strix** system has a span of 3m, a length of 1.17m and uses conformal tip tail surfaces. It is intended to have an operational radius of 12.5km and an endurance of 1.5h. The modular Strix design can be taken apart for transport in a backpack giving it a great deal of operational flexibility.

GBU-39 Small-Diameter Bomb (SDB)

The **GBU-39 Small-Diameter Bomb** (**SDB**) is a 250 pound (110 kg) guided bomb that is intended to provide aircraft with the ability to carry a higher number of bombs. Most US Air Force aircraft will be able to carry a pack of four of these bombs in place of a single 2,000 lb bomb using the BRU-61/A rack.

Two variants are being developed. One version of the SDB is equipped with a GPS-aided inertial navigation system which makes it ideal for fixed/stationary targets such as fuel depots, bunkers etc. The second variant (GBU-40) includes a thermal seeker with automatic target recognition features which makes it ideal for striking mobile targets such as tanks, vehicles, and mobile command posts. The GBU-39 has a circular error probability (CEP) of only 5-8 meters, which means it has a 50% probability of hitting within 5-8 metres of its intended target, which should minimize collateral damage. CEP is reduced by updating differential GPS offsets prior to weapon release.

The small size of the bomb allows a single strike aircraft to carry more of the munitions than is possible utilizing currently available bomb units. The SDB carries approximately 50 lb (23 kg) of high explosive, yet because of its design it has the same penetration capabilities as the 2,000 lb BLU-109. During demonstrations, the SDB has successfully penetrated more than 6 ft (1.8 m) thick reinforced concrete. It also has integrated "DiamondBack" type wings which deploy after release, increasing the glide time and therefore the maximum range.

Under a contract awarded in September 2006, Boeing is developing a version of the SDB I which replaces the steel casing with a lightweight composite casing and the warhead with a focused blast explosive such as Dense Inert Metal Explosive. This will significantly reduce the possibilty of collateral damage when using the weapon for pin-point strikes in urban areas.

GLIMPSES 2007

14th SAARC Summit: India's External Affairs
Minister Sh. Pranab Mukherjee with HE Hamid Karzai, President of Afghanistan

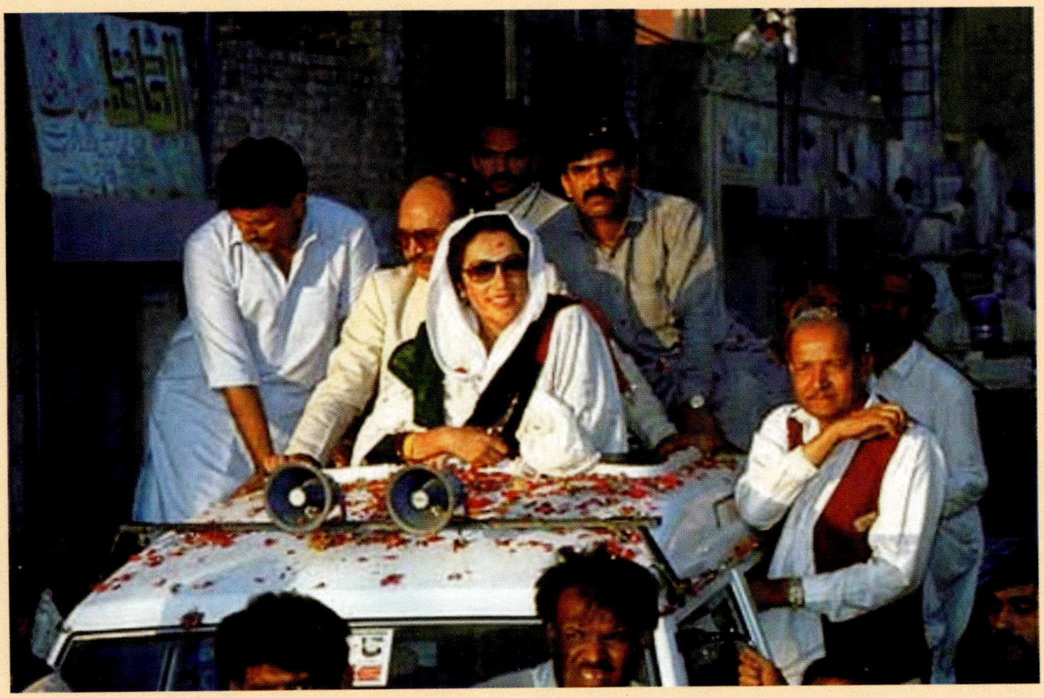

Benazir Bhutto, Ex Prime Minister of Pakistan, shortly before her assassination on 27th Dec 07

CNS and Chairman Chiefs of Staff Committee, Admiral Sureesh Mehta with Naval Chief of France in New Delhi.

Defence Minister Sh AK Antony with legendry Gen Vo Nguen Giap, Vietnam.

'Fourth Military World Games' Hyderabad, October 2007.

Exercise 'hand-in-hand' : Joint Indo-Chinese Army Exercise.